IS ENLIGHTENMENT POSSIBLE?

IS ENLIGHTENMENT POSSIBLE?

Dharmakīrti and rGyal tshab rje on Knowledge, Rebirth, No-Self and Liberation

Introduced, Translated and Annotated

by

Roger R. Jackson

SNOW LION PUBLICATIONS
ITHACA, NEW YORK

Snow Lion Publications
Post Office Box 6483
Ithaca, New York 14851

Printed in the United States of America

Typeset by Gigantic Computing

ISBN 1-55939-010-7 (paper)
ISBN 1-55939-011-5 (cloth)

Textual Studies and Translations in Indo-Tibetan Buddhism Series
ISBN 0-937938-98-X

Library of Congress Cataloging-in-Publication Data:

Is enlightenment possible? : Dharmakīrti and rGyal tshab rje on knowledge, rebirth, no-self and liberation / introduced, translated and annotated by Roger R. Jackson.
p. cm. — (Textual studies and translations in Indo-Tibetan Buddhism series)
Includes the translation of Rgyal-tshab Dar-ma-rin-chen's Rnam agrel thar lam gsal byed.
Includes bibliographical references and index.
ISBN 1-55939-010-7
1. Dharmakīrti, 7th cent. Pramāṇavārttika. 2. Buddhist logic. 3. Buddhism—Doctrines. I. Jackson, Roger, 1950. II. Rgyal-tshab Dar-ma-rin-chen, 1364-1432. Rnam agrel thar lam gsal byed. 1992. English & Tibetan. III. Series.
BQ3237.18 1992
181'.043—dc20 92-28455
CIP

Table of Contents

I think, just as you do, Socrates, that although it is very difficult if not impossible in this life to achieve certainty about these questions, at the same time it is utterly feeble not to use every effort in testing the available theories, or to leave off before we have considered them in every way, and come to the end of our resources. It is our duty to do one of two things, either to ascertain the facts, whether by seeking instruction or by personal discovery, or, if this is impossible, to select the best and most dependable theory which human intelligence can supply, and use it as a raft to ride the seas of life—that is, assuming that we cannot make our journey with greater confidence and security by the surer means of divine revelation.

Simmias, in Plato's *Phaedo*

Can we actually "know" the universe? My God, it's hard enough finding your way around in Chinatown.

Woody Allen

Preface

Enlightenment (Sk. *bodhi*, T. *byang chub*), and such cognates as *nirvāṇa* (T. *mya ngan las 'das pa*), *vimokṣa* (T. *rnam thar*) and *vimukti* (T. *rnam 'grol*), all connote for traditional Buddhists the attainment of a state that radically and finally transcends the unsatisfactoriness that pervades existence in the cycle of rebirths known as saṃsāra. Whether enlightenment is conceived of as "merely" the elimination of attachment, aversion and ignorance, or is invested with such qualities as omniscience, omnibenevolence and miraculous powers, it is a state far beyond anything most of us have ever believed possible, let alone experienced. In the West, in particular, where secular and psychological views of human possibility have by and large replaced religious notions, traditional Buddhist descriptions of enlightenment most often are greeted either with incredulity or with a "demythologized" reformulation along psychological or existential lines more palatable to the agnostic tastes of the late twentieth century.

Westerners usually *must* reformulate traditional descriptions in order to assimilate them at all, and Asian Buddhists often *choose* to so as to ease their communication with an increasingly non-traditional audience. This may be fine, and may simply represent another of the periodic transformations undergone by Buddhism in the course of its adaptation to different cultural circumstances, but it ought to be remembered that the meaning such a concept as "enlightenment" may have for contemporary Westernized Buddhists is *not* the meaning it has had for most Buddhists in most places throughout the centuries. For traditional Buddhists, enlightenment was, and is, precisely the radical transcendence of the suffering of saṃsāra outlined above, no more and no less—for the simple reason that traditional Buddhists still see the cosmos primarily through the lenses of the saṃsāra-nirvāṇa cosmology so pervasive in Asia, particularly among Indians and peoples influenced primarily by India, such as the Sinhalese, Burmese, Thais and Tibetans.

When, therefore, Tibetan lamas expound the four noble truths and describe the enlightenment that is the culmination of the Buddhist path, they are not being fanciful, they are not being metaphorical, and they certainly are not joking; they are describing a set of facts that follow from their paradigmatic assumptions about how the cosmos functions. Now, just as most Westerners do not question the secular-scientific paradigm from which they operate, so most traditional Buddhists have been content to accept the cosmology presented by their culture, satisfied that it bore the weight of tradition, was socially and personally useful, and was not grossly contradicted by experiences they might have. On the other hand, there *have* been a great many Buddhists who recognized that Buddhist beliefs were not necessarily self-evident, could not simply be accepted on faith, and rested on problematic philosophical assumptions that needed to be defended rather than simply asserted. There were, in short, Buddhists who recognized that the Buddhist world-view, to be regarded as "true"—taken in its most common usage, as corresponding to the way things actually are in the cosmos—must be susceptible of validation by an uncommitted observer through the universally accepted means of perception and inference. Not all thoughtful Buddhists have believed that Buddhist religious beliefs can thus be validated—some Mādhyamikas and later "logicians" arguably are exceptions—but there does exist a tradition that takes such validation seriously, stemming from the Indian pandit Dharmakīrti (seventh century C.E.) and continuing to this day in Tibetan schools.

When I began studying Buddhism seriously in Nepal in 1974, with the late Lama Thubten Yeshe and Lama Thubten Zopa Rinpoche (members of the dGe lugs school), the very first thing I was taught is that enlightenment is possible, and that the enlightenment that is possible is the transcendent state described by traditional Buddhist teachers and texts. A few cursory arguments (e.g., the mind is naturally pure) were offered, and we moved on, necessarily, to other topics. The initial assertion, however, that enlightenment is possible, remained in my mind as a sort of koan, sometimes taunting, sometimes promising, usually quite frustrating. Enlightenment, and the world-view on the basis of which it was asserted, simply did not correspond to anything I had known or conceived. The ultimate "proof" of enlightenment, I was assured, lay in "the pudding," i.e., in *experiencing* it. Being, however, for better or worse of a philosophical cast of mind, I sought some sort of prior rational assurance that the object of my quest was not a mere chimera. When, therefore, I persisted in my questions to various Tibetan teachers whom I encountered, I found that, again and again, I was being directed to the same source: the *Pramāṇasiddhi* ("Establishment of Authority") chapter of Dharmakīrti's *Pramāṇavārttika* ("Commentary on Authority," or, alternatively, "Commentary on [Dignāga's Compendium on] Authoritativeness"). Here, I was told, was laid out in systematic fashion a logical proof of the reality of past and future lives, the truth of the four noble truths and the possibility of enlightenment. If I took the trouble to follow the arguments, I—and any reasonable person—would be convinced that the Buddhist view of the cosmos was, in fact, essentially correct.

The 285 verses of the *Pramāṇasiddhi* chapter of the *Pramāṇavārttika* are extant in Sanskrit, and have been translated completely into English by Masatoshi Nagatomi (in his unpublished Harvard Ph.D. dissertation, 1957) and partially into German by F. Tillmann Vetter (1984). On their own, however, as is so often the case with "root-texts," they are concise to the point of obscurity, and require commentary to be truly comprehensible. There are Indian commentaries on the *Pramāṇavārttika* extant in Sanskrit, and there are Indian commentaries extant in Tibetan translation. However, because my entré into Buddhist philosophy was through the Tibetan tradition, specificially the dGe lugs school, I was directed eventually to the *rNam 'grel thar lam gsal byed* ("Elucidating the Path to Liberation According to the Pramāṇavārttika"), written in the fifteenth century by rGyal tshab dar ma rin chen (1364-1432), one of the two spiritual "sons" of the great Tsong kha pa blo bzang grags pa (1357-1419), founder of the dGe lugs tradition. The *rNam 'grel thar lam gsal byed* is considered by most present-day dGe lugs pas to be the greatest Tibetan commentary on the *Pramāṇavārttika,* and is most often the basis of contemporary dGe lugs pa expositions of Dharmakīrti's logical system. In fact, as I worked my way through the *Tshad ma'i grub pa (Pramāṇasiddhi)* chapter of rGyal tshab rje's commentary, I found that it was, indeed, an admirable work, providing a detailed outline of the structure of Dharmakīrti's argument, interpolating discussions on difficult points, and generally presenting the material in a manner detailed enough that the meaning was clear, but not so elaborately that the structure and direction of the argument were lost. It is a moot question whether in every case rGyal tshab rje reflects Dharmakīrti's own viewpoint (it is highly doubtful that he does), but his commentary stands nevertheless as a useful gloss on Dharmakīrti, and has value in its own right as the forerunner of a tradition of *Pramāṇavārttika* interpretation that still has knowledgeable and serious exponents today. It is, therefore, at least as "alive" as, say, Aquinas' *Summa Theologiae,* and ought to be regarded with the same seriousness as other ancient and medieval philosophical works, whose idiom may no longer be our own, but which are not thereby invalidated, and which may, in fact, contain far more truth than we moderns suspect.

This book is a revision of portions of my Ph.D. dissertation, "Is Enlightenment Possible? An Analysis of Some Arguments in the Buddhist Philosophical Tradition, With Special Attention to the

Pramāṇasiddhi Chapter of Dharmakīrti's *Pramāṇavārttika*" (University of Wisconsin, Madison, 1983). It is, centrally, a translation of rGyal tshab rje's commentary on the *Pramāṇasiddhi* chapter of Dharmakīrti's *Pramāṇavārttika*. My primary purpose is to expose Dharmakīrti/rGyal tshab rje's arguments as clearly as possible. Because this is philosophically challenging material, however, it requires considerable contextualization. Thus, I have provided in Part I a lengthy analysis that sets Dharmakīrti's undertaking both within its Indian and Buddhist context and vis à vis Western discussions of truth and religious argument; in Part II I give some indications of this book's relation to other scholarship on Dharmakīrti and rGyal tshab rje, as well as guidelines for reading the translation; and, in Part III, the translation, I provide an extensive set of explanatory notes that, if unworthy of being considered a sub-commentary to the text, nevertheless will, I hope, help make rGyal tshab rje and Dharmakīrti reasonably accessible. In the translation itself, in order to indicate rGyal tshab rje's relation to Dharmakīrti's root-text, I have interpolated translations of the *Tibetan* translation of the verses at the beginnings of the sections in which they are discussed, and I have highlighted phrases from the root-text as they have been incorporated into the commentary. My translation of the Tibetan verses is geared toward rGyal tshab rje's interpretation, which does not always accord with a straightforward reading of the Tibetan verses themselves; I have tried to indicate those places where rGyal tshab rje significantly departs from the straightforward reading. I also have included, in an appendix, a detailed outline of rGyal tshab rje's chapter, keyed to the translation, the edition of rGyal tshab rje's commentary I used, and Dharmakīrti's root-verses.

My overall emphasis here is philosophical, so my introduction and annotations deal more with issues of philosophical context and meaning than with philological or historical matters. Thus, I have not attempted to trace in detail the course of Dharmakīrti studies in India and Tibet, or to provide exhaustive cross-references to *pramāṇa* literature relevant to Dharmakīrti's or rGyal tshab rje's discussions, though I hope such history and references as I do provide (most often geared to material available in Western languages) are useful. Nor do I attempt here a definitive translation of the Sanskrit verses of the *Pramāṇasiddhi* chapter. Such a translation certainly is a desideratum (and we may hope that the lacuna soon will be filled by Prof. Nagatomi), but my focus here is on rGyal tshab rje's Tibetan commentary, which was based on a reading of the Tibetan, not the Sanskrit, version of the *Pramāṇavārttika*. Nor, as a consequence, do I undertake to study, except where there are notable discrepancies, the relation between the Sanskrit original and the Tibetan translation. Furthermore—

and this may frustrate some readers—I do not attempt in any detail an evaluation of Dharmakīrti/rGyal tshab rje's arguments. Thus, I do not presume to answer the book's title question, as to whether enlightenment is possible. I have occasionally interjected philosophical observations into notes, and have devoted a section of Part I to discussing some of the problems raised by the arguments, but I am mainly concerned simply to make available (and, I hope, comprehensible) to readers of English an important source of past and present Buddhist philosophizing, not to render judgment on it; I leave it to readers to decide for themselves whether the koan has a solution.

My stylistic conventions bear only brief notice. I have maintained precise transliterations rather than phonetic spellings in my rendering of both Sanskrit and Tibetan terms. Transliterated Sanskrit presents little problem; Tibetan, on the other hand, is notoriously difficult to pronounce. I apologize in advance for any discomfort the Tibetan transliteration may cause the reader, but would add that it is only thus that precision can be assured. The words, in any case, are meant to be read and recognized visually, not pronounced, and I suspect that only a Tibetan can pronounce them properly, anyway. I have tried to reduce italics by treating as English words Sanskrit terms found in Webster's *Third New International Dictionary*—though I have preserved diacritical marks (for a list of such terms, see R. Jackson [1982]). In Part I, which focuses on Indian Buddhism, I have generally favored Sanskrit terms, although Pali or Tibetan terms, where appropriate, are indicated parenthetically. Sanskrit terms that are conjectural are preceded by an asterisk. I have attempted not to clutter the translation with parenthetical foreign terms, since most of them may be found in the Glossary, under the English words that translate them. A key to the abbreviations used in footnotes may be found at the beginning of the bibliography. My solution here to the still problematic quest for the perfect nonsexist singular pronoun is to adopt the gender-free "they" and "them", which I personally prefer either to "he or she"/"him or her" (which is unwieldy, and certainly never reflected in Sanskrit or Tibetan texts) or to arbitrarily alternating "he"/"him" and "she"/"her" by paragraph or chapter (which can be downright confusing).

Northfield, Minnesota
lNga mchod (1 December) 1991
(572nd anniversary of Tsong kha pa's nirvāṇa)

Dedicated to the memory of my grandmothers,
Christine Challenger Reid (1887-1979)
and
Annie Britton Jackson (1895-1983),
one a skeptic, one a believer,
both fearless and independent questioners.

Acknowledgments

Many people have helped me in the preparation of this book, but I owe by far the greatest debt of gratitude to Geshe Lhundup Sopa, Professor of South Asian Studies at the University of Wisconsin-Madison, who served as my dissertation adviser, and patiently and good-humoredly went through the entire translation with me, clarifying countless difficult passages. Any errors that remain are mine, and mine, too, are any philosophical opinions found in the introductory sections or notes. Without Geshe Sopa's encouragement and help, this work simply could not have been done. I am also greatly beholden to Geshe Namgyal Wangchen (presently of Manjushri Institute, London), with whom I studied the first half of rGyal tshab rje's chapter in Sarnath, India. Further thanks go to the late Pandit Jagannath Upadhyaya of Sanskrit University, Varanasi, who served as my adviser while I was an American Institute of Indian Studies Junior Research Fellow in India; Ven. Samdhong Rinpoche, who put at my disposal the library of the Central Institute of Higher Tibetan Studies in Sarnath; Dr. E. Gene Smith of the Library of Congress, who kindly gave me a copy of dGe 'dun grub's *Pramāṇavārttika* commentary; Drs. Leonard Zwilling and Stephan Beyer, whose skeptical questions helped provide the impetus for my research; and the American Institute of Indian Studies and the U.S. Office of Education, whose fellowship support enabled me to pursue issues that really mattered to me—which is what graduate school ought to be all about. More recently, my colleagues at the University of Michigan, Fairfield University and Carleton College have helped provide the rich intellectual atmosphere in which work like this could continue to be refined. Additionally, Frank Barone, Marilyn Groves and John Newman read through the manuscript in earlier drafts and made important suggestions for its improvement. Dr. Martin Willson made frank and incisive comments on portions of the translation and on the glossary, and Drs. John E. Thiel, Anne Klein and Georges Dreyfus have been most helpful with their observations on the introduction. I am also grateful to Sidney Piburn of Snow Lion Publications for his support and encouragement, to Craig Preston and Bill Magee of Gigantic Computing for overseeing a very difficult typesetting process, and to Susan Kyser for her constant, cheerful help through the editing process. Finally, I am indebted to many, many friends for their passionate conversation over the years, but above all to my wife, Pam Percy, who always has provided sanity and stimulation, criticism and encouragement, just when I needed it most.

Part One

Truth and Argument in Buddhism

1. *Upaka's Shrug and the Sermon at Sarnath*

According to the *Ariyapariyesana Sutta* of the Pāli *Majjhima Nikāya,* when the newly enlightened Buddha has been convinced by Brahmā Sahampati to preach his doctrine, and has decided first to seek out the five ascetics with whom he had formerly practiced austerities, he sets out from Uruvelā—now Bodh Gaya—for Benares. Between the bodhi tree and Gaya, he encounters an Ājīvika ascetic named Upaka, who remarks on Śākyamuni's serene and radiant demeanor. Upaka asks him under whom he has taken vows, who his teacher is, and whose doctrine he professes. The Buddha relpies, in verse:

> All vanquishing am I, all knowing,
> Untainted by any existent.
> All-renounced, I am freed through craving's destruction.
> Self-taught, whom should I declare [my teacher]?
>
> I have no master, my equal is unseen;
> In this world, with its gods, I have no rival.
>
> I, indeed, am sanctified, am the teacher unsurpassed;
> I alone, indeed, am perfectly enlightened; cooled, I have reached nirvāṇa.
>
> I go to Kāsi-town to turn the Dharma-wheel;
> In this world grown blind, I beat the drum of deathlessness.

"Friend," remarks Upaka, "It is as if you claim to be a saint, an unlimited conqueror."

The Buddha replies:

> They are conquerors who, like me, have won the contaminants' destruction;
> I have conquered evil tendencies and so, O Upaka, I am a conqueror.

Shrugging, Upaka replies, "Perhaps, friend," and continues on his way.[1]

At the very outset of his career, then, before he has preached a word, the Buddha's claim to supreme attainment is doubted. In the *Ariyapariyesana* account, the Buddha then proceeds to Sarnath, where his five former companions greet him with the same familiar term of address as had Upaka: *āvuso*, a word used primarily by senior religious persons in addressing their juniors, or clergy in addressing lay people, and best translated as "friend," "sir," or "brother."[2] Unlike Upaka, however, the five ascetics are overwhelmed by the Buddha's charisma, and agree to listen to him. The Buddha announces to the ascetics that he is a tathāgata, that deathlessness has been won, and that he will preach to them the doctrine through which they will learn for themselves and come to possess "that highest good to which the holy life conducts."[3] In the *Ariyapariyesana*, the Buddha then proclaims the importance of overcoming attachment to the pleasures of the senses. He likens those who are attached to pleasure to a deer caught in a hunter's snare; those who are detached from pleasure are like deer free to roam the woods. The Buddha enjoins the practice of the dhyānas, (P. *jhānas*, meditative absorptions) and the subsequent attainment of the wisdom that utterly destroys one's defiling contaminants (*āsrava*, P. *āsava*) and blinds the Evil One, Māra.[4]

A far more famous version of the sermon at Sarnath is the "Discourse on Turning the Wheel of Doctrine,"the *Dhammacakkapavattana* Sutta of the Samyutta Nikāya,[5] wherein the Buddha expounds the "four noble truths."[6] These are: (1) the truth of suffering (duḥkha, P. *dukkha*), (2) the truth of suffering's origination (*samudaya*), (3) the

---

1 From *sutta* no. 26, M, i, 170-71. Translations are found at, e.g., Warren (1970) 342-43; Sīlācara (1924) 153-54; and Chalmers (1926-27) I, 121. For an analysis of the relative antiquity of *sutta* no. 26, cf., e.g., Pande (1974) 123-24. On Ājīvikas, see Jayatilleke (1980) 195-230.

2 See, e.g., Childers (1979) 74.

3 Warren (1970) 344; M, i,172.

4 M, i,172-75.

5 S, v,420. There are many translations of this seminal *sutta*, e.g., Rhys Davids and Woodward (1950-56) V, 350; and Rahula (1978) 92-94.

6 "Noble" is perhaps not the most felicitous translation of *ariya* (Sk. *ārya*), which may convey the rather stronger sense of "holy,"or "sanctified" (see Childers [1979] 57), and the term *satya* can denote not only a "truth,"but a "reality,"or what is the case. However, the expression "four noble truths"as a translation of *caturariyasaccani* (Sk. *caturāryasatyani*)—coined, I believe by F. Max Müller—is so common now that I see no need to quibble with it.

truth of suffering's cessation (*nirodha*), and (4) the truth of the path (*mārga*, P. *magga*) to the cessation of suffering.

The assertion of the truth of suffering entails the fact that there is suffering accompanying birth, aging, sickness, death, sorrow and lamentation, pain, grief, despair, association with the unpleasant, disassociation from the pleasant and unfulfilled desire—in short, that the five aggregates (*skandhas*, P. *khandhas*) that compose what we usually call a person are suffering. The assertion of the truth of origination entails the fact that there is a cause for suffering, namely craving (*tṛṣṇa*, P. *tanha*, literally, "thirst"), which is directed toward sense-pleasure (*kāma*), the annihilation of pain (*abhava*), or further existence (*bhava*), and which generates further "existence," i.e., rebirth. The assertion of the truth of cessation entails the fact that it is possible entirely to leave behind, or stop, craving and its resultant suffering. The assertion of the truth of path entails the fact that there exists a procedure whose outcome is the cessation of craving and suffering, here identified as the eightfold noble path, consisting of right views, right intention, right speech, right action, right livelihood, right effort, right mindfulness and right concentration.

As long, the Buddha notes, as he had not fully comprehended that suffering is to be understood, origination to be abandoned, cessation to be realized and the path to be followed, he was not perfectly enlightened. Once, however, he realized that each of these "truths" was true, that each truth entailed an appropriate action, and that he had performed the appropriate action with regard to each, he knew that he *had* gained perfect enlightenment, and "a vision of true knowledge arose in me thus: My heart's deliverance is unassailable. This is the last birth. There is no more rebecoming (rebirth)."[7]

We never will know, of course, exactly what the Buddha taught the five ascetics at Sarnath, for the Pāli canon (and likewise the corresponding Sanskrit *āgamas* that we have in Chinese translation) are regarded by scholars today not as a precise record of the Buddha's utterances, but as a compilation and edition of various pericopes: stories, formulas and quotations of varying degrees of antiquity and authenticity.[8] Still, virtually all Buddhist traditions, both "Hīnayāna" and "Mahāyāna," have considered the wheel-turning sermon at Sarnath to be the Buddha's first discourse. If there is little historical

7 Rahula (1978) 94.
8 On this issue, see, e.g., Pande (1974); Winternitz (1972) II; and Sangharakshita (1980) chapters 1-4.

warrant for this view,[9] there certainly is poetical warrant, for so concise a formulation of the Buddha's doctrine is difficult to find,[10] and the four noble truths—if they do not have quite the binding force of a Christian creed—*have* served as the basic statement of Buddhist principles wherever the religion has spread.

It is important to note that what is basic to Buddhism is the assertion of "truths" (*satyāni*, P. *saccani*), statements that purport to tell us about "states-of-affairs," "the way things are," "what is the case"—in short, what is "real" (*sat*). The Buddha proclaims his attainment to all he meets, and may be greeted with either the skepticism of Upaka or the reluctant acceptance of the five ascetics, but in neither case is the mere fact of his charisma or his assertion sufficient to compel assent: Upaka disbelieves and does not linger for a sermon; the five ascetics hearken and are presented with four propositions whose truth they are invited to discover for themselves.

Few truths come unattended; they usually are surrounded by a wraith-like host of presuppositions. The four noble truths are no exception, for implicit in them are a number of cosmological and philosophical assumptions. In the most general sense, the four noble truths are posited against the background of a two-fold cosmological vision. The universe, in this vision, holds open two, and only two, possible modes of existence for conscious beings: (1) the beginningless, ignorance-rooted experience—in life after life—of pain, sorrow, the transience of joys, separation from the pleasurable, encounter with the

---

9 For better or worse, it is generally assumed by scholars that the least formulaic and philosophical material in the *nikāyas/āgamas* is likely to be the most ancient. The *Sutta Nipāta*, part of which is regarded as very ancient on the basis of this and other criteria, contains virtually no reference to the four noble truths, the five aggregates, the twelve links of dependent origination, or many other "original" teachings of the Buddha.

10 At least in propositional form; there are, of course, briefer "symbolic" expressions of the whole Dharma, either verbal or non-verbal. Instances of the former include various prayers, dhāraṇīs, mantras or *bījas* (e.g., "Hail to the *Lotus Sūtra*" = praise of the Buddha's greatest sermon = the essence of the Dharma; the letter *a* = voidness = the essence of the Dharma). Instances of the latter include famous "gestures," such as the Buddha's smile while silently holding a flower (the "Flower Sermon" of Zen lore), or the Tibetan yogin Mi la ras pa's display of his buttocks, calloused from endless sitting in meditation. One "propositional" expression of the Dharma that is as concise as the four noble truths is the "Buddhist credo" often inscribed on post-Gupta statuary (but traceable to the Pāli canon): "Of those dharmas produced by causes, the Tathāgata has described the cause; and also their cessation: thus speaks the Great Recluse."

unpleasant and unfulfilled desires; and (2) the incorruptible peace that is the cessation of suffering, and which results from the eradication of the ignorance and craving that perpetuate that suffering. The universe, in short, holds open the possibilities of saṃsāra and nirvāṇa.

This cosmology, in turn, entails certain philosophical assumptions, which are, above all, assumptions about the nature and function of the mind: (1) the reality of past and future lives, which are contingent on the mind's independence of particular bodies; (2) the existence of a universal moral law, karma, that works with the same predictability in the psychological realm as causality does in the physical realm; (3) the fundamental perfectibility of mind, such that when its adventitious defilements have been removed one attains an undecaying liberated state that is beyond suffering, and makes the greatest of worldly joys seem infernal by comparison; (4) the possibility of control of the causal factors related to the universal moral law such that the liberated state can be attained. Assumption (1) bears most strongly on the truth of suffering, assumption (2) on the truth of origination, assumption (3) on the truth of cessation and assumption (4) on the truth of path. Common sense would dictate that if these four assumptions are true, the four noble truths are true, and that if any or all of them are false, then the four noble truths—and thus the Buddha's teaching—are at best partially true and at worst simply false.

Here, however, there is a still more fundamental question that must be asked, namely: In precisely what sense are the four noble truths, along with their cosmological and philosophical presuppositions, "true"? The answer is not as self-evident as common sense might dictate, for the word "true" is in fact ambiguous—a fact recognized not only in the Western, but also in the Buddhist philosophical tradition. Thus, we find that there are, in fact, at least three possible ways of interpreting the statement, "The four noble truths, along with their cosmological and philosophical presuppositions, are true":

1. The facts and processes described by the four noble truths are "literally" true. In other words, such facts and processes as rebirth, karma, nirvāṇa, etc., have a reality independent of the terms that describe them or the conceptual schemes out of which those terms arise. Furthermore, even if the terms that describe such facts and processes are limited by their location in a particular cultural-linguistic system, there nevertheless *do* exist facts and processes corresponding closely enough to those terms that they can be said to be "true"—and true not only for those in the cultural-linguistic world in which the terms are found, but in *all* possible worlds. In short, statements about the four noble truths and their presuppositions are literally and universally true: such facts and processes as rebirth, karma, nirvāṇa, etc., occur

just the way the Buddhist texts indicate they do, and they occur for every possible person, even if that person has never heard of them.

2. The facts and processes described by the four noble truths are only figuratively or symbolically true. In others words, such facts or processes as rebirth, karma, nirvāṇa, etc., either do not reflect realities independent of the terms that describe them, or cannot be ascertained to reflect such realities. Furthermore, such considerations are secondary, for the terms were taught not as a reflection of an inalterable extrinsic reality, but for their utility in providing images, symbols or stories that assist us in finding meaning in our lives, whoever or wherever we may be. Thus, not only is it possible (probable, even) that rebirth, karma, nirvāṇa, etc., are not realities in the literal sense in which they are described in Buddhist scriptures, but this probability is unimportant: their value—indeed the value of any truth-claim—is purely heuristic and utilitarian.

3. The facts and processes described by the four noble truths are true not independently and universally, but only within the context of a particular conceptual scheme, world-view or language-game. In other words, such facts and processes as rebirth, karma, nirvāṇa, etc., may in fact be "true,"but only relative to the particular thought-world out of which they emerge, that of Indian Buddhism. If statements that describe rebirth, karma, nirvāṇa, etc., cohere comfortably within a Buddhist conceptual scheme according to Buddhist standards of rationality, then the statements can be accepted as true, though they may *not* be true within another thought-world that is based on a different set of presuppositions—e.g., that of a Yoruba, Christian or secular humanist. The reason that they *can* be accepted as true is that we never can discover an independent or neutral world outside the conceptual schemes that merely give us versions of the world. If reality thus is viewed as a collection of partially overlapping, non-ultimate conceptual schemes, then truth never can be more than adequacy to a particular conceptual scheme. Thus, statements about rebirth, karma, nirvāṇa, etc., are *relatively* true (and, of course, relatively false), and to expect more of them is to misunderstand the nature of truth-statements, which always are limited by and to the "world" in which they are made.

Readers familiar with Western philosophy will have recognized in each of the preceding interpretations one of the classic theories of truth, namely truth as correspondence, pragmatic utility or coherence. Buddhists, of course, had no exact equivalents to these terms, nor for the majority of terms and issues that have concerned Western philosophers of religion. Nevertheless, I think that it is possible—with all appropriate caution and sensitivity to cultural context—to argue in general that Buddhists, like religious people everywhere, have had to concern themselves with questions of truth, and therefore to develop explicit and implicit criteria for determining how truth is to be found. Thus, to apply Western theories to Buddhist truth-claims is by no means utterly arbitrary, for as we shall see shortly, each is a possible option from a Buddhist point of view as well. Before we examine Buddhist attitudes toward truth, and decide just what Buddhists mean by the claim that the four noble truths are true, we may do well to explore at least generally the modern Western discussion of the problem of truth, and then see how that discussion bears on the more particular problem of the nature of religious truth-claims—of which Buddhist claims are a sub-set.

2. *Truth*

It may well be, as Ambrose Bierce has cynically suggested, that truth is simply "an ingenious compound of desirability and appearance."[1] Though it certainly is the case that "truth"is a term used with decreasing confidence nowadays by philosophers, notions of truth and falsity seem among the most fundamental and universal of human mental structures. Indeed, I would be prepared to argue that the true-false dichotomy, broadly conceived, is a basic aspect of what existentialists like to call "being human": human society—human life, even—is inconceivable without mechanisms for sorting and assessing information, and the most basic method of assessment is to categorize information as reliable or unreliable, i.e., true or false. It may seem as if I am casting the net of truth-and-falsity rather widely, but I would maintain that any information, whether verbalized or not, that can in principle be cast in the form of a statement is subject to truth or falsity. Thus, a once-burned infant's aversion to fire is an instance of the "true-false structure"in action (since the aversion could be recast as a statement, "Fire is harmful"), while a painting by Cézanne or a cantata by Bach is not—a Keatsian argument that the beautiful is the "real"criterion of the true notwithstanding.

So much, a philosopher—and even Bierce in a sober moment—possibly would concede, yet an admission of the centrality of the true-false dichotomy in human existence does not necessarily determine what it is of "true"or "false"information that makes it thus, nor does it help us in deciding whether a given piece of information is, in fact, true or false. The instinctive, "commonsensical"approach to truth is to maintain, simply, that "truth is agreement with reality—that it consists in a correspondence between (for example) a statement and 'the way things are'"[2] and that "a true proposition is one that *corresponds* to a fact—that is, to an actual state-of-affairs."[3] This "commonsensical" definition of truth—upheld in pre-modern phi-

---

1 Bierce (1979) 144.
2 Flew (1979) 73.
3 Hospers (1967) 116.

losophy by such notables as Aristotle and Aquinas, and more recently by, e.g., Bertrand Russell and G.E. Moore—is what has come to be called the correspondence theory. Correspondence theories of truth generally have been marked, implicitly or explicitly, by the assumption that there does, in fact, exist a reality extrinsic to and at least partially independent of our statements about reality, and that our statements can more or less accurately represent that reality. Thus, for me to say that "My cat, Mickey, exists" is a true statement is to maintain that (a) Mickey *does* exist, regardless of whether I make any statement to that effect, and (b) there are reliable methods by which any reasonable person can confirm that Mickey does, in fact, exist. Correspondent truth-claims such as the foregoing, because they claim a kind of universal validity, often are regarded as "strong" or "hard" claims.[4]

The strength of a correspondence theory of truth is that it is firmly "realistic," accepting the existence of independent data the analysis of which can result in a reasonably confident universal determination of whether a statement is true or false. The theory's weakness is that independent, universal data are notoriously hard to find. Indeed, much of the last hundred years of Western philosophy has seen a retreat from traditional certainties regarding the objectivity and clear comprehensibility of the world—beginning perhaps with Nietzsche's espousal of an epistemological and moral perspectivism, which has been echoed in various ways in, e.g., Wittgenstein's contention that language relates not to some extrinsic "reality" but to itself; Gadamer's analysis of the "hermeneutical circle" whereby our "knowledge" of phenomena is structured by the interpretive methods we bring to bear on them; Derrida's "deconstruction" of the essentialist "logocentrism" of Western literary and philosophical theorizing; the attack, by Goodman and many others, on epistemological "foundationalism" Quine's postulation of "ontological relativity"; and Berger and Luckmann's analysis of the degree to which human "reality" is a social construct.[5] Even in the so-called "hard sciences," Einstein's theory of relativity and Heisenberg's uncertainty principle in physics, Gödel's theorem in mathematics, and various physiological studies that demonstrate the

---

4 For a good discussion of the varieties of correspondence theory, see Prior (1967). For an excellent condensed argument for it, see Russell (1959) 134-35.

5 Original sources include Wittgenstein (1958), Gadamer (1975), Derrida (1974), Goodman (1978), Quine (1969) and Berger and Luckmann (1966). Discussions of the issues raised by these and the other seminal thinkers mentioned above may be found in, e.g., Rorty (1979), Culler (1982) and Tracy (1987).

degree to which "conception" informs empirical "perception," as well as the analyses of such philosophers of science as Kuhn and Feyerabend, have made it evident that scientific objectivity is not so easily obtained, either, and that many a statement is accepted as true not because it has finally and irrefutably been shown to be true (definitive experiments often have not even been conceived), but because (a) it has received no decisive refutation and (b) it fits well with accepted theories. Indeed, much of the data that is used to support a truth-claim can be shown to be theory-laden to one degree or another, "made" in accordance with the dictates of a particular theoretical construct as much as it is "found." Thus, it is open to some question whether (a) there is an objective referent to which our statements correspond, and (b) even if there is, we would have any way of knowing or showing the fact.

The weaknesses inherent in the correspondence theory have given rise to alternative attempts to explain truth, the two most notable of which are the pragmatic and coherence theories. These both entail what we might call "weak" or "soft" truth-claims, since both eschew the universal, demonstrable objectivity sought by correspondence theory. Indeed, the two overlap in significant ways, but we shall first consider them separately.

The pragmatic theory of truth—whose most famous exponent was William James, and whose most recent may be Richard Rorty—is based on the premise that a true statement should not, and perhaps cannot, be shown finally to correspond to some extrinsic objective reality that "causes" it, and that what, in fact, characterizes true statements is their "utility" or "efficacy" in promoting particular purposes or effecting particular results—in short, whether they "work" or "pay." Truth-claims thus are seen very much as functions of specific human activities, and will be adjudicated on the basis of their success or failure in furthering either those activities or our overall "satisfaction." Here, the statement "My cat, Mickey, exists," is seen as true not because it "represents" some objective fact about the world, but because a "cat" is comprehensible within a scheme of human purposes, e.g., as a pet whose presence (usually) adds to the pleasure of one's existence. We understand how a cat "works," what its benefit is, and thus can assign to the identification of Mickey both meaningfulness and truth. It appears that—at least in James' version of pragmatism—the "fruit" (as opposed to the "root") is so thoroughly determinative of truth that even if no one else will confirm that I have a cat, my assertion of his existence may be regarded as true if it helps contribute to my overall happiness, i.e., if my "fictional" Mickey fulfills the same function in my life as an "actual" cat would. "Fictional" and "actual" must be set apart in quotes because the distinction between them is introduced as an attempted correspondence "reality-check," and this, of course, the pragmatist considers of secondary importance.[6]

The coherence theory of truth maintains that "a statement is true if it 'fits' or coheres with the system of other statements that we take for granted."[7] The theory traditionally has been associated with rationalism and idealism, and in particular with such figures as Leibniz, Hegel and Bradley. More recently, it has gained renewed respectability, either directly or indirectly, through the work of Wittgenstein and his successors in the analytic tradition. It is the latter-day versions of coherence theory that I will summarize here. According to more recent versions of the theory, a true statement cannot be shown to correspond to some extrinsic objective reality, because there is no reality extrinsic to statements about reality: there is only the reality that is provided by one or another conceptual scheme, world-view, or language-game, and reality as is various as the systems by which it can be described. Thus the statement, "My cat, Mickey, exists," is true in the sense that Mickey can be assigned existence within a given set of parameters: he is real *if* reality is granted to conventional objects whose presence is perceptually confirmed, *if* his presence is confirmed intersubjectively, *if* the term "cat" is meaningful within the linguistic world in question, and *if* observation of Mickey leads to agreement that he fulfills the definition of a "cat." The statement thus is true to the degree that it coheres with a particular set of assumptions about the world, and is true only relative to those assumptions; it will not be true if the word "cat" has no meaning, or Mickey does not fulfill the definition of "cat," or there is doubt as to his observability (perhaps he is a Cheshire Cat!), or we are applying some different criterion of existence, e.g., a Platonic or a quantum or a Mādhyamika criterion, by which his "existence" is provisional at best.

The pragmatic and coherence theories, of course, are not nearly so simple as I have portrayed them—they are subtler, and each term may cover a range of views. The two theories are distinct approaches to the truth, arising out of unique problematics and each possessing its own strengths and weaknesses. Pragmatic theory has the specific strength of showing the pervasiveness of concerns with "utility" in matters

---

6 On the pragmatic theory in general, see Ezorsky (1967). For a contemporary version of pragmatism, see Rorty (1982). On the question whether non-existent entities can be considered "true" according to pragmatic theory, see Russell (1959) 134-5.

7 Bruner and Feldman (1986) 48. See also the discussion in White (1967).

often taken to be "objective," and the weakness of confusing psychological utility with "warranted assertability"—not to mention failing to account for the ambiguity of "utility" at the time of a truth's assertion. Coherence theory has the specific strength of showing the embeddedness of truth-claims, and the weakness of making the arguable assumption that all truth-claims share features of *a priori* systems like mathematics—not to mention failing to explain how mutually incoherent systems might be understood comparatively.

At the same time, though, the pragmatic and coherence theories have a number of features in common, and it is upon those that I will focus here. Their common strengths include (a) the vital realization that the objectivity sought by a correspondence theory is difficult, if not impossible, to attain, because the object is almost impossible to find apart from the purposes and presuppositions that inform the act of finding it; thus, the very processes by which we would find the object are limited, relative, without ultimate foundation; (b) the healthy recognition that there are many ways of approaching and describing the world, and that it is only with great difficulty that we can reduce all others to one description or declare unilaterally and with total confidence that *this* way is "true" and *that* way "false"; and (c) the sensible insistence that truth-claims cannot and should not be understood without reference to the cultural-linguistic and existential matrices in which they appear—for it is according to the axioms of *particular* conceptual schemes that truth or falsity actually is determined. The common weaknesses of the pragmatic and coherence theories can be summarized in a single word: relativism. If the objectivity, universality and ontological and epistemological foundations assumed in correspondence theory are abandoned, then are we not left with a kind of pluralistic insularity, in which "the world" actually consists simply of the totality of possible interpretations and/or descriptions of the world, each of which may be understood and judged, finally, only from within a particular interpretive scheme? Proponents of pragmatic or coherence theories generally deny the charge of relativism: they will claim that statements still can be "true" or "false" to the degree that they contribute to our purposes and/or cohere with a particular meaningful scheme. This sort of truth or falsity, though, clearly is a *relative* matter, and cannot be settled ultimately by recourse to any over-arching set of data or criteria, because no such data or criteria exist: there are no meta-tests for truth or falsity, and so truth is at best provisional. To my mind, this is relativism.[8]

The theories of truth outlined above have been presented as if they were quite incompatible, but in fact they actually are intertwined in complex ways, for it is difficult even to describe the function of one without introducing the others. The correspondence theory may appeal to universality and objectivity, yet we seldom make truth-claims that are not "pragmatic" in the broad sense of the word, i.e., intended to assist in the fulfilment of particular human aims; nor do we *ever* make truth-claims that do not arise within a particular cultural-linguistic—hence conceptual—matrix, and whether or not a truth-claim has universal import it must at the very least cohere with the particular scheme from which it originates. The pragmatic theory may concentrate on a truth-claim's utility in furthering our aims, but whether or not the truth-claim actually furthers our aims ultimately may be understood in terms of its coherence with the conceptual scheme from which it originates and/or its correspondence to realities assumed or demonstrated to be "the way things are."[9] Coherence theory may dispense with the search for universal objectivity, and concentrate on a truth-claim's consistency with the conceptual scheme in which it is found, but a particular "coherent" claim has little importance if it does not further some human aim and—as I shall argue shortly—if one is to discuss, move among and adjudicate contradictory or variant truth-claims from differing conceptual schemes, some over-arching criteria of correspondence would seem to be indispensable.

Thus, all of the traditional theories of truth have significant strengths and weaknesses, and are parasitic upon each other in subtle but important ways. Nevertheless, I believe that the most basic sense of the word "truth" both is and must be as correspondence. It may be, as the more sophisticated proponents of the pragmatic or coherence theory maintain, that there simply is no basis for upholding correspondence, that the theory's epistemological and ontological underpinnings have been stripped away by the contributions of modern physicists, mathematicians, anthropologists, philosophers (both analytic and phenomenological), physiologists and psychologists. However, the tendency to posit some kind of ultimate certainty persists, not just as a psychological need—a "correspondence complex" left over from our philosophical childhood—but as a very real philosophical requirement. Simply put, unless we assume that there actually exists a unique "'real world' that is independent of human

---

8 On the very complex question of the nature of relativism, see Hollis and Lukes (1982), Krausz and Meiland (1982) and Krausz (1989).

9 James himself seems to admit as much when he claims (1955:172) that a useful truth ought to be believed "unless the belief incidentally clashes with ...the rest of our truths."

mental activity and human symbolic language,"[10] we cannot sensibly describe or adjudicate among our various conceptual schemes as we do, nor even alternate among them—whether we make the trivial switch from a checkbook-balancing conceptual scheme to a novel-reading one or make the profound move from one culture to another. It may be argued that the over-arching "real world" that we posit to tie together our multiple worlds is itself either (a) simply another particular conceptual scheme, and *not*, therefore, really over-arching, or (b) if free from such particularity, then virtually empty of meaningful content, hence a basis for adjudicating only trivial questions. It is undeniable that any scheme, even that of a "real world," is still a *particular* scheme—short of that in the mind of God or a buddha, any scheme will be particular. This does not, however, mean that, *a fortiori*, such a scheme is delusory or useless. With appropriate obeisances to the difficulty of attaining objectivity and the pervasiveness of conception in our perception of reality, it still may be possible to derive a set of assumptions universal enough to adjudicate non-trivial cross-schematic truth-claims. Or, perhaps it is less a question of deriving such an ideal set as of observing closely how all of us (pragmatists and coherentists included!) make the distinctions and adjudications that we do—for to function without collapsing into solipsism or relativism, we all must and do posit that there is a way the world is and that there are more or less adequate ways of describing that world. Granted, this world may be "merely posited," but it has priority among the schemes we posit, hence such objectivity as may be possible. As a result, correspondence, however modified and cautiously applied, remains the basic criterion of truth.[11]

In sum, our discussion of truth may seem to issue in a paradox: there is no real basis for believing that a given truth-claim can find universal agreement or foolproof demonstration, but the plurality of truth-systems that results when we abandon the quest for universality and certainty seems finally to entail a relativism that renders the very concepts of truth and falsity meaningless—since in a thoroughgoing relativism, *every* statement is true. Because we cannot function without the true-false dichotomy, we cannot accept relativism, and yet if we are to avoid relativism, we must presume standards by which we can adjudicate variant truth-claims from different systems. Such

---

10 Bruner and Feldman (1986) 46.

11 For a variant and considerably more detailed version of the same argument, see Griffiths (1991) chapter 2.

standards are very difficult to find, but I think that we do and must presume such standards. To do so is to presume over-arching criteria of "reality" and its determination, and therefore to concede, finally, that statements, in order to be "true," must "correspond" to some reality beyond the conceptual scheme in which they are found—even though one must be exceedingly cautious in assuming or describing the existence of such a reality.

3. *Religious Truth*

The foregoing discussion of "the problem of truth" has been an exceedingly general one—there are complexities and ambiguities involved at which I have not even hinted[1]—but it does, I hope, at least provide a relatively clear background against which we can now consider a more specific aspect of the same problem, namely, the question of what we are to make of *religious* truth-claims. Because I will begin discussing Buddhist truth-claims in the next section, I will restrict myself here primarily to examples drawn from the Christian tradition, whose parallels with the Buddhist examples to follow may be inferred by the reader.

If, as has been argued above, most people instinctively adopt the commonsensical definition of truth as correspondence to a reality extrinsic to the truth-claim itself, it seems reasonable to assert that this also is the case in the realm of religion. Thus, the Christian claim that "Jesus was resurrected from the dead" means precisely what it seems to: that the resurrection of Jesus is a historical fact, attested by eyewitnesses, that occurred regardless of whether anyone chooses to believe that it occurred; similarly, the claim "God exists" means that there really does exist an entity not entirely unlike what Christians predicate when they use the word "God," and that God exists quite independently of anyone's assertion of his existence. There is little question that, throughout most of history—and today in places where modern thought has yet to be strongly assimilated—people have made and believed religious claims in the hard sense entailed by cor-

---

1 For informed and stimulating analysis of the issues raised in this and the previous section, see, e.g., Barbour (1974) and Hollis and Lukes (1982), especially the introduction and Lukes' essay, "Relativism in Its Place." Each of these books makes points similar to mine. Barbour defends what he calls "critical realism," ("in both science and religion there are experiential data and criteria of judgment which are not totally paradigm dependent" [172]) over against an "instrumentalism" that assumes that all models are "useful fictions." Hollis and Lukes uphold "rationality"—the acceptance and utilization of universal standards of translation and judgment—against a relativism that denies that there can be such standards.

respondence theory: Jesus "really" rose from the dead, God "really" exists, Allah "really" spoke to Muhammad via the angel Gabriel, a messiah "really" will come to save the Jews, Krishna "really" took form as Arjuna's charioteer, we "really" have lived before and may live again, we "really" may attain someday a peace that passeth understanding.

If the correspondence theory has difficulties even in its everyday application, its problems in the religious arena are even more severe, for religious truth-claims have special characteristics of their own, the most important of which are *universality* and *metaphysicality*. In most places and times, each religious world-view has claimed to be the most adequate possible description of "the way things really are." Competing descriptions have been regarded as either false or incomplete. The actual structure of the cosmos and blueprint for human action have been said to have only *one* truly satisfactory formulation, and fulfilment of one's ultimate purpose as a human being has been dependent on understanding and applying that one formulation. At the same time, a religious world-view almost always has entailed the assertion of realities that transcend the physical plane, and which are not, therefore, susceptible to the same kinds of empirical checking procedures that we might apply to, say, my assertion of the existence of my cat, Mickey. Each of these special characteristics of religious truth-claims creates special problems. The claim of universality is problematic not only because actual or possible evidence for the truth of universal claims is difficult to produce, but also because it is clear that the various religions of the world provide multiple, often conflicting versions of "universal" truth and that, in the absence of absolutely compelling evidence, one's insistence on the truth of one universal claim and the falsity or partial truth of the others is probably arbitrary, a question of dogmatic preference. The claim that metaphysical realms or entities are "real" in some very important but unconventional sense is problematic because evidence for the existence of such realms or entities is likely to be inconclusive if we follow the canons of ordinary empirical or scientific evidence, while the extraordinary evidence supplied by scripture or faith or religious experience is difficult adequately to adjudicate between one religious tradition and another.

Because hard claims to religious truth often result in dogmatism, supernaturalism, or both, and because neither of these tendencies is favored by the scientific world-view that is the touchstone of modern thought, many modern religious people have chosen to abandon the correspondence theory, and have, instead, adopted the softer approach of pragmatism or coherence.

The pragmatic approach to religious statements, not surprisingly, downplays the objective verifiability of their truth, and emphasizes instead their utility in contributing to our happiness or sense of purpose or authenticity. Thus, James writes, "If theological ideas prove to have a value for concrete life, they will be true, for pragmatism, in the sense of being good for so much."[2] One recent trend that I would consider pragmatic regards religious assertions not as confirmable philosophical propositions, but as "stories," or, to employ E.M. Hare's term, "bliks," which are "factually empty statements" that are meaningful "as principles by which one lives and in accordance with which one interprets experience."[3] Similarly, R.B. Braithwaite claims that religious language is "the statement, but not the assertion, of certain stories."[4] Although not "factual,"these stories are more than the mere expression of feelings: they are a declaration of adherence to a policy of action and a way of life. Whether or not they are "actually"true, they tend, like great fiction, to give us psychological support in the form of a meaningful vision of life or certain aspects of life.[5] Like the "story" approach, Rudolf Bultmann's attempt to "demythologize" the Christian tradition is broadly pragmatic. According to Bultmann, we in the modern era no longer can accept the literal veracity of most Biblical statements, for those statements are rooted in an ancient world-view that we have transcended. Rather, we must read the Bible "existentially," for its stories and statements still can provide symbols rich enough to generate meaning in lives lived in a world far in space, time and concept from that of the Bible.[6] In these broadly pragmatic approaches to religion, then, the claim that "Jesus was resurrected from the dead" may or may not be a historical occurrence—what is important is that Jesus' resurrection can serve as a story to inspire us to love God or live a moral life, or as a powerful symbol of our own attempts to move from the "death" of inauthentic existence toward an authentic life. Similarly, the claim that "God exists" may or may not be objectively true, and probably is not verifiable even if it is. But statement (as opposed to assertion) of the existence of God, and acting *as if* God ex-

---

2 James (1955) 170.
3 Quoted in Donovan (1976) 25.
4 Quoted, ibid., 27.
5 I am reminded here of the American poet Wallace Stevens' concept of a "Supreme Fiction." In a post-religious age, Stevens believed, the place of God or the gods will be taken by non-factual poetic myths and symbols, which can give structure and meaning to our lives in the same way that religious myths and symbols once did.
6 See, e.g., Bultmann (1951-55).

isted are (allegedly) generally beneficial both to the individual and society, and thus are pragmatically true.

Coherentist interpretations of religious truth-claims center on the notion that the universality of a particular world-view never can be demonstrated, and that the truth of a religious statement—which always arises within a particular system—must be determined by its consistency (or coherence) with other statements taken to be true in that system. While the application of coherence theory is implicit in many discussions of religion grounded in the language-game theory of Wittgenstein or the analysis of religion as a "cultural system" by such anthropologists as Clifford Geertz (as well as in the attempts of members of different religious traditions to engage in dialogue) one of the more interesting explicit attempts at its application has been made by George Lindbeck. Lindbeck argues that religious doctrines are to be taken "not as expressive symbols or as truth claims, but as communally authoritative rules of discourse, attitude, and action,"[7] and that doctrines "are not first-order propositions, but are to be construed as second-order ones; they make. . . intrasystemic rather than ontological truth-claims."[8] Thus, the statement that "Jesus was resurrected from the dead" is not a universal claim so much as a statement that is true within the set of assumptions governing the conceptual scheme or language-game that is Christian doctrine, and may be involved less with asserting a fact than helping to regulate the thought and action of those who adhere to the Christian scheme of things. Similarly, the assertion that "God exists" cannot be expected to be either true or meaningful within a non-theistic context, while within a theistic framework like that of Christianity, it is meaningful, at least arguably demonstrable, and determinative of thought and action.

The advantages of pragmatic or coherence explanations of religious truth-claims ought to be obvious: they reduce considerably the "cognitive dissonance" entailed by the assertion of universal metaphysical truths in an era marked intellectually by pluralism and materialism. By placing in abeyance questions of the literal truth of religious assertions, modern religious people are able to "eat the cake" of a

7 Lindbeck (1984) 18.

8 Ibid., 80. Lindbeck's very useful division of approaches to doctrine into "propositionalist," "experiential-expressive" and "cultural-linguistic" is similar, though not precisely parallel, to my own division of approaches to truth-claims into those reflected by the correspondence, pragmatic and coherence theories of truth.

science-based world-view, and at the same time "have" the structure and meaningfulness provided by a traditional religious allegiance. Certainty may be sacrificed, but dogmatism is avoided, rationality preserved, and existential relevance assured.

At the same time, the disadvantages of a pragmatic or coherence approach to religion are considerable. Most fundamentally, each entails a relativism that makes meaningful truth-decisions difficult if not impossible, and thus vitiates the true-false dichotomy that we have identified as an integral aspect of human existence. The dilemma encountered by the pragmatist or coherentist seems inescapable: if all stories or conceptual schemes are equally true (as ought to be the case, since there is no meta-test for ranking them outside their own borders), then relativism ensues; if the relativism is denied, then some meta-test or over-arching standard of truth must be assumed, hence a greater or lesser degree of "correspondence" of conceptual schemes to this over-arching standard. As noted before, to argue that this implicit meta-scheme is still "just another scheme" is sophistry, because its degree of universality gives it a reality and objectivity against which all other schemes must be measured; whether or not it ultimately is a construct, it functions as the "real world."

We have noted above that two of the most distinctive traits of traditional religious truth-claims were universality and metaphysicality. One or the other or both of these is abandoned by the pragmatic or coherence approach (the metaphysics rather more prominently by the former, universality by the latter), and the question must be raised whether in the absence of universality and metaphysics, what we are discussing still is "religion."

If universality is abandoned, then one's faith becomes simply one among a vast number of world-views, each of which, it appears, has an equal claim to validity, and none of which, therefore—including one's own—can provide any firmer claim to one's allegiance than any other. This extremely tolerant view is acceptable only as long as one does not pause to consider the fact that many of the "equally valid" systems to which one might adhere are utterly incompatible, since they make conflicting claims about the way things are. As human beings, we inevitably must discriminate between true and false, and this is no less the case in regard to our views of the ultimate nature of things. Each of us—whether or not it can be justified—establishes an epistemological and ontological fulcrum on which to pivot our functioning in the world. We must have a comprehensive or over-arching conceptual scheme, a total world-view, and that world-view will be of no use to us unless we regard it as true, and other views as false or less true. In the broad sense of the term, then—as an account of the structure and meaning of the cosmos—each of us must have a religion.

If metaphysics is abandoned, then how much of "religion" actually remains? If the resurrection, or God, are simply edifying stories or "meaningful" concepts that may as well be fictitious, or only are true within a particular scheme, then it is difficult to say what distinguishes a "religious" person from a secular humanist apart from their choice of symbolic language. If we are to regard *any* all-explanatory symbolic language-system as a religion, then we must admit humanism, Marxism and hedonistic materialism, among others, to the list of religions, and we begin to attenuate the term "religion" so much as to threaten its usefulness.[9] I would argue, therefore, for the rather traditional view that a religion is not fully a religion unless it claims universality and refers to a metaphysical realm and/or entities, and that the compromises wrought in religion by acceptance of a pragmatic or coherence theory of truth rob it of some of its most vital characteristics.

It is entirely possible—probable, even—that, despite the foregoing objections, the term "religion" will in fact undergo a change such that it no longer is tied to claims regarding universality or metaphysical reality—people who call themselves religious, after all, will determine the meaning of "religion" themselves. At the same time, I think it is undeniable that what most people at most places and times have meant by their "religion" is just such an all-explanatory, universal, metaphysically rooted world-view, and that most people, therefore, have believed that the truth-claims of their religion are true in the strongest sense of the term, i.e., as corresponding to actual states-of-affairs. Indeed, if I may be permitted a turn on the ontological argument for God's existence, I would maintain that, given the equal plausibility (or, at least, necessity) of each of the three traditional theories of truth, a religious person perforce will opt for correspondence, for correspondence permits to the realities described by religion the greatest certainty, the greatest universality, the greatest "actuality"—existence that is actual rather than merely imaginary. Thus, as John Hick observes, "In order to render a distinctive style of life both attractive and rational, religious beliefs must be regarded as assertions of fact, not merely as imaginative fictions."[10] Peter Donovan claims that

---

9 James argues—and here I would agree with him—that religion is a "total reaction upon life" that "signifies always a serious state of mind" in relation "to whatever [humans] may consider the divine" (1961:45, 47, 42).

10 Quoted in Donovan (1976) 27. In his most recent work (1989), Hick implicitly

> . . . there is little doubt that religious people themselves do care that their words be taken as the truth, and would be offended at the suggestion that it did not matter whether their language was misleading and their claims dishonest.[11]

Donovan adds that

> . . . despite the great diversity to be found amongst the religions of the world and the obscurity of the claims of even the most thought-over of them, it is simply a misrepresentation of religions to ignore their claims to tell us . . . *what is so*, regardless of whether everybody, or even anybody, acknowledges it to be so, or finds any point in the language in which it is claimed to be so.[12]

Finally, Paul Griffiths argues that there is

> [a] tendency toward absoluteness that makes religious truth-claims of such interest and gives them such power; to ignore it is to eviscerate them, to do them the disservice of making them other than what they take themselves to be.[13]

---

upholds correspondence as a criterion of religious truth, but the "Real" to which he insists religious statements and truth-claims ultimately refer is so nondescript as to be vacuous: Hick purchases tolerance, and the assurance that religious experience does have an object (see, e.g., 249), at the price of abstracting that object to the point where it becomes virtually unrecognizable to any traditionally religious person. I suspect that Hick's argument points the way that many modern people will take in reformulating their sense of "religion," but in its reduction of religion to a virtually contentless lowest common denominator, it deprives particular traditions of the ultimacy of many of their most important claims about the cosmos and, by levelling out any claims other than the assertion of the "Real," effectively approaches the relativism implied by pragmatic or coherence approaches.

11 Donovan (1976) 4.

12 Ibid., 97.

13 Griffiths (1991) 3; cf. Griffiths (1986) xvii ff. See also the stimulating discussion of these issues by Hendrik Vroom (1989), who analyzes the way contemporary philosophers of religion have understood religious truth, and juxtaposes it with the ways in which various religions, includng Buddhism, have regarded truth. He arrives, thereby, at a complex appreciation of the place of truth-claims in religions and of a variety of different things that "truth" may mean in a religious context, but still maintains that "doctrine" is central to most religions and that "true doctrine indicates how things really are . . . . in relation to the transcendent (as it is conceived in various traditions)" (357).

Thus, we can conclude that when Christians assert that "Jesus was resurrected from the dead" or "God exists," they generally mean that these are so in the most literal sense (and that they would be quite disappointed should the opposite be established). The correspondence theory is at the heart of what religious people traditionally have meant by "truth," and—arguably—it must remain at the heart of any comprehensive world-view if that view is to be considered religious.

4. *Truth in Buddhism*

In the light of what we have discovered about the indispensability of correspondence as a criterion of truth, especially where religion is concerned, we should not be surprised if, when we analyze the sorts of truth-claims made in Buddhism, correspondence (though not named as such, of course) turns out to be the most fundamental criterion, and that the Buddha asserted the four noble truths and their cosmological and philosophical presuppositions in a literal or "hard" sense. That the Buddha did adhere to a correspondence criterion has been argued by the philosopher Walter Kaufmann, who maintains in his *Critique of Religion and Philosophy* that the four noble truths are both cognitive and meaningful, and that "the Buddha himself seems to have considered acceptance of four propositions essential for salvation. His Four Noble Truths . . . were clearly meant to be unambiguous,"[1] and "to be taken literally."[2]

If the four noble truths and their presuppositions are to be taken literally, then there "really" are past and future lives at various points on the wheel of rebirth, which means that the mind "really" must be independent of particular bodies; there "really" exists a universal moral law in accordance with which every mental, vocal or physical action will engender an appropriate result; the mind "really" is capable of attaining a state in which all suffering has been eliminated forever; and there "really" do exist extraordinary practices, such as meditation, that can assure the attainment of such a state. In short, saṃsāra and nirvāṇa "really" are the two possible destinies for sentient life. Much like the Christian beliefs outlined in the last section, these Buddhist assumptions are, in their literal form, at considerable variance with modern secular humanist views, according to which, e.g., we only live once; the mind is a perishable function of a perishable organ, the brain; morality is a matter of human convention, not of the structure of the cosmos; no human being achieves either perfection or unsullied

---

1 Kaufmann (1972) 181.
2 Ibid., 190.

happiness; and extraordinary "spiritual" practices are more likely to lead to self-deception and hallucination than beatitude.

A. SOME BUDDHIST REVISIONISTS

Given the sort of cognitive dissonance produced by the literal espousal of the Buddhist world-view in a modern setting, the temptation arises to explain Buddhism, either to oneself or to others, more along the lines of a pragmatic or coherence approach to truth. Thus, the Buddha did not "really" mean the four noble truths to be taken literally—rather, they are stories to help us live our lives better, symbols to give meaning to our existence, statements valid only within the limited conceptual scheme that was the world-view of ancient India. A number of modern Western (or Westernized) commentators have, in fact, adopted this idea. Some early British students of the Pāli canon believed they had found in the Buddha an ancient exponent of the positivism of their own day, and explained away such alien notions as rebirth and nirvāṇa as, at best, metaphors whose real intent was to describe psychological states and, at worst, later interpolations by devious monks who sought to distort the Master's message. Recently, the most egregious—and, unfortunately, influential—exponent of this view has been the late Alan Watts, who writes that

> Buddhists . . . who understand their own doctrines profoundly, who are in fact liberated, do not believe in reincarnation in any literal sense. Their liberation involved . . . a liberation from being taken in by social institutions; it is not a liberation from being alive.[3]

Further, for Watts, "The individual's multitude of lives is interpreted as the multitude of his physical and social relations."[4] This psychological explanation of rebirth and liberation—of saṃsāra and nirvāṇa—is echoed in many of the equally influential works of the late Tibetan lama, Chögyam Trungpa Rinpoche, who writes, for example, that the traditional six realms of saṃsāric existence (those of gods, titans, humans, animals, hungry ghosts and hell-beings) are "psychological states of being . . . different kinds of projections, the dream worlds that we create for ourselves."[5] As for the four noble truths, *duḥkha* is an assertion of our "neurosis," *samudaya* an analysis of "how ego develops

3 Watts (1961) 67.
4 Ibid., 76.
5 Trungpa (1973) 131.

and operates," *nirodha* the recognition that "there is a sane, awake quality within us," and *mārga* "the practice of meditation."[6]

Existentialist terminology is employed frequently in the works of the noted interpreter of Tibetan Buddhism, Herbert Guenther. He writes, for instance, that in Buddhism,

> . . . knowing himself not merely to be an object in time but to be temporality, man is called upon to make a choice as to authenticity or unauthenticity. In Buddhist terms, unauthenticity would be the disruption of unitary reality into the events of Saṃsāra and Nirvāṇa. . . .[7]

Further, each of the six types of saṃsāric existence is

> . . . a fragmentation, positive or negative, we may say, and a disavowal of the unitary nature of man's existence. Stated otherwise, man's experience of himself as, say, a brute or a god, is a neglect of the transcendent in his total nature.[8]

A more recent "existential approach to Buddhism" is provided by Stephen Batchelor, in his *Alone With Others*, where he argues that the traditional "two wings" of the Mahāyāna path, wisdom *(prajñā)* and method *(upāya)* can be taken as providing "authentic" approaches to the two basic "modes" of being human, "being-alone" and "being-with-others," the basic insight of wisdom being a recognition of entities' lack of permanence or substantiality, the basic practice of method being compassion and the perfections that embody it, i.e., generosity (*dāna*), morality (*śīla*), patience (*kṣānti*) and effort (*vīrya*). In the course of providing his existential analysis, Batchelor simply ignores such traditional Buddhist concerns as karma and rebirth, and insists that the Buddha must be understood not as a transcendent or in any way superhuman being, but as "the man who walked through Northern India with a group of disciples, begged for food, gave clear and practical teachings, and finally died of dysentery,"[9] and is extraordinary simply because he is a paradigm of "the optimum possible mode of human life."[10]

---

6 Ibid., 152-3. Another Tibetan lama who has gone far toward accomodating Buddhist ideas with Western ones is Tarthang Tulku, most importantly in his book *Time, Space and Knowledge* (1977).

7 Guenther (1971) 235.

8 Ibid., 247.

9 Batchelor (1983) 120.

None of the authors just cited is trying deliberately to misrepresent Buddhism; each is simply trying to explain it to a Western audience either unschooled in or skeptical of traditional Buddhist cosmology and metaphysics. There always is a danger, however, that explaining may become explaining-away, and that what begins innocently as an attempt to show that Buddhism may be more readily comprehended *via* this or that psychological description or existential analysis may end with the implication that what all Buddhists "really" have meant when asserting their traditional doctrines is *just* this or that psychological description or existential analysis. The implication for truth-theory, then, is that the Buddha did not assert the four noble truths literally, but only figuratively, and that his criterion of truth was pragmatism or coherence rather than correspondence. This interpretation of the Buddha undoubtedly makes him more attractive to contemporary people, and may help to clarify or make palatable such relatively alien notions as saṃsāra and nirvāṇa, but it must be remembered that if the virtue of explaining an alien tradition by recourse to "matching concepts" from our own culture is comprehensibility, its vice is the danger of serious distortion—misrepresenting what people in the alien tradition actually have meant when they have made certain statements.

What, in fact, *have* Buddhists meant by the assertion of the four noble truths? How literally *have* they intended their cosmology to be taken? From the examination of traditional Buddhist attitudes toward truth that follows, we will see that Buddhism *probably* can be asserted to have upheld correspondence as its main criterion, but that the tradition has a greater ambivalence toward truth than might at first seem the case. Indeed, the Buddhist appreciation of the paradoxes involved in truth-claims is as sophisticated in its own way as that of the Western tradition. We shall begin by examining a number of Buddhist sources that seem to point to correspondence as the main criterion of truth, then turn to texts that seem rather more pragmatic or coherentist in orientation.

B. "CORRESPONDENCE THEORY" IN BUDDHISM

The Buddha never overtly propounded a correspondence theory of truth—the term, after all, comes from the Western tradition. There are, however, many indications that he did adhere implicity to such a theory. Thus, in the *Abhayarājakumāra Sutta* of the *Majjhima Nikāya*, the Buddha discusses statements in terms of their (a) truth or falsity, (b) utility or use-

---

10 Ibid., 129.

lessness and (c) pleasantness or unpleasantness. He maintains that he asserts as truths only those statements that are (a) true, useful and pleasant or (b) true, useful and *un*pleasant.[11] The Buddha was concerned chiefly to teach a way to salvation, so it is not surprsing that he should have tended to emphasize those truths that had the greatest bearing on the attainment of this goal, i.e., "useful" or "pragmatic" truths. To teach pragmatic truths and to teach a pragmatic criterion of truth, however, are different matters. As K.N. Jayatilleke puts it, ". . . the truths of Buddhism were considered to be pragmatic in the Buddhist sense of the term, but it does not mean that Early Buddhism believes in a pragmatist theory of truth."[12] A pragmatist theory, as we have seen, may involve, in effect, the supposition that "a belief is true if it is useful and false."[13] Although it is not mentioned specifically, Jayatilleke infers that a proposition that was useful but false would not have been asserted by the Buddha, because

> it was considered self-contradictory to say of a statement that it was false but useful. . . . Since falsehood or the assertion of a statement that is false (*musāvāda*) was considered a moral evil, it would have been held to be logically or causally impossible for what is false, i.e., what is morally evil, to result in what was useful in the sense of being morally advantageous or good. . .[14]

The Buddha, or Tathāgata, repeatedly is described as one who sees and describes "the truth," which may be *satya,* that which is "real" or "actual" (*sat*); *tathatā,* which is "thusness" or "objectivity"[15] or *bhūta,* that which has "happened" or "become." This, says Jayatilleke, "tacitly implies the acceptance of a correspondence theory of truth."[16] The "conscious avowal" of the correspondence theory is found in the *Apaṇṇaka Sutta* of the *Majjhima Nikāya,* where the Buddha makes it clear that falsity is non-conformity with

---

11 M, i, 395; tr. Chalmers (1926-27) I, 282-85. See also D, iii, 135, sutta no. 29; tr. Rhys Davids and Rhys Davids (1951) III, 126-27. See also Jayatilleke (1980) 351-52.

12 Jayatilleke (1980) 358.

13 A.D. Woozley, quoted ibid. The "falsity," in such a case, of course, would only be from the poin view of one upholding the correspondence theory!

14 Jayatilleke (1980) 358, 359. A pragmatist might argue that there is an implicit circularity here, since the determination of what is "objectively" good may in fact be parasitic on assumptions about what is socially useful.

15 See Kalupahana (1976) esp. p. 93: ". . . causation is not merely an idea or thought-construction without any objective validity, but an idea that corresponds to what is found in nature" (i.e., nature is "thus," *tathā*).

16 Ibid., 352.

fact and truth conformity with fact. If, for example, one believes, conceives or asserts that there is no next world, when in fact there is a next world, then one's belief, conception or assertion is false. If one believes, conceives or asserts that there is a next world, when in fact there is one, then one's belief, conception or assertion is true.[17] Here, a clear distinction is made between belief, conception or assertion on the one hand, and actuality on the other, a distinction often ignored in the pragmatic theory of truth and rejected in coherence theory, and therefore truly meaningful only within the framework of a correspondence theory. This same distinction is made—and a correspondence theory thereby implied—in one of the most famous of all *nikāya* passages: "Whether tathāgatas arise or do not arise, this order (*dhātu*) persists: the fixed nature of things, the way things are, conditionality."[18] Thus, there exists a "way things are,"a reality that is *independent* of any perceptions or formulations of it. Tathāgatas, after all, are virtually the only beings who have comprehended and explained things as they actually are, so the assertion that the reality they expound exists whether or not they are around to expound it is a quite unambiguous indication of an attitude toward truth that only can be characterized as correspondence theory.

Further evidence of what counts as "true" in Buddhism may be provided by a brief survey of the ideas considered *false*: the notion of "wrong view" (*mithyādṛṣṭi*, P. *micchadiṭṭhi*)[19] shows a remarkable consistency throughout Buddhist history, Hīnayāna and Mahāyāna; Pāli and Sanskrit; Vaibhāṣika, Sautrāntika, Yogācāra and Mādhyamika. The basic formulation of wrong view is found in a number of different places in the *nikāyas*, e.g., in the *Mahācattārīsaka Sutta* of the *Majjhima Nikāya:*

> What, O monks, is wrong view? [Saying] there are no alms, there is no sacrifice, there is no offering; there is no ripening of the fruit of karma that tends toward happiness or suffering; there is no "this" world, there is no other world; there is no mother, there is no father, there are no miraculously born beings; there are in this world no *samanas* or *brāḥmanas* who have reached the highest point, who live perfectly, and who, having themselves understood and experienced this world

---

17 M, i, 402-3; tr. Chalmers (1927-27) I, 289-97 and Jayatilleke (1980) 352-53.

18 S, ii, 25; see, e.g., Jayatilleke (1980) 448.

19 Wrong view must be distinguished from "ignorance" (*avidyā*), which is most often the term employed for a failure to comprhend the ultimate nature of all phenomena: no-self (*anātman*) or voidness (*sūnyatā*). In this sense, *avidyā* might be considered ontological ignorance, while *mithyādṛṣṭi* is cosmological ignorance.

> and the other world, relate [their experiences to others]. This, O monks, is wrong view.[20]

Vasubandhu, writing early in the first millenium C.E., identifies precisely the same set of ideas as wrong view in his scholastic classic, the *Abhidharmakośa*.[21] The *Laṅkāvatāra Sūtra*, also composed early in the first millenium, but half a continent away, and in the Mahāyāna rather than the Hīnayāna idiom, criticizes those who are

> . . . destructive and nihilistic regarding abiding, activity, generation, dissolution, existence, nirvāṇa, the path, karma and its result, and truth. Why is that? Because they have not cognized these through perception, they have not attained a vision of them.[22]

Nearly a thousand years later, the great Tibetan philosopher, Tsong kha pa blo bzang grags pa (1357-1419), writes that wrong view (T. *log par lta ba*) is essentially nihilism, and that such nihilism is fourfold:

> There is nihilism in relation to cause, effect, activity and what really exists. Nihilism in relation to cause is the claim that there are no good or evil actions. Nihilism in relation to effect is the claim that there is no fruit of these two. Of the three types of nihilism in relation to activity, . . . [the second,] nihilism in relation to the activity of coming and going is the claim that there are no past or future lives. . . . Nihilism in relation to what really exists is the claim that there are no arhants, etc.[23]

Although it is not surprising that there exists such unanimity throughout the length and breadth of a single tradition—since fundamental doctrinal formulas have a way of being encoded and repeated—it is important that so central a formula consistently has

---

20 M, iii, 71-72, in *sutta* no. 117; tr. Chalmers (1926-27) II, 194. Other references include D, i, 27 and 58, and M, i, 402. The definition is found in shorter form at, e.g., D, ii, 316, in the *Pāyāsi Suttanta*, where only three items are mentioned: "there is no other world, there are no miraculously born beings, there is no ripening of the fruit of karma that tends toward happiness or suffering." It is specifically noted at A, i, 268 that wrong view overlaps the beliefs attributed to Ajita Kesakambalī, a materialist contemporary of the Buddha. See Woodward and Hare (1951-55) I, 247-48.

21 AK, iv, 78b-c; tr. Poussin (1923-31) III, 167-68.

22 Vaidya (1963) 9; tr. Suzuki (1978) 36.

23 Tsong kha pa, in PTT, vol. 152, p. 38, folio 90a.

been repeated by Buddhists, regardless of their locale, sectarian differences or diverse notions of the Buddha's most vital teaching. The Buddhist notion of "right view" (*samyagdṛṣṭi*, P. *sammadiṭṭhi*) is simply the opposite of wrong view. Right view, thus, involves the belief that there *are* past and future lives, the causal mechanism of karma *does* function, there *do* exist arhants and other beings who have travelled a path and attained nirvāṇa. These beliefs, in turn, correspond closely to the assumptions that underlie the four noble truths. Right view, therefore, essentially comes to entail acceptance of the four noble truths and their cosmological and philosophical presuppositions as literally true.

That the four noble truths are intended as "propositions about states-of-affairs" is evident not only from the degree to which they inform Buddhist notions of right and wrong view, but also from later, detailed formulations of them in the abhidharma. In the Vaibhāṣika and other Sanskritic traditions, for example, the four noble truths are divided into sixteen "aspects" (*ākāra*), the direct realization of which transforms one from an ordinary being (*pṛthagjana*) into an ārya, destined for enlightenment. A number of different arrangements of the sixteen aspects are found in Vasubandhu's *Abhidharmakośabhāṣya*. One of the most interesting of these, the fourth, explains each of the sixteen aspects in terms of the incorrect philosophical view to which it is an antidote:

1. The truth of suffering: The fact that suffering is impermanent (*anitya*) counters the view that it is permanent. The fact that it is suffering (*duḥkha*) counters the view that it is happiness. The fact that suffering is void (*śūnya*) counters the view that it pertains to a self. The fact that suffering is non-self (*anātmaka*) counters the view that it has a substantial self.

2. The truth of origination: The fact that suffering has a cause (*hetu*) counters the view that it has no cause. The fact that suffering is originated (*samudaya*) by a complex of causes counters the view that it has a single cause, such as God (*īśvara*). The fact that suffering is successively produced (*prabhava*) counters the view that it is merely the transformation of some pre-existent cause, such as the "nature" (*prakṛti*) posited by Sāṃkhyas. The fact that suffering is variously conditioned (*pratyaya*) counters the view that suffering is brought about by some intelligent being.

3. The truth of cessation: The fact of cessation (*nirodha*) counters the view that there is no liberation from suffering. The fact that cessation is peaceful (*śānta*) counters the view that liberation is suffering. The fact that cessation is sublime (*pranīta*) counters the view that such meditative attainments as the dhyānas and *samāpattis* ("equipoises") are sufficient for liberation. The fact that cessation is emergence

(*niḥsarana*) counters the view that liberation is not definitive, and is subject to decline.

4. The truth of path: The fact that there is a path (*mārga*) counters the view that there is no path leading to the cessation of suffering. The fact that the path is reasonable, practical or correct (*nyāya*) counters the view that some false path is the true path. The fact that the path accomplishes (*pratipad*) the goal counters the view that there is another path one might follow. The fact that the path leads to a definite removal (*nairyānika*) of suffering counters the view that one on the path is subject to relapse.[24]

It is obvious even from this skeletal summary that, in asserting the sixteen aspects of the four noble truths a Buddhist is, at the same time, contradicting a number of views central to other schools of Indian philosophy, e.g., the *ātmavāda* of most orthodox (*āstika*) schools, the "transformation theory" (*pariṇāmavāda*) of the Sāṃkhyas, the random causal theory of some materialists, the theism of Naiyāyikas and the soteriological skepticism of materialists and many Mīmāṃsakas. The refutation of others' views and the assertion of one's own is not, presumably, something undertaken idly. One pursues such discussions because one believes that one's own assertions "correspond" to the way things really are, whereas the assertions of one's opponents are false, misleading and spiritually damaging. From the very first sutta of the *Dīgha Nikāya*,[25] the *Brahmajāla*, which refutes sixty-two mistaken views, down to the late "logicians," such as Dharmakīrti and Śāntarakṣita, Buddhists have been concerned to promote their own views and refute those of others; this in itself is further evidence for the "hardness" of Buddhist truth-claims, and of correspondence as the way in which those truth-claims are made.

A final, crucial piece of evidence that Buddhists have asserted the four noble truths as literally true statements corresponding to actual states-of-affairs is found in the *Dīgha Nikāya*, where the Buddha distinguishes statements that can be made categorically from those that can*not* be made categorically. Among the statements that cannot be asserted categorically are the famous "unanswered" (*avyakṛta*, P. *avyakata*) metaphysical questions about the duration and extension of

---

24 Poussin (1923-31) VII, 38-39. The relevant verse is AK, vii, 13a. For a further discussion of the sixteen aspects, particularly as analyzed by Asaṅga and Tsong kha pa, see Wayman (1980). See also below, section III:6.

25 D, i, 1-46; tr. Rhys Davids and Rhys Davids (1951) I. For a study of this important *sutta*, see Bodhi (1978).

the cosmos and a tathāgata's fate after death. Among those that *can* be asserted categorically are the four noble truths.[26] The Pāli term that has been translated as "categorical," *ekaṃsika,* literally means "one-sided, one-edged," and thus, in this context, admitting of only one interpretation, unequivocal, unambiguous. Therefore, when the four noble truths are asserted, they are asserted directly and unambiguously. There is no sense in which their truth could be merely relative or provisional. They correspond to reality whether or not a buddha appears to assert them, and the cosmological and philosophical assumptions behind them must equally be regarded as true. Thus, however modern Buddhists may choose to interpret the terms, most traditional Buddhists seem to have believed that statements regarding saṃsāra and nirvāṇa are true in the most literal sense, as a wheel of rebirths powered by deluded actions and the utter stopping of that wheel through the extraordinary meditative practices of the Buddhist path.

There is, thus, considerable evidence that when the Buddha preached the four noble truths to his ascetic friends at Sarnath, he meant exactly what he said. The evidence of the tradition as a whole, however, is not entirely unambiguous, for there are many passages in Buddhist texts, both Hīnayāna and Mahāyāna, that might be adduced to qualify a categorical insistence that the Buddhist criterion of truth is correspondence, pure and simple.

C. BUDDHIST PRAGMATISM

We already have seen that the Buddha of the *nikāya/āgama* tradition considered "usefulness" nearly as important a characteristic of true statements as their veracity, and there is, indeed, a strong pragmatic thrust in much of the Buddhist tradition—to the point where we may occasionally wonder if Walter Kaufmann was not correct in his remark that Buddhism is essentially "unphilosophical,"because its primary focus is on salvation rather than truth, and "knowledge and understanding are... mere instruments for the attainment of an experience."[27] As noted, the Buddha simply refused to answer certain metaphysical questions about the limits of the universe or the condition of a tathāgata after death, on the grounds that *any* answer was fraught with philosophical pitfalls, and the perplexity resulting from confronting such dilemmas did nothing to advance the questioner spiritually.[28] The Buddha also taught a number of

---

26 D, i, 191, in sutta no. 9, the *Potthapāda;* tr. Rhys Davids and Rhys Davids (1951) 256. See also Jayatilleke (1980) 279.

27 Kaufmann (1972) 261-63, 267.

well-known parables that seem intended to show that there are times when philosophical analysis is pointless. The "arrow" parable, in which it is suggested that a man shot by an arrow must seek medical treatment rather than inquiring as to the particulars of the arrow and bowman, indicates that we who suffer in saṃsāra should be more concerned with leaving it than with an endless analysis of its workings.[29] The "raft" parable compares the Dharma to a raft, and suggests that just as a raft is left behind once we have successfully crossed a river, so the Dharma no longer is necessary when one has reached its goal, nirvāṇa.[30]

The parable of the raft, in particular, can be given an interpretation that is not only pragmatic, but pragmat*ist*: it *may* be taken to imply that the contents of the Buddha's Dharma, including the four noble truths, are taught primarily with their utility, not their truth, in mind, and that they may be dispensed with once one has attained the goal to which an understanding of them conduces. Perhaps, then, they do not really "correspond to states-of-affairs," but are, rather, simply convenient fictions, to be used or discarded entirely on the basis of expediency. This interpretation is tempting, but not, I think, ultimately plausible. We must bear in mind Jayatilleke's insistence above that the Buddha would not have promulgated teachings that were useful but false—since mendacity by definition could not be beneficial, and utility only could be assigned to a statement that was true, i.e., that described things as they actually are. Thus, the fact that the "raft of Dharma" can be left behind by those who have attained the "other shore" of nirvāṇa does not mean that it thereby is falsified; it remains true, but it no longer is useful, since its usefulness is restricted to those who have not yet reached the other shore. Similarly, the fact that the metaphysical and other speculations with which we concern ourselves much of the time "do not tend to edification" does not mean that no truths or knowledge have any importance. It simply means that we should concern ourselves with those truths that bear most directly on our situation in the cosmos. Thus, we should not, perhaps, concern ourselves excessively with "factual" knowledge about details of the world; but we *should* be most concerned with the crucial details of the way in which saṃsāra is perpetuated or discontinued. There *is* information about such matters, in propositions like the four noble truths, and they, in turn, only will be worth exploring if they are true descriptions of how things really are in the cosmos.

---

28 For a lucid discussion of the unanswered questions, see Jayatilleke (1980) *passim*.

29 M, i, 429, in sutta no. 63, the *Cūlamālunkhya*; tr. Chalmers (1926-27) I, 306.

30 M, i, 134, in *sutta* no. 22, the *Alagaddūpama*; tr. Chalmers (1926-27) I, 90-100.

If the pragmatism of the Hīnayāna tradition turns out to be less subversive of a correspondence criterion of truth than might at first appear the case, matters are less clear when we turn to the literature of the Mahāyāna. Here, the malleable concept of the Buddha's skill-in-means (*upāyakauśalya*) is invoked either directly or implicitly to explain both inconsistencies among the Buddha's teachings and apparent breaches of traditional morality by buddhas or bodhisattvas: any act or statement that is conducive to the spiritual welfare of others, even if apparently immoral or false, is an example of skill-in-means, motivated by compassion and guided by wisdom, and is not, in fact, immoral or false.

The *locus classicus* for raising the issue of skill-in-means on the moral level is the famous "burning house" parable of the *Lotus* (*Saddharmapuṇḍarīka*) *Sūtra,* recounted by the Buddha for Śāriputra. A wise father (the Buddha) sees that the house (saṃsāra) in which his children (sentient beings) are playing is on fire (with suffering). He also perceives that they do not realize this (because of ignorance) and must be saved. Rather than panic them with a cry of alarm, he calmly lures them outside, promising to each the sort of animal-cart he most desires (the *śrāvakayāna, pratyekabuddhayāna* or *bodhisattvayāna*). Excited, the children rush out of the house (enter the path). They discover that their father actually has but one type of cart to offer (the one vehicle, *ekayāna,* which is the *bodhisattvayāna*), and has advertised three because he knows that different promises will lure out different children, depending on their dispositions. Having recounted the parable, the Buddha asks Śāriputra whether the father, promising three types of carts but delivering only one, was a liar. No, Śāriputra replies, he was not, because his "lie" had the effect of inducing the children to leave the burning house; a "white lie" such as this is no lie at all.[31] Here, it seems, truth really has been cut loose from factuality. Truth is not a matter of propositions about states-of-affairs, but something "situational": the true statement in a given circumstance is that which is most beneficial spiritually for the person to whom the statement is directed. In a very literal sense, the Buddha becomes a teller of great "stories," in the manner suggested above by Hare and Braithwaite.

This apparently pragmatist approach to truth receives a more systematic basis with the development of the Mahāyāna hermeneutical practice of distinguishing between scriptures of definitive meaning (*nītārtha*) and those whose meaning requires further interpretation

---

31 SP, 53; tr. Kern (1963) 75-76.

(*neyārtha*). The distinction is introduced in the *Saṃdhinirmocana Sūtra,* which is roughly contemporaneous with the *Lotus*. The seventh chapter of the *Saṃdhinirmocana* describes "three turnings of the wheel of Dharma," whose contents, respectively, were the Hīnayāna, Mādhyamika and Yogācāra teachings. The Hīnayāna teachings (including the four noble truths), because of their ontological "realism," were conducive to misunderstanding, and therefore required further explanation (*neyārtha*); the Perfection of Wisdom (*prajñāpāramitā*) and Mādhyamika teachings were similarly in need of interpretation (*neyārtha*) because of their apparent nihilism. Only the Yogācāra teachings, because of their clear discrimination between what "really" exists (the "absolute," *pariniṣpanna,* nature of phenomena) and what does not exist (the "imagined," *parikalpita,* nature), is unambiguous and definitive (*nītārtha*), requiring no further interpretation.[32] Different schools, of course, have differed on which of the Buddha's teachings are definitive and which interpretable, but that some such type of distinction is valid has been assumed by virtually all subsequent Buddhist thinkers[33]—after all, despite its possible circularity and trans-sectarian inconclusiveness, such a hermeneutical principle does give a Buddhist philosopher a way of resolving apparent contradictions in the Buddha's teaching, and of organizing the massive accumulation of received tradition. For our immediate purposes, the principle's most important trait is that it grants at least provisional truth-status to a vast number of teachings that are, at least from an ultimate perspective, false. Because the "lower" teachings are spiritually beneficial for those to whom they are addressed, they are, in their way, true. Their truth, however—much like the *Lotus* father's promise of three animal-carts—only is a function of their utility, and the criterion of truth that seems to be invoked is a pragmatic one.

D. COHERENCE AND INCOHERENCE: HOW TO MAKE SENSE OF NOTHING

If truth as correspondence is undermined by these ethical and hermeneutical applications of Mahāyāna "method" (*upāya*), then it seems utterly to be shattered when we turn to the literature of the Mahāyāna "wisdom" (*prajñā*) tradition, as exemplified by the Perfection of Wisdom

---

32 Lamotte (1935) chapter 7.

33 The Indo-Tibetan tradition has retained the *nītārtha/neyārtha* distinction; the equivalent in the Sino-Japanese tradition is the *p'an chiao* system of ranking teachings from most elementary to most advanced.

sūtras and the Mādhyamika and Yogācāra schools of philosophy. Thus, we read in the Perfection of Wisdom sūtra generally conceded to be the oldest, the *Aṣṭasāhasrikā*, that both buddhahood and nirvāṇa are like an illusion, or a dream, i.e., that they are "unreal."[34] In a similar vein, the most famous Perfection of Wisdom text, the *Heart Sūtra* (*Prajñāpāramitāhṛdaya*), proclaims that "there is no suffering, origination, cessation or path, no gnosis, no attainment. . ."[35] This sort of negative rhetoric suffuses the Perfection of Wisdom literature, as it does the major philosophical works of Nāgārjuna (second century C.E.?), founder of the Madhyamaka. Nāgārjuna writes, for instance, that "As an illusion, as a dream, as a celestial city: thus has generation, thus has duration, thus has destruction been characterized,"[36] that "nirvāṇa is non-existent"[37] and that "nirvāṇa is not in the least distinct from saṃsāra."[38] If the dialectic of the Mādhyamika is aimed primarily at demonstrating the utter vacuity (or "voidness,"or "emptiness": *śūnyatā*) of all entities and concepts, including those truths solemnly asserted by earlier Buddhist traditions, then discussion in the Yogācāra centers on rejecting the existence of any "world"external to perceptions of it, and asserting that the "world"is, in fact, simply a mental construction. In the words of the *Laṅkāvatāra Sūtra*,

> External objects are not admitted; the triple world is taught as not being anything but the Mind [*citta*] itself; multiplicities of external existences are not accepted; there is no rising of the elements, nor their disappearence, nor their continuation, nor their differentiation.[39]

The implication of this sort of rhetoric for truth-theory would seem to be, quite simply, that there *are* no objective truths. All truth-claims are ultimately unwarranted, because the "real" entities that are supposed to "correspond" to the entities described in truth-statements turn out, on closer analysis, to be either non-self-sufficient, hence ontologically vacuous (*śūnya*); or mere mental constructs (*vijñaptimātra, cittamātra*), beyond which there is no extrinsic object. What, then, of the four noble truths, those most fundamental of early Buddhist truth-claims? It would seem, in the

---

34 Vaidya (1963a) 20; tr. Conze (1973) 98-99.
35 See Conze (1958) 89.
36 MMK, vii, 34; text and tr. Inada (1970) 70; tr. only at Streng (1967) 192.
37 MMK, xxv, 4; tr. Inada (1970)154-55; Streng (1967) 215.
38 MMK, xxv, 19; tr. Inada (1970) 158; Streng (1967) 217.
39 Suzuki (1978)180; S. at Vaidya (1963b) 84.

light of a Mādhyamika or Yogācāra analysis, that they lack the sort of "correspondent" reality attributed to them by the *nikāya/āgama* tradition, since the "world" to which they would correspond is denied self-sufficiency and objectivity. Are they true in any sense, then? Can they be said, at least, to "cohere" with a given conceptual scheme, and therefore to be true in some provisional sense, or does their lack of self-sufficiency and/or objectivity render them utterly false?

The latter view, which holds that a critique of ontological self-sufficiency or epistemic objectivity entails nothing short of nihilism, is put forward by Nāgārjuna's hypothetical opponent at the beginning of the twenty-fourth chapter of the *Madhyamakakārikā*: "If everything is void," he maintains, "then there will be neither generation nor destruction, and it follows that the four noble truths are non-existent"[40] furthermore, "through voidness [*śūnyatā*], the true existence of results, right and wrong, and all conventional and worldly [knowledge] is undermined."[41] A nihilistic interpretation of the concept of voidness (or of mind-only) is not, by any means, merely a hypothetical possibility; it consistently was adopted by Buddhism's opponents wherever the religion spread, nor have Buddhists themselves been immune to it, as two examples from the history of the Tibetan tradition will illustrate.

In the first instance, an apparently nihilistic view was propounded by the Chinese Ch'an master Ho-shang Mo-ho-yen (T. Hva shang Mahāyāna), who debated doctrinal matters with a number of Indian pandits at the court of the Tibetan king Khri srong lde btsan, late in the eighth century C.E. Mo-ho-yen propounded an instantaneous path to enlightenment through the elimination of all discursive thought, while the Indians (led by the great ācārya Kamalaśīla) were concerned to preserve the integrity of the traditional sequence of practices, in which wisdom was founded on morality, analysis and concentration. Mo-ho-yen believed that the truth was verbally incommunicable and he was reluctant to debate, claiming that he preferred silence. Compelled nevertheless to debate, he consistently cited scriptural passages that seemed to show that truth had nothing to do with propositions and everything to do with an unmediated insight into reality, and, consequently, that conventional analysis and practices were both irrelevant and spiritually harmful.[42] Whether Mo-ho-yen really rejected

---

40 MMK, xxiv, 1; tr. Inada (1970) 144; Streng (1967) 212.

41 MMK, xxiv, 6; tr. Inada (1970) 146; Streng (1967) 213.

42 See, e.g., Demiéville (1952); Tucci (1958); and Houston (1980). It is as the "bSam yas debate" that the controversy is best known.

all conventional truths and practices, including the four noble truths, is very much open to debate; what is beyond dispute is that he was perceived by his opponents as a nihilist, nor can there be much doubt that the style of rhetoric employed by the Ch'an/Zen tradition—very much like that of the Perfection of Wisdom literature itself—can at times be uncompromisingly "negative," so concerned is the tradition to undercut the mind's habit of clinging to the self-sufficient or objective existence of entities.

Later in the Tibetan tradition, the founder of the dGe lugs school, Tsong kha pa, assails as nihilists unidentified philosophical opponents, who appear to assert that such passages as the *Heart Sūtra*'s denial of the four noble truths are to be taken at face value: conventional entities simply do not exist, so all conventional truth-claims must be false. Similarly, Nāgārjuna's statement, "If I set forth any proposition, then I would be in error; / I do not set forth any proposition, so I am not in error,"[43] is taken to mean that no propositions whatever are to be entertained. Taken literally, these statements appear to rule out cosmology, logic and virtually any sort of philosophical analysis, not to mention various conventional path practices. What, if anything, they *permit* is not clear—though their proponents may have intended, by denying the conventional, radically to open the way to the ultimate—presupposing that the two truths, rather than reinforcing each other, are radically opposed.[44]

In order to obviate nihilism such as this, mainstream Mahāyānists have explained their own negative rhetoric by appealing to the notion that there are, in fact, two types of truth (*satyadvaya*), conventional or "mundane superficial" (*lokasaṃvṛti*) truths, and ultimate truths that are true in the "highest sense" (*paramārtha*). Thus, Nāgārjuna, in replying to his opponent's contention that his dialectic entails nihilism, insists that

43 VV 29. See Bhattacharya (1978) 1st part, 23 and 2nd part, 29; and Streng (1967) 224.

44 Tsong kha pa's discussion is found in, e.g., the *lhag mthong* ("insight," *vipaśyanā*) section of his *Lam rim chen mo* and in the *Drang nges legs bshed snying po*. On the former, see Napper (1989); for a translation of the latter, see Thurman (1984). It is conceivable that Tsong kha pa's unidentified opponent is a Jo nang pa, an upholder of the doctrine of "voidness of the other" (T. *gzhan stong*), whereby the ultimate truth is what remains when the conventional is removed—if not necessarily negated in the way that Tsong kha pa asserts. On *gzhan stong*, see Hookham (1991).

> The buddhas' teaching of the Dharma is based on two truths, mundane superficial truth and truth in the highest sense. Those who do not know the difference between those two truths do not know the profound principle of the Buddha's teaching.[45]

This distinction between two levels of truth became as fundamental to Mahāyāna philosophical discussion as the distinction between definitive and interpretable scriptures did to Buddhist hermeneutics (indeed, they are closely related, since definitive scriptures are generally held to teach ultimate truths and interpretable scriptures teach conventional truths). Thus, for either a Mādhyamika or a Yogācāra,[46] the assertion of such notions as the four noble truths, production and destruction, and saṃsāra and nirvāṇa, is conventionally valid. From an ultimate point of view, however, such "facts" lack self-sufficiency or objectivity; they are merely void and/or mentally constructed. The ultimate truth for a Mādhyamika is, simply, voidness (which is itself void); for a Yogācāra it is mind-only (which may or may not itself be mind-only).

Nāgārjuna is quite emphatic in his subsequent insistence that each of the two truths must be balanced, that *both* are necessary on the Buddhist path: "Without reliance on the conventional, the ultimate is not taught; without approach to the ultimate, nirvāṇa is not attained."[47] Thus, the assertion of voidness is not the negation of either the Buddhist path or conventional reality, for voidness is a different type of truth, a meta-truth that describes the ultimate mode of existence of all entities asserted by conventional truth-claims. It does not nullify the conventional truth of conventional entities; it merely affirms that in an ultimate sense all conventional phenomena and statements lack self-sufficiency, i.e., they arise depending either on other entities, subjective imputation, or both. Thus, conventional truths like the four noble truths may be "ultimately" false but literally true, since their ultimate falsity reflects not their lack of correspondence to states-of-affairs but, simply, their lack of ontological self-sufficiency. Not only is voidness not a negation of the conventional—it actually is the only principle by which the conventional can be understood to work. If phenomena are self-sufficient or "self-exis-

---

45 MMK, xxiv, 8-9; tr. Inada (1970) 146; Streng (1967) 213.

46 Rather than two truths, Yogācāra actually analyzes reality into "three natures" (*trisvabhāva*), the dependent (*paratantra*), the imaginary (*parikalpita*) and the absolute (*parinispanna*), but the concepts are functionally quite similar.

47 MMK, xxiv, 10; tr. Inada (1970) 146; Streng (1967) 213.

tent" (*svabhāva*), they must be unchanging and independent; if they are unchanging and independent, nothing can "work" in the way that it actually does. It is only because phenomena are impermanent and interdependent—void of self-existence—that the processes of the world can occur as we know them to.[48]

Thus, the fundamental mistake made by Mo-ho-yen and Tsong kha pa's unnamed opponents is to ignore the importance of *both* of the two truths, and to subordinate the conventional utterly to the ultimate. To do this is, in fact, to leave oneself with a "one-truth" rather than a "two-truth" theory. Statements in the Mahāyāna wisdom-tradition that appear to negate the conventional thus must be interpreted carefully. When, for instance, the *Heart Sūtra* insists that "there is no cessation" (i.e., nirvāṇa), it does not mean that in a conventional sense none of us ever will attain the cessation of suffering. After all, the very next sentence of the sūtra insists that bodhisattvas who "rely upon the perfection of wisdom" will "in the end attain nirvāṇa."[49] Thus, the "negation" of cessation merely implies that when subjected to an ultimate analysis the concept of "cessation" cannot be found to exist independently of, for example, the concept of "suffering" or the mind that conceives "cessation."[50] Similarly, Nāgārjuna's statement to the effect that he makes no propositions would, if taken literally, be self-contradictory; it is more likely that what he actually means is that he can make no assertions about entities or concepts taken as ontologically self-sufficient—the way in which, he would maintain, most of us take entities or concepts to exist—since no such self-existent entities or concepts exist to be the subject of propositions.[51]

Indeed, the only way in which the "paradoxes" of Mahāyāna (or other Asian) wisdom-literature can be understood is against the background of a two-truth theory—unless, that is, we assume that Mahāyānists actually are content to entertain contradictory theses (if they were, then Mahāyāna critiques of opposing viewpoints, which presuppose the meaningfulness of contradiction, would themselves be meaningless). Thus, we only can make sense of a work that both as-

---

48 MMK, xxiv, 14; tr. Inada (1970) 147; Streng (1967) 213.

49 See Conze (1958) 93.

50 See, e.g., Rabten (1983) 40-41, for such an interpretation.

51 The point is complex and controversial, and much discussed by both Buddhists and Buddhologists. For a recent discussion that states in greater detail the position I have adopted here, see Thurman (1984) 153ff.; for a recent contrasting view, see Huntington (1989), introduction.

serts and denies the same fact on the same page if we take it to mean that from one perspective the fact is true, but that from another it is false. It is very important to note that "true" and "false" have different usages from perspective to perspective. Thus, truth and falsity in the ultimate sense depend on the presence or absence of ontological self-sufficiency or epistemic objectivity. The four noble truths lack such a mode of existence, and so "ultimately" are false. Their truth from a conventional perspective is *not,* however the opposite of their ultimate falsity: they do not have "conventional" ontological self-sufficiency. Conventionally, truth and falsity depend on correspondence to states-of-affairs, and conventionally the four noble truths do reflect the way things are, so they are "true."

We still may be tempted, however, to infer that the ultimate perspective does relativize conventional truths radically, thereby making them true at best in the weaker sense entailed by a pragmatic or coherence criterion of truth. This temptation may perhaps be curbed if we view the levels of discourse in a Mahāyāna text as a set of Chinese boxes. The innermost box in a given text may insist on the reality of, say, the four noble truths; around that, then, will be a box that negates those same truths from the ultimate perspective, apparently denying or relativizing them. There is, however, a box outside even the "ultimate" box, and that is the box that represents the composition of the work itself. If we accept as axiomatic that Buddhist works are written for the purpose of assisting their readers to attain enlightenment, then we see that the "real" perspective from which such "anti-correspondent" doctrines as skill-in-means, voidness and mind-only are offered is a perspective that centers on salvation, hence, at the very minimum, on the assumption that there is a fundamental set of problems that human beings share, and that there exists a potential solution to that set of problems. It may be that the "solution" is to be arrived at through disabusing oneself of the idea that problems and solutions exist self-sufficiently or independent of a problem-solving consciousness, but the problem-solution framework remains the *sine qua non* of the entire "spiritual" exercise, and those who pose the problems and solutions, therefore, must be assumed to be quite serious in their enterprise. They must believe, in effect, that the problems and solutions they pose are meaningful and real—whether or not they withstand the sort of ultimate philosophical analysis favored by the tradition. The "problem" with which all traditional Buddhists begin, of course, is saṃsāra, and the "solution" nirvāṇa, and to the degree that any Buddhist—whatever their subsequent rhetoric—must take these seriously if they are to write a Buddhist work, we can say that for all practical purposes saṃsāra and nirvāṇa must be assumed to be "the way things really are," and thus in some meaningful way to "correspond" to actual states-of-affairs.

Thus, just as those Western philosophical arguments that purport to overturn the correspondence theory of truth still must presuppose it in some way, so, too, Buddhist texts and traditions that seem to overturn all conventional notions of a "real" or objective world still assume that there is a "way things are"—broadly divisible into "saṃsāra" and "nirvāṇa"—that makes the whole enterprise of criticizing "objective reality" meaningful. To that degree, objective reality may be negated from a particular analytical perspective, but as a construct without which human activity would be virtually impossible, it is upheld—and with it, correspondence as the "real" criterion of truth for Buddhists, even those who might deny that this is their criterion.

Therefore, each of the foregoing candidates for a "pragmatic" or "coherence" theory of truth rests on the assumption that the bifurcation of the cosmos into saṃsāra and nirvāṇa, spelled out in the four noble truths, is the real state-of-affairs from which inquiry begins. The concept of ethical skill-in-means, thus, may "pragmatically" loosen the connection between morality and external behavior, or between truth and factuality, but skill-in-means only are applied as a spiritual expedient against the background assumption that saṃsāra and nirvāṇa are the two options "really" open to beings. The distinction between direct and interpretable teachings may relativize many traditional Buddhist truth-statements by describing them as "merely" pragmatic. But even "definitive" teachings are "merely" pragmatic, since they are "definitive" only to the degree that they are the most crucial principles to be understood in one's movement from saṃsāra to nirvāṇa—whose reality is, again, the truly definitive ground for the composition and interpretation of texts. The negative rhetoric of the Perfection of Wisdom and Madhyamaka, the "idealism" of Yogācāra, and the "absurdity" of Zen may all *appear* to establish the four noble truths as true only to the degree that they are coherent with some limited conceptual scheme (called "elaboration," *prapañca*, in Madhyamaka, and "imputation," *vikalpa*, in Yogācāra), but we must recall that the "falsity" of the four noble truths according to these systems is very much relative to a particular philosophical perspective that is pursued only because it is assumed to be "useful" in promoting our movement from saṃsāra to nirvāṇa, which, regardless of whether they ultimately are "void" or "mind-only," do correspond to states-of-affairs. Thus, even though such particulars of Buddhist cosmology as past and future lives, the "law" of karma, or the procedures of the Buddhist path may be "void" or "mind-only," their "reality" in the conventional, "correspondent" sense of the term is not compromised. A Mādhyamika dialectician, a Yogācāra metaphysician and a Zen master will, in fact, maintain—as certainly as their more straightforward "Hīnayāna" co-religionists—that if our karma is bad we "really" may fall to a lower realm in the next life, and that if we practice the Buddhist path we "really" may attain enlightenment.[52]

52 For a more detailed discussion of many of these issues, see R. Jackson (1989).

5. *What Buddhists Claim Is True*

We have seen that in the Buddhist philosophical tradition, as in that of the West, the question of what it means for a statement to be true is a complex one, and that Buddhists—particularly Mahāyānists—have been as cognizant as their Western counterparts that many of the conventions that we consider true must be qualified by the recognition that in some ultimate sense they cannot be found to be realities independent of other entities and/or some conceptual scheme. At the same time, the relativization of conventional truths by an ultimate perspective does not make those truths less real from a *conventional* viewpoint, which still depends on the idea that our truth-claims must in some way correspond to a "real world"—whatever its ultimate nature—if they are to be meaningful. What, then, do Buddhists claim is the case? What is the "state-of-affairs" that the Dharma describes? We already have discussed the four noble truths as the "cornerstones" of the Buddhist world-view, and indicated at least generally the presuppositions that they appear to entail. In this section, we will examine in somewhat greater detail the sort of cosmology and soteriology that these truths involve, taking care to distinguish variations within the tradition. This, in turn, will provide us with the basic set of propositions whose truth-status Buddhists have debated over the centuries, among themselves, and with their non-Buddhist opponents.

A. SAṂSĀRA AND NIRVĀṆA

The proposition that is in some ways the most fundamental of all to Buddhists is that which we uncovered toward the end of the previous section, i.e., the claim that the fundamental structure of the cosmos is twofold, divisible into saṃsāra and nirvāṇa. Saṃsāra, in its broadest sense, is the unsatisfactory or "suffering" cycle of existence that is the lot of sentient beings still under the control of deluded actions. Nirvāṇa, in its broadest sense, is the state or condition, attainable via a spiritual path, that is the cessation of saṃsāra. The degree to which this proposition is fundamental to Buddhism is illustrated by the fact that, before he had enunciated a single item of what would become his Dharma, the Buddha framed his very quest for enlightenment by setting saṃsāra—especially the prospect of endless rebirth—as the "problem" he sought to solve, and nirvāṇa as the hypothetical "solution."[1] In taking saṃsāra and nirvāṇa as the axes of his cosmology, the Buddha was neither unique nor original; by the time he arrived on the Indian scene,[2] it was commonly (though by no means universally) assumed that sentient existence was characterized by a migration from body to body, whose end was devoutly to be wished and earnestly to be sought. On the evidence of the Vedas, the concepts of saṃsāra and nirvāṇa were not a part of the world-view brought to India by the Ārya invaders of the second millenium B.C.E.; indeed, their religion centered primarily on pleasing the gods, *devas*, so that life could be long, productive and prosperous, while their eschatology was hazy at best, centering on the expectation of going after death either to the blessed "world of the fathers"or the tenebrous "house of clay."

Such classical Indian concepts as reincarnation, karma and liberation (mokṣa) and such practices as yoga and meditation (*bhavanā*) developed only slowly, for complex reasons that may be rooted in the disquieting social changes afflicting the eastern Gangetic area from early in the first millenium B.C.E. onward. These changes included the unhappy absorption of many formerly independent "tribes" of Āryas into great imperial states such as Magadha and Kosala; the growth of new economic classes who felt excluded by the brahmanical rituals that had become the center of religious life; and ongoing contacts with people and ideas, outside the Ārya fold, that may have suggested alternative world-views and life-styles. Whatever the reasons, we see in the later Brāhmaṇas and the early Upaniṣads a gradual restatement of India's cosmology and religious agenda. The cosmos increasingly is viewed as a cycle of more or less unsatisfactory rebirths (saṃsāra) that is fueled by deluded actions, karmas. The highest goal of sentient striving is seen as release from that cycle (mokṣa, or nirvāṇa), a condition of eternal and imperishable bliss to be won—most commonly—through the direct realization of some vital metaphysical principle.[3]

Delineations of the particulars of saṃsāra and nirvāṇa and the way one perpetuated the former or reached the latter quite naturally var-

---

1 See especially the various *suttas* in which some semblance of a biography is given by the Buddha, such as *Ariyapariyesana Sutta, Mahāpadāna Suttanta* and *Catusparisat Sutta* of the *Majjhima Nikāya*.

2 The dates for the Buddha commonly accepted by scholars are 563-483 B.C.E., although these are based on an arguable set of inferences from later Aśokan inscriptions and Sinhalese texts.

3 For clear accounts of this crucial period of Indian history, see, e.g., Basham (1959) chapters II and III; Lamotte (1958); Jayatilleke (1980); and Campbell (1962) esp. 183-84.

ied. The early Upaniṣads, for instance, begin to articulate what became a classic Hindu view, namely that saṃsāra is perpetuated by our ignorance of the fact that we have within us an imperishable principle, ātman, that is identical with the immutable ground of the cosmos, brahman, and that only a profound realization of this fact will free us from the vicissitudes of the delusively multiple world in which we have lost ourselves. The group that would come to be known as the Jainas insisted that the suffering and rebirth of the soul (*jīva*) were due primarily to its obscuration by karma, and that if karmas were "shed" through austerities and abstinence from thought and action, the soul once again would shine purely, ascending to the peak of the cosmos to reside in perpetual bliss. There were many other groups, both orthodox (brāḥmaṇa, or *āstika*: proto-Hindu) and heterodox (śramaṇa, or *nāstika*), including the Ājīvikas (of whom Upaka, who first doubted the Buddha, was a member), materialists and various yogins of the sort Siddhārtha Gautama studied under before he became a buddha. Most of these groups embraced the saṃsāra-nirvāṇa cosmology, a few rejected it, but all had in one way or other to respond to it, much as medieval Christian mystics had to respond to theological notions of the relation between God and humanity, and as people in the contemporary world must respond to the world-view stated or implied by science.

Thus, given the cultural and religious background into which the Buddha was born, it hardly can surprise us that he framed his search in terms of the saṃsāra-nirvāṇa cosmology—taken quite literally as the belief in a cycle of rebirths and the prospect of attaining an eternally blissful release from that cycle.[4] Thus, the problem for the Buddha, as for so many of his contemporaries, was to discover the "keys" to saṃsāra and nirvāṇa, and this, clearly, he believed he had done—if tradition be accepted—while sitting under the bodhi tree in Bodh Gaya. The "keys" to saṃsāra and nirvāṇa, in turn, may be formulated as the four noble truths: the *nature* of saṃsāra is described by the truth of suffering, its *causes* by the truth of origination; the *nature* of nirvāṇa is described by the truth of cessation, its *causes* by the truth of path. Let us, then, examine the particulars of these four great truth-claims.

---

4 As Jayatilleke notes (1980: 371), "The conception of *salvation from* is intimately connected in Buddhism with the belief in rebirth. It is therefore an integral part of Early Buddhist belief and much of Buddhism would be unintelligible without it."

B. THE TRUTH OF SUFFERING

The truth of suffering involves the claim that all saṃsāric existence is either implicitly or explicitly unsatisfactory. Birth, sickness, aging, dying, separation from the pleasant, encounter with the unpleasant and not getting what one wants all entail suffering, either physical, mental, or both. This suffering is to be found not only in the human realm, but in the other five realms (*gati*) of saṃsāra, too: hell-beings suffer from extremes of heat or cold; "hungry ghosts" (*pretas*) suffer from thirst, hunger and excruciating forms of indigestion; animals suffer from fear, stupidity and slavery; and even the gods of the two "highest" realms (*devas* and *asuras*), though possessed of longevity, power and pleasure far beyond that of humans, are too absorbed in pleasure to concern themselves with the Dharma, and die miserable, uncontrolled deaths that often are followed by rebirth in a lower realm.[5] Thus, "suffering" involves not only the obvious physical or mental pain that all of us experience at one time or another, but also what we would call "pleasure," which Buddhists refer to as "suffering of change," since pleasure is transient, and sooner or later will be replaced by neutral or painful sensations. In the broadest sense, according to Buddhists, suffering pervades any being that has uncontrollably appropriated the five[6] aggregates (*skandhas*) that form what we usually call a "person": form or matter (*rūpa*), sensation (*vedanā*), conception or recognition (*samjñā*), dispositions or "formations" (*saṃskāra*) and cognition (*vijñāna*).

Buddhists at different places and times obviously have varied in their degree of concern with the "problem" of rebirth. It is, for instance, emphasized little in the "this-worldly" perspective of Zen, while being fundamental to the fully articulated forms of most Tibetan traditions. At the same time, until very recently it has stood at least in the background of virtually all Buddhist traditions, both Hīnayāna and Mahāyāna. Pre-modern Buddhists certainly recognized that the six realms could be seen as symbolic, say, of human psychological states, but there is no real evidence that any of them took the realms as *merely* symbolic, i.e., as *only* denoting psychological states.

---

5 The deva realm, in turn, is subdivided into types of gods inhabiting the desire realm (*kāmadhātu*), in which the other five realms are entirely situated, the form realm (*rūpadhātu*) and the formless realm (*arūpyadhātu*). The latter two are the rebirths that ensue for those who die having achieved one of the four "form" and four "formless" meditative absorptions (*dhyānas*) accepted by Buddhists as attainable by Buddhists and non-Buddhists alike.

6 Four in the formless realm, where there is no matter (*rūpa*).

To the degree that they believed in the six realms in a literal sense, Buddhists have, perforce, believed in past and future lives, i.e., in rebirth. To the degree that they have believed in rebirth, in turn, they have accepted that some aspect of the "mind"(which comprises all aggregates but form) must be independent of particular bodies, hence that some form of mind-body dualism must be the case.[7] To the degree that the realms of saṃsāra—even when they appear to be pleasurable—are seen to be *suffering,* Buddhists have presupposed that there exists a supreme pleasure that does not decay—since it is only in comparison to such a notion of pleasure that transient worldly pleasures can be defined as "suffering."

C. THE TRUTH OF ORIGINATION

The truth of origination describes the causes of the suffering that pervades saṃsāra. The cause of suffering is conventionally asserted to be craving, or "thirst"(*tṛṣṇa*), those compulsions for sense-pleasure, the annihilation of pain, and existence that drive us from rebirth to rebirth. More precisely, we are impelled by defilements (*kleśa*) and actions (*karma*). Actions, whether of body, speech or mind, "plant"in the mental continuum "seeds"that will bear "fruit"in the future as the events and circumstances of this life and future lives. Since results are commensurate with the actions that "seed"them, and since the vast majority of sentient actions spring from defilement, from such basic forces as attachment, aversion and ignorance—it stands to reason that the majority of results are unpleasant, whether in this life or the next. Although craving may be the defilement that propels the wheel of saṃsāra, the "root"defilement generally is seen by Buddhists after the earliest period to be ignorance (*avidyā*), which is, on the one hand, an ignorance of the way in which cause-and-effect functions morally through the "law"of karma, but which is, most importantly, the ignorant grasping after an immutable, independent self (*ātman*), the philosophical or instinctive sense of "I."[8]

---

7 There has been considerable disagreement among Buddhists over just what it is that transmigrates, or takes rebirth; it is sufficient for our purposes to note that it is not an immutable soul, like the Hindu ātman or the Jaina *jīva,* and is some aspect of a being's mental makeup, e.g., its cognition aggregate (perhaps the most common view).

8 It has been suggested that the dual identification of origination with craving and ignorance reflects a basic ambivalence in the early Buddhist movement, where some monks, more inclined to tranquillity (*śamatha*) meditation, tended to identify the passions that could be stilled by such meditation as the yogin's main foe; while others, more inclined to insight (*vipaśyanā*) meditation,

Clinging to such a self, we fail to apprehend the essential transience of all conditioned phenomena (ourselves included), and at the same time generate acquisitiveness and defensiveness for the sake of this self, which in turn become attachment and aversion. Belief in a self, thus, generates the whole complex of defilements that propels us through saṃsāra.[9]

As with the truth of suffering, the general parameters of the truth of origination have remained largely intact since the formulation of the earliest Buddhist traditions. Where there have been variations, they have tended to arise in the interpretation of the "ignorance" that keeps us circling in saṃsāra: each new Buddhist school of thought and practice quite naturally assumed that ignorance of *its* fundamental principle was the ignorance that perpetuates saṃsāra. Thus, a Theravādin might insist that "ignorance" is the belief in an immutable self, a Mādhyamika that it is grasping at the "inherent existence" of any entity or concept, a Yogācāra that it is the acceptance of entities external to the consciousness that cognizes them, a Zen master that it is ignorance of our innate enlightenment, and a Nichiren priest that it is our failure to recognize the supremacy of the *Lotus Sūtra*.

Regardless of their varying notions of ignorance, however, most Buddhists, both Hīnayāna and Mahāyāna, have accepted the basic assumptions underlying the truth of origination, which center on the fundamental principle of dependent origination (*pratītya samutpāda*), i.e., the universal operation of causality. For Buddhist soteriology, perhaps the most important corollary of the "law" of dependent origination is its application to the moral realm, in the form of the

---

identified ignorance as that which had to be opposed.

9 The process of the origination of saṃsāra is described in somewhat greater detail by way of the "twelve links" (*nidānas*): (1) ignorance entails defiled actions, which leave (2) (karmic) formations in the mental continuum, some of which will come to fruition as the initial (3) cognition of a particular rebirth. Cognition entails a particular combination of aggregates, a (4) name-and-form, which itself entails (5) six "entrances," five for sense-objects, one for mental objects. Such entrances imply (6) contact between subject and object, which leads to (7) sensations, pleasant, painful or neutral. Sensations entail, in turn, a (8) craving for their continuance or discontinuance, which turns soon to (9) grasping. Grasping is a fundamental mode of action throughout life, and at the end of life, one grasps for continued existence, thereby (10) becoming still another set of aggregates, which, like all others, undergoes the inevitable processes of (11) rebirth and (12) aging and dying. Since the seeds of ignorant actions are being sown at virtually every moment, the rebirths one is "scheduled" to experience are limitless—especially since this process has been underway beginninglessly.

concept of karma. In other words, it is in the very nature of the cosmos that sentient actions have positive or negative "qualities," and actions of a particular quality or intensity will—given the reality of dependent origination—entail reactions, or results, of an "appropriate" (if not always "equal") quality or intensity.[10] Other corollaries of the principle of dependent origination include the assumption that the set of causes and results that is the cosmos is beginningless—since every result presupposes a cause, and the chain must therefore be infinite—and multiple—since the variety of results cannot be accounted for by a single cause. The beginninglessness and multiplicity of the causal realm, in turn, obviates the possibility that there is a single creator of the sort posited by Jews, Christians, Muslims and most Hindus. A final, important implication of dependent origination is that, since all results have particular causes, to the degree that a cause can be known and controlled, the result can be controlled. This includes the idea that if a cause is eliminated, its effect will be, too; thus, if the cause of saṃsāra has been identified, controlled and eliminated, then saṃsāra will be eliminated, too. Saṃsāra, hence, is subject to cessation.

D. THE TRUTH OF CESSATION

The truth of cessation in its most basic sense is the assertion that there is a state or condition that transcends the suffering cycle of saṃsāra and which, once attained, never is subject to decay. It is the state whose attainment permits the Buddha to proclaim, after his enlightenment, "My liberation is unshakeable, this is my last life, there is no more rebirth for me"[11]; "birth is destroyed, spiritual practice is complete, what is to be done is done, there is no more of this sort of existence"; and "the contaminants are destroyed, what is to be done is done, the burden is laid down, the true goal is attained, the fetters of becoming are destroyed, I am liberated by perfect knowledge."[12] This *summum bonum* is generally known as nirvāṇa, which means, literally, "extinction." Nirvāṇa is said, at

---

10 Thus, to cite a common example, murder in this life will result in one's being murdered in a future life and/or being reborn in a miserable realm, usually hell. The severity of the "reaction" to any action is dependent on the "heaviness" of the karma, i.e., the attitude, frequency, etc., with which an act is committed.

11 M, i, 167; tr. Chalmers (1926-27) I, 165.

12 For complete references on these various "victory formulas" found in the *nikāyas*, see Rhys Davids and Stede (1972) 77; see also Ergardt (1977) 1-8; and Horner (1936) 134-35.

various times, to involve the extinction of contaminants, of ignorance, attachment and aversion, and of the five aggregates, and to be "unborn, unchanging, uncreated, uncompounded."[13] The question naturally has been raised whether nirvāṇa thus is extinction in the sense of utter annihilation. The question is not easily answered, and only can become meaningful when we are careful to distinguish two fundamental usages of the word nirvāṇa: as the state attained by the Buddha under the bodhi tree in Bodh Gaya, and out of which he functioned for the next forty-five years of his life; or as the condition an enlightened one enters at death, their "final" nirvāṇa (*parinirvāṇa*). If we take nirvāṇa as the former, then clearly the "extinction" involved is not total, since, although the Buddha had extinguished all contaminants and defilements, he certainly continued to "exist" in the sense of possessing aggregates. It is nirvāṇa as *parinirvāṇa* that is the more problematic, for once this condition has been attained, the aggregates are extinguished and one ceases to influence or be influenced by the world. This sounds a great deal like complete extinction, and yet we must remember that the question whether the Tathāgata exists, does not exist, both exists and does not exist or neither exists nor does not exist was one that the Buddha refused to answer. It is dangerous on our part to speculate what he "meant" by this refusal, but it is worth noting that to say that the Tathāgata does not exist after death is inappropriate: this at least leaves the door open for his possible existence in some manner very different from our usual sense of "existence," "existence" being excluded as an option because of the misunderstanding its assertion is likely to entail.

If the Buddhist tradition has generally been consistent in its acceptance of the specifics of the truths of suffering and origination, there is far less unanimity on the question of the nature of nirvāṇa: considerable differences exist not only between Hīnayāna and Mahāyāna, but *within* each of these traditional divisions. The *summum bonum* of the Theravāda and, to the degree that we can infer it from the *nikāyas* and *āgamas*, of early Buddhism is seen as a state entirely beyond suffering or change, a sphere of immutable bliss. One who has attained this state is generally characterized as an arhant, a "worthy one." At the very least, an arhant is beyond saṃsāra, free from all defilement and suffering, possessed of the certain "knowledge of the destruction of all contaminants" (*sarvāsravakṣayajñāna*). Depending, then, on the degree of their experience with the dhyānas, they may possess various other "superknowledges" (*abhijñā*), including clairvoyance, clairaudience,

---

13 *Udāna,* 80; tr. Woodward (1948) II, 98.

retrocognition, telepathy and magical powers (such as flying, walking through walls, etc.). Arhants who have experienced the full range of the dhyānas possess all of the superknowledges, but they still lack the historical role and pedagogical skill of the highest of all arhants, a buddha. Buddhas appear at regular intervals in the world-cycle, but they are generally separated by thousands of years. Śākyamuni Buddha, né Siddhārtha Gautama, was the fourth buddha of this particular kalpa; he lived well over two thousand years ago, and it will be many centuries yet before his successor, Maitreya, descends. It is important to note that although a buddha is cognitively and pedagogically superior to other arhants, spiritually they all are equal, since the essential criterion of spiritual "victory" is transcendence of saṃsāra, which has been effected by all arhants. Although the various "Hīnayāna" traditions agree on these basics, as well as on the fact that a buddha no longer is a part of the world-scene once he has left the body in which he attained enlightenment, the Theravāda does depart from "early" Buddhism in its insistence that a buddha is omniscient, an attribute that is expressly denied him by the *nikāyas*.[14]

In the Mahāyāna, the arhant ideal of the Hīnayāna is disparaged, and the *summum bonum* redefined as unexcelled perfect enlightenment (*anuttarasamyaksaṃbodhi*), or buddhahood (*buddhatva*). Arhantship is disparaged for a variety of reasons: its achievement is motivated by a selfish concern with one's own liberation only; arhants are content with a quiescent final nirvāṇa, happy to be off the world-stage; arhants fail to realize the utter voidness (*śūnyatā*) of all phenomena, their realization being restricted to the no-self (*anātman*) of persons; arhants lack the great skill-in-means that ought to be exercised by an enlightened being; arhants have eliminated the gross obstacles to perfection, but not the subtle ones—or at least not the traces of the subtle ones.[15] Mahāyānists did not deny that an arhant was liberated from saṃsāra, but this achievement no longer was regarded as the *summum bonum*. In some versions of Mahāyāna soteriology,[16] *arhants* were doomed to an eternity of "mere" nirvāṇa, having forever lost the opportunity to progress to the greater goal of buddhahood; in other versions—these

---

14 See Jayatilleke (1980) *passim*; and D, i, 17-18, tr. Rhys Davids and Rhys Davids (1952) I, 29; D, iii, 134, tr. ibid. III, 126; and M, i, 482, tr. e.g., Jayatilleke (1980) 468.

15 The *Lotus Sūtra* (see Vaidya [1960a], Kern [1963]) is a particularly rich source of polemics such as the preceding.

16 E.g., the writings of certain Yogācāras, such as Asaṅga.

came to predominate—it was assumed that after a period of selfish indulgence in the bliss of liberation, an arhant would be "awakened" by the power of the buddhas, and would continue the ascent to full buddhahood.[17]

The buddhahood attained at the culmination of the Mahāyāna path was a state considerably more exalted than that attributed to Śākyamuni Buddha by the *nikāya/āgama* or Theravādin traditions. A fully enlightened buddha was eventually said to consist of three "bodies" existing on different levels of subtlety: the Dharma Body (*dharmakāya*), which represents the perfection of mental abilities, is totally free from the slightest trace of even the subtlest obscuration,[18] and at the same time totally omniscient, totally compassionate, and supremely powerful in guiding sentient beings; the Enjoyment Body (*saṃbhogakāya*), which represents the perfection of communicative abilities, is an "ethereal" body, replete with the various "marks" of a great being, that is established in the *akaniṣṭha* heaven, where it teaches the Mahāyāna to high-level bodhisattvas until (if there is such a time) the end of saṃsāra; the Transformation Body (*nirmāṇakāya*), which represents the perfection of bodily activity, is multiple, the countless "physical" forms taken by a buddha in order help sentient beings. Transformation Bodies may be inanimate or animate, animal or human, but the best known are those periodic appearances we call "historical buddhas," such as Siddhārtha Gautama in the past and Maitreya in the future. For the Mahāyāna, it still is theoretically possible for a fully-enlightened being to "disappear" into final nirvāṇa, but it almost never occurs, because the force of compassion will prevent the buddha from doing so as long as there are sentient beings yet to be delivered. Thus, Śākyamuni's "*parinirvāṇa*" was not the utter disappearance of that buddha, but merely the withdrawal of one of his Transformation Bodies. "Śākyamuni" is, in fact, eternal in lifespan, and virtually infinite in his manifestations.[19] This is the classic Mahāyāna

---

17 It ought to be noted that the term *nirvāṇa* sometimes is used by Mahāyānists to denote the limited state achieved by arhants, and sometimes as synonymous with buddhahood.

18 This "negative" aspect of the Dharma Body often is referred to in later traditions as the Essential Body (*svabhāvakāya*).

19 For discussions of the late, fully developed Mahāyāna notions of buddhahood, see, e.g., The Dalai Lama (1985) 99-109 and Williams (1989). The concepts were developed systematically primarily within the Yogācāra, and are fully exposed for the first time in such texts as the *Mahāyānasūtrālaṃkāra*, attributed to Maitreya, and the *Mahāyānasaṃgraha* of Asaṅga.

view of buddhahood; it was modified, at various times, by different traditions that arose within the Mahāyāna. Thus, the tantric traditions elaborate still further by positing such "bodies" as the Body of Great Bliss (*mahāsukhakāya*) or Diamond Body (*vajrakāya*); "mind"-oriented meditative traditions such as the Great Seal (*mahāmudrā*) and Great Perfection (T. *rdzogs chen*) "psychologize" the three buddha-bodies as the voidness, clarity and referentiality (or compassion) of the mind[20]; while the Zen tradition tends to de-emphasize (at least rhetorically) the extraordinariness of buddhahood, seeming at times to equate it "merely" with a direct realization of the nature of reality—itself sometimes simply described as "ordinary mind."

There is considerable divergence among the various versions of the *summum bonum* posited by different Buddhists, but all do agree that the truth of cessation is true, that there does exist some state that transcends the suffering of saṃsāra. To assert this, in turn, is to assert that the nature of the mind is such that its faults can be eliminated—since it is the mind that determines whether one is deluded or enlightened. Thus, the mind is held in some sense to be perfectible, capable of knowledge that is both true and salvific, able to comprehend the truth that "will make you free." Thus, the epistemology posited in Buddhism—for all its analysis of the delusions that we superimpose on reality—is an "optimistic" one, maintaining that we are, in the final analysis, capable of truly and directly knowing reality (how "reality" is defined will, of course, vary from tradition to tradition), and that knowledge of reality can be spiritually liberating.

E. THE TRUTH OF PATH

The truth of path, finally, centers on the assertion that there exists a set of procedures that, ultimately, issues in the cessation of suffering: as the Buddha remarks, the goal and the path flow into each other like the Ganges and Jamuna rivers.[21] It is probably in their definitions of the path that the traditions that call themselves Buddhist are most at variance; in-

---

20 See, e.g., Wang-ch'ug dor-je (1978) 119-20, 144-46; and Jig-me ling-pa (1982) 96. These two traditions, which are important parts of Tibetan Buddhism to this day (emphasized, respectively, by the bKa' brgyud and rNying ma schools) arose in India among the *mahāsiddhas*, great tantric wonder-workers. Rhetorically, and viewed in isolation, the Great Symbol and Great Perfection are similar to Zen; in a larger historical and practical context, however, they are inseparable from tantrism, which has had little influence on Zen.

21 D, ii, 223; tr. Rhys Davids and Rhys Davids (1951) II, 261.

deed, traditions often are distingiuished from one another primarily on the basis of the path upon which they set their followers. To delineate all the varieties of Buddhist paths is far beyond the scope of a work such as this. We shall have to content ourselves with laying out the general parameters of the main Hīnayāna and Mahāyāna versions of the path.

It ought to be noted clearly at the outset that the *nikāyas* and *āgamas* contain a bewildering variety of path-schemes, some of them quite systematic, like the famous "eightfold noble path" that comprises the fourth noble truth in the sermon at Sarnath,[22] or the "thirty-seven limbs of enlightenment" spelled out in the *Mahāparinibbāna Sutta*[23]; others somewhat more loosely strung together, like the progression toward knowledge of the destruction of contaminants by way of detachment, the dhyānas, and various psychic powers, as described in the *Samaññaphala Sutta*.[24] There is not, in fact, any single path-scheme that dominates the *nikāyas* and *āgamas*, and it is more than likely that what is represented there is a great number of different "authentic" traditions handed down from earlier times to the writers of the canon, some emphasizing the dhyānas, others stressing dispassion, still others focusing on the centrality of insight into no-self. Which, if any, of these the Buddha himself stressed, historians never will know.

The Theravāda tradition, especially in the person of its greatest scholiast, Buddhaghosa, organizes the canonical material into a coherent scheme that centers on the "threefold" path of morality (P. *sīla*), concentration (*samādhi*) and wisdom (P. *paññā*). Morality, which consists essentially in refraining from such non-virtues as killing, stealing,

---

22 See above, p. 21. Rod Bucknell (1984) has found a number of places in the *nikāyas* where the path should be ten-fold, with the addition of right insight and right liberation.

23 D, ii, 120; tr. Rhys Davids and Rhys Davids (1951) II, 128-30. The thirty-seven are: the four foundations of mindfulness (of body, sensations, mind and dharmas), four exertions (in preventing non-arisen evil from arising, eliminating evil that has arisen, developing good that has not been developed, and maintaining good that has been developed), four powers (of will, thought, energy and investigation), five faculties (faith, energy, mindfulness, concentration and wisdom), five strengths (identical to the faculties, only intensified); seven factors, or qualities, of enlightenment (mindfulness, discrimination, energy, joy, tranquillity, concentration and equanimity) and the eightfold path. For an account of the doctrine of the Buddha in terms of the thirty-seven limbs, see Warder (1980) chapter 4.

24 D, i, 51ff.; tr. Rhys Davids and Rhys Davids (1951) I, 68ff.

adultery, lying, calumny, slander, gossip, covetousness, malice and heresy, is said to be the foundation of the path, a necessary stabilizer of one's life so that one then may stabilize one's mind in concentration. Minimally, concentration involves the ability to contemplate an object without any distraction for as long as one chooses. Additionally, concentration may involve exploration of the dhyānas (P. *jhāna*) and the superknowledges that result from them. Even total familiarity with the dhyānas, however, is considered a basically mundane achievement; in order to be salvific, concentration must be coupled with wisdom. Indeed, with a concentrated mind, one must examine the nature of reality, developing insight into the body, sensations, mind and dharmas until one directly realizes the "truth"—whether formulated as the four noble truths, the "three marks" of phenomena (impermanence, suffering, no-self), or in some other way. When a concentrated mind realizes the truth directly (as opposed to intellectually), then a radical transformation has occurred: one has become an ārya (P. *ariya*), no longer subject to rebirth in the lower realms, destined for enlightenment within, at most, seven lifetimes. Āryas are classed into streamwinners (*srotāpanna*, P. *sotāpanno*), who will be enlightened within seven lives, once-returners (*sakṛdāgāmin*, P. *sakadāgāmin*), who will be enlightened in the next life, non-returners (*anāgāmin*), who will be enlightened from a heavenly realm after death and, finally, those who actually are enlightened, arhants. Arhants, as we have seen, are divisible in various ways, depending on their experience with the dhyānas; most fundamentally, they are divided into those who are "liberated through wisdom," i.e., have developed one-pointed concentration and combined it with wisdom, and those who are "liberated in both ways," i.e., have experience with the dhyānas and have combined it with wisdom. The former sometimes are referred to as "dry" arhants, the latter as "wet" arhants.[25]

Within the Sanskritic schools of the Hīnayāna, the same basic material was organized into a five-path scheme. At the point where one has become utterly convinced that saṃsāra is a raging inferno from which one must escape, one enters the first of the paths, that of accumulation (*saṃbhāramārga*), where one lives a thoroughly moral life, develops some skill at concentrating the mind, and familiarizes oneself with the four foundations of mindfulness. On the path of application (*prayogamārga*), one further deepens one's concentrative ability, and contemplates the four noble truths in their sixteen as-

---

25 For details on the Theravāda path, see Buddhaghosa (1976).

pects.[26] One ascends through four different stages of the path of application, culminating in the "highest worldly dharma," which leads directly to the "union of tranquillity and insight" (*śamathavipaśyanā-yuganaddha*) that is applied to a *direct* realization of the four noble truths (especially of the central truth of no-self). With the first moment of this realization, one has achieved the path of seeing (*darśanamārga*) and become an ārya. On the path of seeing one "uproots" gross defilements, especially those relating to our habitual misapprehension of reality. On the path of development (*bhavanāmārga*), one uproots defilements of other types and of increasing subtlety, until finally only the subtlest of the subtle defilements remain. When the last of these has been removed, one attains the path of no-more-training (*aśaikṣamārga*), and is an arhant. The different types of ārya described above (streamwinner, etc.) may be correlated with different degrees of progression on the paths of seeing and development, and the different types of arhants are as in the Theravāda.[27]

Like the material in the *nikāyas* and *āgamas*, much of the "path-theory" of the Mahāyāna sūtras is only partially systematized. The Mahāyāna's ideal path-traveller, the bodhisattva, is enjoined to develop faith in the buddhas, expressed in various acts of devotion, and great compassion (*karunā*) for suffering sentient beings, while all the time realizing that neither they, nor sentient beings, nor suffering, nor buddhas exist in an ultimate sense, all being void. The bodhisattva's path often is said to involve six "perfections" or transcendent virtues (*pāramitā*): generosity, morality, patience, effort, concentration and wisdom, to which sometimes are added skill-in-means, aspiration, power and gnosis. Alternatively, the bodhisattva is said to be accumulating two great "stores" (*saṃbhāra*), of merit and gnosis, that will eventuate, respectively, in the Form (*rūpa*, i.e., Enjoyment and Transformation) Bodies and Dharma Body of a buddha. There also developed a scheme of ten stages or "grounds" (*bhūmi*) through which a bodhisattva passes before enlightenment, each involving the perfection of one of the pāramitās, each endowing one with geometrically expanding powers of magical manifestation for the assistance of sentient beings.[28]

---

26 See above, pp. 50-51.

27 The classic source for this path-scheme is AK, esp. chapter vi.

28 For a good account of the Mahāyāna path as described in this paragraph, see Dayal (1970).

The five-path scheme of the Sanskritic *ābhidharmikas* eventually was applied to the Mahāyāna material as well,[29] resulting in a parallel—but quite different—formulation of the path. Here, after first convincing oneself of the futility of saṃsāric existence, one goes on to develop the prime "motive" of the Mahāyāna, *bodhicitta*, the "thought of enlightenment" that aspires to buddhahood so that one may best assist other sentient beings. When *bodhicitta* is utterly spontaneous and natural, one enters the path of accumulation, where, as before, one develops morality, concentration and the foundations of mindfulness. On the path of application, one continues to deepen one's concentration, and to analyze the nature of reality, which is voidness. When calm and insight have been united with voidness as an object, and a direct realization ensues, one enters the path of seeing, having become an ārya. The path of seeing is said to be equivalent to the first of the ten bodhisattva stages. On the path of development, which comprises the nine remaining stages, one uproots all of one's defilements, not only those—uprooted by Hīnayāna śrāvakas and pratyekabuddhas—that inhibit one's liberation, but also those subtle defilements or trace-defilements—uprooted only by bodhisattvas—that keep one from the omniscience of a fully-enlightened buddha. Finally, when the last of the subtlest trace of defilement has been removed, one enters the path beyond training, as a buddha.

In addition to this "mainstream" Mahāyāna path-scheme, which came to dominate the late Indian and the Tibetan tradition, there are, of course, many others. The tantras describe a whole variety of practices, from visualizing oneself as a buddha-deity at the center of a maṇḍala, to the recitation of complex mantras, to working within one's "subtle body" to develop an "illusory body" and a "clear light" awareness—with or without the assistance of a consort of the opposite sex. Zen—as do the Great Seal and Great Perfection traditions—concentrates on the direct realization of the nature of one's mind, seen as essentially luminous and wise. The Pure Land traditions focus on the recitation of the name of Amitābha Buddha so that one may be born after death into his western paradise, Sukhāvatī—there to enjoy great happiness, and thence eventually to proceed to full buddhahood.

---

29 By "Maitreya," in the *Abhisamayālaṃkāra* (fifth century?). See Conze's translation (1954), and E. Obermiller's seminal study, *Analysis of the Abhisamayālaṃkāra* (1933, 1936). The full development of the scheme that was taken over into Tibetan tradition was effected by Haribhadra (eighth century?), in his *Abhisamayālaṃkārāloka*.

The Nichiren schools insist that the "one thing needful"is recitation of a formula praising the *Lotus Sūtra*. The list could go on and on—Buddhist practice is even more varied, perhaps, than Christian—and each new tradition, regarding itself as the highest or most essential of the Buddha's teachings, tends to generate its own path-scheme, which may or may not be assimilable to the over-arching structures outlined above.[30]

However bewildering the variety of Buddhist path-schemes may be, every post-*nikāya/āgama* scheme has one essential characteristic: it insists that attainment of the *summum bonum* is dependent on the profound realization of one central fact, or truth. Different schools, of course, differ on just what that truth is: it may be no-self, or voidness, or mind-only, or one's own innate enlightenment, or the power of Amitābha's name, or the centrality of the *Lotus Sūtra*. There is, however, at least implicit agreement among nearly all Buddhists that there must be a principle whose realization, or effectuation, assures one's liberation, and that there must be a procedure for realizing that principle. For the more "wisdom"-oriented Buddhist schools, the procedure is what broadly would be called "meditation" (the union of tranquillity and insight, of concentration and wisdom) that has the power to effect liberation; for the "faith"-oriented traditions, some "act"is essential—though an act, of course, must be preceded by some sort of decision, hence a realization. In every case, the belief holds that there do exist certain cognitions and/or acts that have the power radically to change the sort of being one is—at the very least, from a saṃsāric into an enlightened being. Thus, just as the truth of cessation entails positing a certain "nature" for the mind (as perfect*ible*), the truth of path entails positing certain "powers" for the mind (as perfect*ing*). Neither of these, of course, bears much resemblance to the modern vision of the mind, any more than the theories of rebirth and karma resemble modern cosmology, but they are at the core of what Buddhists traditionally have believed to be the case.

---

30 The five-path scheme, though not unknown to the Sino-Japanese tradition, has not been nearly as influential there as it has been in Tibetan Buddhism, which subsumes both the varieties of Tantra and the Great Seal and Great Perfection (which themselves are at least quasi-tantric) under the five paths.

6. *Religious Argument*

If, then, Buddhists have been quite serious in their assertion of the four noble truths, how do they go about *arguing* that these truths are true, that, e.g., past and future lives are real and enlightenment possible? Some answers to this question will be forthcoming—indeed, Dharmakīrti's arguments for these truths are the main focus of this book—but before we turn to the matter of how Buddhists argue for the truth of those propositions they consider most fundamental, we must first be certain *whether* they would or should so argue. Whether or not religious truth-claims can or should be demonstrated is a question that has exercised religious people in many places and times, and we shall consider it both generally and with reference to Buddhism.

A. THREE ARGUMENTS AGAINST RELIGIOUS ARGUMENT

It undoubtedly would be too cynical to suggest that the reluctance of religious people to argue for the validity of their truth-claims is inversely proportional to the amount of evidence they are able to present. At the same time, religious truth-claims *are,* as we have seen, often extraordinary, in the literal sense that they describe realities that are beyond the reach of the sensory capacities of ordinary humans. It is not easy to demonstrate the truth of such propositions as "God exists," "past and future lives are real," or "enlightenment is possible." That such propositions *are* true, however, is of great importance to religious people. Given propositions whose truth is vital yet difficult to prove, religious people often find themselves appealing to the notion that religious truth-claims somehow are different from other sorts of truth-claims, and therefore may be accepted as true without recourse to argument or demonstration of the sort demanded of ordinary truth-claims.

One "argument against argument" is the appeal to ineffability, to the notion that both the object and the experience at the core of religion are beyond the capacity of any language to describe. It undoubtedly is true that both the subjective and objective poles of religious experience are complex and often mystifying. However, to claim that a transcendent object is indescribable—and therefore not subject to ordinary checking procedures—because it is transcendent is both tautologous and contradictory. It is tautologous because the "transcendent object" is used as the reason proving its own reality; it is contradictory because if reality is *completely* ineffable, then any designation of it, even as "ineffable"—let alone as "holy" or "void"—is meaningless. As Peter Moore notes, if religious experiences are utterly ineffable, then those who report them must not be believed, for utter ineffability requires silence, while if reports actually are made, they inevitably are *descriptive,* invoking images and terms familiar to the audience, and so presuppose precisely the sort of communicability that the claim to ineffability seems to deny.[1]

Literally, then, ineffability is absurd; taken, however, rather more functionally, we see that it serves at least two purposes: it helps to locate an extreme point on the human experiential continuum, to indicate an experience that is *least* like other experiences; and it underlines the inadequacy of language for describing much of our experience.[2] Neither of these functions establishes religious experience as unique, however, since there are many candidates for the "extremity" of experience, from battle, to sex, to childbirth, to the taste of a fresh baguette; each of these is to *some* degree ineffable, yet each has been described for people who have not had the experience, hence is not, strictly speaking, ineffable; and even if an experience has been described "only" by way of analogies, those analogies assure that the experience finds its way onto the continuum of generally available and comprehensible human experiences. As Renford Bambrough puts it, "To hold that there may be inarticulate understanding is not to hold that there may be any understanding that could not be articulated."[3] In short, then, ineffability claimed absolutely is self-contradictory, for *nothing* then can be asserted meaningfully; while ineffability claimed relatively is not really ineffability, but a statement about the difficulty one is having in explaining a particular experience. Any experience that is described—and even the most recondite mystical experiences have been described—is susceptible of comparison with other experiences that we have had, and is therefore open to judgment and criticism as to, e.g., the appropriateness of the analogies employed or the reliability of the conclusions drawn from the experience.

---

1 Moore (1978) 101, 105.
2 Smart (1978) 17-18.
3 Bambrough (1978) 212.

Another "argument against argument" rests on the claim that religious propositions belong to a different class than, say, scientific propositions, and that they cannot, therefore, be expected to undergo to same sorts of "rigorous" or "empirical" or "rational" confirmation procedures as do the latter. Thus, religious truth-claims must be adjudicated within the "court" of *religious* judgment, which may, in fact, admit as evidence attitudes and experiences that would be deemed inappropriate if a scientific truth-claim were being tested. It certainly is important to recognize that different statements are made within different cultural matrices and conceptual schemes, and that they only can be understood against the background of those matrices or schemes. It is quite another matter, however, to maintain that the *truth* of statements only can be judged from within their respective matrices or schemes—this is tantamount to an acceptance of truth as localized coherence, and we have already seen that the price for this is relativism. If religious people were, in fact, claiming only such local coherence for their truth-claims, then there would be little problem with appealing to different courts of judgment. Since, however, most religious people have intended their truth-claims to be taken literally and universally, i.e., "correspondently," it is disingenuous for them then to try to exempt those claims from the sorts of checking procedures that generally are applied to hard claims of the correspondence sort.

A religious person cannot, in short, make a hard claim and expect to have "soft" evidence accepted. Hard, i.e., correspondence claims must, at the very least, be subject to *some* sort of testing: there must be some way in which they are determined to be true or false. Conversely, insists H.D. Lewis, if a religious assertion cannot be proven or disproven, then "it is without factual significance, and makes no genuine truth-claim."[4] Peter Donovan agrees: "Statements which fail to pay the necessary price for factuality (i.e., being open to confirming or falsifying observations) cannot be counted as statements of fact."[5] W.V. Quine and J.S. Ullian add that "What stands open to fresh verification may merit special confidence, since such a belief has been withstanding greater risk of disproof."[6] It is potential falsifiability that is the key to the meaningfulness of a religious assertion, for, as Ninian Smart notes,

---

4 Quoted in Donovan (1976) 17.
5 Ibid., 20.
6 Quine and Ullian (1970) 39.

> Only a statement which sticks its neck out and runs the risk of being refuted in sense-experience is meaningful. If a supposed assertion does not do this, then it is a fraud. It is empty, meaningless (unless its truth simply arises from the meanings of the terms used in it). Thus, if I say 'There is a fairy at the bottom of my garden,' but it turns out I am thinking of a fairy which cannot be touched, smelled, seen, etc., then no counterevidence could challenge my assertion and so by that very fact it is empty, meaningless.[7]

At the very least, says Donovan, the "empiricist challenge" to religion amounts to the contention that for religious statements "some observations must be agreed to count for or against them, some tests must be accepted as relevant to their credibility."[8]

Each of the "arguments against argument" discussed above presupposes that there *do* exist tests for determining the truth-value of statements, while at the same time seeking to exempt religious statements from those tests. A third, and final, "argument against argument" springs from a fundamental skepticism—already alluded to in chapter 2—about *all* truth-determinations, on the grounds that *no* statement in any realm really can be said to have been decisively verified, or, for that matter, falsified. Observation is limited, context-dependent and often "prejudiced"; logic is only as strong as its own unquestionable presuppositions; and experience is only interesting when the conclusions drawn from it are utterly uncontroversial, hence trivial. In short, the very foundations of knowledge are thrown into question, leaving those who seek certainty in any realm forced to admit defeat.[9] The curious converse of this skepticism is that, since all knowledge—including the scientific—is called into question, there is no realm that enjoys a greater or lesser claim to certainty. Hence, religion, even if undemonstrable, is no more undemonstrable than is science and, in fact, can therefore make an equal claim to truth.[10] Ironically, then, skepticism, which for so long was seen by religious thinkers as vitiating religious truth-

---

7 Smart (1979) 55. It should be pointed out in fairness that Smart beleives there are serious limitations to the application of the falsifiability criterion to religious assertions, the limitations resulting from the limitations of empiricism and its observational techniques. See p. 56 and Ashby (1967) 240-47.

8 Donovan (1976) 24.

9 See Rorty (1979) for a clear exposition of this position.

10 Expressions of this may be found in, e.g., Wolfe (1982) and O'Flaherty (1984).

claims, now is embraced by some, with something like the philosophical equivalent to the attitude that "my enemy's enemy is my friend," i.e., an undermining of the foundations of science opens up the possibility that other—even traditionally religious—explanations of the cosmos may, in fact, be true.

It ought to be evident that the evasion of argumentation on the basis of skepticism is really no more satisfactory than that based on ineffability or "different courts." First of all, there is the paradox of skepticism itself: if no knowledge is to be trusted, then skeptical knowledge is not trustworthy, either; hence, if skepticism is true, it must be false. Second, and more importantly, even if there is reason to believe that the foundations of knowledge may be less secure than we would like them to be, it does not mean that there is no basis for any judgments whatsoever. Neither verifiability nor even falsifiability may be an utterly secure standard on which to judge a scientific hypothesis, but judgment is necessary, and one applies the standards that, relatively speaking, seem least likely to produce misleading results: hence, whatever their ultimate shakiness as epistemological foundations, observation and rational analysis remain important standards for determining scientific truth. By the same token, if religious truth-claims are to be meaningful in the least, there must be some way in which true and false claims can be separated. It is an open question whether the tests that are applied to religious truth-claims ought to be the same as those applied to scientific ones, but that there must be tests there is no doubt, and to the degree that the sorts of truth-claims made by religious people are hard ones, the evidence will have to be commensurate, hence in some way concordant with observation and rationality. Finally, it ought to be noted that a justification of religion on the basis of skepticism is rather a pyrrhic victory, since it leaves one with, at best, a relativism that is contrary to the sort of universality so often sought by religious truth-claimants.

B. ARGUMENTS AGAINST ARGUMENT IN BUDDHISM

Each of these "arguments against argument" has found its champions within Buddhism. Buddhists have been as quick as other religious people to insist that their highest experiences and truths are ineffable—witness the Buddha's imprecision about nirvāṇa and refusal to discuss the tathāgata's fate after death, or the lay bodhisattva Vimalakīrti's famous summation of a dialogue about nonduality by his "thundering silence." The exaltation of ineffability perhaps reaches its zenith in the Zen tradition. We may recall that the Ho-shang Mo-ho-yen preferred silence to debate when called to account by Indian pandits in Tibet, and that one of the paradigmatic Zen tales is of the Buddha's "Flower Sermon," in which, presented a flower by the gods and asked for a discourse, he simply smiled and held the flower aloft silently. Zen at its best is, certainly, refreshingly free of the sort of cant—not to mention contradiction—that can afflict a scholastic tradition, but Zen *does* function within an overall world-view (broadly speaking, a saṃsāra-nirvāṇa cosmology) that is assumed to be true, and it does provide at least a symbol-language by which the ultimate it seeks may be indicated. The fact that a persimmon rather than a proposition may be used to indicate the nature of reality does not make the persimmon any less a form of human symbolization, hence, broadly, of speech. In a similar manner, Nāgārjuna's insistence that he makes no propositions is literally self-contradictory and, in any case, to be understood as indicating the limits of language, or the lack of ultimate nature in what language describes—*not* as eliminating all propositions whatsoever. As in other religions, then, the appeal to ineffability has an important place in Buddhism, but its purpose is to point up the difficulty in communicating or symbolizing certain objects and experiences, not to obviate all discussion of religious truth-claims.

The insistence that religious truth-claims are somehow of a different order than other sorts of truth-claims, hence subject to different criteria of judgment, also is encountered in traditional Buddhist literature, albeit most often implicitly.[11] Thus, ultimate reality often is assumed by Buddhists to be a realm in which conventional epistemology and criteria of judgment do not apply. The ultimate *object*, e.g., voidness, is marked by the absence of ordinary signs and designations, including "true" or "false"; the *experience* of the ultimate object, e.g., via a wisdom consciousness, similarly lacks the characteristics of ordinary sense-perception or inference, hence cannot be described or judged in quite the same way that ordinary knowledge is; and the *experiencer* of the ultimate is held, by virtue of their experience, to be

---

11 While Buddhists certainly recognized that "practicing the buddhadharma" is different from, say, "practicing medicine," and that different sorts of cognition and action were appropriate to each, they did not distinguish utterly different "spheres" of, e.g., religion and science, as have many in the West. It is important to remember that "religion" in the abstract is a Western invention; Asians generally have spoken of their particular Dharma or Tao, which is not a separate sphere of life so much as a "way" of seeing and acting that informs all areas of human existence. Obviously, such distinctions become easier for modern Buddhists, who are familiar with Western categories. See, e.g., Conze (1967) I, 1, and Sangharakshita (1980) for arguments based on this distinction.

beyond ordinary moral judgments, since their every action is informed by a "higher" realization than is available to ordinary people. At the same time, we have seen that the transcendent nature of ultimate reality does not preclude the conventional truth of conventional assertions, and conventional assertions presumably will be judged by conventional means, hence by recourse to "arguments" based on such criteria as observation and rationality. Furthermore, even the ultimate truths that lie beyond conventional signs and designations are asserted to be true, hence subject to some criteria for determining what is and what is not so; are said to be objects of "knowledge," hence to lie *somewhere* on the continuum of states that we conventionally consider cognitive; and are asserted to be both "good" and the basis for "good" actions by enlightened beings, hence to depend on the meaningfulness of the conventional distinction between good and evil. Thus, even if Buddhists seek to place certain truths or cognitions outside conventional judgments of truth or falsity, those judgments still come into play, and so too must standards for judgment, i.e., means for determining truth or falsity. These may not be identical to the standards that would be applied in science, but they must be similar at least to the degree that they are founded on some type of observation and rationality—or, as Buddhists would say, perception (*pratyakṣa*) and inference (*anumāna*).[12]

Finally, challenges to the "foundations of knowledge" are not unknown in Asian philosophy. The Buddha encountered skeptics, such as Pūrana Kassapa, during his own lifetime, and later Buddhists had to contend with the radical skepticism of Cārvākas such as Jayarāśi, who sought in his *Tattvopaplavasiṃha* ("The Leonine Upsetting of All Theories") to refute all possible *pramāṇas*, or sources of authoritative knowledge, including those accepted by all Buddhists, perception and inference.[13] Attacks on the foundations of knowledge came from within Buddhism, too. Perhaps the best-known such attack is found in Nāgārjuna's *Vigrahavyāvartanī* ("Turning Aside Objections"), where he argues that none of the traditional *pramāṇas* is ultimately justifiable, since they cannot, on the one hand, simply be presupposed, but cannot, on the other hand, be validated, since if they are self-validated they are tautologous, while if they are validated by some other *pramāṇa*, then there will ensue an infinite regress of validating

---

12 For a provocative discussion of this idea, see Robinson (1971-1972).

13 See Radhakrishnan and Moore (1957) 236-44, for a translation of Jayarāśi's demolition of inference.

pramāṇas that only can be ended by resorting to circularity or tautology.[14] Whatever traditional Buddhists may have made of this argument, at least one modern commentator[15] has urged that its great value is to overturn any of the possible modes of argumentation that might be used against Buddhist views, hence that Buddhism somehow is more firmly established by the vitiation of conventional epistemology. Once again, however, the skeptic's path is strewn with paradox, for (a) the attack on epistemology is itself carried out within the framework of an attempt to establish what is the case, which only can, ultimately, be an object of "knowledge" and (b) the vitiation of conventional epistemology makes Buddhism equally likely and equally unlikely as any other view to be true. In fact, Nāgārjuna's critique of the *pramāṇas* probably does not entail total skepticism any more than his denial that he makes propositions is an appeal to ineffability; in each case, it is more likely that he is pointing out the limitations (i.e., "voidness") of certain conventional concepts and modes of thought—were he to deny them utterly he not only would lose himself in paradox, but would undercut the basis of the "wisdom" (*prajñā*) that he seeks to establish. Prajñā may transcend the limitations of conventional knowledge, but it still is knowledge, and for Nāgārjuna to assert that it is knowledge, "knowledge" must have some meaning, and so, too, must the "means of knowing," the *pramāṇas.* If, in turn, the pramāṇas have conventional validity, then argumentation is both necessary and desirable in settling matters of conventional truth—nor, for that matter, can ultimate truths be exempted: Nāgārjuna, after all, must argue for voidness, Yogācāras for mind-only, and Zen Buddhists—after their fashion—for the indescribability of it all.

---

14 VV, 30ff.; Bhattacharya (1978) 30; tr. Streng (1967) 224-25.
15 Fenner (1982) 10-22.

7. *Pre-Dharmakīrti Defenses of the Buddhist World-View*

Perhaps it is true that, as Edward Conze remarks, philosophical disputation is "[a]t variance with the spirit of Buddhism . . . . a radical departure from the spirit of *ahimsā* and tolerance which was so characteristic of Buddhism in its heyday."[1] Certainly, many early texts—perhaps most notably the *Sutta Nipāta*—explicitly denounce disputation, opinion-mongering and attachment to particular philosophical views. It also is undeniable that, for most Buddhists at most times and places, philosophical disputation was far from a major concern, and that authority was derived primarily on the basis of the testimony of scriptures or a spiritual teacher. At the same time, it should be evident by now that—at least in their encounters with critical or curious non-Buddhists—Buddhist intellectuals really have little choice *but* to argue, since to make correspondent truth-claims about non-ordinary reality, as Buddhists traditionally have, is necessarily to invite some sort of test of the "accuracy" of one's statements. In fact, a survey of the course of Indian Buddhist thought shows that a small but influential number of Buddhists have argued forcefully and imaginatively for their truth-claims. The texts in which they did so may have been written primarily for a Buddhist audience—most religious texts are written by insiders for insiders—but this does not mean that the arguments reported or framed there did not or could not occur, or that the preoccupations of the authors were entirely *intra*-systemic: there is simply too much *inter*-systemic debate recorded in various texts to believe that it did not occur.

The most interesting and sophisticated defense of the Buddhist world-view (taken as the validity of the four noble truths and the spiritual supremacy of the Buddha) is that of the Indian pandit Dharmakīrti (seventh century C.E.), and it is on his arguments, as commented upon by the fifteenth-century Tibetan scholar rGyal tshab dar ma rin chen, that this book focuses. In marshalling his arguments,

---

1 Conze (1973) 265.

Dharmakīrti had the advantage of working with sophisticated logical and epistemological tools that his predecessors had lacked, although in some cases they helped to develop those tools. At the same time, however, the first thousand years of Buddhist intellectual history hardly are lacking in attempts to justify the Buddhist world-view. They may not be as explicit or systematic as Dharmakīrti's and those of his successors, but they do occur, and a review of a number of these arguments—and the problems they posed—will help us better to understand the background out of which Dharmakīrti's discussion emerged.

It ought to be said at the outset that the *ultimate* Buddhist criterion for unsuccessful or successful argument in religious matters probably is that expressed in the Buddha's famous "advice to the Kālāmas," where he warns against accepting statements as true merely on the basis of report, tradition, hearsay, logic, propriety or respect for the speaker; statements are to be verified, ultimately, *only* through personal experience.[2] This tells us two things about Buddhist confirmatory procedures: they are not, in principle at least, based on reliance on testimony or scripture, i.e., they are non-authoritarian; and they *are* strongly "empirical" in their thrust: even when later thinkers attempted to devise sophisticated inferential demonstrations of Buddhist truths, the final appeal offered by most Buddhists has been to confirmatory *experience*. Thus, the arguments regarded most suspiciously by Buddhist intellectuals are generally those that rely on testimony, while those most favored rely on personal experiential verification. Neverthless, Buddhists have attempted arguments that seem to rest on testimony, or charisma, or analogy, or one or another logical schema, or—perhaps most commonly—applications of the "law" of dependent origination (*pratītya samutpāda*), and we will examine some of them before returning at the end of the section to consider the argument from experience.

In spite of the Buddha's warning to the Kālāmas not to accept statements simply out of respect for the speaker, and his criticism of both opponents and disciples (e.g., Ānanda) who make truth claims not based on personal experience, there seems to be a certain ambivalence, throughout the Buddhist literature, toward the value of testimony, charisma and faith. Faith (*śraddhā*) is, on the one hand, only supposed to be directed toward persons or propositions that have

---

2 A, i, 19; tr. is that of Woodward and Hare (1951-55) I, 173. Cf. also Radhakrishnan and Moore (1957) 345-46.

been partially verified through personal experience. On the other hand, one cannot even undertake a religious practice, such as the Buddhist path, without some prior "faith" that is likely to bear spiritual fruit—if one already *knew* through direct experience that it *would* bear fruit, one's attitude would no longer be faith, but knowledge. Since beginners do *not* yet know with certainty that the path will issue in success, they must by definition undertake it in part on the basis of faith—which is, in fact, one of the five "faculties" (*bala;* the others are effort, mindfulness, concentration and wisdom) to be applied on the Buddhist path. What, then, is the basis of faith? In part, of course, it must be the conformity of statements with our common-sense notions and with previous experience—this fact helps to separate the kind of faith valued in Buddhism from "blind faith." Since, however, the referents of Buddhist religious propositions are matters beyond our ken, we most often will look for other reasons for placing faith in them or the person asserting them. Most often in Buddhist literature the "reason" for which faith is placed in the Buddha and what he teaches is , simply, his charisma, i.e., the fact that his behavior (including posture, countenance, speech, etc.) seems to point to some kind of extraordinary attainment. This is not a bad reason for having faith in someone, but it is not entirely rational, either, for there is no invariable concomitance between inner state and outer behavior: even a cursory look at the history of religions informs us that there are (a) inwardly spiritual people whose behavior is either unremarkable or, occasionally, repellant and (b) inwardly mediocre or evil people whose behavior is charismatic. Charisma, thus *may* be an indicator of spiritual worth, but it hardly is an adequate basis, by itself, for placing faith in a religious teacher.

If a teacher's charisma is not by itself an adequate basis for faith, then what of the reasonableness of what they propound? Despite the Buddha's avowed suspicion of "mere"logic or inference, both the Buddha himself and early Buddhists adduced a number of arguments that are, explicitly or implicitly, based on logical principles of one sort or another.

One of the most frequently used types of argument is that based on analogy. The Pāli *nikāyas* are full of analogies, of similes that illustrate a particular doctrinal point and thereby make it more compelling, from the likening of the Dharma to a raft on which one crosses to the far shore of the river of saṃsāra, to the comparison of idle philosophical speculation to the ill-timed questions of a man shot by a poisoned arrow. Similarly, Mahāyāna sūtra literature abounds in such analogies. The *Lotus Sūtra* alone contains a number of seminal similes: the parable of the burning house, which, as we have seen, illustrates the doctrine of the Buddha's skill-in-means; the story of the phantom city, which describes the provisional nature of the "Hīnayāna"nirvāṇa; the image of the rain cloud, which represents the Buddha's impartial compassion, etc.[3]

The most explicitly argumentative use of analogy is probably that of the post-*nikāya* Pāli text, the *Milindapañhā,* in which the bhikkhu Nāgasena seeks to demonstrate a number of Buddhist truths to King Milinda through analogies. How, for example, Milinda asks, can we know that nirvāṇa, though unconditioned, exists? We know this by mental perception, replies Nāgasena, just as we know the existence of the invisible wind by the sensations it leaves.[4] How can arhants ascertain that they will never be reborn again? By their knowledge that all possible causes of rebirth have been removed, just as a farmer who has quit farming and rid himself of all the grain in his granary knows that there is no further basis for filling the granary.[5] Examples from the *Milindapañhā* could be multiplied greatly, but these two are typical, and they reveal the basic structure of—and problem with—analogical arguments. The structure is simply: unknown *x* is related to unknown *y* just as known *x* is related to known *y*; therefore unknown *x* and *y* are real. There are, however, both particular and general problems with this formulation. The particular problem is that in most of the analogies cited by Nāgasena, the known examples are physical in nature, while the unknown objects that he seeks to prove are mental (or, at least, distinctly non-physical): to speak of nirvāṇa as if it were the wind, or causes of rebirth as if they were grains is, very possibly, to apply inappropriate characteristics to the category of the mental. Granted, Buddhists often apply "material"metaphors to "mental"topics,[6] and may even view the mental through concepts borrowed from physical processes (e.g., causation), but that the boundary can be crossed so easily between the example and its probandum is not so clear. The more fundamental problem with analogical arguments is a general one, namely, that they are not really arguments at all, but, simply, statements of the sort: *if* such-and-such unknown *is* the case, it is *like* such-and-such known; or, such-and such unknown *is* the case, and it is like such-and-such known. The former statement is provi-

---

3 See Vaidya (1960), and the sūtra's numerous translations, e.g., Kern (1963).

4 Rhys Davids (1963) II, 124-27.

5 Ibid., I, 65-66.

6 See Collins (1982) for a particularly interesting analysis of some of Theravāda Buddhism's guiding metaphors.

sional, hence inconclusive, while the latter is dogmatic, hence inconclusive.

A somewhat more rigorous, and decidedly less poetic, mode of logical argument is that employed in the *Kathāvatthu*, another post-*nikāya* Pālī text, which is an account of early Buddhist doctrinal controversies. Here, the form of argument is as follows: "You asssert proposition *x*; proposition *x* contradicts propostion *y*, universally accepted to be true; therefore, proposition *x* is false." It may be argued, for example, that arhants can fall from their spiritual pinnacle. However, the definition of *arhant* is such that they are, by definition, beyond return. Therefore, arhants can*not* fall from their spiritual pinnacle.[7] This represents an early attempt at systematic inference, but it occurs within the limited scope of intra-Buddhist debates. Therefore, the "universally accepted" propositions that are the basis of proof are, in fact, simply bits of Buddhist doctrine, drawn from scripture, whose truth-value still is open to question by outsiders. The argument may be conclusive to another Buddhist, who accepts Buddhist scripture as valid, but it cannot have much value for an uncommitted seeker.

This, in fact, is the fundamental problem with many earlier Buddhist demonstrations of the truth of Buddhist religious assertions: they beg the question by applying to the demonstration principles that either themselves are questionable or simply are too general to have much probative value. Examples of the former include the above-cited arguments from the *Kathāvatthu*, as well as such later Mahāyāna claims as those surrounding the notion of tathāgatagarbha, our potential for enlightenment, which is defended not only by recourse to analogies,[8] but by the argument that we must be able to attain enlightenment because (a) our *desire* to attain enlightenment, which is a "good" desire, must come from a "good" source, which must be the tathāgatagarbha itself[9] and (b) the mind is by nature clear and pure, and its defilements adventitious. Argument (a) fails because the existence of desire for an object does not assure the existence of the object. Argument (b) is problematic because the assertion that the mind is clear and pure by nature is not *self-evidently* true. Rather, it is derived

---

7 Aung and Rhys Davids (1960) 64-70.

8 As, e.g., the ten similes of the *Tathāgatagarbha Sūtra*, cited at RGV i:94-5 (Johnston and Chowdhury [1950] 59ff.), tr. Obermiller (1931) 213ff.

9 RGV i:40 (Johnston and Chowdhury [1950] 35), tr. Obermiller (1931) 176 (cited as i:39). Cf. Wayman and Wayman (1974) 105. In general on this topic, see Ruegg (1969).

from meditative experiences, and must stand or fall depending on the epistemological weight we give those experiences—over against other, perhaps contradictory, philosophical and psychological evidence—in deciding the nature of the mind.[10]

Examples of the latter form of question-begging, in which too broad a principle is applied, revolve around the use in discussion of the critical concept of dependent origination (*pratītya samutpāda*). This concept, which is absolutely fundamental to Buddhist thought, involves the application, to *all* realms of conditioned existence, of the theory of causation: "This being, that occurs; from the arising of this, that arises; this not being, that does not occur; from the cessation of this, that occurs."[11] In other words, if *x*, then *y*; if no *x*, then no *y*. Because this principle applies not only to the physical realm in which it most manifestly is valid, but also to the mental realm, Buddhist soteriology can be stated in straightforwardly causal terms: if craving (*x*), then suffering (*y*); if no craving (*x*), then no suffering (*y*); therefore cessation (*z*). The obvious problem here is that it still remains to be demonstrated that the *particular* causal sequence described by, e.g., the four noble truths, actually obtains. After all, given the general fact of dependent origination, or of universal causality, some causal relations are possible, while others are not; it is entirely possible that craving is *not* the cause of suffering, or the removal of craving the cause of nirvāṇa. It is, of course, equally possible that these relations *do* obtain, but the point is that the mere assertion of the validity of a general principle of causation does *not, ipso facto,* guarantee that this or that particular application of the law is, in fact, the case. Whether particular applications are valid only can be decided on the basis of independent observation or inference. Therefore, dependent origination cannot serve as an *a priori* argument for Buddhist soteriology.

Thus, one cannot argue, as Nāgārjuna seems to in his *Vigrahavyāvartanī*, that (a) all entities are void, (b) all entities thus are dependently originated and therefore (c) the four noble truths are true and enlightenment possible.[12] (a) may entail (b), but (b) does not necessarily entail (c), for dependent origination may be the case without

---

10 For a discussion of some of the epistemological consequences of the idea that the mind is by nature luminous, see R. Jackson (1990).

11 M, i, 257-71 and ii, 29-39, tr. Chalmers (1926-27) I, 183-91 and II, 16-21.

12 VV 70 and commentary: Bhattacharya (1978) text, 52-53; tr. op. cit., translation, 47. Cf. MMK xxiv:14 and xxiv:40 for a similar sequence of argument; tr. Inada (1970) 147, 157 and Streng (1967) 223, 225.

the four noble truths *necessarily* being true.[13] Similarly, one cannot take most *ābhidharmika* descriptions of the path-process as probative of the process they describe, for the simple reason that such accounts presuppose that one or another dharma-classification is valid, and simply go on to describe how the dharmas thus classsified interact according to causal laws. The *ābhidharmika* tradition does *not* seriously question whether the dharmas that make up one or the other scheme correspond to actual features of the cosmos: it is *assumed* that most of the basic elements (including the cessation of suffering) are legitimately included in the schemata, and the problem then simply becomes one of explaining the elements in the most elegant and satisfactory manner.

In a somewhat circuitous manner, therefore, we find ourselves back with the Buddha's advice to the Kālāmas, for we have seen that neither faith, nor testimony, nor analogy, nor narrowly-based inferences, nor *a priori* principles such as dependent origination can suffice to give an uncommitted seeker certainty that the fundamental assertions of Buddhism, the four noble truths and the spiritual supremacy of the Buddha, are actually true. The Buddha's advice, of course, and the advice of countless Buddhist masters since him is, simply, *"ehi passako,"* come and see for yourself whether what I say is true, and once you have, you will have no need for faith, testimony, analogy, inference or *a priori* principles, for then you will know *by direct acquaintance* how things are in the cosmos. In short, the most important pre-Dharmakīrti argument for the truth of Buddhist religious assertions is what in the West would be called the argument from experience.

How conclusive is the argument from experience? To do justice to this complex question would require a separate volume; here, I merely wish to focus on one important line of analysis in recent discussions: the science/religion analogy. It often is suggested by proponents of the argument from experience that to travel a religious path really is no different from undertaking a scientific experiment: one begins with a hypothesis, e.g., enlightenment is possible, or past and future lives exist, and then proceeds to execute a specified sequence of operations (i.e., the path), at the end of which one will have one's answer through direct experience.[14] The analogy seems at first compelling, but there are certain problems with it. Donald Evans claims that there are at least three ways in which religious and scientific assertions are funda-

---

13 For a fuller discussion of this issue, see R. Jackson (1985).

14 See Staal (1975) 51 and Burns (1971) 176.

mentally different: (l) religious assertions are value-colored, while scientific assertions are value-free, i.e., logically neutral. In other words, religious "experiments" are far more likely than scientific ones to involve self-fulfilling prophecies. (2) Religious assertions are not comprehensible impersonally, while scientific assertions are; i.e., religious assertions *always* have a psychological coloration that limits their universality. (3) Religious assertions, unlike scientific ones, are not testable by *inter*subjective observation, i.e., they always must remain to a degree idiosyncratic.[15] A fourth argument that might be made is that religious assertions, unlike scientific ones, are not usually designed to be falsifiable: one sets out to *verify* the hypothesis, and one is not likely to be credited with genuine religious experience by a given tradition if one concludes on the basis of following its path that the initial hypothesis is, in fact, false.[16] This, in turn leads to the further problem of who is qualified to *judge* whether one has followed the experimental procedure (i.e., followed the path) properly and whether one's conclusions are to be taken seriously. An arhant, in Buddhism, is supposed to be able to perceive another arhant, but how is one to be certain that the arhant judging one is really enlightened? If one traces their lineage of recognition back to the Buddha, one begs the question, for it is the validity even of the Buddha's understanding that is at issue. Furthermore, how does one account for the often contradictory (and sometimes demonstrably mad) statements made by religious visionaries at different places and times? If experience alone is sufficient warrant for the truth of their assertions, then they *all* must be true; and we can escape the relativism this implies only by arguing somewhat dubiously that all religious visionaries actually experience the same thing, but simply express it differently,[17] or by appealing to some *other* criterion of validity, which removes us from the realm of the experience alone.

---

15 Evans (1974) 326-27.

16 Cf. Hoffman (1982) and (1987).

17 For several incisive essays attacking this position, see Katz (1978). The basic argument is that we never have access to anything like "pure experience"; we only have expressions, and expressions (particularly when contextualized) differ from case to case, forcing us to conclude that experiences differ, too. For a critique of Katz et al. that also is an attempt to establish the possibility of something like "pure experience," see Forman (1990). An intermediate position is suggested by John Hick (1989), who although he claims (170-71) to side with Katz, might well be regarded as a partial ally by Forman et al., since he insists that there must be a "Real" that is the common basis of various religious experiences—even if it nowhere and never is experienced "purely." It

Proponents of the argument from experience are not without reply. They may note that it has become increasingly clear as the century progresses that science is not nearly so neutral, or value-free, as once believed; that scientific experiments, just like religious quests, often are guided beforehand by what is sought; that many scientific hypotheses are no more conclusively verifiable or falsifiable than are religious doctrines; and that the scientific community is just as liable as the religious to find itself trying to choose between competing paradigms that seem rationally or experimentally justified.[18] In short, science is simply one among a number of discrete and only partially overlapping areas of human inquiry, guided by its own rules and beset by its own problems, and it cannot be taken as final and universally definitive any more than religion can.

There is much to be said in favor of these points, yet they do not, by themselves, clinch the argument from experience. In the first place, the uncertainty surrounding a competing theory is not sufficient to establish the truth of one's own: science may not be as certain as once it was, but that does not mean that religion is thereby rendered more certain. Secondly, although there may not exist the difference of *kind* between religious and scientific assertions claimed by Evans, there still, clearly, is a difference of *degree*: religious experiences are not only subjective experiences, but subjective experiences of a rather uncommon type; not only are they not easily verified intersubjectively, but they are difficult to comprehend even by analogy to more common subjective experiences. Therefore, regardless of whether religious visions involve perception of the truth (and they may very well), claims made strictly on the basis of them cannot have the same general evidential weight as do claims that can be checked either intersubjectively or against more common types of subjective experience—for, unless we are to accept a total relativism that is as unsatisfactory to the religious philosopher as to the scientist, we must (and we do, instinctively) accord greater weight to evidence that is *more* disinterestedly gathered, *more* subject to intersubjective checking, *more* buttressed by ordinary perceptions and the inferences based on those perceptions.

---

seems to me but a short step from the admission of such a "Real" to the admission that, in some way, all religious experiences must intend it in some way, even if on a level inaccessible to speech or understanding.

18 On this issue, see especially Kuhn (1962) and Feyerabend (1975).

Thus, religious experience may convey truth, often helps to buttress the doctrines and beliefs of a particular religious community, and almost invariably conveys certainty to the experiencer, but it is *not* a secure basis for convincing an uncommitted seeker that one's doctrine is, in fact, true. In the arena of public discussion, one must appeal to more commonly accepted perceptual and inferential procedures. Early Buddhists made some attempts at this and, as we have seen, generally raised as many problems as they solved. With Dharmakīrti, a new and far more sophisticated attempt was made to show that those facts about the cosmos experienced as true by Buddhists who had followed the path could be shown *rationally* to accord with common perception and inference, to the point that any person who followed the Buddhist line of argument would be compelled to accept that its conclusions were true, so that the four noble truths were basic facts about the cosmos and the Buddha *was* supremely accomplished in spiritual matters.

8. The Turn to Epistemology and Logic

Though the arguments we reviewed in the last section were treated synchronically rather than historically (since our main interest was in *types* of arguments), we can, at least in general terms, trace an evolution of Buddhist religious arguments. Arguments seem to fall into three main phases, determined primarily by the overall position of Buddhism within the Indian philosophical scene at a given time. The first phase encompasses Buddhism's formative period of two to three centuries. During this period, Buddhism was simply one of a vast number of religious alternatives available in India. The Buddha and his immediate successors were most concerned to differentiate their Dharma from those of Jainas, Ājīvakas, Brahmins, and others. Most early Buddhist defenses of the Dharma do not, therefore, self-consciously presuppose its truth. Implicit or explicit arguments based on testimony, analogy or logic do, as we have seen, occur, but we also have seen that the Buddha was aware of the limitations of such arguments, and his main appeal was to personal verification of the Dharma through actually practicing the Buddhist path. The Buddha—like Buddhists since him—was probably aware of some of the pitfalls of the argument from experience,[1] but he still felt that it provided the surest means of guaranteeing to an outsider that the Dharma was in fact valid.

With Buddhism's increasing institutional stabilization and then, after Aśoka, expansion, Buddhists began to occupy themselves increasingly with *intra*-traditional concerns, with constructing and criticizing various arrangements of the basic elements of the Buddhist world-view—which were, for the purposes of discussion, assumed to be true. Early Buddhists had not had the luxury of such assumptions

1 The Buddha is clearly aware, in the *nikāyas,* that religious experience can give false as well as true information (otherwise, he could not criticize the "limited" visions of non-Buddhist yogins) and various parts of the tradition have applied appropriate checks to the experience-reports of their adherents. For a discussion of the latter issue, see Gimello (1978).

in their initial attempts to justify the Dharma, but the authors of the great abhidharma treatises, the Mahāyāna sūtras, and the early śāstras of Madhyamaka and Yogācāra were less concerned to refute non-Buddhist systems (though they did, of course, discuss them) than to refute errors *within* the Buddhist fold. Such internal discussions could proceed most smoothly when a maximum number of presuppositions were shared by the discussants, and Buddhists, presumably, did not need to question the fundamental validity of their tradition, but simply the way in which it was to be interpreted most effectively. Thus, even as radical a figure as Nāgārjuna, whose Mādhyamika dialectic seems to invalidate all possible philosophical positions, is careful to distinguish the ultimate level, on which his dialectic is utterly destructive, from the conventional level, on which dependent origination and causality still obtain, and on which the Buddhist world-view is presumed (though not proven) to be correct.[2]

Early Buddhists had at their disposal only limited and rather undeveloped modes of argumentation with which to defend the Dharma, which may in part explain their suspicion of logic and appeal to experience. Buddhists of the second phase absorbed advances in logic and epistemology as they occurred, but their concerns were primarily intra-Buddhist, and their efforts directed primarily at better explaining the presupposed elements of the Buddhist world-view or—in the case of someone like Nāgārjuna—using logic to *criticize* the belief that anything can be demonstrated conclusively by such traditional sources of knowledge as perception and inference. Nāgārjuna's critique remains a fundamental one, and in some ways it represents the most sophisticated possible development of the early Buddhist suspicion of logic and argumentation, but it did not spell the end of constructive philosophizing in India.[3] Indeed, it was in the post-Nāgārjuna period,

---

2 See MMK, chapter xxiv and VV verse 70.

3 It is a major point of contention in later Madhyamaka thought whether Nāgārjuna even would have wanted to put an end to constructive philosophy. The Svātantrikas claimed that the use of formal inference (*anumāna*) was justified in some ultimate-level arguments, while the Prāsaṅgikas upheld the use only of the "*reductio*," the *prasaṅga*. See Hopkins (1983) part five and Lopez (1987) 55-82 for detailed analyses. Interestingly, most Tibetan schools claim to be Prāsaṅgika, yet there is disagreement on what this means. The dGe lugs pas, for instance, tend to favor widespread use of formal inference, even in regard to ultimate truth. Other schools, such as the rNying ma, attack them for this, claiming that they are crypto-Svātantrikas—yet the dGe lugs pas steadfastly maintain that *their* version of Prāsaṅgika is the one countenanced by

between the second and sixth centuries C.E., that Indian philosophers representing a number of schools, especially the Mīmāṃsā, Nyāya and Buddhism, developed inference and argumentation to a sufficient degree that it became possible to engage in *inter*-traditional discussion that did not presuppose the validity of one or the other religious world-view. Indeed (ideally, at least), the only assumptions that were to be made were those on which all disputants could agree, although these, of course, had to be the sort of logical and empirical truths that were common and basic enough to be beyond dispute.

The central realization of the third phase of Buddhist argumentation thus was, as A.K. Warder expresses it, that

> We cannot make any assured progress in philosophy or, therefore, in the practice of Buddhism which is founded on knowledge of the truth, unless we first ascertain what sources of knowledge can be accepted. The theory of knowledge, therefore, becomes the basis of all study and all practice...going to the root of all philosophical problems.[4]

In other words, any tradition that concerns itself with "truth" must concern itself with establishing the foundations for secure knowledge, for without such foundations truth cannot be grasped firmly, and it is apprehension of the truth—specifically of critical religious or philosophical truths—that is the basis for liberation in so many Indian religions. Therefore, anyone devoted to religious knowledge *had* to be interested in epistemology, for it was epistemology that provided the basis for understanding how *any* truth, religious or otherwise, could be apprehended and validated. Thus, the major preoccupation of an important segment of Buddhist philosophers, beginning with Dignāga (sixth century) is the problem of *pramāṇa*, authoritative knowledge,[5] revolving around such questions as the number of *pramāṇas*, their relationship, the intrinsic or extrinsic nature of their validity, and the fields of inquiry to which they could properly be applied.

Buddhist philosophers concerned with *pramāṇa* often came to different conclusions on these issues than did their colleagues in other religious traditions, but there *did* develop a substantial body of shared assumptions, which greatly facilitated inter-systemic philosophical

---

tradition. For discussions of the dGe lugs approach to rationality, see, e.g., Sweet (1979) and Klein (1986) 13-89.

4 Warder (1980) 449.

5 For a discussion of my translation of *pramāṇa* as "authority," see below, p. 168, n. 5.

discussion. There was, first of all, agreement (usually unstated) on the fundamental axioms of philosophical thought, which include such notions as "the law of the conservation of being," whereby something can neither come from nor turn into nothing; the definition of existence as existence in space and time; the law of contradiction, whereby contradictory things cannot occupy the same place at the same time; the reality of causality, in which effects must be similar, but not identical, to their causes; the implication of the existence of non-*x* simply on the basis of the existence of x; the inferability of the unseen from the seen; and the law of the excluded middle, whereby a thing must be either *x* or non-*x*.[6]

There was, further, general agreement on rules for argumentation, and a careful cataloguing of the fallacies to be avoided in debate. These included self-residence (*ātmāśraya*), whereby a term is used illegitimately to explain itself, much like question-begging in Western thought; reciprocal dependence (*anyonyāśraya*) and vicious circle (*cakraka*), both examples of circularity in which an initial term is explained by a second or subsequent term, which then is explained by the first term; infinite regress (*anavasthā*), whereby a term's relation to a second term is explained by a third term whose relation to the first and second terms must be explained by a fourth term and so on, *ad infinitum*; and complexity (*gaurava*), whereby either entities or concepts are multiplied needlessly, leading to eventual, if not immediate, explanatory difficulties.[7]

The most important area of agreement was on the nature and process of formal inference (*anumāna*), which has been described by many writers as the Indian "syllogism." The term is not entirely unwarranted: an Indian formal inference differs structurally from an Aristotelian syllogism, and reflects somewhat different emphases, but is at least partially interchangeable with it, for both are instances of deductive processes rooted in universal principles arrived at through inductive generalization or definitional agreement. The Buddhist form of an Indian formal inference is as follows:

---

6 Robinson (1967) 63-65. The terminology he employs is, of course, more Western than Indian, but that there did exist Indian equivalents for the ideas behind the Western terms is difficult to dispute.

7 See, e.g., Potter (1976) 78-84 and Vidyabhusana (1978) chapter 34.

SUBJECT (*dharmin*)
is
PREDICATE (*sādhya, dharma*)
because
REASON (*hetu, liṅga*)
as in
ACCORDANT EXAMPLE (*sajātīya dṛṣṭānta*)
unlike in
NON-ACCORDANT EXAMPLE (*vijātīya dṛṣṭānta*)

The subject and predicate together form the thesis (*pakṣa, pratijñā*). The reason is supported by the accordant and non-accordant examples, whose presence in the "syllogism" grounds Indian formal inference more explicitly in the empirical realm than its Aristotelian counterpart. In order to be "correct," the reason must not only be exemplified, but have the characteristics of (a) relevance to the subject (*pakṣadharma*), (b) invariable concomitance with the predicate (*anvaya*) and (c) being such that its negation is invariably concomitant with the negation of the predicate (*vyatireka*).

The "chestnut" Indian syllogism, in which a cause is inferred from an observed effect is as follows:

(SUBJECT) On the hill
(PREDICATE) there is fire,
(REASON) because there is smoke,
(ACCORDANT) like in a kitchen
(NON-ACCORDANT) unlike in a lake.

The reason used ("because there is smoke") is valid, and the syllogism therefore correct because (a) the reason is relevant to the subject, since there is smoke on the hill, (b) the reason is invariably concomitant with the predicate, since where there is smoke, there is fire and (c) the non-reason is concomitant with the non-predicate, since where there is no smoke, there generally is no fire. The reason's invariable concomitances with the predicate in both positive and negative instances, in turn, serve as the unstated premises (arrived at through inductive generalization) on which an Aristotelian version of the same syllogism would be based. Therefore:

Where there is smoke there is fire.
On the hill there is smoke.
Therefore, on the hill there is fire.

To demonstrate even more clearly the functional similarity between the two forms of inference, let us take the classic Western "chestnut" example:

All men are mortal.
Socrates is a man.
Therefore, Socrates is mortal.

This can be restated as an Indian-style inference based on synonymy (or "own-nature": *svabhāva*):

(SUBJECT) Socrates
(PREDICATE) is mortal
(REASON) because he is a man,
(ACCORDANT) like Pericles
(NON-ACCORDANT) unlike Zeus.

The syllogism is correct because (a) the reason is relevant to the subject, since Socrates is a man, (b) the reason is invariably concomitant with the predicate, since men are mortal and (c) the non-reason is invariably concomitant with the non-predicate, since if a being is not mortal he will not be a man. The addition of the accordant and non-accordant examples does mark the syllogism as peculiarly Indian, and the interchangeability of the two forms should not be overstated, but there is at least enough similarity that the rough translation I have suggested becomes plausible.There are countless other details of Indian logical theory, some of which will be encountered later in the introduction or in the translation. This general account should suffice for now.[8]

With the acquisition of a common "language"for conducting intersystemic philosophical discussion, there existed for the first time the possibility that the different Indian traditions could debate among themselves the fundamental truth-claims that each system made, whether about epistemology, ontology, or even the path to spiritual liberation. Indeed, one's opponents were far more likely to criticize one's fundamental beliefs than one's commentarial glosses on received tradition, so we should not be surprised that the inter-religious debate in India became lively indeed. Buddhist philosophers used to intra-traditional discussions of abhidharma categories that did not re-

---

8 For more detail, see, e.g., Stcherbatsky (1962) I:II:III, Mookerjee (1980) chapters XXII-XXIV, Potter (1976) 59-78, Solomon (1976-78), Vidyabhusana (1978) chapter 95, Perdue (1992) and various articles in Matilal and Evans (1986).

quire justification to other Buddhists suddenly found themselves defending the existence of past and future lives against Cārvāka materialists, the possibility of liberation against both materialists and Mīmāṃsakas, their denial of universals aginst the Vaiśeṣikas, their rejection of a creator God against the Naiyāyikas, the theory of momentariness against the Sāṃkhyas and Jainas—and the theory of no-self (*anātman*) against virtually everybody.

It should be evident from this that religion and religious truth-claims were not granted some special exemption from the need to conform to the newly developed canons of evidence and validity. Quite the contrary: to the degree that religion has always been a central part of Indian philosophical traditions, the justification of religious truth-claims became a major concern of many of those who developed new logical and epistemological tools, for religious truths were the most existentially significant of all possible truths, and therefore the truths most urgently in need of clear demonstration. That Indian philosophers genuinely believed that they could, and attempted to, prove religious assertions shows the confidence they felt in the rational techniques that had been developed. It shows, too, their implicit realization that, whatever evidential value personal religious experience may have for the experiencer, it carries considerably less weight in public discussions, where the evidence of greatest value is that which is common to all participants.

The basic axiom on which most later Indian philosophical discussions rest is beautifully stated by Dharmakīrti at the outset of his *Nyāyabindu* ("Drop of Reasoning"), where he writes, simply: "All human accomplishment is preceded by correct cognition."[9] The focus on "human accomplishment" locates the philosophical enterprise within the projects, humble or exalted, that are so central to human existence. We are, quite simply, beings with goals, and the goals may vary from walking into the kitchen to make a cup of tea, to learning a mathematical theorem, to achieving total peace of mind. Our goals are valuable to us, and we consider them in some sense "good," yet we cannot accomplish them unless we know what to do and what not to do in trying to achieve them. To go into the kitchen to brew tea, I have

---

9 NB i:1, reconstructed as: *samyagjñānapūrvikā sarvapuruṣārthasiddhir*. The original and Dharmottara's commentary are found at Śāstri (1954) 1. These are translated at Stcherbatsky (1962) II, 1-11. The verse and Vinītadeva's commentary are found at Gangopadhyaya (1971) 79-86. For further discussion of the implications of the verse, see Phillips (1987) 238ff. and R. Jackson (1988).

to know the direction to walk, how to open the door, where the tea is kept, etc., and I must know *not* to go into the bathroom, *not* to take out the coffee can. To learn a mathematical theorem I must know certain operations by which numbers are combined, and must know *not* to calculate incorrectly or skip steps in reasoning. To achieve total peace of mind I must, if a Buddhist, know which virtues to practice and which vices to avoid, which views to shun and which to cultivate. In short, then, the accomplishment of human goals requires "correct cognition." We must *know* what to adopt and what to reject, what to practice and what to avoid in the completion of our projects. If knowledge is so utterly vital even to the simplest human activity, then the ascertainment of what is knowledge and what is not, of which assertions are reliable and which are not, becomes fundamental. One must, therefore, strive to understand the way in which knowledge functions, and come to know what is to be accepted and what rejected in the realm of epistemology itself—for once this has been determined, one can have greater confidence in one's knowledge in other areas of human endeavor. Finally, then, Dharmakīrti's axiom states that *all* human accomplishment is preceded by correct cognition. Thus, secure knowledge is required not only for ordinary human projects, but for "ultimate" ones, as well, and for most human beings, the "ultimate" project is the achievement—here or hereafter—of some religious *summum bonum*. Religious statements, thus, cannot be exempted from the sort of checking procedures that must be applied to other kinds of truth-claims, and so some may not stand up to scrutiny. By the same token, however, just as ordinary truth-claims can be confirmed or refuted through commonly accepted perceptual and inferential processes, so may religious claims. The door, therefore, is open to the secure establishment of the validity of this or that religion, as a result of which one ought to be able to conclude that the people who subscribe to the religion will, in fact, accomplish the goals described for them by the teachers and scriptures of the tradition. It is important to note that neither Dharmakīrti nor most other religiously affiliated Indian logicians believed that the *summum bonum* described by a religious tradition was actually *accessible* through rational argumentation—to achieve, e.g., nirvāṇa, one had to enter the path and experience liberating insights directly—but they nevertheless felt great confidence that the existence of such a *summum bonum* was *demonstrable* through argumentation.

Whether the confidence of Dharmakīrti and others, that logic and epistemology could settle truth-claims in all but the most hidden matters, is justified or not is not for us to decide here. As we have seen, there are thinkers within both Indian (e.g., Nāgārjuna) and Western thought (e.g., Nietzsche, Wittgenstein, Derrida) who question seriously whether we *ever* can establish the foundations of utter certitude, and who believe the beginning of wisdom to lie in the abandonment of the quest for fool-proof logic and epistemology and in the acceptance of the provisional nature of *all* expressible truths. Such a view may have a great deal to be said for it philosophically, but, rightly or wrongly—as we also have seen—it often is felt to entail a relativism that is both philosophically and psychologically discomfiting; it certainly runs very much counter to both the intuitions and the arguments of Dharmakīrti, whose works are among the greatest expressions of the epistemological self-confidence felt by so many Indian philosophers in the middle and late first millenium C.E.[10]

10 Their confidence is not unlike that of medieval Christian theologians who, armed with the newly discovered Aristotelian syllogism, felt most religious and philosophical issues to be amenable to clear rational adjudication.

9. *Dharmakīrti: Life, Work, and Influence*

Dharmakīrti is not the first of the great Buddhist "logicians"—that distinction is Dignāga's—but he is the most interesting for our purposes because it is he whose works form the basis of the study of logic and epistemology in the various Tibetan schools and, most importantly, it was he who first attempted a systematic demonstration of the truth of such basic Buddhist assertions as the four noble truths and the supremacy of the Buddha's spiritual attainment. He did so in the *Pramāṇasiddhi* ("Establishment of Authority") chapter of what is generally regarded as his *magnum opus*, the *Pramāṇavārttika* ("Commentary on Authority," or alternatively, "Commentary on [Dignāga's *Compendium on*] *Authority*"). It is a translation of rGyal tshab rje's Tibetan commentary on the *Pramāṇasiddhi* chapter that forms the main part of this book.

As is the case with so many ancient Indians, we have little reliable historical information about Dharmakīrti. There is general agreement that he lived during either the sixth or, more probably, seventh century C.E., but for details of his life, we must rely on the histories written in Tibetan by Bu ston rin chen grub (fourteenth century) and Tāranātha (early seventeenth century), who had in turn to rely on a mixture of fact and legend in their reconstructions of the lost Indian past.[1]

According to the Tibetan histories, Dharmakīrti was the son of a south Indian Brahmin philosopher. He was steeped early in the traditional sciences and in Hindu thought, but was converted to Buddhism by reading Buddhist śāstras while in his teens. He became a Buddhist layman (*upāsaka*), and eventually travelled to northern India, where he received ordination as a monk from the ācārya Dharmapāla. He went on to study with a direct disciple of Dignāga, Īśvarasena, who exposed him to Dignāga's masterwork, the *Pramāṇasamuccaya* ("Compendium

---

1 For English translations, see, respectively, Obermiller (1931-32) and Chattopadhyaya (1970). Modern scholarship is divided on Dharmakīrti's dates. Long accepted was Frauwallner's (1961) suggestion of 600-660. Lindtner (1980) has recently suggested 530-600.

on Authority"). Dharmakīrti quickly surpassed Īśvarasena in his understanding of the work, correcting many errors of interpretation. Īśvarasena accepted Dharmakīrti's superiority graciously, and asked him to write a definitive commentary on the *Pramāṇasamuccaya*. This would be the *Pramāṇavārttika*, very possibly the earliest and certainly the most important of the "Seven Treatises on Authority" attributed to Dharmakīrti by Tibetan tradition. The others are the *Pramāṇaviniścaya* and *Nyāyabindu* (both general treatises on logic and epistemology), along with the *Hetubindu* (on logical reasons), *Sambandhaparīkṣā* (on the relationship between logical reasons and predicates), *Santānāntarasiddhi* (on perception and the problem of other minds) and *Vadanyāya* (on debate technique).[2] Dharmakīrti became a renowned debater, dedicated enough to the refutation of his opponents that he supposedly lived for two years with the great Mīmāṃsaka Kumārila, disguised as a servant so as to learn his system and eventually defeat him in debate. He also is supposed to have defeated the Advaita Vedāntin Śaṅkara in three of the latter's incarnations—Śaṅkara drowned himself in the Ganges after his first two defeats, and converted to Buddhism after the third.

Had Dharmakīrti been as great a debater as the legends suggest, Hinduism barely could have survived his onslaught. If his forensic legacy must be regarded with a bit of caution, there is no doubting the immense intellectual legacy he left the Buddhist philosophical tradition, most importantly in his masterwork, the *Pramāṇavārttika*. As noted above, it was written as a commentary on Dignāga's pioneering *Pramāṇasamuccaya*. In fact, however, the Pramāṇavārttika is far more than a gloss on Dignāga's work: it follows it only generally, and reformulates old issues and raises new ones.[3] It is divided into four chapters

---

2 Of Dharmakīrti's works, the *Pramāṇavārttika, Nyāyabindu* and *Vādanyāya* survive *in toto* in Sanskrit. The others are found in Tibetan translation, though Sanskrit fragments of all remain, and some have been reconstructed in Sanskrit. Few have been translated *in toto* into Western languages. For more complete references, see Potter (1977), Warder (1980) 539-540, Lindtner (1980) 27-28, Phillips (1987) 238, Dreyfus (1991) and the entries under the various works in my bibliography. Lindtner (1980) suggests that two other (lost) works be added to the Dharmakīrti canon: the *Tattvaniṣkarṣa* and the *Laukikapramāṇaparīkṣā*, though this suggestion has not yet received general acceptance. Also, see the discussion below, section II:1.

3 Warder (1980) 470. Hayes (1984), making a similar point, suggests that Dignāga and Dharmakīrti are essentially different sorts of philosophers, the former "critical" and the latter "dogmatic." See also van Bijlert (1989) 170-71,

(all in verse), which cover inference for oneself (*svārthānumāna*), the establishment of authority (*pramāṇasiddhi*), perception (*pratyakṣa*), and inference for the sake of others (*parārthānumāna*). There is some dispute as to the proper ordering of the chapters. Tibetan scholars accept the ordering just given, while the editors of recent Sanskrit editions have favored the ordering: establishment of authority, perception, inference for oneself and inference for the sake of others.[4] The *Svārthanumāna* chapter discusses the general structure and types of formal inference (or syllogism), and the *apoha* theory of meaning. The *Pramāṇasiddhi* chapter, with which this book is centrally concerned, seeks to define authority and to demonstrate that the Buddha, both because he is genuinely accomplished and because he speaks the truth, is uniquely authoritative for those intent on spiritual freedom. The *Pratyakṣa* chapter establishes that there are two, and only two, sources of authoritative cognition (*pramāṇas*), perception and inference, and goes on to discuss the four types of perception that are to be accepted (sensory, mental, apperceptive and yogic). The *Parārthānumāna* chapter discusses the ways in which logical reasons are correct or incorrect.

Like many Indian Buddhist philosophers, Dharmakīrti never gave an explicit name to his own philosophical standpoint. The tradition that has been most deeply influenced by him, the Tibetan, usually identifies him (as well as Dignāga) as a "Cittamātrin ('mind-only-ist' = Yogācāra,[5] a Mahāyāna school) Following Reasoning" in contrast to such "Cittamātrins Following Scripture" (and positing a storehouse consciousness, *ālaya vijñāna*) as Asaṅga and (in his later treatises) Vasubandhu.[6] At the same time, some Tibetan writers on tenet-systems (*siddhānta*, T. *grub mtha'*) specify that the Sautrāntika—a Hīnayāna school—includes those who "follow Dharmakīrti's *Seven Treatises on Valid Cognition*."[7] If Dharmakīrti influenced Sautrāntikas, might he have been one himself? Some scholars have examined Dhar-

---

n. 6. The *Pramāṇasamuccaya* is available *in toto* only in Tibetan translation. The best Western work on it to date is Hattori (1968).

4 The two most recent editions, those of Shastri (1968) and Miyasaka (1972-77) follow the ordering just enumerated, but there is by no means scholarly consensus or uniformity. In order to overcome the confusion, I have referred throughout Part I to the chapters of *Pramāṇavārttika* by their Sanskrit titles. For further discussion, see p. 167, n. 1.

5 Some Tibetan analysts see Cittamātra and Yogācāra as only partially overlapping terms, but for our purposes here, they may be treated as synonymous.

6 See, e.g., Sopa and Hopkins (1976) 111 and Klein (1986) 24-25.

7 Sopa and Hopkins (1976) 92.

makīrti's work and declared him to be, in fact, a Sautrāntika.[8] A major part of the problem here is that we have extant virtually no self-proclaimed "Sautrāntika"literature, which makes defining the tenets and parameters of the school extremely difficult. Thus, we find among modern scholars of Buddhism some who limit the term to an anti-abhidharma Hīnayāna tradition with no literary remains, others who insist that the school at least may be exemplified by Vasubandhu's *Abhidharmakośabhāṣya,* and still others who define the school primarily in terms of the works of Dignāga and Dharmakīrti.[9] Nor are the Tibetans entirely in accord on the parameters of Sautrāntika. Most agree that (a) no purely Sautrāntika texts were translated into Tibetan and (b) that there were in India Sautrāntikas who followed the style and outlook of Vasubandhu's *Abhidharmakośabhāṣya*—though this need not entail that the text itself was Sautrāntika. The dGe lugs pas assert, uniquely, that there also were in India Sautrāntikas who followed the style and outlook of Dignāga and Dharmakīrti—though presumably, as Hīnayānists, they would ignore those elements of his writing that seemed too religiously Mahāyānist or philosophically idealistic.[10]

What are we to make of this welter of views? Is Dharmakīrti a Hīnayānist or Mahāyānist? Sautrāntika or Cittamātrin? It is undeniable that, with his predominant interest in logic and epistemology, he writes little that is suggestive of either the style or themes of the great Mahāyāna sūtras or śāstras, and that his one major description of Buddhist religious doctrines, in the *Pramāṇasiddhi* chapter of the *Pramāṇavārttika,* is largely in "Hīnayāna"terms, with external objects treated as real existents and arhantship (not omniscient buddhahood) posited as the goal of a path that is completed through the direct realization of no-self (as opposed to voidness, the more common Mahāyāna term). Further, the specific ways in which he explicates his religious and philosophical views, there and elsewhere, are quite close to those found in Vasubandhu's *Abhidharmakośabhāṣya*—considered by all Tibetan traditions to represent the "Sautrāntika"standpoint. On the other hand, it is entirely possible that Dharmakīrti may simply

---

8 See Singh (1984); cf. Hayes (1986) for a highly critical review. For a discussion, and rejection, of the unusual view that Dharmakīrti was a Mādhyamika, see Steinkellner (1990).

9 Versions of the first and second positions are represented by, e.g., Bareau (1955) 155-59 and Dutt (1970) 186-89. The last position is reflected in, e.g., Singh (1984) and Mookerjee (1980).

10 See, e.g., Sopa and Hopkins (1976) 111, Klein (1986) 24-25 and (1991) 26-27.

have reduced Buddhism to its "lowest common denominator" in the *Pramāṇasiddhi* chapter so as more effectively to counter the general criticisms of the Buddhist world-view made by his opponents. The view he defends, therefore, need not be his own in every detail. Indeed, Dharmakīrti clearly holds views associated with Cittamātra, as, for instance, in the *Pratyakṣa* chapter of the *Pramāṇavārttika* (e.g., verses 320ff. and 532ff.), where he explicitly refers to the ultimate non-difference between the epistemic subject and the epistemic object, i.e., the true nature of reality as "percept-only" (*vijñaptimātra*).[11] Furthermore—though this cannot be counted as strong evidence—Dharmakīrti is said by the traditional histories to have been a tantric practitioner, appealing on one occasion to the deity Heruka for inspiration, and on another occasion reciting a powerful mantra in order to escape his house, which had been set afire by his opponents.[12] Thus, if the denial of external objects is Cittamātrin (or Yogācāra), and if Cittamātrin ideas (not to mention tantric practices!) are Mahāyānist, then Dharmakīrti must have been both a Cittamātrin and a Mahāyānist. It still might be possible to argue that Dharmakīrti is a Sautrāntika *if* Sautrāntika is defined in such a way that it does not exclude a mind-only perspective on reality, but this then would leave the problem of how "Sautrāntikas" who did not accept mind-only could be covered by the term. The best solutions seem to be the acceptance either of the Tibetan idea that Dharmakīrti is indeed a "Cittamātrin Following Reasoning," in effect a "Sautrāntika-Yogācāra" (in this case, assertion of mind-only is taken as definitive of Cittamātra) or the suggestion of some modern scholars[13] that Dharmakīrti, along with Dignāga, be assigned to an epistemologically oriented school of his own, the "*Pramāṇavāda*" (in this case, assertion of the storehouse consciousness, as well as various cosmological and psychological speculations, is taken as definitive of Cittamātra).

Whatever Dharmakīrti's actual position, he came deeply to influence late Indian Buddhist philosophy, both through his commentators and through those who made use of his theories for their own purposes, such as Svātantrika Mādhyamikas, whose greatest representatives

---

11 For a persuasive discussion of this issue, see Dreyfus and Lindtner (1989).

12 Chattopadhyaya (1972) 230, 235. It is curious that, if Dharmakīrti really was a *tāntrika*, we see this nowhere reflected in his writings, especially in his accounts of the rebirth process—a topic discussed extensively in tantric traditions.

13 For instance, Warder (1971, 1980).

included Jñānagarbha, Śāntarakṣita and Kamalaśīla (all eighth century), and whose philosophical perspective combined a Mādhyamika approach to ultimate reality with a Dharmakīrtian analysis of the conventional world.[14] Partly through Svātantrika Mādhyamika influence on early Tibetan scholasticism, Dharmakīrti would become the "conventional" philosopher par excellence for Tibetan tradition, too.[15] The *Pramāṇavārttika* was the most influential of Dharmakīrti's texts, and has received either direct or indirect commentary from almost every important Indian or Tibetan philosopher after Dharmakīrti's time. Ironically, though, if the legends be believed, Dharmakīrti despaired of finding any disciple who could understand it. At the same time, Dharmakīrti himself composed a commentary to only one chapter of the *Pramāṇavārttika*, the *Svārthānumāna* (whether because it was the first chapter or the most difficult is uncertain). He permitted his most important disciple, Devendrabuddhi (ca. 630-690), to write a commentary on the other three chapters. Dissatisfied with the first draft, Dharmakīrti effaced it with water; dissatisfied with the second, he burned it. He finally accepted the third draft, damning it with the rather faint praise that it did, at least, manage to convey the literal meaning—although it had missed the deeper significance.[16] Devendrabuddhi's *Pañjikā* to the *Pramāṇavārttika* was followed by the *Alaṃkāra* (or *Bhāṣya*) written by Prajñākaragupta (ca. 850?), who criticizes Devendrabuddhi's interpretations in a number of places and comments at length on the religious (particularly the Mahāyāna) implications of Dharmakīrti's work. Devendrabuddhi and Prajñākaragupta are considered by Tibetan tradition to be the twin fountainheads of *Pramāṇavārttika* commentary, an opinion that is borne out by the proliferation of sub-commentaries to their works: an extensive commentary on Devendrabuddhi's commentary was written by his disciple Śākyabodhi (who may also have studied directly with Dharmakīrti), and subcommentaries on Prajñākaragupta's by Ravigupta (ninth century?) and Yamāri (eleventh century).[17]

---

14 See, e.g., Eckel (1987).

15 On the other hand, he has had very little influence in East Asian Buddhism, both because the texts that proved most influential in East Asia generally predate Dharmakīrti, and (perhaps more arguably) because the forms of logical and epistemological analysis favored by later Indian Buddhists found little precedent—hence a cool reception—among East Asian Buddhists.

16 Chattopadhyaya (1972) 239.

17 For discussions of Dharmakīrti's commentators, see Stcherbatsky (1962) I, 39-47 and Vidyabhusana (1978) II:II:III. The only two commentaries extant *in toto*

Tibetan interest in Dharmakīrti was evinced by Sa skya pa scholars like rNgog lo tsā ba bLo ldan shes rab and Phya pa chos kyi seng ge as early as the twelfth century, and the great thirteenth-century polymath, Sa skya paṇḍita Kun dga' rgyal mtshan (1182-1251), wrote independent treatises on logic that drew heavily from the *Pramāṇavārttika,* thereby establishing Dharmakīrti as the authoritative logician and epistemologist for the Tibetan tradition and the *Pramāṇavārttika* as the most authoritative of his works. The first actual commentary on the *Pramāṇavārttika* was written in the thirteenth century, by 'U yug pa Rig pa'i seng ge (d. 1253). Sa skya pa influence extended to other schools. In the fourteenth century, the 'Bri gung bKa'brgyud pas explicitly sought to ally study of *pramāṇa* with practice of a Mādhyamika-oriented path to liberation, and in the fifteenth century, Tsong kha pa, the founder of the dGe lugs, studied the *Pramāṇavārttika* with such Sa skya pa masters as Red mda' ba. Tsong kha pa passed on his respect for the work to his major disciples, rGyal tshab dar ma rin chen (1364-1432), mKhas grub dge legs dpal bzang po (1385-1438) (who were themselves ex-Sa skya pas) and dGe 'dun grub pa (1391-1475)—each of whom went on to write a commentary on the *Pramāṇavārttika.* dGe lugs pas consider rGyal tshab rje's *rNam 'grel thar lam gsal byed* ("Elucidating the Path to Liberation According to the *Pramāṇavārttika*"), which draws on the commentarial traditions founded by both Devendrabuddhi and Prajñākaragupta, to be the greatest of these. It is the basis for later dGe lugs pa monastic *yig chas* (textbooks) on the *Pramāṇavārttika,* and is studied to this day by virtually all dGe lugs pa monks. Among the five major subjects studied by aspirants to the dGe lugs pa rank of *dge bshes,*[18] *tshad ma (pramāṇa)* is based chiefly on the *Pramāṇavārttika,* and understanding of the *Pramāṇavārttika* based chiefly on rGyal tshab rje's commentary. rGyal tshab rje's commentary was sufficiently important that it drew the critical attention of latter-day Sa skya pas, most notably Śākya mchog ldan (1427-1507). Other Tibetan writers who have commented on the *Pramāṇavārttika* include the Sa skya pa Go ram pa bsod nams seng ge

---

in Sanskrit are Prajñākaragupta's *Pramāṇavārttikālakāra* (or *-bhāṣya*) and Manorathanandin's *Pramāṇavārttikavṛtti.* Devendrabuddhi's *Pramāṇavārttika-pañjikā,* Śākyabodhi's *Pramāṇavārttikavṛtti,* Ravigupta's *Pramāṇavārttikavṛtti* and Yamāri's *Pramāṇavārttikālaṃkāraṭīkā* are available in Tibetan translation. For more information, see the appropriate author-entries in the bibliography.

18 Logic and Epistemology (T. *tshad ma*), Vinaya (*'dul ba*), Abhidharma (*mngon rtogs*), the Perfection of Wisdom (*sher phyin*) and Madhyamaka (*dbu ma*).

(1429-1489), the 'Brug pa bKa' brgyud pa polymath Padma dkar po (1527-1592) and the nineteenth-century rNying ma pa exponent of the "non-sectarian" (*ris med*) movement Mi pham rgya mtsho.[19]

19 Sa skya paṇḍita's major work on *pramāṇa* is the *Tshad ma rigs pa'i gter*; 'U yug pa rig pa'i seng ge's commentary is the *rNam 'grel rig mdzod chen mo* (see van der Kuijp [1983] 116), rGyal tshab rje's the *rNam 'grel thar lam gsal byed,* mKhas grub rje's the *rGyas pa'i bstan bcos tshad ma rnam 'grel gyi rgya cher bshad pa rigs pa'i rgya mtsho,* dGe 'dun grub pa's the *Tshad ma rnal 'grel legs par bshad pa,* Śākya mchog ldan's the *rGyas pa'i bstan bcos tshad ma rnam 'grel gyi rnam bshad kun bzang chos kyi rol mtsho,* Go ram pa's two commentaries the *rGyas pa'i bstan bcos tshad ma rnam 'grel gyi rnam par bshad pa kun tu bzang po'i 'od zer* and the *rGyas pa'i bstan bcos tshad ma rnam 'grel gyi ngag don kun tu bzang po'i nyi ma,* Padma dkar po's analysis the *Tshad ma'i mdo sde bdun dang bcas pa'i spyi don rig pa'i snying po,* and Mi pham rgya mtsho's commentary the *Tshad ma rnam 'grel gyi gzhung gsal por bshad ma rnam 'grel gyi rgya chen bshad pa rigs pa'i rgya mtsho.* For further information on the development of *pramāṇa* study in Tibet and detailed bibliographic references, see especially van der Kuijp (1983) and (1987), Steinkellner (1983) and D. Jackson (1987). For bibliographic details on the works listed, see van der Kuijp (1983), Chandra (1963) and Kanakura et al. (1953). Fukuda and Ishihama (1986 ref.) list (in Tibetan) the complete text-divisions (*sa bcad*) of the commentaries by 'U yug pa, rGyal tshab rje, mKhas grub rje, dGe 'dun grub pa, Go rams pa (the second listed above) and Śākya mchog ldan.

10. *Basic Assumptions of Dharmakīrti's Thought*

As noted above, the *Pramāṇasiddhi* chapter of the *Pramāṇavārttika* is devoted to the "establishment of authority," i.e., to establishing the definition of epistemic authority (*pramāṇa*), and then to establishing that the Buddha is uniquely authoritative for those seeking spiritual liberation. The latter, in turn, is established through a demonstration that (a) the Buddha *can*, in fact, have achieved the supremely enlightened state that Buddhist tradition claims (this is shown in large part through a proof of the existence of a multitude of lives in which the necessary causes of enlightenment can be cultivated) and (b) the four noble truths, the core of the Buddha's teaching, are true (the bulk of the discussion here revolves around a proof of the unique spiritual efficacy of the Buddhist insight into no-self).

We also noted earlier that Dharmakīrti, like others in the *pramāṇa* tradition, was confident (a) that the development of generally accepted inferential procedures assured that the "correct cognition" that necessarily preceded any successful human action could be securely grounded, and (b) that human *religious* knowledge could thus be grounded, strictly through chains of inferential reasoning that, in every case, would ultimately be founded on perceptions and principles common to all humans. One need not, therefore, appeal to principles or experiences unique to one's own religious tradition, for they were of little value in *inter*-traditional discussions and, furthermore, proof could be provided without them. In the *Pramāṇasiddhi* chapter, therefore, Dharmakīrti does not try to demonstrate past and future lives by claiming that if they did *not* exist, there would be no strong foundation for the Buddhist notion of karma. Rather, he attempts to show that they are possible because the mind-body relation is such as to permit them. Similarly, he does not attempt to argue that the Buddhist insight into the no-self of persons has unique spiritual value because it is stated thus in Buddhist scripture, or because Buddhist meditators have thus experienced it. Rather, he frames a philosophical and psychological demonstration that belief in a self entails suffering, and that the elimination of that belief entails the elimination of suffering. Thus,

Dharmakīrti is quite sensitive to the problems of what we today call "philosophy of religion," and he strives to set forth an argument for the truth of Buddhist religious assertions that relies as little as possible on idiosyncratically Buddhist assumptions. There *are,* however, certain assumptions that inform the arguments in the *Pramāṇasiddhi* chapter—many of them demonstrated elsewhere in Dharmakīrti's work or in the writings of other Buddhist philosophers—and it may be worthwhile to note some of the more important ones.

The assumptions that I will detail might cautiously be described as "Sautrāntika" (as opposed to Cittamātrin)—though we must bear in mind the definitional difficulties described in the previous section. Before we turn to these, however, something ought to be said about the assumptions borrowed by Dharmakīrti from the pre-Sautrāntika abhidharma tradition. It sometimes is assumed that because Sautrāntikas generally are assumed to have been critical of aspects of the Vaibhāṣika (or Sarvāstivāda) abhidharma, and gave much of their attention to logical and epistemological matters, that they "rejected" abhidharma categories. Quite to the contrary, however, Dharmakīrti is heavily indebted to the abhidharmists who preceded him. Indeed, they gave him much of the "language" with which he describes reality. Thus, Dharmakīrti makes the central assumption that—questions of their ultimate status as "external" or "percept-only" notwithstanding—it is legitimate to describe the cosmos in terms of dharmas, elementary units of existence whose conjunction, opposition and interaction are the process we call the universe. The dharmas are like "numbers" in a universal equation that is, in fact, calculated in quasi-mathematical terms. Dharmas are divided in various ways, e.g., into conditioned (forms, cognitions, mental factors and non-associated compositional factors) and unconditioned (space and cessations, including nirvāṇa), or the five aggregates (matter, sensation, recognition, formations and cognition), or the twelve "entrances" (*āyatanas:* six faculties and six objects), or the eighteen fields (*dhātus:* six faculties, six objects and six cognitions). The sphere of the physical (or "form": *rūpa*) is divisible into the five "elements" (*bhūta*): earth, water, fire, air and ether (or "space"). The sphere of the mental is described in terms of (a) the primary, bare cognitions (*citta*) through which an object is initially apprehended and (b) the constellation of mental factors (*caitta*), some fixed and some variable, that give a particular quality, or tone, to a mental moment.[1]

---

1 Discussions of these basic categories can be found in most basic works on

The central doctrine of Dharmakīrti's ontology is the theory of momentariness, whereby the "objective" and "continuous" world we believe we experience is actually a subsequent imposition onto the actual nature of things, which truly is discontinuous events (*kṣaṇa*) of infinitesimal extension and duration. The theory of momentariness is closely connected with two even more fundamental Buddhist assertions, impermanence and no-self, of both of which it is in a sense a corollary. The theory seems to have arisen among the Sautrāntikas, at least in part as a critique of the Vaibhāṣika account of impermanence, which divided an "event" into moments of arising, subsistence, decay and cessation. According to the Sautrāntikas, such a description makes a mockery of the notion of a momentary event, which ought by definition to be irreducible. Furthermore, if such a division is made, then it might be argued that each of an event's sub-moments *also* ought to be thus divisible, and so on, in infinite regress. The Sautrāntikas arrive at their own theory through a forceful application of the law of the excluded middle, maintaining that phenomena must be utterly permanent or utterly impermanent. In other words, if events are granted the slightest duration, then there is no reason to believe that they ever would cease, for duration would be their *nature*, and thus ineradicable. Thus, their duration must be *no* duration, or, rather, a duration so brief that an event's cessation is virtually simultaneous with its arising. To allow duration is to open the door for permanence, and where there is permanence—a subsisting self, or ātman—there can be no change. Manifestly, the world is one in which change obtains, so, finally, the world only can be explained on the basis of momentariness.[2]

The most common criticism of the theory of momentariness (as of the theory of no-self, *anātman*) is that it makes causality unintelligible, since causality implies some sort of continuity, while the momentary events posited by the Buddhist are *dis*continuous. The Buddhist response is that momentariness does *not* vitiate causality, because every

---

Buddhist philosophy, e.g., Warder (1980), Stcherbatsky (1970), Sopa and Hopkins (1976) and The Dalai Lama (1985).

2 The most complete account of the doctrine of momentariness remains that of Stcherbatsky (1962) I, 79-203, though as both Zwilling (1975) and Klein (1986 [29-30]) have pointed out, Stcherbatsky's interpretation of the Sautrāntika notion of ultimate truth is open to criticism for his failure to consider that composite impermanent objects may have as much "reality" as the "events" that compose them. Cf. also Zwilling (1976) Introduction, Mookerjee (1980) *passim*, Koller (1970) 154-55 and Steinkellner (1968-69).

momentary event (*kṣaṇa*) is marked by causal "efficiency" (*arthakriyatva*) whereby it "impresses" its particular characteristic (or "own-mark," *svalakṣaṇa*) on a subsequent event (which then is designated as "the same"), or whereby it serves as the cooperative condition for the arising of an event of a different type. Just as the smallest particles known to physics are hard to distinguish on an ultimate level, and yet are the basis of the diverse world we know, so too the momentary events posited by Buddhism are difficult to characterize in their barest sense, and yet they combine in different ways to form the composites of the known world. We know these composites to have particular characteristics and causal efficiency, and logical rigor demands that the elements out of which composites are made be of a non-contradictory nature. Therefore, momentary events must be efficient and have particular characteristics, and so causality must, in fact, obtain.[3]

For a proponent of momentariness, then, the apparently continuous "things" that we observe in everyday life are, in fact, *series* of infinitesimal events, in which an event of a particular type lasts but the shortest instant, to be replaced in the next instant by an event of a similar type. Each event in a series is both the effect of the event (and other cooperative-condition events) that preceded it, and the cause (along with other cooperative-condition events) of the event that succeeds it. A "seed" or a "jar," then, is not a continuous thing, but a series of seed-events or jar-events, in which the "continuity" is provided by a "constant" constellation of causes and conditions. The "changes" we describe on the macroscopic level, then, simply are changes in the constellation of events. A seed actually "becomes" a sprout in infinitesimal increments through subtle shifts in the effect on the seed of such conditions as moisture and sunlight. A jar is "destroyed" when

---

3 At PV *Pratyakṣa*:3 and 50b-51b, Dharmakīrti intimates that whatever is efficient, or able to perform a function, is (a) ultimately existent and (b) possessed of an own-mark. This, of course, leaves open the question of whether efficient, "own-marked" phenomena are *just* momentary events (as maintained by Stcherbatsky and a number of Tibetan—especially rNying ma pa—commentators) or also include impermanent composites such as are encountered in "everyday" perception (as maintained by the dGe lugs pas). For an excellent discussion of these issues, see Klein (1986) 28-32 and chapter 1. The PV verses are cited by her on pp. 35 and 60. For an analysis of Tibetan interpretations of *Pratyakṣa*:3, see Zwilling (1981). For more on *arthakriyatva*, see, e.g., Nagatomi (1967-68), as well as the discussions in Stcherbatsky (1962) and Mookerjee (1980).

a hammer-series suddenly interrupts the condition of cohesion on the basis of which we call a particular arrangement of matter a "jar." Conventionally, then, we may talk about "transformation" or "destruction" as "processes" that "things" undergo, but in point of fact there is *only* an ever-shifting constellation of events that are irreducibly instantaneous, and the "processes" we impute to "things" are, except at the most basic level, mental constructions.

From the earliest abhidharma treatises, Buddhists have attempted to enumerate and classify the various causes and conditions that apply in different causal situations. These *hetus* and *pratyayas* have varied in number and distribution from system to system. I will not discuss here all the causes and conditions posited by Dharmakīrti, but will touch only on his general definition of a cause and those specific causes and conditions that are central to his arguments. In general terms, Dharmakīrti views a cause negatively as that factor in the absence of which a result cannot arise, and positively as that factor a variation in which will assure a variation in the result. His specific discussions seem to presuppose a basic division into, on the one hand, the entity under discussion, which is a result of a homogeneous substantial cause, and the cooperative conditions that contribute to its generation. The *upadāna hetu* (or *karaṇa*) is, literally, the "obtaining cause," but it is better characterized as the "substantial cause," for it is that "substance" or entity-moment whose disappearance or "transformation" is followed in the next moment by an event of the same type, which is designated as the substantial result. Thus, on the microscopic level, a seed-event is the substantial cause of the seed-event that—conditions permitting—follows it; on the macroscopic level, a seed is the substantial cause of a sprout, or milk of butter. *Sahakāriya pratyayas* are the "cooperative" conditions that aid in the generation of a given result, either macroscopic (the transformation of the seed into a sprout) or microscopic (the moment-to-moment "existence" of the seed). Cooperative conditions may be either indispensable (as in the case of, e.g., the *adhipatipratyaya*, the principal condition) or assistant (*upakārya*). Indispensable cooperative conditions are those conditions in the absence of which a substantial cause cannot generate its result. Sunlight and moisture are indispensable to a seed's generation of a sprout, because without them there can be no sprout. Assistant cooperative conditions are those conditions that may contribute toward a particular result, but are not essential to it. In the case of the generation of a sprout, assistant cooperative conditions might include, e.g., the particular mineral content of the soil, extra watering done by the farmer, particular methods of planting, etc. It might be noted parenthetically that Dharmakīrti's discussion of the mind-body problem revolves around his attempt to show that the body is neither the substantial cause nor an indispensable condition of the mind, but is merely an assistant condition.

One further aspect of Dharmakīrti's theory of causality worth mentioning, especially for its importance in discussions of the mind-body problem, is his insistence that an entity's substantial cause must be "homogeneous" (*svajāti*) with it, i.e., of the same "type." Thus, a seed-event only can be preceded by a seed-event; it cannot be preceded by a jar-event (although it may be contained within a jar-event!). By the same token, Dharmakīrti will argue, a mind-event simply cannot be generated by an event fundamentally different from it in nature, i.e., a body-event, which is even more different from a mind-event (the one being physical, the other not) than a jar-event is from a seed-event (both of which are material). The insistence on the homogeneity of causal series is an attempt to insure that there is an orderliness to causality such that causes and effects remain compatible. The insistence on homogeneity, incidentally, does not, as it may first appear, rule out "novelty" in the universe, for what we describe as "novelty," a Buddhist simply will call a compatible homogeneous transformation (where the lines of compatibility are to be drawn, then, becomes a further issue to be decided).[4]

How, then, do we come to know the world thus described, with its momentary events coordinated according to discernible causal laws? We know it through valid cognitions, those epistemic authorities known to the Indians as *pramāṇas*. Enumerations of types of authority vary in Indian philosophy from the one (perception) of some materialists to the eleven of the Vaiśeṣika thinker Caraka. Dharmakīrti, like other Sautrāntikas and most Buddhists, accepts only two authorities: perception (*pratyakṣa*) and inference (*anumāna*). The argument against counting such means of knowledge as testimony, comparison and negation as authorities is that they actually can be subsumed under inference. Testimony, for instance, is not an independent source of knowledge, but actually induces knowledge in us throught the following inferential process: *x* must be true, because *y* says so, where *y* is known (probably through inductive generalization) to be authoritative on subjects like *x*. Knowledge arrived at through comparison also is inferential, for when we see for the first time an *x* that we have been told is like a *y* that we already know, we must infer not only that what

---

4 For accounts of Buddhist causal theory, see, e.g., Stcherbatsky (1962) I:II:II, Kalupahana (1976), Mookerjee (1980) I:I-V and Karunadasa (1967).

we see *is* similar to *y*, but that the speaker of the comparison is a reliable source. The knowledge of negation, similarly, must involve an inference, for an *absence* cannot be known directly, but, rather, is inferred from a change in the constellation of what is present.[5]

Dharmakīrti regards authoritative perception as a non-deceptive cognition that is free from any conceptual construction. Perceptions are of four types. (1) A sense perception (*pratyakṣa*) directly cognizes a sensory object (form, sound, smell, taste, tangible) through the medium of a sense-faculty (*indriya:* eye, ear, nose, tongue, body). (2) A mental perception (*mānasa pratyakṣa*) is, in most people, a brief non-conceptual, non-sensory perception that follows upon and cognizes the object of a previous moment of sense perception. Also counted as mental perceptions are instances of extra-sensory perception, such as clairvoyance, clairaudience, retrocognition, telepathy, etc. (3) An apperceptive perception (*svasaṃvedanā pratyakṣa*) is a perception of perception: each perception has a substantially identical concomitant perception that perceives it, thereby enabling the Sautrāntika to explain how perceptions can be remembered. (4) Yogic perceptions (*yogi pratyakṣa*) are the direct "realizations" of āryas, who perceive a salvific truth (e.g., the four noble truths or no-self) and thereby begin to uproot defilements from their mindstreams. It is useful to remember that "the mind," just like a material object, is for Buddhists composed of a quantifiable, qualifiable constellation of events: at the "center" is a "principal mind," or bare cognition (*citta*), "around" which are arrayed various mental factors (*caitta*), some ever-present (such as sensation, discernment, intention, contact and attention), others variable (such as various positive and negative mental attitudes).

The least commonly accepted of the four types of perception is apperception, which is rejected even by a majority of Buddhist schools (let alone by non-Buddhists) on the grounds that a perception is by nature "subjective," and cannot, thus, ever become an object. Mental perception (especially of the extra-sensory type) and yogic perception are accepted by all Buddhists and by most non-Buddhists, as well. Most Hindu schools agree that mental and material events *can* be perceived without direct sensory contact, and most agree, too, that there exists a kind of perception—usually the direct realization of a key religious or philosophical principle—that can serve as the basis of

---

5 On the numbers and types of inference, see, e.g., PV *Pratyakṣa*:1ff. and NB I:2-3. On the question of the knowledge of absences, see, e.g., Klein (1985), chapters 5-7, 9.

spiritual liberation. Both mental and yogic perceptions vary from tradition to tradition, however, and they are not (for all their authoritativeness *within* a tradition) the sort of perceptions that can be accepted as independent evidence for truth-claims made on the basis of them. Dharmakīrti, thus, does *not* appeal to them, for some of his opponents will disagree with the conclusions drawn from such experiences, while others (the materialists) will deny that such perceptions can be veridical.

The one type of perception to which appeal can be made with confidence, then, is sense-perception. Sense-perception, for a Sautrāntika, begins with an instant of direct sensory perception. This is followed by an instant (usually unnoticed) of direct mental perception, and then by a "subsequent"sense-perception that still is direct, but no longer is an authority, since it does not ascertain its object independently, but in the wake of the initial direct perception. Moments following the subsequent direct perception no longer involve *directly* apprehending the object. Rather, such moments involve the apprehension of a "generic image" (**arthasāmānya*, T. *don spyi*) of the object, and hence mental construction—which cannot be involved in *any* kind of perception.[6]

The second authority, inference, is said by Dharmakīrti to be a process of reasoning from an evident particular (e.g., there is smoke on the hill) to a non-evident particular (there is fire on the hill) by way of a generally accepted principle of concomitance (where there's smoke, there's fire). In other words, one establishes a particular predicate in a particular subject through knowledge of a particular reason that has particular relation to the subject and a general relation of causality or synonymy to the predicate. Unlike perception, inference involves conceptual construction, and because it involves apprehension of *general* principles, i.e., universals, it proceeds at least in part on the basis of negative apprehension, for Buddhists in general reject the existence of real "universals,"claiming that we come to know class characteristics of particular phenomena through the "exclusion of what is other than" the class characteristic in question, a process known as *apoha*. By thus arguing that we know a particular entity to be, e.g., a cow through an instantaneous process of excluding everything that is *not* a cow, the Buddhist is able to avoid claiming—as do, for instance, the Nyāya-

---

6 On perception, see, e.g., Stcherbatsky (1962) I:II:III and II, 1-47, Mookerjee (1980) chapters XVII-XXI, Rabten (1978) 11-17 and Lati Rinbochay (1980) 49-75. See also the specialized analyses in Nagatomi (1980) and Matilal (1986).

Vaiśeṣikas—that we know class characteristics through direct apprehension of a real, permanent universal that inheres in particulars. The Buddhist rejection of universals is closely related to a theory of "meaning,"whereby words denote entities not by virtue of some absolutely inherent relation, but rather by a kind of indirection: words *exclude* everything but the entity intended by the speaker. Because there is no absolute relation between word and object, the existence of a word need not entail the existence of its (or any!) object, as it does in naively realistic theories of meaning. On the other hand, the fact that a word expresses an entity at least indirectly means that there is *some* relation that obtains, and that Buddhism therefore avoids extreme nominalism.[7] Indeed, it is important to recognize that for Dharmakīrti and for most Buddhist epistemologists following him, inferences are "effected by the force of actual entities," or "objectively impelled" (*vastubalapravṛtta*), and thus grounded in "actuality"or "the way things really are" (*bhūtatā*, T. *gnas lugs*).

The actual inferential procedure accepted by Dharmakīrti is the same as outlined above in chapter eight: subject is predicate, because reason, as in accordant example, unlike in non-accordant example, where the reason is relevant to the subject and positively and negatively concomitant with the predicate. Dharmakīrti also specifies three ways in which a reason can be fallacious: as unproven (*asiddha*), where it is *not* relevant to the subject; as uncertain or inconclusive (*anaikāntika*), where its positive and negative concomitance with the predicate is doubtful; and as contradictory (*viruddha*), where it directly contradicts the predicate. There are other topics covered by Dharmakīrti in his many discussions of inference, e.g., the classification of reasons into those based on causality, synonymy or negation; and elaborations on the ways in which reasons can be fallacious. Some of these will arise in the course of the translation, and will be dealt with there; for now, a general understanding of the structure of syllogism and the marks of correct and incorrect reasons should suffice.

These, then, are the major philosophical underpinnings of Dharmakīrti's arguments in the *Pramāṇasiddhi* chapter of the *Pramāṇavārttika*. It ought to be noted again that there are no real *religious* assumptions

---

7 On *apoha*, see Shah (1967) chapter III, Zwilling (1976), Stcherbatsky (1962) II, Appendix V and Mookerjee (1980) chapter VII. Klein ([1986] 206-14) gives a good overview of the similarities and differences between Western and dGe lugs pa scholars' analyses of the Sautrāntika view of the relation between words and objects.

made by Dharmakīrti, at least in principle, and this is precisely as it should be, since it is religious truths that must be proven in the *Pramāṇasiddhi* chapter. Thus, although Dharmakīrti works with a "lowest-common-denominator" description of the Buddhist path as a progression from delusion to enlightenment through the direct, salvific realization of a critical principle (no-self), he sets out to demonstrate—and does not presuppose—that the path can succeed. And, although his arguments presuppose the truth of the doctrine of no-self (indeed, they rest upon it: "all human accomplishment is preceded by correct cognition"), no-self presumably can be demonstrated by independent reasoning. (Indeed, rGyal tshab rje, recognizing this, interpolates a proof of no-self into his commentary on Dharmakīrti's discussion of the truth of cessation.) To his own mind, then, Dharmakīrti enters the *Pramāṇasiddhi* chapter begging no questions, for all his arguments are based on valid inferences or on assumptions, such as those outlined in this section, that can be proven by valid inferences.

11. *Dharmakīrti's Defense of the Buddhist World-View*

Just as the *Pramāṇavārttika* as a whole is conceived as a commentary to Dignāga's *Pramāṇasamuccaya*, yet in many ways goes beyond the original, so the *Pramāṇasiddhi* chapter begins from Dignāga, yet is entirely Dharmakīrti's. Indeed, the departure from the *Pramāṇasamuccaya* is perhaps most marked in the case of the *Pramāṇasiddhi* chapter, for its 287 complex ślokas comment on just one verse of Dignāga's text, the first:

> To the one who has become an authority, the one who desires to benefit beings, the teacher, the sugata ("well-gone"), the savior, I bow down.
>
> In order to establish authority, I make here a single compendium of my various scattered writings.[1]

The greater part of the *Pramāṇasiddhi* chapter is, in fact, devoted to explicating just the first half of the verse, for it is there that Dignāga lists the five epithets of the Buddha that provide Dharmakīrti with the framework of his arguments: (1) the one who has become an authority (*pramāṇabhūta*), (2) the one who desires to benefit beings (*jagadhitaiṣin*), or, alternatively, the compassionate one (*dayāvan*), (3) the teacher (*śāstṛ*), (4) the sugata and (5) the savior (lit., "protector," *tāyin*).

Dharmakīrti's primary purpose in the *Pramāṇasiddhi* chapter is to demonstrate that the Buddha is an authority for those intent on spiritual freedom, or liberation. To do so, he first must define authority, then show how the Buddha fulfills the definition. To demonstrate *that* the Buddha fulfills the definition, he shows the *cause* of his authoritativeness, namely the way in which his attainment of buddhahood was

---

1 *pramāṇabhūtāya jagadhitaiṣine pranamya śāstre sugatāya tāyine / pramāṇasiddhyai svamatāt samuccayaḥ kariṣyate viprasṛtād ihaikataḥ*. The original Sanskrit is preserved in Vibhūticandra's notes to Manorathanandin's *Pramāṇavārttikavṛtti*: see Saṃkṛtyāyana (1938) 108. See also Hattori (1968) 23f., 74ff., Nagatomi (1959) and Steinkellner (1982) 7ff. Cf. also below, p. 169, n. 8.

both possible and actual. This demonstration entails showing that the Buddha is the compassionate one, and that therefore he is the teacher, the sugata and the savior. To demonstrate *why* the Buddha fulfills the definition of authority, Dharmakīrti establishes that he is qualified to be the savior, and that therefore he is the sugata, the teacher and the compassionate one. The demonstration of the *cause* of the Buddha's authoritativeness, much of which is devoted to proving that there exist a multiplicity of lives in which compassion can be "accustomated," was called by later commentators the "forward system of explanation." The demonstration of the reason for the Buddha's authoritativeness, most of which is devoted to a proof of the four noble truths (especially the truth of path), is known as the "reverse system of explanation."[2]

Though Dignāga undertook no extensive discussion of the five epithets such as Dharmakīrti would attempt, he does seem to have been generally aware of their implications. He indicates in his own commentary to the first verse of the *Pramāṇasamuccaya* that the latter four epithets (compassionate one, teacher, sugata and savior), which are probative of the fact that the Buddha is the one who has become an authority (the first epithet), correspond to a set of "excellences" (*sampat*) that a buddha develops. Generally, a buddha possesses excellence of causes (*hetu*) and excellence of results (*phala*). These, then, are subdivided into the four excellences that correspond to the last four epithets. Excellence of causes includes excellence of intention (*aśaya*), i.e., the Buddha's *compassionate* intention to assist all beings, and ex-

---

2 There is some disagreement as to precisely which verses are covered by the forward system and which by the reverse. Nagatomi ([1959] 266, note 26) holds that the forward system covers the entire chapter through verse 281 (= Miyasaka's 279), the reverse system only verses 282-285a (280-283a). Tibetans, by and large, believe that the reverse system begins at verse 146b, with the discussion of the four noble truths. This system has been presented by Inami and Tillemans (1986), following dGe 'dun grub pa. The point at issue is whether the long proof of the four noble truths is the last argument in the forward system or the first in the reverse. I tend to side with the Tibetans in holding the former. Since Dharmakīrti sees *compassionate one, teacher, sugata* and *savior* as terms in an inferential chain, it is vital for him to prove the *first* epithet in each sequence in detail; the others then follow easily. Thus, the forward system is rooted in the proof of "compassionate one,"proof of which takes up much of the first part of the chapter. The reverse system is rooted in "savior," which is a characteristic of the Buddha because of his knowledge of the four noble truths. The correctness of these, then, must be proved in detail, as Dharmakīrti attempts to do from verses 146b-280a. Dharmakīrti's arguments as a whole are summarized in greater detail in R. Jackson (1983) I:255-415.

cellence of application (*prayoga*), which is his *teacherhood,* mostly in the sense that he possesses the teaching that results in liberation, the doctrine of no-self. Excellence of results is divided into excellence of one's own aims (*svārtha*) and excellence of others' aims (*parārtha*). The former is the Buddha's sugatahood, his complete liberation from saṃsāra; the latter is his status as *savior,* both willing and able to show others the way to liberation.[3] Schematized, the excellences and epithets appear thus:

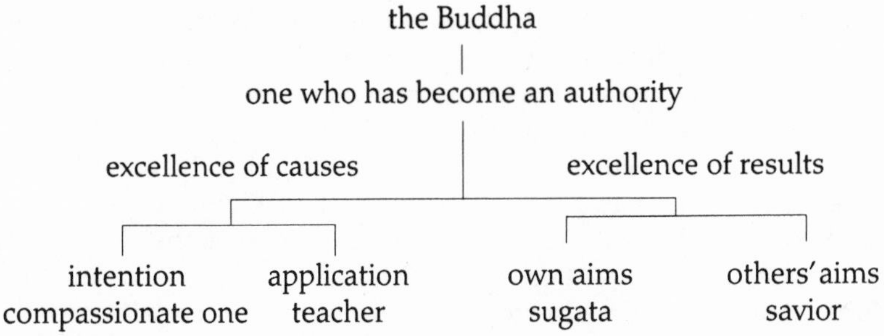

The excellences and epithets that, for Dignāga, simply indicate the Buddha's superiority are, for Dharmakīrti, the basis of an ambitious attempt systematically to prove the truth of the Buddhist world-view.

In order to prove in a general way that the Buddha merits the epithet "one who has become an authority," Dharmakīrti first must define authority. Authority, he argues, is awareness that is: (1) nondeceptive, i.e., uncontradicted by either perception or valid inference; (2) cognitive, i.e., a mental act rather than the activity of, e.g., some sense-faculty; and (3) new, i.e., a cognition that draws certainty toward its object independently rather than on the basis of a previous authoritative cognition.[4] Having established a definition of authority, Dharmakīrti turns to non-existent and existent examples of beings who may be authoritative for those intent on freedom. The negative instance is furnished by the Hindu (especially Nyāya-Vaiśeṣika) con-

---

3 See Nagatomi (1959) and van Bijlert (1989) for discussions of Dignāga's autocommentary.

4 PV (Miyasaka ed.) *Pramāṇasiddhi*:1-7a; see below, section III:2:A. For a translation and discussion of some of the relevant verses, see Katsura (1984) and van Bijlert (1989). It ought to be noted that verse references here are to the Sanskrit, while those in the translation are to the Tibetan, so there may be some discrepancy in line-lettering, since the Sanskrit verse usually is divided into two lines (a and b), while the Tibetan is divided into four (a, b, c and d).

cept of *īśvara,* a permanent, omniscient creator God. Dharmakīrti demonstrates that such an entity cannot be authoritative because authority entails cognition, and cognition, being of the impermanent, cannot be predicated of a permanent entity. Furthermore, *īśvara* cannot be proven to be the creator of the phenomenal world, because (a) his permanence makes interrelation with the impermanent impossible and (b) arguments for his creatorship, such as the Indian version of the argument from design, are logically flawed, since the "creation" of the world cannot be shown to be analogous to the creation of a human artifact, such as a pot. In fact, *īśvara* is a superfluous concept, unnecessary for explicating the known world, the Buddhist concepts of karma and dependent origination being perfectly adequate to the task.[5] The positive instance of an authoritative being is the Buddha, who is generally known to be thus because he, uniquely, knows what is to be rejected (ignorance and other saṃsāric defilements) and what is to be adopted (the path to nirvāṇa, at whose core is the realization of no-self) by those intent on spiritual freedom. Whether or not the Buddha's authoritativeness extends to an omniscient cognition of all objects of knowledge is, here at least, moot; what makes him authoritative is his direct, experientially verified knowledge of what is to be done or shunned by a religious practitioner.[6]

Dharmakīrti next turns to a specific demonstration (via the forward system of explanation) of the way in which the Buddha could and did become an authority. He seeks first to prove that the Buddha is the compassionate one. To do so, he must establish that the extraordinary compassion possessed by a buddha really can be "accustomated," or developed. *Extraordinary* compassion really can be developed only if there exists a multiplicity of lives in which to develop it. Dharmakīrti realizes, in turn, that a multiplicity of lives is possible only if the mind-body relation is such as to permit it. He therefore seeks to show that a materialism that reduces the mental to the physical is flawed, and that the true mind-body relation is what in the West would be called an interactionist dualism, whereby mind and body both are causal entities, and therefore capable of at least indirect interaction, but substantially different enough that the physical cannot be the substantial cause or indispensable condition of the mental, as they are *not* invariably con-

---

5 *Pramāṇasiddhi*:3-28; see below, section III:2:B. For further translations and discussion, cf. R. Jackson (1986) and Vattanky (1984) 34-35.

6 *Pramāṇasiddhi*:29-33; see below, section III:2:C. See also R. Jackson (1987) and Jaini (1974) 86-87.

comitant. Dharmakīrti analyzes a number of materialist attempts to argue that mind depends upon an invariably concomitant physical basis, and finds that neither the sense-faculties (whether severally or individually), nor the body (whether as a whole or partially), nor atoms (whether collectively or individually), nor breaths (whether permanent or impermanent) are thus concomitant. The physical, therefore, may serve as an assistant condition of the mind, but cannot be its substantial cause or indispensable condition. Events only can arise out of previous events of the same type, so the basis of mind must be previous mind. Thus, the first mind-moment of this life must have been preceded by a previous mind-moment, which must have been in a past life, and the last mind-moment of this life—if still dominated by self-grasping—will be succeeded by a mind-moment that will be in a subsequent life. Rebirth thus is proved, and with it (a) the general concept of saṃsāra, the reality of which is required for nirvāṇa to be fully meaningful and (b) the multiplicity of lives in which an aspiring buddha may develop extraordinary compassion.[7] Dharmakīrti completes his discussion of the Buddha's status as compassionate one by replying to charges that, even if there are many lives, compassion may be "naturally limited," like human jumping ability, or boiling water. He argues in response that compassion (and, by implication, other virtues, such as wisdom) differs from the physical examples cited by the opponent, and need not be limited, because it has a stable basis, namely a non-material, concentrated mind, and therefore can increase cumulatively—and even geometrically.[8]

The Buddha's compassion prompts him in turn to seek an antidote to the suffering of others. He realizes that he can provide only an antidote that he himself has tested and validated, so he comes into possession of the teaching, literally "the teacher," that is the antidote: the wisdom directly realizing no-self. This wisdom enables one actually to uproot the defilements that perpetuate one's stay in saṃsāra, and when developed to the fullest, it issues in liberation. The Buddha's liberation, his absence of any and all defiling tendencies, is his sugatahood. Sugatahood is glossed by Dharmakīrti as entailing goodness (for it represents the true uprooting of all defilements, hence the highest good), irreversibility (for one who has attained it never will lapse

---

7 *Pramānasiddhi*:34-119; see below, section III:3-4. Cf. also Jha (1937-39) vol. I and Mookerjee (1980) XV for Śāntarakṣita and Kamalaśīla's discussion of the same issue.

8 *Pramāṇasiddhi*:120-131; see below, section III:5:A.

into saṃsāra) and remainderlessness (for there exists in it not even the trace of a defilement or fault). Understanding the antidote that has resulted in his own spiritual "cure," and desiring to benefit others, the Buddha is prompted to pass on what he knows. He is able to in such a way that others follow in his wake, and therefore he is fit to be considered the savior.[9]

Since "all human accomplishment is preceded by correct cognition," the Buddha's attainment (traced causally in the forward system of explanation) can be real, and his authoritativeness assured, only if what he teaches is, in fact, true, i.e., if he really has correctly cognized the nature and solution of the problem of saṃsāra. Thus, there arises the question of the validity of the Buddha's central teaching, the four noble truths. The truth of suffering involves a description of the nature of saṃsāra. The truth of origination describes the causes of the resultant suffering analyzed by the first truth. The truth of cessation asserts the existence of a purified, nirvāṇic state that transcends saṃsāra. The truth of path describes what must be known and done in order to effect the cessation described by the third truth. A demonstration that these four propositions are true should clinch the argument that the Buddha is worthy of being regarded as "the one who has become an authority" by those intent on freedom, so Dharmakīrti sets out to prove the four noble truths in order.[10]

The truth of suffering is proven (a) through identifying suffering with the five aggregates that, without control, take birth after birth in saṃsāra and (b) by showing that the suffering experienced by sentient beings cannot be explained strictly in physical terms (e.g., as an imbalance among the bodily humors, or as changes in one's physical elements), but must be seen as stemming from *mental* causes. The discussion of the truth of suffering, therefore, dovetails with the earlier demonstration of interactionist dualism as the mind-body relation; some of the earlier arguments may be applied here, and some of the arguments adduced here may be applied to the earlier discussion. The general outlook is the same: the physical cannot be shown to be the invariably concomitant basis of the mental—which only can be based on homogeneous causes.[11]

---

9 *Pramāṇasiddhi*:132-146a; see below, section III:5:B.

10 This is the section of the *Pramāṇasiddhi* chapter translated into German by Vetter (1984).

11 *Pramāṇasiddhi*:147-179a; see below, section III:7.

The truth of origination is proven through an examination of the way in which ignorance and craving function together to generate the suffering we universally experience. Ignorance is the fundamental cause: the ignorant belief in the existence of a self of persons, and the ignorant belief that future pleasures or rebirths somehow will entail an improvement over present sufferings. This ignorance leads to the "efficient" cause of suffering and suffering rebirths: craving, whether for sense-pleasure, existence, or annihilation. Quite simply, the presence or absence of craving in a being's mindstream determines whether or not conditions are ripe for a suffering result to arise.[12]

The truth of cessation is proven at least partially by the fact that if there exists an identifiable cause originating suffering, then, given the general validity of the notion of dependent origination, the elimination of that cause ought to entail the elimination of the resultant suffering. Dharmakīrti also answers various criticisms raised against Buddhist arhants, e.g., that they are subject to desire or anger, or that their liberation is reversible. The question of the reversibility of liberation is crucial, for if liberation *is* reversible, then the truth of cessation—which asserts a *complete* stopping of suffering—is untrue. rGyal tshab rje will expand on Dharmakīrti's discussion by arguing that liberation (hence cessation) is possible because the direct realization of no-self entails generation of a recognition that is both true and profound. Because it is true (and rGyal tshab rje adduces arguments for its truth, drawn from Madhyamaka), it can precede religious accomplishment. Because it is profound, direct realization of it has a *power* that simply does not permit the arising of the contradictory view, namely that there *is* a self. In the absence of this view, defilements simply cannot arise, and they do not.[13]

The truth of path is proven primarily through a discussion of the salvific value of the realization of no-self. Dharmakīrti first argues that the mind is clear and cognitive by nature, capable of accurately apprehending objects, and that an accurate, or true, representation of an object, once established, cannot be supplanted. Once it is firmly established, then, the realization of no-self—given that it is true—cannot be supplanted by its contradictory. Therefore, it *is* the antidote to saṃsāric suffering; it *is* the path to nirvāṇa.[14] Its value as a path, however, must be upheld not only against those who deny the possibility

12 *Pramāṇasiddhi*:179b-190a; see below, section III:8.
13 *Pramāṇasiddhi*:190b-205a; see below, section III:9.
14 *Pramāṇasiddhi*:205b-226a; see below, sections III:10:A-B. See also R. Jackson (1990).

of liberation (such as materialists and some Mīmāṃsakas), but against alternative paths to liberation proposed by other schools. Dharmakīrti, therefore, undertakes detailed refutations of a number of these alternative paths. He argues, against such Hindu schools as the Vaiśeṣika, Sāṃkhya and (perhaps) Vedānta, that the attempt to disassociate one's perfect, unchanging self (whether it be called ātman or puruṣa) from the defiled, changing body and/or cosmos cannot succeed, in part because the concept of such a self is unproven, in part because desire for such a self inevitably will turn into *selfish* desire, and thus will entail the generation of defilements.[15] He argues against such theist and/or ritualist traditions as the Nyāya that neither divine injunctions nor rituals for which one has been empowered can possibly serve to uproot the myriad afflictions suffered by sentient beings; indeed, they are more likely to perpetuate them.[16] Finally, he argues against the Jainas that self-mortification and other forms of austerity cannot be the basis of liberation because such activities seek to eliminate either karma or the body, which may be causes contributing to suffering, but are not (as ignorance and craving are) the real key to it. Austerities, therefore, may eliminate particular sufferings, or particular karmic seeds, but they do not attack the problem at the root.[17]

With the four noble truths thus proven, the Buddha has been shown to be a savior, for he teaches truths that are conducive to salvation. A savior must teach from experience, so the Buddha must have completed the path he teaches; he must, therefore, be a sugata. If he is a sugata, he must have developed to the fullest the antidote to suffering, the "teacher"that is the wisdom realizing no-self. He will have found and developed the antidote only if he had a motive for doing so. His motive was compassion which, developed through countless lives, induced him to discover the teacher/antidote that he could test on himself and—when he had validated it through becoming the sugata—pass on to others as the savior.[18]

Thus, Dharmakīrti has shown to his own satisfaction, and to the satisfaction of generations of Indian and Tibetan Buddhists, that the Buddha is, indeed, the one who has become an authority for those intent on freedom, for (a) he has been shown to possess the necessary causes of such authoritativeness and (b) his analysis of those causes

---

15 *Pramāṇasiddhi*:226b-257a; see below, sections III:10:C-11:A.
16 *Pramāṇasiddhi*:257b-273a; see below, section III:11:B.
17 *Pramāṇasiddhi*:273b-280a: see below, section III:11:C.
18 *Pramāṇasiddhi*:280b-283a: see below, section III:12.

has been shown to be true. If Dharmakīrti's arguments are successful, then the Buddhist world-view truly has been upheld: the saṃsāra-nirvāṇa cosmology has been justified, the four noble truths have been validated and, in particular, it has been proven that past and future lives must exist and that the Buddhist identification of self-grasping as saṃsāra's cause and the direct realization of no-self as its antidote are correct, and ought to be accepted by any reasonable individual. In short, if Dharmakīrti's arguments succeed, any rational person ought to become a Buddhist forthwith.

12. *On Evaluating Dharmakīrti's Arguments*

I have already said that I do not intend to enter here into a detailed evaluation of Dharmakīrti's arguments in defense of the Buddhist world-view. On the other hand, many readers undoubtedly will want to evaluate the arguments for themselves, whether out of personal or philosophical interest, so it seems worthwhile at least briefly to discuss some of the problems faced by anyone attempting such an evaluation.

The first question that must be asked is whether such an evaluation even is possible. Is not the Indian (or Tibetan) philosophical context so different from our own that any attempt on our part to evaluate Buddhist arguments will fail virtually by definition? Obviously, there *are* great differences between the cultural contexts and philosophical language-systems of the Indo-Tibetan and Western traditions. One must, as a Westerner approaching Asian texts, remain as sensitive as possible to these differences, being careful to evaluate unfamiliar arguments in their own terms as much as possible, while importing one's own instinctive prejudices as little as possible. At the same time, I do not think that such an evaluation is in principle impossible.We already have seen that the logically inclined tradition of which Dharmakīrti was a part rested its discussions primarily on common perception and formal inference, and that its criteria of validity, therefore, did not differ, so greatly as to be incomprehensible, from the criteria applied by Western philosophers. Indeed, we have seen that the Indian Buddhist formal inference can tentatively be translated into Aristotelian terms. Furthermore, Indian philosophers in general and Buddhists in particular have *invited* evaluation: they are convinced that their argumentative procedures are universally comprehensible and applicable, and that anyone who takes the time to understand the principles involved will be able to follow—and eventually agree to—the arguments proffered. They *make* their arguments seriously, and we owe it to them to *take* them seriously.[1]

Once we have agreed that arguments such as Dharmakīrti's *can* be evaluated, however cautiously, we face the problem of how we are to go about the evaluation. It seems to me that there are three different levels on which evaluation must be made: (1) the level of the arguments themselves, where we must ask: are they compelling in the light of the logical canons accepted by Indian philosophers?; (2) the level of the assumptions informing the discussion, where we must ask: are the Buddhist ontological and epistemological doctrines presupposed by Dharmakīrti, and undergirding his discussion, valid? and (3) the level of the whole epistemological exercise, where we must ask: are logic and epistemology in fact sufficiently grounded in certainty to permit us to base generally valid ontological statements upon them? We will consider each of these problems briefly in turn.

(1) Dharmakīrti's actual arguments must be evaluated by examining whether they violate any of the logical canons described earlier, in section 8, i.e., whether they are properly constructed inferences to which any reasonable person ought to assent because (a) the reason is correct in all three respects, (b) the rules of argumentation regarding question-begging, circularity, infinite regress, etc., are respected and (c) the fundamental axioms of Indian philosophy regarding causality, existence and non-existence are upheld. Though much of Dharmakīrti's discussion does follow these canons, there are at least two general types of problem that may arise, with respect to (a) hidden assumptions and (b) representation of opponents' positions.

(a) Two of the central arguments in the *Pramāṇasiddhi* chapter are, first, the refutation of materialism and establishment of an interactionist dualism as the mind-body relation and, second, the demonstration of the salvific power of the direct realization of no-self. These two arguments comprise nearly two-thirds of the chapter, and clearly are crucial to Dharmakīrti's case. In each instance, however, it is possible to argue that Dharmakīrti may have imported assumptions not shared by all of his readers. In his mind-body discussion, at least part of his argument seems to be that mind and body cannot be as closely related causally as claimed by the materialist because they obviously are different types of entity, the one subjective and immaterial, the other objective and material (not entirely unlike Descartes' *res cogitans* and *res extensa*). There clearly is such a fundamental difference in common-sense experience and parlance, and yet is not the whole purpose of the mind-body discussion to ascertain whether the com-

---

1 See the discussion above, in section I:3. Incidentally, readers who are interested in a more "evaluative" discussion of Dharmakīrti's arguments may consult R. Jackson (1983) I:255-428. I would not now stand by every criticism made there, but a considerable number of them still seem to me cogent.

mon-sense division is a legitimate one?[2] May not, therefore, an argument that *presupposes* that division beg the question? In the discussion of the salvific efficacy of a direct realization of no-self, Dharmakīrti relies heavily on the notion that a truth, profoundly realized, is ineradicable from the mind, and, furthermore, that there are some truths (or *a* truth) sufficiently crucial that their assimilation will entail the total eradication of suffering. That there is any realization sufficiently profound to eradicate suffering is not vouchsafed by common experience or psychological observation. How, then, is it vouchsafed? Only, I think, through meditative experience. Meditative experience, as noted earlier, may give truth, and usually imparts certainty to the experiencer, but its extraordinariness makes it less reliable as a criterion of validity in public discussions. Dharmakīrti generally avoids basing arguments on appeals to extraordinary experience, yet he seems to have imported an unstated appeal to it in this crucial instance. I do not think that these two instances of imported assumptions are sufficient to topple the edifice of Dharmakīrti's arguments, but they (and others that the reader may detect) may make it a bit less steady than it first appears.

(b) Philosophers are notorious for setting up their opponents as straw-men easily blown away by the rhetorical wind of "truth," and we must ask, in all fairness, whether Dharmakīrti falls prey to this temptation. He appears to make great efforts to represent his opponents' positions in detail, yet some doubts must persist. In the case of his refutation of materialism, we simply cannot be certain that Dharmakīrti is representing his opponents accurately, for the simple reason that we do not have enough Indian materialist literature to make a comparison. Many of the materialist arguments seem foolish, and hardly worthy of response, yet we must remember that (a) they *may* actually have been held by someone and (b) even if they were not, Dharmakīrti is attempting to consider and refute all *possible* materialist views. We *do* have independent literature from the various non-Buddhist schools whose soteriologies Dharmakīrti criticizes, and here it seems that he does not always succeed in being completely fair. He rarely *misrepresents* an opponent's position, but he does not often permit the opponent a response that elucidates the subtleties of their position. Thus, in his concern to show that *any* system that posits a self automatically entails selfishness, hence the perpetuation of saṃsāra, Dharmakīrti does not really allow his opponents to explain that *they*

2 For a clear discussion of this point, see Shaffer (1967).

are as radically opposed to self-grasping as he is, but that they seek to transcend it through subsumption by a universal self, whereas the Buddhist seeks to transcend it by recognizing that there is no self anywhere, period. The existence or non-existence of a universal self then would become a further topic for debate.

A corollary problem that arises from the preceding is whether, even if Dharmakīrti is being utterly fair to *his* opponents, he has refuted *all possible* opponents. For instance, the materialists whom he refutes argue for the invariable concomitance of mind with such material entities as the body, the sense-faculties, the breath, the humors or the elements. None of these would be argued seriously by a present-day materialist, who would claim, instead, that it is the properly functioning brain that is the basis of what we call mind. It is uncertain whether Dharmakīrti's arguments would have as much force against contemporary materialism, for (a) much stronger arguments can be made for brain-mind concomitance than for the types of concomitance proposed by Dharmakīrti's opponents[3] and (b) compelling (though not conclusive) materialist "models"of the physical basis of consciousness have been offered by cognitive scientists working with computers and artificial intelligence.[4] (And, of course, there also remains the question whether Dharmakīrti's or *any* interactionism can be adequately defended against charges that it is self-contradictory to describe something as both causal and immaterial.) It might also be urged that Dharmakīrti would have more difficulty refuting a Christian or Muslim soteriology than those of the Indian traditions he explicitly addresses. A Buddhist undoubtedly would argue that, as long as we can translate philosophical terms adequately across traditions, Christian and Muslim soteriologies could be restated in terms of the self/no-self distinction deemed so crucial by the Buddhist, and therefore be accepted or rejected unequivocally.[5]

---

3 See, e.g., Blakemore (1977), Rose (1976) and Place (1964). A contemporary version of interactionist dualism is proposed in Popper and Eccles (1978). For remarks on Buddhist arguments for the existence of past and future lives, see Willson (1984).

4 See, e.g., the various suggestions in Hofstadter and Dennett (1981), Dennett (1978) and, most recently and interestingly, Edelman, as discussed in Hellerstein (1988).

5 The most ambitious recent attempt to do this, with respect to the question of God, is Dharmasiri (1974); for at least the beginnings of an engagement on the question of self/soul, see Griffiths (1991) chapter 6.

(2) The question whether Dharmakīrti would or could refute a Christian or Muslim world-view takes us to the second general level on which his arguments must be addressed: that of the assumptions that underlie his discussion. His arguments for past and future lives, for instance, rest upon the assumption that the Buddhist analysis of the world into durationless events is, in fact, valid, while his arguments for the salvific value of a realization of no-self presuppose that no-self is, in fact, the way things ultimately are. Yet these, and most other Buddhist doctrines assumed by Dharmakīrti, have been subjected to attack by various non-Buddhist schools. The doctrine of momentariness (as noted earlier) has been criticized in general for vitiating causality and, in the particular instance of rebirth from life to life, for failing to account for personal continuity and karmic responsibility. In the eyes of the critic, for all the Buddhist's attempts to qualify momentariness by dependent origination, the dilemma seems absolute: either events are utterly momentary, and no continuity can be posited, or there is some carry-over from moment to moment, in which case some type of permanence—hence a self—is being admitted. The doctrine of anātman comes under attack for similar reasons, then: without positing a self, the critic argues, we cannot account for the continuities that obviously exist in the world, so it is Buddhists who are not reporting reality "truly,"and *they*, therefore, who are spiritually doomed.

Similarly, Buddhist accounts of the initial non-conceptual immediacy of perception may be criticized on the grounds that, regardless of how it seems to the perceiver, *all* perceptions are in fact determined at least in part by physiological, psychological and cultural factors that rule out the pure immediacy posited by the Buddhist. The Buddhist rejection of the existence of universals may be criticized as requiring the very entities it seeks to refute, for whether one discovers that an animal is a cow "positively" or "negatively," one still has encountered a quality that must be accounted for. At a fundamental level, the Buddhist division of the world into dharmas of various types may be criticized as a selection, from experience, of categories as arbitrary as any others. And, most basically, it may be that Buddhist descriptions of the world are based on unstated assumptions about, e.g., the ultimate "impersonality" of reality that simply would not be shared by those who select "personal" metaphors, like agency, as a way of understanding things.[6] All these issues are moot, and I do not intend to

---

6 For reflections on this issue in relation to the question of the existence of God,

discuss them here. However, the very fact that they are moot begins to hint to us that perhaps the grounds of agreement among disputants in Indian philosophical discussions were *not* as broad as they, or we, would like to think, and that many arguments simply cannot be understood without the background of tradition-specific ways of thinking that are themselves problematic. Thus, it is entirely likely that a Hindu or Jaina (let alone a Christian or Muslim) will have difficulty accepting Dharmakīrti's arguments not only because they may find the arguments themselves problematic, but because there are assumptions—some logical and some pre-logical—informing those arguments with which they fundamentally disagree.

(3) Thus, we arrive at the third, and most general, level on which Dharmakīrti's arguments must be assessed. Here, what is questioned is not the validity of particular arguments (level 1) or the validity of particular ontological or epistemological assumptions (level 2), but, rather, the validity of the entire enterprise in which Dharmakīrti and so many others were engaged: the attempt to arrive at certain, universal knowledge through securely founded avenues of authoritative cognition. In short, we arrive again at the question of truth. We already have seen that questioning along these lines has been increasingly common in the "post-modernist" Western tradition, and that such questioning is present in the Indian tradition, too, e.g., in the works of Nāgārjuna. Nāgārjuna's critique of philosophical concepts and the ways in which we arrive at them did not appreciably affect the development of constructive philosophy in India, nor is it clear that this was his intent. When, however, we begin to realize the difficulty we have in attempting to justify even the most *basic* truth-claims (let alone whole world-views), we begin to wonder whether Nāgārjuna should not have been taken more literally, for the entire edifice of constructive philosophy *does* seem wobbly. We think that we have developed universal methods of agreement based on inference and worldly perception, yet at every turn we find our "neutral" perceptions and inferences structured by presuppositions and assumptions that are themselves problematic—and our very methods of cognition are problematic, too. There seems to be *no* proposition (even the axioms, or "laws of thought"that undergird philosophical discussion) that can be asserted unambiguously or without qualification, no epistemological fulcrum on which dispassionately to balance competing truth-claims. Indeed, as we have seen, the corollaries of the sort of skeptical ques-

---

see R. Jackson (1986).

tioning outlined here are (a) the abandonment of a correspondence criterion of truth and its replacement by a pragmatic or coherence criterion and (b) the acceptance of a relativism whereby truth is determined within particular "communities of discourse."

A Buddhist adopting this position thus would not claim that Dharmakīrti's (or any other) arguments for the Buddhist world-view can be decisively proven—for inference, religious experience, and even common perception all are problematic to a degree. They probably would maintain modestly that the Buddhist world-view can be verified within a *Buddhist* frame of reference, and that the world-view thus is "true," for there is no over-arching set of truths that could falsify it. Neither religion nor science may any longer claim universality or exclusivity, yet neither thereby forfeits its claim to truth, for truth means not correspondence to some "objective" reality, but simply what is coherent and effective within a particular community of discourse. Thus, whereas traditional and post-modern Buddhists both will insist that the answer to the question "Is enlightenment possible?" is "yes," this "yes" will mean very different things to each. For the former, it will mean that there exist and have existed people who have attained an actual psychological state corresponding to one or another description of the Buddhist *summum bonum*. For the latter, it will mean that a given Buddhist community—or crucial members of the community—agree that certain persons are to be recognized as "enlightened." For the former, enlightenment is a "real" state; for the latter, it is a social construction that may enhance individual and collective well-being, but its "truth" is utterly undemonstrable—and perhaps irrelevant—outside the Buddhist community. We cannot, the latter insist, nor should we care to, ask for more.

And yet, as the reader no doubt will surmise by now, I doubt that the degree of relativism implied by the post-modernist position would gain total assent from many of us, let alone from the traditionalist, for whom the universality of a religion's claims are, almost by definition, vital. Are we not, as I have argued before, able to translate from one community of discourse or "language game" to another, and does this not imply areas of agreement among us that may be the basis for establishing some truths as "correspondent" beyond any taint of subjectivity or self-contradiction? Does not the logical demolition of logical and epsitemological certainty itself imply a certainty? Do not questions remain about how broadly or narrowly "communities of discourse" are to be defined and what their areas of overlap are? Are religion and science, for example, simply two barely overlapping, largely incommensurable language games, resistant to serious comparison? Did Dharmakīrti waste his time attempting to refute skeptics and materialists, and do we waste our time studying him? I think not. There probably is a way the universe really exists, and rationality is the most generally reliable method our species has developed for approaching what the universe might actually be like. What is more, it is entirely possible that some particular tradition actually has come closer to describing the way the universe is than others have. Most Christians have believed this about their tradition; Dharmakīrti certainly believes it about his. Religious people make existentially significant truth claims that they take to correspond to the real nature of the universe, and as long as they do, we owe it to them and to ourselves to try to clarify and evaluate those claims, for the simple reason that, whether we admit it or not, truth matters. Although we cannot ignore the limitations of our very tools of clarification and evaluation, we nevertheless must attempt judiciously to weigh the evidence presented to us, in the hope that, even if "final" certainty never will be ours, the world may on some matters move towards becoming a single "community of discourse," and on those others where total agreement is impossible, a community of tolerance and sympathetic understanding.[7] Perhaps in the end Dharmakīrti's project, and our own struggles with "truth," may simply have to be accepted as paradoxical: unpromising, yet urgent; unfounded, yet a foundation of human life; probably impossible, undeniably necessary—to paraphrase a character from Samuel Beckett's *Happy Days*: we can't go on; we must go on. I hope I have made at least somewhat plausible the claim that, paradox notwithstanding, "we must go on" in our pursuit of truth. In any case, Dharmakīrti—in spite of an ontology that denies either a substantial self or real external objects—went on, and it his pursuit of truth, as exposed through his Tibetan commentator rGyal tshab rje, to which the remainder of this book is devoted.

The journey through Dharmakīrti and rGyal tshab rje's arguments may convince some that enlightenment is in fact possible; others will conclude that the arguments fail, and so enlightenment is impossible;

7 For a thoughtful discussion of these issues, particularly as pertains to the relationship between religion and science, see Barbour (1974), which defends "critical realism" (cf. above, p. 35, n. 1). It is interesting to note that "critical realism" is the designation given to Sautrāntika thought by Mookerjee (1980). An epistemological position less skeptical than Barbour's is found in Popper (1963). A more skeptical position (hence, ironically, one that opens the door more widely to religious truths) is represented by Feyerabend (1975); see also the application of this sort of approach to the Indian context, by O'Flaherty (1984).

still others will insist that, even if rational arguments fail, we still can ascertain that enlightenment is possible by the method that the Buddha—and Dharmakīrti—finally insist upon: entering the path and experiencing enlightenment for oneself. My own sense is that the arguments are unlikely to yield a final answer to the question, Is enlightenment possible? Nevertheless, readers who follow them all the way—even if to an uncertain end—will be rewarded by the knowledge that they have explored some of the most sophisticated arguments ever framed by Buddhists. Convincing or not, the arguments are an invitation to "come and see" for oneself the depths of the Buddhist philosophical tradition, and whether the acceptance of such an invitation leaves one a skeptic, a believer, or wanting to explore the possibilities in ways that lie beyond the scope of rationality, to accept is worthwhile, because we admit thereby that we take truth and its claimants seriously, and are willing ourselves to "come and see" where it is they propose to lead us.

Part Two

About the Translation

1. *Scholarship on Dharmakīrti*

Dharmakīrti is indisputably one of the greatest and most influential philosophers of Indian Buddhism's classical period, yet the study, translation and understanding of his work is still, relatively speaking, in its infancy. I do not intend to provide here a complete account of Dharmakīrti scholarship, but simply to indicate some of the main trends and works in the field—primarily as a way of more clearly locating my own effort. Readers who wish more complete bibliographic information on Dharmakīrti or any other figure or movement discussed below are advised to consult Karl Potter's exhaustive and clearly cross-referenced *Bibliography of Indian Philosophies* (1983: e.g., 114-117, 621-623)—not the least of whose virtues is its inclusion of Japanese scholarship—as well as the more recent bibliographies found in, e.g., Hayes (1988a), van Bijlert (1989) and Dreyfus (1991).

Dharmakīrti is classed by most writers on Indian philosophy as a "logician" or "epistemologist," so his works often are discussed within the broader context of works on Indian logic and epistemology. Works that deal with this area have been appearing for over a half-century now, but reliable monographs still are few and far between. S.C. Vidyabhushana's *History of Indian Logic* (1920; rpt. 1978) is an early effort that gives a useful survey of the range of figures and texts, though a fair amount of its historical information must be considered suspect. Reliable guides to modes of inference and argumentation in Indian philosophy include Karl Potter's *Presuppositions of India's Philosophies* (1967; rpt. 1976) and Esther Solomon's *Indian Dialectics: Methods of Philosophical Discussion* (1976-78). Useful general works on Indian epistemology include Jadunath Sinha's *Indian Psychology* (1934) and Bimal Matilal's *Perception* (1986). Nyāya-Vaiśeṣika approaches to logic and epistemology may be gleaned from standard works on Indian philosophy, such as those of Surendranath Dasgupta (rpt. 1975) and Sarvepalli Radhakrishnan (1929), as well as Potter's superb volume on Nyāya-Vaiśeṣika in the *Encyclopedia of Indian Philosophies* (1977). Last, but by no means least, the works of E. Frauwallner, whose masterpiece is his *Geschichte der Indischen Philosophie* (1953), remain a treasury of information on Indian and Buddhist logic and epistemology.

As a subcategory of Indian logic and epistemology, Buddhist *pramāṇa* literature has received its share of attention, too. If we leave aside the works of those who treat Buddhist logic as a formal logical system—Richard Chi (*Buddhist Formal Logic* [1969]) and Douglas Daye (*Metalogical Studies in Sixth-Century Buddhist Protologic* [1972]) are two prominent examples—we still find a number of important works that examine the tradition either broadly or through one or more of its representative figures. F.Th. Stcherbatsky's two-volume *Buddhist Logic* (1930; rpt. 1962) remains in many ways a classic work. Certainly, one must be wary of Stcherbatsky's tendency to confuse Vaibhāṣika and Sautrāntika viewpoints (a difficuly noted by both Leonard Żwilling [1975] and Anne Klein [1986]), or to generalize about the whole tradition on the basis of its later representatives (especially Śāntarakṣita and Kamalaśīla), or to apply inappropriate or outdated comparisons from Western philosophy. However, the work as a whole remains a rich source of information and insight, and its second volume, centered on Stcherbatsky's translation of portions of Dharmakīrti's *Nyāyabindu*, together with Dharmottara's commentary, remains an important source for scholars. Also still of use is Satkari Mookerjee's *The Buddhist Doctrine of Universal Flux* (1935; rpt. 1980), which considers the whole tradition, but focuses most on the contributions of Śāntarakṣita and Kamalaśīla; by the same token, Ganganatha Jha's translation of Śāntarakṣita's *Tattvasaṃgraha*, together with Kamalaśīla's *Pañjikā* (1937-39), remains one of the finest and most useful sources for our understanding of late Buddhist ontology and epistemology. Other figures in the Buddhist logical tradition who have received serious scrutiny include Dharmakīrti's precursor, Dignāga (most notably by M. Hattori [1968] and Richard Hayes [1988]), and one of the last great Indian Buddhist philosophers, Ratnakīrti (by A.C. Senape McDermott [1970]). The only general text on Buddhist thought that contains reliable information on the *pramāṇa* tradition is that of A.K. Warder (1980).

Dharmakīrti probably has received the most attention of any Buddhist logician, though monographs devoted to him still are few and far between. Leaving aside the *Pramāṇavārttika* for the moment, we find that most of his works—whether extant in Sanskrit or not—have by now been issued in critical editions, and a number have been translated, too. Thus, for example, the *Nyāyabindu* has been edited by C. Śāstri (1954), the *Hetubindu* (in part, 1967) and *Pramāṇaviniścaya* (in part, 1973-1979) by Ernst Steinkellner, and the *Vādanyāya*[*prakaraṇa*] by Dwarikadas Shastri (1972). In addition to the portions of the *Nyāya-*

bindu translated by Stcherbatsky, other works in translation include the parts of the *Hetubindu* and *Pramāṇaviniścaya* edited by Steinkellner, as well as the *Sambandhaparīkṣā* (by Frauwallner [1934]) and *Santānāntarasiddhi* (by Kitagawa [1955]). General discussions of Dharmakīrti and his philosophy are found primarily in a few monographs and in articles too numerous to mention, but among the most noteworthy are Frauwallner's article on the formation and organization of Dharmakīrti's work (1954), Tillman Vetter's book on the problem of knowledge in Dharmakīrti (1964), Steinkellner's article on reality and concept in Dharmakīrti (1967) and Chr. Lindtner's article on Dharmakīrti's date and corpus (1980).

The *Pramāṇavārttika*, a Sanskrit text of which was discovered in Tibet over half a century ago by Rahula Sāṅkṛtyāyana, has undergone a number of editions, either partial or complete (by, e.g., Sāṅkṛtyāyana himself, Raniero Gnoli (1960), Satkari Mookerjee (1968), and Dalsukh Malvaniya and Dwarikadas Shastri (1968)), but the edition generally used nowadays is that of Y. Miyasaka (1972-77), which, in addition to the care with which it was prepared, has the advantage of placing the Sanskrit and Tibetan texts together in the same volume. If we except the *Pramāṇasiddhi* chapter (on which more below), we find that translations from the *Pramāṇavārttika* into Western languages have mostly been sporadic and partial. Frauwallner (1930-36), Gnoli (1960) and Zwilling (1976) have translated significant portions of the *Svārthānumāna* chapter, Georges Dreyfus and Lindtner (1989) small portions of the *Pratyākṣa* chapter and Tom F.J. Tillemans (1986) a small portion of the *Parārthānumāna* chapter. The works just cited contain excellent discussions of a number of elements of the *Pramāṇavārttika*, as does Dreyfus's recently completed dissertation (1991).

The *Pramāṇasiddhi* chapter is, with the *Svārthānumāna*, the section of the *Pramāṇavārttika* that has received the most attention. It has been translated from the Sanskrit *in toto* only by Masatoshi Nagatomi, in his still-unpublished dissertation (1957). The second half of the chapter (Miyasaka verses 146c-287) has been translated into German by Vetter (1984). Smaller portions of the chapter have been translated by Katsura (1984: verses 1-7), van Bijlert (1989: verses 1-7) and by me (1986: verses 7-13, 21-28; 1990: verses 205b-211a). Analyses of various aspects of the *Pramāṇasiddhi* chapter include Nagatomi's article on the chapter's framework and its relation to Dignāga's *Pramāṇasamuccaya* (1959), Steinkellner's ground-breaking analysis of the relation between epistemology and soteriology (1982), van Bijlert's examination of the definition of *pramāṇa* (1989), analyses by Steinkellner (1983) and me (1988) of the concept of an "authoritative person," and discussions by me of Dharmakīrti's attitude toward theism (1986), omniscience (1987) and the nature of the mind (1990).

The Tibetan tradition of logic and epistemology, for which Dharmakīrti and the *Pramāṇavārttika* are so important, has only in the last decade begun to receive serious study. In terms of historical analysis, the most important contributions have come from Leonard W.J. van der Kuijp (esp. 1983, 1987) and David Jackson (1987), who have painstakingly researched the Sa skya pa roots of the Tibetan study of logic and epistemology. The way in which the logical tradition was understood by dGe lugs pas—both among themselves and in contradistinction to other schools—has been studied in detail by Anne Klein (1986, 1991). The Tibetan tradition of debate has been discussed by, among others, Lobsang Tharchin (1970) and Daniel Perdue (1992). Outlines of Tibetan commentaries on the *Pramāṇavārttika* have been furnished by van der Kuijp (1983: that of the fifteenth-century Sa skya pa Go ram pa bsod nams seng ge), Fukuda and Ishihama (1986 ref.: several; see p. 116, n. 19) and Inami and Tillemans (1986: that of the fifteenth-century dGe lugs pa dGe 'dun grub).

I shall say more below about my reasons for translating, and annotating so extensively, rGyal tshab rje's commentary to the *Pramāṇasiddhi* chapter of the *Pramāṇavārttika*. Let me say by way of conclusion to this survey, however, that my translation is indeed intended as a contribution to Dharmakīrti studies (as well, I hope, as to our understanding of Indian philosophy, both in its own context, and in relation to relevant Western discussions), but that its contribution is somewhat indirect. Because I have focused on a Tibetan commentary and the Tibetan version of Dharmakīrti's text, I am not transposing Dharmakīrti unalloyed from his original language and context. I have said before that my primary purpose is to expose a significant vein of Indo-Tibetan philosophical thought. Thus, although I hope I have remained sensitive to the various contexts in which different discussions may have originated or evolved, the unending discussion of such matters has *not* been foremost among my concerns. If I have provided for interested readers—whether Buddhological or philosophical in their interests—a reasonably accessible and comprehensible example of Indo-Tibetan philosophizing, I will be satisfied; if readers find that the translation contributes in ways beyond this, so much the better.

2. *rGyal tshab rje and His World-View*

rGyal tshab dar ma rin chen (1364-1432), author of the commentary on Dharmakīrti's arguments translated in part below, was, as already noted, one of the great disciples of Tsong kha pa blo bzang grags pa (1357-1419), the founder of the dGe lugs, the Tibetan Buddhist tradition that eventually, under the Dalai Lamas, came to dominate both religious and political life in Tibet (as well as Mongolia).

Like another of Tsong kha pa's great disciples, mKhas grub dge legs dpal bzang po (mKhas grub rje), rGyal tshab rje originally was a Sa skya pa, a learned student of the lama Red mda' ba (who also was a teacher of Tsong kha pa). Accounts of rGyal tshab rje's first meeting with Tsong kha pa stress his arrogance and pride. In one version, he and mKhas grub rje go to a hall where Tsong kha pa is to lecture. When they enter, mKhas grub rje is impressed immediately by Tsong kha pa's aura of holiness and erudition, and removes his pandit's hat and sits at his feet. rGyal tshab rje, however, insists not only on keeping his hat on, but on sitting on the teaching throne with Tsong kha pa. As Tsong kha pa's lecture proceeds, however, rGyal tshab rje begins to realize that he is in the presence of genius. By the end, he too has removed his hat and is sitting at Tsong kha pa's feet.

In another version, rGyal tshab rje and mKhas grub rje have decided to listen to Tsong kha pa, but do not know where to find him. Walking along the road, they encounter a woman drawing water. They approach her and ask derisively where they might find "the big-eared Khampa."The woman does not answer, but goes to her house, and returns a minute later reverently holding incense between folded palms. She points down the road and says, "The holy one can be found there." Amused, but hardly chastened, mKhas grub rje and rGyal tshab rje proceed to the small hall where Tsong kha pa is to speak. They decide ahead of time not to remove their pandit's hats. mKhas grub rje enters first and, neglecting to stoop under the low door-frame, he loses his hat. rGyal tshab rje, following, remembers to duck, but has his hat knocked off by the door-curtain, which slaps him in mKhas grub rje's wake. The symbolism is not lost on them, and they listen respectfully to Tsong kha pa, eventually becoming his greatest disciples. Before Tsong kha pa's death in 1419, he passed on his robe and hat to rGyal tshab rje, who succeeded his guru as the head of dGa'ldan monastery, near Lhasa. rGyal tshab rje remained as dGa' ldan *'khri pa* until his death, at the age of 68, in 1432. He was succeeded by the younger mKhas grub rje. The two are now so closely identified with Tsong kha pa, and so thoroughly said to embody his teaching, that they almost invariably are pictured with him on thangkas and in statuary in dGe lugs pa temples: the three together are referred to by dGe lugs pas as the *yab sras gsum*, the threesome of father and sons.[1]

rGyal tshab rje did not, of course, acquire his reputation simply by being a loyal disciple to Tsong kha pa; he was a great scholar in his own right. Like those of other great scholars in the Tibetan tradition, his writings cover a wide range of Buddhist subject-matter, from the arcane mysteries of the *Kālacakra Tantra*, to the subtleties of the Perfection of Wisdom and *pramāṇa*, to details of various "profane" sciences. It seems safe to say, however, that his reputation among dGe lugs pas rests primarily on his commentaries to Mahāyāna śāstra literature. Among the works that seem to enjoy particular esteem are his commentaries to: Maitreya's *Abhisamāyālaṃkāra*, the *rNam bshad snying po rgyan*; Maitreya's *Uttaratantra* (as the *Ratnagotravibhāga* usually is known in Tibet), the *Theg pa chen po rgyud bla ma'i ṭikka*; Śāntideva's *Bodhicaryāvatāra*, the *sPyod 'jug rnam bshad*; and Dharmakīrti's *Pramāṇavārttika*, the *rNam 'grel thar lam gsal byed*.[2]

On a superficial reading, the *rNam 'grel thar lam gsal byed* ("Elucidating the Path to Liberation according to the *Pramāṇavārttika*") appears seamless and coherent, as if rGyal tshab rje's mind had been melded to Dharmakīrti's. This certainly was the impression rGyal tshab rje wished to convey, but it is important that we remember that two works are involved, and that their authors are from different cul-

---

1 Little biographical information on rGyal tshab rje is available in either English or Tibetan. Readers are, however, referred to Thurman (1981) section I:a, *passim* and Gelek (1980) Preface to vol. I.

2 All these are, of course, contained in Gelek (1980). In addition, most, if not all, have been issued in book form by the Pleasure of Elegant Sayings Press, Tibetan Monastery, Sarnath. The *Abhisamayālaṃkāra* commentary has been discussed in Bastian (1980); the *Uttaratantra* commentary is featured prominently in Obermiller's translation of that "Maitreya" text (1931). The sequence and dating of rGyal tshab rje's works has yet to be clearly established. Thus, we can locate the *rNam 'grel thar lam gsal byed* no more precisely than to estimate that it was composed in the first quarter of the fifteenth century.

tures, different centuries and different philosophical traditions: one was a seventh-century Indian Sautrāntika-Yogācāra, the other a fifteenth-century Tibetan Prāsaṅgika Mādhyamika. Many of the differences between the two will be brought out in the notes to the translation, but at least a broad sketch of the sort of assumptions informing rGyal tshab rje's world-view is not out of place here.

The overall framework of rGyal tshab rje's thought has four crucial characteristics, in descending order of generality. It is: (a) Mahāyāna, (b) *lam rim,* (c) Prāsaṅgika Mādhyamika and (d) dGe lugs pa.

(a) As Mahāyāna, rGyal tshab rje's system accepts as virtually axiomatic certain ideas about the goal and path of Buddhism. I have discussed many of these in section I:5, but will briefly recapitulate some of them here. The goal is assumed to be full buddhahood, a condition of complete omniscience, infinite compassion and virtually unlimited power. Buddhahood is divisible into three "bodies": the Dharma Body (*dharmakāya*), which is, roughly, enlightened mind; the Enjoyment Body (*sambhogakāya*), which is, roughly, enlightened communication; and the Transformation Body (*nirmāṇakāya*), which is, roughly, enlightened form, or enlightened action. The path, traversed by the aspirant buddha, or bodhisattva, is assumed to consist generally of two stores (*sambhāra*): that of gnosis and that of merit. The former, which results in a buddha's Dharma Body, is equivalent to the Mahāyāna perfection of wisdom; the latter, which result in a buddha's Enjoyment and Transformation Bodies, is equivalent to the Mahāyāna perfections of generosity, morality, patience, effort and concentration. More specifically, the path is itself divisible into ten bodhisattva stages (*bhūmi*) and/or five subsidiary paths. Of the latter, two, the paths of accumulation and application, are "mundane." On them, one practices the various Mahāyāna virtues, develops one's one-pointed concentration and analyzes the nature of reality discursively. On the path of seeing, one combines one-pointed concentration with insight into the nature of reality in such a way that reality is seen directly. Defilements are at last uprooted and the supramundane paths entered. The process of the elimination of subtler and subtler defilements continues through the path of development, until, when no more defilements—or their residues—remain, one achieves the path of no-more-training, the first moment of buddhahood.[3]

---

3 On Mahāyāna, see, e.g., Dayal (1970), Warder (1980), The Dalai Lama (1985), Williams (1988), etc.

(b) As *lam rim*, rGyal tshab rje's system is rooted in the common sūtra-level meditative structures accepted by virtually all Tibetan Buddhist schools. Based on the *Bodhipathapradīpa* of the eleventh-century Bengali traveler Atiśa, the *lam rim*, or "stages of the path" to enlightenment is a graded series of meditations that condenses and organizes the mass of material inherited by the Tibetans from Indian Buddhism. The *lam rim* is structured most generally by psychological types: beings of lesser, intermediate and great "scope," or aspiration. Beings of lesser scope are capable only of aspiring to a higher rebirth in a future life, and so must become aware of the rarity, preciousness and fragility of a human rebirth, the nature of the lower realms of saṃsāra, and the way in which positive and negative actions (*karma*) lead to positive and negative results. Aware of these points, they will strive to act virtuously and thus achieve the higher rebirth to which they aspire. Beings of intermediate scope must be aware of all this, but, aspiring to transcend any saṃsāric existence (i.e., achieve "Hīnayāna" nirvāṇa), they also must be aware of the subtle ways in which the higher saṃsāric realms are suffering and the way in which, through the twelve links of dependent origination, ignorance leads to suffering in saṃsāra. Aware of these points, they will renounce all ignorance, attachment and aversion, meditate one-pointedly on the absence of any self, and achieve the nirvāṇa to which they aspire. Beings of great scope, the bodhisattvas, must be aware of all of the preceding, but, because they aspire to full buddhahood, they also must develop great compassion; the altruistic aspiration to enlightenment, *bodhicitta;* and the particular Mahāyāna wisdom that sees phenomena as void and/or mind-only. Having developed one-pointed concentration on this final nature of phenomena, they are ready to practice the more advanced, swifter path laid out in the tantras. It should be noted that, as a "latter-day" *lam rim* system, rGyal tshab rje's entails the assumption that the "logical" system of Dignāga and Dharmakīrti had necessarily to be understood as part of one's training in wisdom, and the converse assumption that the major purpose of learning logic was to assist one toward one's ultimate spiritual goals.[4]

(c) As Prāsaṅgika Mādhyamika, rGyal tshab rje's system is rooted philosophically in the dialectic of Nāgārjuna as interpreted in the śāstras of Candrakīrti (seventh century), especially the *Prasannapadā*

---

4 On *lam rim*, see, e.g., Atiśa (1983), sGam po pa (1970), Dhargyey (1974), Rabten (1984) and Thurman (1981). On the relation of *lam rim* to the "logical" tradition, see the references in p. 116, n. 19, above.

and the *Madhyamakāvatāra*. As Mādhyamika, Candrakīrti's system rejects not only such Hīnayāna positions as Vaibhāṣika and Sautrāntika, but also the Yogācāra description of reality as ultimately mind-only, claiming that this description tends toward a kind of absolutization of mind. In its place, the Mādhyamika will insist that the ultimate nature of all phenomena (including dharmas, mind, and anything else) is voidness (*śūnyatā*) of substantial existence. As Prāsaṅgika, Candrakīrti's system specifies that the ultimate nature of phenomena is not only voidness, but, specifically, voidness of *inherent* existence (T. *rang bzhin gyis grub pa*). This specification supposedly results in a more subtle understanding than that of the other Mādhyamika school, the Svātantrika, which merely specifies that phenomena are void of true existence (T. *bden par grub pa*), and maintains (erroneously, Prāsaṅgikas assert) that on a conventional level phenomena are established by their own-marks, or specific characteristics (T. *rang gi mtshan nyid kyis grub pa*). Prāsaṅgika also rejects the Svātantrika's faith in independent syllogisms (S. *svatantra*), preferring to argue via consequences (S. *prasaṅga*), and asserts, uniquely, that *all* practitioners (Hīnayāna and Mahāyāna) realize the same object—voidness of inherent existence—prior to achieving liberation.[5]

(d) As dGe lugs pa, rGyal tshab rje's system is rooted in the writings and perspectives of Tsong kha pa. Tsong kha pa accepted the Mahāyāna, *lam rim* and Prāsaṅgika Madhyamaka, but in a manner that often set him apart from other Tibetan thinkers who accepted the same structures. Thus, he arranged the "stages of the path" in a particular way, such that guru-devotion was the "root of the path," prior even to the contemplation of the preciousness and rarity of a human rebirth. Further, he interpreted the various philosophical systems in a manner that sometimes placed him at odds with his contemporaries. At the root of this was his profound concern with and respect for rationality. Thus, he emphasized a "strong" relation between the conventional and the ultimate, insisting on the indispensability of a rational understanding of voidness before one can apprehend it non-conceptually. He also tended to view conventional reality through lenses shaded crucially by Sautrāntika concepts, and to interpret Sautrāntika itself in a more realistic, less nominalistic manner than was common.[6]

---

5 See references in the bibliography to the works of Nāgārjuna and Candrakīrti. Also, see, e.g., Hopkins (1983), Thurman (1984) and Lopez (1987).

6 On the particular perspectives afforded by dGe lugs, see, e.g., Sweet (1979),

These are some of the more important aspects of rGyal tshab rje's world-view. The way in which it is different from Dharmakīrti's will be brought out in some detail in the notes to the translation, but at least a few of the more important points of difference may be summarized here. First, rGyal tshab rje assumes that full omniscience is a fruit of the Buddhist path, and therefore reads Dharmakīrti as attempting to prove omniscience in the course of the *Pramāṇasiddhi* chapter; in fact, Dharmakīrti nowhere explicitly says that this is what he is trying to do. Second, rGyal tshab rje assumes the applicability of the five-path system common to many Indian Buddhist schools, and often reads Dharmakīrti as making reference to one or another of these paths; in fact, Dharmakīrti nowhere in the *Pramāṇasiddhi* chapter mentions any of the five paths. Third, rGyal tshab rje assumes a basic distinction between a no-self of persons and a no-self of dharmas, and claims that Dharmakīrti treats the former in the *Pramāṇasiddhi* chapter and the latter in the *Pratyakṣa* chapter; in fact, Dharmakīrti appears nowhere to recognize this distinction explicitly. Fourth, rGyal tshab rje assumes that the most advanced practitioners are Mahāyānists, and therefore he reads Dharmakīrti as asserting the superiority of Mahāyāna over Hīnayāna techniques and practitioners; in fact, Dharmakīrti nowhere in the *Pramāṇasiddhi* chapter makes it clear that this is his point. In short, rGyal tshab rje, as a Mahāyānist, assumes that Dharmakīrti, as a "Cittamātrin Following Reasoning," is a Mahāyānist, and therefore embracing a Mahāyāna soteriology. We have seen above, however (section I:9), that it is not evident that Dharmakīrti is doing this. To reiterate: Dharmakīrti's work shows clear traces of Yogācāra epistemology and ontology, but very little evidence of a specifically Mahāyāna soteriology—especially not of the elaborate kind taken for granted by rGyal tshab rje.

Hopkins (1983), Thurman (1981, 1984) and Klein (1986).

3. *The Translation: Whys and Wherefores*

I have already noted that rGyal tshab rje's *rNam 'grel thar lam gsal byed* is considered by dGe lugs pas to be their tradition's most important *Pramāṇavārttika* commentary. In attempting to expose the *Pramāṇasiddhi* chapter of that great work to readers of English, I have settled on translating rGyal tshab rje's commentary for a number of reasons:

1. Dharmakīrti's verses are terse in the extreme, and cannot easily be read without a commentary to provide needed interpolations and explanations. As noted, Masatoshi Nagatomi translated the *Pramāṇasiddhi* chapter directly from the Sanskrit as his dissertation for Harvard in 1957, but the work has yet to be published. Nagatomi provides excellent cross-references and a useful bilingual glossary, but his occasional interpolation of glosses from the commentaries of Manorathānandin and Prajñākaragupta does not go far enough toward making the philosophical meaning of Dharmakīrti's verses accessible. Nagatomi and, more recently, Richard Hayes, have been working on translations of the entire *Pramāṇavārttika*. These will be important landmarks in Buddhist studies when they appear, but in the meantime it seems useful to expose at least part of the Dharmakīrti corpus to readers interested in either Buddhism or philosophy of religion, for any of whom the *Pramāṇasiddhi* chapter ought to be of basic interest. Any commentary, especially one separated from its root-text by seven centuries, several philosophical systems and the highest mountains in the world, necessarily distorts the original, but this distortion is a price that must be paid for comprehensibility—and the commentarial process of distortion is itself interesting, and will be noted where necessary.

2. rGyal tshab rje's commentary has the specific virtue of having been written after all the great Indian commentaries, and with all of them at hand and under consideration. Thus, rGyal tshab rje—though not, of course, without his prejudices—was able to separate the wheat from the chaff in the commentarial tradition and to give the most weight to the explanations that seemed to him the most reasonable. He has relied most heavily on the commentaries of Devendrabuddhi

and Prajñākaragupta.[1] Devendrabuddhi, as we have seen, wrote his *Pramāṇavārttikapañjikā* under the direct supervision of Dharmakīrti himself, and thus can be assumed closely to have captured the literal meaning, if not the depth and breadth, of his intention. Prajñākaragupta's *Pramāṇavārttikālaṃkāra,* besides being a knowledgeable exposition of the text, is important for its spelling out of many of the Mahāyāna themes left implicit in the *Pramāṇasiddhi* chapter by Dharmakīrti himself.

3. Unlike most Indian commentaries, rGyal tshab rje's commentary structures the *Pramāṇasiddhi* chapter according to an extremely detailed outline. The Tibetan scholastic habit of providing elaborate textual divisions (*sa bcad*) for commentaries undeniably has proven a mixed blessing. There are times when the *sa bcad* threaten fairly to strangle the text under study—particularly when the work is not perhaps as neat and systematic as the scholastic mind would like to imagine. There is the further danger, of course, that the *sa bcad* will represent not the intentions of the work's author but the imagination of the commentator. These dangers must be borne in mind, but *sa bcad* do, in the right hands, possess the enormous advantage of laying bare the structure of a work whose meaning would be far less accessible without such elucidation. I believe that the *Pramāṇasiddhi* chapter of the *Pramāṇavārttika* is such a work, and that rGyal tshab rje's division of the text, while by no means the only one possible (and while clearly going beyond Dharmakīrti's explicit intention in a number of instances) is a considerable boon to anyone who wishes seriously to study the chapter.

4. Unlike many (though not all) Tibetan commentaries, rGyal tshab rje's commentary not only elucidates the meaning of Dharmakīrti's root-verses, but provides in addition extremely helpful summaries and/or extended discussions at a number of points. Of particular inter-

---

1 Ruegg (1966 [37-38, note 1]), citing kLong rdol bla ma and Stcherbatsky (1962 [I, 42]), assigns rGyal tshab rje to the Kashmiri "critical" school of PV commentators, founded by Dharmottara and Śāṅkārānanda, rather than to the "philological" school of Devendrabuddhi or the "religious" school of Prajñākaragupta (to which mKhas grub rje's commentary is assigned). I confess that I do not understand this assignment. There is scant mention of either Dharmottara or Śāṅkārānanda in the *rNam 'grel thar lam gsal byed;* both Devendrabuddhi and Prajñākaragupta, on the other hand, are quoted often. My own sense is that rGyal tshab rje follows most closely on the "religious" school, but I admit that there may be subtleties in the scheme of classification that I do not understand.

est are the discussion of the compatibility between the notion that a *pramāṇa* must be "new" and the Mahāyāna concept of omniscience (III:2), a summary of arguments on the mind-body problem (III:4), and the proofs of liberation and omniscience interpolated into the discussion of the truth of cessation (III:9). Of other Tibetan commentaries, I have looked most closely at those of dGe 'dun grub pa (fifteenth century, dGe lugs) and Mi pham rgya mtsho (nineteenth century, rNying ma). The former has the virtue of being a concise, syllogistically-framed gloss on Dharmakīrti's verses. The latter, despite its prolixity, spells out Dharmakīrti's meaning in considerable detail. To my mind, however, neither of them digresses as interestingly or as clearly as rGyal tshab rje's commentary.

5. Finally, precisely because the *rNam 'grel thar lam gsal byed* is the basis of dGe lugs pa *Pramāṇavārttika* interpretation, it is part of a large, living philosophical tradition that still has many knowledgeable exponents. Students who ask dGe lugs pa teachers for proofs of rebirth or enlightenment or the four noble truths sooner or later will be referred to rGyal tshab rje's commentary, and it has been my good fortune to be able to study the text with Tibetan teachers to whom its details and meaning are very familiar.

Before unleashing the reader on the translation—or perhaps it is better expressed the other way around!—I want to point out a number of stylistic and other idiosyncracies worthy of brief mention.

1. The numbered, capitalized verses that inaugurate each section are, as noted in the preface, translated from the *Tibetan* version of the *Pramāṇavārttika,* since this was the version used by rGyal tshab rje in composing his commentary. The capitalized words and phrases within the commentary highlight rGyal tshab rje's incorporation of Dharmakīrti's verses. Because I have tried to translate the root-text in the light of rGyal tshab rje's particular reading of the Tibetan, my rendition is in some cases two stages removed from the original Sanskrit. Let me simply reiterate what I said in the preface: this book is a translation of rGyal tshab rje's commentary, with a translation of Dharmakīrti's verses interpolated for the sake of clarity; it is *not* a definitive translation of Dharmakīrti's original text. I have followed the numbering and text of Miyasaka's edition (1972-77). The corresponding verse in Shastri's edition (1968) may be found by adding 2 to Miyasaka's number. By and large, lines *a* and *b* of the Tibetan verse will correspond to the first line, and lines *c* and *d* to the second line, of the Sanskrit śloka. Because of the peculiarities of Tibetan syntax (here reflecting the Sanskrit rather closely), translation order often is the reverse of text order. Furthermore, rGyal tshab rje's commentarial choices often dictate

reversals where translation would not. Therefore, although I have broken the translation of each verse into four lines, seldom does the first line correspond exactly to line *a* of the Tibetan, the second line to line *b*, etc. Indeed, as often as not, one of my translated lines includes elements from more than one Tibetan line—such are the exigencies of translation.

2. I have not included the Tibetan text of rGyal tshab rje's commentary, since (a) the book would become even larger than it already is and (b) the *rNam 'grel thar lam gsal byed* is available in book form in a two-volume in-print edition (1974) published by the Pleasure of Elegant Sayings Press (Tibetan Monastery), Sarnath, Varanasi 221007, India.

3. I have tried to translate rGyal tshab rje's Tibetan into English as readable as possible, but I fear that some turgidity remains. This is unavoidable, for both the style and subject-matter of rGyal tshab rje's discussion are quite technical. The structuring of much of the material in either syllogistic or *reductio* form, as well as the frequent use of technical philosophical vocabulary, make mellifluous rendering rather difficult. I have, I hope, somewhat mitigated the stylistic difficulties by translating the text as a philosophical treatise, not a debate manual—one way in which it may be read and used. Thus, I have translated the work into sentences rather than syllogisms. I have left untranslated such "markers" as *chos can*, which invariably sets off the logical subject, but I trust that my sentences are clear and regular enough that the syllogistic structure is evident. I have tried to mitigate the difficulty of the subject-matter by providing a rather large apparatus of notes. These are used partially for bibliographic and linguistic observations, but their primary purpose is to elucidate the meaning of the text. It would be presumptuous of me to treat them as a "sub-commentary," but I do hope they will help make Dharmakīrti and rGyal tshab rje's often complex thought somewhat clearer to the reader.

4. In my translation of Tibetan terms and words into English, I have tried to maintain an overall but by no means slavish consistency. Some single English word may translate several different Tibetan terms, as, e.g., "mind," which variously renders the Tibetan *blo*, *yid*, or *sems*, etc.; and "nature," which renders, among others, the Tibetan *rang bzhin* or *chos nyid*. Conversely, some single Tibetan word may be given different English equivalents in different contexts, as, e.g., *bde ba*, which can be either "happiness" or "pleasure"; *'dzin pa*, which means either "apprehension" or "grasping"; *grub pa*, which is either "accomplishment" or "proof"; and *don*, which is a "goal," an "aim" or an "object." I have attempted to make variant translations clear by cross-references in the glossary.

5. I have translated into their Sanskrit forms a number of words that are most familiar thus, e.g., saṃsāra, nirvāṇa, arhant, sūtra, Mahāyāna and the names of Indian personages and philosophical schools.

6. Much of rGyal tshab rje's commentary is in "dialogue" form, with questions or objections from real or hypothetical opponents setting the stage for the exposition of the "correct" position on a given matter. Some of the opposing points actually are contained in Dharmakīrti's verses; most of them must be supplied by commentaries. I have demarcated the sections that usually conclude with the Tibetan *zhe na* ("if it is said. . .") as: [OPPONENT:], with the understanding that many of the views expressed by "opponents" are merely possible positions, rather than positions actually held by Dharmakīrti's or rGyal tshab rje's contemporaries. I have demarcated the "reply" sections as [RGYAL TSHAB RJE:]. I realize that in the vast majority of cases rGyal tshab rje is simply fleshing out Dharmakīrti's meaning, but the ordering and phrasing nevertheless remain rGyal tshab rje's, and it seems fairer to attribute the "correct" side of the dialogue to him. In those cases where rGyal tshab rje has significantly departed from the most straightforward reading of the root-verses, I have attempted so to indicate in the notes.

7. Brackets in the course of the translation indicate either interpolations that clarify the meaning of a sentence or nominal phrases that replace pronouns and therefore identify their antecedents.

8. In the body of the translation, I have included all of rGyal tshab rje's section titles, and have numbered them consecutively; the number is indicated parenthetically after the title. Since these sections actually comprise a complex scheme of divisions and subdivisions that is, in effect, rGyal tshab rje's outline of the chapter, an Appendix is devoted to a listing of all section titles. There, the title is preceded by the consecutive number assigned to it in the body of the translation, and its more detailed enumeration in rGyal tshab rje's outline. Each title is followed by (a) the verse(s) it covers in the Miyasaka edition of the *Pramāṇavārttika,* (b) the pages it covers in the Sarnath edition of the *rNam 'grel thar lam gsal byed* and (c) the pages it covers in my translation.

The *Pramāṇasiddhi* chapter of the *Pramāṇavārttika* presupposes an understanding of a great deal of Indian philosophy, both Buddhist and non-Buddhist, touching as it does at various times on theology, causal theory, the structure of inference, soteriology, epistemology and metaphysics. My knowledge of these areas is woefully inadequate, but I have attempted nevertheless to supply what clarification I could, in many cases on the basis of explanations provided by my mentor and friend, Ven. Prof. Geshe Sopa. Whatever imperfections occur in both the translation and notes are my own fault, and I hope that eventually they may be eliminated. I hope, too, that in the meantime those imperfections do not negate the value of any correct translations and interpretations that I may have provided.

Part Three

A Translation of rGyal tshab rje's Commentary on the *Pramāṇasiddhi* Chapter of Dharmakīrti's *Pramāṇavārttika*

1. *Introductory*

I bow down to the holy gurus

The second [chapter],[1] an explanation of what is to be known [logically],[2] i.e., liberation and omniscience and the path leading to them, [is divided into]: (1) The general meaning [sequential section 1] and (2) The meaning

---

1 There has been considerable debate over whether the *Pramāṇasiddhi* (*tshad ma'i grub pa*) chapter of the *Pramāṇavārttika* is the second or the first. The Tibetan commentarial tradition considers it the second, and holds the *Svārthānumāna* chapter to be the first, because (a) Dharmakīrti is said to have written the *Svārthānumāna* chapter first, to have considered it the most difficult, and to have written his own commentary only on it and (b) because it is necessary to establish at the outset the structure of syllogisms, which will be used as the argumentative framework throughout the remainder of the *Pramāṇavārttika*. Modern scholars who observe the Tibetan ordering include Frauwallner (1954) and Inami and Tillemans (1986). All three modern editors of the *Pramāṇavārttika,* as well as Nagatomi (1959 [263, note 1]) and Stcherbatsky (1962 [I, 38-39]), consider the *Pramāṇasiddhi* as the first, reasoning that, since the *Pramāṇavārttika* is constructed as a commentary on the *Pramāṇasamuccaya*, the *Pramāṇavārttika* chapter that comments on the first verses of the *Pramāṇasamuccaya* must be the first. It ought to be noted, however, that the first "chapter" of the *Pramāṇasamuccaya* covers perception (*pratyakṣa*), which has never been considered the topic of the *Pramāṇavārttika*'s first chapter, being relegated to either second (by modern editors) or third (by most Tibetans). Thus, relationship to the precise topic-ordering of the *Pramāṇasamuccaya* would seem not to be a manifest determinant of the *Pramāṇavārttika's* order, a fact that might lend slightly more weight to the Tibetan ordering. Furthermore—and perhaps most importantly—early Indian commentaries on the *Pramāṇavārttika* favor the Tibetan ordering; the ordering favored by most modern editors seems to date from the rather later commentary of Manorathanandin (see van Bijlert [1989] XXII, n. 2).

2 In light of the Tibetan ordering of the *Pramāṇavārttika*'s chapters, *rtogs bya* refers to "what is to be known" or understood through application of the type of syllogism whose structure has been established in the *Svārthānumāna* chapter, namely "liberation and omniscience and the path leading to them."

of the limbs [2].[3]

The general meaning [1][4]

[This is divided into:] (1) Setting forth the explanation of ācārya Dignāga [2], (2) The way [Dignāga's] meaning was arranged by the author of the *Pramāṇavārttika* [3] and (3) The intention of [Dignāga and Dharmakīrti] [4].

Setting forth the explanation of ācārya Dignāga [2]

> To the one who has become an authority,[5] the one who desires to benefit beings,[6]
> The teacher, the sugata, the savior,[7] I bow down.

---

3 Sections covering "the general meaning" (*spyi'i don*) here denote introductory discussions composed by the commentator, while sections covering "the meaning of the limbs" (*yan lag gyi don*) explain the actual root verses being commented upon. The discussion of the four noble truths (sections II:6-11) is structured similarly.

4 For a table of correspondences between the sequence of section numbers employed here and rGyal tshab rje's outline of the text (as well the root verses in the Miyasaka edition of the *Pramāṇavārttika* and the page numbers in the *rNam 'grel thar lam gsal byed),* see the Appendix.

5 I have chosen to translate *tshad ma* (*pramāṇa*) nominally as "authority" and adjectivally as "authoritative." Although strictly speaking *tshad ma* always is a cognition, and is not wrongly translated as, e.g., "means of knowledge" (Warder), "valid knowledge-instrument" (Nagatomi), "avenue of validity" (Sopa), "prime cognizer" (Hopkins) or "valid cognizer" (Klein), nevertheless I have chosen "authority"/"authoritative" because it carries particularly well the ambiguity involved in discussions, central to the *Pramāṇasiddhi* chapter, of the Buddha as *tshad ma:* he is an authority in the double sense that his cognitions themselves are valid and that he is a source of valid cognition for "those intent on freedom." Because for Buddhists authority always is a cognition, a person—even the Buddha—cannot technically be considered an authority. Nevertheless, it is admitted by Tibetan tradition (see Inami and Tillemans [1986] 127-28) that a person may be an authority at least by metaphorical extension. This, then, enables the Tibetans to refer to the Buddha as an "authoritative person" (*tshad ma'i skyes bu*), a term for which there seems to have been no Sanskrit prototype, yet which has helped considerably to shape Tibetan perceptions of the soteriological role of *pramāṇa*-study. On this term, see Steinkellner (1983) and van der Kuijp (1987).

6 The Tibetan *'gro ba* tends usually to connote "sentient beings," or, more literally, "transmigrators"; the Sanskrit *jagat,* though derived from the verbal root *gam,* ("go") often is translated rather more abstractly as "the world."

7 *skyob pa* (*tāyin*) is probably more accurately rendered as "protector," which seems to me, however, too weak to convey the force of the idea: that the Buddha is one who enables others to be freed from saṃsāra. I realize that "savior"

Out of compassion for beings deluded by faulty reasoning,
I will explain properly the establishment of authority.[8]

The meaning of this quote:

The first half shows the homage, the second half shows the promise to explain. The homage praises the teacher for his excellence in causes and excellence in results.

[His] excellence in causes is twofold: excellence of intention and excellence of application.[9] Intention is the great compassion that desires to benefit beings to the utmost. Application is the "teacher"[10] that for the sake of others accustomates[11] the wisdom realizing no-self.

[His excellence in] results is also twofold: excellence of his own aims and excellence of others' aims. [Excellence of] his own aims is his possession of the three special qualities of the sugata,[12] whose nature is abandonment and realization. [Excellence of] others' aims is his having the characteristics of one who is a savior of beings by way of showing to others the path that he has seen himself.

---

has some rather strong Christian connotations, but it is an effective word, and, as long as we recognize that it does not imply that the Buddha "saves," as Jesus does, through divine grace or fiat, I think it can serve our purposes.

8 The first half of the verse corresponds to the first half of the opening verse of Dignāga's *Pramāṇasamuccaya.* The second half of Dignāga's verse, however, reads in Tibetan: *tshad ma bsgrub phyir rang gi gshung kun las / btus te sna tshogs 'thor rnams 'dir gcig bya* ("In order to establish authority, I make here a single compendium of my various scattered writings"). The second half of the verse as quoted by rGyal tshab rje appears to be taken from Prajñākaragupta (PVA p. 3): *rtog ge ngan 'khrul 'gro ba la brtse bas / tshad ma grub pa tshul bzhin bshad par bya*). Cf. above, p. 127, n. 1.

9 Although *sbyor ba* (*sampat*) denotes "application," or "activity," it refers here primarily to a particular mental activity, namely the realization of no-self. Within a Mahāyāna framework, therefore, it corresponds to wisdom (*prajñā*), while "intention" corresponds to method (*upāya*).

10 "Teacher" is placed in quotes because of its ambiguity: it can refer to the human being who is a teacher, but its primary referent is the wisdom realizing no-self.

11 I am not happy with "accustomates" and "accustomation" for *goms* and *goms pa* (*abhyāsa*)—they verge on neologism or what Paul Griffiths has called "Buddhist Hybrid English"—but they are legitimate English words, and I prefer them to "habituates" and "habituation," which tend, I think, to have somewhat negative connotations for most of us.

12 Like "teacher," "sugata" is ambiguous: it can refer to the person who is "well-gone," but technically denotes the sets of abandonments and realizations that are the characteristic qualities of the "well-gone."

Therefore, the Buddha, the Blessed One, who from excellence in causes has arisen as an authority who has as his nature excellence of the two resultant aims, must be described as perfectly authoritative.

The expression "one who has become an authority":

There is a purpose necessitating [this]: [Dignāga] will explain [the phrase] in order to lead the way for beings who are mistaken about actuality because they apply inverted definitions of "authority," etc., [arrived at through] faulty reasoning.[13]

The way [Dignāga's] meaning was arranged by the author of the Pramāṇavārttika [3]

The first half of the verse is shown to be summarized in five topics: (1) the one who has become an authority, (2) the one who desires to benefit beings, (3) the teacher, (4) the sugata and (5) the savior. Furthermore, the first is the basis of the four particular qualities that are to be established; the remaining [four] are the particular qualities that establish that [authoritativeness predicated of the Buddha].

The way of explaining that is divided into the forward system of explanation, which accords with the order of the verse, and the reverse system of explanation, which is the reverse of that.

There is a reason for making such a division. [Some, e.g., Mīmāṃsakas,] saying, "Because there exists no proof[14] / That there is an authority cognizing hidden objects,"[15] argue that someone's accustomating a method for obtaining the omniscience of one who has become an authority is not a cause producing omniscience that would

---

13 In other words, our failure to understand the essentials of epistemology, i.e., what authority is and who is authoritative, contributes to our misapprehension of the "actuality" (*gnas lugs*) of things. Our most fundamental error, of course, is the mistaken apprehension of a self, but our failure to understand what knowledge is contributes mightily to our confusion.

14 *sgrub byed* in its broadest sense means "accomplishment." It is used in logic to denote the "proof" of a thesis by a reason, and more broadly to refer to the accomplishment of any state or goal. The Mīmāṃsaka, therefore, is arguing that omniscience is a condition susceptible of neither logical proof nor actual accomplishment. This dual sense of *sgrub byed* occurs quite frequently.

15 Phenomena are divided by the Tibetan scholastic tradition into three types of objects, classified according to their accessibility to the observer: manifest (*mngon gyur, *abhimukhī*), hidden (*lkog gyur, *parokṣa*) and very hidden (*shin tu lkog gyur, *atyantaparokṣa*). The first is accessible to sense perception, the second to inference, the third only to a being who perceives yogically. See, e.g., Lati Rinbochay (1980) 77-80.

occur in that [person]. Also, [others object that] there is no cause informing [us] of omniscience in such [Buddhist] statements as, "Such omniscience exists, because we see its results or [something] of similar nature."[16]

The forward system of explanation is effected in order to refute the inverted understanding of the first objectors. The reverse system of explanation is effected in order to refute [the inverted understanding in] the second.

Excellence of intention is shown directly by [Dharmakīrti's] first proof to be great compassion [and shown] by implication to be the thought of enlightenment.[17] Excellence of application has as its chief activity accustomation, for the sake of others, of the wisdom realizing no-self; it is shown by implication to be the training in generosity, morality, etc.[18]

The first mode of explanation demonstrates the way the teacher arrived [at his goal] via some path. The second mode of explanation first

---

16 As will be noted below, in notes to section III:2:D, it is very much open to question whether Dharmakīrti even accepted, let alone was intent on demonstrating, the Buddha's omniscience—especially in the full sense of the omniscience cognizing every aspect of reality (*rnam pa thams cad thams cad mkhyen pa, sarvākarajñāna*). Explicitly, he seeks to prove only the Buddha's authoritativeness. For both Prajñākaragupta and the Tibetan tradition, though, the Buddha's authoritativeness is synonymous with his omniscience, hence rGyal tshab rje's conflation of the two in these introductory remarks. See R. Jackson (1987 and 1988).

17 Dharmakīrti does not himself mention the thought of enlightenment (*byang chub sems, bodhicitta*), which is rooted in compassion and is itself, in the *Abhisamāyālaṃkāra* path-system followed by rGyal tshab rje, the "doorway" through which one enters the Mahāyāna. The thought of enlightenment is generally glossed as the altruistic aspiration to enlightenment, though it is divisible in many ways, and has been a topic of much discussion by Mahāyāna writers.

18 The six transcendent practices, or perfections (*pha rol tu phyin pa, pāramitā*) of a bodhisattva are: (1) generosity (*spyin pa, dāna*), (2) morality (*tshul 'khrims, śīla*), (3) patience (*bzod pa, kṣānti*), (4) effort (*brtson 'grus, vīrya*), (5) concentration (*bsam gtan, dhyāna*) and (6) wisdom (*shes rab, prajñā*). They are transcendent because they are coupled with a realization of the voidness of any inherently existing aspects of the practice involved. For a discussion, see, e.g., Dayal (1970), and two great Mahāyāna poems, Candrakīrti's *Madhyamakāvatāra* (fully translated by Huntington [1989], partially translated by Poussin [1907-11] and Rabten [1983]) and Śāntideva's *Bodhicāryāvatāra* (translated by Batchelor [1979] and commented upon by Gyatso [1980]), both of which are structured along the lines of the perfections.

establishes the four noble truths; then, having proven by reasoning that because of them [the teacher] must have excellence of realization, and from that that there must be preceding [causes], [this second mode] also correctly shows how he arrived [at his goal] by way of that path.[19]

The intention of [Dignāga and Dharmakīrti] [4]

The purpose of proving the teacher, the Blessed One, to be an authority, through proving that his teaching is flawless, is [to effect] the accomplishment of the goal manifestly desired by those intent on freedom.

[OPPONENT:] It follows that it is pointless to prove the *muni* to be an authority in order [to effect] the accomplishment of a person's desired goal, because [goals] are accomplished through authoritative perception and inference.

[RGYAL TSHAB RJE:] The *muni* is proven to be an authority not for the sake of the accomplishment of just any goal, but in order to show that the *muni* is an authority in having the method for [accomplishing] high rebirths and the definitive good.[20]

[OPPONENT:] Even if it is for the sake of those goals, it [still] follows that it is pointless to prove the *muni* to be an authority, because you accept that past and future lives, the four noble truths, etc., are proven by objectively impelled inferences.[21]

---

19 In short, the forward system explains the *cause* of the Buddha's authoritativeness, i.e., the way in which he became an authority; the reverse system explains the *reason* for his authoritativeness, i.e., the authoritativeness of what he teaches, the four noble truths. This point is made clearly by Mi pham rgya mtsho (n.d.) 257. On the question of which of Dharmakīrti's verses cover which system, see above, p. 128, n.2.

20 High rebirths (*mngon tho, abhyudaya*) and the definitive good (*nges legs, niḥśreyasa*) are, respectively, the temporary and ultimate goals of religious striving. High rebirths comprise the human, titan (*asura*) and god (*deva*) realms of saṃsāra, which, though at least as pleasurable as painful, still can issue in rebirth in any of the three lower realms, those of animals, hungry ghosts and hell denizens. The definitive good is a level of attainment from which there is no return to saṃsāra. From the Mahāyāna point of view, this includes both the nirvāṇa of a Hīnayāna arhant and the omniscient enlightenment of a buddha. Within the *lam rim* anthropology that rGyal tshab rje derived from Tsong kha pa and Atiśa, higher rebirths are the goal of persons of small scope, while the definitive good is the goal of persons of medium and great scope. On this, see Atiśa's *Bodhipathapradīpa* and Tsong kha pa's *Lam rim chen mo*, or any of his shorter *lam rim* texts, as translated in, e.g., Thurman (1982) part II.

[RGYAL TSHAB RJE:] There is no problem. Without relying intitially on the scriptures of the Blessed One, one will not even think of no-self or subtle momentariness, not to mention understand them inferentially. Thus, when they see initially that the Blessed One's teachings on high rebirths and the definitive good, and the reasons proving them, are connected uninterruptedly to worldly authoritative perception,[22] those who possess [the power of] investgation will investigate whether [things] exist just as they are taught or whether they do not, and they will understand inferentially the way in which those [teachings are true].[23]

---

21 Objectively impelled inferences (*dngos stobs rjes dpag, vastubalapravṛttānumāna*) are inferences literally "effected by the force of actual entities." They are, in other words, inferences validated by ultimate reference to the actual own-marks, or specific characteristrics (*svalakṣaṇa*), possessed by phenomena. This crucial concept, which grounds inference in the commonly observable nature of things, and is a token of Dharmakīrti's epistemological realism (perhaps even foundationalism), is discussed by him in the *Parārthānumāna* chapter of the *Pramāṇavārttika*, verses 48-71. See Tillemans (1986) 147, note 17. According to dGe lugs tradition, objectively impelled inferences relate to hidden phenomena; they are contrasted with conclusions drawn on the basis of confidence, or belief (*yid dpyod, āraddhā*) toward an authority who claims to perceive very hidden phenomena yogically. The distinction is drawn by Lati Rinbochay (1980) 78: "[Hidden phenomena] are those which must be established for common beings in dependence on a sign by the power of the fact [*dngos stobs kyis*], such as liberation and omniscience, the selflessness of the person, the subtle impermanence of sound, and so forth. Very hidden phenomena are such things as the subtle features of the cause and effect of actions, as taught in the scripture,. . . [which are] accessible to inference, but only through belief, which is called scriptural inference." Dharmakīrti's main concern, as will be evident, is with hidden phenomena, and the objectively impelled inferences that establish them.

22 In other words, no matter how "other-worldly" or "hidden" the phenomenon subjected to inferential proof, it can be established conclusively because the final step in a logically connected series of inferences will appeal directly to intersubjective perceptual knowledge. Although far more steps will be involved in inferring the Buddha's authoritativeness than in inferring, e.g., that there is fire on a particular hill, all objectively impelled inference operates in this way.

23 In the foregoing, the opponent has tried to establish the pointlessness of proving the Buddha an authority, on the grounds that (a) authority accomplishes its goals adequately without such particular proofs and (b) the Buddha's teachings already are asserted to be objectively proven, so no new proof is required. rGyal tshab rje replies that (a) a particular type of person, the authoritative person, must be established for those with the particular interest in spiritual freedom and (b) the truth of the teachings is not self-evident, and

so it must be demonstrated, and one must have some confidence beforehand that the being whose teachings are to be investigated is worthy of attention.

2. *Definition and Examples of Authority*

A. THE DEFINITION OF AUTHORITY

The meaning of the limbs [5]

[This is divided into:] (1) Proving the *muni* to be an authority [6] and (2) The purpose of praising him for his authoritativeness [324].

Proving the muni *to be an authority [6]*

[This is divided into:] (1) Showing through the forward system the way in which the teacher arrived [at his goal] via some path [7] and (2) Demonstrating through the reverse system that he arrived at such [a goal] [176].

Showing through the forward system the way in which the teacher arrived [at his goal] via some path [7]

[This is divided into:] (1) Identifying the definiendum, the authoritative person, through explaining the meaning of "has become an authority" [8] and (2) Defining the authoritative person through the four remaining [epithets] and identifying the path that leads to that authoritativeness [52].

Identifying the definiendum, the authoritative person, through explaining the meaning of "has become an authority" [8]

[This is divided into:] (1) The general definition of authority [9] and (2) Showing that the *muni* also possesses the characteristics [of authority] [18].

The general definition of authority [9]

[This is divided into:] (1) The essential definition [10] and (2) Particulars [17].

The essential definition [10]

[This is divided into:] (1) The definition [11], (2) The definiendum [15] and (3) Ascertaining the definition in the definiendum [16].

The definition [11]

[This is divided into:] (1) Identifying non-deceptiveness [12], (2) Disposing of [the objection that the definition is] too narrow [13] and (3) Disposing of [the objection that the definition is] too broad [14].

Identifying non-deceptiveness [12]

(1) AUTHORITY IS NON-DECEPTIVE COGNITION;
[NON-DECEPTIVENESS] ABIDES WITH REGARD TO [CAUSAL] EFFICIENCY.

[OPPONENT:] Since cognizing authority-objects—such as high rebirths and the definitive good, together with the methods [thereto]—depends on authority, and since only the *muni* is an authority regarding every such object, what then are the general characteristics of authority such that by possessing those characteristics one becomes an authority?

[RGYAL TSHAB RJE:] Perceptual AUTHORITY apprehending blue is an authority, because it IS a new, NON-DECEPTIVE COGNITION.

[OPPONENT:] If cognition is an authority, it follows that discussions of the characteristics of authority found in the śāstras are pointless, because when a cognition is established by apperception, the non-deceptiveness that exists [simultaneously] with, and is substantially identical to, [that cognition] is already proven.[1]

[RGYAL TSHAB RJE:] It does not follow that a knowledge-object is completely and non-deceptively cognized merely by an experience of its own essence, because how could there ABIDE an auto-comprehension WITH REGARD TO the [CAUSAL] EFFICIENCY of cooking, burning, etc.? Non-deceptiveness is in regard to [potential confirmatory] ac-

1 Apperception (*rang rig, svasaṃvedanā*), or cognition of the contents of consciousness, is one of the four types of perception accepted by Dharmakīrti. It is posited in part to explain memory. Apperception invariably accompanies, is substantially identical to, and is authoritative regarding the content of any of the six types of cognition (or consciousness: *rnam par shes pa, vijñāna*), i.e., the five types of sense-cognition and mental cognition. See p. 123, above. The opponent is arguing that, since apperception is authoritative regarding cognitions, nondeceptiveness is self-evidently a characteristic of authority, and need not, therefore, be proven or explained by recourse to the śāstras. A further—and more important—implication is that, since any authoritative cognition already is established as nondeceptive by the apperception accompanying it, there is no need for recourse to subsequent confirmation via such criteria as efficiency.

tion; it definitely is not cognized merely by an experience of [a cognition's] own essence.[2]

Disposing of [the objection that the definition is] too narrow[3] *[13]*

(1c) NON-DECEPTIVENESS ARISES FROM WORDS, TOO,
BECAUSE THEY SHOW A MANIFEST DESIRE [TO SPEAK].
(2) WORDS IN THE [ŚĀSTRAS] ARE NOT CAUSE-POSSESSING REAL
OBJECTS, AUTHORITIES; THEY BRING ABOUT
IN THE MIND A CLEAR [APPEARANCE OF] SOME OBJECT
THAT IS THE OBJECT THE SPEAKER [DESIRES TO EXPRESS].

[OPPONENT:] Since NON-DECEPTIVENESS regarding [potential confirmatory] action has the meaning of [cognitive] attainment of an object, and since no one can attain [anything by] words, etc., aural cognition does not fit the definition of authority.

[RGYAL TSHAB RJE:] The aural cognition that ARISES FROM objectifying WORDS that have been apprehended does not have the problem of unsuitability as an authority, BECAUSE IT *is* a cognition that newly SHOWS A MANIFESTly DESIREd object [i.e., the words] as its own authority-object.[4] The word "TOO" [indicates] the inclusion of the visual perception of lightning, etc.[5]

---

2 Apperception cannot guarantee the authoritativeness of all cognitions, because not all authoritative cognitions are immediately and self-evidently authoritative. A cognition of a patch of blue is immediately and self-evidently authoritative, so the apperception of that cognition cognizes not only the cognition's contents, but its non-deceptiveness, too. On the other hand, a cognition of fire on a distant hill is subject to subsequent confirmation or disconfirmation, and thus is not immediately and self-evidently authoritative. Thus, the apperception of that cognition *cannot* cognize the cognition's non-deceptiveness, because the non-deceptiveness—although it is actual—has yet to be confirmed.

3 The Tibetan actually reads *ma khyab*, or "nonpervasion," which translates the Sanskrit *avyāpti*, but its sense is *khyab chung*, underpervasion, a condition in which a definition fails to cover all possible instances of the phenomenon defined, and therefore is inadequate. *Ma khyab* or *khyab chung* is contrasted with *khyab ches pa* (*ativyāpti*), in which the definition "overpervades," or covers more instances than truly are relevant to the phenomenon defined. *Ma khyab*, then, is excessive narrowness of a definition; *khyab ches pa* is excessive broadness. These concepts are crucial to dGe lugs pa discussions of the object to be negated (*dgag bya*) in the demonstration of no-self: the self for which one is searching must be defined with utter precision, not too inclusively, not too exclusively. See, e.g., Thurman (1982) III:b.

4 An aural cognition is an authority simply because it nondeceptively appre-

[OPPONENT:] Since the śāstras are authorities regarding all knowledge-objects, they should [effect the] accomplishment of one's goal. What, then, is gained by proving the muni to be an authority?

[RGYAL TSHAB RJE:] It follows that the expressive WORDS IN THE śāstras, etc., ARE NOT correct CAUSE-POSSESSING reasons that demonstrate [the reality of] high rebirths and the definitive good,[6] which are the REAL OBJECTS expressed [by the words], because words expressing that are AUTHORITIES—i.e., they are correct reasons—in BRINGing ABOUT IN THE MIND of the listener A CLEAR [appearance of] SOME OBJECT THAT IS THE OBJECT THE SPEAKER desires to express. [That object] is [the logical subject that is] the basis of the reason's relevance to the subject.[7] Alternatively, the meaning of the previous [interpretation] should be applied so as to accord with the words of the latter.[8]

---

hends a word, or sound, that a speaker desires to express. It attains its object in this sense, not in the sense that it necessarily apprehends anything beyond the mere word, such as, e.g., the word's referent object—which, the opponent correctly notes, one cannot attain through a mere word.

5 Thus, all types of sense-cognitions are covered by the auditory example. A visual cognition that may or may not authoritatively ascertain lightning still is authoritative in its apprehension of a visual object (as opposed, say, to a hallucination).

6 We cannot infer the reality of a phenomenon simply from the fact that there exist words that express it, for there is no absolute connection of either causality or synonymy (the two chief logical relations in Buddhist epistemology) between words and things. Not everything for which we have a name actually exists. In the case under discussion, the words "high rebirth" and "definitive good" are verbal entities, and so have as their cause not the reality of the conditions described, but simply the speaker's desire to express them.

7 The reason's relevance to the subject (*phyogs chos, pakṣadharma*) is one of the three characteristics required of a correct logical reason. The other two are the reason's invariable concomitance with the predicate (*rjes khyab, anvaya*) and the reason's invariable non-concomitance with the non-predicate (*ldog khyab, vyatireka*). I have generally translated the latter two, respectively, as positive and negative concomitance. The syllogism rGyal tshab rje is discussing might be stated thus: "High rebirths and the definitive good (subject) are objects a speaker desires to express (predicate), because they are meaningful sounds (reason)." The syllogism is correct because the reason is relevant to the subject, i.e., high rebirths and the definitive good are instances of meaningful sound; because the reason is invariably concomitant with the predicate, i.e., the utterance of a meaningful sound always is observed to follow upon a speaker's desire to express the referent of the sound; and because the reason is invariably non-concomitant with absence of the predicate, i.e., in any case without meaningful sound, there is an observed absence of the desire to express.

Disposing of [the objection that the definition] is too broad [14]

(3) A CONVENTIONAL [MIND] CANNOT BE ACCEPTED [AS AN AUTHORITY],
BECAUSE IT APPREHENDS THE [ALREADY] APPREHENDED; . . .

OPPONENT:] It follows that subsequent cognition also is an authority, because it is non-deceptive.

[RGYAL TSHAB RJE:] A CONVENTIONAL mind, a memory, a subsequent cognition, CANNOT BE ACCEPTED as really being an authority, BECAUSE IT is a cognition that by memory APPREHENDS again an object already APPREHENDED and cognized by a previous authority that induced [the memory] and has not diminished.[9]

The definiendum [15]

(3b) . . . MIND IS AUTHORITY,
BECAUSE IT IS THE CHIEF [CAUSE] OF ENGAGING
ENTITIES THAT ARE TO BE ADOPTED AND REJECTED, AND
(4) BECAUSE IF THAT IS SO, THIS BEING THE CASE,
SINCE THERE ARE DIFFERENT ASPECTS OF THE OBJECT,
THERE ARE DIFFERENT COGNITIONS OF MENTAL [OBJECTS].

[OPPONENT:] Because one attains objects in dependence upon them, are not the clear visual and other faculties authorities?

[RGYAL TSHAB RJE:] Only a MIND that is new and non-deceptive about the arisen aspect of its own object IS AN AUTHORITY, because it is

---

8 rGyal tshab rje has offered two possible interpretations for PV 2c-d: (a) aural cognition is an authority because it attains its desired object, which is a word or sound and (b) aural cognition is an authority because it shows us authoritatively that a speaker wishes to express an object. The "meaning of the previous interpretation" only will "accord with the words of the latter" when *ston*, which generally means "shows" or "demonstrates," is glossed to mean "attains," and when *mngon par 'dod pa* is taken to mean the object we desire to apprehend, rather than the object the speaker desires to express.

9 A *bcad shes* (**paricchinnajñāna*), or subsequent cognition, is, literally, "cut off," i.e., cut off from the immediacy of an authoritative cognition, which apprehends its knowledge-object newly and independently. Following on a previous authoritative cognition, it is, as the opponent points out, nondeceptive, but because it is not new, it fails to fulfill the definition of authority. See Rabten (1978) 41-43. It ought to be noted that Dharmakīrti here denies authority-status to a *sāṃvṛtta*, a "united cognition" or "verbal identification" (Nagatomi [1957] 7), which is translated into Tibetan here as *kun rdzob*, a "conventionality," hence read by rGyal tshab rje thus and glossed to mean a subsequent cognition.

cognition that chiefly accomplishes indirect and direct results, through authority.

An authority accomplishes indirect results, BECAUSE IT IS THE CHIEF cause OF a person's ENGAGING in adoption or rejection of ENTITIES THAT ARE TO BE ADOPTED AND REJECTED. AND, that authority accomplishes direct results, BECAUSE IF THAT [definition is true], THIS BEING THE CASE, one is able to establish directly the [definition of] authority [as] cognition of an object.[10] This follows, because, SINCE THERE ARE DIFFERENT ASPECTS OF THE OBJECT appearing to the mind that is newly able to cut off superimposition,[11] one is able to establish DIFFERENT [authoritative] COGNITIONS OF MENTAL objects.

Ascertaining the definition in the definiendum [16]

(4d) COGNITION [EXPERIENCES] ITS OWN ESSENCE FROM ITS OWN [SIDE];
(5) AUTHORITATIVENESS [IS COGNIZED] THROUGH DESIGNATION;
ŚĀSTRAS EFFECT A REVERSAL OF DELUSION.

[OPPONENT:] Authority, defined as new and non-deceptive, is either (a) ascertained by itself or (b) dependent on another, subsequent [authority]. If (a), then no one will be confused in distinguishing the authorities from the non-authorities. If (b), that ascertaining authority will also require ascertainment as non-deceptive by another, subsequent [authority], and since that [authority] will depend on still another, there will be an infinite regress.

---

10 In other words, authority accomplishes direct results because, as above in the case of aural cognition, authority sometimes resides simply in the nondeceptive cognition of a knowledge-object. Direct knowledge of non-deceptiveness entails direct knowledge of authoritativeness.

11 Superimposition (*sgro 'dogs, āropa*) generally refers to philosophical hypostatization, the superimposition of a metaphysical entity where there is none. It is used frequently in Mādhyamika texts, where it refers to the view that there exists an inherent self in the aggregates or dharmas. Here, the term simply refers to a cognition that is the contradictory of an authoritative cognition. If I am to cognize authoritatively that a lamp is white, I must have a mind that newly cuts off, or is able to cut off, the possibility that it is non-white. Thus, my authoritative cognition of the lamp as white is actually a cognition of it as non-non-white. This is in accord with the Buddhist theory of *apoha,* whereby we cognize qualities in objects not by virtue of any universal that inheres in them, but by elimination of everything that is not the quality of that object. See above, pp. 124-25.

[RGYAL TSHAB RJE:] It is not the case that all authorities are ascertained exclusively by themselves or [exclusively] by another [subsequent authority], because [some authorities] are ascertained by themselves and some, too, can be ascertained by another [subsequent authority]. This follows, because we see that when a self-experiencing apperceptive authority cognizes its own essence, by its own power it induces certainty of the part of non-deceptiveness that exists simultaneously with and is substantially identical to it; and because we see that some authorities require ascertainment as non-deceptive authorities by an authoritative designation that arises subsequent to the [original] cognition of its own authority-object.[12]

Alternatively, in the direct cognition that investigates the ultimate, one cannot distinguish between authorities and non-authorities, because in that case it is a COGNITION that is a non-dual experience that experiences ITS OWN ESSENCE FROM ITS OWN [SIDE], cognizing only the voidness of substantial difference between subject and object. [Even] if [there is no distinguishing in an ultimate cognition], it follows that there is no problem such that it cannot be accepted that one makes distinctions, because an authority that functions *without* analyzing [the ultimate] *is* proven to distinguish the authorities from the non-authorities.[13]

[Some] assert that the first [part of the] passage shows that [authoritativeness] is proved by apperception of the part that experiences its own essence; and that the second [part of the] passage shows that authoritativeness is proven with regard to its own authority-object by a subsequently arising authority that shows [the object's] efficiency. This is *not* a complete definition of self-ascertainment and other-ascertainment.[14]

---

12 At issue here is the way in which we become aware of the non-deceptiveness of an authoritative cognition. Sometimes we are directly aware of it: it is, as it were, directly given in cognition itself. Other times, we must be informed by subsequent "designations" (*tha snyad, vyavahāra*) supplied by ourselves or others. Cf. above, p. 176, n. 1 and p. 177, n. 2.

13 The Tibetan here reads: *rang las rang gi ngo bo rtogs / tha snyad las ni tshad ma nyid*. The most evident interpretation is the first one rGyal tshab rje gives, i.e., that some authorities are self-ascertaining, while others require subsequent designation for ascertainment. However, since *tha snyad* (*vyavahāra*) also can mean "conventional,"rGyal tshab rje makes the further point that it is a conventional mind, not a mind cognizing the ultimate nature of reality (which is, after all, non-conceptual), that is able to distinguish authoritative from non-authoritative cognitions.

Alternatively, one can apply the explanation of ācārya Devendrabuddhi: Even if through a self-experiencing apperception one cognizes merely the existence of a perceptual cognition like that that apprehends blue, it does not follow that there is certainty that one cognizes the part of authoritativeness that is simultaneous with and substantially identical to it, because we see that the AUTHORITATIVENESS part must be cognized THROUGH authoritativeness that is a DESIGNATION that has an apparent object that arises at a later time.[15]

[OPPONENT:][16] What is [the meaning of] the terms "self-ascertaining" and "other-ascertained"? There are objects and there are cognitions. In relation to objects, one distinguishes either (a) by virtue of whether a cognition does or does not draw independent certainty toward its object or (b) by [virtue of an apperceptive] subject.[17]

If (a), it follows that the [other-ascertained] authority will be a subsequent cognition, and the [self-ascertaining] authority will not draw independent certainty toward even a part of its own object, so there will be only doubt. If that is the case, because neither is suitable [to be considered] an authority, not even a little perplexity will be cut off.

(b) In relation to subjects, it is ascertained that there are three [topics]: the definition, the definiendum and the example. An example of

---

14 The definitions are incomplete because they fail to mention the crucial factor that differentiates self-ascertainment from other-ascertainment: a cognition's power or lack of power to induce certainty toward its knowledge-object independently (*rang thob gyis*). Self-ascertaining authorities have such power; other-ascertained authorities lack it. Furthermore, the hypothetical definition of self-ascertainment is insufficient because it fails to specify that a self-experiencing apperception must experience not only its own essence but, specifically, non-deceptiveness. The hypothetical definition of other-ascertainment is insufficient because it fails to specify the need for a subsequent *designation* (*tha snyad*) to assist in confirming the cognition that cannot induce certainty by its own power.

15 Devendrabuddhi's point (PVP 220/3-4: rGyal tshab rje has paraphrased) seems to be that the authoritativeness of any cognition (even an apperception) is dependent upon a subsequent designation for its *ascertainment* as authoritative.

16 The following paragraphs are an attempt by the opponent to show the incoherence of the concepts of self- and other-ascertainment, through a highly specific analysis of the various options entailed by the concepts, which are seen to lead, inevitably, to dilemmas. rGyal tshab rje will not comment in detail on the dilemmas posed by the opponent, but will, rather, restate their definitions.

17 The Tibetan actually reads *yul can*, "object-possessor."

authority, such as [the cognition] apprehending blue, is either able or unable to ascertain itself independently, [yet] it is unreasonable to distinguish between these two, because it is impossible that an externally directed cognition, such as [the cognition] apprehending blue, could know itself; and because unless a self-experiencing apperception that just exists [simultaneously with the cognition of blue] independently [ascertains the cognition as authoritative], that [cognition] will be unsuitable [to be considered] an authority.

It is also unacceptable to distinguish between independent and non-independent ascertainment [through applying] the designation of an "authoritative" example in the definiendum, [because] inference will not be self-ascertaining in the mindstreams of fools and Lokāyatas, who do not understand the term "authority."

Also, when one investigates whether the characteristic, "non-deceptiveness," is or is not independently ascertained, [one sees that] inference will not be self-ascertaining in the mindstream of Lokāyatas, because they necessarily assert [inference] to be deceptive.[18]

[RGYAL TSHAB RJE:] There is no problem. When one investigates the authority that ascertains the ["non-deceptive"] characteristic of authoritativeness in the definiendum, [one sees that] it is impossible that an authority not draw independent certainty toward some part of its own authority-object. Therefore, when the non-deceptive part is ascertained independently, that is self-ascertainment; and when it is ascertained by the power of another [subsequent authority], that is other-ascertainment.[19]

---

18 Originally, a Lokāyata seems to have been a kind of sophist (see Jayatilleke [1980] 46-57). By the time of Dharmakīrti, however, the term seems to have been used interchangeably with "Cārvāka" to refer to that system of philosophy that was metaphysically materialist and epistemologically positivist. Lokāyatas were credited by their opponents with holding the self-contradictory view that the only authority is perception, and that inference, as rGyal tshab rje puts it, is "deceptive." See Radhakrishnan and Moore (1957) 231-33 and TS 1460-67 (tr. Jha [1937-1939] 718-20). On the other hand, we also learn from Kamalaśīla (TSP to TS 1481, tr. Jha [1937-39] 726) that there were Lokāyatas who accepted inference in worldly matters but denied its applicability to metaphysical problems, such as the existence of past and future lives. Cf. Dasgupta (1975) III, 536.

19 See Lati Rinbochay (1980) 121ff. and Rabten (1978) 35-39 for fuller discussions of self-ascertaining and other-ascertained authorities, which are, as rGyal tshab rje stresses here, distinguished primarily by their ability or inability independently to induce certainty with regard to what one wishes to know.

[OPPONENT:] Well, then, inference will not necessarily be self-ascertaining.

[RGYAL TSHAB RJE:] There is no problem. When Lokāyatas understand by authority that there is fire in a smoky place from the reason, smoke, it is well proven that they are undeceived about the object, because they draw independent certainty toward attaining the object they have cognized.[20]

[OPPONENT:] If authoritativeness and non-authoritativeness are, respectively, ascertained by an authority itself and [an authority] that arises later, then the composition of śāstras will be pointless.

[RGYAL TSHAB RJE:] Śāstras are not pointless, because it is necessary to EFFECT REVERSAL OF the DELUSION that the Vedas, etc., are authoritative methods of [attaining] liberation—and it is thus that śāstras are composed. Alternatively, [the line] can be applied to the words of the Omniscient One [i.e., the sūtras].[21]

Particulars [17]

(5c) [AUTHORITY] ALSO IS THE ELUCIDATION OF AN OBJECT NOT COGNIZED [BEFORE].
AFTER ONE HAS COGNIZED THE OWN-NATURE [OF AN OBJECT],
(6) ONE ATTAINS THE COGNITION OF THE GENERIC [IMAGE].
"SOME COGNITION OF AN OWN-MARK
NOT COGNIZED [BEFORE]"—THE QUOTATION'S INTENT IS THAT
INVESTIGATION [REVEALS] THE OWN-MARK.

Merely "non-deceptive" does not fulfill the definition of authority; there must be THE ELUCIDATION OF AN OBJECT NOT COGNIZED before, because it is ALSO necessary to speak of a first, or new, cognition as part of the definition of [authority]. This shows in particular that the phrase "non-deceptive" or "new, non-deceptive" [must] first accord

20 In other words, whether or not Lokāyatas assert inference as an authority, they *use* it, and it is as certain for them as it is for someone who does accept it as an authority. The Lokāyata's dilemma is a bit like that of the radical skeptic of Western philosophy, who cannot defend their position without contradicting it.

21 The opponent is attempting to argue, much as they did in the introductory chapter, that the relative adequacy of our notions of authority obviates the need for explanatory śāstras. rGyal tshab rje's reply here is that śāstras are required, if by nothing else, by the need to counter non-Buddhist scriptures that claim authority in ultimate matters. Again, therefore, rGyal tshab rje counters a philosophical point with a practical explanation. Whether this answers the substance of the opponent's objection is unclear.

with the explanation of the etymological definition of the term *pramāṇa*.[22]

Some say that ["non-deceptive"] and ["new, non-deceptive"] are the same definition of authority. This is unacceptable, because their respective arising generic images are dissimilar—the definienda necessarily have different opposites of the negative.[23]

It also is unacceptable to say that ["non-deceptive"] shows a definition of conventional authority and ["new, non-deceptive"] shows a definition of ultimate authority, for it would follow that an ultimate authority is a conventional authority, because it is a non-deceptive cognition. It also would follow that a conventional authority is an ultimate authority, because it elucidates an object not cognized before.

[OPPONENT:] What [then] is the meaning of the statement, "It is an ultimate authority, because it newly elucidates an object not cognized before"?

[RGYAL TSHAB RJE:] ["Non-deceptive"] also is a definition of ultimate authority; it is sufficient to quote the statement, "It is an authority regarding the ultimate, because it is non-deceptive regarding the ultimate."[24] Therefore, since it is necessary to accept that ["new, non-deceptive"] also shows a definition of conventional authority, it is unacceptable to separate [the two phrases].

[OPPONENT:] Well, then, what about Prajñākaragupta's explanation to that effect?

[RGYAL TSHAB RJE:] He shows that the words of the definition [are applicable] to a definiendum that is ultimate, but he does not claim to show that the [two] phrases have opposite meanings, because merely by showing the general definition of authority he is able [to cite such a definiendum].

---

22 The Sanskrit term *pramāṇa* is explained as *pra* + *māṇa*. The *pra* is said to connote the newness or freshness of an authoritative cognition. The *māṇa* means "measurement," which in epistemological terms means "comprehension," i.e., a state in which one understands, or is undeceived. Hence, *pra* + *māṇa* = "new, non-deceptive."

23 Saying that two definienda have "different opposities of the negative" (*ldog pa tha dad*) is, in Buddhist epistemology, a way of saying that the words may be semantically similar, or synonymous, but are, in fact, lexically different. It is often said of synonyms, or substantially identical items, that they are *ngo bo gcig dang ldog pa tha dad*, "essentially identical, but with different opposities of the negative." On generic images, see below, p. 186, n. 25.

24 PVA 14/4 conveys the sense of the passages cited by rGyal tshab rje and his opponent, but the quotations appear not to be verbatim.

[OPPONENT:] If authority is the new elucidation of an object, then a subsequent cognition ascertaining blue also is an authority, because it newly elucidates a generic image.[25]

[RGYAL TSHAB RJE:] There is no problem such that it follows that a subsequent cognition is an authority, because AFTER a perception apprehending blue HAS COGNIZED THE uncommon OWN-NATURE of blue, by the power of that [authority] ONE ATTAINS THE COGNITION apprehending THE GENERIC image, but [that subsequent cognition] is powerless to judge the object on its own.

[OTHER OPPONENT:] After the cognition of the own-nature of blue, that very cognition that arises to apprehend the generic image will attain [status] as an authority.

[RGYAL TSHAB RJE:] The following passage should be applied to this statement: "An authority grasps either (a) a generic image that is not based on or connected to an own-mark[26] or (b) a generic image that is the arisen aspect of an own-mark. If (a) [is asserted], it [nevertheless] follows that it is impossible that there be an authority that apprehends an independent generic image, because if [a cognition is] an authority, it must necessarily be either a new cognition of an own-mark not cognized before, or based on that [cognition]. If (b) [is asserted], since [a cognition] apprehending a generic image is an authority, it follows that there is no problem such that it follows that a subsequent cognition is an authority, [because] those intent on a resultant object ultimately will attain SOME new COGNITION OF AN OWN-MARK NOT COGNIZED before, together with the object [of that cognition]."[27]

---

25 A generic image (*don spyi, *arthasāmānya*), sometimes translated as "meaning-generality," is both an after-image of an object that follows on a moment of direct perception and an image in the memory that assists in the identification of objects. In Sautrāntika "representationalism," it is the medium through which much of our experience occurs, though it is based on an actual, directly perceived object. It is not the same as the "universal" of Western philosophy, in that it is neither inherent in objects nor eternal. See Sopa and Hopkins (1976) 94-95 and Klein (1986) chapter 4 and *passim*.

26 An own-mark, or specific characteristic (*rang gi mtshan nyid, svalakṣaṇa*), is used by Sautrāntikas to refer to the final, existent object that is the real basis of our mental judgments. An own-mark invariably possesses "efficiency" (*don byed nus pa nyid, arthakriyatva*), which is the major criterion of "reality" for Sautrāntikas. See above, section I:10 and p. 120, n. 3.

27 I have been unable to locate the source of this quotation, which appears in neither PVP nor PVA. Because Dharmakīrti's verse includes reference to a quotation, it may be that the passage is found in the *Pramāṇasamuccaya*,

This QUOTATION'S INTENT IS to speak [directly] of an authority that apprehends a generic image, and indirectly of the characteristic of authority that is elucidation of an object not cognized before. Those intent on a resultant object ultimately have to engage the authority that encounters the own-mark, together with its object, because they must investigate [on the basis of] having analyzed the two positions, viz., that there is or is not an own-mark that is chiefly to be intended.

In this regard, ācārya Devendrabuddhi says that the purpose of this passage is to criticize directly [the idea that] if there is an authority-object, it necessarily is an own-mark, and [to assert] that an authority necessarily *is based upon* an own-mark.[28]

[OTHER OPPONENT:] [If] the explanation runs thus, then since entities exist with the two fundamental natures—of own-marks and generic images—and since subsequent cognition elucidates the nature of generic images, [then subsequent cognition] is an authority.

[RGYAL TSHAB RJE:] There is this extract:

> For one who cognizes the own-mark [of reality],
> Any cognition [of an external] is nescient; [externals are discussed] due to [the Buddha's compassionate] intention.
> [There is nonduality,] BECAUSE INVESTIGATION [reveals nonduality as] THE OWN-MARK [of reality].[29]

It follows that there is no problem such that it follows that [a cognition] encountering an independent generic image is an authority, because when one investigates the own-mark of any cognition, one does not cognize two dissimilar [entities], but only the uncommon, abiding, nondual reality.[30]

---

though it also is possible that the section referred to by Dharmakīrti is nested within rGyal tshab rje's quotation without separate attribution.

28 PVP 221/1. The main point is that if only own-marks themselves are the objects of authoritative cognitions, and that which is *based upon* an own-mark is not such an object, then memory and recognition, which are based on generic images, never could be authoritative, which, in fact, they are. The cognition of a generic image may be a subsequent cognition, and therefore non-authoritative, but it need not be: a subsequent cognition always is of a generic image, but cognition of a generic image is not always a subsequent cognition.

29 I am unable to locate the source of this quotation, which is found in neither PVP nor PVA.

30 The opponent has maintained that both own-marks and generic images really exist, and that if a subsequent cognition cognizes that which really exists, it must be an authority. rGyal tshab rje counters by pointing out that when one meditates in the Yogācāra manner, neither own-marks nor generic images are

[OPPONENT:] Well, then, how is it that we can speak of external objects, etc.?

[RGYAL TSHAB RJE:] There is a purpose in speaking thus, because [such ideas are] spoken of by virtue of [the Buddha's compassionate] intentions toward his disciples, in order to lead them to reality. There are no two dissimilar uncommon fundamental natures, because when one investigates the abiding own-mark of entities, there is no reality other than the nondual voidness of a substantial difference between object and subject.[31]

B. OMNISCIENCE AND THE DEFINITION OF AUTHORITY

Showing that the muni *also possesses the characteristics [of authority] [18]*

[This is divided into:] (1) Applying (to the *muni*) the meaning of authority already explained [19] and (2) Explaining the meaning of "has become" [an authority] [20].

Applying [to the muni*] the meaning of authority already explained [19]*

(7) THE BLESSED ONE IS AN AUTHORITY [BECAUSE] HE POSSESSES THAT.

The *muni*, THE BLESSED ONE, IS AN AUTHORITY with regard to all conventional and ultimate objects, because HE POSSESSES THAT new, non-deceptive cognition of all those, and *is* that [authoritativeness]. If [the verse is read] according to Devendrabuddhi, then one must apply to the example the words ["the Blessed One is an authority] LIKE THAT."[32]

---

found "really" to exist: all there is is "the uncommon, abiding nondual reality" (*de kho na nyid*). It might be noted that by negating own-marks and generic images equally via non-dual wisdom, rGyal tshab rje has failed to negate the ontological and epistemological *equivalency* of the two posited by the opponent.

31 From the Yogācāra point of view, the Buddha's framing discussions in terms of subject and object—when no such differentiation ultimately exists—is an instance of his skill-in-means (*upāya kauśalya*), a heuristic device to assist his disciples, who are incapable of thinking clearly without a conventional differentiation between subject and object.

32 The Tibetan reads: *de ldan bcom ldan tshad ma nyid*. The *de ldan* translates the *tadvat* of the original Sanskrit (*tadvat pramāṇaṃ bhagavān*) in a possessive sense, while Devendrabuddhi takes it in a comparative sense, expressed in Tibetan by *de bzhin*, which makes the verse read: "The Blessed One is an author-

An investigation: [33]

[OPPONENT:] An omniscient one either is or is not an authority regarding all knowledge-objects. If he is not, then all these exhausting [attempts] to prove that the *muni* is an authority through proving that his teaching is authoritative are pointless, and it is unacceptable to distinguish our own teacher from other teachers as [especially] worthy of being followed. If he *is* [an authority], then the first omnisicence-moment is an authority, because it newly sees by direct perception all knowledge-objects, but it follows [then] that the second and subsequent omniscience-moments are not authorities, because there is nothing new to be cognized. If there is [something new to be cognized], then, since it is necessary [that the *muni*] exert himself for the method of analyzing a new authority-object that has not been cognized before, he will not already have eliminated the knowledge-obstacles,[34] because there is a new path to be accomplished. If you think that [the second-moment cognition] is an authority merely be-

---

ity like that."Monier-Williams (1974 [434, col. 2]) gives instances of both possessive and comparative uses of *tadvat*.

33 The following analysis is found neither in Dharmakīrti's root verses nor in Devendrabuddhi's commentary. Rather, it reflects the particular concern of rGyal tshab rje and other commentators (e.g., Prajñākaragupta) for whom the Buddha's authoritativeness is coextensive with his omniscience. The analysis seeks to establish that the Buddha's omniscience fulfills the definition of authority as *new*, nondeceptive cognition. The problem the opponent will pose is that since a newly omniscient mind cognizes all phenomena of the past, present and future directly and simultaneously in its very first moment, all subsequent moments must be subsequent cognitions, hence not authoritative. The essence of rGyal tshab rje's reply will be that subsequent omniscience-moments are authorities because phenomena continually change their status, and those changes of status are cognized newly.

34 According to Mahāyāna soteriological writings, there are two classes of obstacles to be eliminated before buddhahood is attained: defilement-obstacles (*nyon sgrib, kleśāvaraṇa*) and knowledge-obstacles (*shes sgrib, jñeyāvaraṇa*). Elimination of the former—and with them the roots of ignorance, attachment and aversion—is a prerequisite for *any* liberated state, be it that of a śrāvaka, pratyekabuddha or a buddha. Knowledge-obstacles, which are merely the subtle traces of uprooted defilements, must be eliminated before one can gain the full omniscience of a buddha; they still remain in śrāvakas and pratyekabuddhas. In most accounts of the Mahāyāna path, a bodhisattva has eliminated defilement-obstacles by the end of the seventh stage (*sa, bhūmi*), and from that point through the end of the tenth stage, progressively eliminates the knowledge-obstacles. On these and the other "path"issues raised below, see, e.g., Sopa and Hopkins (1976) *passim* and Dhargyey (1974) 195-218.

cause it is non-deceptive, then it is pointless to make the particular statement that [authority] is "first, or new, and non-deceptive," and it also is impossible to refute [the idea that] a subsequent cognition is an authority.

[RGYAL TSHAB RJE:] This is the reply to be made to that: The second omniscience-moment either (a) arises or (b) does not arise immediately after the first omniscience-moment. If (b), then it is necessary to accept [the first moment] as permanent. If (a), then since the second and subsequent moments cognize newly [what was cognized by the first moment], it is necessary to accept that they are authorities.

[OPPONENT:] Since the first omniscience-moment cognizes [the content of] the second and subsequent omniscence-moments as yet-to-arise,[35] there is nothing to be cognized again [newly by the second and subsequent moments].

[RGYAL TSHAB RJE:] When there is such cognition, the second and subsequent moments either have or have not already arisen. If they have already arisen, then it is pointless to specify that they are yet-to-arise. If they have not yet [arisen], then since the part that has already arisen must be newly cognized [as already-arisen, the idea that the second and subsequent moments] are not authorities is undermined.

If it is impossible that there be new knowledge-objects after the first omniscience-moment has arisen, then every entity will be permanent. If it is possible, then since that new existent must be newly cognized, [the idea that the second and subsequent moments] are not newly-cognizing authorities is undermined.

Also, an eighth-level bodhisattva[36] either (a) is or (b) is not a buddha. If (a), then there will exist a buddha who has not abandoned the small and medium [defilements] to be abandoned on the path of development.[37] If (b), then it is either possible or impossible for them to

---

35 I have opted for a rather literal reading of *'byung 'gyur*. It also may simply be translated as "future."

36 The eighth level of the bodhisattva path, known as the "unmoving" (*mi g-yo ba, acala*) is, as noted above, the point at which bodhisattvas begin to uproot knowledge-obstacles. They are no longer in saṃsāra by the eighth stage, but not yet buddhas.

37 The path of development (*sgom lam, bhāvanāmārga*) is the fourth of the five successive paths to enlightenment posited by the traditions based on either the *Abhidharmakośa* of Vasubandhu or the *Abhisamayālaṃkāra* of Maitreya. It is the second of three supramundane paths, following the initial direct realization of the truth on the path of seeing (*mthong lam, darśanamārga*) and preceding the achievement of enlightenment on the path of no-more-training (*mi*

become a buddha. If it is impossible, then because it is impossible that a sentient being become a buddha, there will be no new buddhas, so it is pointless [to speak] in particular of a first omniscience-moment. If it is possible, then when [someone], not [a buddha] before, later newly becomes a buddha, it is definitely necessary to accept that it is a second or subsequent omniscience-moment [by which the "old" buddha] cognizes the new one.

[OPPONENT:] When [an omnisicient one] directly cognizes the present, it is impossible that they not be able to cognize implicitly all past and future [phenomena] as the cause and result of the present, so we accept that it is impossible for second and subsequent [omniscience-] moments to cognize a new authority-object.

[RGYAL TSHAB RJE:] It follows that in the first moment of the Mahāyāna path of seeing[38] there will be no new *dharmatā*[39] to be newly

---

slob lam, aśaikṣamārga). It is the path on which most of the work of uprooting defilements is accomplished, via deep meditation (*sgom*) on the nature of reality. In the Mahāyāna tradition initiated by the *Abhisamayālaṃkāra*, the path of development coincides with the last nine bodhisattva stages, the first coinciding with the path of seeing. Incidentally, a "path" in this sense comprises a series of mental states of a particular type.

38 The path of seeing consists of sixteen "moments," or time-divisions, and marks the point at which a meditator first applies the union of tranquillity and insight (*gzhi gnas lhag mthong gzung 'jug, śamathavipaśyanāyuganaddha*) toward the salvific truth emphasized in their system. In Mahāyāna, this salvific truth is voidness (*stong pa nyid, śūnyatā*), which is interpreted in Yogācāra to be the voidness of a substantial difference between subject and object, and in Madhyamaka to be voidness of any inherently or naturally existing substance in either persons or dharmas. It is only at the point where one cognizes the truth directly that one begins to uproot—as opposed to suppress—the defilements that, together with karma, keep us circling in saṃsāra. Attainment of the path of seeing makes one an ārya, or "noble," possessing the "eye of Dharma." It should be noted that in the Sautrāntika system, with which Dharmakīrti was associated, one cannot directly perceive a negation, or absence, such as that of inherent existence. Thus, the attainment of āryahood is marked for a Sautrāntika not by a direct cognition of no-self, but by a direct cognition of, e.g., the aggregates as no longer qualified by a self; no-self thus is realized implicitly, not directly. For rGyal tshab rje, who is a Prāsaṅgika Mādhyamika, there is no such qualification: voidness, no-self, or any other negation *can* be cognized directly. See Sopa and Hopkins (1976) 105 and Klein (1986) *passim.*

39 *Dharmatā* is a venerable and malleable term, whose general sense is simply "the way things are." Since different Buddhist schools have differed on "the way things are," the term has been used in many ways. rGyal tshab rje here is using the term in its Prāsaṅgika Mādhyamika sense, as voidness of inherent

cognized, because there is no diminution of the cognition of *dharmatā* already effected during the path of application,[40] which is [the path of seeing's] cause. What is your answer?

[OPPONENT:] Although there is nothing other than just *dharmatā* to be newly cognized, the part of *dharmatā* that is a manifest phenomenon must be newly cognized, so [the first moment of the path of seeing] is an authority.[41]

[RGYAL TSHAB RJE:] Well, then, even if the first omniscience-moment has already cognized an entity as yet-to-arise, that [entity] must be newly cognized as already-arisen by the second and subsequent moments.

[OPPONENT:] Since it is impossible that there exist in the past anything that is yet-to-arise, when there ["exists"] something that is yet-to-arise, it necessarily must already have arisen.[42]

[RGYAL TSHAB RJE:] Well, then, it follows that a bodhisattva on the path of application already has abandoned the seeds of the knowledge-obstacles, because they *will* abandon them. It [also] follows that they are already a buddha, because they *will* become a buddha.

---

existence. Dharmakīrti, were he to employ the term, would more likely use it to refer to no-self, or perhaps to the lack of a substantial difference between subject and object.

40 The second path, that of application, or linking (*sbyor lam, prayogamārga*), is that which leads one to the threshold of the direct cognition of reality afforded by the path of seeing. It consists of four stages, which mark the increasing intensity of one's analytical understanding of reality. The path of application is preceded by the path of accumulation (*tshogs lam, sambhāramārga*), on which one familiarizes oneself with the basic types of meditation, both concentrative and analytical. Entrance into it is marked in the *Abhidharmakośa* system by attainment of a spontaneous desire to be fully separated from saṃsāra, and in the *Abhisamayālaṃkāra* system by attainment of a spontaneous desire to achieve enlightenment for the sake of all sentient beings, i.e., *bodhicitta*.

41 One way to describe the path of seeing is to say that it is the point at which *dharmatā* becomes a manifest phenomenon for one, rather than a hidden phenomenon; on the path of application, it is merely inferred, while on the path of seeing, it is directly realized.

42 This rather sophistic argument by the opponent plays on the definition of "exists." A future object cognized by an omniscient mind is seen to *exist* as future; since to say that something "exists" is to say that it has already arisen, it follows that a future object has already arisen. The simplest reply is to point out that a future object *has* already arisen—as future, not present. If the distinction is not maintained, then the meaningfulness of the distinction among the three times will collapse, with consequences that rGyal tshab rje now will point out.

[OPPONENT:] In general, if there is [an entity] that is yet-to-arise, it necessarily must already have arisen, [but an entity] yet to arise in the mindstream of a [particular] person has not necessarily already arisen.[43]

[RGYAL TSHAB RJE:] Well, then, since there necessarily will later exist in the mindstream of that person an already-arisen [entity] that previously had not already arisen, there necessarily must be a new cognition. If it is possible that sentient beings eliminate new obstacles at a later time, then it is necessary that a second or subsequent omniscience-moment [of one already a buddha] newly cognize that elimination of new obstacles, and [the idea that the second and subsequent moments] are not newly cognizing authorities is undermined. Other [cases] should be known by implication [from this].[44]

However we consider within and without, we do not find an omnisicient [cognition] that is not an authority, or an authority that is not by necessity a new cognition.

C. A REFUTATION OF THEISM

Explaining the meaning of "has become" [an authority] [20]

[This is divided into:] (1) The purpose of saying "has become" [21] and (2) Disposing of objections to that [22].

The purpose of saying "has become" [21]

(7b) BECAUSE SAYING "HAS BECOME" IS
FOR THE SAKE OF REVERSING [THE IDEA] THAT HE DOES NOT ARISE,[45]
[SINCE] AUTHORITATIVENESS DEPENDS ON ACCOMPLISHMENT, IT IS
REASONABLY [ASSERTED OF HIM].

---

43 The opponent here attempts to rescue himself by distinguishing between metaphysical and psychological ways of speaking. In general, because of the meaning of the word "exists" as "already arisen," an object that exists in the future has already arisen; it may not, however, be "already arisen" *for* a particular person.

44 An example of another case is that of a seed and sprout: as long as there still are seeds that newly will become sprouts at some future moment, an omniscient mind cognizing that event will cognize newly, and thus fulfill one of the criteria of authoritativeness.

45 The Tibetan here reads *ma skyes pa,* rather than *ma gyur pa,* the expected translation of the Sanskrit *abhūta*.

Saying "has become" [an authority] in the verse of homage has a negative purpose, BECAUSE SAYING that the Omniscient One "HAS BECOME" [an authority] IS FOR THE SAKE OF REVERSING [THE IDEA THAT] HE DOES NOT ARISE from his own causes. It has positive purpose, because the purpose of saying that be "has become" omniscient is to demonstrate that he has arisen as AN AUTHORITY IN DEPENDENCE UPON his having completely accustomated the special ACCOMPLISHMENT of method and wisdom. Also, IT IS REASONABLY [ASSERTED] that the Omniscient One is an Authoritative Person, because when we depend upon the perfect reasoning that proves his omniscience, we see that he is one who has become an authority.[46]

Disposing of objections to that [22]

[This is divided into:] (1) Refuting [the idea that someone] who knows how to create all knowledge-objects is omniscient [23] and (2) Proving as omniscient the one who knows by perception how all [knowledge-objects] really exist [46].

Refuting [the idea that someone] who knows how to create all knowledge-objects is omniscient [23]

[This is divided into:] (1) Refuting [the idea] that the nature of God[47] is such that he is the maker of all [knowledge-objects] [24] and (2) Refuting the proofs [of a creator God's existence] [27].

---

46 Throughout this whole section, rGyal tshab rje will identify omniscience and authority in a way that Dharmakīrti nowhere explicity does. The assertion that the Buddha is one who "has become" an authority implicitly launches the critique of theism to follow, for God (*dbang phyug, īśvara*), as a self-existent, immutable entity, cannot "become" anything.

47 I render *dbang phyug* (*īśvara*) as "God" because the attributes imputed to the deity—creativity, power and omniscience—by those Indian schools that posit him are generally similar enough to those of the Christian God to warrant the use of the same term. Further, as we will see below, arguments for the existence of *dbang phyug* bear a remarkable resemblance to certain Western arguments for the existence of God. For explorations of Indian theism, see, e.g., Potter (1977), Vattanky (1984), R. Jackson (1986) and Hayes (1988b). Incidentally, I use the masculine pronoun whenever "God" is mentioned because this is the gender "he" possesses in Sanskrit.

Refuting [the idea] that the nature of God is such that he is the maker of all [knowledge-objects] [24]

[This is divided into:] (1) Refuting [the idea] that he is permanent [25] and (2) Refuting [the idea] that he is impermanent [26].

Refuting [the idea] that he is permanent [25]

(8) [THERE] CANNOT EXIST A PERMANENT AUTHORITY,
BECAUSE AN AUTHORITY COGNIZES EXISTENT ENTITIES,
BECAUSE, SINCE KNOWLEDGE-OBJECTS ARE IMPERMANENT,
THAT [AUTHORITY] IS UNSTABLE,
BECAUSE THINGS THAT ARISE SUCCESSIVELY
(9) CANNOT BE ACCEPTED TO ARISE FROM A PERMANENT [ENTITY],
[AND] BECAUSE IT IS UNSUITABLE THAT [A PERMANENT ENTITY] DEPEND [ON CONDITIONS].

[OPPONENT:] That God who is the maker of all [knowledge-objects] is an authoritative person who is permanent and self-originated.

[RGYAL TSHAB RJE:] It follows that God CANNOT EXIST as A PERMANENT AUTHORITY, because whatever is him necessarily would be AN AUTHORITY that COGNIZES objects that are EXISTENT as ENTITIES.[48] [The reason] pervades [the predicate], BECAUSE, SINCE objects that are KNOWLEDGE-OBJECTS ARE IMPERMANENT, THAT authority that comprehends them necessarily IS UNSTABLE.[49]

Some presumptuous [commentators] on the Buddha's scriptures say that this [verse] refutes a permanent conventional authority, but does not refute a permanent ultimate authority.[50] This is an opinion

---

48 The term *dngos po* (*vastu*) is most often translated as "entity." Its connotation for Buddhists is of an entity that is causally efficient and impermanent. The assumption that whatever is existent must be efficient and whatever is efficient must be impermanent is a fundamental Buddhist axiom, and may lead to a certain amount of difficulty in discussions with proponents of other systems, since they may rightly point out that, *a priori*, the Buddhist never will admit the reality of any entity that is not impermanent, while the possible existence of such an entity (God) is precisely the point in dispute.

49 "Unstable" (lit. "instability": *mi brtan nyid, adhrauvya*) here is synonymous with "impermanent."

50 The "presumptuous" Buddhist commentators attacked here are not identified, but they may be Jo nang pas, a Tibetan school founded in the twelfth century, and held by Tsong kha pa and his followers to stray dangerously close to the extreme of eternalism, since they were held to assert that an enlightened consciousness is (a) void of what is other than enlightenment (*gzhan stong*) and (b) possesses its enlightened characteristics inherently and unchangingly.

[whose proponents] have not the slightest mastery of the logical system that refutes permanence. If there exists a permanent conventional authority, then that authority is permanent. If that is the case, then you must consider: what ultimate or conventional distinction is there between that [permanent conventional authority] that is the object of refutation here and the ultimate [authority] asserted by you?[51]

[OPPONENT:] An eye, which remains motionless, apprehends forms successively; the function of the eye does not change into something dissimilar. Just so, knowledge-objects are impermanent and God's cognition is unstable, but he [himself] is a permanent cognizer God.[52]

[RGYAL TSHAB RJE:] It follows that, BECAUSE his earlier and later [cognitions] are THINGS THAT ARISE SUCCESSIVELY, God's cognition CANNOT BE ACCEPTED TO ARISE FROM A PERMANENT God.[53] [A permanent God] cannot generate [cognitions] in dependence upon conditions, BECAUSE IT IS UNSUITABLE THAT a permanent [entity] DEPEND on conditions.[54] Also, if the function of the eye does not [change into] something dissimilar, it must already apprehend a later [object] when it apprehends an earlier one.[55]

---

51 In other words, if the opponent admits that there is a permanent conventional authority that is to be refuted, and that that conventional authority is, e.g., a permanent authoritative cognition such as that attributed to God, then what permanent authority could there be that is different from this such that it could be called "ultimate"and stand unrefuted? The question is rhetorical, because the opponent cannot, in fact, specify a permanent "ultimate"authority that is any different from what is admitted to be conventional and refutable.

52 This argument seems to appeal to a notion somewhat like that of the Aristotelian "unmoved mover": God is essentially unmoving, but there is an aspect of himself that, in contact with the contingent universe, moves. In Indian terms, the argument is that God is essentially permanent but that his cognitions are impermanent.

53 It is a contradiction in terms that impermanent cognitions arise from a permanent source.

54 If the opponent argues that God is permanent and his impermanent cognitions generated not directly from him but in dependence on conditions, they are open to the reply that God cannot be subject to external conditions, or he loses his self-sufficiency. Furthermore, impermanent conditions cannot affect a permanent God any more than impermanent cognitions can arise from him.

55 This argument is typically and fundamentally Buddhist, and is crucial to the establishment of the doctrine of momentariness. Its basic formulation is clearly stated by Koller (1970 [154-155]): "... both terms of the following disjunction are false: either the action of causation is instantaneous and complete, or else it is temporally extended. The action of causation cannot be instantaneous and complete, for then all the effects would be produced at

Refuting [the idea] that he is impermanent [26]

(9c) BECAUSE HE HAS NOT BEEN AIDED IN ANY WAY,
IF [THAT GOD] IS IMPERMANENT, HE IS NOT AN AUTHORITY.

[OPPONENT:] If that God IS IMPERMANENT, it is not the case that he has previously experienced attachment, etc., in saṃsāra and then depended on achieving accustomation to generosity, etc., as an antidote to that; it *is* the case that he has arisen beginninglessly from previous homogenes[56] as detached and omniscient.

[RGYAL TSHAB RJE:] It follows that God IS NOT AN AUTHORITY proven to be an omniscient being arising from previous homogenes, BECAUSE never before, at any previous saṃsāric moment, HAS HE BEEN harmed or AIDED IN ANY WAY by conditions on the side of utter defilement or purification.[57]

---

once and reality would, except for that moment, be static. Furthermore, if the action were instantaneous and complete, the question would arise as to whether the permanent exists after the first moment of change—if it does, then it should give rise to the same effects as it did in the first moment, and the same for each succeeding moment. But this is absurd, for it results in an infinity of complete universes. If the permanent continues to exist after the first moment of causation but not as a cause, then apparently it changed from a cause to a non-cause. Since it is not possible for a self-contradictory thing to exist, such a reality is not possible. The alternative to instantaneous and complete causal action is temporally extended causal action. This view is untenable also, for if it were the case that the permanent cause produced first x, then y, and then z, etc., it could be asked whether or not y or z could have been produced while x was being produced. If the answer is affirmative, it would turn out that all the effects were producible at once, and this alternative would be indistinguishable from the first. But if the first cause could not produce effects y, z, etc., at any given time, say when x was being produced, it would be impossible for it to cause them at any later time, for what is not capable of producing a given effect at a given time cannot produce that effect at any other time, except by assuming other causal activity.... Even if it is admitted that certain modifications in the cause are required, the Buddhist argument is successful, for this is an admission that the cause has changed. But if the cause has changed, then there are really two things: the cause prior to change and the cause after change. To admit that the substance changes as it produces effects is to deny permanence and to admit different existences at different moments. And this is in accord with the doctrine of momentariness which the Buddhists wish to support." If one substitutes "cognition" and "object" for "cause" and "effect" in the preceding passage, its applicability to the problem at hand is clear.

56 "Homogenes" (*rigs 'dra, svajāti*) are previous and subsequent instances of the same type of entity as that being discussed. It will figure centrally in discussions, below, of the mind-body problem.

Alternatively, according to Devendrabuddhi's explanation, these lines should be applied toward proving the previous [refutation, of permanence].[58]

Refuting the proofs [of such a God's existence] [27]

[This is divided into:] (1) Showing that the proofs are false [28] and (2) Showing that the existence of a maker of all [knowledge-objects] is confuted by authority [43].

Showing that the proofs are false [28]

[This is divided into:] (1) A brief demonstration [29] and (2) An extensive explanation [30].

A brief demonstration [29]

(10) "[BECAUSE] THEY ACT INTERMITTENTLY, HAVE A PARTICULAR SHAPE,
AND ACHIEVE PURPOSES," ETC.: [THIS INVOLVES]
A PROVEN ASSERTION, OR THE EXAMPLE IS UNPROVEN;
ALTERNATIVELY, THE STATEMENT IS DOUBTFUL.

---

57 The flaw in the opponent's argument is the contention that God has arisen beginninglessly from previous homogenes. To arise thus is to be impermanent, but to be impermanent is also to be subject to helping and hindering causes and conditions, yet the opponent insists that their God is both impermanent and free from causes and conditions such as those found in saṃsāra, and that he always has been so. rGyal tshab rje is arguing that it is meaningless to use the terms "arisen" and "impermanent" of an entity and then deny to that entity those characteristics that in part define being arisen and impermanent, i.e., susceptibility to hindrance or assistance by external causes and conditions. It might be noted parenthetically that a Western conception of an impermanent God that might escape the net of Buddhist criticism is the "process" theology exposed in the works of, e.g., Alfred North Whitehead and Charles Hartshorne. In process theology, God is an ever-changing, non-omnipotent force that requires the assistance of particular entities for the unfolding of its divine nature and purposes—a conception not entirely different from the Mahāyāna conception of a buddha.

58 The reason cited by rGyal tshab rje as proving that an impermanent God cannot be an authority, namely, "because he has not been aided in any way" (*rnam 'gas phan gdags bya min phyir = kathañcinnopakāryatvād*), is taken by Devendrabuddhi as a proof that permanence is impossible: if the opponent argues that God is permanent but generates impermanent cognitions assisted by causes or conditions, this is simply another way of saying that he is dependent, and a permanent being cannot depend on anything. The syntactical structure of PV 9c would seem to support Devendrabuddhi, yet rGyal tshab rje was preceded by Prajñākaragupta in his interpretation.

[OPPONENT:] "Worldly abodes, bodies and enjoyments are preceded by the mind of a maker, because THEY ACT INTERMITTENTLY, like an axe; because they HAVE A PARTICULAR SHAPE, like a pot; AND because they ACHIEVE PURPOSES, like a battle-axe."[59] From this and other statements, it is proven that [abodes, bodies and enjoyments] have a maker whose mind preceded them, and also that that [maker] is God.

[RGYAL TSHAB RJE:] If it is proven in general merely that [abodes, bodies and enjoyments] are preceded by a mind, it follows that this is not a correct proof [of a syllogism] not already A PROVEN ASSERTION of the Buddhist, because the Buddhist has already proven— and not forgotten—that [abodes, bodies and enjoyments] arise from karmic intentions that are their causes.[60] The word "OR"refers to the following analysis.

If it is proven that [knowledge objects] are produced by a *permanent* mind, then it follows that THE EXAMPLE of that reason IS UNPROVEN, because it is impossible that there exist a permanent functioning entity.[61]

---

59 This is an Indian statement of what is known in the West as the teleological argument, or the argument from design. It is similar, if not identical, to syllogisms developed in the Nyāya-Vaiśeṣika system of Indian philosophy. For the best analysis of Nyāya-Vaiśeṣika theology, see Vattanky (1984). For a lucid discussion of the Western form of the argument, see Hospers (1967) 455-78. The second of the three reasons, "because they have particular shape, like a pot," closely resembles Western arguments from design, with the pot serving the same analogical function as a watch has in some Western arguments. The third reason, "because they achieve purposes, like a battle-axe,"seems to echo a more strictly teleological argument, of the sort proffered by Aquinas as the fifth of his "five ways." The first reason seems linked to the third. The argument from particular shape is refuted in verses 11-20, the argument from intermittence in verses 21 and 23, and the argument from purpose in verses 22-26.

60 A syllogism, in order to be a true syllogism, must demonstrate something not already demonstrated; if it merely restates what has become axiomatic, it is adding nothing to our store of knowledge. The Buddhists maintain, and are content to have proven already, that worldly abodes, bodies and enjoyments are preceded by mind, i.e., by the karmic intentions (*sems pa'i las, cetanā*) of those beings who use them, so if the theist is merely proving in a general way that they are mind-preceded, nothing new has been proven, and the syllogism is irrelevant. How the Buddhists have proven it, rGyal tshab rje does not say, but it is possible that they must do so at least in partial dependence on the authoritative word of the Buddha (who alone is an authority regarding the subtleties of karma). Since the Buddha's authoritativeness is at issue, it is possible that rGyal tshab rje is begging the question. If, on the other hand, intentionality can be demonstrated to precede abodes, bodies and enjoyments through an objectively impelled inference, the question is not being begged.

Alternatively, if it is proven merely that [knowledge-objects] are preceded by another maker, it follows that pervasion is uncertain, because—since it is not ascertained that [creation is] specifically by God—THE STATEMENT IS DOUBTFUL [with regard to logical] pervasion.[62]

If you say that it is unproven that God acts intermittently, [we reply that] since we see that the results occur successively, it is proven that the direct cause of those [results] must be successive.[63]

There must be a specific analysis of the predicate: it is impossible to undertake a destructive [analysis] of all three fallacies [of the reason][64] in one simultaneous application.

An extensive explanation [30]

[This is divided into:] (1) A refutation through an analysis of the meaning [of the words used in] the proof [31], (2) Refuting other similar [arguments] through that [41] and (3) The aim that is accomplished by those [refutations] [42].

---

61 If the syllogism states that all objects are preceded by a permanent mind, because they are intermittent, shaped and purposive, like an axe, pot and battle-axe, then the examples are unproven (*ma grub, asiddha*)—not established as relevant to the subject (abodes, bodies and enjoyments)—because no impermanent object can be preceded by a permanent mind, yet all three examples are of impermanent objects. The predicate here is too restrictive, because it specifies "permanent."

62 In this case, the predicate is too broad, and therefore the reason is uncertain, or inconclusive (*ma nges, anaikāntika*), because it merely states that all objects are preceded by another maker; it does not specify clearly enough that that creator is, e.g., a mind, or God, and there is no clear concomitance between, on the one hand, intermittence, shape and purpose (the reason) and "another maker" (the predicate).

63 Further, the reason is contradictory (*'gal ba, viruddha*), because an intermittent result must have an intermittent cause. An intermittent cause is by definition impermanent, and so it is contradictory to cite the fact that objects are intermittent as a reason proving that they are preceded by a permanent mind (the predicate).

64 The three fallacies (*ltar snang, abhāsa*) of the reason are those just encountered: unproven (where relevance to the subject is in doubt), uncertain (where positive and/or negative concomitance with the predicate is in doubt) and contradictory (where the predicate is contradicted).

A refutation through an analysis of the meaning [of the words used in] the proof [31]

[This is divided into:] (1) The unsuitability of the meaning of "shape"as a reason [32] and (2) The unsuitability of the word "shape" as a reason [38].

The unsuitability of the meaning of "shape" as a reason [32]

[This is divided into:] (1) [The fact that] particular shape is unproven in the subject [33] and (2) [The fact that] mere shape is uncertain [34].

[The fact that] particular shape is unproven in the subject [33]

(11) A SHAPED [OBJECT], ETC., THAT IS POSITIVELY AND NEGATIVELY RELATED
TO A DESIGNER: [IF EVERYTHING] EXISTS IN THAT WAY,
THEN SOME INFERENCE FROM THAT —
THAT WILL BE REASONABLE.

It follows that A SHAPED [OBJECT], ETC., THAT IS POSITIVELY AND NEGATIVELY RELATED TO the assistance of A person who is its own DESIGNER is not a correct reason proving that worldly abodes, bodies and enjoyments have preceding them the mind of some person, because if everything EXISTS IN THAT WAY that a pot does, THEN SOME such INFERENCE FROM THAT — THAT WILL BE REASONABLE; but [in fact] it is unproven that the reason is present in the subject of that proof.[65]

[The fact that] mere shape is uncertain [34]

[This is divided into:] (1) An example of uncertainty [35], (2) Extreme consequences if that is the case [36] and (3) Disposing of [the objection that] it follows that the argument rebounds [37].

An example of uncertainty [35]

(12) "BECAUSE [THEY] ARE NOT DIFFERENT" — IT IS NOT REASONABLE
TO INFER [FROM THIS, BECAUSE] IT IS PROVEN THAT ENTITIES
ARE DIFFERENT, [EVEN IF ONE CAN APPLY] THE SAME WORD;
IT IS LIKE [INFERRING] FIRE FROM A GREY SUBSTANCE.

---

65 The reason is unproven in the subject because it is unproven that all objects are shaped in the way that a pot is: there are other possible explanations for the shapes of things, explanations that do not depend on deliberate design. Cf. TS 63.

"BECAUSE the shape of a pot and mere shape ARE NOT DIFFERENT." IT IS NOT REASONABLE TO INFER from such a reason that [mere shapes] are made by a person, BECAUSE IT IS PROVEN THAT those shapes arise as ENTITIES that ARE such as to have DIFFERENT kinds of causes from those shapes made by a person. As "mere shape," these latter are not different [from the former], since one can apply [to them] THE SAME WORD, "shape." IT IS LIKE inferring FIRE FROM A GREY SUBSTANCE on the basis of [just the grey substance's] existence.[66]

Extreme consequences if that is the case [36]

(13) IF THAT IS NOT SO, THEN EVEN AN ANT-HILL
WILL BE PROVEN TO HAVE BEEN MADE BY A POTTER,
BECAUSE THE POT, ETC., [IS SIMILAR BY VIRTUE OF]
SOME TRANSFORMATION OF MUD.

IF THAT [preceding observation] IS NOT SO, it follows that EVEN AN ANT-HILL WILL BE PROVEN TO HAVE BEEN MADE BY A POTTER, BECAUSE THE POT, ETC., made by the potter is similar [by virtue of] SOME TRANSFORMATION OF MUD.[67]

Disposing of [the objection that] it follows that the argument rebounds [37]

(14) EVEN THOUGH PROOF OF A RESULT IS IN GENERAL,
THE EXPRESS FAULT OF [OVER-]DIFFERENTIATING DISTINCTIONS
IN THE RELATOR WHEN IT PERVADES THE PREDICATE—
WE ASSERT THAT THIS IS A REBOUNDING ARGUMENT.

[OPPONENT:] When you analyze in general and particular what we have set forth as reasons, [we find that] there is the express flaw of a rebounding argument, [because] your analysis [applies] equally to [the reasons] *you* have asserted as probative.[68]

---

66 Here, the reason's pervasion of the predicate is uncertain because it is too broad (*khyab ches ba*): there are instances of objects that "merely have shape" (reason) that are not "shaped by a person" (predicate), e.g., natural objects. Similarly, one cannot infer the presence of fire on a hill merely from the perception of a grey substance, because there are many grey substances that are not smoke.

67 Here, a further counterexample is offered: an ant-hill, which (especially in India) is shaped like a pot, but known to have a maker that is multiple and (perhaps) non-intelligent. Thus, pot-like shapes do not even entail creation by a potter—nor, thus, do shaped objects necessarily entail one intelligent designer.

68 A rebounding argument (literally, "equal results": *'bras mtshungs, kāryasama*) is a form of sophistry, wherein one analyzes a reason with excessive specificity, and

[RGYAL TSHAB RJE:] [The cases] are not the same. When one sets forth a general reason that is able to prove a thesis and that [proof] is confuted by a particular analysis, the applicability to the confuter of the fault [they have found] in the setting forth of the proof [makes theirs] a rebounding argument. Expressing a confutation of a fallacious proof that has been set forth is not a rebounding argument.

In proving that a conch-sound is a result, when one sets forth as a reason "[because] it arises by effort," it can be objected: "If you set forth as your reason '[because sound] clearly exists before the effort,' [the reason] is uncertain.[69] If you set forth [as your reason] 'because it arises from a new, unprecedented [effort],' [the reason] is unproven."[70] It is reasonable to assert this [objection] as a rebounding argument, because EVEN THOUGH the reason set forth as PROOF OF the conch-sound's being A RESULT IS "arises from effort" IN GENERAL, [the objector has given] a wrong reply that has THE EXPRESS FAULT OF [OVER-] DIFFERENTIATING through an analysis of DISTINCTIONS IN THE RELATOR.[71] The [general] reason is able to prove the thesis WHEN IT PERVADES THE PREDICATE and is proven in the subject. When the Akṣipādins set forth the [above general] reason, the Naiyāyikas ASSERT THAT THIS IS the express flaw of A REBOUNDING ARGUMENT. The ācārya [Dharmakīrti] also has explained it thus.

The meaning of the term "rebounding argument" is this: When one has made "is a result" the predicate and set forth just "arises from effort" as the reason, and a confutation is expressed through a particular analysis, then the proof expressed by the confuters themselves—such as "is the conch-sound a result of a fresh, unprecedented effort or

---

thereby finds it wanting. The argument "rebounds," or has equal results, because the same specific analysis can be employed to invalidate the syllogism of the objector. Here, the opponent is arguing that the Buddhist's specific analysis, of the use of "shape" as a reason proving that objects are created by God, is a rebounding argument, a sophistry. rGyal tshab rje rejects the contention, for reasons cited below. For a discussion of *kāryasama* that employs the same example as cited by rGyal tshab rje, see Vidhyabhusana (1978) 81. Cf. also TS 69.

69 The reason is uncertain because something that is a result cannot be said to exist before its cause. In this case, the conch-sound would pre-exist the effort that is its cause.

70 The reason is unproven because for the Sāṃkhya (who is the opponent here), sound exists prior to its manifestation, in unmanifest prakṛti. Hence, it is unproven that sound arises from a fresh, unprecedented effort. Vidyabhusana, loc. cit., gives a somewhat different explanation of the dilemma posed by the opponent.

71 The relator (*'bral ba can*) is another name for the logical reason. It is the relator in the sense that it relates the subject of a syllogism to the predicate.

does it clearly [arise] from pre-existent effort?"—can be applied equally to the analyzed and the analyzer. That, in brief, is the meaning of a "rebounding argument."

Alternatively, when [someone has made] a "perfect" confutation and the reasons they themselves have set forth have the same results for them, that is called a rebounding argument.[72] Accordingly, when one sets forth "[because it is] a product" as a reason proving [the thesis] "sound is impermanent," someone else may object: "If you set forth 'the product of a [permanent] sound' as a reason, it is contradictory;[73] if you set forth 'the product of a pot,' it is unproven;[74] and if you say 'that does not exist in a permanent existent either,' there is the fallacy of an uncommon uncertain [reason]."[75] This [objection] is a rebounding argument.[76]

The unsuitability of the word "shape" as a reason [38]

[This is divided into:] (1) An example of the unreasonableness of seeing the mere word "shape" as a reason [39] and (2) Extreme consequences [40].

An example of the unreasonableness of seeing the mere word "shape" as a reason [39]

> (15) [ALTHOUGH] A PARTICULAR CLASS IS PROVEN [BY SOME WORD],
> IT IS UNREASONABLE, FROM SEEING THE GENERAL WORD [APPLIED],
> [TO ATTEMPT] TO PROVE [SOME OTHER PARTICULAR]; FOR EXAMPLE:

---

72 This is a slightly more general statement of the definition than that made in the previous paragraph, but the import is the same.

73 The reason is contradictory because a product (reason) cannot arise from a permanent existent: products are impermanent, and so must their causes be.

74 The reason is unproven because the product of a pot (reason) bears no necessary relation to a sound (subject).

75 An uncommon uncertain reason (*thun mong ma yin pa'i ma nges pa*) is one in which the reason "abides in nothing homogeneous with and in nothing heterogeneous from" the predicate (Vidyabhusana [1978] section 96A). There is no certainty that a sound exists as either permanent or impermanent; indeed, its impermanence is what is at stake in the syllogism.

76 The argument rebounds because the same detailed analysis could be applied to the objector's statements. The result of arguments endlessly rebounding is that nothing ever can be established rationally, not a situation relished by Dharmakīrti—thus his important proviso, to be elaborated below, that a reason is related to subject and predicate in a *general* sense, for an overly specific critical analysis can undermine any syllogism, with epistemological chaos as the result.

"WORDS, ETC., HAVE HORNS, BECAUSE [THERE IS A WORD] '*GOTVA*.'"

It follows that, although A PARTICULAR CLASS of shaped objects, such as pots, etc., IS PROVEN [to be made by a person] through application of the word "shaped object," IT IS UNREASONABLE, FROM SEEING the application of THE same GENERAL WORD, "shape," [to attempt] TO PROVE that abodes, bodies, etc., are made by a person, because [the reason's] pervasion [of the predicate] is uncertain. FOR EXAMPLE, it is unreasonable to infer thus: "WORDS, ETC., HAVE HORNS, BECAUSE we see that there is a word "*GOTVA*" [= cowness and wordness].[77]

Extreme consequences [40]

(16) ALL [PERSONS] SHOULD ACCOMPLISH ALL [GOALS],
SINCE THEY WOULD ATTAIN THEIR OBJECTS BY THE EXISTENCE [OF WORDS FOR] THOSE;
THERE ARE NO THINGS FOR WHICH THERE ARE NOT WORDS,
BECAUSE [WORDS] ARE UNDER THE POWER OF [SOMEONE'S] DESIRE TO EXPRESS.

It follows that ALL persons SHOULD ACCOMPLISH ALL desired goals without effort, BECAUSE THEY WOULD ATTAIN THEIR OBJECTS [merely] BY THE EXISTENCE OF the words for THOSE [objects]. [This reason] pervades [the predicate], because THERE ARE NO THINGS FOR WHICH THERE ARE NOT WORDS THAT EXPRESS [them]. This follows, BECAUSE [words] are merely UNDER THE POWER OF [someone's] DESIRE TO EXPRESS.[78]

---

77 The point here is that a word cannot serve as a correct logical reason in just *any* syllogism, simply because it serves thus in *one*. "Shaped" is a valid reason proving that, e.g., a pot is created by a person, because a shaped object is created by a person. One cannot, however, simply take the word "shaped," which belongs to the first proof, and apply it to proving that abodes, etc., are created by God. Similarly, one cannot say that words are cows just because we see that there is a Sanskrit word, *gotva*, that denotes both "wordness" and "cowness." No such confusion is possible in Tibetan, so the Tibetan translation gives, for the Sanskrit *gotva, go nyid* (= *go-tva*), rather than, e.g., *glang nyid* (cowness) or *tshig nyid* (wordness), either of which would lose the ambiguity of the Sanskrit. The very important logical point made here is that a general reason's applicability to a particular class of objects does not assure the applicability to that same class of a lexically similar but semantically different reason.

78 Words exist simply because someone desires to express them. There is no guarantee that the existence of a word entails the existence of its referent. If it did, then merely by uttering the word, we should attain its referent. Alternatively, the mere existence of a word would lead to the *proving* of an object in the logical sense and to the accomplishment of a goal in the existential sense.

Refuting other similar [arguments] through that [41]

(17) THIS [REASONING] CAN ALSO INVESTIGATE [PROOFS] OF THE SĀṂKHYAS, ETC.:
[MINDS] ARE NON-MENTAL, BECAUSE THEY ARE IMPERMANENT, ETC.
ALSO [THE JAINAS CLAIM THAT A TREE] POSSESSES MIND,
BECAUSE IT DIES WHEN ITS BARK IS STRIPPED.

This reasoning confuting the reasons [purporting to] prove [the existence of] God CAN, when relied upon, ALSO INVESTIGATE and refute other fallacious proofs, such as those of the Sāṃkhyas, Jainas, etc.[79]

The Sāṃkhyas say that mind, pleasure, etc., since they ARE NON-MENTAL, etc., are material, BECAUSE, since THEY ARE IMPERMANENT, ETC., they have a birth. ALSO, the Jainas say that a tree POSSESSES MIND, BECAUSE IT DIES WHEN ITS BARK IS STRIPPED. Analyzing these [syllogisms], we are able to refute them.[80]

The aim that is accomplished by those refutations [42]

(18) IF THE GENERAL ENTITY [REASON] IS UNPROVEN IN THE SUBJECT,
THIS IS A WAY [OF DISPROVING IT]; IF IT IS PROVEN, THEN EVEN IF PARTICULARS ARE UNPROVEN,
THE [REASON] IS NOT DAMAGED [BY SPECIFICATIONS]
SUCH AS "SOUND DEPENDS ON SPACE."
(19) EVEN IF THE WORD IS UNPROVEN, [THE REASON]

Dharmakīrti already has pointed out above (PV 1c-2) that words do not establish their referents, but only the speaker's desire to express them.

79 The other schools' syllogisms are refutable in the general sense that logical faults will be found in their reasons, not in the specific sense that arguments against the existence of God will be applied to them. Indeed, neither the Jainas nor many Sāṃkhyas are theists.

80 The Sāṃkhya syllogism is invalid because it is using as a reason a doctrine not accepted by the Sāṃkhyas themselves, namely that of impermanence as momentariness, i.e., instantaneous arising and destruction. The Sāṃkhya is attempting to show that the evolutes of prakṛti are insentient, and does so by arguing that they are evanescent—yet this sort of evanescence is not accepted by the Sāṃkhyas themselves, since for them evolutes are modifications of an eternal substance, and cannot therefore be impermanent in the sense in which Buddhists use the term. The Jaina syllogism is invalid because it is using as a reason a doctrine not acceptable to another school: the Buddhists do not accept that death is related to the removal of bark, and have a different notion of sentience. One cannot merely assume one's own doctrine; it is a cardinal rule of logical disputation that the disputants must agree on the terms. See Stcherbatsky (1962) I, 329-30 and II, 173-76.

CAN BE PROVEN BECAUSE THE ENTITY IS PROVEN.
FOR EXAMPLE, THE BUDDHISTS EXPLAIN
TO THE VAIŚEṢIKAS: "[BECAUSE] THEY ARE PHYSICAL."
(20) IF JUST THAT [MEANING] IS MISTAKEN, ETC.,
THEN EVEN IF THE WORD IS UNMISTAKEN,
THE PROOF MUST BE KNOWN AS FLAWED,
BECAUSE ONE CAN PROVE AN ENTITY
[ONLY] FROM AN ENTITY.
(20[B]) [FOR EXAMPLE, ONE MAY PROPOSE] PROOFS SAYING: "[A VARIEGATED COW] IS A HORNED ONE [COW], BECAUSE IT IS A GOER,"
[AND "AN ELEPHANT CALF] IS AN ELEPHANT, BECAUSE IT IS AN 'ARM-POSSESSOR'";
THE WORDS OF THESE TOPICS
ARE [APPLIED] BY COMMON OPINION; THEY ARE ASSERTED AS TOPICS NOT [APPROPRIATE TO THEIR PREDICATES].

An example [showing] that, of the general and the particular, the general is primary:

Of general and particular reasons, the general are primary, because IF the way THE GENERAL ENTITY of a reason has been proposed in relation to a subject one desires to know IS UNPROVEN to be appropriate, it is accepted that THIS IS A WAY OF DISPROVING [THE REASON]; BUT IF [the general reason] IS PROVEN [in relation to the subject], then EVEN IF PARTICULAR details ARE UNPROVEN in relation to the subject, [the general reason] IS NOT DAMAGED.

For example, if one proves that "[because it is] a product" is a reason approporiately applied to [the subject] sound in general, then even if it is unproven of the product, sound, that it is synonymous with a particular quality of space, [the general reason] is not damaged. Alternatively, it is AS when, ["product"] being proven in relation to SOUND, even if ["product"] is unproven in relation to a [particular] sound that DEPENDS ON a particular SPACE, [the general reason] is not damaged.[81]

---

81 The point here is similar to that made with regard to the rebounding argument: reasons are general, and to burden them with excessive precision or with artificial dilemmas is merely sophistry. Indeed, it is precisely the generality of a reason that gives it the ability to be relevant to the subject and pervasive of the predicate, hence correct and probative. Here, unproven specifications about a sound's relation to space do not vitiate the syllogism proving sound's impermanence. If such specifications were applied, there would be no end to them, hence no reason could ever be proven relevant to any subject.

An example [showing] that of word and meaning, meaning is primary:

A product, EVEN IF THE WORD for the object expressed by the verbal expression [of the reason] IS UNPROVEN, CAN BE PROVEN to be a reason present in the subject of a proof that sound is impermanent, BECAUSE THE ENTITY IS PROVEN to have the actual meaning that is appropriately proposed [as a reason] in relation to the subject one desires to cognize, sound.[82]

FOR EXAMPLE, THE BUDDHISTS EXPLAIN TO THE VAIŚEṢIKAS[83] [the following] PROOF: "The atoms of the four elements are impermanent because THEY ARE PHYSICAL, ETC.," and it is grasped that "tangible" [is implied]. Although the word "physical" is applied by one of the disputants, it is unproven that it is commonly agreed upon by the disputants.

The Vaiśeṣikas assert that all knowledge-objects are collected into six categories: substance, quality, generality, particularity, action and inherence. Substance [is divided into] non-ubiquitous substances, viz., the four elements and mind; and four ubiquitous substances, viz., self, time, direction and space. Of the six categories, it is quality [that includes] size. If we divide size, there are big and small and long and short. Big [is divided into] permanent and impermanent. The permanent big is a quality based on a substance that has parts and is composed of three or more atoms. The small is divided [in the same way]. The permanent small is the quality characterized by an atom's appearing to the mind as round. The impermanent small is the quality based on [a substance] that has parts and is composed of [one or two] atoms. Long and short are similar to impermanent big and small.

It is accepted that the word "physical" is applicable to all the sizes except the permanent big. The meaning of "physical" is "touchable," which is accepted by both disputants as [a reason] in relation the [the subject], the four elements. Accordingly, although the Vaiśeṣikas assert that atoms are unimpeded, they assert, like the Buddhists, that the meaning of "tangible" is [that atoms can] have their way blocked by

---

82 In other words, the absence of the specific *word* "product" from a syllogism proving that sound is impermanent will not invalidate the syllogism, as long as the specific *meaning* expressed by "product" is supplied by some other word, e.g., "composite." It is the actual natures of entities that finally are probative, not words.

83 The usual Tibetan term for Vaiśeṣika, *bye brag pa,* is replaced here by *'ug pa pa,* which refers to Ulūka, another name of Kaṇāda, traditionally considered the author of the *Vaiśeṣika Sūtras.* See Dasgupta (1975) I, 71.

other formed objects. The word "touchable" means "physical." Although, according to the Vaiśeṣikas, ["physical"] is unproven in relation to the four elements, according to them there is no flaw such that ["physical"] is unproven in the subject of the proof that the atoms of the four elements are impermanent, because even if that [word] is unproven, according to them it is certain that the *meaning* of ["physical"] is an appropriate reason to propose in relation to the subject one desires to cognize, [and] which will be proven thus.[84]

The reason the meaning of [verses 19-20] is acceptable:

IF JUST THAT meaning IS MISTAKEN or contradictory or unproven, ETC., THEN EVEN IF THE WORD IS UNMISTAKEN, THE PROOF MUST BE KNOWN AS FLAWED, BECAUSE ONE CAN PROVE A pervading causal ENTITY FROM a pervaded resultant ENTITY, but one cannot prove an object from a mere word.[85]

For example, [one may] propose the following PROOFS, SAYING: "A variegated cow IS A HORNED ONE [cow], BECAUSE IT IS A GOER"; AND "an elephant calf IS AN ELEPHANT, BECAUSE IT IS AN 'ARM-POSSESSOR.'" THE WORDS "goer" and "arm-possessing," which are terms [for the proving] OF THESE [predicates], "is a cow" and "is an elephant," are not applied as terms [for proving those predicates merely] by reason of their being unmistaken in relation to the bovine and elephantine objects that are the [subject] TOPICS one wishes to know, but because they ARE applied BY force of COMMON OPINION that is mistaken about its objects. "Goer" and "arm-possessing," which ARE ASSERTED AS [relevant] to the [subject] TOPICS, are NOT unmistaken in relation to [the predicates] "is a cow" and "is an elephant," because we see that there are living beings that are not those two [elephants and cows, yet have those qualities].[86]

---

84 This is simply a detailed demonstration that—as the sub-heading states—words are subordinate to meaning. The actual nature of an entity is what ultimately validates a syllogism, and it is the meaningful expression of that actual nature—not a particular verbal formulation—that is crucial to a syllogism's correctness.

85 This merely states the corollary of what was demonstrated above. Not only can a correct meaning that lacks a specific word be probative, but an incorrect meaning, even where the word is "correct," cannot be probative. A reason's probative power comes not from the word or words of which it may consist, but from the observable relation between what is symbolized by the word or words of the reason and what is symbolized by the word or words of the subject and predicate —i.e., by the meaning.

86 PV 20[b] is found only in Tibetan. It presents two examples of cases where a "correct" word is misunderstood, and cannot, therefore, serve as a correct rea-

Showing that [the existence of] a creator of all knowledge-objects is confuted by authority [43]

[This is divided into:] (1) [God's] unsuitability as a permanent cause [44] and (2) Disposing [of the idea that our objections apply] equally to us [45].

[God's] unsuitability as a permanent cause [44]

(21) THAT ENTITY IS NOT ASSERTED FOR ANY REASON
AS A NON-CAUSE [WHEN IT] IS ASSERTED TO BE A CAUSE, [YET IF] IT IS THUS, SUCH AS TO BE A CAUSE,
IT IS AT THAT SAME [TIME] A NON-CAUSE.[87]
(22) WHY [SHOULD] AN UNCONNECTED POST,
NOT COGNIZED AS BEING A CAUSE, [CURE NAGPA'S WOUND],
[WHEN] THE WOUNDING AND HEALING OF NAGPA
[ARE KNOWN TO ARISE] FROM CONNECTION WITH A WEAPON AND MEDICINE, ETC.?
(23) [GOD] ALSO IS UNSUITABLE AS THE MAKER,
BECAUSE HE CANNOT CHANGE HIS NATURE;
IT IS DIFFICULT TO COGNIZE EVEN HIS ABILITY [TO ASSIST]
BECAUSE ABSENCE IS NOT [CHARACTERISTIC] OF A PERMANENT [ENTITY].
(24) THERE WOULD BE AN INFINITY OF CAUSES
FOR EVERY [RESULT], BECAUSE THEN [IT WOULD BE ACCEPTABLE] TO THINK
THAT WHEN SOME [CAUSES] ARE [THE CAUSE] OF SOME [RESULT]

---

son. In each case, the reason set forth is in common usage a synonym for the animal that is the subject of the syllogism: *'gro ba* (*jagat*), or "goer,"is another word for cow; and *lag ldan* (*hathi*), or "arm (= trunk-) possessing,"is another word for elephant. These cannot serve as correct reasons because they are merely common expressions, liable to be misunderstood by anyone unaware of their popular usage. The words "goer"and "arm-possessing"are ambiguous, and when they are applied in their more general, non-idiomatic sense, their pervasion of their respective predicates is uncertain, because there are goers that are not cows, and arm-possessors that are not elephants. Even if this ambiguity were not present, the syllogisms still would be incorrect, for they would merely use synonyms as reasons, and thereby supply definitions rather than proofs: the resultant syllogism would be tautologous.

87 A somewhat more straightforward reading of the Tibetan (*ji ltar dngos de rgyu yin pa / de lta de nyid gang gi tshe / rgyu min gang gis de ni rgyur / 'dod la rgyu ma yin mi 'dod*) yields: "If an entity is a cause just as, at the same time, it is not a cause, why is it not asserted that what is asserted as a cause is [in fact] not a cause?"

[SOME THINGS] OTHER THAN THOSE ARE THE CAUSES OF THAT.

Setting forth the consequences:

It cannot be accepted that THAT ENTITY that IS God NOT be ASSERTED FOR ANY REASON AS A NON-CAUSE at the same time as he IS ASSERTED TO BE A CAUSE, because if he IS THUS, although he does not change from SUCH nature AS TO BE A CAUSE, he IS AT THAT SAME time asserted sometimes to have the nature of being A NON-CAUSE.[88]

If this reason does not pervade, then WHY, it follows, is it not reasonable to think that AN UNCONNECTED POST, NOT COGNIZED AS BEING THE CAUSE generating [the cure], heals a wound? It would be reasonable, because the former [reason] does not pervade. It follows that this [latter] assertion is unreasonable, BECAUSE IT is accepted that the infliction of A WOUND AND its HEALING on the body OF NAGPA [arise respectively] FROM CONNECTION WITH A WEAPON AND MEDICINE, ETC.; it is not accepted otherwise.[89]

[God] ALSO IS UNSUITABLE AS THE MAKER of all results, BECAUSE he [is asserted sometimes] not to generate results, and HE CANNOT CHANGE HIS NATURE. IT IS DIFFICULT TO COGNIZE EVEN HIS ABILITY to assist the cause [in bringing about] the result, BECAUSE his ABSENCE as an assistant IS NOT the basis for the prevention OF the arising of the result, and because he is A PERMANENT entity.[90] If he is a permanent entity, since

---

88 God might be asserted as an occasional non-cause because objects arise intermittently, and it might be said that when they do not arise, God is their non-cause; but if God is permanent he cannot change his nature, and if he is a cause, he cannot become a non-cause, or vice versa.

89 If God is asserted to be a non-cause, then, because he is permanent and cannot change his nature, he must always be a non-cause. For the opponent to insist that he still is a cause as well is to say that a non-cause is a cause. Why, then, not say that a post, which has no connection to either the infliction or healing of a wound, is the cause of the infliction and healing? The statement is absurd, but reasonable in light of the absurdity the opponent is asserting. Incidentally, Dharmakīrti (and, following him, Devendrabuddhi) attributes both the wound *and* its healing to the weapon, an instance of what Nagatomi ([1957] 33) calls "homeopathic magic." Cf. Dante's *Inferno*, XXXI: 4-6, for a Western equivalent, Achilles' lance.

90 The basic argument here is that, quite apart from the logical impossibility of a permanent being's assistance in bringing about an impermanent result, God cannot be said to cause, or assist in the causation of, particular results because his presence or absence is not observed to be relevant to the workings of causality, which are in almost all cases subject to satisfactory *natural* explanations ("natural," in a Buddhist sense, including karma). God, in short, is an unnec-

it is impossible that he prevent [results from occurring], it cannot be ascertained that there is positive or negative concomitance [between God and particular results].

Showing by authority that the [last] pervading reason is flawed:

It follows that THERE WOULD BE AN INFINITY OF CAUSES FOR EVERY result, BECAUSE THEN it would be acceptable TO THINK THAT WHEN SOME causes ARE assistant to [a result], the causes OF THAT [result] are some unseen things OTHER THAN THOSE which ARE [THE CAUSES OF] the arising of SOME result.[91]

Disposing [of the idea that our objections apply] equally to us [45]

(25) SOIL, ETC., HAVING TRANSFORMED THEIR NATURE,
BECOME A CAUSE GENERATING A SPROUT,
BECAUSE WE SEE THAT WHEN THAT [PLOWING, ETC.]
HAS BEEN DONE WELL, THERE IS A CHANGE.
(26) YOU MAY SAY: JUST AS OBJECT [AND] FACULTY,
THE CAUSES OF COGNITION, DO NOT CHANGE
WHEN THEY HAVE MET, SO, TOO, THIS [GOD]. [WE REPLY:] NOT SO,
BECAUSE IN THOSE THERE *ARE* CHANGES.
(27) EVEN WHEN THEY HAVE MET, THEY WILL NOT HAVE THE POWER [TO GENERATE COGNITION],
BECAUSE THEY DO NOT HAVE THE POWER INDIVIDUALLY,
AND THEY DO NOT CHANGE THEIR NATURE;
THEREFORE, IT IS PROVEN THAT THERE IS A CHANGE IN THOSE [CONDITIONS].
(28) GOD, ETC., IS NOT [A CAUSE], BECAUSE
HE DOES NOT CHANGE; SOME [FACTORS] THAT HAVE NO POWER
INDIVIDUALLY ARE, WHEN THEY MEET, THE CAUSE
OF THE QUALITY THAT COMES INTO EXISTENCE.

---

essary, "metaphysical"entity. rGyal tshab rje adds a bit to the most straightforward reading of the Tibetan here, which simply states that God's causal ability is difficult to cognize because a permanent entity cannot ever be absent. Because he never is absent, God is present in *all* circumstances, and what explains absolutely everything comes very close to explaining absolutely nothing.

91 If some unseen factor, such as God, is asserted to be a cause, even though his presence or absence makes no discernible difference to the operation of causality, then *any* unseen factor can be asserted to be the cause of any observed result, an idea that—if not absurd—is quite useless, because it makes causality so general as to be meaningless, and therefore irrelevant to any purpose, worldly or religious. Cf. TS 90.

[OPPONENT:] Well, then, according to you, when soil, etc., do not generate a sprout, they cannot change their nature, so there will be no generation of a sprout.

[RGYAL TSHAB RJE:] It follows that SOIL, ETC., while not changing, will not be the cause of a sprout, because WHEN THEY TRANSFORM THEIR NATURE from the time they are not generating a sprout, *then* they BECOME A CAUSE GENERATING A SPROUT. This follows, BECAUSE WE SEE THAT WHEN THAT plowing and sowing of a field HAS BEEN DONE WELL, THERE IS A perfect TRANSFORMATION of it [such that there is] an autumn harvest.[92]

[OPPONENT:] JUST AS OBJECT, FACULTY, etc., are THE CAUSE OF sense-COGNITION, even though they DO NOT CHANGE their aspect between [the time] when they have not met and [the time] WHEN THEY HAVE MET, SO, TOO, is THIS God [both a cause and a non-cause, although he does not change his aspect].[93]

[RGYAL TSHAB RJE:] It is NOT SO that the faculties, etc., do not change, BECAUSE IN THOSE THERE *ARE* CHANGES, according to the clarity or unclarity [of the sense-faculties].

If such is not the case, it follows that EVEN WHEN the three conditions HAVE MET, THEY WILL NOT HAVE THE POWER to generate sense-cognition, BECAUSE THEY DO NOT HAVE THE POWER [to generate it] INDIVIDUALLY when they have not met, and THEY DO NOT CHANGE THEIR NATURE at the time when they do meet. THEREFORE, IT IS PROVEN THAT THERE IS A CHANGE IN THOSE three conditions [between] when they have met and when they have not met, because we see the difference that there is the arising or the non-arising of sense-cognition [respectively] when they have met or have not met.[94]

---

92 The well-worked field that produces a good autumn harvest is a general example of the change in nature undergone by the elements. Before the fields have been properly sown, neither the earth nor the seed is a cause of a sprout; when, however, they have met under the proper conditions, they will result in the sprouts that are the beginning of a bountiful harvest.

93 The opponent argues that sense-objects and faculties do not change from the time when they have not met to cause a sense-cognition to the time when they have met, and actually cause a sense-cognition. If this is so, then we may infer that an entity such as God, even though he does not change from the time when he is not a cause to the time when he is a cause, still may serve as a cause.

94 In this example, as in the one above, the simple inference is that the factors causing a particular result must have a different nature when they meet as when they are separate, because when they are separate they are not causes, and when they meet they are, and to be a non-cause is to have a different na-

GOD, ETC., IS NOT the cause of all results, BECAUSE HE DOES NOT CHANGE his nature [from when] he does not generate results. It follows that [this reason] pervades, because SOME [factors] THAT HAVE NO POWER to generate a common result INDIVIDUALLY ARE, WHEN THEY MEET, THE CAUSE OF that common result, since [when they meet] THE QUALITY of the result COMES INTO EXISTENCE.

D. WHY THE BUDDHA IS AN AUTHORITY

Proving as omniscient the one who knows by perception how all [knowledge-objects] really exist [46]

[This is divided into: (1) Objections [47] and (2) Refuting those (objections) [48].

Objections [47]

(29) SOME SAY: "AN AUTHORITY IS A COGNIZER OF HIDDEN OBJECTS;
BECAUSE THERE IS NOT ANY ACCOMPLISHMENT OF THAT,
THERE DOES NOT EXIST [ANY]ONE WHO MAKES AN EFFORT [FOR IT]."
THIS THEY CLEARLY EXPRESS.

SOME Hedonists, Mīmāṃsakas, etc., SAY: "As you have refuted [the existence of] God, so there is equal fault in your omniscient one, because if he is AN AUTHORITY-person, he necessarily IS A COGNIZER OF HIDDEN OBJECTS without exception.

"(a) BECAUSE THERE IS NOT in the least ANY method for the ACCOMPLISHMENT[95] OF THAT state of omniscience by some [sort of mental] development, THERE DOES NOT EXIST [any] ONE WHO MAKES AN EFFORT for that method.

"(b) Not only is there no cause generating [such omniscience], but because there is not the least bit of proof that demonstrates it, there does not exist, either, anyone who strives for the sake of cognizing it." [This] is CLEARLY EXPRESSED [by those critics].

---

ture from a cause. Of course, only an impermanent entity can thus change its nature: seeds and sprouts, and sense-faculties and their objects are impermanent, and thus capable of changing nature; God, as a permanent entity, is not.

95 As in a number of previous instances, the Tibetan *sgrub byed* carries the double sense of "accomplish" and "prove." Because there is no way of "accomplishing" omniscience, omniscience has no identifiable cause. Because there is no way of "proving" omniscience, there is no means by which we could identify an omniscient one.

Thus, they say that (a) it follows that one cannot accomplish omniscience by unimaginable mantras or medicines, because those are used by Buddhists and non-Buddhists [alike], and it would follow that everyone is omniscient; and (b) it follows that sense-cognition cannot cognize all hidden phenomena, because it is powerless to function where there are obstacles. It follows that mental cognition cannot be [omniscient], because it follows on sense-cognition. It follows that even if the mind relies on scripture it cannot cognize all hidden phenomena, because [words] are not necessarily related to meaning — and even if they are, one will not cognize [the meaning] directly.[96]

Moreover, it follows that it is unacceptable that one cognize all knowledge-objects successively, because if that is the case, you must accept that there is an exhaustive limit [to phenomena]. If [all knowledge-objects are said to be] cognized simultaneously, it follows that there is a beginning to saṃsāra, because such a cognition is completely limiting.[97]

One cannot cognize the existence of such an omniscient one through logical reasons, because there are no reasons apart from words and [because] since all persons are undeceived regarding some words, it would follow that if some person were undeceived regarding [the word] "all" they would be omniscient.[98]

---

96 The existence of a word, as we have seen, does not guarantee the existence of the word's referent. There is no absolute ontological connection between words and things, and even if there were such a connection, knowledge gained through words still would be indirect, and thus not of the most certain kind.

97 The Mīmāṃsaka is driving home the logical consequences of claiming that *all* phenomena can be cognized. To say that *all* phenomena are cognized successively is to imply that there is a limit to phenomena. If phenomena are—as generally believed in Indian philosophy—infinite, then it is theoretically impossible to cognize all phenomena successively, for there always will be a new phenomenon to cognize. Similarly, to claim that all phenomena are cognized simultaneously is to claim that all phenomena can be delimited by a single cognition, and so must be finite in space and time. Saṃsāra, therefore, must have a beginning, contrary to what a Buddhist would maintain.

98 The Mīmāṃsaka here argues against the relevance of logical reasons to the demonstration of omniscience on two grounds: (a) reasons are invariably connected with words, and words are not necessarily bound up with the reality of their referents and (b) if everyone is correct in their use of some words—i.e., everyone has had the experience of using a word that *does* really have an object corresponding to it—then if some person is correct in their use of the word "all," they should be omniscient. It is not likely that the Buddhist would

If it is proven by perception, then the one [so proving] must also be omniscient, for without oneself cognizing all knowledge-objects, one cannot ascertain, "This being cognizes all knowledge-objects."

[In short,] there is neither a cause generating omniscience nor a reason demonstrating [its existence].[99]

Refuting those [objections] [48]

[This is divided into:] (1) The reason for seeking an omniscient one [49], (2) The way of seeking him [50] and (3) Identifying the omniscient one [51].

The reason for seeking an omniscient one [49]

(30) [THE] IGNORANT, HAVING CHOSEN A TEACHER [AND]
BEING CONCERNED THAT THEY ARE MISTAKEN [IN THEIR CHOICE],
SEEK SOMEONE WHO KNOWS [A METHOD OF PACIFYING SUFFERING],
SO THAT THEY MAY MAKE AN EFFORT TOWARD THAT [GOAL] EXPLAINED BY THAT [PERSON].[100]

IGNORANT of the method of pacifying suffering, HAVING TAKEN as A TEACHER someone who [allegedly] effects a demonstration of that [method], and BEING CONCERNED THAT THEY ARE MISTAKEN [in believing] that that person is a perfect teacher, THOSE intent on freedom have a reason to SEEK SOMEONE WHO KNOWS well the method of paci-

---

disagree with either observation, but the Buddhist still would maintain that omniscience is subject to logical demonstration, because logical reasons rest ultimately not on mere words, but on commonly accepted invariable concomitances among phenomena.

99 These arguments against omniscience, typical of the Mīmāṃsakas, are interpolated by rGyal tshab rje and other later commentators. They are present neither in Dharmakīrti's verses nor in Devendrabuddhi's commentary (PVP 224-225). Explicitly at least, Dharmakīrti is concerned not with proving the Buddha's omniscience, but his authoritativeness. On the evidence of Dharmakīrti's writings, his attitude toward omniscience seems to have been ambivalent at best. Indeed, it is possible to construe the following section as an attack on the idea of universal omniscience (*sarvākārajñatā*); at the very most, it is an attempt to establish knowledge of what is to be adopted and what rejected as the sufficient condition of a being's authoritativeness for those intent on freedom. For further discussion of this issue, see R. Jackson (1987) and (1988).

100 A somewhat more straightforward reading of the Tibetan (*mi shes ston par byed pa la / 'khrul bar dogs pa can rnams kyis / des bshad nan tan bya ba'i phyir / shes ldan 'ga' zhig tshol bar byed*) yields: "Those who are anxious about being deceived in taking an ignoramus as a teacher seek someone wise so as to make an effort toward what has been explained by him."

fying suffering, because they are seeking SO THAT THEY MAY MAKE AN EFFORT TOWARD THAT goal EXPLAINED BY a person such as THAT. The verse does *not* mean that when those intent on freedom do not know [the method of pacifying suffering] they seek a virtuous friend [because] they are concerned that they will err when teaching others.[101]

The way of seeking him [50]

(31) THEREFORE, [WITH REGARD TO] WHAT [SPIRITUAL] PRACTICE OUGHT TO BE,
ONE MUST INVESTIGATE WHETHER THIS [TEACHER] HAS THE KNOWLEDGE [THAT KNOWS THAT];
FOR US, THEIR KNOWLEDGE OF HOW MANY INSECTS THERE ARE
IS NOT AT ALL USEFUL.

[THEREFORE,] one must consider whether this teacher knows or does not know [the methods whereby] one engages with and exits from saṃsāra, WHAT the [spiritual] PRACTICE OUGHT TO BE that is manifestly desired by those intent on freedom. ONE MUST INVESTIGATE WHETHER or not THIS [TEACHER] HAS THE KNOWLEDGE that knows that. One should not first investigate whether or not they know how many insects there are, because FOR those of US intent on freedom, THEIR KNOWLEDGE OF HOW MANY INSECTS THERE ARE IS, for the time being,[102] NOT AT ALL USEFUL, because we are intent on freedom.

[OPPONENT:] Well, then, when we investigate thus, before we take [a person] as a teacher, we either know or do not know that they have the quality of knowing the path to enlightenment and freedom. If we know, then since we ourselves already know the method of pacifying suffering, seeking [an omniscient one] is pointless. If we do not know, then, unable to distinguish who is to be trusted from who is not to be trusted, we should trust the first [teacher] we meet.[103]

---

101 The reply to the Mīmāṃsaka objection, thus, is that there is a reason for seeking an omniscient (or authoritative) person, namely spiritual need, and the fear that an ignorant teacher will lead us astray from our spiritual goals.

102 The Tibetan *re zhig,* "for the time being," is neither contained nor implied in Dharmakīrti's verse or Devendrabuddhi's commentary. The implication of its interpolation is that knowledge such as that of the number of insects is not *now* useful, but such knowledge is possible, will be part of a buddha's omniscience, and may, in fact, someday be useful. Dharmakīrti does not deny the possibility of such knowledge, but his denial of its usefulness is, apparently, categorical, without any temporal modifier.

103 The opponent is, in their own way, posing the paradox of spiritual commitment: we cannot have any basis for choosing a spiritual guide, for we cannot,

[RGYAL TSHAB RJE:] There is no problem. This is the way a virtuous friend is sought by the intelligent: From the very beginning, one knows the object[104] roughly by authority; also, one comes to know the existence of its subtle qualities through faith, and one also will understand partially from questioning others, through reports, etc.[105]

Identifying the omniscient one [51]

(32) [WE] ASSERT THAT SOMEONE IS AN AUTHORITY
WHO HAS COGNITION OF WHAT IS TO BE ADOPTED AND REJECTED, TOGETHER
WITH THE METHODS [THERETO];
COGNITION OF ALL [PHENOMENA] DOES NOT [DEFINE AUTHORITY].
(33) WHETHER OR NOT THEY CAN SEE A GREAT DISTANCE,
THEY SEE THE PRINCIPLE THAT IS DESIRED [BY SENTIENT BEINGS];
IF IT IS THE CASE THAT [YOU DEFINE] AUTHORITY [BY] SEEING A GREAT DISTANCE,
RELY ON THE VULTURE [AS YOUR TEACHER]!

It is reasonable to ASSERT THAT the *muni*, the Blessed One, IS AN AUTHORITY for those intent on freedom, because he is one WHO HAS complete perceptual COGNITION OF WHAT IS TO BE ADOPTED AND WHAT REJECTED — [inversely,] engagement with and exit from saṃsāra — TOGETHER WITH THE METHODS [thereto]. Just by HAVING COGNITION OF ALL the numbers of insects there are, he DOES NOT fulfill the desires of those intent on freedom, because that [detailed knowledge] alone is not useful.[106]

---

by our deluded nature, know with certainty that a possible guide has the ultimate knowledge they claim. If we were certain, we would not need a guide!

104 The Tibetan word *don* carries here the double sense of an "object" in general and, in particular, the "goal" that is sought by those intent on freedom.

105 "Faith," *yid dpyod*, is one of seven types of dispositions toward objects (*blo rigs bdun*). It is the belief, without direct certainty, that something is the case when, in fact, it *is* the case. More certain than *yid dpyod* are authoritative perception and inference and subsequent cognition. Less certain are uncertainty regarding an appearance (*snang la ma nges*), doubt and wrong cognition. rGyal tshab rje's argument appears, on one level at least, to be circular, since one only can develop faith on the basis of good reasons, while he is asking that some of the reasons (i.e., the existence of various subtle qualities) be taken on faith. The problem of choosing a guide is complex, and although rGyal tshab rje's dismissal of it seems a bit cavalier, his implication that the solution is partly pragmatic certainly makes sense on a non-philosophical level. See Rabten (1978) 43-46 and Lati Rinbochay (1980) 92-99.

Accordingly, [the Buddha] is reasonably [considered] the teacher of those intent on freedom, WHETHER OR NOT HE CAN SEE A GREAT DISTANCE, because HE completely SEES the actuality of the four noble truths, THE PRINCIPLE THAT IS DESIRED [by those intent on freedom]. Without that being the case, IF IT IS THE CASE THAT one fulfills the definition of an AUTHORITY-person merely by SEEING A GREAT DISTANCE, then it follows that it would be reasonable to instruct those intent on freedom: "Come here! RELY ON THE VULTURE as your teacher!"[107]

Furthermore, others assert that the meaning of omniscience is knowing how to create all things, as we use the term "omniscient" in a conventional worldly sense in relation to those who know how to do many things, such as painting, smithing, tailoring, etc. If someone who can make anything because of their knowledge of the sciences is omniscient, then they also have made the sufferings of the lower realms, etc. Thus, one should take as one's teacher someone who is omniscient regarding karma and the defilements and who, having accomplished the elimination of every last fetter, is omniscient regarding how all knowledge-objects really exist.[108]

---

106 This passage is the key identification of the qualities necessary to a teacher who would teach those intent on freedom, and it is authoritativeness, not omniscience, that is at issue. Indeed, it is with this observation that the discussion of the Buddha as "one who has become an authority" concludes. Whether or not a buddha's authoritativeness is coextensive with omniscience is problematic. Such an assumption is not obvious in Dharmakīrti and Devendrabuddhi, but it is assumed by Prajñākaragupta and rGyal tshab rje, on the grounds that what is to be adopted and what rejected comprises all dharmas of, respectively, saṃsāra and nirvāṇa. Since these two categories are exhaustive of all phenomena, knowledge of what is to be adopted and rejected in regard to them will be knowledge of everything.

107 Dharmakīrti here seems to be clearly distinguishing between omniscience and authority—in Western terms, he is pointing out the difference between "knowledge" and "wisdom."

108 This discussion, which is added by rGyal tshab rje, not only describes another type of "omniscience," that is useless for those intent on freedom, but raises what in Western philosophy is called the "problem of evil": why should we follow a teacher whose creative abilities extend to the manufacture of tortures? rGyal tshab rje, of course, is assuming that the omniscience of the teacher in question is limited to their creative prowess, and that they do *not* know, e.g., how all things really exist and how saṃsāra is engaged and disengaged. The Christian God, on the other hand, is omniscient and omnipotent in the most complete sense, so he not only creates (or, depending on one's theodicy, permits) the tortures of hell, but also knows the way to salvation—indeed, he *is* salvation, and his grace the only assurance of its attainment.

3. *The Mind-Body Problem: A Refutation of Materialism (1)*

A. INTRODUCTORY

Defining the authoritative person through the four remaining [epithets][1] *[52]*

[This is divided into:] (1) Proving the four particular qualities [53] and (2) Showing from that that [the Buddha] is one who has become an authority [175].

Proving the four particular qualities [53]

[This is divided into:] (1) Identifying the excellence of intention [54], (2) The way in which excellence of application arises from [excellence of intention] [158] and (3) [Based on] those two, the way of proving excellence of results [168].[2]

Identifying the excellence of intention [54]

[This is divided into:] (1) Showing initial proof of the excellence of intention [55] and (2) Disposing [of the objection that] it is unproven [56].

Showing initial proof of the excellence of intention [55]

(34) ACCUSTOMATION WITH COMPASSION IS THE ESTABLISHER.

When the Greatly Compassionate One accomplished [the state of] an authoritative person, [his accomplishment] necessarily first was

---

1 To this point, the characterization of the Buddha as "the one who has become an authority," or the "authoritative person," has been proven only generally, via the assertion that he is one who knows what to adopt and what to reject on a spiritual path. In the remainder of the chapter, the characterization will be proven in detail, through a forward and reverse demonstration of the four remaining epithets given to the Buddha by Dignāga: the one who desires to benefit beings (i.e., the compassionate one), the teacher, the sugata and the savior.

2 For a discussion of these terms, see above, section III:1.

preceded [by great compassion], because it was necessary that, having first generated the compassion that desires to free [sentient beings] from all their sufferings, he then accustomated a method of pacifying suffering, and from that he became the teacher.[3] Great compassion does not arise causelessly or from inappropriate causes, because it is accomplished through ACCUSTOMATION WITH previous homogenes. Great COMPASSION IS THE ESTABLISHER of the beginning of meditation on the Mahāyāna path,[4] and [similarly] when one has made "he is the savior" the thesis [requiring] a reason, then ["compassion"] is the first [reason used] in proving it.[5] The way in which this is necessary will be explained below.

Disposing [of the objection] that that is unproven (56)

[This is divided into:] (1) The objection [57] and (2) The refutation of that [58].

---

3 Compassion (by which I translate both *brtse ba* [*kṛpā*] and *snying rje* [*karuṇā*]) is the chief quality of one who desires to benefit beings. To prove that the Buddha is the teacher for those intent on freedom, one must establish a motive, which is the compassion out of which he seeks and finds a method for pacifying suffering, which method he then is able to teach to others.

4 Compassion is the seed from which the entire Mahāyāna path flowers. In Candrakīrti's *Madhyamakāvatāra,* for instance, the initial homage is directed not—as is customary—to a deity, such as Mañjuśri, but to compassion itself. See Poussin (1907-11), Hopkins (1980) 101ff. and Huntington (1989). The term "Mahāyāna path" is used by rGyal tshab rje in a general sense: in order to enter the first of the five "paths" of the *Abhisamayālaṃkāra* path-system (that of accumulation), it is necessary not only to have generated compassion (the desire to see others freed from suffering), but great compassion (the desire to free them oneself) and, ultimately, the thought of enlightenment (*byang sems, bodhicitta*), which is the aspiration to highest enlightenment so that one may assist other beings. It might be noted parenthetically that, in line with the "generic" Buddhism being presented here, Dharmakīrti nowhere specifies that he is discussing "great" compassion.

5 "Savior" is the last of the five epithets, so in the forward system of explanation, "he is the savior" becomes the logical thesis, for which "compassion" will serve as the first in a chain of "establishers," or reasons. From the Buddha's compassion, we will be able to infer that he is the teacher, and from his teacherhood, we may infer that he is a sugata, which, in turn, will inform us that he is the savior—as well as the one who has become an authority, which is here the unstated thesis of the syllogism that underlies this entire chapter: the Buddha (subject) is the one who has become an authority (predicate), because he is the compassionate one, the teacher, the sugata and the savior (reasons, to be traced in both forward and reverse order).

The objection [57]

(34b) [THE LOKĀYATAS] SAY: "[COMPASSION] IS NOT ACCOMPLISHED THROUGH ACCUSTOMATION,
BECAUSE MIND IS BASED ON THE BODY."

The Lokāyatas SAY: "Compassion IS NOT ACCOMPLISHED BY ACCUSTOMATION through many lives, because those many past and future lives do not exist. This follows, BECAUSE, since MIND IS BASED ON THE BODY, when the body is destroyed, [mind] is also destroyed. For example, [mind] is a result of the body, as light [is the result] of a lamp; or it is a quality of the body, as capacity to intoxicate [is a quality of] liquor; or it is naturally based [on the body, and the relation is] like that between a wall and the drawing that depends on it."[6]

The refutation of that [58]

[This is divided into:] (1) Refuting [the idea] that it is impossible to accustomate [compassion] through many lives [59] and (2) Refuting [the idea] that, even if such accustomation is possible, its infinite increase cannot be accepted [148].

Refuting [the idea] that it is impossible to accustomate [compassion] through many lives [59]

[This is divided into:] (1) A brief demonstration [60] and (2) An extensive explanation [61].

---

6 Dharmakīrti merely states that some say that mind (*blo, buddhi*) is based on the body (*lus, deha*). The probative reasons and examples are supplied by rGyal tshab rje. The examples, in particular, are stock Lokāyata similes. The "capacity to intoxicate," for instance, is cited in Mādhava's account of the Cārvāka system in the *Sarvadarśanasaṃgraha* (tr. Radhakrishnan and Moore [1957] 229). Because there is virtually no original materialist literature extant, it is difficult to know whether the examples cited referred to one or several materialist theories of mind. The likening of mind to the light given off by a lamp or to a picture on a wall sounds somewhat like what is called epiphenomenalism in the West. Mind's similarity to liquor's capacity to intoxicate could be taken as like the "category-mistake" discussion initiated by Ryle (1949): i.e., we talk about the intoxicating power of liquor as if it were a separate substance above and beyond the liquor, but it is, in fact, a quality of the liquor, and to speak of it as if it were a substance is to commit a category mistake. Similarly, then, mind is a "quality" of the body or brain—a certain set of dispositions, as Ryle would put it—and *not* a substance. See Ryle's book and the lucid discussion of it in Passmore (1970 [445-450]).

A brief demonstration [60]

(34d) NOT [SO], BECAUSE THAT [THE BODY] IS THE BASIS [OF MIND] IS REFUTABLE.

Mind[7] does NOT have the body as its basis as either substantial cause or special cooperative condition, BECAUSE [the thesis] THAT [body] IS THE BASIS in such a way IS REFUTABLE by authority, and we will refute it. Alternatively, it does not follow that by giving reasons for the non-existence of past and future lives [one proves that] it is unsuitable that one accustomate compassion through many lives, because the non-existence of [past and future lives] is [a thesis] refutable by authority, and we will refute it.[8]

Having well proven through authority that there are past and future lives, [Dharmakīrti] relies on the [the concept of] karma and its result, which will be explained below, and proves just that [one can attain] a high-level rebirth in the next and subsequent worldly lives. Based on that, he establishes the reality of the four noble truths, and from that he proves [the existence of] just the cause and result of the definitive good, which are to be meditated upon in common by beings of all three classes.[9] He proves that, after one has adorned those [four noble truths] with an infinite increase in compassion, [there is] a way in

---

7 rGyal tshab rje actually has *yid blo rtog pa* (*manas-buddhi-kalpanā*), three separate terms for aspects of "the mind."In a Buddhist context, *yid* may refer either to mind in general or, more specifically, to "mental cognition"(*yid kyi rnam par shes pa, manovijñāna*), from among the six types of cognition (the other five being sensory). *blo* seems to be a general term that encompasses what we would call "mind." *rtog pa* is often translated as "thought,"and seems usually to entail conceptuality. These distinctions are not central to the argument. Furthermore, Dharmakīrti refers the vast majority of the time to either *citta* (*sems*) or *buddhi* (*blo*); *citta* may in some contexts refer to a "principal" mind as distinguished from mental factors (*caitta*), but Dharmakīrti seems to be using both it and *buddhi* to refer to mind in general. Therefore, I have generally translated rGyal tshab rje's expressions simply by the term "mind." It must be remembered, incidentally, that "mind"for a Buddhist is not an abstract phenomenon, but one momentary cognition in a series. Indeed, the reader might want to supply "-moment" internally whenever such words as "mind,""cognition"or "knowledge"appear.

8 rGyal tshab rje is taking Dharmakīrti's verse to imply not only that the proposition that mind has the body as its basis is refutable, but that arguments for the non-existence of past and future lives (which are based on the first proposition) are equally refutable.

9 Śrāvakas, pratyekabuddhas and bodhisattvas.

which [that compassion is conjoined with] a complete realization of the four noble truths, and from that, he proves omniscience.[10] Thus, the way of proving by objectively impelled reasoning just[11] that [it is possible to attain] a high rebirth in a future life, liberation into the definitve good and omniscience is extensively demonstrated in this chapter.

The desire-realm gods in a particular heaven, such as Brahmā, etc., are very hidden phenomena, so they must be inferred in dependence upon scripture. The perfect reasons proving them are shown in the first chapter.[12] The perceptual authority that confirms their existence is shown in the third chapter.[13] If one includes the subject-matter [of the *Pramāṇavārttika*] in three chapters, as [Dharmakīrti did] in the *Pramāṇaviniścaya*, then this is included in the chapter on perception, because that is the part that extensively discusses yogic perception.[14]

---

10 There are, thus, two different levels of direct realization of the four noble truths, especially in the aspect of no-self: (a) that realization common to all beings who attain the definitive good, i.e., nirvāṇa and (b) that realization attained only by bodhisattvas through conjoining realization with compassion (or wisdom with skill-in-means) on the Mahāyāna path. The implicit formula for the proof of omniscience (see below, pp. 396-397) is: realization of the four noble truths + infinite compassion = omniscience.

11 That the *Pramāṇasiddhi* chapter shows "just"(*tsam*) that high rebirths, the definitive good and omniscience are possible means that it demonstrates their possibility in a general sense, or in principle. Particular details of particular attainments are considered to be very hidden phenomena and not, therefore, knowable through inference. They must be taken on faith from authoritative scriptures. Eventually, it is presumed, one will be able to cognize them oneself.

12 GT I, 175-180, discusses reliance upon scripture, which is considered a form of inference. Reliable or authoritative scripture must not contradict: (1) perception, (2) inference or (3) authoritative scripture. José Cabezón (1981) has argued that the last requirement is not circular, because it presupposes different levels of scripture, divided into those of direct meaning (*nges don, nītārtha*) and those of interpretable meaning (*drang don, neyārtha*). A scripture will not contradict authoritative scripture as long as it does not contradict scriptures of direct meaning. See also Lati Rinbochay (1980) 78-80.

13 The third chapter, in the scheme used by dGe lugs pas, is that on perception (*mngon sum, pratyakṣa*). The type of perception that would confirm past and future lives is a direct *mental* perception (*yid kyi mngon sum, mānasapratyakṣa*) in the mindstream of one who has developed their concentrative abilities to a high degree. They need not be an *ārya* (attainment of which condition is synonymous with the gaining of yogic perception). See Lati Rinbochay (1980) 54-55.

14 Yogic perception here is used figuratively as the perception of a yogin, not precisely as one of the four types of perception, since, as just noted, perception of past and future lives is included under mental perception.

An extensive explanation [61]

[This is divided into:] (1) Setting forth proof of the existence of past and future lives [62] and (2) Refuting proofs of their non-existence [65].

Setting forth proof of the existence of past and future lives [62]

[This is divided into:] (1) Setting forth the reason [63] and (2) Disposing of [the objection that that proof] is faulty [64].

Setting forth the reason [63]

(35) BREATHING, SENSE-FACULTIES AND MIND ARE,
WHEN [ONE] TAKES BIRTH,
[NOT] INDEPENDENT OF THEIR HOMOGENES;
[THEY] DO NOT ARISE FROM JUST THE BODY ALONE,
(36) BECAUSE OF THE EXTREME CONSEQUENCES. LATER CONNECTION[15]
[WILL NOT FAIL THROUGH] SOME [CAUSAL] LACK:
WE HAVE SEEN THAT THAT [EARLIER HOMOGENE] HAS THE ABILITY
TO CONNECT [WITH LATER HOMOGENES].
(37) [IT FOLLOWS FROM THE MATERIALIST THESIS THAT] ALL
[ELEMENTS] HAVE THE NATURE OF BEING SEEDS [OF LIFE]:
WHERE IS THERE A PART OF THE EARTH
THAT COULD NOT BECOME AT SOME TIME THE SOURCE
OF HEAT AND MOISTURE [BIRTH], ETC.? NOWHERE.
(38) THEREFORE, JUST AS ONE [ELEMENT] TRANSFORMS,
SO MUST THEY ALL TRANSFORM,
BECAUSE IF SENSE-FACULTIES ORIGINATE INDEPENDENTLY,
THERE IS NO SPECIFICATION [OF THE SOURCES OF LIFE].
(39) WHEN THE SENSE-FACULTIES ARE INDIVIDUALLY DAMAGED,
THE MIND IS NOT DAMAGED,
[WHEREAS] WE SEE THAT WHEN THIS [MIND] IS TRANSFORMED,
THOSE [SENSE-FACULTIES] ALSO ARE TRANSFORMED.
(40) THEREFORE, BASED ON JUST A MIND,
MIND HAS AS THE BASIS OF ITS EXISTENCE SOME [PREVIOUS MIND];
THE SENSE-FACULTIES ARE [ORIGINATED] FROM MIND,

---

15 The term I have translated as "connection," *mtshams sbyor* (*pratisandhāna*), also can refer to the process of taking rebirth, though its more general sense is of a joining together, hence connection. It must be noted that the connection discussed here is not always an immediate one: body, for instance, may "connect" (*sbyor*) with body across an interval (*mtshams*) of lives in the formless realm, or cognition with cognition across an interval of sleep or unconsciousness.

BECAUSE [MIND] IS THE CAUSE OF THE SENSE-FACULTIES.
(41) ALSO, LATER, [THE RESULT] IS SIMILAR,
BECAUSE THERE EXISTS A SIMILAR CAUSE.

A just-born ordinary being's BREATHING, clarity of the SENSE-FACULTIES AND particular inclinations of MIND are not, WHEN [that being] TAKES BIRTH, INDEPENDENT OF THEIR previous HOMOGENES, because [the being] has breathing, etc.[16] It is proven by the ascertainment of positive and negative concomitance that mental inclinations, etc., arise from accustomation with their own causes.[17] If we do not [know positive and negative concomitance], then there follows the extreme consequence that there is no cause and result, because no authority could ascertain them.[18] Also, [mental inclinations, etc.,] DO NOT ARISE FROM JUST THE elemental BODY ALONE, BECAUSE they arise from previous homogenes of mind, etc. If such is not the case, there follows the EXTREME CONSEQUENCE that all the elements are living beings, because mind arises from the elements alone.[19]

---

16 A moment of breath, sensation or thought is known in general to be preceded (directly or indirectly) by a moment of the same type: indeed, all things have as their substantial cause (*nyer len gyi rgyu, upadānahetu*) a preceding event of an appropriate or similar type. Thus, the syllogism proposed is correct, because breathing, sense-clarity and mental inclinations all are phenomena that are known to follow on homogeneous causes. Thus, even the "first" moment of breath in this life must be preceded by a breath-moment from a previous or intermediate-state existence.

17 That breath, etc., arise from homogeneous causes is demonstrated by the fact that (a) except at the time of birth, whenever there is a breath-moment, it has been observed to have been preceded by a breath-moment (positive concomitance) and (b) except at the time of death, whenever there is no breath-moment, no previous breath-moment has been observed (negative concomitance). The fact that homogeneity has obtained during life should insure that it obtains before birth and (in most cases) after death.

18 The observation of positive and negative concomtance (*rjes su 'gro ldog*) between the reason and predicate is fundamental to the inductive generalizations that form the basis of correct reasoning. Without positive and negative concomitance, neither general nor particular conclusions may be drawn about causal relations, so all causal inference would be pointless.

19 If mind arises from the elements, and mind is characteristic only of what is living or sentient, it follows that the elements must be sentient. Panpsychism, which is accepted by Jainas and some Hindus, is rejected by Buddhists, for whom there is a clear line of demarcation between sentient beings and "dead" matter (including plants), and, within the realm of sentience, between the physical body and the mind that is associated with it. This dualism, to be

It also is unacceptable [to assert] that LATER, at the time of an ordinary being's death, their sense-faculties, etc., do not make a CONNECTION with subsequent homogenes because of SOME reason such as the LACK of some part of the cause, because at that time the homogeneous causes are complete; and in the past WE HAVE SEEN THAT THAT previous homogene HAS THE ABILITY TO CONNECT with a subsequent [homogene] and that it is unacceptable that there exist any other additional cause.[20]

In summary, the mind of a just-born ordinary being follows on previous homogenes, because it is a mind.[21] The death-time mind [of] that [ordinary being] connects with a subsequent mind, because it is an attached mind.[22]

---

spelled out in greater detail below, is a hidden presupposition of this and many other Buddhist attacks on materialism.

20 If breath, etc., are observed during this life to follow in a homogeneous causal series, then not only is it legitimate to infer that the first breath of this life must have been preceded by a homogeneous cause, a breath, but also that the last breath of this life must be followed by a homogeneous effect, a breath. As rGyal tshab rje notes, the validity of these inferences is based on the fact that, apart from the observed homogeneous cause of a breath, we do not see any other additional cause. This being so, what is good enough for this life ought to be good enough for previous and subsequent lives. The assertion that there is no additional cause—even in the form of a necessary condition—seems problematic: functioning lungs, for example, seem at least as indispensable to breath as a "previous breath." Of course, if homogeneity is required, and the lungs and breath are considered to be heterogeneous, this objection cannot apply—but this heterogeneity has not yet been established, so the Buddhist may not be able to appeal to it without begging the question.

21 This syllogism follows the same form as that of which breath, etc., were subjects. The initial syllogism merely paved the way for this one, by establishing an observable example of a homogeneous causal series. Once the notion of a homogeneous causal series has been established, it can be applied to a subject somewhat less open to general inspection: the mind. Essential to this view, of course, is the notion that mind, like matter, can be logically analyzed into instantaneous, efficient events. If this is the case, then mind too must consist of a homogeneous causal series. Whether mind is, in fact, in the same ontological category as matter (what might be called "substance" [*rdzas, dravya*]), and thus analyzable "atomistically," is not a question that seems to have been explicitly raised in Indian philosophy, though as indicated above, there may be suggestions of it in some materialist analyses.

22 The qualification, "attached" mind, will be explained in greater detail below. It is necessary to specify "attached," because the mind of an arhant, who is detached, does not, according to the Sautrāntikas, connect at death with a subsequent mind, because the arhant will enter *parinirvāṇa,* which for the Sautrāntikas is a totally negative state.

[OPPONENT:] All the elements are not living beings, because those that are unable to generate sense-faculties and mind in stone, etc., are not living beings.[23]

[RGYAL TSHAB RJE:] It follows that ALL the elements HAVE THE NATURE OF BEING SEEDS of living beings, because WHERE IS THERE A PART OF THE EARTH and other elements THAT COULD NOT BECOME AT SOME TIME THE SOURCE OF HEAT AND MOISTURE-born beings, ETC.? NOWHERE.[24] Since something is a living being merely by being the cause of a living being, the same extreme consequences still remain.[25]

Alternatively, it follows that when one has filtered and left uncontaminated water, it could not be accepted that there be inside that living beings with red heads and yellow bodies *and* those born differently, with opposite characteristics, because they arise from a cause that is just the element.[26] Our system does not have the flaw of [this] unacceptable [consequence], because [we hold that] all living beings have a nature such that they have karma as their seed.[27]

---

23 The opponent is attempting to argue that the elements are divided into those that are able to generate life and those that are not. They do not, however, provide any criterion for distinguishing life-bearing from inanimate elements, and therefore leave themselves open to refutation. A modern, scientifically trained materialist is able to appeal to the notion of different levels of organization of matter, and thereby to provide a plausible—if not indisputable—explanation of how some "elements" generate life while others do not.

24 Moisture-birth is one of four different types of birth recognized in Buddhism, the others being birth from the womb, birth from an egg and miraculous birth, such as is taken by the gods. Birth from moisture is similar to the now-discredited Western concept of spontaneous generation. rGyal tshab rje is arguing against his opponent that it is impossible to divide something as fundamentally simple as the elements into life-bearing and inanimate parts: if some parts of the elements are life-bearing, then all must be.

25 What is living, rGyal tshab rje maintains, only can come from what is living. If the elements are the cause of a living being, then they must be living to begin with. It should be noted that once again rGyal tshab rje appeals implicitly to the strong Buddhist demarcation of the living/sentient from the inanimate/insentient.

26 rGyal tshab rje argues that because of the simplicity and uniformity of the elements, the elements alone are insufficient as an explanation of the variety of beings found, e.g., in a drop of water. One could not, as he puts it, find beings with red heads and yellow bodies *and* beings with yellow heads and red bodies in the same drop.

27 According to the Buddhist view, the varieties we encounter among living beings are due to non-physical karmic causes. The general philosophical problems it raises quite aside, karma in this instance is invoked as a

THEREFORE, it follows that JUST AS ONE element TRANSFORMS into a living being, SO MUST THEY ALL TRANSFORM into [living beings], BECAUSE THE SENSE-FACULTIES, etc., ORIGINATE merely from the elements, INDEPENDENTLY of their homogenes. It follows that this [reason] pervades, because if [sense-faculties, etc.] originate thus, THERE IS NO SPECIFICATION of the causes and conditions for the arising or non-arising of living beings.[28]

[OPPONENT:] Well, then, do you or do you not also assert that mind arises continually from the sense-faculties?

[RGYAL TSHAB RJE:] In general, something that is merely assistant [to a result] is not [that result's] special indispensable cause. [On the other hand,] when mind is absent, it is the basis of the absence of the sense-faculties. Mind does not have THE eye and other SENSE-FACULTIES as its special basis, because WHEN THESE ARE INDIVIDUALLY DAMAGED, by, e.g., cataracts, [MIND] IS NOT DAMAGED.[29] [On the contrary, mind] is the special basis of the eye and other sense-faculties, because it is the basis of their [recognition of] other objects, and [because] WE SEE THAT WHEN THIS [mind] IS TRANSFORMED by sorrow, etc., THOSE [sense-faculties] ALSO ARE TRANSFORMED.[30]

---

non-materialist explanation of phenomena that in the last century have come to be explained materialistically through genetic theory. Whether genetic theory can account for *all* physiological and behavioral traits is problematic. Karma, on the other hand, *can* explain all such traits, but the obscurity of its mechanisms and its ubiquity make its usefulness as an explanatory principle something less than ideal, even for those scientists well-disposed toward non-materialistic explanations. In this sense, karma poses explanatory problems not unlike those posed by the concept of God, who is equally obscure and ubiquitous.

28 This summarizes the Buddhist view: appealing to the elements alone as causes of living beings does not provide us with adequate criteria for distinguishing the living from the non-living—and the distinction must be made, as it is evident from observation that there are in the world both animate and inanimate objects.

29 rGyal tshab rje is arguing against the idea that the mind is directly dependent on the activities of the senses. He cites as proof the fact that we see many cases where a person whose sense-faculties have been impaired suffers no impairment of their higher mental functions. This observation, of course, predates the recognition that mind is associated with a particular *physical* organ, the brain—and of course it is well established that there is a concomitance between the impairment of the brain and the loss of mental functioning. Some Buddhist arguments can, of course, be recast by substituting "brain"for "body" or "senses" (as in Wangchen [1980]), but others have been rendered archaic.

30 Conversely, rGyal tshab rje argues, we see that the senses *are* affected by states

[OPPONENT:] Well, then, what *is* the special basis of mind?

[RGYAL TSHAB RJE:] There is no problem such that this mind, which is included in the present [karmic] ripening, exists without a basis, because, BASED ON JUST A previous MIND of the same type, this MIND of the present ripening HAS AS THE BASIS OF ITS EXISTENCE SOME previous intentional act.[31] THE SENSE-FACULTIES ARE ORIGINATED FROM MIND BECAUSE some previous intention that exists together with craving for a body IS THE projecting CAUSE of the eye and other SENSE-FACULTIES.[32]

ALSO, LATER, the death-time sense-faculties of an ordinary being will connect with a subsequent homogene that is similar to the preceding [homogene], BECAUSE THERE EXISTS A SIMILAR projecting CAUSE of the same type.

Disposing of [the objection that that proof] is faulty [64]

(41c) [SCRIPTURE] EXPLAINS THAT [MENTAL] COGNITION IS BASED ON THE BODY
BECAUSE A [BODY-] COGNITION ASSISTS [THE MIND].
(42) IF [YOU CLAIM THAT] THERE IS NO MIND WITHOUT SENSE-FACULTIES,
THEN THOSE [FACULTIES] ALSO DO NOT [OCCUR] WITHOUT [MIND];
[IF YOU ASSERT] THUSLY, THEY WILL BE IN MUTUAL CAUSATION,

---

of mind, as when one is, e.g., "blinded by anger." It is, in fact, possible to cite counter-instances to both of his assertions—the mind *is* often affected by what happens to the sense-faculties, and there are many cases in which one's state of mind does *not* affect the functioning of the sense-faculties—but rGyal tshab rje is concerned to establish a general point: that there is no *invariable* relation between states of the sense-faculties and states of mind.

31 A present mind-moment, which is by definition a result, is the result of some previous intentional act (*sems pa, cetanā*) that is appropriate as its cause, and that, in turn, is the result of still another previous intention, and so forth, ad infinitum. For example, a moment of desire—whatever the proximate external conditions—has as its antecedent some previous moment of desire or attachment. Even the first instance of desire after birth, e.g., for the mother's breast, must have a homogeneous cause, and therefore must be traced to instances of desire or attachment in a previous life.

32 A "projecting cause" (*'phan byed kyi rgyu*) is, in effect, an indirect substantial cause or indispensable condition. A projecting cause usually is a karmic "seed," planted at the time of a particular action, and bearing fruit with the coincidence of certain conditions. The sense-faculties have mind not as their substantial cause, but as their indispensable condition—whereas mind does not have the faculties as *its* indispensable condition.

BECAUSE THEY HAVE CAUSES THAT ARE MUTUAL.
(43) [A PERMANENT BODY] DOES NOT [HAVE MIND ORIGINATE] FROM IT SUCCESSIVELY, FOR IT IS NON-SUCCESSIVE,
[AND THUS] NOT DEPENDENT AND NOT SUBJECT TO CHANGE;
[SINCE] MINDS WILL BE [ORIGINATED] SUCCESSIVELY FROM THE BODY,
CLEARLY, THAT [BODY] ALSO HAS STAGES.
(44) IF [YOU ASSERT THAT] VARIOUS PREVIOUS MOMENTS
ARE THE CAUSES OF EACH SUBSEQUENT
MOMENT, [THEN] BECAUSE OF THAT, AT ALL TIMES
WE SHOULD SEE [BODY AND MIND] AS [MUTUALLY] CAUSATIVE.

Disposing of [the objection that] it contradicts scripture:

[OPPONENT:] Well, then, this contradicts the teacher's explanation that [mental] cognition depends on the body: "Body and mentality are mutually successive."[33]

[RGYAL TSHAB RJE:] There is no problem. There is a reason why scripture EXPLAINS THAT [mental] COGNITION IS BASED ON THE BODY, BECAUSE it is said that it means that A BODY [-cognition] is assistant to [mental] cognition; it does not mean that [the body is mind's] direct special basis.[34]

---

33 I have been unable to locate the source of this quotation, which presumably is from the *Sūtra Piṭaka*.

34 Body-cognition (*lus kyi rnam par shes pa, kāyavijñāna*) is consciousness of touch. A physical sensation of touch is followed by an awareness of that sensation. The awareness of the sensation can lead to a mental cognition, e.g., the thought, "I am being touched,"but the sensation does not lead directly to the mental cognition. Mental cognition only can be preceded by another mental cognition or by a sense-cognition; these are considered to be the "faculty"or "organ" (*dbang, indriya*) of mind. Further, even sense-cognitions do not have the sensations as their substantial cause: they arise on the basis of cognitive capacity when a sense-faculty encounters a sense-object and attention is applied. It might be noted that in Theravāda *abhidhamma,* mental cognition, like the sense-cognitions, has a material basis, the *hadayavatthu* (lit., "heart-substance"). See Karunadasa (1967) 62ff. Whatever the basis of a mental cognition, Buddhist views of the mind-body relation tend to be interactionist, maintaining that the mental and physical are alike in being causally conditioned types of phenomena, but heterogeneous enough in nature that the one cannot be the "direct special basis" (i.e., substantial cause or indispensable cooperative condition) of the other—rather, they interact indirectly. The dualism seems rather more pronounced in Dharmakīrti's system than in Theravāda, but *some* sort of dualism is fundamental to the establishment of past and future lives (after all, the body dies, while the mind, in some sense, continues), and few Buddhists will want to disavow it entirely.

Disposing [of the objection that] it contradicts reason:

[OPPONENT:] IF THERE IS NO occurrence of MIND without the sense-faculties, it must be based on the body.

[RGYAL TSHAB RJE:] It follows that THOSE sense-faculties ALSO are based on mind, because the sense-faculties do NOT occur WITHOUT mind.[35] Also, if you assert THUSLY, it follows that they will be continually in MUTUAL CAUSATION, because of their being mutually assistant. If you assert that, it follows that THEY HAVE CAUSES THAT ARE continually MUTUAL, because of that [prior] assertion.[36]

Alternatively, if [mind] is based on the body, it must be based on either (a) a permanent body or (b) an impermanent [body]. (a) is unacceptable, because it follows [from it] that the body DOES NOT have mind originating FROM IT SUCCESSIVELY, because IT IS permanent and NON-SUCCESSIVE.[37] [Mind] also IS NOT generated successively [from a permanent body] DEPENDENT on successive conditions, because [a permanent body] IS NOT SUBJECT TO CHANGE by conditions.[38]

[OPPONENT:] [Mind] arises not from a [permanent] body alone; rather, later MINDS WILL BE originated SUCCESSIVELY FROM A [permanent] BODY that is associated with a previous mind.

[RGYAL TSHAB RJE:] It follows that it is CLEARLY demonstrated that THAT body HAS earlier and later STAGES, because it is demonstrated that the body generates a later mind in dependence on a previous mind.

If you assert that, it follows that the VARIOUS PREVIOUS body-MOMENTS that are the cooperative conditions of mind ARE THE CAUSES OF

---

35 rGyal tshab rje is simply reversing the opponent's argument: if mind and the sense-faculties are seen to be concomitant, it is just as valid to argue that "the sense-faculties do not arise without mind"as that "mind does not arise without the sense-faculties."

36 The prior assertion is that mind and sense-faculties are mutually dependent. The establishment of mutual dependence is undesirable for the materialist, because such a situation goes against the unidirectional (material to mental) causality they wish to establish.

37 This argument parallels almost exactly the one used above (section III:2:C) to refute the existence of a permanent God who is the cognizer or creator of impermanent phenomena. It is, quite simply, a contradiction in terms for a non-successive entity to produce successive phenomena, whether that non-successive entity be God or a body.

38 This argument, too, is similar to one used against the idea of a permanent creator God, who cannot be said to depend on conditions, because dependence on conditions is impossible for a permanent entity.

EACH SUBSEQUENT, later MOMENT of [both] mind and body, BECAUSE OF THAT assertion and [our previous] objection. If you assert that, it follows that at death-time, just after birth, and AT ALL TIMES, WE SHOULD SEE body and mind AS mutually CAUSATIVE, because of what you have asserted.[39]

Refuting proofs of their non-existence [65]

[This is divided into:] (1) A brief demonstration [66], (2) An extensive explanation [76] and (3) Summary [147].

A brief demonstration [66]

[This is divided into:] (1) [Showing that] the reason is uncertain [67] and (2) [Showing that] the example is unproven [68].

[Showing that] the reason is uncertain [67]

> (45) IT IS NOT IN ANY WAY CONTRADICTORY THAT A FINAL MIND CONNECT TO ANOTHER MIND.

[OPPONENT:] "A death-time mind necessarily does not connect with a subsequent homogene, as, for example, a detached one's [arhant's] death-time mind [does not so connect]. An ordinary being's death-time mind also is a death-time mind [with no sequel]."[40] The non-existence of past and future lives is proven through reasons like the above-quoted. If you claim that it is not a [correct] reason because it can

---

39 rGyal tshab rje here points out that by making their assertion the opponent lays the groundwork for a proof of the Buddhist view. Since minds are seen to occur at every moment, there must be a continual pre-association of the permanent body with a mind. This is tantamount to a description of a momentary body and mind cooperating in the generation of subsequent mind. Even if a body does *cause* mind in the way described by the opponent, that body cannot possibly be permanent, as rGyal tshab rje's *reductio* argument has shown. Nothing can be said in defense of rGyal tshab rje's opponent, though it might be noted that an opponent who actually argued for the existence of a permanent body might be rather difficult to find—unless in a Buddhist caricature of another school's position. Certainly it is an argument that seems to have little contemporary relevance.

40 Restated syllogistically, the proposition is as follows: an ordinary being's death-time mind does not connect with a subsequent homogene, because it is a death-time mind, like a detached one's death-time mind. The materialist, of course, is taking death to mean cessation, which is not an adequate definition for the Buddhist. Cf. TS 1863.

be damaged by its opposite, then we reply that the opposite equally is not a [correct] reason, because it can be damaged by [our reason].[41]

[RGYAL TSHAB RJE:] It follows that such reasons are not correct reasons with inverse pervasion, because IT IS NOT IN ANY WAY CONTRADICTORY THAT an ordinary being's FINAL, death-time MIND CONNECT TO ANOTHER [subsequent] MIND of the same type.[42]

[Showing that] the example is unproven [68]

[This is divided into:] (1) [Showing that] there is no authority proving the example [69] and (2) Refuting [the idea] that there exists an authority [proving the example] [70].

[Showing that] there is no authority proving the example [69]

(45c) ALSO, THAT AN ARHANT'S MIND BE ASSERTED
NOT TO CONNECT [IS UNJUSTIFIABLE] THROUGH ANY [AUTHORITY].

It follows ALSO THAT "AN ARHANT'S final MIND" cannot reasonably BE ASSERTED as a correct accordant example, possessing both a reason and a predicate,[43] and proving an ordinary being's death-time mind NOT TO CONNECT with a subsequent homogene, because that [arhant's existence] is unproven [for the opponent] THROUGH ANY authority. If

---

41 The opponent is saying that the Buddhist can argue in their turn that "An ordinary being's death-time mind necessarily *does* connect with a subsequent homogene, because it is a death-time mind," but that such an argument can be countered by a reassertion of the opponent's syllogism. Such trading of syllogisms, like a stalemate in chess, could go on indefinitely, as long as there remained the fundamental disagreement over the meaning of "death-time mind."

42 rGyal tshab rje counters that the Buddhist does *not* assert the opposite of the opponent's syllogism, because the Buddhist will not use "death-time mind" as a reason proving that an ordinary being's mind continues, since—for the (Sautrāntika) Buddhist—not all death-time minds connect to a subsequent homogene (an arhant's does not). The reason the Buddhist uses is, of course, "attached mind." Because there is, nevertheless, no inherent contradiction in the idea of a death-time mind's connection with a subsequent mind, the opponent's reason is uncertain. "Inverse pervasion" refers to positive and negative concomitance, in the absence of which a reason is uncertain.

43 An accordant, or appropriate, example (*mthun dpe*) must—like the reason itself—be applicable to both the subject and predicate of a syllogism, and must be accepted by both proponent and opponent. The example of an arhant fulfills neither of these criteria, as (a) it is not accepted by the opponent and (b) from the Buddhist point of view, it is not applicable to the subject, since an arhant is not an ordinary being.

that last [reason] is unproven, then any effort to refute [our assertion of the existence of liberated beings] is contradictory.[44]

[OPPONENT:] Now[45] in your system, you either (a) accept or (b) do not accept that there is a final mind of an arhant. If (a), then [the syllogism], "The death-time mind of an ordinary being connects with a subsequent mind because it is a mind," has an uncertain reason.[46] (b) is unreasonable, because it contradicts what is clearly stated in the *Pramāṇaviniścaya*.

[RGYAL TSHAB RJE:] There is no problem. In our system it is not the case that we do not accept that there is a final mind of an arhant. If the Buddhist writings of the ācāryas Devendrabuddhi and Ravigupta are authoritative, then it is necessary to accept that the death-time mind of an ordinary being connects with a subsequent homogene. If those writings are not authoritative, then, since the final mind of an arhant also is unproven, it is unsuitable as an accordant example.[47]

It is not the case that in our system we do not accept that there is a final mind of an arhant. When the *Pramāṇaviniścaya* sets forth the definition of "entitylessness that is void of efficiency," it expresses [the idea] that an arhant's final mind is an uncertain [example]. [An arhant's final mind] is final because it is not the substantial cause of any other moment that is counted as a sentient-being moment. It is not the case that it does not produce even the slightest result, because

---

44 If the opponent insists that the arhant is an appropriate example, they must deny that the arhant's existence is unproven for them. If they deny that it is unproven, they must accept that it is proven, in which case they accept the existence of an arhant, and cannot any longer seriously object to the Buddhist concept of a liberated being. Granted, the existence of a liberated being is not the point at issue here, but the opponent's acceptance of one aspect of the Buddhist world-view would—assuming its essential coherence—tend to make acceptance of other aspects of it more likely. In this case, the concept of an arhant cannot be understood without recourse to a concept of saṃsāra from which liberation is possible, and saṃsāra entails past and future lives.

45 The remainder of this section is taken up with a digressive discussion of various problems involved in the acceptance of the finality of an arhant's death-time mind, a topic not covered by Dharmakīrti.

46 The reason, as already noted, is uncertain because not all minds connect with a subsequent mind, the death-time mind of an arhant being the exception.

47 One must, in other words, either take or leave Buddhist writings. If one accepts them, one must accept both the existence of arhants and the continuation after death of an ordinary being's mind. If one rejects them, one is able to deny future lives, but one cannot then cite the arhant as an example supporting that denial.

it is explained as assisting in [the production of] the gnosis of an omniscient one, etc.[48] [The passage says:] "Since it is not the substantial cause of a mind that is counted as a sentient being, it is clear [why] it is explained that it does not connect with a subsequent homogene."[49]

Ācārya Prajñākaragupta explains that "In our system of tenets, it is shown only that an arhant's final mind contradicts [the idea of] connection [with a subsequent homogene]; not all death-time minds are [thus contradictory]."[50]

Ravigupta [explains that] "On the basis of the acceptance of external objects, one explains the termination of the physical and the mental as being like the extinction of a lamp. Since we do not accept [external objects, we assert that] minds purified of defilement will connect only with subsequent homogenes."[51]

All those commentators [adhere to] the system that explains that there are three final vehicles, and if one asserts that these passages definitely show that there is one final vehicle, then [one's] assertion shows no familiarity with tenet-systems.[52]

---

48 An arhant's final mind does not produce a subsequent homogeneous result, but it does have effects: it is, for example, perceived by the mind of an omniscient one, and therefore assists in the generation of a mind—though obviously not as a substantial cause or indispensable condition. It cannot, therefore, serve as an appropriate example of entitylessness that is void of efficiency, because it *does* have a result of some type.

49 PVn, second section, pp. 108-116.

50 PVA 28/2-4. Thus, an arhant's final mind scarcely is suitable proof that *no* minds connect with subsequent homogenes at death; it is at best merely one exception to a general rule.

51 PVVṛ 138/1-3. If one accepts the reality of external objects, it is possible to describe an arhant's final mind as being like a lamp that goes out when its fuel (karma and the defilements) is exhausted. Ravigupta, as a Yogācāra, does not accept external objects, and so does not apply that example. Nor, for that matter, does he accept an arhant's final mind: he believes that, after death, an arhant's mind continues, endlessly purified of defilement, never taking birth again, but not ceasing, either.

52 The belief in "three final vehicles"is characteristic of some Yogācāras. It entails the assumption that each of the three spiritual goals—śrāvakahood, pratyekabuddhahood (which two together comprise arhantship) and buddhahood—is an end in itself. According to this doctrine, neither a śrāvaka nor a pratyekabuddha ever will become a buddha. The belief in "one final vehicle" (*ekayānā*) is upheld by most Mādhyamikas, of whom rGyal tshab rje is of course one. The one final vehicle is the *bodhisattvayāna*, whose end, full buddhahood, is the destiny of all sentient beings. Even śrāvakas and pratyekabuddhas eventually will become buddhas, so their minds neither are extin-

[OPPONENT:] Well, then, how can you avoid [the objection] that the reason proving a future life is uncertain?[53]

[RGYAL TSHAB RJE:] As it says in the *Tattvasaṃgrahapañjikā* of Ācārya Kamalaśīla, "Any attached mind is able to generate another mind that is its substantial result, [because,] just like any previous attached mind, the death-time mind of an ordinary being is an attached mind."This statement [sets forth] a reason [based on] synonymy.[54]

Refuting [the idea] that there exists an authority [proving the example] [70]

[This is divided into:] (1) The unacceptability of proof through scripture [71] and (2) The unacceptability of proof through reasoning [72].

---

guished at death (as many Hīnayānists maintain) nor do they simply generate homogenes ad infinitum (as three-final-vehicle proponents insist). Their minds do continue, and for a very long time remain "homogeneously" entranced by the bliss of liberation, but sooner or later they will be stimulated by a fully enlightened buddha to rouse themselves and complete the bodhisattva path that alone conduces to full enlightenment. Of the three positions reflected here, it seems most likely (though the evidence is not conclusive) that Dharmakīrti represents the first (that an arhant's death-time mind is final), Ravigupta (and the other commentators cited) the second (three endless, independent vehicles) and rGyal tshab rje the third (one final vehicle).

53 The objection has been raised that the existence of a future life is uncertain when one sets forth the syllogism, "The death-time mind of an ordinary being connects to a subsequent homogene because it is a mind,"for not all minds connect to a subsequent homogene—the arhant's, again, being the counterexample.

54 An attached mind (*chags dang bcas pa'i sems*) is not necessarily a mind that is specifically attached to a particular object; it is, rather, any mind in the continuum of a being who has not yet eradicated attachment. Thus, even a virtuous mind in the continuum of an ordinary being falls under the general rubric of "attached mind." A "reason based on synonymy,"or, more literally, own-nature (*rang bzhin gyi rtags, svabhāvahetu;* see above, p. 104) might be restated: "The death-time mind of an ordinary being is able to generate another mind that is its substantial result, because it is an attached mind."This syllogism is satisfactory for Buddhists, and, by excluding the troublesome example of the arhant, helps resolve the problems raised by the uncertainty of the reason, "because it is a mind."It is not, however, self-evident to an opponent that an attached mind is synonymous with the production of a subsequent homogene, for they have yet to be convinced that mind is its own substantial cause, nor do they accept the Buddhist division of minds into those that continue (those of ordinary beings) and those that do not (those of arhants).

The unacceptability of proof through scripture [71]

(46) WHAT, ARE YOU A FOLLOWER OF THE TENET-SYSTEM
[WHOSE] SUBJECT-MATTER IS [FOR YOU] UNPROVEN BY AUTHORITY?

[OPPONENT:] A faultless one's death-time mind is established [and therefore is an appropriate example] because it is explained in your own scriptures.

[RGYAL TSHAB RJE:] WHAT, ARE YOU A FOLLOWER OF THE Buddhist TENET-SYSTEM? It follows that [this objection] is unsuitable for proving [the appropriateness of the example], because you assert (a) that that tenet-system has a SUBJECT-MATTER UNPROVEN BY AUTHORITY and (b) that Buddhist scriptures are an object of refutation [for you].[55]

The unacceptability of proof through reasoning [72]

[This is divided into:] (1) Refuting the reason [73], (2) Disposing of objections [74] and (3) Identifying the special cause indispensable to the result [75].

Refuting the reason [73]

(46c) IF [YOU CLAIM THAT AN ARHANT'S FINAL MIND DOES NOT CONNECT] BECAUSE IT IS SEPARATED FROM ITS CAUSES,
[THEN] WHY DON'T YOU EXPRESS PRECISELY THAT [AS PROOF] IN THIS INSTANCE, [OF AN ORDINARY BEING]?
(47) MENTAL COGNITION DOES NOT [ARISE] FROM [THE BODY] TOGETHER WITH THE SENSE-FACULTIES,
BECAUSE [THEN THE MIND] WOULD APPREHEND JUST AS THAT [SENSE-] COGNITION [DOES].
IT ALSO IS NOT THE THE CASE THAT [MIND ARISES] FROM ALL [THE SENSE-FACULTIES,]
BECAUSE THEY HAVE DIFFERING ABILITIES FOR GENERATING COGNITIONS.
(48) [MIND ALSO DOES] NOT [ARISE] OTHERWISE, [E.G., FROM A BODY WITHOUT SENSE-FACULTIES], BECAUSE THAT IS MINDLESS.

[OPPONENT:] An arhant's death-time mind does not connect with a [subsequent] homegene, BECAUSE IT IS SEPARATED FROM breathing, the sense-faculties, etc., which are ITS CAUSES.

---

55 This is a final, clear assertion of the contradiction involved when the opponent cites the arhant as an example of non-continuing minds: not only is the opponent implicitly accepting the reality of the arhant, but they are quoting Buddhist scriptures in order to bolster their case!

[RGYAL TSHAB RJE:] WHY DON'T YOU EXPRESS PRECISELY THAT [reason] as proof IN THIS INSTANCE that an *ordinary being's* death-time mind does not connect [with a subsequent homogene]? It follows that it is reasonable to do so, because you want to assert this reason [in] either this or the previous [syllogism], and the reason is uncertain [in the] previous [syllogism].[56]

Showing that if [the latter][57] *is asserted, [the reason] is unproven:*

If the visual and other sense-faculties are the special indispensable causes of mind, they cannot be either the substantial cause or the principal condition. [That they are] the former will be refuted below. If they are the principal condition, it follows that MENTAL COGNITION DOES NOT arise FROM a principal condition that is the body TOGETHER WITH THE SENSE-FACULTIES, BECAUSE if such were the case, [the mind] WOULD clearly APPREHEND form just as [THAT] visual COGNITION apprehends a form.[58]

IT ALSO necessarily IS NOT THE CASE THAT [mind] is ascertained to arise FROM a principal condition that is the collection of ALL the sense-faculties, BECAUSE the sense-faculties HAVE DIFFERING ABILITIES, which are the principal conditions FOR GENERATING COGNITIONS of their respective objects. The word "also" means that a [further] reason [must be applied] to the foregoing thesis, viz., "because it would follow that if even one sense-faculty were not present, [mind] could not arise."[59]

---

56 rGyal tshab rje's tone is sarcastic here. The opponent continues to speak of an arhant's death-time mind, when what they really are seeking to prove is the non-continuation of an ordinary being's mind. Since it is uncertain that separation from breathing, etc., necessarily entails the mind's inability to connect with a subsequent homogene, rGyal tshab rje suggests that the opponent try to apply "separation from breathing, etc.," to a syllogism that has "an ordinary being's death-time mind" as its subject.

57 The "latter" syllogism is the one proposed for his opponent by rGyal tshab rje: "The death-time mind of an ordinary being does not connect with a subsequent homogene, because it is separated from breathing, the sense-faculties, etc., which are its causes."

58 Mind cannot have as a principal condition (*bdag rkyen, adhipatipratyaya*) the body together with the sense-faculties, because then mental cognition would have to cognize as sense-cognition does, or vice versa, in which case the mental and the sensory are being (according to the Buddhist, at least) illegitimately conflated.

59 There are two problems, then, inherent in claiming that the collection of sense-faculties is the principal condition of mind: (a) the individual functions of the various faculties would be eliminated and (b) if even one member of the

Since mind clearly apprehends all six [types of] objects, if it is generated by [just] one sense-faculty, the other sense-faculties are pointless.

Mind also does NOT arise OTHERWISE, with a dead body as its principal condition, BECAUSE the substantial cause of that, [the corpse,] IS MINDLESS.[60]

Disposing of objections [74]

(48b) [THE MIND AND SENSES] CO-EXIST, BECAUSE [THEY ARISE] FROM A SINGLE CAUSE,
AS DO THE SENSES, AND FORM AND TASTE;
[MIND] IS TRANSFORMED THROUGH OBJECTS.

[OPPONENT:] Well, then, what about the co-existence [of mind and the sense-faculties]?[61]

[RGYAL TSHAB RJE:] It is suitable that the sense-faculties and mind of a single collection, which are included in the [present karmic] ripening, CO-EXIST, BECAUSE they arise from A SINGLE CAUSE, previous karma. For example, it is just AS THE five SENSES also co-exist without being [related] as basis and based, AND as do FORM AND TASTE.[62]

---

collection, e.g., the visual faculty, were absent, the mind could not arise—a suggestion that is patently absurd.

60 These last two paragraphs dispose of two other possible materialist options, only the latter of which is covered by Dharmakīrti: (a) mind cannot be generated with just one sense-faculty as its principal condition, because in that case—given that mind clearly cognizes multiple types of object—*one* sense-faculty would suffice for the mind's cognition of *any* object, and the other four sense-faculties would be unnecessary and (b) some other possibility, such as mind's generation from a non-living body, is impossible, because there clearly is no mind in a corpse.

61 How, the opponent wants to know, can we account for the co-existence of the mind and sense-faculties in the same individual if they are not related as basis and based?

62 rGyal tshab rje points out that different qualities can inhere in a whole without having an essential causal relation, as, e.g., the whiteness (or roughness) and the sweetness of sugar. The sense-faculties can act as an *immediately-preceding* condition (*de ma thag rkyen, samanantarapratyaya*), but they cannot be mind's *principal* condition, because a principal condition must be a directly efficient cause, and mind is generated not directly from the sense-faculties, but from either a previous mind or from sense-cognitions—which latter have the sense-faculties as their principal conditions. See Kalupahana (1976) 165-66. rGyal tshab rje explains the co-existence of different qualities in the same whole as being due to their derivation from a common seed. In the case of an

[OPPONENT:] Because the mind is also sometimes transformed by poison, etc., the body is its principal condition.

[RGYAL TSHAB RJE:] The mind is not transformed through the body as a principal condition, because IT IS TRANSFORMED merely THROUGH having made those OBJECTS [poison, etc.,] its intentional objects.[63]

Identifying the special cause indispensable to the result [75]

(49) SOMETHING, BY BEING ASSISTANT
[WHEN THE RESULT] ALWAYS SUCCEEDS IT,
IS [THAT RESULT'S] CAUSE. THEREFORE [ONE SŪTRA] EXPLAINS
[USING] THE SEVENTH CASE, AND [ANOTHER, USING THE FIFTH,] SAYS:
"BECAUSE [X] HAS ARISEN, [Y ARISES]."
(50) GRANTED, [THE BODY] SOMETIMES
IS ASSISTANT TO THE MINDSTREAM,
[BUT IT DOES] NOT [FOLLOW] MERELY FROM THAT [BODY'S ABSENCE] THAT [MIND] WILL BE ABSENT,
AS FIRE, ETC., ARE [ASSISTANT] TO A POT, [BUT DO NOT, BY THEIR REMOVAL, DESTROY THE POT].

[OPPONENT:] What is a special indispensable cause?

[RGYAL TSHAB RJE:] Lamp-light has the lamp as its special indispensible cause, because SOMETHING [e.g.,] a lamp,merely BY BEING replaced by [lamp-light] is directly ASSISTANT to that [lamp-light]. This follows, BECAUSE [lamp-light] ALWAYS SUCCEEDS ITs direct substantial CAUSE, the lamp.[64]

---

oak tree, all of its qualities are inherent in the acorn; in the case of the mind and sense-faculties, both are inherent in a particular karmic seed sown sometime in the past. A materialist might agree with the principle, but argue that the co-existence of mind and the sense-faculties is inherent in the genetic coding in the combined sperm and egg at the moment of conception. This position is in some ways the inverse of the Buddhist view, which assumes that co-existence stems from an essentially *mental* circumstance, an intentional act, that is the actual karmic seed.

63 The opponent is implying (correctly) that a principal condition can be defined as that condition whose alteration invariably effects the alteration of the result, and that since the mind invariably is affected by poison in a body, the body must be mind's principal condition. rGyal tshab rje's reply is that it is the *cognition* of poison, not the poison itself that alters the mind: poison effects internal sensations, which are the objects of a body-cognition, which then can be cognized conceptually by a mental cognition. Thus, the physical affects the mental only indirectly.

64 A special indispensable cause (*ldog byed gyi rgyu khyad par can*)—whether

THEREFORE, there is a reason why [one] sūtra EXPLAINS [by] saying, "When *x* exists, *y* occurs," [using] THE SEVENTH, locative CASE, and [why another sūtra] says, "BECAUSE *x* HAS ARISEN, *y* arises," [using] the fifth, ablative case; it is because it is explained [thus] so that we may know: "The special indispensable cause is like *x*."[65]

Therefore, when there exists an attached mind, there necessarily definitely will occur a subsequent homogene. If one proves that this applies to the death-time mind of an ordinary being, one has definitely proved a future life, and one cannot by any possible inference entertain the objection that the existence of a future life is not definitely proved.[66]

GRANTED, the body SOMETIMES acts as, or IS, ASSISTANT TO THE MIND-STREAM. It does NOT follow, MERELY FROM THAT, THAT by virtue of the absence of body, mind WILL BE ABSENT, because [one entity] cannot have as its special indispensable cause [an entity] substantially different from it. For example, it is just AS FIRE, ETC., ARE assistant TO A clay POT, etc., [when it is being made, but do not, by their removal, entail the removal of the pot].[67]

---

taken as a substantial cause or principal condition— is a factor, *x*, such that its absence necessitates the absence of result *y*. The *khyad par can* here is a bit ambiguous: I have translated it as "special,"but it also connotes change or transformation, hence a cause a change in which will entail a change in the result. A moment of lamp-light invariably follows a moment of lamp, and should there be no lamp, there can be no lamp-light. Alternatively, a change in the lamp entails a change in the lamp-light. Notice that the light *succeeds* the lamp that is its cause. It is the Sautrāntika view that an effect only can arise when the cause has ceased to function. Thus, moments of lamp and lamp-light may exist simultaneously, but they cannot, in that instant, have a causal relationship. A particular moment of lamp-light will have as its cause the previous moment of the lamp.

65 The two unidentified "sūtra" passages cited are standard general formulations of the law of dependent origination (*pratītya samutpāda*), which might more fully be formulated: if *x*, then *y*; therefore, if non-*x*, then non-*y*.

66 In other words, an attached mind has as its special indispensable cause a previous attached mind; and if attached mind leads to attached mind in this life, then there is no reason why the last attached mind of this life should not connect to an attached mind in a subsequent life, since no other indispensable condition has been or can be proved by the opponent.

67 Fire assists an earthen pot by baking it to completion. When the pot is complete, the fire no longer is present. Similarly, the argument runs, body assists mind, but is not indispensable to it, and mind can continue to exist when the body has ceased to function. Just as fire cannot be the indispensable cause of a pot because it is substantially different from it, so body cannot be the indis-

An extensive explanation [76]

[This is divided into:] (1) Refuting [the idea] that the body is the special basis of mind [77] and (2) Disposing of [the attempt to] damage our refutation [139].

Refuting [the idea] that the body is the special basis[68] *of mind [77]*

[This is divided into:] (1) Refutation through an analysis of the way in which the body acts as the basis of mind [78] and (2) Refutation through an analysis of the essential aspect of the body that acts as the basis [of mind] [107].

Refutation through an analysis of the way in which the body acts as the basis of mind [78]

[This is divided into:] (1) Refuting [the idea] that it acts as the substantial cause [79] and (2) Refuting [the idea] that it is the special cooperative condition [97].

B. WHY THE BODY IS NOT MIND'S SUBSTANTIAL CAUSE

Refuting [the idea] that it acts as the substantial cause [79]

[This is divided into:] (1) Refutation through an analysis of their [alleged] successive [existence] [80] and (2) Refutation through an analysis of their [alleged] simultaneous [existence] [90].

---

pensable cause of mind, because it is substantially different from it. It is problematic whether the analogy is entirely apt, for not only could it be argued that the fire *is* indispensable to the *completion* of the pot—although substantially different from it—but also that mind and body are different in a different way than fire and a pot: fire and a pot are both material, so their interaction is not problematic, whereas mind and body are substantially different in a much more fundamental sense, and the assertion of their interaction raises the familiar problem of how something immaterial can interact with something material. See Hofstadter and Dennett (1981) 388. I do not, of course, mean to imply that materialism is without its own severe problems; I merely wish to indicate a possible discrepancy here between the example and its exemplar.

68 The special basis (*rten khyad par can*) is similar to the principal condition and special indispensable cause (discussed above) and comprises both the substantial cause and the special cooperative condition (both of which will be discussed in greater detail below).

Refutation through an analysis of their [alleged] successive [existence] [80]

[This is divided into:] (1) Setting forth the consequences [81], (2) Refuting the reply to that [82] and (3) Explaining the definition of substantial cause [87].

Setting forth the consequences [81]

(51) IT FOLLOWS THAT IN A [DEAD] BODY, MIND
WILL NOT BE ABSENT, SINCE [ITS CAUSE, THE BODY] REMAINS.

IT FOLLOWS THAT IN A dead BODY, MIND WILL NOT BE ABSENT, because the body, the substantial cause [of mind] REMAINS complete.[69]

Refuting the reply to that [82]

[This is divided into:] (1) Refuting the reply that the appropriate conditions are not complete [83] and (2) Refuting the reply that there is destruction by a contradictory condition [84].

Refuting the reply that the appropriate conditions are not complete [83]

(51c) BREATHING [ORIGINATES] FROM [MIND, AND] NOT [VICE VERSA],
BECAUSE [BREATH] EXISTS BY [VIRTUE OF] THE EXISTENCE OF THAT [MIND], AND [BECAUSE] IT IS UNDER THE POWER OF THAT;
(52) EXHALATIONS AND INHALATIONS OF BREATH
CANNOT EXIST THROUGH ANY [CAUSE] EXCEPT EXERTION.
[IF THEY DID,] THEN THE INCREASE AND DECREASE OF [MIND]
WOULD BE OBTAINED THROUGH THE INCREASE AND DECREASE OF THOSE [BREATHS].
(53) IT FOLLOWS EQUALLY THAT THOSE [BREATHS] ARE ALSO [PRESENT] IN THAT [DEAD BODY];
[THAT CONSEQUENCE DOES] NOT [FOLLOW] EQUALLY IF MIND IS THE CAUSE [OF MIND],
BECAUSE IT IS ASSERTED THAT OTHER [KARMAS] PROJECTING
THE [CO-]EXISTENCE [OF BODY AND MIND] ARE THE CAUSES [OF CO-EXISTENCE].

[OPPONENT:] Although body, the substantial cause of mind, exists [in the case of a dead body], since such conditions as breath are absent, it is not the case that [the appropriate conditions] are not absent

---

69 The absurd consequence of maintaining that body is the mind's substantial cause here is stated first; the definitions that set the stage for this absurdity will follow.

[from a dead body], just as [the appropriate conditions are absent] in a fainting spell.[70]

[RGYAL TSHAB RJE:] It follows that the BREATHING that originates FROM THAT mind is NOT the special principal condition of mind, BECAUSE breath EXISTS BY virtue of THE EXISTENCE OF THAT mind, and [because] its strength and weakness IS UNDER THE other-POWER of [mind's] efforts at movement.

This follows, because a person's EXHALATIONS AND INHALATIONS OF BREATH originate preceded by [mental] exertion, and it CANNOT be accepted that they EXIST having originated THROUGH ANY cause EXCEPT that [mental exertion].[71]

[OPPONENT:] It follows that during deep sleep there is no breathing, because there is no mental effort.

[RGYAL TSHAB RJE:] There is not even the slightest problem. Although there *is* breathing during present deep sleep, it necessarily is projected by the previous mental intention known as karma.[72] [It is accepted that] if there is smoke it necessarily is preceded by fuel; but why should it follow that at the time when smoke exists fuel must necessarily exist there?[73]

---

70 As so often in rGyal tshab rje, the double negatives here can be a bit bewildering. The opponent is simply arguing that a dead body cannot be conscious because the appropriate conditions of mind, e.g., breathing, are absent, just as they are in a fainting spell. (What, then, would differentiate a fainting spell from death is not indicated.)

71 If rGyal tshab rje is arguing that individual breaths are dependent on conscious individual mental exertions, e.g., "I will breathe, I will breathe. . .,"then it is an odd argument, indeed. I suspect that he actually is making the more general point that breathing is projected by previous mental karma. Incidentally, a modern materialist might argue that breathing is, of course, a result of the autonomic nervous system, but a Buddhist might reply that although there is a relationship, the order of priority has not been established: the nervous system, after all, might necessitate "mind"for its functioning, rather than the other way around.

72 Breathing is possible during deep sleep precisely *because* breathing in general is projected by previous mental karma. Conscious thought is *not* necessary for breathing to occur. If each breath necessitated an immediately preceding thought, there could *not* be breathing during deep sleep, but since such immediacy is not the nature of the relation between mind and breath, there is no problem.

73 rGyal tshab rje here makes the general point—in support of his specific observations on breathing—that a cause and effect need not—indeed, they *cannot* co-exist: a cause always precedes an effect; when the cause is present, the effect has not yet arisen, and when the effect has arisen, the cause is no longer

It would follow [from your previous assertion] that THE INCREASE AND DECREASE of mind WOULD BE OBTAINED THROUGH THE INCREASE AND DECREASE OF THOSE breaths, because [breaths] are the special principal condition of [mind].[74] Further, IT FOLLOWS EQUALLY [from your assertion] THAT THOSE breaths ARE ALSO not absent IN THAT dead body, because the substantial cause [of breath], the body, remains complete. Therefore, the consequence remains that since the [appropriate] conditions are present, mind is not absent [from a dead body].[75]

[OPPONENT:] Well, then, it follows that according to your position, too, mind is not absent from a dead body, because of the existence of [mind's] substantial cause, the mind.

[RGYAL TSHAB RJE:] It does NOT follow that it follows EQUALLY that IF MIND IS THE CAUSE of mind, then [mind] is not absent from a dead body, since BECAUSE of [our position] IT IS ASSERTED THAT OTHER karmas projecting the co-EXISTENCE of body and mind ARE THE CAUSES of the co-existence of the two.[76]

Refuting the reply that there is destruction by a contradictory condition [84]

[This is divided into:] (1) Setting forth the consequences [85] and (2) Refuting the reply to that [86].

---

present. Therefore, it is not necessary that when an effect, breathing, is observed, its cause, mind, still be present. Hence, breathing during deep sleep is not impossible.

74 This involves the absurdity that mind would fluctuate exactly as breathing does. There may be some connection between the two, but from the Buddhist point of view, the causal direction is the opposite of that posited by the materialist: it is mind that is the special principal condition of breathing.

75 Quite simply, if breath is the substantial cause of mind, and the body is the substantial cause of breath, then the presence of the body in the case of a corpse should necessitate the presence of breath, and the presence of breath should necessitate the presence of mind. rGyal tshab rje has added numerous glosses to the original Tibetan, which simply says that the consequences (*thal ba*) would be the same (*mtshungs*) with regard to those (*de dag*), i.e., breathing and mind.

76 The opponent argues that if mind's presence can be projected by previous karma, it can be present in a dead body. rGyal tshab rje replies that this is not the case, because the karma that projects the co-existence of mind and body ceases to function at the time of death.

Setting forth the consequences [85]

(54) IF [YOU ASSERT THAT] JUST AS A STICK-PILE, ETC. [CANNOT IGNITE IF IT IS CHARMED BY MANTRAS],
SINCE THERE ARE DEFECTS [IN IT], A [DEAD] BODY IS INCOMPATIBLE [WITH MIND], IT HAS NO CAUSE [OF MIND IN IT],
[WE REPLY THAT A BODY] WILL BE REVIVED
AT DEATH-TIME, [SINCE] THE DEFECTS [ALSO] DETERIORATE.

[OPPONENT:] You cannot apply those consequences: JUST AS fire cannot ignite A STICK-PILE, ETC., charmed by mantras, so, SINCE THERE ARE DEFECTS [of] wind, bile [and phlegm],[77] a dead BODY, which IS INCOMPATIBLE with the persistence of mind, HAS NO CAUSE of mind [in it]; you also accept that a result cannot be generated when it is destroyed by a contradictory condition.[78]

[RGYAL TSHAB RJE:] It follows that a body WILL BE REVIVED AT DEATH-TIME, because its substantial cause, the body, remains, and the contradictory conditions, the defects [of the humors], are in equal part non-existent. Alternatively, one can add as a reason to the prior consequence, "because THE DEFECTS DETERIORATE [in a dead body]."[79]

---

77 Wind, bile and phlegm are the three "humors" recognized in Indian and Tibetan medicine. Good health is said to depend upon a proper balance among them, and disease to result from their imbalance. Since the term for "humor" (*nyes pa, doṣa*) is the same as for "defect," or "fault," it sometimes is ambiguous which is intended. Here, "defect" seems to accord better with the sense of the passage.

78 Although rGyal tshab rje will refute this objection, the general point seems well taken: it is not simply the body that is the indispensable condition of mind; it is the body's proper functioning, represented by a proper balance among the humors. A modern materialist might argue in the same vein that mind has as its indispensable condition a *properly functioning* brain.

79 rGyal tshab rje here is raising the point that, in effect, death is the end of disease. If disease—in this case, a severe imbalance among the humors—is said to cause death, then when the result, death, exists, the cause must be absent, so disease will, as it were, "deteriorate" in a dead body. Though technically correct, this reply seems a bit sophistic, playing as it does with definitions of cause and effect. There is nothing to indicate that the humors are either balanced or unbalanced in a dead body; indeed, the concept of humors only is relevant to a living body, as is the concept of disease. The fact that death "eliminates" disease or imbalances among the humors does not mean that "health" or a balance among the humors has been restored, because what has been eliminated is only the applicability of a concept.

Refuting the reply to that [86]

(55) IF YOU SAY THAT JUST AS THE ABSENCE
OF FIRE [DOES NOT ENTAIL] THE ABSENCE OF THE TRANSFORMATION OF WOOD [INTO ASH],
[SO THE ABSENCE OF THE DEFECTS IN A DEAD BODY] DOES NOT [ENTAIL] THE ABSENCE OF [THE TRANSFORMATION OF SICKNESS], THAT [DEATH],
[WE REPLY THAT] IT IS NOT [SO], BECAUSE THERE IS [A POINT TO] APPLYING CURES.
(56) [THIS IS SO,] BECAUSE, AS [FIRE AFFECTS] WOOD, SOME [AGENTS]
GENERATE IRREVERSIBLE TRANSFORMATIONS;
AND, AS [THAT WROUGHT ON] GOLD BY FIRE,
SOME [TRANSFORMATIONS] ARE REVERSIBLE.
(57) THE FORMER, EVEN IF SMALL, CANNOT BE REVERSED,
[WHEREAS] SOME TRANSFORMATION SUITABLE TO BE REVERSED
WILL BE REVERSED,
LIKE [THE LIQUEFACTION OF] SOLID GOLD.
(58) [A SICKNESS] SAID NOT CURABLE IN THE SLIGHTEST
[IS THUS] BECAUSE PREPARATIONS ARE DIFFICULT TO ACQUIRE
OR [BECAUSE OF] THE EXHAUSTION OF THE LIFE-SPAN; IF DEFECTS ALONE [ARE THE CAUSE OF DEATH],
THERE IS NO INCURABLE [SICKNESS].
(59) HOW [THEN IS IT THAT A DEAD BODY] WILL NOT BE REVIVED?
[ON YOUR VIEW, IT WILL BE,] SINCE THE DEADLY POISON, ETC., WHICH ARE THE CAUSE,
OF THE TRANSFORMATION, CAN BE REMOVED [THROUGH MANTRAS] OR
THROUGH CUTTING [THE WOUND] OF THAT [PERSON] WHO HAS BEEN BITTEN.[80]

[OPPONENT:] JUST AS THE ABSENCE OF FIRE does not [entail] THE ABSENCE OF THE TRANSFORMATION OF WOOD [i.e., ash] that is generated by it, so the absence of the cause transformed by sickness, i.e., the defects that are the contradictory conditions, DOES NOT [entail] THE ABSENCE OF the great transformation of sickness, THAT death.[81]

---

80 The Sanskrit of the last line (= last part of 59a) here (*daṃsac chedato 'pi vā*) differs somewhat from the Tibetan, and may be taken (as by Nagatomi [1957] 77) to mean that the teeth (of the snake, which contain poison) can be extracted, or cut out.

81 The opponent argues that a dead body cannot be revived because the body's passage from sickness to death is an irreversible transformation, like the burning of wood: even when the fire that burned the wood is removed, the ash that

[RGYAL TSHAB RJE:] It follows that IT IS NOT unsuitable that the transformation of sickness [death] be absent, BECAUSE THERE IS a point to APPLYING CURES to sickness.

It follows that the transformation of wood [ash] wrought by fire and the transformation of sickness [death] are not equivalent examples, BECAUSE when, AS [in the example of the transformation] of WOOD wrought by fire, it is reasonable [to assert] that SOME transforming agents GENERATE IRREVERSIBLE TRANSFORMATIONS, then it is impossible to reverse even a small transformation; and because when, AS [in the example of the transformation] of GOLD BY FIRE, it is reasonable [to assert] that SOME [transforming agents generate] a REVERSIBLE [transformation], then it is reasonable [to assert] that even a great transformation is reversible.

If wood is an equivalent [example], then it is impossible that the slightest transformation wrought by a disease be reversible. It follows that THE FORMER transformation, EVEN IF SMALL, CANNOT BE REVERSED, because if wood has even just been blackened, it cannot turn back into wood. It is reasonable [to assert] that SOME TRANSFORMATION, SUITABLE TO BE REVERSED, even if great, WILL BE REVERSED, because SOLID GOLD, even if it has been liquefied, can be turned back into a solid.[82]

[OPPONENT:] Well, then, it follows that the great transformation of sickness [death] necessarily is reversible, because [even] a small transformation is reversible. If you assert that, it contradicts the explanation [to the effect that] there are incurable sicknesses.[83]

[RGYAL TSHAB RJE:] A sickness SAID NOT CURABLE IN THE SLIGHTEST is not explained to be thus by reason of its incurability, but BECAUSE the medicinal PREPARATIONS and doctor ARE DIFFICULT TO ACQUIRE, OR because it is explained to be thus by force OF THE [karmic] EXHAUSTION OF THE LIFE-SPAN of the sick person.[84] IF the cause of death is a sickness

---

is left does not revert to wood.

82 rGyal tshab rje rightly points out the subtlety of the matter and the inadequacy of the opponent's example. If disease is said to be an irreversible process, like the blackening of wood, then no disease should be curable, which manifestly is not the case. The appropriate example for disease, rGyal tshab rje points out, is that of a reversible transformation, like that of solid gold into liquid. Note that the opponent has set themselves up for rebuttal here by describing death as the transformation of disease, thereby pairing a reversible condition with an irreversible one.

83 The opponent counters with the contention that, if disease is said to be a reversible transformation, then any disease must be curable, so there cannot be any incurable diseases, a patent absurdity.

84 The curability or incurability of a disease, rGyal tshab rje holds, is not due to

[consisting] of DEFECTS of wind, bile [and phlegm] ALONE, without [having as a cause] the non-presence of such appropriate conditions [for cure], then it follows that THERE IS NO INCURABLE sickness, because if the appropriate conditions [for cure] are present without other contradictory conditions, then the sickness definitely can be cured.[85]

HOW, it follows, can it not be accepted that a body killed by poison WILL NOT BE REVIVED? [It must be so accepted,] BECAUSE the substantial cause, the body, remains, and the contradictory condition, the DEADLY POISON, ETC., [WHICH ARE THE CAUSE OF THE TRANSFORMATION of sickness (death)] CAN BE REMOVED by mantras, etc.; or because the cause of the transformation of sickness [death] can be extracted THROUGH CUTTING the poisoned wound OF THAT person WHO HAS BEEN BITTEN by a poisonous snake.[86]

Explaining the definition of substantial cause [87]

[This is divided into:] (1) The definition of substantial cause [88] and (2) [Showing that] the body is not [the substantial cause] of mind [89].

The definition of substantial cause [88]

> (60) A SUBSTANTIAL [CAUSE IS SUCH THAT] WITHOUT A TRANSFORMATION [OF IT],

---

any intrinsic curability or incurability, but to the presence or absence of the conditions necessary for a cure, which are a doctor and/or medicines. When those are present but death still results, then it is due to "the karmic exhaustion of the life-span of the person"—an explanatory principle that is convenient, if a bit elusive, to say the least.

85 rGyal tshab rje points out that it is actually the opponent's position that implies that there are no incurable sicknesses, because if the absence of curative conditions, especially of the karmic determinant, is *not* the cause of death, then any disease must be curable, because disease has been redefined as a reversible transformation. Without the admission of factors other than the disease itself, the opponent cannot assert that *any* disease cannot be cured.

86 This is a way of making the same point as above: if the cause of mind is the body, and the cause of the body's death, poison, can be removed, then the body ought to be revived and mind present in a corpse from which the poison has been removed, because the substantial cause is present and the contradictory conditions absent. As above, rGyal tshab rje's argument seems a bit sophistic, but as long as the opponent identifies the causes and conditions as they do, their position will be vulnerable. Their best tactic, I suspect, might be to refine their definitions of reversible and irreversible transformations, specifying, e.g., that disease is reversible until the point of death and, after death, either irreversible or, quite simply, an inapplicable concept.

THERE CANNOT BE A TRANSFORMATION
OF THE SUBSTANCE-POSSESSOR, AS, FOR EXAMPLE, WITHOUT A TRANSFORMATION
OF THE CLAY [THERE CAN BE NO TRANSFORMATION OF] THE POT, ETC.

A lamp is the SUBSTANTIAL [cause] of lamp-light, because WITHOUT an essential TRANSFORMATION of [the lamp], THERE CANNOT BE an essential TRANSFORMATION OF THE SUBSTANCE-POSSESSOR, the lamp-light, [and because the lamp] directly establishes an uncommon imprint of just its essence upon the light. FOR EXAMPLE, WITHOUT A TRANSFORMATION OF THE CLAY, there cannot be a transformation of a POT, ETC.[87]

[Showing that] the body is not [the substantial cause] of mind [89]

(61-62) BODY AND MIND ALSO, ACCORDINGLY, ARE [NOT THUS RELATED]:
WITHOUT A TRANSFORMATION OF SOME ENTITY,
IT IS UNREASONABLE THAT THAT [EXISTS IN RELATION TO] THE TRANSFORMATION
OF SOME [OTHER] ENTITY AS THE SUBSTANTIAL [CAUSE],
AS A COW [IS NOT THE SUBSTANTIAL CAUSE OF] A WILD OX, ETC.
[DIFFERING] RESULTS SUBSIST SIMULTANEOUSLY: THEY ARISE
FROM [EACH] TAKING THE CAUSE [OF THE OTHER]AS COOPERATIVE,
AS IN THE CASE OF FIRE AND THE LIQUIDITY OF COPPER.

It follows that BODY AND MIND ALSO are not [related as] substantial cause and substantial result, because a change in a cow does not follow ACCORDINGLY from a change in a wild ox [or vice versa]. This [reason] pervades, because WITHOUT A TRANSFORMATION OF SOME ENTITY that is the cause, IT IS UNREASONABLE to classify THAT cause of THE TRANSFORMATION OF SOME ENTITY that is the result AS THE SUBSTANTIAL [cause], JUST AS A COW [is not the substantial cause of] A WILD OX.[88]

---

87 Defined, as are all other types of cause, in terms of the fundamental Buddhist doctrine of momentariness, a substantial cause is an entity-moment that is transformed in the very next moment into a substantial result that is essentially, or naturally, related to it. The most important quality of a substantial cause is transformation. A transformation in some substance, such as a lamp or clay, will inevitably and immediately effect a transformation of the appropriate "substance-possessors,"lamp-light or a pot, so the latter may be regarded as substantial results, and the former as substantial causes. Cf. the discussion above on the special indispensable cause and note 66, above.

88 Because a substantial cause must be an entity whose modification or transformation invariably modifies or transforms an essentially similar entity that is

[OPPONENT:] Well, then, it is contradictory that [body and mind] subsist in the same collection.

[RGYAL TSHAB RJE:] It is suitable that body and mind, which are RESULTS, SUBSIST SIMULTANEOUSLY, because each of THOSE two ARISES FROM TAKING THE substantial CAUSE of the other AS its COOPERATIVE condition, AS IN THE CASE OF FIRE AND THE LIQUIDITY OF COPPER.[89]

Refutation through an analysis of their [alleged] simultaneous [existence] [90]

[This is divided into:] (1) Refuting [the idea] that [the body] is the simultaneous basis [of mind] [91], (2) Refuting other syllogisms through that [95] and (3) Summary [96].

---

thus regarded as its substantial result, an entity whose transformation does *not* entail the transformation of a particular entity posited as its substantial result cannot be the latter entity's substantial cause. A change in a wild ox does not entail a change a change in a cow. Just so, argues rGyal tshab rje, a change in the body does *not* invariably entail a change in the mind: not only do we observe that this is the case, but, also, mind and body are substantially different enough that the one cannot "establish an uncommon imprint of just its essence" on the other. It is problematic whether this refutation can as easily be applied to the brain, for, as far as neurophysiologists are aware, there is no mental event that is not—at the very least—correlative with neural activity in the brain; a transformation in the brain invariably will produce transformations of "mind," and no mental event can occur without the "transformation of"—i.e., without activity in—the brain. The problem of the substantial relation between mind and brain also raises problems, it not being at all obvious how mind can be described in "substantial" terms. On the other hand, the materialist position is not without its difficulties, too, the most obvious being how mental functioning can be explained purely on the basis of physiology. Here, as elsewhere in this section, fundamentally opposed concepts of "mind" and "substance" are at work, and it is not clear that either position is incontestably demonstrable.

89 Molten copper, though seemingly "one" collection, in fact consists of a fire element and a copper element. Since fire and copper are substantially different, the one cannot be the substantial cause of the other. On the other hand, they co-exist because the one acts as the cooperative condition (*lhan cig byed rkyen, sahabhūpratyaya*) of the other. Fire, thus, has a previous moment of fire as its substantial cause and a previous moment of copper as its cooperative condition. Copper has previous copper as its substantial cause and previous fire as its cooperative condition. Similarly, mind has previous mind as its substantial cause and previous body as a cooperative condition. Note that the body is a cooperative condition, but not a special or indispensable cooperative condition—mind, after all, according to Buddhists, *can* exist without it.

Refuting [the idea] that [the body] is the simultaneous basis [of mind] [91]

[This is divided into:] (1) Setting forth the consequences [92], (2) Refuting the reply to that [93] and (3) Disposing [of the objection that our position] contradicts perception [94].

Setting forth the consequences [92]

(63) [THE BODY IS NOT MIND'S SIMULTANEOUS BASIS,] BECAUSE, WHETHER [SUBSTANCES ARE] EXISTENT OR NON-EXISTENT, THERE IS NO BASIS [SUBSTANTIALLY DIFFERENT FROM THEM].

Mind does not have the body as its simultaneous basis, BECAUSE WHETHER substances are EXISTENT OR NON-EXISTENT, THERE IS NO point in their having a simultaneous BASIS that is substantially different [from them].[90]

Refuting the reply to that [93]

(63b) IF YOU SAY: "THAT IS NOT SO; THE BASIS IS THE CAUSE OF ABIDING
OF AN EXISTENT," [WE REPLY:] THAT IS NOT THE BASIS [OF AN EXISTENT'S ABIDING];
BECAUSE [THE ABIDER ARISES] FROM THE ABIDER [ITSELF], WITHOUT ANOTHER [CAUSE].
(64) IF [YOU SAY THAT THE ABIDER] IS DIFFERENT [FROM THE ABIDING ENTITY, WE REPLY:] HOW COULD THAT
EFFECT THE ENTITY AS ITS CAUSE?
IT WILL FOLLOW THAT [ENTITIES] ARE INDESTRUCTIBLE.
IF YOU ASSERT THAT THAT IS DESTROYED THROUGH A DESTRUCTIVE CAUSE,
(65-66b) [WE REPLY THAT] THERE IS ALSO THE SAME CONSEQUENCE,
[FOR] WHAT, IT ALSO FOLLOWS, CAN A CAUSE OF ABIDING DO?
IF [YOU ASSERT THAT] THAT [CAUSE OF ABIDING MAKES AN ENTITY] ABIDE UNTIL IT MEETS ITS DESTRUCTIVE

90 A non-existent entity does not have *any* basis, so the question of whether its "basis" is substantially identical to or substantially different from it, or whether that basis precedes it or is simultaneous with it, is irrelevant. An existent entity cannot have a substantially different simultaneous basis because it already has come into existence, and so does not *need* any simultaneous basis for its existence. Thus, a mind that has not yet arisen cannot have any basis for its existence, because it does not exist; a mind that *has* arisen does not need a basis for its existence because it already exists. Furthermore, two simultaneous, substantially different entities cannot be related causally, for causality obtains between entities existing at different moments.

CAUSE, [THEN] THERE IS NO DENIAL THAT THIS EXISTENT
HAS THE NATURE OF [BEING] A DESTRUCTIBLE ENTITY, BECAUSE
[AGAIN,] WHAT CAN A CAUSE OF ABIDING DO?

[OPPONENT:] THAT IS NOT SO; THE meaning of "BASIS"IS THE CAUSE OF THE ABIDING OF AN already EXISTENT mind.

[RGYAL TSHAB RJE:] An already existent [mind] does NOT have that body as THE BASIS of its abiding, BECAUSE the abider arises FROM [THE ABIDER] itself, in its own nature from its own cause, WITHOUT ANOTHER [cause].[91]

[OPPONENT:] The reason is unproven; [the abider] IS substantially DIFFERENT [from the abiding].

[RGYAL TSHAB RJE:] HOW, then, COULD THAT body in any way EFFECT the abiding of THE ENTITY [mind]? It follows that it cannot be accepted that it could effect it, because the body IS [posited as] THE CAUSE OF THAT abiding that is objectively separate from it.[92] IT WILL FOLLOW THAT [mind] IS INDESTRUCTIBLE, because it already exists, and abides in a second moment.[93]

[OPPONENT:] Since WE ASSERT THAT THAT [mind] IS DESTROYED THROUGH A DESTRUCTIVE CAUSE, it is not permanent.

[RGYAL TSHAB RJE:] It follows that it is unacceptable that an already existent and abiding [mind] be destroyed by a destructive cause acting later, because when we analyze, [we find that] whether the destructive cause of that [mind] is substantially identical to or different from [mind], THERE IS ALSO THE SAME flaw as in the previous CONSE-

---

91 The Vaibhāṣikas posit four characteristics of a "moment"—arising, abiding, decaying and destruction—and hold that these characteristics are different from that which possesses the characteristics, the "moment."The Sautrāntikas, Yogācāras and Mādhyamikas, however, maintain that a moment cannot thus be divided without ceasing to be a moment, i.e., the shortest conceivable unit of time. They also deny that the moment itself is in any way different from its characteristics. Thus, if a moment possessed a quality such as abiding (which the Sautrāntikas, etc., do not admit), that quality would *not* in any way be different from that which abides, the moment itself.

92 If abider and abiding are substantially different entities that exist at the same time, then there can be no causal connection between them, and one cannot be considered the "basis"of the other. Further, if a body and its abiding are different entities, what relates them? *don gzhan*, "objectively separate,"is synonymous with *rdzas tha dad*, "substantially different."

93 If a mind-moment exists, and in addition has abiding as an intrinsic characteristic, then how could it ever end? It would seem that it could not, and that it would be permanent.

QUENCE.[94] WHAT, IT ALSO FOLLOWS, CAN A CAUSE OF ABIDING DO? It is pointless, because when [mind] does not meet a destructive cause, it is already existent and abiding; when it does meet [a destructive cause], a cause of abiding cannot make it abide.[95]

[OPPONENT:] IF there is no cause of abiding, then before meeting its destructive cause, [mind] already will have been destroyed; since THAT cause of abiding makes [mind] ABIDE UNTIL IT MEETS ITS DESTRUCTIVE CAUSE, there is no flaw [in our position].[96]

[RGYAL TSHAB RJE:] It follows that THERE IS NO DENIAL THAT THIS EXISTENT HAS THE NATURE OF being A DESTRUCTIBLE ENTITY, BECAUSE it is possible that it already be destroyed without meeting a destructive cause. If that is asserted, then WHAT, it follows, CAN A CAUSE OF ABIDING DO? It cannot make an already existent [mind] abide, because of that assertion.[97]

Disposing [of the objection that our position] contradicts perception [94]

(66c) IF YOU SAY, "[THE BODY SUPPORTS MIND] JUST AS, FOR EXAMPLE, [EARTH IS]

---

94 The flaw is the same as before, because a destructive cause must be either identical to or different from that which is destroyed (e.g., mind). If destructibility is identical to—and therefore the nature of—mind, then a cause of abiding can do nothing to make it abide; if destructibility is different from mind, then it is impossible to see how mind could be destroyed. Above, we saw that if abiding is inherent in mind, it cannot be destroyed; whereas if abiding is not inherent in mind, it cannot persist.

95 An already existent mind that does not meet a destructive cause will abide on its own, without need of a cause of its abiding. A mind that *does* meet a destructive cause could not abide even through the power of a cause of abiding. Therefore, a cause of abiding is, on the one hand, unnecessary and, on the other, powerless. Cf. TS 357-62.

96 The opponent claims that it is necessary to posit a cause of abiding. If there were no cause of abiding, then mind would be destroyed before it has a chance to meet its destructive cause; as it is, a cause of abiding makes an entity abide until it meets its destructive cause.

97 rGyal tshab rje is not upset in the least by the problem the opponent is attempting to solve, for he admits that entities have destruction as their very nature. Thus, they will not persist until they meet a destructive cause, because there is no destructive cause other than the entity itself. Since entities are inherently destructible, they do not abide at all, so a cause of abiding is both irrelevant and impotent, and must be dismissed as an unnecessary postulate. See Stcherbatsky (1962) I, 95.

THE SUPPORT OF WATER, ETC.,"THIS ALSO [HAS] THE SAME [FAULTS AS BEFORE].

(67) [A VESSEL] IS THE SUPPORT OF THAT [WATER INSIDE IT] BECAUSE AT EACH MOMENT,
IT IS THE CAUSE OF THE ARISING, [IN THE SAME PLACE] AS THE [PREVIOUS] ENTITY,
OF A [SUBSEQUENT] CONTINUUM OF DESTRUCTIBLE ENTITIES.
IF IT IS NOT THUS, IT [NEVERTHELESS] IS NOT REASONABLE [TO EXPLAIN THINGS OTHERWISE].

(68) [A VESSEL] IS THE SUPPORT OF WATER, ETC.,
BECAUSE IT BLOCKS IT FROM SPILLING;
WHAT IS THE PURPOSE IN QUALITY, GENERALITY AND ACTION
HAVING A SUPPORT, [SINCE] THEY ARE NON-PROCESSIVE?

[OPPONENT:] JUST AS, FOR EXAMPLE, it is proven by perception that earth is THE SUPPORT[98] for the abiding OF already existent WATER, ETC., so also is the body [the support] of the mind.

[RGYAL TSHAB RJE:] It follows that already existent water is not made to abide by a vessel, because THIS assertion ALSO possesses THE SAME faults cited in the previous case.[99]

[OPPONENT:] Well, then, why is it common worldly opinion that [a vessel] is the support [of water]?

[RGYAL TSHAB RJE:] A water-vessel IS THE SUPPORT OF THAT water inside it, BECAUSE AT EACH MOMENT IT IS THE CAUSE OF THE ARISING, in the same place AS THE previous ENTITY, OF A subsequent CONTINUUM OF THE naturally destructible ENTITIES of water inside it. IF IT IS NOT THUS assistant, it follows that IT IS NOT REASONABLE [to assert] that there exists a support that is objectively separate [from] what is supported.[100]

---

98 Although the Tibetan *rten*, translated above as "basis,"is used in the next section without qualification, in fact the Sanskrit term that it translates has changed, from *āśraya*, "basis,"to *ādhāra*, "support."

99 The opponent has attempted to cite an instance in which an object (an earthen pot) acts as the support for something substantially different from it, water. rGyal tshab rje maintains, however, that the same consequences apply as in the case of a "cause of abiding."In this case, if water has as a support something substantially different from but simultaneous with it, it is impossible to establish a causal connection. If its support is substantially identical to it, it must always be supported, with or without an earthen vessel.

100 Thus, an earthen vessel is the "support"of water only in a conventional sense. Water consists of a "stream"of water-moments. Each of these is the substantial cause of its successor. An earthen pot is merely the assistant, immediately preceding cooperative condition, which assures that the water-moment-

Although it is acceptable that an impermanent [entity] have a support, it is unacceptable that a permanent [entity] have one. [A water-vessel] IS THE SUPPORT OF THE WATER, ETC., inside it, BECAUSE IT BLOCKS IT FROM SPILLING down. WHAT, it follows, IS THE PURPOSE IN QUALITY, GENERALITY or ACTION[101] having an objectively separate SUPPORT? There is no purpose, because THEY ARE such as to be NON-PROCESSIVE from previous to subsequent moments.[102]

Refuting other syllogisms through that [95]

> (69) THIS CLEARS AWAY [THE IDEA THAT] THERE IS
> INHERENCE AND THE CAUSE OF HAVING INHERENCE,
> BECAUSE [THESE] DO NOT HAVE A BASIS [OF ABIDING],
> [AND] UNIVERSALS, ETC., DO ABIDE [INDEPENDENT OF PARTICULARS].[103]

---

stream is continually generated in the same place; the pot certainly is not necessary to the continued existence of the water itself. Similarly, body may act as the support of mind in the sense that it assures mental continuity in the same "place," and is an immediately preceding cooperative condition of mind, but it is by no means indispensable to mind's existence, and therefore is not a simultaneous causal support of the kind envisioned by the opponent. The explanation given by the Buddhist—in terms of successive moments—is the only one that can account for two substantially different entities acting as support and supported.

101 These are three of the six *a priori* categories (*padārtha*) recognized in the Vaiśeṣika system. The six are: substance (*dravya*), quality (*guṇa*), action (*karma*), generality (*sāmānya*), particularity (*viśeṣa*) and inherence (*samavāya*). See *Vaiśeṣika Sūtra* I:1:4 (tr. Radhakrishnan and Moore [1957] 387), Dasgupta (1975) I, 313ff. and Koller (1970) chapter 6. These concepts are introduced here because the Vaiśeṣikas maintain that, e.g., qualities are related to substances as supported to support.

102 The Vaiśeṣika categories, therefore, cannot even be said to be supported in a conventional sense, for a pot, e.g., acts to prevent the spilling, falling, or flowing of the water inside it. Something that spills, falls or flows necessarily is impermanent, and thus conventionally can be said to require a support. The Vaiśeṣika categories, however, are permanent. They do not change from moment to moment, let alone spill, fall or flow, so they cannot be described as supported, even by the entities in which they are said to inhere. Furthermore, as we have seen above, there cannot be a connection between a permanent and an impermanent entity, so it is impossible for the Vaiśeṣika to explain how the categories can inhere in impermanent entities.

103 A somewhat more straightforward reading of the Tibetan of the verse (*'dis ni 'phrod pa 'du ba yang / 'phrod pa 'du ba can rgyu dang / rigs la sogs pa rnam gnas nyid / rten med phyir na gsal ba yin*) yields: "This clears away [the idea that] there is inherence, inherent cause and the abiding of generality, etc., because

THIS reasoning,[104] which refutes the existence of a basis for the abiding of an already existent entity, also CLEARS AWAY[105] [the idea] that there is INHERENCE [connecting] substance and quality, AND that substance is THE CAUSE OF HAVING the [co-]INHERENCE of qualities, BECAUSE it has been shown that something that already exists DOES NOT HAVE A BASIS of its abiding.[106] It follows that it is unacceptable to say that if there is no cause of having inherence, then there cannot be inherence, because even without a refutation of [particulars], UNIVERSALS, ETC., DO ABIDE.[107]

Alternatively, one can apply the first reason [in the previous paragraph] to the statement, "There is no basis of the abiding of an already existent universal."[108] This also clears away [the idea] that there is a cause of inherence [connecting] body and mind, [for] one can apply to that [idea] the reason set forth in relation to substance and quality.[109]

[one] cannot be the basis [of the other]."

104 "This reasoning" refers to the statement (above, PV 63) to the effect that there is no point in either a non-existent or an existent entity's having a simultaneous cause of abiding.

105 In GT, *bsal* probably is preferable to *gsal*.

106 Inherence is conceived—at least in the Buddhist reading of Vaiśeṣika—as an essentially causal factor, for it "causes" universals to inhere in particulars. However, if it exists as substantially different from but simultaneous with the categories that it relates, it cannot "cause" anything, and would require a further factor to relate it to the categories that it is supposed to connect, a requirement that leads to an infinite regress. Similarly, substance is considered the cause of qualities' co-existence in the same collection; but, since it is held to exist simultaneously with and to be substantially different from those qualities, it cannot "cause" them at all. Additionally, the Vaiśeṣika categories cannot function causally because they are conceived as permanent, non-successive "entities." (Whether a Vaiśeṣika would accept the Buddhist's analysis of their categories in terms of "entities" is open to question. They might insist that by doing so the Buddhist is committing—pardon the expression—a category mistake.)

107 The opponent attempts to claim that if there is no simultaneous, substantially different cause of inherence, then there can be no inherence at all. Yet, rGyal tshab rje points out, the Vaiśeṣikas themselves assert that universals exist independently of their particulars, so it is unnecessary for them even to posit the existence of inherence.

108 The syllogism thus would read: "The particulars are not the basis of the abiding of an already existent universal, because even without particulars, universals do abide." Since the existence of universals is not dependent on their connection with particulars, the particulars cannot be said to be the basis of the universals' abiding.

Summary [96]

(70) WHAT CAN THE CAUSE OF ABIDING OF THAT DO,
SINCE THERE IS DESTRUCTION OF THE ENTITY THROUGH A SEPARATE CAUSE?
SINCE [ENTITIES] ARE DESTROYED WITHOUT [ANY] SEPARATE [CAUSE],
IT IS NOT THE CASE THAT CAUSES OF ABIDING CAN [PERPETUATE ENTITIES].
(71) [IF THERE WERE A CAUSE OF ABIDING,] NO ENTITY
COULD BE DESTROYED AT ANY TIME,
[FOR] ALL ARISEN [ENTITIES] WOULD POSSESS A SUPPORT,
[AND] ALL THAT HAVE A SUPPORT ABIDE.
(72) IF [AN ENTITY] HAS A NATURE SUCH THAT IT IS ITSELF NATURALLY
DESTRUCTIBLE, [WHAT] OTHER [ENTITY] CAN EFFECT ITS ABIDING?
IF IT DOES NOT HAVE A NATURE SUCH THAT IT IS ITSELF NATURALLY
DESTRUCTIBLE, WHAT OTHER [ENTITY] CAN EFFECT ITS ABIDING?

When we analyze a destructive cause that originates later, it is unacceptable that there be a cause of abiding of an already existent [entity]:

WHAT, it follows, CAN THE CAUSE OF ABIDING OF THAT [already existent] ENTITY DO? It has no purpose, SINCE its purpose is THE DESTRUCTION OF THE ENTITY THROUGH A SEPARATE CAUSE, but [an already existent entity] has not arisen as essentially destructible. SINCE [an entity] IS DESTROYED by its own nature, WITHOUT ANY SEPARATE cause that destroys it, it follows that IT IS NOT THE CASE THAT CAUSES OF ABIDING ARE ABLE to make an already existent [entity] abide.[110]

If there exists a support for the abiding of an already existent [entity], it follows that there is no destruction:

It follows that NO ENTITY COULD BE DESTROYED AT ANY TIME, because ALL ARISEN [entities] ultimately WOULD POSSESS A SUPPORT that is a permanent entity, such as a self, etc. It follows that this [reason] pervades, because ALL [entities] THAT HAVE as their SUPPORT a permanent entity necessarily ABIDE, without being destroyed.[111]

---

109 Body and mind, as substantially different, cannot be related by some third entity, such as inherence, for the reasons outlined above.

110 This recapitulates arguments offered above. If an entity is not inherently destructible, it does not need a cause of abiding to make it abide, for it will do so naturally. If it *is* naturally destructible, then a cause of abiding can do nothing to make it abide.

111 If there does exist a cause of abiding, then no entity ever can be destroyed, for it will have continuously present a cause of its perpetuation. rGyal tshab rje

When we analyze [how an entity exists] in its own nature, [we see that] it is unacceptable [that there exist a basis of abiding]:

IF an entity HAS A NATURE SUCH THAT IT IS ITSELF NATURALLY DESTRUCTIBLE, then what OTHER [entity] CAN EFFECT ITS ABIDING? None, it follows, has the power to make an already existent [entity] abide. IF IT DOES NOT [HAVE A NATURE SUCH THAT IT IS ITSELF NATURALLY DESTRUCTIBLE], WHAT OTHER [entity] CAN EFFECT THAT [entity'S] ABIDING? It follows that there is no need [for such an effector].[112]

C. WHY THE BODY IS NOT MIND'S SPECIAL COOPERATIVE CONDITION

Refuting [the idea] that [the body] acts as the special cooperative condition[113] [of mind] [97]

[This is divided into:] (1) The actual refutation [98], (2) Refuting [the idea] that the body and mind are substantially identical [103] and (3) Identifying the cause of saṃsāra [104].

The actual refutation [98]

[This is divided into:] (1) Refuting [the idea] that the body is the principal condition of wisdom, etc. [99] and (2) Refuting [the idea] that it is the principal condition of attachment, etc. [100].

Refuting [the idea] that the body is the principal condition of wisdom, etc. [99]

(73) WISDOM, ETC., HAVE THEIR
INCREASE AND DECREASE TAKE PLACE

---

specifies here that a cause of abiding would be *permanent,* and points out that any entity with a permanent support, such as, e.g., the ātman, cannot perish. Whether an impermanent cause of abiding could be posited is problematic, because the very concept of "abiding" precludes impermanence for the Buddhist.

112 Finally, if an entity *is* inherently destructible—as Buddhists maintain—then nothing can make it abide; if it is not inherently destructible, then no cause of abiding is necessary, but neither is destruction possible. Such, in any case, is the dilemma posed by Dharmakīrti's reasoning, which clearly relies heavily on an application of the Indian equivalent of the "law of the excluded middle"—entities are either naturally destructible and momentary or abiding and permanent; there is no "middle" alternative.

113 A cooperative condition (*lhan cig byed rkyen, sahakāripratyaya*) is in general an assistant condition, as soil, moisture and sunlight are to the growth of a plant. A special (*khyad par can*) cooperative condition is one that is essential to the result.

THROUGH CHANGES IN MENTAL FORMATIONS,[114] WITHOUT
FOLLOWING THE INCREASE AND DECREASE OF THE BODY.
(74) THIS [WISDOM] DOES NOT EXIST AS
DEPENDENT, [LIKE] LAMP-LIGHT, ETC.;
IT IMPROVES THROUGH [IMPROVEMENT OF] THAT [BODY],
[BUT THE BODY] DOES NOT ASSIST [DIRECTLY IN GENERATING] MIND, SO IT IS NOT [MIND'S SPECIAL BASIS].

Setting forth the reason:

WISDOM, compassion, ETC., do not HAVE the body as their special basis, because THEIR INCREASE AND DECREASE TAKE PLACE THROUGH CHANGES IN previously accustomated MENTAL FORMATIONS, WITHOUT FOLLOWING THE INCREASE AND DECREASE OF THE BODY['s health].[115]

THIS [reason] pervades, because this reason [demonstrates] that [wisdom] DOES NOT EXIST AS DEPENDENT on the body, [as] LAMP-LIGHT, ETC., [depend on] their substantial causes. Because we see that there is an improvement in wisdom, etc., when the body is strengthened through elixirs, etc., it is the case that THIS wisdom, etc., ALSO IMPROVE a little THROUGH improvement in THAT body, but it does not follow that the body is their special basis, because the body assists wisdom through directly assisting [in the generation of] the body-cognition, but DOES NOT ASSIST [directly in the generation of] MIND, SO IT IS NOT [the special basis of mind].[116]

---

114 The Tibetan *blo yi byed pa* (*buddhivyāpāra*) simply means "[changes in] the exercise or activity of mind."rGyal tshab rje, however, glosses the *byed pa* as *'du byed* (*saṃskāra*), those mental "formations," attitudes or propensities that comprise the fourth of the five aggregates of the "person,"and which serve as the basis of much that happens to us, both mentally and physically.

115 rGyal tshab rje's basic point is that mental qualities vary through a combination of their degree of previous accustomation and present external circumstances (including the vigor of the body), but that the projecting cause or special basis of a moment of wisdom is some previous instance of wisdom, not the vigor of the body, which is merely assistant.

116 rGyal tshab rje argues here, as he has before, that the body *indirectly* affects the mind, by generating a body-cognition that is, then, the cause of a mental cognition, and thus of a variation in wisdom, etc. The body is not, however, the special basis of mind or its wisdom, so one cannot maintain that wisdom varies with the condition of the body as the intensity of lamp-light varies according to the condition of the wick. Undoubtedly, a better case can be made that there is a remarkably close correlation between the condition of the *brain* and mental abilities, but the Buddhist *still* would deny that the physical organ is the special basis of mind, because they would maintain that there still inter-

Refuting [the idea] that it is the principal condition of attachment, etc. [100]

[This is divided into:] (1) [Proof that] attachment, etc., do not directly arise from the body, together with an example [101] and (2) Summary [102].

[Proof that] attachment, etc., do not directly arise from the body, together with an example [101]

(75) ATTACHMENT, ETC., WHICH INCREASE THROUGH THE STRENGTH [OF THE BODY]
AT TIMES, HAVE ARISEN FROM PLEASURE AND PAIN;
IN TURN, THESE [SENSATIONS HAVE ARISEN] FROM PROXIMITY TO AN INTERNAL
OBJECT THAT IS A BALANCE [OR IMBALANCE] OF THE ELEMENTS.
(76) IN THIS [WAY], IT IS EXPLAINED HOW MEMORY-LOSS, ETC.,
[ORIGINATE] FROM TYPHOID, ETC.,
BECAUSE [MEMORY, ETC.] ARE JUST TRANSFORMED BY A COGNITION
THAT ARISES FROM A CHANGE IN AN INTERNAL OBJECT,
(77) FOR EXAMPLE, CONFUSION, ETC.,
WILL OCCUR THROUGH SOME CHANGES IN A [PERSON'S] CONTINUUM
WHEN THEY HEAR A TIGER
OR SEE BLOOD.

[OPPONENT:] Attachment, etc., follow on the increase and decrease of the [strength of] the body, [because] we see that attachment increases in a strong body and anger in a weak body.

[RGYAL TSHAB RJE:] ATTACHMENT, ETC., WHICH INCREASE THROUGH THE STRENGTH or weakness of the body AT TIMES when [the mind] is separate from the wisdom realizing reality,[117] do not have the body as their direct principal condition, because they HAVE ARISEN directly FROM sensations of PLEASURE AND PAIN. IN TURN, THOSE feelings of pleasure and pain do not have the body as *their* principal condition, because they have arisen FROM PROXIMITY TO AN INTERNAL tangible OBJECT THAT IS THE BALANCE or imbalance OF THE ELEMENTS, ETC.[118]

---

venes a "body-cognition"—or perhaps "brain-cognition"—between the physical and the mental events. Whether the Buddhist description of the relationship among body, body-cognition and mental cognition is defensible, or whether it simply is an *ad hoc* account formulated in order to maintain the traditional distinction between the physical and the mental, is a separate question.

117 "Reality" here is *so sor,* the actual natures of individual entities.

118 The point here is similar to that made above: a particular physical condition, i.e., the balance or imbalance of the elements (*khams, dhātu*) (or, perhaps, hu-

IN THIS way, IT also IS EXPLAINED HOW MEMORY-LOSS, ETC., originate FROM TYPHOID fever, ETC., BECAUSE THEY ARE JUST TRANSFORMED BY a sensory COGNITION THAT ARISES FROM A CHANGE IN AN INTERNAL tangible OBJECT. FOR EXAMPLE, the mental CONFUSION, ETC., that WILL OCCUR THROUGH SOME CHANGES IN A timid [person's] CONTINUUM WHEN THEY HEAR the words, "A TIGER is coming!" OR SEE the BLOOD of some other [being] who has been killed, are not based directly on the body, because they are merely intensified by internal feelings.[119]

Summary [102]

> (78) THEREFORE, MIND IS BASED ON MIND,
> BECAUSE WITHOUT IT, IT WILL NOT [OCCUR];
> IT DEFINITELY SUCCEEDS ON
> THE FORMATIONS OF SOME [PREVIOUS MIND].

[THEREFORE,] MIND IS BASED ON previous MIND, BECAUSE WITHOUT THAT as its substantial cause, IT WILL NOT OCCUR. It is not based on the body as its substantial cause, because IT DEFINITELY SUCCEEDS ON THE accustomated FORMATIONS OF SOME appropriate previous mind.[120]

Refuting [the idea] that body and mind are substantially identical [103]

> (79) [IF MIND IS SUBSTANTIALLY IDENTICAL TO THE BODY, THEN] JUST AS THE FORMATIONS OF LISTENING, ETC.,
> ARE BASED ON MIND, SO WHEN, IN THE MIND [THERE IS AWARENESS],
> [THOSE] QUALITIES SHOULD [APPEAR] AS CLEARLY
> IN THE BODY, BECAUSE [BODY AND MIND] ARE NOT DIFFERENT.

---

mors), generates particular bodily sensations of comfort or discomfort. These sensations then are apprehended by a body-cognition, which in turn effects a mental cognition that may be represented as an increase or decrease of attachment, anger and other vices. Only in this very indirect sense can the health of the body be said to affect mental states which, just like wisdom, have as their principal condition some previous mental formation of the same type.

119 Again, the condition of the mind is affected only indirectly by occurrences in the body, for at the very least, a body-cognition will intervene between them.

120 This simply restates the basic Buddhist position—that a type of mind must be preceded by a similar component of the complex of mental formations. This may, in fact, be correct, but it ought to be reiterated that it presupposes (a) the existence of a past mental formation that can continue in latent form and "manifest" in the present under appropriate conditions, (b) that a particular description of perception and consciousness, i.e., in terms of object, sensation, sense-cognition and mental-cognition, is valid and (c) that mind and body can, in a general sense, be described as substantially different.

[OPPONENT:] Because we see that a child's body succeeds the parents' bodies, so [we say that a child's body] arises from [the parents']; and mind also [arises from the body], because it [too] is not different [from it]. When you prove that [mind] follows previous mental formations, you do not prove that it is not based on body.[121]

[RGYAL TSHAB RJE:] It follows that JUST AS THE FORMATIONS OF LISTENING, reflection, creativity, ETC., which ARE accustomated BASED ON previous MINDS of their own type, [appear clearly to a conscious mind,] SO, at the time WHEN there is awareness [of them] IN THE MIND, [those QUALITIES] should appear as CLEARLY IN THE BODY as they are clearly manifest [to the mind], BECAUSE THEY ARE mental qualities, definitely suitable to be classified as mind, and body and mind are NOT substantially DIFFERENT.[122]

Identifying the cause of saṃsāra [104]

[This is divided into:] (1) Identifying the cause of taking birth in a womb [105] and (2) Disposing of objections to that [106].

Identifying the cause of taking birth in a womb [105]

(80) ONE WHO DESIRES TO OBTAIN HAPPINESS AND AVOID SUFFERING
TAKES [BIRTH IN] A LOWER ABODE
BECAUSE OF HAVING ATTACHMENT TO SELF,
WITHOUT BEING LED BY OTHER SENTIENT BEINGS.
(81) THE INVERTED COGNITION [THAT SEES] SUFFERING [AS HAPPINESS],
AND CRAVING, ARE COMPLETE BONDAGE,
THE CAUSES OF BIRTH; SOMEONE WHO DOES NOT [DISTORTEDLY CRAVE]

---

121 The opponent argues that just as a child's body succeeds on but is not substantially different from its parents' bodies, so mind succeeds on but is not substantially different from body. Also, the fact that past mental formations may affect present mental states does not mean that the present mental states are not dependent on the body. It might, for example, be argued that the mental formations require a physical basis for storage, and cannot manifest unless that "storage-system" is working properly.

122 rGyal tshab rje replies that if the mind is substantially identical to the body, then mental qualities should appear in the body and physical qualities in the mind, which is absurd. He points out that to describe body and mind as identical is to confuse two different types of events. However, it remains open to question whether mind and body differ exactly as the Buddhists maintain they do. It may show logical absurdity and linguistic confusion simply to "reduce" mind to body, but it is not clear that the Buddhist way of explaining "the ghost in the machine" is not itself susceptible to linguistic carelessness or the commission of a category mistake. On the latter, see Ryle (1949) chapter 1.

WILL NOT BE BORN [IN SAṂSĀRA].

An ordinary being, by craving that DESIRES TO OBTAIN HAPPINESS AND AVOID SUFFERING, TAKES [birth in] A LOWER ABODE, such as the womb, etc., because they take those [births] BECAUSE OF HAVING ATTACHMENT TO SELF, independently, WITHOUT BEING LED BY OTHER SENTIENT BEINGS, such as God, etc.[123]

[OPPONENT:] [If rebirth occurs] because of a desire to attain happiness, it is unacceptable that one willingly take [birth in] a suffering abode.

[RGYAL TSHAB RJE:] It follows that there is no contradiction [in our position], because THE INVERTED COGNITION that apprehends SUFFERING as happiness, AND the CRAVING that desires to attain happiness, ARE the causes of a person's COMPLETE BONDAGE, THE CAUSE OF BIRTH in saṃsāra. This follows, because SOME arhant, WHO DOES NOT invertedly crave anything, WILL NOT BE BORN in saṃsāra, by virtue of having utterly abandoned [that craving].[124]

Disposing of objections to that [106]

(82) IF YOU SAY [THAT THERE IS NO] COMING FROM OR GOING TO [OTHER LIVES BECAUSE] WE DO NOT SEE [THEM],
[WE REPLY THAT] YOU DO NOT SEE THEM BECAUSE YOU HAVE UNCLEAR SENSE-FACULTIES;

---

123 This is an assertion of the basic Buddhist notion that we, and only we, are responsible for our destinies. As the *Dhammapada* (I:1) says, "all that we are is a result of what we have thought"—not only our present states of mind, but our present bodies and external circumstances are the result of actions of body, speech and mind committed earlier in this life or in some previous life. Because actions ultimately are under the sway of the mind, "all that we are" has its origin there. The idea that there exists a God who could control our destinies already has been refuted above. The basic cause of birth in "lower abodes," i.e., anywhere in the six realms of saṃsāra, then, is our own attachment to self (*bdag la chags pa, ātmasneha*).

124 rGyal tshab rje points out that we willingly take birth in a suffering abode because we do not realize that it is suffering. We ignorantly, "invertedly," mistake it for an abode of happiness (as we also take the non-self for the self, the ugly for the beautiful and the impermanent for the permanent) and therefore crave it. Ignorance compounded by craving equals saṃsāra's continuation. Note that, at this point, the fact that ignorance and craving perpetuate saṃsāra and that there exists a being, an arhant, who abandons ignorance and thereby transcends saṃsāra, is simply asserted—it is not proved. The proof will come later, in the section on the four noble truths.

FOR EXAMPLE, AN UNCLEAR EYE
WILL NOT SEE A MINUTE AMOUNT OF SMOKE.
(83) SOME [BEINGS] ARE EMBODIED BEINGS,
BUT ARE INTANGIBLE BECAUSE THEY ARE SUBTLE,
AS WATER [ENTERING CLAY] AND AS MERCURY [ENTERING] GOLD;
IT IS NOT THE CASE THAT [OTHER LIVES] ARE NON-EXISTENT BECAUSE [YOU] DO NOT SEE [THEM].

[OPPONENT:] There is no GOING TO OR COMING FROM other lives, because WE DO NOT SEE them.

[RGYAL TSHAB RJE:] It follows that the fact that [YOU] Lokāyatas DO NOT SEE [other lives] does not prove that they are non-existent, BECAUSE [you] Lokāyatas HAVE UNCLEAR SENSE-FACULTIES. FOR EXAMPLE, AN UNCLEAR EYE WILL NOT SEE A MINUTE AMOUNT OF SMOKE, even though it is present.

[OPPONENT:] But [the smoke], even if it is not seen by the eyes, can touch the body; since [other lives] are not the intentional objects [of any sense-cognition], they are non-existent.

[RGYAL TSHAB RJE:] SOME embodied beings in the intermediate state, etc., ARE EMBODIED BEINGS, BUT ARE INTANGIBLE, BECAUSE THEY have bodies that ARE SUBTLE and pass through [solid objects] without resistance, AS WATER enters fresh clay and AS MERCURY [enters] GOLD WITHOUT RESISTANCE. THEREFORE, IT FOLLOWS THAT it is not the case that [other lives] ARE NON-EXISTENT just BECAUSE [you] Lokāyatas DO NOT SEE [them], because even if they do exist, it is impossible that [you] Lokāyatas see them.[125]

---

125 rGyal tshab rje's general point is quite well taken: the non-perception of something does not assure its non-existence (cf. TS 1938), and there are subtle features of the world not accessible to superficial perception. In this instance, beings in the intermediate state (*bar do, antarābhava*), definite perception of whom would considerably bolster Buddhist claims about the existence of other lives, are said to be subtle in the way that a minute amount of smoke is, and to pass through objects in the way that water enters clay or mercury enters gold. rGyal tshab rje is arguing on the basis of analogy here, but—the question of the usefulness of analogies in rational argument quite aside—there is some question whether the analogy is entirely apt, since a minute amount of smoke, or water's entering clay and mercury gold, are subtleties in principle cognizable by a more careful application of sense-perception, whereas intermediate state beings only are perceivable through the concentration-born mental perception of an advanced yogin. A Lokāyata, being essentially a positivist, will not admit such extra-sensory perception as authoritative. Or, if they accept E.S.P., they may argue on the basis of their own experience that there are no inter-

mediate-state beings, in which case an uncommitted observer must decide between two claims based on instances of E.S.P. that are not accessible. This highlights the epistemological problems involved in truth-claims based on religious experience in general and E.S.P. in particular. See above, pp. 97-100.

4. *The Mind-Body Problem: A Refutation of Materialism (2)*

A. PARTS AND WHOLES

Refutation through an analysis of the essential aspect of the body that is the basis of [mind] [107]

[This is divided into:] (1) Refuting [the idea] that there is a partless gross body that is the special basis of mind [108] and (2) Refuting [the idea] that subtle atoms are that [special basis] [126].

Refuting [the idea] that there is a partless gross body that is the special basis of mind [108]

[This is divided into:] (1) Refuting [the idea] that there is a partless whole [109] and (2) Disposing of [objections alleged to] damage that refutation [112].

Refuting the idea that there is a partless whole [109]

[This is divided into:] (1) Proving the reason [110] and (2) Setting [the conclusion] forth [111].[1]

---

1 In this case, proving the reason involves establishing the validity of the reason to be set forth formally in the next section as a disproof of a partless whole: the necessity of attributing contradictory qualities to an ontologically unique entity. The opponent in this section will be not the Lokāyata, but the Vaiśeṣika, who posits the existence of partless wholes that are distinct from the parts said to comprise them (see *Nyāya Sūtra* II:1:32). The discussion bears only indirectly on the mind-body problem: rGyal tshab rje seeks to disprove one possible material source of mind, a body that is a partless whole like that posited by the Vaiśeṣikas.

Proving the reason [110]

(84) IF THE HAND, ETC., MOVES, THEN ALL [THE BODY]
WILL MOVE; BECAUSE OF [THIS], AND BECAUSE IT IS UNSUITABLE THAT
A ONE [SUPPORT] CONTRADICTORY ACTIONS,
IT WILL BE PROVEN OTHERWISE, [THAT THE BODY HAS] DIFFERENT [PARTS].
(85) [ACCORDING TO YOUR REASONING], IF ONE [PART] IS COVERED, THEN ALL
WILL BE COVERED, OR, IF IT IS NOT COVERED,
THEN [ALL] WILL BE SEEN [AS UNCOVERED]; IF ONE [PART] IS PAINTED,[2]
[ALL] WILL BE PAINTED, OR WE WILL COGNIZE [THE WHOLE AS] UNPAINTED [IF JUST A PART IS UNPAINTED].

It is contradictory on the basis of action:

IF THE HAND, ETC., of a person's body, to which the whole is proven to be connected, MOVES, it follows that ALL the body WILL MOVE, BECAUSE those two [hand and body] are a partless one. It follows that this reason [pervades], BECAUSE IT IS UNSUITABLE THAT a partless ONE be an appropriate basis for the CONTRADICTORY ACTIONS of movement and non-movement. If the reason is unproven, then it follows that [the body] WILL BE PROVEN OTHERWISE, to have DIFFERENT parts, because of the contradictory [actions] of movement and non-movement.[3]

It is contradictory on the basis of seeing:

IF ONE [part], a person's face, IS COVERED by a cloth, it follows that ALL, the whole body, WILL appear to be COVERED by cloth, because [the body] is one whole, without two parts.[4]

---

2 The Tibetan *tshon gyis bsgyur na* (lit., "when transformed by paint," or "when transformed by color") translates the Sanskrit *rakte,* which means "when reddened," or "when red."

3 If the whole is indivisible, then its "parts" cannot be considered in isolation from it, for the whole becomes a unique ontological unit, of which contradictory qualities cannot be predicated. Thus, if the whole has quality *x,* then the parts all must share this quality, for they cannot be considered apart from that whole. If it is *not* the case that a whole cannot combine contradictory qualities, then it must possess parts that *are* conceptually independent of the whole, which is what the Vaiśeṣika seeks to deny.

4 This makes the same point as above: if the body is a partless whole, then what is true for "part" must be true for the whole, because no ultimate distinction between them is possible.

[OPPONENT:] The word "OR" [in the root-verse refers] to covering a *part* with a cloth, but since the whole IS NOT COVERED, it cannot have two parts, covered and uncovered.[5]

[RGYAL TSHAB RJE:] Well, then, it follows that at that time the whole face WILL BE SEEN as uncovered, because it is suitable that it be seen as uncovered.[6]

It is contradictory on the basis of qualities:

IF ONE [part], the face, IS PAINTED blue, it follows that the entire body WILL appear to BE PAINTED, because [the body] is one whole, without two parts.[7]

[OPPONENT:] The word "OR" [in the root-verse means] that the part is painted, but the whole is not.[8]

[RGYAL TSHAB RJE:] Well, then, it follows that WE WILL COGNIZE individually two faces, one that has been painted blue and one that is UNPAINTED, because when we see by perception the face painted blue, it is also suitable that we see as unpainted the whole face, which is the basis of the connection [of the parts].[9]

---

5 Here, there is a conflict between the Buddhist and the Vaiśeṣika in the reading of verse 85a-c (*gcig bsgribs pa na thams cad dag / bsgribs par 'gyur ba'am ma bsgribs na / mthong 'gyur*). The Buddhist reads it as: "If one [part] is covered, then all will be covered, or, if it is not covered, then [all] will be seen [as uncovered]." The opponent's reading is: "If one part is covered, then will all appear covered? We see that it will not [appear] covered." Using their particular interrogative reading of *'am*, the opponent is trying to maintain that the whole-part distinction still is valid, and that only a *part* has been covered, not the whole.

6 rGyal tshab rje pursues *his* logical line, and maintains that if a whole is not divisible into parts, then what describes the one must describe the other. Thus, if the opponent claims that the whole is not covered, then none of the parts can be covered, either, because they are not substantially different from the whole.

7 Again, a partless whole cannot be the basis for contradictory qualities, so a body can be either blue or non-blue, but not both. Through this section, the Buddhist is relying on a version of what in the West is called the law of contradiction to expose the weakness of the opponent's position: an analytically indivisible unit cannot possess contradictory qualities.

8 The opponent repeats in a slightly different context the point made above, i.e., that a part can be described as covered while a whole is not, but they fail to perceive how the Buddhist has used their own position to catch them in contradiction. For a discussion of the import of "or" (*'am*) see above, note 5.

9 Once again, if one says that a part (the face) has been painted blue but the whole has not, then it would be reasonable to see two faces, a blue and a non-

Setting [the conclusion] forth [111]

(86) THUS, A COLLECTION DOES NOT EXIST AS A ONE.

[THUS,] A person's body-COLLECTION DOES NOT EXIST AS A gross, partless ONE, because [the body] combines many contradictory qualities, such as movement and non-movement, etc.[10]

If, as the Vaiśeṣikas [assert], there exists a gross external object having parts, then when one investigates the division of parts, [one sees] that [the gross external object] is nothing more than a mere collection of subtle atoms. If that is the case, then since it is impossible that [the atoms] be a resistant, tangible entity, it is accepted that any partless whole must be objectively separate from its parts.[11]

Some assert that if there is a gross object, it necessarily does not exist substantially, or assert that a collection and the collection's [parts] are substantially different. [These assertions] only [reflect] the distorted understanding that misconstrues how a collection is formed.[12]

This "whole"is a fundamental assertion of the Vaiśeṣkas, but when the Lokāyatas assert that the body is the special basis of mind, they are partly refuted by an analysis of the essential [aspect of] body that acts as a basis, [so] the Lokāyatas are the opponents in this verse.[13]

---

blue, the former on the basis of the fact that a part has been painted, the latter on the basis of the fact that the whole has not—for by the opponent's own admission, the whole is partless, and thus not logically separable from any parts.

10 This, then, is the Buddhist position: there is no whole above and beyond the sum of its parts, for if there were, then the consequences outlined above would ensue.

11 Even if there exists a gross external object with parts, one discovers upon analysis that the ultimate parts of a gross external object are atoms. A gross object is visible and tangible, and thus has qualities that are contradictory to those of its parts, atoms, which are invisible and non-resistant. For the Vaiśeṣika, then, a whole must be substantially different from its parts.

12 rGyal tshab rje criticizes two views: (1) that a gross object does not have substantial existence and (2) that a collection and its parts are substantially different. A gross object *does* have substantial existence, because it can be an object of cognition. At the same time, the collection and its parts are *not* substantially different, because if they were, then the problem of the co-existence of contradictory qualities in a unitary collection, raised above, would remain unsolved.

13 The actual position being refuted in this section, rGyal tshab rje reminds us, is that of the Lokāyatas. The Vaiśeṣika view has been singled out for discussion because one of the types of body that a Lokāyata might assert as the basis of mind is the body as a partless whole, so the notion must be shown to be in-

Disposing of [objections alleged to] damage that refutation [112]

[This is divided into:] (1) Disposing of the [alleged] consequence that an external object cannot be cognized by a sense-cognition [113], (2) Refuting other syllogisms through that [114] and (3) Refuting [the existence of] a whole and, in particular, the qualities based upon it [115].

Disposing of the [alleged] consequence that an external object cannot be cognized by a sense-cognition [113]

(86b) IF YOU SAY: IF [AN OBJECT] IS JUST [ITS] MANY [ATOMS],
THEN JUST AS THE PREVIOUS [ATOMS ARE INVISIBLE, SO THE OBJECT] WILL NOT BE COGNIZED, BECAUSE
THEY ARE NOT SEPARATELY [VISIBLE] AND BECAUSE THEY ARE EXTREMELY SUBTLE; [WE REPLY:] IT IS UNPROVEN THAT
(87) [AN OBJECT] IS NOT SEPARATE [FROM ITS ATOMS], BECAUSE OBJECTS OF SENSE
ARE SEPARATE; [AN OBJECT] IS NOT ITS ATOMS.

[OPPONENT:] IF a gross external object is not substantially different from its atoms, then IT IS nothing more than JUST an occasion of MANY atoms. If that is the case, then it follows that JUST AS THE PREVIOUS atoms are not [visible as] separate, [so] a subsequent external object [composed of those atoms] WILL NOT BE COGNIZED by a sense-cognition, BECAUSE (a) the previous atoms ARE NOT [visible as] SEPARATE, AND (b) BECAUSE the atoms ARE EXTREMELY SUBTLE.[14]

[RGYAL TSHAB RJE:] (a) is unproven. IT IS UNPROVEN THAT the form that acts as the objective condition of a sense-cognition IS NOT SEPARATE from an occasion that does not act as an objective condition, BECAUSE necessarily, those [things that] are OBJECTS OF SENSE-cognition, i.e., forms, ARE SEPARATE from the previous [invisible atoms].[15]

---

coherent. Whether anyone ever actually has tried to argue that a partless whole body is the basis of mind, I do not know—the position certainly has no recent parallels in Western thought (though a discussion involving the role of parts of the brain and the "whole"brain is at least conceivable).

14 The opponent argues that if a gross object is not substantially different from its atoms (as the Buddhist maintains), then the object must be as invisible as the atoms of which it is composed.

15 rGyal tshab rje replies that atoms *do* change from a state of invisibility to a state of visibility, because in the former there is no objective condition (*dmigs rkyen, ālambanapratyaya*) for a sense-cognition, while in the latter there is. Thus, there is a functional—if not an ontological—difference between atoms

(b) is unproven. It follows that a pot IS NOT ITS ATOMS, because it is an object that can induce certain knowledge independently, via a sense-perception authority.[16]

Ācārya Devendrabuddhi says in his commentary on this that "At that time, those atoms are not the designated object."The explanation of this is that [the atoms] are not objects that are cognized and designated by an independent sense-cognition, because a sense-cognition designates roughly, saying, "this is form," etc.[17]

According to those who assert that if there exists a gross object it does not exist substantially,[18] this verse shows that it is impossible that atoms be seen by a sense-cognition. This statement is very unreasonable, because it follows, then, that blue is atoms, because an external object [need] not be gross. If the reason is unproven, then the previous thesis is contradicted. If it is asserted, then it follows that there are no atoms, because [blue] is seen by a sense-cognition.[19] It follows, then,

---

and the objects they form. The implication is that atoms are "different"individually or collected, just as (above, PV 25-28) a seed, soil and moisture, or an object, sense-faculty and cognition are different separately or in combination.

16 Furthermore, a pot is not *conceptually* identical to its atoms. We may not be able to make an ultimate distinction between the whole and its parts, but we certainly do distinguish conceptually. If we did not distinguish conceptually, then no one could perceive a pot without knowing of the existence of atoms—a manifest absurdity. A pot and its atoms are substantially identical, but have different opposites of the negative (*ngo bo gcig dang ldog pa tha dad*).

17 PVP 236/1/4. Atoms, though they are the basis of the sense-cognition that recognizes a "pot,"and are therefore perceived in some sense (as a collection), are not the designated object (*tha snyad kyi yul*) of that cognition, because one designates an object roughly, not in terms of its ultimate components.

18 The opponent is not clearly identified here, but may be a representative of one of the other Tibetan lineages, e.g., the Sa skya, that deny any kind of ultimacy to gross objects, or collections, but, rather, consider such collections merely to be imputations upon their atomic components. On this dispute, see Klein (1986) 84-88.

19 The criticism here is directed at the idea that gross objects alone are perceptible, and that that which is perceived is not substantially existent. Not all external objects are necessarily gross objects. "Blue,"for instance, is external but not gross. Since, according to the opponent, only a gross object can be perceived, blue would be imperceptible. By extension, then, blue would have to be atoms. If blue is atoms, it is substantially existent, but cannot be perceived. If blue is perceived, it cannot be made of atoms, so it must be a gross object, but if it is a gross object, it must be non-substantially existent. What is non-substantially existent is non-efficient. How, then, can it effect a cognition? rGyal tshab rje is attempting to establish an ultimate—if not conceptual—

that [when] one accepts that a visual cognition does not see blue, if there *is* an object of sense-perception, it is contradictory that it be an [efficient] entity, because it is impossible that its atoms be an object; and if it is a gross object, it is contradictory that it be an [efficient] entity.[20]

Alternatively, [if] the phrase "if it is just many"is set forth as the objection, [then] the phrase "as before"becomes the answer. If this body is many atoms, since it is impossible that it be gross, it follows [by the Vaiśeṣika view] that when there exist separate atoms, a sense-cognition will cognize the atoms individually.[21] You may think that if it is impossible that there be a partless whole, then since [an object] is nothing more than its atoms, it follows that the atoms are cognized individually. We say that because of the above refutation of a partless whole, it follows that [according to *you*] one does cognize thus.[22]

Refuting other syllogisms through that [114]

(87c) THIS ALSO CLEARS AWAY [THE IDEA] THAT
[OBJECTS] DO NOT COVER [EACH OTHER,] ETC.

THIS proof of [the aggregate visibility of] atoms — since a partless gross object is impossible — ALSO CLEARS AWAY [the idea] THAT external objects DO NOT have the ability to COVER [each other], ETC.,

---

equivalence between gross objects and the atoms of which they are made, by pointing out the difficulties involved in separating perceptibility from substantial existence: the two must be posited of the same entities. Hence, both atoms (compositely) and gross objects are perceptible *and* substantially existent.

20 The opponent's assertion of the substantial non-existence of gross objects, coupled with their denial of the perceptibility of atoms, leads to the undesirable conclusions (a) that an object of sense-perception is a non-efficient entity, because it is not atoms, which alone ultimately are efficient and (b) that an object is non-efficient because, as a gross object, it has no substantial existence, and that which lacks substantial existence cannot be an efficient entity.

21 The verse (PV 86b) reads: *du ma nyid na snga ma bzhin* (*...smādanekatve 'pi pūrvavat*). The opponent's original objection comprised both. Here, the objection is that if the body is composed of many atoms, then from moment to moment one's ultimate object of cognition is, simply, the many atoms of the body. The reply is that the fault is "as before."

22 The Vaiśeṣika is disturbed by the implication that if there is no partless whole, then there is no object that is "more"than the sum of its atoms, and all we ever perceive is individual atoms. The Buddhist, who believes that atoms are invisible individually, but visible in composite, does not face this dilemma, but recognizes that the Vaiśeṣika does.

because although there are no [partless gross objects], there are collections of atoms, and it is shown that they act [in such a way as to cover objects].[23]

Refuting [the existence of] a whole and, in particular, of the qualities based upon it [115]

[This is divided into:] (1) Extreme consequences if it is necessary that there be an objectively separate whole for there to be seeing by a sense-cognition [116] and (2) Refuting [the existence of] an objectively separate number that is based on that [117].

Extreme consequences if it is necessary that there be an objectively separate whole for there to be seeing by a sense-cognition [116]

(88) HOW COULD MERCURY APPEAR
MIXED WITH GOLD OR A STONE [APPEAR] PAINTED?[24]
HOW COULD THE [SENSE-] FACULTY, ETC., [GENERATE] COGNITIONS,
[WHEN] THEY ARE UNABLE [TO DO SO] INDIVIDUALLY?
(89) IF YOU SAY THAT [COGNITION ARISES] FROM CONJUNCTION, HERE THE CONSEQUENCES ARE THE SAME;
IF YOU SAY THAT IN THE CASE OF GOLD AND MERCURY
THE CONJUNCTION APPEARS,
[WE REPLY:] HOW COULD [SENSE-COGNITION] COGNIZE [THE CONJUNCTION] WHEN IT DOES NOT SEE THE BASIS?
(90) IT IS [BY YOUR THEORY] CONTRADICTORY THAT [E.G., DRINKS] POSSESS TASTE *AND* COLOR, ETC.
IF YOU ASSERT THAT [THIS OCCURS] THROUGH
IMPUTATION, [WE REPLY THAT THEN] THERE WILL BE DIFFERENT MINDS;
HOW, [FURTHER,] COULD IT BE SAID [THAT THERE IS] "A LONG GARLAND?"

HOW, it also follows, COULD MERCURY APPEAR to a sense-cognition as MIXED WITH GOLD, OR A STONE, ETC., [appear] PAINTED? It is unacceptable that they could, because they are objectively separate wholes, and because they are collections of inharmonious types of atoms.[25]

---

23 In the Vaiśeṣika view, which admits only of the possibility of individually visible atoms if there does not exist a gross, partless whole, no object could cover any other. Buddhists, however, assert that atoms in aggregate are different from atoms not in aggregate; thus, although individual atoms cannot cover objects, aggregates of atoms can.

24 The Tibetan here is *rdo tshon* ("painted stone"), while the Sanskrit is *taptopala* ("heated stone").

25 A mixture of mercury and gold, or paint and stone, though known to exist,

Based on this text, it is unreasonable to assert that, when iron is molten red, the fire and the iron are substantially different, [because] it is the case, as proven in the *Pramāṇaviniścaya*, that those two are substantially identical, and Dharmottara extensively explains in his [*Pramāṇaviniścaya*] commentary that the case of [the painted stone and mercury-gold] and that of [molten iron] are quite dissimilar.[26]

How, it follows alternatively, COULD the meeting of the three conditions, [sense-] FACULTY, [object and cognition], generate even the common results, COGNITIONS of form? It is unacceptable that it could, because THEY ARE UNABLE [to generate cognitions] INDIVIDUALLY, when they have not met, and even when they do meet, there is no objectively separate whole.[27]

[OPPONENT:] Sense-cognition arises FROM the CONJUNCTION among the three conditions when they meet.[28]

[RGYAL TSHAB RJE:] It follows that it also is unacceptable that the three conditions generate the conjunction, because although you assert HERE the generation of the conjunction, THE CONSEQUENCES ARE THE SAME whether [the three conditions] meet or do not meet.[29]

---

could not, on the Vaiśeṣika view, be cognized as a mixture, because (a) each disparate element is a partless whole that cannot combine with other partless wholes and (b) atoms of disparate elements cannot have any basis for their combination.

26 Thus, painted stone and mercury mixed with gold are appropriate examples of composites that would be inadmissible under Vaiśeṣika theory. Molten iron, on the other hand, would not be an appropriate example, because when iron is molten, there is a substantial identity between fire and iron, and it is a mixture of substantially *different* elements that Vaiśeṣika theory renders impossible.

27 The three conditions of sense-cognition—faculty, object and cognition— are individually unable to generate their common result. Yet, if there is no whole that is substantially different from them, as the Buddhist has proven there cannot be, then their aggregate generation of sense-cognition cannot be explained, because, again, the Vaiśeṣika is unable to explain aggregates other than by recourse to the concept of an objectively separate whole.

28 The Vaiśeṣika explains that disparate substances form aggregates through a quality known as "conjunction" (*ldan pa, saṃyoga*). Thus, a sense-cognition is a result of the object, sense-faculty and cognition, all of which are brought together by conjunction. See *Vaiśeṣika Sūtra* I:1:16 and Robinson (1967) 37.

29 The Vaiśeṣika asserts that sense-cognition is generated from conjunction, but the generation of conjunction itself is inexplicable. The factors individually cannot generate it, and since there is no principle by which they can combine, there is no basis for asserting that there is a change in their situation such that they could generate conjunction—any more than they could generate a

[OPPONENT:] IN THE CASE OF the mixture of GOLD AND MERCURY, although there is no whole, THE CONJUNCTION APPEARS to sense-cognition when inharmonious types of atoms meet.

[RGYAL TSHAB RJE:] HOW COULD sense-cognition directly COGNIZE a meeting of what is based on atoms? It follows that it is impossible that it could, because IT DOES NOT SEE the atoms that are THE BASIS. This well refutes those who say that sense-cognition does not see atoms [but] sees collections of atoms.[30]

It follows that IT IS CONTRADICTORY that drinks made of various inharmonious types of substances POSSESS such qualities as sweet TASTE, good COLOR, ETC., because there is no objectively separate whole that is the basis of their possessing [such qualities].[31]

[OPPONENT:] Even IF there is no objectively separate whole, we ASSERT THAT IT IS THROUGH IMPUTATION on the taste and color parts that we designate that it is a sweet-tasting drink, etc.

[RGYAL TSHAB RJE:] It follows that when the individual tastes and colors are not mixed into the drink, THERE WILL BE the arising of DIFFERENT appearing MINDS, but it is impossible that there arise a cognition of taste and color originating from their [mixture], because the imputation [that the taste or form] is sweet-tasting, etc., is merely [made] when the taste and color parts are not mixed into the whole.[32]

Alternatively, it follows that it is unacceptable that in a drink made of various substances one experience another taste different from the mentally experienced taste of particular drinks [that comprise the

---

sense-cognition.

30 The Vaiśeṣika claims that atoms are invisible, so anything that is based on atoms, such as their conjunction, must be invisible as well. According to the Buddhist view, atoms are invisible individually, but visible in composite, and although they are not the designated object of a sense-cognition, they are an object nonetheless.

31 If there is no whole substantially different from its elements, the Vaiśeṣika cannot explain how a drink that combines different qualities of color and taste can be said to possess its *own* color and taste, because, in the absence of a substantially different whole, it remains atomic, hence unconnected and invisible.

32 The opponent tries to argue that, although what we actually taste are merely individual tastes and what we see are individual colors, we *impute* a taste and color to the combination of them. The Buddhist, however, maintains—correctly—that the taste and color of the combination of individual substances is different from that of any of the individual substances, and so cannot be known simply through a knowledge of the qualities of all the individual substances.

mixture], such as milk, etc., because one merely imputes that a *part's* taste is "sweet-tasting" not that the whole's taste is.[33]

HOW, it follows, COULD IT BE SAID that a properly arranged garland of a hundred flowers is "A LONG GARLAND"? It is unacceptable that it could, because there is no objectively separate whole; and even if there is [alleged to be] conjunction, a second quality cannot be based on a quality.[34]

Refuting [the existence of] a substantially different number based on that [117]

[This is divided into:] (1) Setting forth the reason [118] and (2) Disposing of [objections alleged to] damage that [119].

Setting forth the reason [118]

(91) ESSENCES SUCH AS NUMBER, CONJUNCTION,
ACTION, ETC., THAT ARE DIFFERENT IN OWN-NATURE
FROM WHAT POSSESSES THEM AND [FROM VERBAL] EXPRESSION
DO NOT APPEAR TO THE MIND.

There are no ESSENCES SUCH AS the NUMBER, CONJUNCTION, ACTION, ETC., of the pot that exist as substantially DIFFERENT IN OWN-NATURE FROM the pot THAT POSSESSES THAT number, etc., AND [from] the words that are THE EXPRESSION of "the pot," because if such [essences] existed, they should appear to an unmistaken mind, but they DO NOT APPEAR TO THE unmistaken MIND.[35]

---

33 See previous note. Nagatomi (1957 [105]) reads the passage somewhat differently, maintaining that the Buddhist's point is that an "imputed" or "figurative" (*upacāra*) conjunction (as that between sweetness and color) would be different from an actual conjunction (as between milk and water).

34 If there is no objectively separate whole, a Vaiśeṣika cannot explain how we can speak of "a long garland," because (a) as we have seen, they have no other principle by which to explain collections and (b) by their own principles, a quality cannot depend on another quality, so if conjunction is invoked to explain the fact that the garland is long, the principle is violated, because conjunction and length both are qualities.

35 An unmistaken mind is any authoritative cognition. rGyal tshab rje maintains that such objectively separate "essences," or notions, as number, etc., do *not* appear to an unmistaken cognition, and that there is as a result no basis for positing the existence of such entities. It is possible, of course, that the opponent may have a different idea of what appears to an "unmistaken cognition"—though by demonstrating the concept's incoherence, rGyal tshab rje presumably intends to show that it could *not* appear to an unmistaken cogni-

Disposing of [objections alleged to] damage that [119]

[This is divided into:] (1) Refuting [the idea] that since we apply different words there exist substantially different objects [120] and (2) Disposing of [the idea that] if that is unproven it follows that [applying] different words is pointless [121].

Refuting [the idea] that since we apply different words there exist substantially different objects [120]

(92) WORDS AND COGNITIONS HAVE OBJECTS IMPUTED
BY CONCEPTUAL COGNITIONS THAT FOLLOW ON DIFFERENT ENTITIES.
FOR EXAMPLE, IT IS LIKE QUALITIES, ETC.,
THAT HAVE BEEN DESTROYED OR HAVE NOT YET ARISEN.
(93) IF YOU ASSERT [THAT] IMPUTING [IS THE CAUSE] IN THIS CASE,
THEN WHY NOT ASSERT THAT [THE IMPUTER] OF THOSE
[IS THE IMPUTER] TO ALL ENTITIES?
THROUGH ANY REASONING, THAT SHOULD BE ASSERTED.
(94) IF YOU SAY THAT ONE IS NOT IMPUTING ALL [ENTITIES],
[BECAUSE] ONE SPEAKS PRINCIPALLY OF PARTICULAR
DIFFERENT [ENTITIES], [WE REPLY:] FOR WHAT [REASON] IS [THIS STATEMENT] MADE?...

[OPPONENT:] There exist number, etc., that are objectively separate from the pot, because we see that there are words for "one pot," "two pots," etc.

[RGYAL TSHAB RJE:] Merely because we see that there are different WORDS AND COGNITIONS, it does not follow that there exist substantially different objects, because although there is no "one" of the pot that is objectively separate from the pot, [the word or cognition of number] HAS AN OBJECT that is IMPUTED BY A CONCEPTUAL COGNITION THAT FOLLOWS ON clearing away [the idea] of any other [entity] DIFFERENT from the ENTITY that is a non-one pot.[36]

---

tion, since it is a mistaken concept.

36 Once again, the Buddhist raises the point that there is no necessary connection between verbal designations and the ontological status of what is designated. Of course, we say "one pot,""two pots,"etc., but that does not mean that there is an essential "number"existing somewhere that corresponds to our numerical specification. The Buddhist, in a wholesale repudiation of universals, maintains that when we specify that there is *one* pot, we simply are eliminating the possibility that this pot can be characterized as non-one. The process, thus, is thoroughly negative and exclusionary, and need not admit the existence of an ontologically distinct "number."For an interesting discussion

FOR EXAMPLE, although there is no second quality that is based on the QUALITY blue, ETC., we see that we say "one blue thing"; or, although there is no separate quality to pots THAT HAVE BEEN DESTROYED OR HAVE NOT YET ARISEN, we see that there are such designations [for these pots] as "one," "two," etc.[37]

[OPPONENT:] In applying the designation of number to past and future [objects], we ASSERT that one [applies] an IMPUTING name IN THIS CASE.[38]

[RGYAL TSHAB RJE:] THEN WHY NOT ASSERT THAT [the imputing name] that is the conventional imputer OF THOSE [past and future entities is the imputer] TO ALL ENTITIES? It follows that it is reasonable so to assert, because THROUGH WHATEVER REASONING [it is shown] that there does not exist a special quality that is objectively separate, and that THAT term "number," etc., as applied to past and future [objects], IS ASSERTED to be an imputing name, [through that we also should assert that] that lack of separate objectivity [predicated] of [past and future] number, etc., should [be predicated] equally of all entities.[39]

[OPPONENT:] One does NOT apply an IMPUTING name to ALL [entities], because then it follows that it is impossible that there be an objective name. Thus, when ONE SPEAKS PRINCIPALLY of the existence of a PARTICULAR substantially DIFFERENT quality, that is an objective name; the name applied to what is not that is an imputing name.

---

of the Buddhist attitude toward universals, see Shah (1967) chapter III. See also above, pp. 124-25.

37 The fact that we can speak meaningfully of a combination of more than one quality (an impossibility on Vaiśeṣika principles) or can ascribe qualities to objects not presently existent demonstrates the independence of linguistic designations from ontological facts.

38 An imputing name (*btags ming*) is distinguished from an objective (or "entitative") name (*dngos ming*). The latter is the name given an entity on the basis of its actual nature, the former is the name given figuratively, or by convention. Thus, past and future objects do not actually exist, so they cannot possess number, but we can conventionally designate that they do, or would if they existed.

39 rGyal tshab rje argues sarcastically that if the Vaiśeṣika is going to apply imputing names to unreal entities, then they should apply them to all those substantially separate qualities the Buddhist has already shown to be non-existent. Since virtually everything is asserted by the Vaiśeṣika to be a substantially separate whole or quality, everything should be designated by an imputing name—leaving virtually nothing to be designated by an objective name.

[RGYAL TSHAB RJE:] FOR WHAT reason IS THIS statement MADE, i.e., that an objective name is the name applied to a particular substantially different quality and that an imputing name is applied to what is not that? It follows that it cannot be accepted, because this is merely imputed without any reason by the Vaiśeṣika.[40]

Disposing of [the idea that] if that is unproven it follows that [applying] different words is pointless [121]

[This is divided into:] (1) Disposing of the consequence that [applying] different words is pointless [122] and (2) Disposing of the consequence that it is unacceptable that there be a sixth [genitive] case [123].

Disposing of the consequence that [applying] different words is pointless [122]

(94c) . . .IF [YOU SAY THAT], THERE BEING NO
DIFFERENT [OBJECT], DIFFERENT [WORDS] ARE POINTLESS,
(95) [WE REPLY THAT] THERE ALSO IS NO REASON FOR [POSITING] AN OBJECTIVELY SEPARATE [NUMBER];
WORDS FOR WHITE [OBJECTS], ETC., AND
NUMBER-POSSESSING [WHITE OBJECTS], ETC., ARE NOT REDUNDANT.
IF [YOU SAY THAT] THAT ALSO HAS OBJECTIVELY SEPARATE [NUMBER],
(96) [WE REPLY THAT] THEN THERE WILL BE NO DISTINCTION BETWEEN SUBSTANCE AND QUALITY;
EVEN THOUGH THERE IS NO OBJECTIVELY SEPARATE [SUBSTANCE], THERE IS
AN ANALYTICAL DIFFERENTIATION OF OPPOSITES,
AS [IN] THE PHRASES, "NOT ACTION"AND "NOT SUBSTANCE."

[OPPONENT:] THERE BEING NO substantially DIFFERENT object that is to be expressed, applying DIFFERENT words IS POINTLESS, because even if they are applied, they will merely be redundant.[41]

---

40 The Vaiśeṣika maintains that objective names are applied to substantially separate qualities (since these are real, hence "objective"), while imputing names are applied to something that is not actually that separate quality, but is designated as if it were. rGyal tshab rje replies that this application of the notions of objective and imputing names is purely arbitrary on the part of the Vaiśeṣika, dependent as it is upon the validity of Vaiśeṣika metaphysics. The Buddhist, accepting their own metaphysics, will obviously define the referents of the two types of name quite differently.

41 The Vaiśeṣika argues that if there are no substantially separate entities corresponding to our verbal distinctions, then there would be no difference be-

[RGYAL TSHAB RJE:] If there are different words for topics that are not objectively separate, then it follows that they necessarily are *not* redundant, because THERE ALSO IS NO REASON for [positing] a number that is OBJECTIVELY SEPARATE from a white object, for there are number-WORDS expressing one WHITE object, two white objects, ETC., AND the words for the NUMBER-POSSESSING white [object], ETC., ARE NOT REDUNDANT.[42]

[OPPONENT:] THAT white object ALSO possesses an OBJECTIVELY SEPARATE "one"-ness.

[RGYAL TSHAB RJE:] It follows that THERE WILL BE NO DISTINCTION BETWEEN SUBSTANCE AND QUALITIES, because of the basing of some second substantially separate quality on a [first] quality.[43]

Therefore, because we apply different words to different cognitions, it follows that it is not necessarily ascertained that there are different substances, because EVEN THOUGH THERE IS NOT in existence AN OBJECTIVELY SEPARATE substance, THERE IS an application of different words, merely through AN ANALYTICAL DIFFERENTIATION OF OPPOSITES. AS, for example: although there is in action no objectively separate quality, "non-substance," or in substance [a quality called] "non-action," THERE ARE THE PHRASES, "this substance is NOT ACTION," AND "action is NOT SUBSTANCE."[44]

---

tween saying "cow," and "one cow," and the predication "one" would add nothing to what we already know when we say "cow."

42 rGyal tshab rje replies that the predication "one" *does* give us non-redundant information, even if it does not correspond to an ontologically distinct entity such as the Vaiśeṣika believes necessary.

43 The Vaiśeṣika cannot argue that a white object has an additional, ontologically distinct quality of "oneness," because they themselves have said that a quality cannot be based on another quality, and in this case, "oneness" would be based on "whiteness." Or, if they *do* base oneness on whiteness, then they are treating one or the other as if it were a substance, since a quality must be based on a substance, yet to do this would undermine the distinction between substances and qualities that the Vaiśeṣika has striven to establish.

44 The fact that we *can* apply predications without there being an ontologically distinct entity to which the predications apply is shown by our ability to speak of "non-action" in relation to substance, and vice versa: certainly, there is no substantially separate quality called "non-action" or "non-substance" that can be predicated of substance or action, yet there is no question that the predications are applied appropriately. In general, predicates do not name an ontologically distinct entity, but eliminate (via *apoha*) all predicates other than the one we wish to specify. Cf. TS 1043-44.

Disposing of the consequence that it is unacceptable that there be a sixth [genitive] case [123]

[This is divided into:] (1) Distinguishing between predicate-expressions and subject-[expressions] [124] and (2) Distinguishing between genus-expressions and collection expressions [125].

Distinguishing between predicate-expressions and subject-[expressions] [124]

(97) THE VERBAL EXPRESSIONS [FOR] AN ENTITY,
WHICH ALSO SEEM TO SHOW THAT NUMBER, ETC.,
ARE DIFFERENT FROM WHAT POSSESSES THEM
ARE TO MAKE THE DISTINCTION BETWEEN [NUMBER AND] THE OTHER PREDICATES [OF THE ENTITY].
(98) THE SAYING, "THE CONJUNCTION OF FINGERS":
ONE EXPRESSES IT AS IF [THE FINGERS] WERE A PREDICATE THAT IS DIFFERENT [FROM THEIR CONJUNCTION],
FOR [SOMEONE] DESIRES TO KNOW JUST THAT,
WITHOUT PROJECTING ANY OTHER [PREDICATE].
(99) THE SAYING , "THE FINGERS ARE CONJOINED,"IS KNOWN
TO EXPRESS THE SUBJECT, BECAUSE ALTHOUGH
IT EXPRESSES THE SINGLE MEANING, IT [CAN] PROJECT ALL [OTHER PREDICATES];
THEREFORE, THERE IS THE EMPLOYMENT OF [DIFFERENT] SIGNS.

[OPPONENT:] Well, then, it is unacceptable [to use] the expression, "the number of the pot," because there is no number that is objectively separate from [the pot].[45]

[RGYAL TSHAB RJE:] [The reply is as follows:]

The purpose of applying the sixth [genitive] case:

THE VERBAL EXPRESSION [for] the predicate, "ENTITY," WHICH ALSO SEEMS TO SHOW THAT NUMBER, ETC., ARE [substantially] DIFFERENT FROM the pot THAT POSSESSES THEM, have a purpose, because THEY ARE applied in order TO MAKE us understand THE DISTINCTION between the number of the pot and the OTHER particular PREDICATES of the pot.[46]

---

45 The Vaiśeṣika argues that if there is no substantially separate quality of, e.g., number, then we cannot legitimately use the genitive, or possessive case, because possession expresses a relation between two ontologically distinct entities.

46 The Tibetan (PV 97a) talks of "the verbal expression [for] 'entity'" (*dngos po brjod pa'i sgra rnams*). rGyal tshab rje glosses this to mean the verbal expression of the predicate. Words genitively expressing the predicate, such as "the

Showing that predicate-expressions exclude other [possible] particular [predicates]:

THE SAYING expressing "THE CONJUNCTION OF FINGERS," has the purpose of EXPRESSING IT AS IF the fingers WERE A PREDICATE THAT IS a [substantially] DIFFERENT quality than "the conjunction of fingers," because WHEN [someone] DESIRES TO KNOW JUST THAT row of fingers, [the words, "the conjunction of fingers,"] express just that in order that they may know it, WITHOUT PROJECTING as a mental object ANY OTHER opposed [predicate].[47]

Showing that by expressing the subject one does not exclude other particular [predicates]:

THE SAYING expressing that "THE FINGERS ARE CONJOINED" IS KNOWN TO EXPRESS THE SUBJECT, BECAUSE ALTHOUGH from among the many particular predicates of "fingers," IT EXPRESSES THE SINGLE MEANING of a row [of fingers], IT is an expression that [can] PROJECT as mental objects ALL other particular predicates of fingers, and does not exclude them.[48] THEREFORE, although there are no objectively separate particular predicates, THERE IS a purpose in THE EMPLOYMENT OF different SIGNS for one object, because one does so in order to [generate cognition] through excluding or not excluding other particular [predicates] of a single object.[49]

---

number of the pot," *appear* to relate two ontologically distinct entities, but they do not. They only serve to set one predicate or quality apart from other possible predicates or qualities. Specifying the "form" of the pot, therefore, excludes as a possible predicate any other quality of the pot.

47 The phrase, "the conjunction of fingers," has the specific purpose of identifying one predicate of "fingers" for someone who wishes to know just *that* predicate of "fingers" and no other. There is no other way that this can be expressed except genitively, yet it does not entail an ontological distinction between the fingers and their conjunction.

48 Expressions in which the predicate is the base, e.g., "the conjunction of fingers," exclude all other possible predicates by making *one* predicate the grammatical subject. Expressions in which the subject is the basis—and therefore also the grammatical subject—e.g., "the fingers are conjoined," do *not* exclude other possible predicates, for fingers just as easily can be long, short, white or black.

49 Thus, the general purpose of applying different predicates and types of predicate-sentences to an object is to enable one's listener to know either one or a number of predicates of an object, depending on what the listener desires to know and/or the speaker desires to communicate. rGyal tshab rje's approach here is a very "pragmatic" one—he simply does not share the Vaiśeṣika's ob-

Distinguishing genus-expressions and collection-expressions [125]

(100-101) THE WORD "POT" IS APPLIED
TO CUT OFF [THE IDEA THAT IT IS] THE NON-CAUSE
OF THE COMMON RESULT OF THOSE [SUBSTANCES COMPRISING THE POT]. THUS,
THE UTTERANCE "THE FORM OF THE POT"
IS NOT A PHRASE THAT HAS ONE [AND THE SAME] BASIS [AS "POT"],
BECAUSE IT EXCLUDES THE PARTICULARS WITH THE ABILITY [TO EVOKE] THE FORM, ETC. [OF THE POT].
THEREFORE, THIS IS THE DIFFERENCE BETWEEN
GENUS- AND COLLECTION-EXPRESSIONS.
(102) THE SAYING "THE FORM OF THE POT," ETC.,
[SHOWS] AS THE PARTICULAR [PREDICATE] THE GENERAL [POT],
AND SHOWS AS THE PARTICULAR [BASIS] WHAT HAS ABILITY [TO PRODUCE COGNITION OF THE FORM OF THE POT];
THIS POSITION ALSO IS EXPRESSIBLE IN OTHER [CASES].[50]

[OPPONENT:] If there merely exist parts, without there being an objectively separate whole, then one merely can use the expressions "the pot is formed" and "the form of form," etc., but it will not be suitable to use the expression "the form of the pot."[51]

[RGYAL TSHAB RJE:] The expression "a pot" is not applied to some objectively separate whole, because THE WORD expressing "POT" IS APPLIED as an objective name to the collection that is CUT OFF from being THE NON-CAUSE OF THE water-holding that is the COMMON RESULT OF [the conjunction of] those eight atomic substances of the pot.[52]

---

session with positing a "real" entity to correspond to every semantic shading.

50 The verse (*de spyi yan lag tu byas te / bum pa yi no gzugs sogs zhes / de nus khyad par ston par byed / phyogs 'dis gzhan la'ang brjod par bya*) is interpreted by Nagatomi (1957 [115]) as saying that (a) expressions like "the form of the pot," etc., express the various abilities (*nus khyad par*) of form (*de*) as "subordinate to a generic character" (*spyi yan lag tu byas*) and (b) "different types of designation are made in different ways" (*gzhan la'ang brjod par bya*).

51 The Vaiśeṣika here raises in a slightly different form the objection voiced above. If there is no substantially separate whole pot, it is claimed, then we may be able to speak predicatively of a substance's qualities ("the pot is formed"), or genitively when the entity is the same as itself ("the form of form"), but we cannot speak genitively of two different entities ("the form of the pot"), since the Buddhist denies the existence of a substantially separate pot to which form could "belong."

52 The word "pot" does not refer to some whole that is substantially different from its parts. It is a collection-expression, applied to that combination of

[THUS,] in the expression "THE FORM OF THE POT," "the pot" and "the form of the pot" have two [bases]; ["the form of the pot"] IS NOT A PHRASE that [implies] HAVING ONE BASIS, [i.e.,] the same basis, BECAUSE the expression "POT" excludes as topics [other] PARTICULAR [predicates] WITH THE uncommon ABILITY to generate a self-apprehending cognition of the FORM, smell, ETC., of the pot.[53]

Therefore, since the expression "a pot" expresses a collection from the point of view of "the form of the pot," etc., and expresses a genus from the point of view of "a golden pot," etc., the former excludes [other particular predicates] as topics, while the latter does not exclude [other particular predicates].[54] Therefore, one must apply the "four-cornered" [analysis] to collection-expressions and genus-expressions. There is (1) collection without genus, as in the expression "Mt. Vindhya"; (2) genus without collection, as in the expression "form"; (3) both collection and genus, as in the expression "a pot"; and (4) neither collection nor genus, as in anything not covered by [the above].[55]

---

eight atomic substances that is able to contain water. Because it is able to contain water, it is causally efficient, hence "real" according to Dharmakīrti's criterion. The fact that it is "real," or that there is an expression that identifies it, however, does not mean that it is a substantially separate whole, because the expression that points to it is a collection-expression, connoting something made up of parts.

53 Thus, the expression "the form of the pot" can be broken down into *two* bases, "pot" and "form of the pot." The latter specifies one quality of the pot, namely, its form, while the general collection-expression "pot" excludes all predicates, and merely includes the collection, pot, itself. Since these two bases are identifiable, it is *not* the same thing to say "pot" and "the form of the pot," but the difference between these does not entail the existence of ontologically distinct referents.

54 Depending on one's point of view, "pot" is either a collection-expression or a genus-expression. In the expression "the form of the pot," it excludes any predication other than the pot's form, and thus is a collection-expression. In the expression "the golden pot," it does not exclude particular attributes, for it is known to be golden. In the latter case, then, "pot" is a genus-expression.

55 (1) "Mt. Vindhya" is a name we apply to a concatenation of rocks, trees, etc., and it is, thus, a collection. At the same time, it excludes the parts that comprise the collection—which semantically, if not ontologically, is different from the sum of its parts. (2) "Form" is not the concatenation of any parts, but is, rather, a general term—a genus-expression— of which there can be many particular instances, e.g., the form of the pot, the form of fingers, etc. (3) "A pot," as noted above, is both a collection-expression and a genus-expression. It is a collection-expression because it names a particular concatenation of

THEREFORE, it does not definitely follow that an objectively separate genus is the topic of a genus-expression and a substantially separate whole [the topic] of a collection-expression, because a genus-expression does not exclude particulars, while a collection-expression does exclude parts — THIS IS THE DIFFERENCE BETWEEN GENUS-expressions AND COLLECTION-EXPRESSIONS.[56]

Although there does not exist any objectively separate whole, such expressions as THE SAYING "THE FORM OF THE POT," ETC., have a purpose, because, by showing thus that there are [two] parts, viz., the particular basis, which is the form of the pot and THE PARTICULAR predicate, which IS THE GENERAL collection, pot, they SHOW as the mental object THE PARTICULAR [object] THAT HAS ABILITY to generate a self-apprehending cognition of the form of the pot.[57]

THIS POSITION that has just been explained ALSO IS EXPRESSIBLE [in the idea] that even though there is no objectively separate whole IN such OTHER expressions as "the smell of sandal," there is nothing contradictory in the expression "the smell of sandal." When [one employs] such an expression, sandal is the particular predicate and its smell is the particular base.[58]

---

material elements that cannot be confused semantically with its parts or qualities. It is a genus-expression because it names a *type* of entity of which any number of particular instances are possible, e.g., a golden pot, a formed pot, etc. (4) An example of a word that expresses neither a collection nor a genus is a proper name, such as "John."

56 Because of the definitions of collection- and genus-expressions in terms of the exclusion of parts and the non-exclusion of particulars, there is no simple one-to-one correspondence between the application of collection- and genus-expressions and the existence of ontologically distinct entities that the expressions denote. The two types of expression function in different ways and, being purely semantic distinctions, they need have no ontological overtones such as the Vaiśeṣika would like to import.

57 To reiterate, then, the purpose of an expression such as "the form of the pot" is to distinguish—for someone who wishes to know— a specific quality (the form) of a general collection (the pot).

58 Again, in an expression such as "the smell of sandal," the smell is the grammatical subject, i.e., the "particular base" (*khyad gzhi*), and the sandal is its "particular predicate" (*khyad chos*). The phrase is a particular grammatical arrangement that fulfills a particular grammatical need, i.e., the need to specify the smell of sandal from among all other possible predicates. As always, the Buddhist insists that the process of arriving at a cognition of the smell of sandal is an exclusionary, negative one, not therefore requiring the "positive" referents for all nuances of expression that are entailed by a realist metaphysics like that of the Vaiśeṣika.

B. ATOMS AND BREATHS

Refuting [the idea that] subtle atoms are that [special basis of mind] [126]

[This is divided into:] (1) Refuting [the idea] that atoms collectively are necessarily the cause of mind [127] and (2) Refuting [the idea] that they are able individually [to act as the basis of mind] [128].

Refuting [the idea] that atoms collectively are necessarily the cause of mind [127]

(103) IF EVEN ONE PART IS MISSING, [MIND] WILL NOT [ARISE],
BECAUSE THE CAUSE [MUST HAVE] EVERY [PART].

Also, IF EVEN ONE subtle PART IS MISSING, it follows that mind WILL NOT arise, BECAUSE that which is THE CAUSE of that definitely must have EVERY single part [present].[59]

Refuting [the idea] that they are able to act individually [as the basis of mind] [128]

[This is divided into:] (1) Setting forth the consequences [129] and (2) Refuting the reply to that [130].

Setting forth the consequences [129]

(103c) MANY [MINDS] WILL OCCUR SIMULTANEOUSLY,
BECAUSE THEY HAVE THE ABILITY INDIVIDUALLY [TO GENERATE MIND].

It follows that MANY minds WILL OCCUR SIMULTANEOUSLY in the mindstream of one person, BECAUSE atoms HAVE THE ABILITY INDIVIDUALLY independently to generate mind.[60]

Refuting the reply to that [130]

[This is divided into:] (1) Refuting [the idea] that with breath as a condition there would not arise many simultaneous [minds] [131] and (2) Refuting [the idea] that even if mind arises simultaneously from

---

59 A collection is not a collection unless all of its parts are present. If the body's collection of atoms is asserted to be the cause of mind, it is necessary that every single atom of the body be present. Yet, if one were to lose, say, a finger, some of the atoms of the body's collection of atoms would be missing. Thus, the collection would be "incomplete,"and since the complete collection is the cause of mind, mind could not arise.

60 If atoms are said to be able to generate mind individually—the logical alternative to their generation of mind collectively—then in theory there could be as many minds as there are atoms in the body, a patent absurdity.

the body at first, later it only arises successively from its homogenes [137].

Refuting [the idea] that with breath as a condition there would not arise many simultaneous [minds] [131]

[This is divided into:] (1) Refuting [the idea that mind] arises from a permanent breath [132], (2) Refuting [the idea that mind] arises from an impermanent breath [133] and (3) Refuting [the assertion of] fault in our position [136].

Refuting [the idea that mind] arises from a permanent breath [132]

(104) BREATHS DO NOT DETERMINE [THE ARISING OF MIND],
BECAUSE THEY ARE EQUALLY AS MULTIPLE [AS THE BODY];
IF THERE IS A SINGLE [PERMANENT BREATH], IT IS CLEAR THAT THERE WILL BE MANY [MINDS],
BECAUSE THEIR PERMANENT CAUSE IS PRESENT.
(105) IF [A PERMANENT BREATH] IS NOT THE CAUSE OF MANY [MINDS],
THEN IT IS NOT THE CAUSE [OF MANY MINDS] SUCCESSIVELY, EITHER, BECAUSE IT DOES NOT CHANGE;
FROM IT [JUST INDIVIDUAL MINDS] ARE NOT ASCERTAINED [TO ARISE], BECAUSE
IN [THE SPACE OF] ONE BREATH, THERE WILL BE [MANY MINDS] APPREHENDING MANY OBJECTS.
(106) IF ONE MIND COGNIZES MANY [OBJECTS],
THEN THAT WILL BE A SIMULTANEOUS COGNIZER,
BECAUSE THERE IS NOTHING PREVENTING [SIMULTANEOUS COGNITION]; IT WILL NOT
[COGNIZE] SUCCESSIVELY, BECAUSE THERE IS NO CHANGE.

It follows that BREATHS not having many parts DO NOT DETERMINE the arising only of individual minds, BECAUSE [breaths] ARE EQUALLY AS MULTIPLE in atomic portions as is the body.[61]

[OPPONENT:] [The reason] is unproven; THERE *IS* A SINGLE, permanent breath.

[RGYAL TSHAB RJE:] It follows that IT IS CLEAR THAT THERE WILL BE MANY simulatneous minds, BECAUSE THEIR PERMANENT CAUSE IS always PRESENT.[62]

---

61 The argument that individual minds are generated by a single, partless, permanent breath is undermined by the fact that breath has extension; it is accepted in Indian thought as pervading the entire body, and thus it has as many parts (or atoms) as the body itself.

[OPPONENT:] [A permanent breath] is the cause of just one mind at a time; IT IS NOT THE CAUSE OF MANY.

[RGYAL TSHAB RJE:] It follows that the [permanent] breath IS NOT the cause of many minds SUCCESSIVELY, EITHER, BECAUSE something that cannot [generate] simultaneous [minds] DOES NOT CHANGE so that it has a dissimilar ability.[63] Even if a permanent breath is possible, it is unacceptable that it be the cause only of individual minds: it follows that FROM THAT breath THERE ARE NOT ASCERTAINED to arise only individual minds, BECAUSE IN the space of any ONE inhalation and exhalation [of BREATH], THERE WILL arise many minds that APPREHEND MANY earlier and later OBJECTS.[64]

[OPPONENT:] ONE MIND COGNIZES MANY earlier and later objects, but there are not many minds.

[RGYAL TSHAB RJE:] Well, then, mind cognizes many earlier and later objects either (a) with [various] aspects, or cognizes them (b) without [various] aspects. If (a), it is proven that there are many minds. If (b) it follows that THAT mind WILL BE A SIMULTANEOUS cognizer of many past and future objects, BECAUSE THERE IS NOTHING PREVENTING its cognizing thus. Alternatively, it follows that [mind] also WILL NOT BE a cognizer of SUCCESSIVE [objects], BECAUSE THERE IS NO CHANGE of its aspects.[65]

---

62 The opponent asserts that there *is* a permanent partless breath that is the cause of mind. If that is the case, rGyal tshab rje replies, then many minds must exist in simultaneous overlap, because the cause of each is continuously present.

63 The opponent argues that the permanent breath is the cause of just one cognition at a time. rGyal tshab rje replies that it is only conceivable that a permanent breath generate minds simultaneously, because what is permanent cannot act successively. Furthermore, because it is permanent, it cannot change its nature, so it never could alter so as to generate minds successively.

64 A breath has not only extension but duration, so it is unreasonable to assert that a single breath generates only one mind, for during the course of a breath, many objects are cognized. Furthermore, if a permanent breath is theoretically capable of generating one mind, there is no reason why it should not generate many.

65 The contention that one mind cognizes many objects is absurd. If the mind is said to cognize objects *with* their aspects or qualities, then multiple cognitions must be involved, for an object and its aspects cannot be cognized by one and the same mind. If the mind is said to cognize objects without their aspects, then there must be no limit to the number of objects cognized by a single mind. Further, cognition without aspects lacks the basis for distinguishing earlier from later, so such a cognition cannot be aware of succession. Cf. TS 197-198.

Refuting [the idea that mind] arises from an impermanent breath [133]

[This is divided into:] (1) Refuting [the idea] that just individual minds are generated by many successively occurring breaths [134] and (2) Refuting [the idea] that one mind is generated by many simultaneously occurring breaths [135].

Refuting [the idea] that just individual minds are generated by many successively occurring breaths [134]

(107) IF [YOU SAY THAT] THOSE MANY MOMENTS OF BREATH,
WHEN THEY DO NOT [ORIGINATE] FROM HOMOGENES,
ARE KNOWN TO BE THE CAUSES
OF MINDS LIKE THOSE,
(108) [WE REPLY:] HOW WILL THOSE HAVE SUCCESSION
WHEN THEY DO NOT HAVE HAVE CAUSES THAT [OCCUR] IN ORDER?
[IF YOU SAY THAT] THE CAUSES ARE PREVIOUS HOMOGENES,
[WE REPLY THAT] AT FIRST [THEN, BREATH] WILL NOT OCCUR,
(109) [FOR] SUCH A CAUSE DOES NOT EXIST [FOR YOU, THE MATERIALIST].
THAT BREATH, EVEN IF IT HAS [PREVIOUS HOMOGENES],
IS ASCERTAINED AS MANY, BECAUSE IT [PERVADES] DIFFERENT PLACES;
THEREFORE, [MANY] MINDS WILL ARISE SIMULTANEOUSLY.

[OPPONENT:] THOSE MANY MOMENTS OF BREATH that originate successively from the body WHEN THEY DO NOT originate FROM previous HOMOGENES ARE KNOWN TO BE THE direct CAUSES OF[66] individual MINDS LIKE THOSE that arise earlier and later; many minds do not occur simultaneously.

[RGYAL TSHAB RJE:] HOW, it follows, WILL THOSE breaths even originate [so as] to HAVE SUCCESSION of earlier and later? It is unacceptable that they can, because THEY DO NOT HAVE CAUSES that can generate them IN ORDER, because they arise from a permanent body.[67]

[OPPONENT:] [The reason] is unproven; they originate from CAUSES that ARE PREVIOUS HOMOGENES.

[RGYAL TSHAB RJE:] It follows that AT FIRST, immediately after birth from the womb, breath WILL NOT OCCUR, because at that time

66 In GT, read *kyi* rather than *kyis*.

67 The opponent's contention, that the body generates successive breaths which, in turn, generate successive thoughts, is futile, because the body, which is constantly present, and thus permanent, cannot generate a successive result, the breaths. If the generation of successive breaths cannot be adequately explained, then the generation of successive minds cannot be, either.

such a previous homogeneous CAUSE DOES NOT EXIST. If this is unproven, then [the assertion] that there are no past or future lives is contradicted.[68]

It follows that the inhalation and exhalation [of] BREATH immediately after birth, EVEN IF IT HAS a previous homogeneous cause, IS ASCERTAINED AS having MANY parts, BECAUSE it pervades many [DIFFERENT] PLACES in different locations. [THEREFORE,] if that is asserted, [it follows that] many MINDS WILL ARISE SIMULTANEOUSLY, because their substantial cause, the permanent body, and their conditions, the many breaths, are present with undiminished ability.[69]

Refuting [the idea] that one mind is generated by many simultaneously occurring breaths [135]

(110) IF [YOU SAY THAT] MANY [BREATHS] ALSO ARE THE CAUSE
OF ONE MIND AT ONE TIME,
[WE REPLY THAT] WHEN BREATH IS MOVING WEAKLY, ETC.,
IF EVEN A SINGLE [BREATH] IS INCOMPLETE, [MIND] WILL NOT OCCUR.
(111) [IF YOU SAY:] WHAT? HOWEVER [STRONG OR WEAK BREATH] IS, IT IS THE CAUSE [OF MIND],
[WE REPLY:] COGNITION ALSO WILL BE CHANGED,
[FOR] ANYTHING THAT IS NOT ALTERED THROUGH
THE ALTERATION OF SOME [ENTITY] IS NOT ITS RESULT.

[OPPONENT:] MANY breaths ALSO ARE THE CAUSE OF ONE MIND AT ONE TIME, but not the cause of many [minds at one time].

[RGYAL TSHAB RJE:] Well, then, it follows that WHEN BREATH IS MOVING WEAKLY, ETC., if even a single strongly moving BREATH IS INCOMPLETE, then mind WILL NOT OCCUR, because the collection of all those is necessary as the cause of mind.[70]

---

68 If the opponent amends their argument by contending that breaths arise not from a permanent body but from previous homogenes, then they face a dilemma: if they hold to their contention that the first breath of this life cannot have a predecessor because there are no past lives in which a predecessor could have existed, then they are undermining their admission that all breaths arise from previous homogenes. If, on the other hand, they concede that *all* breaths arise from previous homogenes, then the first breath of this life cannot be an exception, which means that it must have a predecessor in a previous life, a state of affairs that undermines the denial of past and future lives.

69 Any breath, even the first of this life, has extension, so by definition its various parts must generate various minds, so that even at the moment of first breath, many minds should exist simultaneously. See above, p. 291, n. 62, for a similar argument.

[OPPONENT:] WHAT? [The reason] is unproven; HOWEVER strong or weak [breath] IS, IT IS THE CAUSE of mind.

[RGYAL TSHAB RJE:] It follows that the clarity or non-clarity of mental COGNITION ALSO WILL BE CHANGED by the force of the breath, because however weak or strong the breath is, it is the substantial cause of mind. [This reason] pervades, because ANY result that is NOT ALTERED THROUGH THE ALTERATION — the increase and decrease — OF SOME [entity] IS NOT THE direct RESULT of that [entity].[71]

Refuting [the assertion of] fault in our position [136]

(112) ONE COGNITION IS THE CAUSE
OF ONE [RESULT], BECAUSE IT IS ASCERTAINED TO BE ABLE [TO GENERATE RESULTS INDIVIDUALLY],
BECAUSE COGNITION THAT IS ATTACHED TO SOME OBJECT
DOES NOT APPREHEND ANY OTHER OBJECT; THE ABILITY DOES NOT EXIST.

[OPPONENT:] In your system, you assert that mind arises from homogenes, so many [minds] will arise simultaneously.

[RGYAL TSHAB RJE:] ONE previous mental COGNITION IS THE direct CAUSE of just ONE [homogeneous] result, BECAUSE IT IS ASCERTAINED TO BE ABLE to generate just individual homogenes.[72] This follows, BECAUSE when mental COGNITION is strongly ATTACHED TO SOME OBJECT, [e.g.,] a form, IT DOES NOT simultaneously APPREHEND [some] OTHER OBJECT, [e.g.,] a sound. This follows, because at that time THE ABILITY of

---

70 If the breaths existing simultaneously are asserted collectively to be the cause of mind, then the failure or absence of even a single breath—as, e.g., in the case of asthma—should insure the absence of mind, for when a collection is invoked as a cause, it only can act as a cause when it is complete.

71 If the opponent doggedly continues insisting that mind is caused by breath, then they must face the consequence that mental clarity will vary directly as the strength or weakness of breath varies, because in general an event cannot be said to be the result of a particular cause unless it varies in accordance with the variations of the alleged cause. The opponent's attempt to establish breath as the cause of mind clearly fails on this score, but it is not as obvious that the argument would fail if for "breath" they substituted "brain."

72 The opponent asserts that simultaneously existing minds also are entailed by the Buddhist position, because there have occurred a number of previous homogeneous causes that could, theoretically, issue in numerous homogeneous results at the same time. rGyal tshab rje replies with a statement of the Buddhist doctrine that one mind-moment is capable of generating only one homogeneous result.

the immediately preceding [mental] condition that would apprehend that [other object], having diminished, DOES NOT EXIST.[73]

Refuting [the idea] that even if mind arises simultaneously from the body at first, later it only arises successively from its homogenes [137]

(113) IF [YOU SAY THAT] MINDS [FIRST] ARISE SIMULTANEOUSLY
FROM THE BODY AND LATER, IT IS ASCERTAINED, FROM THEIR
OWN HOMOGENES, [WE REPLY THAT] THE BODY'S ABILITY
IS [NOT THEN] ABSENT — WHY SHOULD IT BE?

[OPPONENT:] At first, immediately after birth from the womb, many MINDS WILL ARISE SIMULTANEOUSLY FROM THE BODY. LATER, IT IS ASCERTAINED, minds will arise successively FROM THEIR OWN HOMOGENES; many minds will not arise simultaneously later.[74]

[RGYAL TSHAB RJE:] It follows that it is unacceptable that THE BODY'S ABILITY to generate many minds simultaneously IS ABSENT even later; WHY SHOULD IT BE?, because it is something that generates many [minds] simultaneously, and is permanent.[75]

---

73 The opponent might still suggest that the single results of various single causes might theoretically be able to co-exist. Such is not the case, however, because our minds are known to function through attachment to particular objects. Attachment involves attention, and attention to one object precludes attention to other objects that may co-exist with the object of attachment. In specific causal terms, it is asserted that the immediately preceding condition of potential attachment to, e.g., a sound is robbed of its power by the intensity of the attachment to, e.g., the visual object.

74 The opponent is attempting to argue that it is only at first that the various types of cognition are generated from the body; once they have come into existence, they generate their own subsequent homogenes. This reproduces on an ontogenetic scale the argument that mind is an emergent property of matter, as argued by, e.g., Alexander, Broad and Popper. The basic contention is that mind has material origins but, once established, has quasi-independent existence within its own realm.

75 The Buddhist reply is to point out that there is no reason why the body, if it once has the capacity to generate mind, should, at a certain point, cease to generate it, particularly since it is constantly present and the conditions that enabled the initial generation of mind have not been removed. The capacity to ensure a particular result should guarantee the result. If a cause with such capacity does not change, then the capacity remains, so the result should be generated continually.

C. SUMMARY

Showing a summary of the foregoing explanations [138]

Mind either (a) does or (b) does not have a cause that generates it. (b) is unacceptable, as shown by such passages from the reverse system of explanation as:

> [Something] INDEPENDENT OF OTHER [ENTITIES] BECAUSE IT IS UNCAUSED
> Is either a permanent existent or will be non-existent.[76] (180a-b)

[and:]

> . . .THEY ARE NOT JUST ACCIDENTAL,
> Because [if] they have no cause, it is contradictory that they arise. (147c-d)

and:

> It will follow that [a being might] not be ascertained as attached, etc.,
> BECAUSE THEY ORIGINATE WITHOUT PRECEDENT. (167c-d)

If [mind] has a cause, it arises from either (a) a permanent [cause] or (b) an impermanent [cause]. (a) is unacceptable. It is unacceptable that [mind] arise from a pervasive permanent [cause]; it should be known implicitly from such passages as:

> It also is not possible [that suffering originates] from GOD,
> ETC., [because these] are unable [to produce], and permanent [entities]
> Have been refuted. . . . (183a-c)

that it is unacceptable that it arise from an infinite and eternal [cause]. It is unacceptable that it arise from a non-pervasive permanent [cause], as shown by such above passages as:

> [A PERMANENT BODY] DOES NOT [HAVE MIND ORIGINATE] FROM IT SUCCESSIVELY, FOR IT IS NON-SUCCESSIVE,
> [And thus] not dependent and not subject to change. (43a-b)

---

76 In this summary section, rGyal tshab rje supplies only short excerpts from the verses he is citing. I have tried to make them clearer by filling them out somewhat. In this and the citations that follow, the material in small capitals is that actually supplied by rGyal tshab rje; the rest is my contextualizing interpolation.

If [mind] arises from an impermanent [cause], then the own-nature of mind is either (a) permanent or (b) impermanent. (a) is unacceptable, as will be shown extensively below, in the section where a permanent self is refuted.[77]

Since [mind's] own-nature is impermanent and it arises from an impermanent cause, body and mind are either (a) substantially identical or (b) [substantially] different. (a) is unacceptable, as shown by such passages as:

> [If mind is substantially identical to the body, then] just as the formations of listening, etc.,
> Are based on mind, so when, in the mind [there is awareness],
> [THOSE] QUALITIES SHOULD [APPEAR] AS CLEARLY
> IN THE BODY, because [body and mind] are not different. (79)

If (b) is the case, [mind] must either (a) arise from insensible matter or (b) arise from mind. If (a) is the case, then, since it is already established that the body acts as a cooperative condition of mind, [that body and mind are thus related] will not be refuted. If the body acts as the special [indispensable] cause, then it acts as either (a) the substantial cause or (b) the special principal condition. (a) is unacceptable, as shown by the analysis of whether body and mind exist successively or simultaneously,[78] and then by such passages as:

> IT FOLLOWS THAT IN A [DEAD] BODY, MIND
> Will not be absent, since [its cause, the body] REMAINS. (51a-b)

and:

> [The body is not mind's simultaneous basis,] because,
> WHETHER [SUBSTANCES ARE] EXISTENT OR NON-EXISTENT, there is no basis [substantially different from it]. (63a)

(b) is unacceptable, as shown by such verses as:

> Wisdom, etc., have their
> Increase and decrease take place
> Through changes in mental formations, WITHOUT
> FOLLOWING THE INCREASE AND DECREASE OF THE BODY. (73)

Alternatively, this verse can be applied to the refutation of [the idea that the body is] the substantial cause, because the same reason appears in

---

77 See sections III:10-11.
78 Above, section III:3:B.

both [assertions].[79] If it refutes [the idea that the body is] the principal condition, then it can be applied to the refutation of [the idea that the body] is the basis [of mind] in the way that the visual faculty assists in [the generation of] visual cognition.[80]

Also, the body that acts as the special basis of mind is either (a) possessed of sense-faculties or (b) without sense-faculties; and either (c) a gross, partless one or (d) many subtle [atoms]. (a) and (b) are unacceptable, as shown by such passages as:

> Mental cognition does not [arise] from [the body] together with the sense-faculties,
> Because [then THE MIND] WOULD APPREHEND JUST AS THAT [SENSE-] COGNITION DOES. (47a-b)

(c) is unacceptable, as shown by such passages as:

> IF THE HAND, ETC., MOVES, then all [the body]
> Will move; because of [this], and because it is unsuitable that
> A one [support] contradictory actions,
> It will be proven otherwise, [that the body has] different [parts]. (84)

Many reasons are shown there refuting the existence of a substantially [separate] whole. Ācārya Devendrabuddhi's discussion set forth in this connection is related to the refutation of an objectively separate universal, which [refutation] is established in the first chapter [of the *Pramāṇavārttika*], where the relation between word and concept is discussed.[81] It is unacceptable (d) that the body of many atoms act as the special basis of mind, as shown by such passages as:

> If even one part is missing, [mind] will not [arise],
> BECAUSE THE CAUSE [MUST HAVE] EVERY [PART]. (103a-b)

Although the text does not directly and clearly teach a refutation [based on] investigating whether the body [arises] from its own body or the parents' bodies, this [refutation] is implied. Thus, as soon as the

---

79 The verse can be taken as a reason refuting the idea that the body's relation to mind is that of *either* substantial cause or special cooperative condition, because each of those is a causal factor that is indispensable to the result, so neither can be altered without the result being altered.

80 The visual faculty, a special cooperative condition of visual cognition, will affect the clarity of the cognition by its strength or weakness. Since the body's strength or weakness does not thus affect mind, the body is not a special cooperative condition of mind.

81 See PV *Svārthānumāna*:39-184, and Zwilling (1976).

parents bodies exist, the previous-life body [of the child] should exist.[82]

If mind arises from previous homogenes, one must ascertain whether [it arises from] (a) its own previous mind[stream] or (b) the previous mind of another mindstream, such as the parents'. If (b), then since [the parents'] minds act as either the substantial cause or the special cooperative condition, it follows that if the parents are creative or very learned, the child should also be thus, and that by virtue of the parents' being mentally unclear, the child should also be thus. This is the implicit meaning of such passages as:

> Therefore, mind is based on mind,
> Because without it, it will not [occur];
> IT DEFINITELY SUCCEEDS ON
> THE FORMATIONS OF SOME [PREVIOUS MIND]. (78)[83]

If (a) [mind] arises from its own previous cognitions, then our assertion is well proven.

A summary of that:

(1) The mind immediately after birth is preceded by a previous cognition, because it is a cognition. For example, it is said that we see that from present attachment, aversion will originate. (2) The death-time mind of an ordinary being connects with a subsequent mind, because it is an attached mind; the previous example [also applies]. Since it is well proven that those reasons are relevant [to the subject] and [positively and negatively] pervasive [of the predicate], it is proven that past and future lives exist.[84]

---

82 If the parents' bodies are the substantial cause of the child's body, then the child's body should come into existence as soon as the parents' bodies exist, for if something has the capacity to produce a result, it must do so immediately. Of course, the present-life child's body could not come into existence at the same time as the parents' bodies, but the child's previous-life body might be held to. Either possibility is absurd. An opponent might, of course, raise a qualification not covered by rGyal tshab rje: the parents' bodies are the substantial cause of the child's body only under certain circumstances, namely, when a sperm and egg unite during intercourse; and, of course, it is not the parents' bodies as a whole that are the cause, but specialized substances combining under particular conditions.

83 The argument here is that if the child's mind has the parents' minds as its substantial cause, then the qualities and fluctuations of their minds should exactly be mirrored in the child's, which obviously is not the case.

84 This is simply a reiteration of the basic syllogisms asserted as proof of past and

D. ANSWERING OBJECTIONS

Disposing of the attempt to damage our refutation [139]

[This is divided into: (1) Objection [140] and (2) Reply [141].]

Objection [140]

(114) IF YOU SAY: "IF [AT DEATH] THE BODY IS ABSENT,
THEN ONLY MIND WILL REMAIN, BECAUSE
[BODY] IS NOT THE BASIS [OF MIND]"...

IF YOU SAY, "At the time of death, IF THE BODY IS ABSENT, it follows that ONLY MIND WILL REMAIN, BECAUSE body IS NOT THE BASIS of mind," [our reply is as follows].[85]

Reply [141]

[This is divided into:] (1) Investigating that and giving an answer [142] and (2) Identifying the substantial cause of a future life's body [143].

Investigating that and giving an answer [142]

(114c-115a) ... [THIS IS SO ONLY] IF THE CAUSE OF THE MINDSTREAM'S
CONTINUATION WILL NOT BE THE AUXILIARY [CONDITION]
WHOSE PURPOSE IS TO BE THE CAUSE OF THAT [NEXT-LIFE BODY].

IF there is a person of the desire realm who will be born in the *formless* realm immediately after death, they will have a death-time mind that continues without being based on an elemental body, because the death-time mind that is THE CAUSE OF THE MINDSTREAM'S subsequent CONTINUATION WILL NOT BE THE AUXILIARY cooperative condition WHOSE PURPOSE IS to enable the death-time body TO BE THE CAUSE OF THAT subsequent body. A person of the desire realm who will be born in the *desire* realm immediately after death does *not* have a mind that continues freely, without depending on a body, because their death-

future lives, and a reiteration of their correctness by way of their possession of the three characteristics of a correct syllogism—which the foregoing section has been devoted to establishing. The closest Dharmakīrti comes to explicitly stating these as syllogisms is in verses 40-41b.

85 The opponent is suggesting that the Buddhist contention that mind and body are ultimately independent of each other leads to the conclusion that there is no reason to believe that a future life's mind would affiliate with a new body.

time body and mind are mutually assistant and generate the co-existence of the future body and mind.[86]

Identifying the substantial cause of a future life's body [143]

[This is divided into:] (1) Identification [144], (2) Disposing of damaging [objections] [145] and (3) Setting forth the proof [146].

Identification [144]

(115b) THE FIVE *ĀYATANAS* OF THIS LIFE
ARE THE CAUSE GENERATING THE OTHER [LIFE'S] BODY.

The final eye and other of THE FIVE *ĀYATANAS*[87] OF THIS LIFE ARE THE substantial CAUSE GENERATING the five āyatanas of THE OTHER, subsequent BODY of a person, [in a] subsequent life, because, from between the essential and the particular, it is the uncommon [substantial] cause that directly applies the essential imprint.[88]

---

86 As we have seen (above, PV 62) it is the Buddhist view that mind and body, while not causally indispensable to one another (for there exist bodies without minds, such as corpses, and minds without bodies, such as formless-realm beings), *can* act as mutually assistant cooperative conditions. They need not do so, however. If a being is about to be born into the desire realm again, their previous karma assures that their death-time mind does have the capacity to act as the cooperative condition for the next life's body. If, on the other hand, they are to be born into the formless realm, their previous karma will assure that their death-time mind does not have the capacity to act as the cooperative condition of a next-life body, because there will be no body in the formless realm. It might be noted that rGyal tshab rje's discussion of these issues in terms of the form and formless realms goes beyond Dharmakīrti's explicit point, which is simply that mind would continue without a body *only* if the body that acted as its auxiliary condition were such as to permit it—but it does not, because mind and body function as mutually assistant cooperative conditions.

87 The *āyatanas* (*skye mched*), sometimes translated as "entrances,"usually number twelve, divided into six subjective extrances (eye, ear, nose, tongue, body and mind) and six objective entrances (form, sound, smell, taste, touch and dharmas). Since the question here is of *physical* continuation, the mental *āyatanas* have been disregarded, and since the question, further, is of the *subject's* physical continuation, the objective *āyatanas* have been disregarded, leaving only the five subjective (or internal) physical *āyatanas* under consideration. The *āyatanas* here are used more or less synonymously with the five sense-faculties (*dbang po, indriya*).

88 We have seen above (PV 60 and commentary) that a substantial cause is that cause that leaves its "essential imprint"(or "likeness") on its result, and can-

This must now be investigated.[89] When someone has [gone] from the desire realm to the formless realm and then [back] to the desire realm, it cannot be accepted that the death-time mind in the formless realm acts as the direct substantial cause of the material sense-faculties [arising] immediately after their [subsequent] birth [in the desire realm], because we have already refuted [the idea] that matter and mind are mutual substantial causes.[90] It cannot be accepted that form acts [as the substantial cause of the subsequent desire-realm faculties], because a formless-realm being is involved.[91]

[OPPONENT:] Well, then, the material sense-faculties at the [original] death-time in the desire realm are the direct substantial cause.

[RGYAL TSHAB RJE:] Well, then, it follows that it is unacceptable that that person be born in the formless realm immediately after death, because their material faculties at death-time are the direct substantial cause of subsequent desire-realm material sense-faculties. If that is accepted, it follows that one will take birth in the desire realm and the formless realm simultaneously.[92]

---

not be transformed without there occurring a transformation in the result. Only the physical can be the substantial cause of the physical, so the cause of the arising of sense-faculties, whether immediately, or across a span of non-physical formless-realm lives, must be physical.

89 The remainder of this section is rGyal tshab rje's expansion upon and justification of Dharmakīrti's assertion, especially in terms of the problem of explaining the way in which desire-realm sense-faculties can arise after an interval, in the formless realm, in which there have been no such faculties.

90 See above, PV 60-62.

91 Mind cannot be the substantial cause of the body any more than body of mind, so the final mind of a formless-realm being cannot be the substantial cause of the first moment of a subsequent desire-realm birth. Indeed, since a formless-realm being is involved, there cannot be any matter present in its final moment. How, then, can material (literally, "form-possessing," *gzugs can*) sense-faculties be generated in the next moment? On the other hand, sense-faculties *do* arise in a form-realm being who has come from the formless realm, a fact that must be explained.

92 If the opponent claims that the material sense-faculties of the previous desire-realm life are the *direct* substantial cause of the material sense-faculties of the subsequent desire-realm life, they will face the absurd possibility that one will be born into *both* the desire and formless realms immediately after the first desire-realm life. One will be born into the formless realm because the direct substantial cause of a formless-realm mind—a final mind that has the capacity immediately to generate a formless-realm mind—is present. One will be born into the desire realm because the direct substantial cause of desire-realm sense-faculties—a final sense-faculty moment that has the capacity immedi-

[OPPONENT:] There is no flaw [in our position]. If the direct cooperative condition or the direct substantial cause [of the subsequent desire-realm faculties] were present, the final material sense-faculties of the previous [desire-realm life would act] thus, but since the direct cooperative condition, the death-time mind in the formless realm, is not [present] at the previous [desire-realm death-time], they do not act thus.[93]

[RGYAL TSHAB RJE:] Well, then, the final material sense-faculties of the previous desire-realm life remain until the arising of the death-time mind in the formless realm, and collect at the same time as that mind [arises]. They either (a) directly generate the first-moment material sense-faculties of the subsequent desire-realm life or (b) stop before the final mind of the formless-realm birth. If (a), then they are a permanent cause. If (b), then it follows that the first-moment material sense-faculties of the subsequent desire-realm life do not have the final material sense-faculties of the previous desire-realm life as their direct substantial cause, because at the time of the arising of the direct cooperative condition that is [ready to generate the subsequent] life, [the final sense-faculties of the previous desire-realm life] have [already] stopped.[94] If this [reason] does not pervade, one should clearly

---

ately to generate desire-realm sense-faculties—is present. The key is the assertion that the previous desire-realm birth's final sense-faculties are the *direct* substantial cause (*dngos kyi nyer len*). A direct substantial cause invariably will generate its result in the very next moment, so if the previous life's final sense-faculties are the direct substantial cause, they must by definition generate the sense-faculties of another desire-realm body in the next moment.

93 The opponent argues that the final faculties of the previous desire-realm life *are* the direct substantial cause of the faculties of the subsequent desire-realm life, but that they cannot bring about their result unless they are accompanied by a direct cooperative condition, the final mind of the intervening formless-realm life. The causal efficiency of the final faculties of the previous desire-realm life somehow continues through the formless-realm life until its final moment when, in combination with the final mind-moment of that existence, it generates the faculties of the subsequent desire-realm life.

94 The opponent's position is unreasonable, because if the causal efficiency of the final faculties of the previous desire-realm life is said to persist through the formless-realm life, then a permanent cause is being asserted. If the efficiency does *not* persist, then the final faculties of the previous desire-realm life cannot be the direct substantial cause of the faculties of the subsequent desire-realm life, because they already have ceased before the final moment of the formless-realm life, when they would have to be present in order to act as a *direct* substantial cause.

interpret the passage found below: "Because [the object] is absent at that time, [a result] does not [arise] from that object."[95]

[OPPONENT:] Since the final material sense-faculties of the previous [desire-realm life] exist as [ready to generate] the first-moment material sense-faculties of the subsequent [desire-realm] life, the reason is unproven.[96]

[RGYAL TSHAB RJE:] Well, then, it is necessary to consider: How do you explain the fact that at the time of birth from the desire realm into the formless realm, the mind continues independent of the body, as demonstrated by [the fact that] that death-time body does not obtain a renewed direct capacity to generate a subsequent body?[97]

[OPPONENT:] Therefore, the substantial cause of the subsequent [desire-realm] body still remains in doubt.

[RGYAL TSHAB RJE:] "Even if the [two desire-realm bodies] are interrupted by many different types of [non-physical moments of the formless realm], since they are not interrupted by any other types of [body-moments, the last body-moment of the previous desire-realm life must be the direct substantial cause of the first moment of the subsequent desire-realm life]" — even if one tries to answer thus, one cannot in the least avoid the damaging [objections cited] before.[98]

Thus, the substantial cause of the material [sense-faculties of the subsequent desire-realm life] is the matter-generating *seed* in the

---

95 PV *Pratyakṣa*: 375a: *de tshe med phyir don las min (nārthād bhāvas tadā 'bhāvāt).*

96 The opponent claims that the final faculties of the previous desire-realm life *do* have the capacity eventually to generate subsequent desire-realm faculties, even if a formless-realm life intervenes: there is, perhaps, a momentary "potency" that carries through the formless-realm life until its final moment.

97 rGyal tshab rje reiterates the fact that if something is a direct substantial cause, it *must* generate its result in the following moment—yet the final faculties of the previous desire-realm life obviously do *not* generate faculties in the next moment, for the next moment is that of a formless-realm life. If faculties have not arisen, the preceding-moment faculties must *not* have had the capacity to generate faculties, so they cannot have been the direct substantial cause of any subsequent faculties.

98 If one argues that, since the final faculties of the previous desire-realm life and the first faculties of the subsequent desire-realm life are not separated by any other *physical* moments, then the former can be the direct substantial cause of the latter, then the same objections as above apply: the final faculties of the previous desire-realm life must be either a permanent cause or have ceased before they can directly generate the initial faculties of the subsequent desire-realm life; and, in any case, since they do not generate faculties in the next instant, they cannot be described as a direct substantial cause.

mind of the formless-realm being. Although there is no matter in the formless realm, [because the seeds] are non-associated compositional factors, there no [flaw in our position such that there would be] matter in the formless realm.[99]

Likewise, one should accept that, as explained by the discerning Kamalaśīla, since there exists an unclear mental cognition during deep sleep that is the immediately preceding condition of the [clear] mental cognition [arising] immediately after awakening from a deep sleep, [so it is with the formless and desire realms].[100]

Disposing of damaging [objections] [145]

(116) WHEN [THE LOKĀYATAS] REFUTE [THE IDEA] THAT [PREVIOUS BODY AND MIND] ARE THE AUXILIARY ENTITY
AND THE [SUBSTANTIAL] CAUSE OF THAT [FUTURE-LIFE MIND, THEY SAY] THAT THEY DO NOT SEE [THINGS THUS];

---

99 rGyal tshab rje's position is that there exists in the mind of the intervening formless-realm being a "seed" that has the capacity to generate faculties under the right circumstances—e.g., combination with a final formless-realm mind with the capacity to generate a desire-realm mind as its own substantial result and with the capacity to serve as the direct cooperative condition for the generation of desire-realm faculties. This seed is momentary throughout the formless-realm life, but its capacity is undiminished from moment to moment. It is not material—despite its capacity to be the substantial cause of something material—because it is classified as a "non-associated compositional factor" (*ldan min 'du byed, viprayuktasaṃskāra*), which is neither mental nor material, but can, in any case, exist in the formless realm. See AK ii:35-48 (tr. Poussin [1923-31] I, 178-244) and, e.g., Sopa and Hopkins (1976) 70-71.

100 The problem that rGyal tshab rje has outlined is similar—but not exactly parallel—to that of explaining how awareness is possible after deep sleep. Just as the final faculties of the previous desire-realm life cannot be regarded as the direct substantial cause of the first faculties of the subsequent desire-realm life, so the final moment of awareness before deep sleep cannot be regarded as the immediately preceding condition of the first moment of awareness after waking, because, quite simply, it does not immediately precede it. What *is* the immediately preceding condition of the first moment of awareness after waking is an "unclear" or subtle consciousness that continues—momentarily, of course—through deep sleep. The unclear cognition that is an immediately preceding cognition has the same function as does the "seed" of the sense-faculties that continues through the formless-realm life. The philosophical problems posed by the two cases are somewhat different, and two slightly different types of causes are involved, but the analogy nevertheless is illuminating. For a discussion of related issues (especially that of continuity during meditative "cessation"), see Griffiths (1986).

WE HAVE CLEARLY EXPLAINED THAT THIS DOES NOT EFFECT CERTAINTY [THAT THINGS ARE NOT THUS].
SENSE-FACULTIES ALSO [ARE INCONCLUSIVE, BECAUSE] THEY ARE INCOMPLETE [REASONS].[101]

WHEN THEY REFUTE [the idea] THAT the death-time body and mind ARE [respectively] THE AUXILIARY ENTITY acting as the cooperative condition AND THE substantial CAUSE OF THAT mind of a subsequent life, the Lokāyatas' saying merely THAT THEY DO NOT SEE things thus is not a perfect demonstration,[102] because WE HAVE already[103] CLEARLY EXPLAINED THAT the fact that the opponents do not see things thus DOES NOT EFFECT with CERTAINTY the understanding that [such things] are not the case. "Because they are SENSE-FACULTIES, ETC.," ALSO are not correct reasons refuting future lives, because THEY ARE INCOMPLETE with regard to positive [and negative] concomitance.[104]

Setting forth the proof [146]

(117) WE SEE THAT SENSE-FACULTIES
ARE ENABLED THROUGH PREVIOUS HOMOGENES,
BECAUSE WE SEE A TRANSFORMATION; IT ALSO IS PROVEN
THAT [FUTURE-LIFE FACULTIES] ARE SUCCESSIVE ARISINGS [FROM THOSE OF THIS LIFE].
(118) IF [YOU SAY THAT] THEY ARISE FROM THE BODY,
THEN THE FAULTS [POINTED OUT] EARLIER WILL FOLLOW;
IF YOU SAY THAT THEY ARISE FROM MIND, THEN OTHER BODIES ALSO
WILL ARISE FROM THAT [MIND, AS WE MAINTAIN].

---

101 Nagatomi (1957 [125]) reads *lhag ldan* (*śeṣavat*) in PV 116d as "like the rest" — i.e., the sense-faculties are, like the other reasons cited above, uncertain.

102 In GT, read *sgrub byed* for *ga byed*.

103 PV 82 and commentary.

104 One cannot assert, "There are no future-life sense-faculties, because they are sense-faculties,"because it is not certain that sense-faculties cannot generate homogenes in another life. Indeed, the entire thrust of rGyal tshab rje's previous section has been to show that they can—even with the intervention of a formless-realm life. In general, if Buddhist notions of the momentariness and homogeneity of substantial causes and results are accepted, sense-faculties *must* be capable of generating homogenes that are the faculties of a subsequent life, just as the first faculties of this life must be the results, in turn, of the faculties of some previous life. In short, the arguments used to establish the continuity of the mind also can be applied to proving the continuity of the material sense-faculties.

WE SEE by authority THAT THE SENSE-FACULTIES of this life ARE ENABLED to be be assisted THROUGH PREVIOUS HOMOGENES, BECAUSE WE SEE A TRANSFORMATION from previous clear or clouded faculties into subsequent clear or clouded faculties. IT ALSO IS PROVEN THAT the sense-faculties of subsequent [lives] ARE SUCCESSIVE ARISINGS from their homogenes, because they arise in the same way as the present life's faculties.[105]

Refuting [the idea] that they arise from another cause:

[OPPONENT:] The fact that the sense-faculties of this life ARISE FROM THE BODY does not prove that the sense-faculties of a future life arise from a body.

[RGYAL TSHAB RJE:] If we analyze that, it follows that it is unacceptable, because if [the sense-faculties] originate from a body that *has* sense-faculties, then it is proven that they arise from a homogene; and if they arise from a substantial cause other than that, THEN THE FAULTS [pointed out] EARLIER WILL FOLLOW.[106] The analysis of [body] with and without sense-faculties is as before, in the brief demonstration.[107]

[OPPONENT:] The sense-faculties of this life arise from mind.

[RGYAL TSHAB RJE:] It follows that OTHER BODIES, of subsequent [lives], ALSO WILL ARISE FROM THAT mind, because the sense-faculties of this life arise from mind, and previous and subsequent bodies must have the same type of cause. If that is asserted, future lives are proven.[108]

Summary [147]

(119) SO, "ALL MINDS OF ORDINARY BEINGS
DO NOT CONNECT [WITH SUBSEQUENT HOMOGENES] BECAUSE THEY ARE

---

105 See previous note.

106 The sense-faculties of a previous life must arise from a body, because if they are said to arise from a body that *has* sense-faculties, then homogeneous causes are being accepted. If they are said to arise from a body that does not have sense-faculties, then non-homogeneous causes are being asserted, and this entails the various problems that have been discussed above in relation to the mind.

107 PV 47-48 and commentary.

108 If the opponent asserts that this life's sense-faculties arise from mind, rGyal tshab rje will have no objection, because he already has claimed that sense-faculties arise with mind as an auxiliary condition, and if causal continuity is assumed, then that causal relationship will continue across the boundary of death.

SEPARATED FROM THE CAUSE [OF CONNECTION]." [THIS] IS NOT [A CORRECT REASON], BECAUSE OF THAT [WHICH HAS BEEN PROVEN ABOVE];
SUCH [PROOFS] ARE ASSERTED TO BE INCOMPLETE.

"The body is not the substantial cause or special cooperative condition of mind, SO ALL final MINDS OF ORDINARY BEINGS and arhants DO NOT CONNECT with subsequent homogenes, BECAUSE THEY ARE SEPARATED FROM breath, which is THE CAUSE of connection, and because they are death-time minds." The reasons set forth ARE NOT [correct], BECAUSE OF THAT proof to that effect above. SUCH statements as "because they are death-time minds" ARE correctly ASSERTED TO BE INCOMPLETE PROOFS, because the reason is proven to exist in the subject, [but] merely by the fact that we do not see the non-accordant, there is said to be doubt about negative concomitance.[109]

---

109 In logical terms, the opponent's proofs of the non-existence of past and future lives are fallacious. Although the reason is relevant to the subject (for final minds are both death-time minds and separated from breath), and the accordant is appropriate (i.e., there is positive concomitance) because we observe that death-time minds separated from breath do not appear to continue, there still remains doubt about the non-accordant (i.e., negative concomitance), because we do not observe non-continuation, either.

5. *The Buddha's Qualities*

A. HIS INFINITE ACCUSTOMATION TO COMPASSION

Refuting [the idea] that, even if such accustomation is possible, its infinite increase cannot be accepted [148]

[This is divided into:] (1) The argument [149] and (2) The answer [150].

The argument [149]

(120) IF YOU SAY: "ALTHOUGH THROUGH ACCUSTOMATION
ONE CAN ATTAIN EXCELLENCE [IN VARIOUS QUALITIES], THEY CANNOT TRANSCEND THEIR NATURES [INFINITELY],
JUST AS JUMPING AND BOILING WATER [ARE NOT INFINITE]."

[OPPONENT:] ALTHOUGH THROUGH a little ACCUSTOMATION to compassion, wisdom, etc., ONE CAN ATTAIN EXCELLENCE [in them], THEY CANNOT TRANSCEND THEIR limited NATURES and increase infinitely. FOR EXAMPLE, although by accustomation to JUMPING one can develop limited excellence, [the length of one's jumps] will not increase infinitely; AND BOILING WATER will not ultimately ignite.[1]

---

1 The opponent is arguing that the impossibility of infinite increase is demonstrated by two examples: jumping ability, which cannot be increased infinitely because there is no carry-over from one jump to another, because each jump requires renewed effort; and boiling water, which never will "ignite"—i.e., become infinitely hot— because as it boils, its heat ever increasing, its basis, the water, is evaporating. Once the water is gone, there is nothing more to boil, so both boiling and heat will cease. The examples are to be applied to compassion, wisdom and other mental qualities, which cannot be increased infinitely because (a) they require repeated effort and (b) their basis, the body, is ultimately unstable, and when it disappears, the mental states will, too. Cf. TS 3168.

The answer [150]

[This is divided into:] (1) [Showing why] jumping ability and boiling water do not have the particular mark [such that they can increase infinitely] [151], (2) [Showing that] compassion, etc., do [have the particular mark such that they can increase infinitely] [154] and (3) Disposing of objections to that [155].

[Showing why] jumping ability and boiling water do not have the particular mark [such that they can increase infinitely] [151]

[This is divided into:] (1) Identifying the particulars of the mark and [showing why] they do not exist in the two examples [152] and (2) [Showing that] if there exist such particulars, it follows that there can be infinite development of them [153].

Identifying the particulars of the mark and [showing why] they do not exist in the two examples [152]

(120d) IF THAT [STATEMENT] IS MADE, WE REPLY:
(121) IF [MENTAL QUALITIES] WERE DEPENDENT ON REPEATED EFFORT
OR HAD AN UNSTABLE BASIS,
THEN THEIR EXCELLENCE COULD NOT INCREASE;
BUT THEIR NATURE IS NOT LIKE THAT.
(122-123b) [JUMPING ABILITY IS LIMITED] BECAUSE WHAT IS ABLE TO
ASSIST IT [EARLIER] IS UNABLE TO PROVE [HELPFUL]
IN LATER [ATTAINMENT OF] EXCELLENCE;
ALTHOUGH [THE BOILING OF WATER] CAN INCREASE IN INTENSITY, IT DOES NOT HAVE
A NATURE [SUCH AS TO BE INFINITE], BECAUSE THE BASIS
DOES NOT REMAIN. . .

[IF THAT (statement) IS MADE, WE REPLY:] Compassion, wisdom, etc., do not have a nature such that they cannot increase infinitely, because IF THEY WERE such that previous accustomation generated subsequent moments DEPENDENT ON REPEATED EFFORT OR [such that] they HAD AN UNSTABLE BASIS, THEN THEIR EXCELLENCE COULD NOT INCREASE infinitely; BUT THEIR NATURE IS NOT LIKE THAT.

Jumping ability, although it can be increased a little in excellence through accustomation, does not have a nature such that it can be increased infinitely, BECAUSE the effort THAT IS ABLE TO ASSIST IT at a previous moment IS UNABLE TO PROVE helpful IN LATER [achievement of] EXCELLENCE.

Boiling water, ALTHOUGH IT CAN INCREASE a little IN INTENSITY, DOES NOT HAVE A NATURE such that it can increase [its heat] infinitely, BE-

CAUSE when THE BASIS, the water, NO LONGER REMAINS, then it has dried up, and [the boiling] is terminated.[2]

[Showing that] if there exist such particulars, then it follows that there is infinite development [153]

(123b) . . . ONCE THERE HAS BEEN [ACCUSTOMATION],
EFFORT WILL MAKE OTHER [LATER EFFORTS MORE] EXCELLENT,
WITHOUT BEING DEPENDENT ON REPEATED EFFORT.

It follows [from your argument] that it is possible that jumping ability and boiling water be increased infinitely, because ONCE THERE HAS BEEN accustomation, a previous EFFORT WILL MAKE OTHER subsequent homogenes more and more EXCELLENT, WITHOUT BEING DEPENDENT ON subsequent REPEATED EFFORT. If that reason is accepted, then one can also take compassion, etc., as the subject and make an independent syllogism.[3]

[Showing that] compassion, etc., do have [the particular mark such that they can increase infinitely] [154]

(124) COMPASSION, ETC., ARISE [THROUGH] ACCUSTOMATION IN THE MIND;
THEY WILL NATURALLY ENTER [THE MIND],

---

2 rGyal tshab rje agrees that neither jumping ability nor boiling water is capable of infinite increase, but he claims here—and will go on to prove—that they are not examples that can be appropriately applied to mental qualities, for the characteristics of jumping ability and boiling water—respectively, the need for repeated effort and the existence of an unstable basis—that render their infinite increase impossible are *not* characteristics of mental states—particularly of the sort of positive mental states under discussion. Cf. TS 3421.

3 Dharmakīrti's verse here seems to be a fairly straightforward introduction to the general notion that where repeated effort is not required, infinite development is possible. rGyal tshab rje, on the other hand, imbeds these ideas within a consequential statement (*thal ba, prasaṅga*) that underlines the absurdity of the opponent's position, and says that if that consequence is reasonable, then it can be turned into an independent (*rang rgyud, svatantra*) syllogism, of which "compassion"is the subject. rGyal tshab rje may be approaching the verse in this manner so as to establish negative concomitance between the opponent's examples (jumping and boiling water) and his own predicate (infinite development), thereby clearing the way for his own syllogism, which would be: "Compassion can be developed infinitely, because once there has been accustomation, a previous effort will make subsequent homogenes more excellent, without being dependent upon repeated effort,"with jumping ability and boiling water serving as non-accordant examples.

AS FIRE, ETC., [ENTERS] WOOD, AND
MERCURY [ENTERS] GOLD, ETC.[4]
(125) THEREFORE, WHAT ARISE THROUGH THAT [MENTAL ACCUSTOMATION]
ARE QUALITIES ARISING AS THE NATURE [OF MIND];
THUS, EACH SUBSEQUENT
EFFORT PRODUCES [EVEN GREATER] EXCELLENCE.
(126) HOW CAN THOSE MINDS OF COMPASSION, ETC.,
REMAIN [LIMITED] WHEN THEY ARE ACCUSTOMATED,
BECAUSE THEY INCREASE FROM THE SEED
OF PREVIOUS APPROPRIATE HOMOGENES?

A brief demonstration:

COMPASSION, wisdom, ETC., have a stable basis, because they ARISE FROM the ACCUSTOMATION of their own previous homogenes, based on clear cognition IN THE MIND. They are not dependent from moment to moment on a [new] different effort, because when they are accustomated, THEY WILL NATURALLY ENTER the mind, AS FIRE, ETC., naturally enters WOOD until [the wood] is reduced to ashes, AND well-refined MERCURY naturally enters GOLD, ETC. Alternatively, it is like well-refined mercury or gold, which naturally generate subsequent homogenes free from tarnish, and [whose] purity from stains does not need to depend on a second application of a scouring shard.[5]

---

4 A more straightforward reading of the Tibetan here (*me la sogs pas shing dag dang / dngul chu dang ni ser sogs bzhin*) yields: "As fire enters wood, mercury and gold, etc." The reference (see Nagatomi [1957] 131-32) seems to be to different stages of transformation that do not require the repetition of earlier stages: fire that has partially burned wood need not re-burn the burned wood on a second application; fire that has partially refined mercury or gold need not repeat the initial stages of refinement. rGyal tshab rje's interpretation focuses on the "naturalness" of accustomation, and therefore he looks to examples of natural activity, such as wood burning fire or mercury mixing with gold.

5 Compassion, etc., are said to have a stable basis because they are generated from homogenes that have a clear mental cognition as their basis. A clear mental cognition is assumed to be a stable basis because it is capable of virtually indefinite repetition, particularly by persons with great mental control—and, if this effortless repetition continues through an indefinite number of lives, its infinite development may be postulated. rGyal tshab rje's alternate reading here reflects the stricter reading of the Tibetan discussed in the previous note. Cf. TS 3422.

An extensive explanation:

A stable basis: [THEREFORE,] compassion, etc., WHICH ARISE THROUGH THAT accustomation, have a stable basis, because THEY ARE QUALITIES ARISING AS THE NATURE of mind.[6]

Accustomation independent of repeated exertion: [THUS,] compassion, [etc.,] do not depend for their subsequent moments of accustomation on a separate effort, because EACH SUBSEQUENT EFFORT at accustomation PRODUCES a greater and greater growth in the EXCELLENCE of many homogenes.[7]

Summary: HOW CAN THOSE MINDS OF COMPASSION,wisdom, ETC., REMAIN limited WHEN THEY HAVE BEEN ACCUSTOMATED through the two applications?[8] It cannot be accepted that they can, BECAUSE THEY have the quality of mind that INCREASES more and more FROM THE SEED OF PREVIOUS APPROPRIATE HOMOGENES.[9]

Disposing of objections to that [155]

[This is divided into:] (1) Disposing of the objection that [compassion, etc.,] increase only through the accustomation of conditions

---

6 As noted above, it is a Buddhist assumption that a clear mental cognition provides a stable basis for the development of various mental qualities, because a clear cognition does not have a nature such that its continuation assures its exhaustion. On the contrary, given that mind is endless, there is no reason why clear cognitions should not be endless, too. A buddha, of course, is a being whose every cognition is perfectly clear and stable. It should be noted that the validity of the Buddhist hypothesis rests on two assumptions: an infinity of lives in which mental qualities can be developed (presumably demonstrated just above), and the natural increase of positive qualities, based in turn on the assumption that stability and clarity are/can become the mind's natural states. Stability and clarity *are* the mind's natural state (cf. PV 207-8 and R. Jackson 1990) in that they are the fundamental nature of mind, adventitiously obscured by defilement. They *can become* the mind's natural state in that one can — on the basis of accustomation through meditation — thoroughly imbue the mindstream with them.

7 It is assumed that because they are generated with a stable basis, instances of various positive mental qualities have the capacity to generate increasingly intense, or "excellent"instances of the same quality. Thus, the process of mental development is geometrical rather than merely arithmetical: mental qualities are "expandable"in much the same way that karma often is said to be. Cf. TS 3414.

8 The two applications *(sbyor ba gnyis)* are two qualities that one brings to one's efforts: consistency (*rtag*) and intensity (*gus*). Any effort assisted by the two applications is bound to be a long-term success.

9 See above, note 7.

[156] and (2) Disposing of the objection that [compassion, etc.,] increase only from [accustomation of] a homogeneous substantial [cause] [157].

Disposing of the objection that [compassion, etc.,] increase only through the accustomation of conditions [156]

> (127) IT IS NOT THE CASE THAT JUMPS [ORIGINATE] FROM JUMPS AS [COMPASSION FROM COMPASSION];
> A JUMP HAS A NATURE SUCH THAT IT IS LIMITED,
> BECAUSE ITS CAUSES, STRENGTH AND EXERTION,
> HAVE LIMITED ABILITY.
> (128) THAT [BEING] DOES NOT AT FIRST JUMP AS FAR
> AS THEY LATER WILL, BECAUSE OF PHYSICAL IMBALANCES;
> ONE CLEARS AWAY IMBALANCES THROUGH GRADUAL
> EFFORT, [BUT JUMPING] REMAINS [LIMITED] BY [THE LIMITS OF] ONE'S OWN STRENGTH.

[OPPONENT:] It follows that jumping ability, etc., also can be increased infinitely, because they increase through accustomation.

[RGYAL TSHAB RJE:] It follows that IT IS NOT THE CASE THAT later JUMPS, etc., originate FROM previous homogeneous JUMPS, AS compassion, etc., [originate from compassion], because however [great] one's physical strength and exertion, only [that great will the jump] be. Therefore, A JUMP HAS A NATURE SUCH THAT ITs extent IS LIMITED, BECAUSE ITS CAUSES, physical STRENGTH AND EXERTION, HAVE the LIMITED ABILITY to generate [only] a measured jump.[10]

[OPPONENT:] Well, then, no matter how much jumping is practiced, it is impossible that steadily applied physical strength can increase [ability] any more. If you assert that, then you contradict perception.

[RGYAL TSHAB RJE:] [When] THAT ordinary being first practices jumping, they DO NOT, from the FIRST, JUMP AS FAR AS THEY LATER will [be able to] jump, BECAUSE even if the appropriate conditions are fulfilled, PHYSICAL weakness and IMBALANCES are induced by [excess of] phlegm, etc. ONE CLEARS AWAY the phlegm and other IMBALANCES THROUGH GRADUAL EFFORT, but even when one is purified of them, one

10 Jumping ability cannot be increased infinitely—as compassion, etc., can—because its conditions, physical strength and physical exertion, necessarily are limited. In general, physical conditions are limited, while mental conditions are capable of infinite increase. This, in turn, presupposes that mind is beginningless and endless, as supposedly ascertained in the previous section. Cf. TS 3424.

will not be able to increase [one's jumping ability] infinitely, because even then, one's [jumping ability] REMAINS limited BY the extent of ONE'S OWN physical STRENGTH.[11]

If jumping ability arises from previous homogenes, then it follows that merely by lifting one's foot to jump, one will jump a long way, and it also follows that if mere practice is the cause of an infinite increase, then birds and monkeys should have equal jumping ability, since they are equally practiced.[12]

Disposing of the objection that [compassion, etc.,] increase only from [accustomation of] a homogeneous substantial cause [157]

(129) COMPASSION ORIGINATES FROM ITS OWN SEEDS;
IT HAS A NATURE SUCH THAT [IT NATURALLY ENTERS] INTO THE MIND
WHEN IT POSSESSES A CAUSE THAT IS ITS OWN SEED
[AND] IS NOT DAMAGED BY OPPOSING FACTORS.
(130) THUS, [AS FOR] THOSE OTHER [SUBSEQUENT] MINDS,
THE MENTAL DHARMAS OF COMPASSION
AND DETACHMENT: THE ROOT OF THEIR CLARIFICATION
IS PREVIOUS ACCUSTOMATION.[13]
(131) A COMPASSIONATE NATURE [OCCURS] THROUGH
ACCUSTOMATION,
LIKE DETACHMENT, ATTACHMENT AND AVERSION.[14]

---

11 Jumping ability never will reach infinity, because its conditions, such as the body and strength, invariably are finite. On the other hand, jumping ability is capable of increase and development, because its conditions will vary with the condition of the body, as determined, e.g., by the balance among the humors. Development occurs when there is a progressive elimination or neutralization of the contradictory conditions preventing such development.

12 Jumping ability must have particular conditions as well as homogeneous causes to explain it, for without the limiting conditions, one step (the substantial cause) *could* result in an infinitely long jump. Also, mere practice at jumping cannot lead to its infinite increase, because "practice" merely is an index of how long and hard one has tried. If practice alone were a factor, and limiting physical conditions did not play an important role, the monkeys and birds (and, for that matter, humans) who were equally practiced in "jumping" (the word must be used advisedly in the case of birds) should be able to jump equal distances, which manifestly they cannot.

13 An alternative reading of the Tibetan (*'di ltar goms pa snga ma dang / snga ma'i sems chos brtse ba dang / chags bral blo sogs gzhan dag gi / gsal ba yi ni rtsa ba yin*) yields: "Thus, previous mental dharmas of compassion and detachment that have been accustomated are the root of the clarification of other [subsequent] minds [of the same type]."

[OPPONENT:] It follows that all sentient beings have great compassion, because compassion is beginningless and arises from its own homogenes.

[RGYAL TSHAB RJE:] There is no flaw [in our position]. Compassion and great compassion, which ORIGINATE FROM THEIR OWN homogeneous SEEDS, HAVE A NATURE SUCH THAT they naturally enter INTO THE MIND of a bodhisattva on the path of seeing, because compassion developed by a bodhisattva [WHEN they are] on the path of seeing POSSESSES A CAUSE THAT IS ITS OWN homogeneous SEED in their mindstream, [a seed] THAT IS NOT DAMAGED BY such OPPOSING FACTORS as anger, etc. The consequential flaw that [compassion, etc.,] abide [always] in all sentient beings is not present, because although [compassion, etc.,] arise in the mindstreams of some sentient beings, they are destroyed by anger, etc. Taking as one's intentional object one's relatives who are born as ordinary sentient beings, and thinking, "If only they could be free from suffering," is merely compassion; it is not *great* compassion.[15]

It is impossible that each sentient being not experience in their mindstream [compassion, etc.,] toward all other sentient beings, because it is impossible that there be a sentient being who has not experienced each [other] sentient being as their parents [at some point] in beginningless time. If [compassion, etc.,] are not destroyed by anger, etc., it is impossible that there be a sentient being who will

---

14 The Tibetan here has *chags bral chags dang yid log bzhin*, whose translation is as indicated; the Sanskrit is *ghṛṇāvairāgyarāgavat*: "Like kindness, detachment and attachment."

15 Just as jumping ability varies with the conditions (particularly the opposing ones) found in each individual, so compassion varies with the degree to which its possessor also has in their mindstream those factors that tend to limit or destroy compassion, such as anger. A being with some proclivity toward compassion, but who still is afflicted by various negative conditions, such as anger, is likely only to be able to generate compassion toward a limited number of sentient beings. Contrary conditions make it impossible for them to generate the great compassion that is the desire utterly to free all sentient beings from saṃsāra through one's own effort. The distinction between compassion and great compassion differs between Hīnayāna and Mahāyāna: the former (e.g., at AK vii:33) regards great compassion simply as that greater degree of compassion felt by a buddha; the latter considers compassion to be the desire to see others freed from suffering, and great compassion to be the desire to free them from suffering oneself. In any case, the distinction here is imported by rGyal tshab rje; Dharmakīrti appears to be concerned simply with the conditions that preclude any type of compassion.

not at some point take all sentient beings as their intentional object and [generate] the great compassion that desires to free all sentient beings from suffering. However, if just compassion toward one sentient being arises, that disappears when destroyed by anger.[16]

If one is not cut off from accustomating the appropriate conditions, increase can be infinite:

THUS, the consequential flaw that there would exist in all sentient beings THOSE OTHER [subsequent] MINDS that are THE MENTAL DHARMAS OF COMPASSION AND DETACHMENT, etc., is not present, because [compassion and detachment's] natures arise from homogenes, but THE ROOT OF the generation of increasing excellence in THEIR CLARIFICATION IS PREVIOUS ACCUSTOMATION, and [accustomation] even previous to that—and [such accustomation] is not present in every sentient being.[17]

An example:

By possession of the two applications, one will have A COMPASSIONATE NATURE that naturally enters the mindstream THROUGH ACCUSTOMATION, because we see LIKEwise that in an arhant's mindstream DETACHMENT arises naturally, and that in [the mindstreams of] the attached there [naturally arises] ATTACHMENT AND [in the mindstream of a yogin] meditating on the unpleasant [there naturally arises] AVERSION.[18]

---

16 Because mind is beginningless, all sentient beings have been mother and father to all other sentient beings. There is, therefore, not a single sentient being who is not in principle capable of contemplating the past kindnesses that other sentient beings have shown them, as well as the present sufferings those beings are undergoing. Thus, there is no sentient being who, in the absence of contrary conditions, will not generate the great compassion that is the desire to free all their ex-parents from their present sufferings. Should only ordinary, limited compassion arise, however, it is fragile and easily destroyed by its contradictory condition.

17 It is only when the appropriate positive conditions (previous accustomation seriously pursued) are present and the opposing negative conditions (anger, etc.) absent that mental qualities such as compassion and wisdom can be expanded to the ultimate degree. It is evident from a simple observation of human (and other sentient) behavior that most beings do not fulfill one or the other or both of these conditional criteria.

18 Again, mental qualities, whether positive or negative, come to arise "naturally" in sentient mindstreams through accustomation and possession of the two applications (see above, p. 313, n. 8).

Summary:

At first, taking all sentient beings as one's intentional object, one generates through effort a forceful compassion that desires to free them from suffering. When one has generated that [compassion] by great effort, each effort is able to generate many homogenes of compassion. Through such accustomation, one comes to have a nature such that great compassion naturally enters [the mindstream] without depending on such effort, but [such accustomation] is not independent of effort from the first. Jumping [on the other hand] requires the assistance of effort for each moment the body is moving apart from the ground, and whenever the effort slackens, the body will fall to the ground.[19]

B. THE BUDDHA AS TEACHER, SUGATA AND SAVIOR

The way in which excellence of application arises from [excellence of intention] [158]

[This is divided into:] (1) A brief demonstration [159], (2) An extensive explanation [160] and (3) Summary [167].

A brief demonstration [159]

(132)[20] A COMPASSIONATE ONE DIRECTLY EFFECTS
APPLICATION OF METHODS TO DESTROY SUFFERING;
METHODICAL OCCURRENCES AND THEIR CAUSES
ARE HIDDEN PHENOMENA; THEY WILL BE DIFFICULT TO EXPLAIN.

It is reasonable that a COMPASSIONATE ONE, a bodhisattva on the path of application, initially [DIRECTLY] EFFECTS accustomation via the

---

19 Once again, rGyal tshab rje relates Dharmakīrti's concerns to the Mahāyāna interpretation of the distinction between compassion and great compassion, and shows how the latter can arise out of the former because of the force of Dharmakīrti's arguments. He also makes the important point that, although repeated application will not be necessary for the accustomation of compassion, effort *is* necessary at the beginning.

20 The Tibetan translation here lacks half a verse, 131c-d, the Sanskrit of which is: *niṣpannakaruṇotkarṣaparaduḥkhākṣamer itaḥ* ("one who has risen to perfect compassion is unable to endure the suffering of others; thus. . . ") This verse probably was meant to be read with verse 132, which flows logically from it, and introduces the discussion of the Buddha's teacherhood. Nagatomi (1957 [137]) reads it thus.

two APPLICATIONs in order to see by perception THE METHODS for pacifying their own suffering, because they are an ordinary being who desires TO DESTROY THE SUFFERING of all sentient beings.[21] It follows that this [reason] pervades, because if the truths of suffering and cessation, which are METHODICAL OCCURRENCES, and the truths of origination and path, which are their causes, ARE HIDDEN PHENOMENA, THEY WILL BE DIFFICULT TO EXPLAIN or cognize undistortedly.[22]

Also, [the existence of] a bodhisattva on the path of application is proved by objectively impelled reasoning. The cognition of impermanence and [other of] the sixteen [aspects of the four noble truths] by way of their generic images is divided into two: clear and unclear appearances [of the generic image]. The clear appearances of the generic image are proved by objectively impelled reasoning to be two: those held by the generation of the Mahāyāna thought [of enlightenment] and those not held [by the generation of the Mahāyāna thought]. A person who is distinguished by possessing a clear appearance of a generic image of no-self through being held by the generation of the Mahāyāna thought, is called a bodhisattva on the path of application.[23]

---

21 Having completed the general proof of the Buddha as authoritative and the detailed proof of him as compassionate, Dharmakīrti goes on to demonstrate that he is the teacher. The "compassionate one" (*brtse ldan, dayāvān*) is taken by rGyal tshab rje to be a bodhisattva on the second of the five paths, that of application. Such a bodhisattva still is an ordinary being, but meditates consistently and intensively (i.e., with the two applications: see p. 313, n. 8) in order to reach the path of seeing, where they will cognize the truth directly and begin definitively to uproot the defilements that are the basis of their own suffering. Directly understanding the way to end their own suffering, they then will be able to assist other beings in ending their suffering—it is, after all, the desire to help others that is the bodhisattva's primary motive.

22 "Methodical occurrences" (*thabs byung*) are regular, caused phenomena, or phenomena that arise through "methods" (*thabs*), either skillful (conducing to cessation) or unskillful (conducing to suffering). They are not obvious, hence they must be sought, so that one may cognize them undistortedly and explain them to others out of the compassion that moves one.

23 As long as one has not attained the path of seeing, one does not cognize the truth (whether it be the four noble truths or voidness) directly. As long as one does not cognize it directly, one cognizes it via its generic image (*don spyi*). Generic images appear clearly or unclearly. They are relatively unclear to a bodhisattva on the first path, that of accumulation; they are relatively more clear to a bodhisattva on the path of application. Clear generic images either are or are not associated with, or "held by" the thought of enlightenment (*bodhicitta*). A being whose cognition of clear generic images is associated with the thought of enlightenment is said to fulfill the

An extensive explanation [160]

[This is divided into:] (1) The method of cognizing what is to be abandoned [161], (2) The way of cognizing the antidote [162] and (3) The purpose of such an analysis [163].

The method of cognizing what is to be abandoned [161]

(133-134b) THROUGH SCRIPTURE AND REASONING, ONE INVESTIGATES
THE ASPECTS [OF THE TRUTHS]:
ONE EFFECTS COGNITION OF THE CAUSE OF SUFFERING
AND THE NATURE OF THAT [SUFFERING] AS IMPERMANENT, ETC.,
BECAUSE IF, THEREFORE, THE CAUSE [OF SUFFERING]
ABIDES, ONE WILL NOT SEE HOW TO COUNTERACT THE RESULT;
[ONE WILL UNDERSTAND] SUFFERING ITSELF BY ITS CHARACTERISTICS.

It is not the case that there is no method for investigating the actuality[24] etc.; of the four noble truths, because, cognizing [them] initially THROUGH the wisdom of study, which is based on SCRIPTURE, AND then through the REASONING that is the wisdom of reflection, ONE INVESTIGATES THE ASPECTS [of the truths].[25]

Alternatively, one must investigate in terms of the methods [applied] to the three types of authority-objects, because one investigates very hidden phenomena by scripture that is [ascertained as] pure by the three tests, and [manifest and hidden phenomena] by reasoning that does not depend on scripture for its refutation or proof.[26]

---

definition of a bodhisattva on the path of application. When they reach the path of seeing, they will cognize the truth not through a generic image, but directly.

24 I have, throughout, translated *gnas lugs* (*bhūtārtha*) as "actuality." It also may be rendered as "reality," "truth," "ultimacy," etc.

25 The text speaks only of investigation through scripture and reasoning; rGyal tshab rje explains these as the first two of the three types of "wisdom," or methods of investigation, i.e., through hearing, or study (*thos pa, śruti*) of scripture; critical reflection, or reasoning (*bsam pa, yukta* or *cinta*); and meditation (*sgom pa, bhāvanā*). The three are held to be successive phases in one's understanding of a particular truth or topic. The aspects, of course, refer to the sixteen aspects of the four noble truths, which will be analyzed in considerable detail in section III:6.

26 A second way of "investigating through scripture and reasoning" is described in terms of attempting to cognize manifest, hidden or very hidden phenomena. Very hidden phenomena, such as the details of karma, must be understood through reliance on authoritative scripture. Scripture is determined to be authoritative if it contradicts neither perception, nor inference, nor other authoritative scriptures. Hidden phenomena may be known through correct

When one has understood the nature of suffering, it is reasonable that ONE EFFECT COGNITION [OF whether] there is or is not A CAUSE OF that SUFFERING AND [whether] THE NATURE OF THAT cause IS permanent or IMPERMANENT, ETC., BECAUSE IF, THEREFORE, suffering is causeless or THE CAUSE ABIDES permanently, then someone who desires to destroy suffering WILL NOT SEE HOW TO COUNTERACT THE suffering RESULT through the power of the antidote. When one analyzes thus, one is able to understand that suffering has a cause and that that cause is impermanent, because SUFFERING ITSELF will be understood BY ITS visible CHARACTERISTICS as arising occasionally and subject to increase and decrease. That [verse, then,] demonstrates how one successively generates the mind that desires freedom from suffering, [the mind that] desires to abandon origination [of that suffering] and the mind that desires to attain the cessation of suffering.[27]

The way of cognizing the antidote [162]

(134c) ONE UNDERTAKES AN ANALYSIS OF THE OPPOSING FACTOR
TO THAT [ORIGINATION], IN ORDER TO DESTROY THE CAUSE OF THAT
[SUFFERING].

---

reasoning. Manifest phenomena are known through sense, mental or yogic perception. On the path, ordinary beings generally will rely on scripture in order to understand the broad outlines of what is to be done. Then they will rely on reasoning independent of scripture to ascertain the truth of various important doctrinal points. Correct reasoning will help take them to a point where they can directly cognize what before had only been known inferentially, or through generic images. Eventually, when beings are enlightened, even very hidden phenomena will be manifest to them. Incidentally, this stress on the vital sequential connection between reasoning and direct realization is a hallmark of the dGe lugs school of Tibetan Buddhism. Reasoning is limited, and is not itself liberating cognition, but it is indispensable to the attainment of that liberating cognition that is direct and unmediated. On this issue, see, e.g., Thurman (1985) and Klein (1986).

27 Thus, the investigation of the nature of suffering entails a concern for the truth of the first three of the four noble truths, the recognition that (a) there is suffering, which is undesirable, (b) there are identifiable causes for suffering and (c) if there are identifiable causes of suffering, then the elimination of the causes should entail the cessation of the suffering. The four noble truths are examined in greater detail below, sections III:6-11. The key assumption, of course, is that suffering can be adequately understood on the basis of the law of dependent origination, such that its causes can be discovered and subsequently eliminated.

(135) ONE ALSO ASCERTAINS THE OPPOSING FACTORS TO THAT [ORIGINATION]
IN ORDER TO COGNIZE THE NATURE OF THE CAUSE.
DESIRE HAVING AS ITS OBJECT THE COMPOSITES
EFFECTED BY GRASPING AT "I" AND "MINE"
(136) IS THE CAUSE; SEEING NO-SELF
IS THE DESTROYER OF THAT, IT CONTRADICTS THAT.

It is reasonable that ONE UNDERTAKE AN ANALYSIS OF the antidote that is THE OPPOSING FACTOR TO THAT origination [of suffering], BECAUSE one desires TO DESTROY [suffering] through reliance upon the antidote to THE orginating CAUSE OF THAT suffering. When one analyzes thus, ONE ALSO ASCERTAINS through authority THE OPPOSING FACTORS TO THAT origination, IN ORDER TO COGNIZE that THE NATURE OF THE CAUSE is self-grasping, and that the antidote to that is the gnosis that grasps [phenomena] in a manner opposite to [self-]grasping. That [verse, then,] demonstrates that the path is to be relied upon.[28]

The craving [mind of] DESIRE for suffering HAVING AS ITS OBJECT-field THE five COMPOSITE aggregates EFFECTED BY GRASPING AT "I" AND grasping at "MINE," IS THE CAUSE of one's resultant suffering, because it is the cooperative condition.[29] The wisdom directly SEEING NO-SELF IS THE DESTROYER OF THAT self-grasping, because IT is able to eradicate that [self-grasping] through a manner of grasping [phenomena] that CONTRADICTS THAT self-grasping. Alternatively, one sees that no-self

28 The search for an antidote to suffering entails a concern for the truth of the fourth noble truth, i.e., the path, the method that is to be applied to the elimination of suffering. The cause for the origination of suffering is said to be self-grasping (or "apprehending a self": *bdag 'dzin, ātmagraha*), which is at the root of craving (*sred pa, tṛṣṇa*); the removal of the cause of the origination should assure the removal of suffering. The cause of origination only will be removed by a way of considering phenomena that is diametrically opposed to self-grasping, i.e., grasping phenomena as neither being nor having self. This point will be discussed in greater detail below, in sections III:10-11.

29 Craving is, in a sense, an omnipresent factor in the minds of ordinary beings, assuring that any act committed while under its sway will have a suffering result—suffering being taken in the broadest sense, as that which pertains to all "contaminated" (*zag bcas, sāsrava*) phenomena. Craving is, specifically, the indispensable cooperative condition for the generation of acts that will have suffering results. The five aggregates (or constituents, or categories: *phung po, skandha*) that are the objects of craving compose the psycho-physical individual. They are: form (or matter), sensation (or feeling), recognition (or perception), formations (or dispositions) and cognition (or consciousness).

damages that craving, and [one] applies the words, "in order to destroy the cause of that."[30]

The purpose of such an analysis [163]

[This is divided into:] (1) [The Buddha's] complete clarity about the flaws and good qualities of objects [164], (2) [How the Buddha] is a subject free from all faults [165] and (3) [How the Buddha] acts specially for the liberation of others [166].

The Buddha's complete clarity about the flaws and good qualities of objects [164]

> (136c-137b) IN [THE BUDDHA] THERE HAS COME TO BE GREAT
> CLARITY [REGARDING] THE FLAWS AND GOOD QUALITIES [OF OBJECTS],
> FROM [HIS] ACCUSTOMATING MANY METHODS
> IN MANY WAYS FOR A LONG TIME.

[OPPONENT:] If the way of investigating through scripture and reasoning is thus, what is the way of manifesting [reality] by meditation?

[RGYAL TSHAB RJE:] There is a reason why IN HIM, the *muni*, the Blessed One, THERE HAS COME TO BE an ultimate GREAT CLARITY of mind that has as its intentional objects THE FLAWS to be abandoned AND the GOOD QUALITIES of the antidotes, because he is thus FROM ACCUSTOMATING all the MANY METHODS of pacifying suffering IN MANY repeated WAYS FOR A LONG TIME, through three countless eons.[31]

[OPPONENT:] He has become a detached one [arhant] by abandoning self-grasping, but how does he become omniscient? If he is [omniscient], then all detached ones are omniscient.[32]

---

30 If the root of craving, hence of continued suffering in saṃsāra, is self-grasping, the cause of the cessation of suffering, i.e., the path, must be the contradictory of self-grasping, the wisdom realizing no-self. These two are the keys to saṃsāra and nirvāṇa, and their establishment is vital to Dharmakīrti's proof of the Buddha's authoritativeness.

31 It already has been proven to Dharmakīrti's and rGyal tshab rje's satisfaction that there are countless past and future lives, and that mental qualities are capable of infinite development, or accustomation, over the course of these lives. Hence, it is not at all unreasonable to assert that the Buddha, who has taken so many different births for the sake of beings over the three great countless eons traditionally required for traversal of the Mahāyāna path, should have developed a complete knowledge of what is to be adopted and what rejected. This knowledge, as we saw above (section III:2:D), is definitive of the Buddha's authoritativeness.

32 The opponent accepts that arhantship may be attainable through the elimina-

[RGYAL TSHAB RJE:] When one sets as the [thesis], "There is a reason why [the Buddha] is *omniscient*, with complete clarity regarding the extent of [flaws and good qualities]," then the reason is: "Because he is thus from accustomating for a long time many specific methods of transcending saṃsāra, having taken many births in saṃsāra by virtue of previously[-accustomated] compassion."[33]

[How the Buddha] is a subject free from all faults [165]

(137c) THUS, HE IS ONE WHO HAS ABANDONED THE PROPENSITIES
TO [CREATE] THE CAUSE, BECAUSE OF HIS CLARITY OF MIND.

THUS, [the Buddha] IS ONE WHO also HAS ABANDONED utterly THE PROPENSITIES TO [create] THE CAUSE of suffering, BECAUSE HE HAS complete CLARITY OF MIND in his analysis of cause and result. One must also counter [the idea] that his [ordinary] speech is impure.[34]

[How the Buddha] acts specially for the liberation of others [166]

(138) THE GREAT *MUNI* [ACTS] SPECIALLY FOR THE RHINOCEROS[-LIKE PRATYEKABUDDHAS], ETC.,
APPLYING [HIMSELF] TO THE AIMS OF OTHERS.

---

tion of self-grasping, and that the elimination of self-grasping must perforce involve knowledge of what is to be adopted and what rejected, but they argue that this in no way entails the omniscience that Mahāyānists attribute to the Buddha. Neither this objection nor rGyal tshab rje's reply is contained or implied in Dharmakīrti's root-verse.

33 According to rGyal tshab rje, the Buddha may rightly be regarded as omniscient because (unlike arhants) he has been able to familiarize himself over the course of countless lives not only with the essential details of saṃsāra and nirvāṇa, but with all the details. Since saṃsāra and nirvāṇa (= what is to be rejected and what adopted) are categories exhaustive of all phenomena, if the Buddha knows saṃsāra and nirvāṇa in all their details, he is by definition omniscient. Cf. above, section III:2:D and R. Jackson (1987) for material relating to Dharmakīrti's attitude toward omniscience.

34 Because his mind is utterly clear and purified, the Buddha may be said to have eliminated not only the causes of suffering, but also the latent dispositions or propensities (*bag chags, vāsanā*) to originating the cause. This distinction, basic to Mahāyāna, is not spelled out explicitly by Dharmakīrti's verse. The subsequent point, also added by rGyal tshab rje, is that since qualities of body and speech are determined by qualities of mind, the Buddha's actions of body and speech must be regarded as pure, right down to and including "ordinary" speech and "everyday" actions.

THE GREAT *MUNI* acts SPECIALLY FOR the liberation of others, such as THE RHINOCEROS[-like pratyekabuddhas], ETC., because he has completed the method of APPLYING [himself] TO THE AIMS OF OTHERS.[35]

Summary [167]

(138c) ONE ASSERTS AS BEING THE TEACHER JUST THAT
ACCUSTOMATION TO METHOD, BECAUSE IT IS THE OBJECT OF THAT [TEACHER];
(139) THESE TWO [COMPASSION AND TEACHERHOOD] ARE EXPLAINED AS CAUSES,
BECAUSE THEY ORIGINATE PRIOR TO ACCOMPLISHMENT [OF SUGATAHOOD AND SAVIORHOOD].

[OPPONENT:] It follows that it is unreasonable to explain as the teacher someone who has accustomated methods, because the ācārya [Dignāga] says, "Application is the teacher because it is the teacher of transmigrators."[36]

[RGYAL TSHAB RJE:] The verse that [so] describes application does not show as the teacher only the ultimate teacher, because it was written thus with a DESIRE to show AS THE TEACHER JUST THAT situation on the path where there is ACCUSTOMATION TO the wisdom realizing METHOD and no-self. There is a reason why the wisdom directly real-

---

35 The Buddha is able to act for the sake of others (including such "lower" enlightened beings as śrāvakas and pratyekabuddhas) because he has attained his own aim, i.e., liberation, and is motivated by compassion to assist others in attaining the same goal. Indeed, he would not attain his own aim were he not already compassionate, for, in Mahāyāna theory, full buddhahood only can be attained when motivated by the altruistic aspiration to enlightenment (*bodhicitta*). This seems to raise a paradox: one only can attain one's own aim by considering the aims of others; yet in considering the aims of others, one may be said to be considering one's own aim, so one may be selfish and thus unable to attain one's own aim! Undoubtedly, the paradox can be partially resolved by the simple observation that compassion may be forced at first, but later will become genuine, or "natural" (cf. above, PV 129)—indeed, it only will become liberating to the degree that it is "naturalized." One must accustomate, or condition oneself (*goms pa, abhyāsa*) to it over a long period of time.

36 The opponent is arguing that "one who has accustomated methods" (such as compassion) cannot be regarded as the teacher, because Dignāga, in his commentary to the *Pramāṇasamuccaya*'s verse of homage (see Nagatomi [1959] 265), identifies application as the teacher; and application, as we have seen, is synonymous with the wisdom realizing no-self, hence with the wisdom (*shes rab, prajñā*) wing of the Mahāyāna path to enlightenment rather than the method (*thabs, upāya*) wing.

izing no-self during the training-path,[37] which is accustomated for the sake of others, is designated as the teacher, BECAUSE IT IS THE OBJECT that is the cause OF THAT ultimate teacher. The reason why THESE TWO excellences explained before, of intention and application, ARE EXPLAINED AS CAUSES of that ultimate teacher, is BECAUSE it is necessary that [sugatahood and saviorhood] ORIGINATE from the accustomation of those methods that originate at the time of the path, PRIOR TO the sugata and savior who [perfect] ACCOMPLISHMENT of their own and others' aims.[38]

Alternatively, "originating from accomplishment" and "originating first" mean that the excellences of intention and application are accomplished first, and that they come first in the verses of homage; they are explained as the cause.[39]

---

37 A "training path" (*slob lam, śaikṣamārga*) is any of the first four spiritual paths, i.e., of accumulation, application, seeing or development—on any of which one is not yet entirely free. Loosely speaking, these paths are the "causes" of the cessation of suffering that is identified with the fifth path, that of no-more-training (*mi slob lam, aśaikṣamārga*).

38 rGyal tshab rje replies to the opponent's objection about the identification of the teacher by pointing out that one must distinguish between conventional and ultimate teachers. Granted, the ultimate teacher is one who has completed their training in method and wisdom. However, the method and wisdom that are developed while one is still on training-paths are the causes of the ultimate teacher, hence may themselves figuratively be spoken of as teachers. Among the four epithets that demonstrate the Buddha's authoritativeness, those that represent the excellence of results are the sugata (which is excellence of one's own aims) and the savior (which is excellence of others' aims). The causes of these results are the excellence of intention (which is compassion) and the excellence of application (which is the wisdom realizing no-self). The description of "method" as the teacher is intended to include both method *and* wisdom. Thus, "method" includes the excellences of both intention and application, thereby fulfilling Dignāga's definition.

39 The Tibetan of PV 119a reads: *grub las dang po 'byung ba. . . .* The reading of the line depends on whether one takes as the subjects the excellences of intention and application or of one's own and others' aims. In the former case, the first two excellences are said to originate first, or *prior to the accomplishment* of the second two. In the latter case, the second two excellences are said to originate *from the prior accomplishment* of the first two excellences. The grammar of the line would seem to support the former interpretation.

[Based on] those two [excellences], the way of proving the excellence of results [168]

[This is divided into:] (1) The excellence of one's own aims [169] and (2) The excellence of others' aims [174].

The excellence of one's own aims [169]

[This is divided into:] (1) Showing that [the Buddha] is a sugata with three special qualities [170] and (2) Disposing of objections to that [173].

Showing that [the Buddha] is a sugata with three special qualities [170]

[This is divided into:] (1) A brief demonstration [171] and (2) An extensive explanation [172].

A brief demonstration [171]

(139c) ABANDONMENT OF THE CAUSE IS THE SUGATA, POSSESSING THREE QUALITIES:

The abandonment that is the ABANDONMENT OF THE CAUSE of suffering together with the propensities thereto, IS THE SUGATA, because it is an ultimate abandonment, POSSESSING THREE QUALITIES.[40]

This chapter shows as the sugata just the abandonment of the two obstacles, (a) the defilement-obstacle and (b) the knowledge-obstacle[41] taken as non-defiled ignorance regarding impermanence and other of the sixteen aspects [of the four noble truths]. It does not teach [as the sugata] the abandonment of the knowledge-obstacle taken as the cognition attached to a substantial difference between object and subject.[42] The reason for that is that [Dharmakīrti] wishes to show the

---

40 The three qualities of a sugata, to be discussed below (PV 139d-142), are goodness, irreversibility and remainderlessness. Cf. below, PV 280c-281, for the three qualities of a sugata in the reverse system of explanation.

41 In Mahāyāna theory, there are two obstacles that lie between oneself and full buddhahood, the obstacle consisting of one's defilements (*nyon sgrib, kleśāvaraṇa*), and the obstacle to full knowledge of what is to be known (*shes bya'i sgrib, jñeyāvaraṇa*), which is equivalent to the subtle propensities to defilement that remain (like the smell of garlic on one's fingers) once the defilements themselves are gone.

42 Sugatahood, which is the excellence or fulfillment of one's own aims, is defined as the abandonment of the two obstacles. Dharmakīrti, as a Sautrāntika-oriented Yogācāra, should ultimately define the knowledge-obstacle to be abandoned as non-defiled ignorance regarding the substantial identity of

definition of the common teacher who is most necessary to all three lineages [of practitioners]; he does not show the definition of the uncommon Mahāyāna teacher. Therefore, the no-self he teaches is just the no-self of persons; the no-self of dharmas will be explained below.[43]

[OPPONENT:] Well, then, it is unreasonable [to assert that] the Greatly Compassionate One is shown [here].[44]

[RGYAL TSHAB RJE:] Although he is the root-teacher who is most necessary to those of the śrāvaka lineage, it is also necessary to show that his accomplishment definitely [arises] from his being the Greatly Compassionate One.[45]

---

subject and object. Here, however, he limits his discussion to ignorance of the four noble truths, especially of the truth of suffering's aspect of no-self. A Prāsaṅgika Mādhyamika, such as rGyal tshab rje, would define the knowledge-obstacle as non-defiled ignorance regarding the inherent voidness of all phenomena. The ignorance involved in a knowledge-obstacle is "undefiled" because defilement already has been abandoned. It is ignorance that has understood the essential to be understood, but not all the details. The ignorance involved in the defilement-obstacle, incidentally, would be identified just as above by the various schools, but with the proviso that it is *defiled* ignorance, wherein one has *not* grasped the essential point.

43 Because Dharmakīrti is interested in establishing the lowest common denominator for liberation, he discusses no-self in terms of the no-self of persons, and the obstacles in terms of ignorance of the four noble truths—with the aspect of no-self the most crucial. Yogācāras (like Dharmakīrti) and Svātantrika Mādhyamikas hold that Hīnayāna practitioners realize only the no-self of persons, while Mahāyāna practitioners also realize the no-self of dharmas. Prāsaṅgika Mādhyamikas (like rGyal tshab rje) hold that *all* practitioners realize the no-self of dharmas, and that the distinctions among them are based on the extensiveness of the *methods* in which they are trained—particularly in the degree of their compassion.

44 The opponent argues that if Dharmakīrti is content to describe the "minimal" path, i.e., that which will lead to arhantship, then it is inappropriate to speak of the Buddha as the Greatly Compassionate One, for great compassion is primarily a Mahāyāna concern, and unnecessary for basic liberation.

45 The Buddha *must* be described as greatly compassionate, for not only could he not have attained his full enlightenment without being motivated by compassion, but if he were not compassionate once he had attained his goal, then he would not teach, and neither śrāvakas nor any other practitioners would have the opportunity to attain liberation. The being whose authoritativeness is being proven is not just any arhant, but the Buddha, who has trodden not just the "minimal" path of those "liberated by insight," but the "maximal" path of those who have been liberated by both concentration and insight and, in addition, fulfill unique historical roles as world-teachers. One who has trodden the "maximal"

An extensive explanation [172]

(139d) . . . [1] BECAUSE IT IS NOT THE BASIS OF SUFFERING,
(140) IT IS GOOD; IT IS A SEEING
OF NO-SELF OR [SOMETHING ARISING] THROUGH [MEDITATIVE] APPLICATION.
IT IS EXPLAINED THAT [IN] ONE WHO WILL REVERT [TO SAṂSĀRA]
BIRTH AND FLAWS WILL ORIGINATE.
(141) [2] SUGATAHOOD IS IRREVERSIBLE,
BECAUSE ONE HAS ABANDONED THE SEED THAT IS THE SELF-VIEW
BY WAY OF HAVING A [MENTAL] NATURE DIFFERENT [FROM SELF-GRASPING, WHICH APPREHENDS WHAT IS] TRUE.
[3] [IN SOME] THERE ARE REMAINING TRACE-FAULTS OF BODY, SPEECH AND MIND;
(142) THERE ARE NO DEFILEMENTS AND THERE IS NO SICKNESS,
[BUT] THERE IS LEFT OVER A LACK OF CLARITY [IN HOW TO] EXPLAIN THE PATH;
[SUGATAHOOD] IS AN ABANDONMENT WITHOUT REMAINDER, BECAUSE OF ACCUSTOMATION [OF SUFFERING'S ANTIDOTE].

[OPPONENT:] What are the three qualities?

[RGYAL TSHAB RJE:] That abandonment is a good abandonment, BECAUSE IT is an ultimate abandonment that is NOT THE BASIS OF [any further] SUFFERING. Although those in other schools [achieve] abandonments, since they are connected with suffering, they ARE not GOOD abandonments. THAT [good abandonment] is preceded by a good method, because there IS A new SEEING, by perception, OF the NO-SELF of persons, and that is attained THROUGH [meditative] APPLICATION and accustomation.[46]

---

path necessarily is greatly compassionate, hence the appropriateness of designating the Buddha thus.

46 Thus, the Buddha's abandonment is good (*legs, śastam*), because it has utterly dispensed with the origination of suffering and the propensities thereto. The reason why it has dispensed with the origination of suffering is that it results from an application of the antidote to the origination of suffering, namely the wisdom realizing no-self. Non-Buddhist teachers, since they do not realize no-self, do not possess the true antidote, so their abandonment of the defilements that are the causes of the origination of suffering cannot be a complete one. They cannot cut the root of saṃsāra, and so are not liberated. This will be proven in greater detail below, sections III:10-11. The reason given for the abandonment's "goodness," namely, *bdag med pa / mthong ba'am sbyor ba las yin no* (= *nairātmyadṛṣṭes tad yuktito 'pi vā*) is susceptible of three different in-

The word "or" [in the root-text] includes as abandonments the respective abandonments on the paths of seeing and development.[47] According to ācārya Devendrabuddhi, when one interprets the quotation as "because of seeing no-self and [because of] *reasoning*," reasoning is praised because it is through the accustomation of the wisdom realizing no-self by the method that sees [no-self] through reasoning, that [the Buddha] is the sugata.[48]

[OPPONENT:] What is the irreversible abandonment by abandoning which one does not revert [to saṃsāra]?

[RGYAL TSHAB RJE:] A streamwinner who will have seven [more] existences is EXPLAINED AS someONE WHO WILL REVERT to saṃsāra, because it is explained that the suffering of continuous BIRTH, AND FLAWS such as attachment, etc., WILL ORIGINATE for seven more existences. The foregoing [ultimate] abandonment is a SUGATAHOOD that IS IRRE-

---

terpretations. The first, listed here, is that the Buddha's abandonment is good and retains no basis for further suffering because it is the result of a good method, i.e., the seeing of no-self, which is synonymous with the excellence of application. The key to this interpretation is the rendering of the Sanskrit *yukti* (usually T. *rigs pa*) as *sbyor* (which usually translates *prayoga*). If *yukti* = *sbyor*, then it is possible to interpret it as referring to the excellence of application (*prayogasampat, sbyor ba'i phun tshogs*), which is, of course, synonymous with the realization of no-self, and is the connotation of the Buddha-epithet, "teacher."

47 A second way of interpreting the basis of the Buddha's abandonment's goodness is to say that it is a result of the abandonments of defilement- and knowledge-obstacles that occur on the path of seeing (*mthong*) and development; the latter is implied by the word "or" (*'am, vā*). It must be noted, however, that the Tibetan *mthong* here translates *dṛṣṭva*, lit., "having seen," not *darśana*, which is the Sanskrit term used when the path of seeing is the topic. The five paths are nowhere in the *Pramāṇasiddhi* chapter explicitly mentioned by Dharmakīrti.

48 A third way of interpreting the basis of the Buddha's abandonment's goodness is that of Devendrabuddhi (PVV 244/4/6), who takes *yukti* as "reasoning," in other words, as *rigs pa* rather than *sbyor ba*. Thus, the goodness of the Buddha's abandonment derives from the fact that it results from the accustomation of the antidote, the wisdom realizing no-self. No-self first is cognized by reasoning. This cognition eventually leads to a direct, non-conceptual realization of no-self. The direct, non-conceptual realization of no-self is the excellence of application, and is the basis for the abandonment of defilements. Accustomated on the paths of seeing and development, that realization eventually issues in buddhahood, in which all obstacles have been abandoned. The wisdom realizing no-self through reasoning thus is an indirect cause of the sugata, or of the abandonments that comprise sugatahood.

VERSIBLE, BECAUSE [in it ONE] HAS utterly ABANDONED THE SEED THAT IS THE SELF-VIEW, together with the propensities thereto.[49]

[OPPONENT:] How does the wisdom realizing no-self damage self-grasping? If it is merely by contradicting [self-grasping's] manner of grasping, then [conversely,] self-grasping should be able to damage [the wisdom realizing no-self].[50]

[RGYAL TSHAB RJE:] The wisdom realizing the no-self of persons directly damages the grasping at a self of persons, because it is directly contradictory BY WAY OF HAVING the NATURE of a DIFFERENT manner of grasping [reality], one THAT IS a subject that has a TRUE and right manner of grasping [reality].[51]

---

49 A second special quality of the Buddha's abandonment is that it is irreversible (*slar mi gshegs pa, apunarāgama*). One who has the abandonment of a buddha never again will return to saṃsāra, whereas there are beings whose abandonments are such that, although they are destined for enlightenment, they have not yet run the course of their saṃsāric existences, for they have not abandoned all defilements. Examples of the latter are the three lower classes of Hīnayāna āryas, the streamwinner (*rgyun zhugs, srotāpanna*), who will attain arhantship after a maximum of seven more saṃsāric existences; the once-returner (*len cig phyir 'ong ba, sakṛdāgamin*), who will attain arhantship after at most one more saṃsāric existence; and the non-returner (*phyir mi 'ong ba, anāgāmin*), who will attain arhantship from a divine abode after the end of their present saṃsāric existence. According to the *Abhidharmakośa* path-system (AK vi), the "fruits" of the streamwinner, once-returner and non-returner are attained on the paths of seeing and development, while the first moment of the fourth fruit, arhantship, coincides with the path of no-more-training. Neither bodhisattvas nor those with the three lower Hīnayāna fruits have irreversibly abandoned saṃsāra; arhants and buddhas have.

50 The opponent is arguing that if self-grasping and non-self-grasping are defined as contradictories, then each should be able equally to damage the other. Thus, there should not be any reason why self-grasping—once replaced by non-self-grasping—might not in turn replace the non-self-grasping that replaced it. The objection presumably is not just a philosophical appeal to symmetry; it is based, too, on the observation of the mental states of ordinary beings.

51 The very important reply here is that although self-grasping and non-self-grasping are contradictories, they are not symmetrical, or equally weighted, because the former is a *false* manner of grasping reality, while the latter is a *true* manner of grasping reality, and where the truth has become securely established, falsehood cannot again take root. Thus, non-self-grasping can replace self-grasping, but self-grasping cannot replace non-self-grasping. Note that this argument presupposes (a) an asymmetrical relation between truth and falsehood and (b) the truth and soteriological value of non-self-grasping. Thus, (b) presupposes the correctness of the Buddhist identification of the

[OPPONENT:] What are the remaining abandonment-objects, by abandoning which an arhant has abandoned every [obstacle]?

[RGYAL TSHAB RJE:] [In] śrāvaka and pratyekabuddha arhants THERE ARE REMAINING TRACE-FAULTS OF BODY, SPEECH AND MIND left over, because they possess trace-faults of the three doors that are not defilement-related. Therefore, they do not revert to saṃsāra, because THERE ARE NO DEFILEMENTS, the cause [of saṃsāra], AND because THERE IS NO SICKNESS of a mind tormented by saṃsāric suffering. THERE IS LEFT OVER [in śrāvakas and pratyekabuddhas] A LACK OF mental CLARITY on [how to] EXPLAIN THE PATH to liberation to others, because they have abandoned just the defilements; they have not utterly abandoned remaining trace-faults. The aforementioned [sugata's] abandonment IS AN ABANDONMENT WITHOUT REMAINDER, BECAUSE it is an abandonment that is attainment [of one's goal] THROUGH a complete ACCUSTOMATION of the antidote [to the cause of suffering][52]

Disposing of objections to that [173]

(142d-144) SOME SAY: "HE HAS NOT ELIMINATED ALL FLAWS,
BECAUSE HE IS A SPEAKER, ETC.; [THE REASON] HAS MISTAKEN
NEGATIVE CONCOMITANCE, SO THE STATEMENT [ENTAILS] DOUBT.
"BECAUSE THE FLAWS ARE PERMANENT" OR "BECAUSE
THERE IS NO METHOD," [OR] ALTERNATIVELY, "BECAUSE [THE METHOD]
IS NOT KNOWN": IF WE ENUMERATE COMPLETELY AN ANALYSIS
OF THESE STATEMENTS [AS TO WHY FAULTS] ARE INCAPABLE OF
ELIMINATION,

---

cause of the origination of suffering and of the antidote to that origination. The correctness of assumptions (a) and (b) will be demonstrated later, during the discussions, respectively, of the truths of cessation and path.

52 The third special quality of the Buddha's abandonment, one that is exclusive to the Mahāyāna, is that it is without remainder (*ma lus, niḥśeṣa*). Śrāvaka and pratyekabuddha Hīnayāna arhants have abandonments that are good (because they result from the accustomation of the antidote to suffering, the wisdom realizing no-self) and irreversible (because they will not revert to saṃsāra), but they have not abandoned all the subtle stains, or trace-faults (*gnas ngan len, vaiguṇya = bag chags, vāsanā*), left by the defilements they have destroyed. Thus, they have not eliminated all knowledge-obstacles, and are not omniscient with regard to all dharmas to be adopted and rejected; thus, they cannot teach the path to liberation to others with utter clarity. A buddha, on the other hand, has completely eliminated all faults, and thus has entirely achieved their own aim. On the basis of the complete attainment of their own aim, they are able to teach others the path to liberation with complete clarity.

[WE FIND THAT: THEY ARE NOT PERMANENT], BECAUSE THEY HAVE CAUSES, AND [THERE IS A METHOD,] BECAUSE ONE ELIMINATES THEM
THROUGH ACCUSTOMATING THE ANTIDOTE TO THEIR CAUSE.
(145) IT IS ALSO PROVEN THAT THERE EXISTS A KNOWLEDGE OF THAT [METHOD],
[BECAUSE] THERE IS KNOWLEDGE OF THE NATURE OF THE CAUSE.

Some rGyal dpog pas[53] and others say: "The *muni* HAS NOT ELIMINATED [ALL] FLAWS, BECAUSE HE IS A SPEAKER, [or] because he has sense-faculties, ETC., like people you meet on the road."[54]

Showing that the reason is uncertain:

THIS reason HAS MISTAKEN NEGATIVE CONCOMITANCE, because THE STATEMENT [entails] DOUBT about the opposite [of the predicate]. When they refute [the existence of] a person who has eliminated faults, on the basis of whether [such a person] is a speaker or not, there is no proof at all, for our opponents are in doubt themselves, and even according to our opponents, one does not generate a right cognition if one has any doubt.[55]

[OPPONENT:] This reason can be set forth for the Buddhists, because they have already proven, and have not forgotten, that a speaker may have eliminated faults. How is it that [the reason] "induces doubt"?

---

53 The rGyal dpog pas apparently are synonymous with the Mīmāṃsakas.

54 The rGyal dpog pa objection is basically a common-sense one, namely that conventional observation does not give us a basis for distinguishing the attainments (or abandonments) of a buddha from those of other people. All we really can observe of other people, such as those we meet on the road, is that they speak and have bodies and sense-faculties. We know that most people who have bodies and sense-faculties and speak have not abandoned suffering, and there is no additional information provided by observation of alleged buddhas that would guarantee that they are any different from other people we encounter.

55 The opponent's argument is uncertain for the simple reason that there is no invariable concomitance between speakership and the possession of sense-faculties on the one hand and the quality of having eliminated or not eliminated flaws on the other. To argue that the Buddha has not eliminated flaws because he has body and speech is to cite insufficient evidence, for it is not impossible (a) that someone with an "impure"body or speech have a mind that has eliminated flaws or, more importantly, (b) that there exist someone whose body and speech are not flawed in the slightest. That the Buddha is an example of the former is a Vaibhāṣika contention; that he is an example of the latter is a Mahāyānist contention.

[RGYAL TSHAB RJE:] Saying, "This *muni* has not eliminated [all] flaws, because he speaks purely [only on the basis of] the Dharma taught him by past teachers," or, "He has not eliminated flaws, as he speaks with attachment," our opponents have set forth doubtful reasons. We answer that [the reasons] do not prove with certainty that there is negative concomitance, other than by merely repeating [the assertion].[56] Those who say that the Buddha's physical form is not the Buddha are welcomed by the rGyal dpog pas.[57]

Investigating the extremes through reasoning and refuting them:

The reasons [adduced] for the impossibility of eliminating faults [are], e.g., (1) "BECAUSE THE FLAWS of attachment, etc., ARE PERMANENT, they cannot be abandoned"; or (2) "Even if they can be, [they will not be,] BECAUSE THERE IS NO METHOD of abandoning them"; or, ALTERNATIVELY, (3) "Even if there really exists a method, [flaws cannot be eliminated,] BECAUSE [THE METHOD] IS NOT KNOWN by anyone"; or (4) "Even if [someone] knows [the method, faults cannot be eliminated,] because it is impossible that one make others strive for their goals"; or (5) "Even if there arises [the desire to make] others strive for their goals, [one does not,] because one does not have the compassion that [leads one] to explain how it is [to be done]."

---

56 When one analyzes the opponent's possible arguments in greater detail, their uncertainty becomes even clearer. If one argues that the Buddha has not abandoned flaws because his speech is pure only on the basis of what he has been taught by past teachers, or because he speaks with attachment, the syllogism lacks negative concomitance (*ldog khyab, vyatireka*), for there is no invariable concomitance between one's having eliminated flaws and one's not being a speaker, or one's being non-attached. Generally speaking, the fact that one possesses body and speech does not automatically entail that one's body or speech are either pure or impure, for instances of both are held to be possible.

57 "Those who say that the Buddha's physical form is not the Buddha" include the Vaibhāṣikas, who claim that only the Buddha's mind is truly the Buddha, and that his body and speech are the impure residue of past karma. This position opens the way for the rGyal dpog pa objection just raised. In general, Mahāyānists accept that the Buddha is his body, speech and mind, and that all aspects of him are pure. His mind, which is equivalent to the Dharma Body, is the pure result of the storage of gnosis (*ye shes kyi tshogs, jñānasambhāra*); his speech and body, which are (roughly) equivalent to the Enjoyment and Transformation Bodies, are the pure result of the storage of merit (*bsod nams kyi tshogs, puṇyasambhāra*). These two stores correspond, respectively, to the wisdom and method wings of Mahāyāna practice. Cf. TS 3369b-3370a.

IF WE ENUMERATE COMPLETELY AN ANALYSIS OF THESE STATEMENTS as to why faults are INCAPABLE OF ELIMINATION, [it is thus:] (1) The faults of attachment, etc., are not permanent, BECAUSE THEY HAVE CAUSES that generate them. (2) It is not the case that there is no method of abandoning [faults], BECAUSE ONE ELIMINATES THEM BY ACCUSTOMATING THE ANTIDOTE to their CAUSE, self-grasping. (3) IT IS ALSO PROVEN THAT THERE EXISTS KNOWLEDGE of a method for abandoning them, because THERE IS KNOWLEDGE OF THE NATURE OF THE CAUSE of [those faults], as it really is. Reasons (4) and (5) and their answers are not set forth here, because they are understood from the earlier quote, "A compassionate one. . . ." and from the section below on the savior.[58]

The excellence of others' aims [174]

(145c) [THE BUDDHA] IS THE SAVIOR, [FOR] HE HAS SEEN THE PATH AND TEACHES IT;
HE DOES NOT TEACH FALSELY, BECAUSE THERE IS NO [GOOD] RESULT [IN DOING SO].
(146) ALSO, ALL UNDERTAKINGS WERE APPLIED TOWARD THE AIMS
OF OTHERS, BECAUSE OF HIS POSSESSION OF A COMPASSIONATE MIND.

The *muni*, the Blessed One, IS THE SAVIOR of those intent on freedom, because he himself has completely SEEN THE PATH to liberation, and because he undistortedly TEACHES to others that path that he has seen, without regard to payment or fame. He has completely seen [the path], because he has utterly abandoned stains. That [verse] shows the way of proving him the savior from the fact he is the sugata.[59]

---

58 These five points, extrapolated by rGyal tshab rje from Dharmakīrti's verses, are essential points of difference between Buddhists and their critics. The first three are clear, and need no further comment. Reasons (4) and (5) would affirm that there does exist someone who *can* assist others in eliminating their flaws, and that such a person *would*, in fact, assist others in so doing. The proof of this is said to be contained in PV 132, which discusses a compassionate bodhisattva's striving for a perfect accomplishment on the basis of which to explain the path to others, and PV 145c-146b, which asserts the Buddha's truthful and compassionate teaching to others of the path that he has seen and traversed by himself.

59 Since the Buddha has utterly abandoned all flaws, he has a complete understanding of all dharmas to be rejected (saṃsāra) and all dharmas to be adopted (nirvāṇa). Thus, he is in a position to explain to others the path that he has travelled. The fact that he possesses an ultimate abandonment, i.e., that he is a sugata, enables him to teach and otherwise assist others, i.e., to be a savior. Indeed, it is only because of the ultimacy of his abandonment that he

Well, then, [it might be argued that] he either (a) does not teach the path to liberation to others at all or (b) he teaches it distortedly. (a) is unacceptable, as proven by the explanation that the fact that he is the teacher proves that he is the sugata.[60] If (b) is the case, then either (i) he claims to teach undistortedly, but [in fact] understands entities distortedly or (ii) he desires to teach distortedly. (i) is unacceptable, as proven by the proof that [the fact that he is] the sugata proves that he is the savior.[61] If (ii) is the case, then either (a) like a bad doctor, he is attached to self and is perplexed as to whether he can accomplish his own desires or (b) he does not possess great compassion that has others as its intentional object. (a) is unacceptable, as in the previous proofs. (b) is unacceptable, as proven by setting forth great compassion [as the reason] proving he is the teacher.[62]

Therefore, [the *muni*] DOES NOT TEACH the path to liberation FALSELY or distortedly, BECAUSE he directly sees that in teaching thus [he will bring about] NO desirable RESULT regarding either his own aims or others' aims. Those verses prove that he is the savior, and shows ["sav-

---

can teach and assist others in every possible way. At this point, rGyal tshab rje launches on another parenthetical explanation, which comprises the rest of the section on "the excellence of others' aims."

60 It cannot be the case that the Buddha does not teach the path at all, because it already has been proven that he is the teacher, with a knowledge of the cause and antidote of saṃsāric suffering. His search for and accustomation to the antidote (the wisdom realizing no-self) is motivated by his desire to help free all beings. His successful development of the antidote issues in his abandonment of all faults, or sugatahood, a condition from which he actually is able to help free all beings, just as he had originally intended—and one of the methods by which he helps free beings is teaching the path.

61 It cannot be the case that the Buddha teaches distortedly (or invertedly: *phyin ci log par*), because he has been shown to have abandoned all flaws. He has been shown to have abandoned all flaws because he has accustomated to the ultimate degree the antidote to the origination of suffering. As one who has abandoned all flaws, i.e., as a sugata, he is free from error. Thus, when he teaches the path to others in his capacity as savior, he cannot possibly do so distortedly.

62 It cannot be the case that the Buddha does not possess the great compassion that has others as its intentional object, because it already has been shown that great compassion can be accustomated infinitely over a series of rebirths, and that it is the motive on the basis of which bodhisattvas exert themselves in the discovery and development of the antidote to the origination of suffering. The antidote, as we have seen, is the wisdom realizing no-self, which is, in turn, called "the teacher." Thus, great compassion is the cause of the teacher.

ior"] as the predicate of the two [reasons], "teacher" and "compassionate."[63]

[The *muni*] undistortedly teaches others the path to liberation he has seen by himself, because earlier, on the training-path, all meditative undertakings regarding impermanence, no-self, etc., were applied toward the aims of all other sentient beings, and he has completed the accustomation [of those]. This shows the way of proving him the sugata from the fact that he is the teacher.[64]

There ALSO is a reason why ALL UNDERTAKINGS WERE APPLIED TOWARD THE AIMS OF OTHERS, BECAUSE earlier, on the training-path, he was in complete POSSESSION OF the great COMPASSIONATE MIND that has as its intentional object all sentient beings. This shows the way of proving him the teacher from the fact that he is compassionate.[65]

Therefore, in this section on the forward system, "savior" is made the predicate of the reason, and the other three [epithets] are proven in succession.[66] Compassion is the ultimate proof, and when one en-

---

63 The syllogism thus would read: "The *muni* is the savior, because he is compassionate and because he is the teacher." The fact that he is the (ultimate) teacher assures that he has complete knowledge of all that is to be rejected and adopted; the fact that he is compassionate assures that he will teach what he knows.

64 See above, note 59.

65 See above, note 61.

66 Thus, the forward-system syllogism might read: "The *muni* is the savior, because he is compassionate, which leads to his becoming the teacher, which leads to his becoming the sugata, which enables him to be the savior of others."Alternatively, it can be said that: "The *muni* is the savior, because he is the sugata, which results from his being the teacher, which results from his compassion." The entire proof might be schematized as follows:

compassion ——>	teacher ——>	sugata ——>	savior
excellence of cause	excel. of cause	excel. of result	excel. of result
(intention)	(application)	(own aims)	(other's aims)
bodhicitta	wisdom realizing no-self	adandonment good irreversible remainderless	buddha-activities
path of: accumulation	application seeing development	no-more-training	

ters the path gradually in order to become an authoritative person, then that is the threshold for first entering the uncommon Mahāyāna path; since great compassion is the method and the proof, [Dharmakīrti] shows compassion as the proof by the words, "Compassion is the establisher."[67]

Showing from that that [the Buddha] is one who has become an authority [175]

(146c) THUS, HE IS AN AUTHORITY....

[THUS, the *muni*] IS AN AUTHORITY-person with regard to those intent on freedom, because through showing the path to liberation to those intent on freedom, he becomes their savior, and he has complete ability to save [them]. If he *can*not save them, then he does not fulfill the definition of a savior, and if he *does* not save them, he does not accomplish what is needed by those seeking salvation. In this teacher, ability and necessity meet.[68]

---

67 Above, PV 34a. Even prior to one's development of compassion, one enters the paths so as to become an authoritative person, i.e., in order to become knowledgeable about what is to be rejected and what adopted for religious purposes. Still, compassion is the *first* in the chain of reasons that demonstrate that one actually *can* become a savior, which is equivalent to an authoritative person for those intent on freedom. Furthermore, from rGyal tshab rje's perspective, compassion is the *first* point on the Mahāyāna path that leads through teacherhood (paths of seeing and development) to sugatahood (path of no-more-training and Dharma Body) and saviorhood (Form Bodies).

68 Thus, the Buddha is an authoritative person for those intent on freedom, because he can and does teach the path to liberation unmistakenly. He is able to teach the path unmistakenly because he has completely abandoned all faults that would hinder his complete knowledge of what is to be rejected and what accepted on the path. He has abandoned all the faults because he has cognized and fully accustomated the antidote to all faults, the wisdom realizing no-self. He has cognized and accustomated the antidote because he wishes to aid all sentient beings. He develops the desire to aid all sentient beings after first having set out to become an authoritative person so as to know how to free himself from saṃsāra. Thus, although savior is the basic predicate and compassion the basic reason used in the forward system of explanation, "the one who has become an authority" may be regarded as equally fundamental, for it is a predicate framing even "savior," and a reason preceding even "compassion." (After all, the *Pramāṇasiddhi* chapter as a whole *is* finally concerned with establishing that the Buddha is an authority: this is the most important of the five epithets.)

6. *The Four Noble Truths in General*

Demonstrating through the reverse system that he arrived at such a goal [176]

[This is divided into:] (1) The way of proving the special dharmas from latter to former [177] and (2) The way of proving from all those that [the Buddha] is an authority [323].

The way of proving the special dharmas from latter to former[1] *[177]*

[This is divided into:] (1) Proving that [the Buddha] has the nature of a savior [178], (2) The way of proving from that that he is the sugata [320], (3) The way of proving from that that he is the teacher [321] and (4) The way of proving from that that he is the compassionate one [322].

Proving that [the Buddha] has the nature of a savior [178]

[This is divided into:] (1) Showing that he is the savior by showing independently the actuality of the four noble truths [179] and (2) Establishing the four noble truths that are the object of scriptural teaching [180].

Showing that he is the savior by showing independently the actuality of the four noble truths [179]

(146c) . . . ALTERNATIVELY, HE IS THE SAVIOR
[BECAUSE] HE TEACHES THE FOUR NOBLE TRUTHS.

Having shown by the forward system the way in which the teacher proceeded [to liberation] via some path, we must show ALTERNATIVELY through the reverse system the perfect reasons demonstrating that he

---

1 In other words, the procedure now will be to prove that the Buddha is the savior, and to deduce from that that he is the sugata, from which we can determine that he is the teacher, compassionate, and the one who has become an authority. In the forward system of explanation it was proved that he is the compassionate one, and deduced from that that he is the teacher, sugata and savior.

proceeded thus [to liberation].[2] The *muni*, the Blessed One, IS THE SAVIOR for those intent on freedom, because for those intent on freedom he is one who completely TEACHES undistortedly the actuality of THE FOUR NOBLE TRUTHS.[3]

Establishing the four noble truths, which are the object of scriptural teaching [180]

[This is divided into:] (1) The general meaning [181] and (2) The meaning of the limbs [188].[4]

The general meaning [181]

[This is divided into:] (1) Ascertaining the number of the four noble truths [182], (2) Ascertaining their ordering [183], (3) Examples [184] and (4) The authority that ascertains that [185].

Ascertaining the number of the four noble truths [182]

The chief [matters] to be established for those intent on freedom are ascertained to be classified on two sides, that of saṃsāra and that of nirvāṇa. It is ascertained that within saṃsāra there are two: the truth of origination, which is the binding cause; and the truth of suffering, which is the resultant bondage. Within purification there are also two: the truth of path, which is the causal method that frees one

---

2 The "alternatively" (*yang na, vā*) is read by rGyal tshab rje as introducing the reverse system of explanation. It also may be read as supplying an alternative reason why the Buddha is a savior, it already having been established that he is one because he is compassionate, the teacher and the sugata.

3 By definition, a savior is someone who can lead others to freedom or salvation. The Buddha has attained freedom himself, has formulated his knowledge of the cosmos in the four noble truths, and teaches those truths to others. If the four noble truths are, in fact, true, they will be the basis of the attainment of freedom for those who subscribe to them. If they are true, they will stand up to the tests of perception and inference. If they stand up to those tests, then the status of savior will reasonably have been attributed to their teacher, the Buddha. Thus, the reverse system of explanation will concentrate on establishing the truth, or actuality (*gnas lugs*) of the four noble truths as the way of establishing that their propounder teaches saving knowledge, and thus is a savior. The *cause* of the Buddha's authoritativeness has been shown by the forward system, which described his progress from compassionate one to savior. The reverse system will show the *reason* for the Buddha's authoritativeness, the truth of his basic teachings.

4 As before, the "general meaning" consists of introductory material furnished by rGyal tshab rje, the "meaning of the limbs" of commentary on Dharmakīrti's text.

from saṃsāra; and the truth of cessation, which is the essential result, freedom. Because this has been ascertained, the cause and result of entering or leaving saṃsāra can be ascertained as fourfold.[5]

Ascertaining their ordering [183]

[If the teaching were] based on objective succession, the truths of origination and path would be taught first and suffering and cessation would be taught later. In this case, [however, the truths] are taught in another order, that which accords with the succession in which they are cognized by a subject, i.e., the truths of suffering, origination, cessation and path.[6]

Through initially thinking of the general and particular disadvantages of saṃsāra, one must generate the mind that desires to be free from that, because if that [desire] does not come first, it is impossible that there will arise the desire to abandon the cause [of suffering].

When the desire to be free from suffering has arisen, one realizes that one either can or cannot be free from this suffering, and that [the suffering] either does or does not have a cause, and [one realizes] that, in relation to origination, that cause is considered either permanent or impermanent—one sees that one cannot dispose of the essence of suffering the way one pulls out a thorn.[7] When one analyzes thus, one

---

5 The accuracy of this fourfold classification, of course, presupposes the correctness of the twofold classification on which it is based, i.e., the division of the cosmos into saṃsāra and nirvāṇa. The assumption of such a division appears at first to beg certain questions, for the establishment of its validity would seem to hinge upon the validity of the four noble truths, which remains to be decided. Perhaps the difficulty can be overcome by arguing that the *validity* of the twofold division is not presupposed, and that the division represents in a general way the categories, hence the line of inquiry, that would naturally occur to anyone who was concerned with suffering and its elimination.

6 If one were to teach the truths in the order in which they actually occur, i.e., with cause preceding result, then one first would describe origination; then its result, suffering; then the path; then its outcome, cessation. Traditionally, of course, the truths are taught from result to cause, in the pairs suffering-origination and cessation-path. This accords with the way in which they are actually cognized, for their discovery is an inferential process, and inferences proceed from result to cause, not the other way around.

7 One realizes upon even superficial investigation that the desired elimination of suffering is no simple matter, like the plucking out of a thorn. It is subtle and complex, and requires sophisticated analysis—it is far more deeply imbedded than the broken tip of a thorn in a finger, to which, if we extend the metaphor, it might be likened.

understands that the cause of [suffering] is twofold, karma and defilements, and when there arises a mind that desires to abandon those, that is origination, taught second.

When one sees that one is able to abandon the origination, then one sees that one is able [to effect] the cessation of suffering, and therefore, when one sees the active power of the cessation that stops suffering, this is cessation, taught third.

That which directly effects that [cessation] is taught as the path, and when one roughly sees what is to be accustomated, that is the path, taught fourth.[8]

[OPPONENT:] One sees in the first place that one is able [to effect] the cessation of suffering. Since one necessarily sees the active power that stops suffering, it would be reasonable to teach cessation second, and when one has seen that one is able to abandon origination, since one must see that one is able [to effect] the cessation of suffering, it would be reasonable to teach [cessation] before suffering's origination. Since initially one is to be taught roughly that a realization of no-self is seen to enable one to abandon the origination [of suffering], then the ordering of the truths as explained is uncertain.[9]

[RGYAL TSHAB RJE:] [The matter] is to be explained [as follows]. In general, one sees the benefits of entering into some actions and sees roughly the disadvantages of the reverse of that. When one thinks about the general and particular disadvantages of saṃsāra, then one sees saṃsāra as a fiery pit. One generates first just the mind that desires to be free from that, but one does not realize that one is able to be free from it. Thus, secondly, one sees by authority that one is able to abandon the origination. When one sees that, since one sees the active power of cessation, it is reasonable to teach origination second and cessation third. As before, path is to be taught last.[10] Thus, when the path of

---

8 Each of the truths has been preceded by the specification "when one sees" (*mthong bas* or *mthong ba na*), which emphasizes the "cognitive"basis of their usual ordering.

9 The opponent is arguing that there is some doubt about the cognitive order of the truths, for it might be maintained that as soon as one has realized that there is suffering, one recognizes in a general way that there must be a cessation of suffering, and the order then must be: suffering, cessation, origination, path.

10 rGyal tshab rje points out that the *desire for* the cessation of suffering, which does, indeed, arise after the recognition of the truth of suffering, is not the same as a recognition that cessation is possible. The latter is the truth of cessation, which only can be accepted if one first has investigated suffering's

seeing that has as its intentional object the four noble truths arises in the mindstream of a yogin, it arises in accordance with that ordering.[11]

Examples [184]

Now, the sensation of pain, etc., in the kidneys is the suffering of suffering. The sensation [resulting] from an excessive craving for delicious food is the suffering of change. All contaminated aggregates on which are placed the imprints of karma and defilements are the suffering [pervading] formations. All those are the truth of suffering.[12] All contaminated karma and defilements are the truth of origination. The freedom that is the stopping of suffering is the truth of cessation. The wisdom directly realizing no-self is the truth of path.[13]

---

causes, the elimination of which should entail the elimination of suffering. Thus, before one can recognize the truth of cessation, one must discover the fact and manner of suffering's origination, since if suffering does not have an identifiable and controllable cause, its cessation will be impossible. Cf. *bhāṣya* to AK vi:2, tr. Poussin (1923-31) IV, 120ff.

11 The path of seeing that has as its intentional object the four noble truths (specifically in its sixteen aspects) is that of a śrāvaka or pratyekabuddha in the path-system set forth in the *Abhidharmakośa* (e.g., AK vi:28). The path is divisible into fifteen "moments": one realizes one aspect of each of the truths explicitly (the others are realized implicitly); each of these four explicitly realized aspects is realized with respect to the desire and "upper" (form and formless) realms of saṃsāra; each realm-realization is divided into an uninterrupted "path" and a "path" of liberation (or accomplishment). Four aspects with respect to two realms each in a sequence of two paths each yields *sixteen* "moments," but the path of liberation with regard to the upper realms in respect of an aspect of the truth of path is counted as the first moment of the path of development.

12 Only the suffering of suffering (*sdug bsngal gyi sdug bsngal, duḥkhaduḥkatā*) covers what in the West is usually thought of as suffering, for only it is manifestly painful. The suffering of change (*'gyur ba'i sdug bsngal, pariṇāmaduḥkhatā*) seems to be pleasure, such as that derived from the anticipation and consumption of a huge meal, but it is suffering because it eventually will be replaced by the suffering of suffering. For example, our hunger and greed will lead us to overeat, which will result in indigestion, an instance of the suffering of suffering. The suffering pervading formations, also known as pervasive suffering (*khyab pa'i 'du byed kyi sdug bsngal, saṃskāraduḥkhatā*) is, in effect, the suffering nature of all beings (or aggregate-possessors) whose actions still are contaminated (*zag bcas, sāsrava*) by defilements, and who therefore will continue to take uncontrolled rebirth in saṃsāra. Obviously, this broad definition of suffering presupposes the validity of the division of the cosmos into saṃsāra and nirvāṇa, for only in a cosmos thus structured would the second and third types of suffering be regarded as suffering. See AK vi:3 and *bhāṣya* (tr. Poussin [1923-31] IV, 124ff.).

The authoritative reasoning that ascertains that [185]

[This is divided into:] (1) Identifying the sixteen distorted ideas [186] and (2) Identifying the sixteen aspects of the four noble truths that contradict those [187].

Identifying the sixteen distorted ideas [186]

Distorted ideas about suffering are four: holding it to be (1) pure, (2) pleasurable, (3) permanent and (4) [related to] a self.

Distorted ideas about origination are two: (1) holding that suffering is causeless and (2) holding that the cause is something inappropriate [to be a cause]. With regard to the latter, [one may wrongly] (a) hold that [the result] is produced by only one cause, (b) hold that [the result] is produced when preceded by the mind of some other [being], such as God, etc., and (c) hold that something whose nature is permanent can change [according to] circumstances.[14]

Distorted ideas about cessation are: (1) holding that liberation never comes about,[15] (2) holding as liberation some particular contaminated [state], (3) holding as liberation the sublimity [that is release from] some particular suffering and (4) holding that even if suffering is eliminated, it can return.

Distorted ideas about the path are: (1) holding that the path to liberation never comes about, (2) holding that it is unreasonable [to assert] as the path the accustomation of no-self, (3) holding as the path to liberation some mere particular absorption and (4) holding that there is no dharmic path that cannot revert to suffering.[16]

Identifying the sixteen aspects of the four noble truths that contradict those [187]

The suffering of suffering is (1) impermanent, because it occurs occasionally. It is (2) suffering, because it is dependent on karma and

---

13 The four noble truths are, thus, one way of exhaustively classifying phenomena, for everything in saṃsāra and nirvāṇa can be included under one of the four truths. These definitions of the second, third and fourth truths will be expounded in greater detail below, in the appropriate section on each.

14 Thus, views 2a, 2b and 2c are the second, third and fourth distorted ideas about origination—the first being that suffering is causeless.

15 The Tibetan for "never comes about" is *ye med,* which literally means "does not have an origination," and which implies "is non-existent"—since anything that exists must have an origination.

16 For variant accounts of the sixteen distorted ideas and the sixteen aspects that are their opposites, cf. AK vii:12c-d and *bhāṣya,* tr. Poussin (1923-31) V, 28ff.; AS II:I, tr. Rahula (1971) 59-130; and Wayman (1980).

defilement. It is (3) void, because there is no objectively separate self that controls it. It is (4) without self, because it does not exist in the nature of an independent self.[17]

The aspects of origination: Contaminated karma and craving have the aspect of (1) cause, because they are the root of one's own resultant suffering. They are (2) the origination of all [suffering], because they are generated in all their aspects again and again. They are (3) strongly arising, because they are generated forcefully. Craving for existence has the aspect of (4) condition, because it is the cooperative condition of one's own resultant suffering.[18]

---

17 (1) The fact that suffering is impermanent counters the idea that it is permanent. (2) The fact that suffering is suffering counters the idea that it is pleasurable—a mistake one is unlikely to make about the suffering of suffering, but one commonly made about the sufferings of change and the formations. (3) The fact that suffering is void counters the idea that suffering is somehow *controlled by* an extrinsic self. (4) The fact that suffering is without self, or no-self, counters the idea that suffering *is* an independent essential self. Note that the four aspects of suffering listed by rGyal tshab rje do not correspond exactly to the four distorted ideas he has listed above. The four distorted ideas he has listed correspond exactly to the four inverted views (S. *viparyāsa*) that one may entertain toward phenomena in general. However, the distorted idea that suffering is pure has no aspect that corresponds to it. Thus, the third and fourth aspects must be seen as contradicting two different aspects of one distorted view, that suffering is (or is controlled by) a self. In Vasubandhu's enumeration of the four distorted views about suffering, "purity"does not appear. "Pertaining to a self" (*ātmīya*) and "a self" (*ātman*) do appear, and they are countered by the third and fourth aspects, void and without self.

18 (1) The fact that suffering's origination has the aspect of cause counters the idea that there is no cause originating suffering. (2) The fact that suffering's origination has the aspect of repeated origination counters the idea that there can be just one cause of suffering, for multiple and various results imply multiple and various causes. (3) The fact that suffering's origination has the aspect of being strongly generated counters the view that it can be generated by some other being, such as God, since another being—particularly a permanent one, such as God—cannot persuasively be shown to be able to effect all of one's suffering. rGyal tshab rje's interpretation of *rab tu skye ba* (*prabhāva*) as *forceful* generation is a departure from Vasubandhu's version, which takes *prabhāva* in the general sense of "generated."For Vasubandhu, the fact that suffering's origination is generated implies that it is successive, which, in turn, counters the idea that *any* entity comes into existence as the transformation of a pre-existent cause, as in the *pariṇāmavāda* of the Sāṃkhyas, in which all results are a transformation of a prime stuff, prakṛti. (4)The fact that suffering's origination has the aspect of conditioning counters the view that something permanent can change according to circumstances. In other words, because

The aspects of cessation: The freedom that is the elimination of the basis of suffering by force of the antidote has the aspect of (1) cessation, because it is a freedom that has abandoned suffering. It has the aspect of (2) peace, because it is a freedom that has abandoned defilements. It has the aspect of (3) sublimity, because it is a liberation that is beneficial and pleasurable. It has the aspect of (4) definitive emergence, because it is a dharmic liberation that is irreversible.[19]

The aspects of path: The wisdom directly realizing no-self has the aspect of (1) path, because it is a path that leads to liberation. It has the aspect of (2) reasonableness, because it acts as a direct antidote to defilement. It has the aspect of (3) accomplishment, because it is the gnosis that perceptually cognizes the ultimate actuality of mind. It has the aspect of (4) definitive removal, because it is a dharmic antidote that cannot revert to suffering.[20]

---

the origination of suffering is in part under the sway of particular cooperative conditions, such as craving for existence, it cannot be asserted to result from any sort of permanent being, such as God, because such a permanent being could not generate particular sufferings in accordance with varying conditions and still remain a permanent being. According to Vasubandhu, the aspect of condition counters the view that things come into being preceded by an intelligent creator—when, in fact, they come into being through a multiplicity of causes and conditions.

19 (1) The fact that cessation is cessation, and therefore is the abandonment of suffering, counters the idea that cessation never comes about. (2) The fact that cessation is peace, and therefore is the abandonment of defilements, counters the view that some state in which defilements (*nyon mongs, kleśa*) or contaminants (*zag pa, āsrava*) still remain can be the cessation that is sought. According to Vasubandhu, the aspect of cessation as peace counters the view that cessation somehow entails suffering. (3) The fact that cessation is sublime, and therefore beneficial and pleasurable, counters the idea that just the cessation of some particular suffering can be the supreme cessation. The Sanskrit term for this aspect, *praṇīta*, simply means "supreme," and thus is taken by Vasubandhu as countering the idea that particular cessations, such as those entailed by the dhyānas and *samāpattis* (in which, in fact, all defilements have *not* been eliminated) are the supreme cessation. The Tibetan translation of *praṇita, gya nom pa,* is somewhat more ambiguous, as it implies both superiority and pleasure. Thus, it may be taken not only as countering the view that a cessation in which defilement remains is the supreme cessation, but also as countering the view that the cessation that is nirvāṇa is merely an absence, devoid even of pleasure. This latter wrong view, incidentally, is like that attributed to some Sautrāntikas; it is unclear whether Dharmakīrti subscribed to such a view.

20 (1) The fact that the path has the aspect of being a path counters the idea that

The eight aspects of suffering and origination are taught by individual divisions in the text [of the *Pramāṇavārttika*]. If one [wants to make] individual divisions of the eight aspects of cessation and path, it appears that one can do so, but ācārya Devendrabuddhi explains that the aspect of cessation and the aspect of path are taught directly, while the remaining six [aspects of cessation and path] are not directly and clearly taught, [but] can be understood as intended.[21]

I will explain in brief the method whereby the intelligent contemplate the details of engaging [saṃsāra] and the way of reversing engagement with saṃsāra, renounce all of saṃsāra, and generate a mind intent on liberation. This text appears to be uniquely important, and those scholars who think about studying this text should not direct [their minds] only to externals, but should contemplate well the general and particular disadvantages of saṃsāra, and there will arise a mind renouncing [saṃsāra]—and there will arise to an equal degree a mind intent on liberation.[22]

When [those attitudes] have arisen, they are taken as the basis of the training in higher morality. Also, having striven in the higher mental training as much as is suitable to one's mind, one should establish

---

there is no path that leads to the cessation of suffering. (2) The fact that the path is reasonable, or correct, counters the idea that it is unreasonable to assert that the wisdom realizing no-self *is* the path. Because the wisdom realizing no-self sees reality as it actually is, it has the power to eliminate defilements, and so it reasonably is asserted to be the path, for the path is simply the process of eliminating defilements until the cessation of suffering is attained. According to Vasubandhu, the aspect of reasonableness counters the idea that a false or unreasonable path is the path to cessation. (3) The fact that the path entails accomplishment counters the idea that some particular samādhi is the path, for an "accomplished" realization is a complete one, and only a complete realization will have the power to eliminate defilements and thus merit identification with the path. (4) The fact that the path entails definitive removal of suffering counters the idea that there is a dharmic path that leads to suffering rather than to the cessation of suffering. The path is the wisdom realizing no-self, and that wisdom permanently abandons the defilements. Thus, once attained, the path is irreversible.

21 PVP 246/4/4-5.

22 rGyal tshab rje points out that "studying" (*thos pa*) this chapter involves more than merely studying syllogisms. It requires of a scholar internalizing what they learn, and taking to heart the viciousness of saṃsāra and the necessity for liberation from it. Thus, an understanding of this chapter requires study (*thos*), reflection (*bsam*) and meditation (*sgom*), which latter is literally interpreted by Tibetans as the accustomation (*goms*) of one's mind to a particular object.

through reasoning the no-self of persons explained in this chapter and the no-self of dharmas explained below, then meditate on it.[23]

If [practitioners] act thusly, their study of and reflection upon the śāstras will be very meaningful, and they will "seize well the essential" in the [human existence] that is the basis of leisure and opportunity.[24] If they think otherwise, that they [should] obtain possessions and respect and fame, then their mindstreams will be considerably impaired by their vices and the downfall [of their vows].[25] [Thus,] when they memorize, they cannot retain the words; when they reflect, they do not understand the meaning; and when they meditate, [the object] does not arise in their mindstreams. Therefore, even if they claim to have been striving to study and understand [the Dharma] for their whole lives, [in fact,] the way their minds ordinarily run will be no different as regards the degree of their desire and the degree of their renunciation of saṃsāra than the way [the mind of] a farmer ordinarily runs. Not simply making the path an *object* of their minds, they should strive earnestly to generate it as the *nature* of their minds.[26]

---

23 Study of this chapter eventually involves development of all of the "three higher trainings" (see, e.g., The Dalai Lama [1985] chapters 4-6), for once one has taken to heart the fact that saṃsāra is vicious and liberation from it to be sought, one will be moved to perfect one's morality, concentration and wisdom, which are the basis of that liberation.

24 "Seizing well the essential" (*snying po legs par len pa*) involves gaining an acquaintance with the basic truths and procedures of the Buddhist path. The basis from which one strives for the great aim is a "perfect" human rebirth, which is, negatively speaking, free from certain hindrances, such as being born in the divine or lower realms where Dharma practice is difficult, being born on earth in places or times where the Dharma is unknown, or being oneself a heretic or idiot. Positively speaking, a perfect human rebirth involves being human, being born where the Dharma is known, possessing clear faculties, having committed no inexpiable crimes, having confidence in the moral practices enjoined by the Vinaya, practicing the Dharma assiduously at a time when it still is taught purely, and developing compassion. For this basic category of Tibetan *lam rim* thought, see, e.g., Sgam po pa (1970) chapter 2 and Dhargyey (1974) 42-52.

25 The vices, sometimes called "sins" (*sdig pa*) are: killing, stealing, sexual misconduct, lying, harsh speech, slander, gossip, covetousness, malice and heterodoxy. The downfalls (*ltung ba*) involve breaking any precepts or vows that one may have taken: those of a lay practitioner or of a novice or fully-ordained monk or nun, which are taken for life; or those of a bodhisattva or tāntrika, which are to be observed until one attains enlightenment.

26 rGyal tshab rje is simply reiterating the importance of internalizing, i.e., meditating upon, what one studies, for mere scholarship will bring us no closer to liberation than will farming.

Having identified the four [paths] distortedly imputed as paths to liberation by others, [which] are the opposing factors to the [actual] path to liberation, the ācārya will explain below the reasons refuting them, and the way of proving liberation and omniscience through objectively impelled reasoning.

The meaning of the limbs [188]

[This is divided into:] (1) The truth of suffering (189), (2) The truth of origination [223], (3) The truth of cessation [233] and (4) The truth of path [249]. [Proof of these will follow.]

7. The Truth of Suffering

A. THE NATURE OF SUFFERING

The truth of suffering [189]

[This is divided into:] (1) Proving the example of the truth of suffering [190] and (2) Explaining the definition [of the truth of suffering] [222].

Proving the example of the truth of suffering [190]

[This is divided into:] (1) Proving that saṃsāra is beginningless [191] and (2) Refuting [the idea that saṃsāra] has a beginning [212].

Proving that saṃsāra is beginningless [191]

[This is divided into:] (1) Identifying suffering [192] and (2) The reason proving that [suffering] is beginningless [193].

Identifying suffering [192]

(147) SUFFERING IS THE SAṂSĀRIC AGGREGATES.

The five appropriated aggregates are the truth of SUFFERING, because they are SAṂSĀRIC AGGREGATES that are [appropriated] in saṃsāra under the power of karma and defilements.[1]

Those who do not know how to establish collections and continuums say: "A person who has just died and enters the next life will be permanent, and it is unacceptable that the first cognition of the subsequent existence be saṃsāra, because that [cognition] has never

---

1 The five aggregates (form, sensation, recognition, formations and cognition), which together constitute what we usually call a person, are said to be suffering because they are under the control of karma and defilements (*kleśa*) such as attachment, anger and ignorance. These karma and defilements, usually negative and always uncontrolled, impel one from life to life—and each life is essentially suffering because the one who lives it is not liberated, but is subject to the three types of suffering (see above, p. 343).

occurred before. Therefore, so-called saṃsāra is merely a mistaken appearance, and does not exist in the least."[2] Others assert a permanent person as saṃsāra.[3] These are the chief objects of refutation of the reasons to be explained below.

Proving that [suffering] is beginningless [193]

[This is divided into:] (1) Proving that it arises beginninglessly from homogenes [194], (2) Refuting [the idea] that it arises causelessly [195] and (3) Refuting [the idea] that it arises from inappropriate causes [196].

Proving that it arises beginninglessly from homogenes [194]

(147b) ATTACHMENT, ETC., [ARISE FROM HOMOGENES,] BECAUSE WE SEE
THAT [THEY ARISE WITH GREATER] INTENSITY
THROUGH ACCUSTOMATION. . . .

ATTACHMENT, anger, ETC., are preceded by previous homogenes, BECAUSE WE SEE THAT they arise naturally with greater and greater INTENSITY THROUGH their own ACCUSTOMATION.[4]

---

2 The rather dubious point made by the opponent is that the first moment of a next life, because it is a first moment, never has occurred before, while the meaning of saṃsāra is an ever-returning circle of births that we have experienced before countless times. Thus, a moment that never has been experienced before must not be saṃsāra. The opponent, of course, misunderstands saṃsāra's "repetitive" nature. One certainly repeats types of experiences—those of a particular realm, and even particular experiences within those realms—but one never repeats experiences in all their particulars. The conditions of particular "repeated" experiences invariably will be somewhat different from one instance to another. At the very least, an experience will be unique because it occurs when it does, and not at some earlier or later time.

3 The assertion that a permanent person is, or is the basis of, saṃsāra, is made by most non-Buddhist schools. A Buddhist will reject it on the grounds that a permanent entity cannot undergo the transformations that suffering is observed to entail.

4 Attachment, anger and other defilements are just like the positive qualities of compassion, wisdom, etc.: their substantial causes are previous instances of the same sort of mental attitude. This is shown by the fact that—just like the positive attitudes—they increase or decrease depending chiefly upon the degree to which they are accustomated. If defilements increase or decrease through accustomation, and if mind is independent of body, then defilements must have existed beginninglessly. Hence, the saṃsāra through which they impel the aggregates must be beginningless. Cf. PV 124.

Refuting [the idea] that it arises causelessly [195]

(147c) . . . THEY ARE NOT JUST ACCIDENTAL,
BECAUSE [IF] THEY HAVE NO CAUSE, IT IS CONTRADICTORY THAT THEY ARISE.

[Attachment, anger, etc.,] ARE NOT JUST ACCIDENTAL occurrences, not dependent on anything, because they occur occasionally. It follows that the [reason] pervades, BECAUSE IF THEY HAVE NO CAUSE, IT IS CONTRADICTORY THAT THEY ARISE.[5]

Refuting [the idea] that it arises from inappropriate causes [196]

[This is divided into:] (1) Refuting [the idea] that it arises only from wind, etc. [197] and (2) Refuting [the idea] that it arises only from the elements [207].

B. SUFFERING AND THE HUMORS

Refuting [the idea] that it arises only from wind, etc. [197]

[This is divided into:] (1) A brief demonstration that [humors and defilements] are not proven [to have] the characteristics of cause and result [198] and (2) An extensive explanation [201].

A brief demonstration that [humors and defilements] are not proven [to have] the characteristics of cause and result [198]

[This is divided into:] (1) Setting forth the consequences [199] and (2) Refuting the reply to that [200].

Setting forth the consequences [199]

(148) [ATTACHMENT, ETC.,] ARE NOT QUALITIES OF WIND, ETC., BECAUSE [THE ASSERTION OF CONCOMITANCE] IS MISTAKEN.

---

5 It is commonly observed that particular defilements do not arise continually, but only occasionally. Something that only arises occasionally must have certain conditions necessary and sufficient for its arising—for there must be a difference between occasions when it arises and occasions when it does not. The conditions in the absence of which something will not arise must be considered its "causes." Therefore, entities that arise occasionally must be caused. Indeed, to apply to them the very word "occur" is to imply that there are occasions when they do not exist (i.e., prior to their occurrence). The fact that at one time they do not exist, while at another they do, can only be explained by the absence or presence of certain conditions. The critical conditions are, again, the "causes." Cf. TS 1948.

[OPPONENT:] Attachment arises from phlegm, anger from bile and ignorance from wind.[6]

[RGYAL TSHAB RJE:] It follows that attachment, etc., ARE NOT QUALITIES that are the direct result OF WIND, ETC., BECAUSE [the assertion of] positive or negative concomitance IS MISTAKEN, because we see that a phlegmatic person may have little attachment and much anger.[7]

Refuting the reply to that [200]

(148b) IF YOU SAY "BECAUSE [BILE] IS NATURALLY MIXED [WITH PHLEGM],
THERE IS NO FLAW," [WE REPLY:] WHY DO WE NOT ALSO SEE,
ASIDE FROM THAT [ANGER, OTHER] QUALITIES OF THAT [BILE]?
(149-150b) ALL [BEINGS] WILL HAVE EQUAL ATTACHMENT,
BECAUSE THIS FOLLOWS [FROM EQUALITY OF THE HUMORS]; [BUT ATTACHMENT, ETC.,] ARE NOT QUALITIES OF ALL [THE HUMORS].
IF YOU SAY THAT THERE IS NO FLAW, [BECAUSE THE CASE IS] LIKE BODY [SIZE, WHICH VARIES DESPITE AN EQUALITY OF CAUSES],
[WE REPLY:] THE [SAME] OBJECTION ALSO EQUALLY [APPLIES] TO THAT—
UNLESS THE PRINCIPAL [CONDITIONS], KARMAS
THAT CHANGE THAT [BODY SIZE, ARE CONSIDERED].

[OPPONENT:] Because the bile that causes anger IS NATURALLY MIXED with the phlegm [in a phlegmatic person], anger increases, and THERE IS NO FLAW of a mistaken [assertion of concomitance].[8]

[RGYAL TSHAB RJE:] Well, then, WHY DO WE NOT ALSO SEE, ASIDE FROM THAT anger, that person's prematurely white hair, jaundice, perspiration and mental clarity, [other] QUALITIES that are the direct result OF THAT bile? It follows that it would be reasonable to see them, because the direct cause, bile, is fully present.[9]

---

6 It was the view of traditional Indian physicians that defilements or negative states of mind (such as the "three poisons" cited here) simply result from an imbalance among the humors (*nyes pa, doṣa*). For a discussion of the medical tradition, see, e.g., Dasgupta (1975) vol. II.

7 The opponent's reason is uncertain, because there is no invariable concomitance between the preponderance of a particular humor and the expression of a particular defilement. Thus, a person who shows clear physical signs of being dominated by phlegm should be expected to be lustful or attached all the time. In fact, however, we observe that such people often may display little desire and much anger—which we would expect only of a bilious person.

8 The opponent argues that their reason is *not* uncertain, because anger occurs in a phlegmatic person when a certain amount of bile is mixed with the phlegm.

[OPPONENT:] Bile generates all three poisons, and so, accordingly, do the other two [humors].

[RGYAL TSHAB RJE:] It follows that ALL beings, who have the three humors[10] in equal proportions, WILL HAVE an EQUAL amount of ATTACHMENT, etc., BECAUSE [attachment's] cause is the same in all. Therefore, IT FOLLOWS that all three poisons ARE NOT QUALITIES that are the direct result OF ALL the humors, because of the consequential fault just explained.[11]

[OPPONENT:] THERE IS NO FLAW [in our position], since this case is LIKE that of people's unequal BODY sizes, which [result] even though [people] arise from equal causes, the elements.

[RGYAL TSHAB RJE:] It follows that THE previous OBJECTION, i.e., that there is no [difference] in the amount [of humors], can ALSO EQUALLY be applied TO [the case of] THAT person's body size, because people's body sizes *would* arise as the same from the equality of the direct causes—unless [one considers] THE PRINCIPAL conditions, previous KARMAS THAT CHANGE THAT [subsequent body size].[12]

---

9 The opponent's qualification is inadequate, because the preponderance of each humor has a number of different physical and psychological results. Indeed, it is by these various results that the preponderance of a particular humor is diagnosed. Thus, a preponderance of bile has among its results not only anger, but prematurely white hair, jaundice, excessive perspiration and a certain mental clarity. If the opponent asserts that anger in a phlegmatic person results from the mixture of bile with the phlegm, then they must be ready to concede that not only anger, but also the other results of bile, should be manifest. Such results are not, of course, manifest, because if they were, the person would no longer be phlegmatic, but bilious, and the opponent would be left with their original proposition (that there is an invariable concomitance between physical types and the expression of one or the other of the three poisons), which already has been refuted. Cf. TS 1960.

10 The Tibetan has *nad gsum*, "three sicknesses,"implying the three humors that are prone to sickness or imbalance. Recall that the term for humor, *nyes pa* (*doṣa*) also can mean "flaw,"or "fault."

11 The opponent argues that each of the three humors is capable of generating all three poisons, and that the fact that each humor-type manifests all three poisons is thus explained. The problem with this, as rGyal tshab rje points out, is that everyone then would have the same psychological make-up, since everyone has the same three humors. Furthermore, if one's defilements were caused by *all* of the humors, then one would expect each person to display the physical and psychological effects of *all* of the humors, an obvious impossibility.

12 The opponent attempts to support their case with an analogy: just as people have different body-sizes, even though their bodies are composed of the same

An extensive explanation [201]

[This is divided into:] (1) [Showing that] because their increases and decreases do not have similar [causes, humors and defilements] are not cause and result [202], (2) Extreme consequences if [humors and defilements are cause and result] [205] and (3) Disposing [of the objection that the consequences] apply equally to us [206].

[Showing that] because their increases and decreases do not have similar [causes, humors and defilements] are not cause and result [202]

[This is divided into:] (1) Setting forth the reason [203] and (2) Proving [that the reason is correct in all three] ways [204].

Setting forth the reason [203]

(150c) THIS IS BECAUSE—EVEN IF THERE IS AN INTENSIFICATION [IN HUMOR-FAULTS]—
IT IS NOT [CERTAIN] THAT FAULTS WILL INTENSIFY. . . .

The faults of attachment, etc., are not the direct result of wind, bile, etc., BECAUSE EVEN IF THERE IS AN increasing INTENSIFICATION in [faults] of wind, etc., IT IS NOT certain THAT those [FAULTS] WILL increasingly INTENSIFY, because we see that [sometimes] when phlegm has increased and the body weakened, attachment *decreases* in intensity.[13]

---

elements, so people's dispositions differ, even though their bodies include the same three humors. rGyal tshab rje replies that in either case, the equality of the causes (elements or humors) only can entail the equality of the results (body size or mental states), and that, in fact, neither is a complete causal explanation: one also must take into account the particular karmas that act as the principal conditions for a particular body size or the disposition toward particular states of mind. Put in somewhat more modern terms, rGyal tshab rje's argument amounts to this: the mere fact that one has a body cannot explain why one's body is the size it is; that must be explained through additional factors, such as heredity (in this case, karma) and nutrition (or conditions). Similarly, the fact that one expresses particular emotions cannot be explained by the general fact that one has the potential to express various emotions; that one expresses various emotions only can be explained by other conditions, such as one's previous expression of them—and also perhaps by heredity.

13 rGyal tshab rje here is repeating the same general point he has made before, that there is no invariable concomitance between the humors and the defilements, and he cites as a demonstration the fact that an increase in phlegm, which should automatically entail an increase in attachment, sometimes weakens the body, and that in that case, attachment is observed to decrease.

Proving [that the reason is correct in all three] ways[14] *[204]*

(150d) . . . [IF YOU SAY THAT] THIS IS UNPROVEN,
(151) [WE REPLY:] IT IS NOT THE CASE, BECAUSE BY A TRANSFORMATION
OF ALL, THERE WILL BE [ANGER]; ALSO IT IS NOT THE CASE THAT [ONE] ARISES FROM ALL.
IF THERE IS AN INCREASE IN THE CAUSE,
IT IS UNSUITABLE THAT THERE BE A DECREASE IN THE RESULT,
(152) AS, FOR EXAMPLE, FEVER, ETC. TRANSFORMATIONS
OF ATTACHMENT, ETC., ARISE FROM PLEASURE AND PAIN;
IF [YOU ASSERT THAT] ATTACHMENT IS NOT GENERATED
BECAUSE OF THE SUFFERING ARISING FROM A DISEQUILIBRIUM [OF THE HUMORS],
(153) [WE REPLY:] TELL US, HOW IS IT GENERATED? [IF YOU ASSERT THAT] ATTACHMENT
[ARISES] FROM AN INCREASE IN SEMEN, WHICH [ARISES] FROM AN EQUILIBRIUM [OF THE HUMORS],
[WE REPLY: IN SOME CASES,] WE SEE ATTACHMENT WHEN THERE IS A DISEQUILIBRIUM,
IN OTHERS, THERE IS NO [ATTACHMENT], EVEN WHEN THERE IS EQUILIBRIUM.
(154) [SOME] OTHER, EVEN THOUGH HE HAS LOST BLOOD FROM [SEMEN] DEPLETION, [MAY BE ATTACHED].
THAT [ATTACHED PERSON] WILL NOT HAVE INTENSE ATTACHMENT TO ONE [PARTICULAR WOMAN];
WHEN [HE SEES] ONE [PARTICULAR] WOMAN, SEMEN IS NOT CERTAIN [TO INCREASE].
IF [ATTRACTIVE] FORM, ETC., IS [SAID TO BE] THE FACTOR,
(155) [WE REPLY:] IT IS NOT, BECAUSE IT IS NOT CERTAIN TO [ATTRACT] ALL;
ALSO [ATTACHMENT] WOULD NOT OCCUR WITHOUT THE ASCERTAINMENT [OF ATTRACTIVE FORM],
[YET WE KNOW THAT] THERE WILL BE [ATTACHMENT] EVEN IN [SOMEONE] WHO DOES NOT APPREHEND THOSE [ATTRACTIVE] QUALITIES.
IF [YOU SAY THAT] THAT APPREHENSION OF QUALITIES ALSO
(156) IS A FACTOR, [WE REPLY:] THEN ALL

---

14 A reason correct in all three ways possesses the *tshul gsum,* or three aspects, of any correct reason: relevance to the subject and invariable positive and negative concomitance with the predicate. A reason's incorrectness is refuted by showing that it is neither unproven, uncertain, nor contradictory.

SHOULD APPREHEND THE QUALITIES,
BECAUSE THE CAUSE WOULD BE INVARIANT.

[OPPONENT:] [The reason] IS UNPROVEN, because when bile increases, then anger arises through the discomfort of the body.[15]

[RGYAL TSHAB RJE:] It follows that IT IS NOT THE CASE that the reason is unproven merely by that, BECAUSE we see that BY A TRANSFORMATION OF ALL the humors, THERE WILL BE the arising of anger, so it follows that anger is the result of all of those [humors]. ALSO, it follows that IT IS NOT THE CASE THAT anger arises from all those humors, because of the flaw that the three humors should then have an equilibrium of anger, [attachment and ignorance].[16]

Proving [that the reason] pervades [the predicate]:

It follows that the previous basic reason[17] pervades [the predicate], because IF THERE IS AN INCREASE IN THE CAUSE, phlegm, IT IS UNSUITABLE THAT THERE BE no increase—or A DECREASE—IN THE RESULT, attachment. FOR EXAMPLE, when bile increases, the FEVER, ETC., of a disease increase.[18]

[OPPONENT:] Well, then, what is the cause of those [defilements]?

---

15 The Buddhist's syllogism is basically: "Defilements do not result from the humors, because their invariable succession on the humors is uncertain." The opponent claims that the reason is unproven, because the uncertainty of concomitance is *not* a quality that the opponent accepts as being relevant to the subject—since the opponent believes that it *is* certain that defilements invariably follow on the humors.

16 rGyal tshab rje defends the Buddhist contention, that the invariable concomitance between defilements and humors is uncertain, on the grounds that anger can result from the "transformation," or predominance, of any of the humors, so anger must be asserted to result from any of the humors, not just bile. It cannot be that anger is generated from all the humors, though, because then each of the humors should be capable of generating all of the defilements, and the predominance of one humor then would entail the generation of all the defilements, which manifestly does not occur.

17 The previous basic reason is the assertion that defilements do not result from the humors because their invariable succession on the humors is uncertain.

18 There *are* results that directly follow an increase in one of the humors: fever, for instance, will increase following an increase in bile. If a defilement is to be so direct a result, then it must invariably increase when the humor asserted to be its cause increases—and it has been shown that there is no such invariable concomitance.

[RGYAL TSHAB RJE:] TRANSFORMATIONS OF ATTACHMENT, ETC., do not arise directly just from the elements, because they ARISE FROM the sensations of PLEASURE AND PAIN that are their own cause.[19]

[OPPONENT:] [Well, then,] ATTACHMENT IS NOT GENERATED, as it is blocked BY THE SUFFERING sensation ARISING FROM A DISEQUILIBRIUM among the three humors. If we only see the non-generation of a result because of the occasional presence of a contradictory condition, then there follows the extreme consequence that [the relationship between] cause and result is undermined.[20]

[RGYAL TSHAB RJE:] Well, then, by way of an answer we say: TELL US, how is attachment GENERATED?

[OPPONENT:] ATTACHMENT [arises] FROM AN INCREASE IN SEMEN, WHICH [arises] FROM AN EQUILIBRIUM of the three humors.

[RGYAL TSHAB RJE:] Well, then, it follows that attachment has mistaken negative concomitance in relation to the equilibrium of the humors, because WE SEE THAT [ATTACHMENT] also arises WHEN THERE IS A DISEQUILIBRIUM of the three [humors]. It follows that [attachment] is [also] mistaken with regard to positive concomitance, because we see that IN the case of OTHERS, who possess the wisdom realzing [the natures of] various phenomena, THERE IS NO arising of [attachment], EVEN WHEN the three [humors] ARE IN EQUILIBRIUM.

It follows that [attachment] has mistaken negative concomitance with the increase of semen, because we see that there may be [some] OTHER attached being in whom [attachment] arises EVEN THOUGH HE HAS LOST BLOOD FROM THE DEPLETION of semen. It follows that THAT attached being,when he sees one [particular] beautiful woman, WILL NOT HAVE INTENSE ATTACHMENT TO [just that ONE], because WHEN he sees [just] that ONE WOMAN, HIS SEMEN IS NOT CERTAIN to increase.[21]

---

19 rGyal tshab rje argues, as he has before, that a mental event, such as a defilement, cannot arise directly from a physical cause, such as the elements. Rather, it arises from a principal condition that is an internal sensation brought about by transformations in the humors or elements. In this sense, the physical is only an indirect, assistant cause of the mental.

20 The opponent, who holds that attachment is generated from an equilibrium among the three humors, argues that the Buddhist could not observe a particular cause of attachment, because they assert that defilements result from painful or pleasurable sensations that follow on the *dis*equilibrium of the humors, and in the case of attachment there is no such disequilibrium. On the other hand, we know that attachment arises, so the Buddhist has simply failed to account for it.

21 Here, the opponent has made their position explicit: the equilibrium of the

[OPPONENT:] ALSO, in the case of beauty of FORM or charming behavior, ETC., it is [form or behavior] that IS THE FACTOR that generates attachment, because we see that it is from changes in [attractive qualities] that changes in attachment arise.

[RGYAL TSHAB RJE:] It follows that [form or behavior] IS NOT a cause that is ascertained to be positively or negatively concomitant with attachment, BECAUSE IT IS UNCERTAIN THAT it is the cause OF ALL [attachment]. It ALSO follows that attachment WOULD NOT OCCUR WITHOUT THE ASCERTAINMENT of physical beauty, etc., because it is ascertained that [physical beauty, etc.,] necessarily is the cause of attachment. It also follows that attachment WILL BE arising EVEN IN [someone] WHO DOES NOT APPREHEND THOSE QUALITIES of physical beauty, etc., because merely by one's seeing physical beauty or [charming] behavior, attachment will arise.[22]

---

three humors entails an increase in the production of semen, which, in turn, leads to attachment. (Note that "semen"need not be used strictly in the sense of the male seminal fluid, but in the more general sense of sexual secretions contributed by the father at conception [as "drops"]. Thus, females are capable of attachment and lust, too—though Dharmakīrti and rGyal tshab rje clearly intend males in this section.) According to rGyal tshab rje, the opponent's reason is uncertain, for there is no invariable concomitance between an equilibrium of the humors and attachment, or semen and attachment. First, attachment is known to arise not only when the humors are in equilibrium, but also when they are in disequilibrium—as in the above-cited case of an excess of phlegm. Second, there are beings whose humors are in equilibrium—such as āryas—who do not develop attachment. Third, attachment is not observed automatically to decrease in people whose semen has been depleted through, e.g., the loss of blood (the connection between blood and semen is an ancient Indian medical notion). A man who has lost semen through the loss of blood should not, by the opponent's theory, feel lust for a beautiful woman, but this is not observed to be the case. Fourth, semen is not certain to increase in every case of attachment. Therefore, attachment must be the result of something other than semen. In modern terms, lust is as much a matter of mind as of hormones.

22 The opponent's attempt to argue that *beauty* is the cause of attachment also fails, because—again—the concomitance between the supposed cause and result is uncertain: there are cases in which men do not generate attachment to women acknowledged to be beautiful, and also cases in which they generate attachment to women *not* acknowledged to be beautiful. By the opponent's theory, however, *all* beautiful women should generate attachment in *all* men, and no non-beautiful women should generate any attachment in any men. The opponent is making an external, "objective" quality the cause of attachment, while the Buddhist maintains that beauty is in the eye of the beholder:

[OPPONENT:] THAT APPREHENSION OF QUALITIES in that [woman] ALSO IS A FACTOR that generates attachment.[23]

[RGYAL TSHAB RJE:] What need is there for that as a cause? If you say that the object just remains [beautiful], then it follows that ALL persons who see a woman's physical beauty and [charming] behavior SHOULD APPREHEND her as having THE QUALITIES [of physical beauty, etc.,] BECAUSE THE CAUSE [i.e., object] of such apprehension WOULD BE complete and INVARIANT.[24]

Extreme consequences if [humors and the defilements are cause and result] [205]

(156d) IN ANY CASE, [A PERSON] LIKE THAT WILL NOT BECOME
ANGRY, [AS] IT IS ASSERTED THAT THEY ARE ATTACHED,
(157) BECAUSE THOSE TWO ARE ESSENTIALLY DISSIMILAR;
ALSO, WE DO NOT SEE [ANGER NOT OCCURRING] AS A RULE IN THIS CASE.

IN ANY CASE, it follows that a person LIKE THAT in whom phlegm increases excessively WILL NOT then BECOME intensely ANGRY, because IT IS reasonably ASSERTED THAT THEY ARE intensely ATTACHED. It follows that this [reason] pervades, BECAUSE of the contradiction that THOSE TWO, attachment and anger, ARE ESSENTIALLY DISSIMILAR ways of apprehending [phenomena]. It follows that the assertion [that a predominance of phlegm precludes anger] is unreasonable, because WE ALSO DO NOT SEE that anger AS A RULE does not occur IN THIS CASE, because anger *does* occur occasionally [in such cases].[25]

---

attachment results from internal, mental events.

23 The opponent retreats somewhat, conceding that it is one's *attitude* toward a beautiful woman—i.e., apprehending her to be beautiful—that generates attachment.

24 The opponent's concession is inadequate, because they still hold that beauty is an objectively existing quality of an external object. As long as they maintain that, in effect, a beautiful woman is objectively and always beautiful, then anyone who looks at her automatically will hold her to be beautiful, and thus automatically will become attached. Thus, the problem is not resolved, but merely removed one step. Cf. TS 1952.

25 Another consequence of the opponent's original contention—that there is an invariable concomitance between an increase in a particular humor and the increase of a corresponding defilement—is that someone who is phlegmatic could not *ever* be angry, because the predominance of phlegm should assure constant attachment, and attachment and anger are contradictory qualities: one cannot exist in the same time and place as the other. The consequence is an absurd one, however, because we do, in fact, observe that "phlegmatic" people can grow angry. Therefore, there is no invariable concomitance be-

Disposing [of the objection that the consequences] apply equally to us [206]

(157c-158b) IT DOES NOT FOLLOW THAT IN THAT [SYSTEM] OF THOSE WHO ARE [LIKE US]
THERE IS THAT FAULT; [IN OUR SYSTEM,] ATTACHMENT, ETC., WILL PROCEED
IN DEPENDENCE UPON CHANGES
IN PROPENSITIES THAT ARE OF THE SAME TYPE.

IT DOES NOT FOLLOW THAT IN THAT system OF THOSE WHO ARE rationalists[26] THERE IS THE FAULT whereby a phlegmatic person will not get angry, because [in the rationalist system] ATTACHMENT, ETC., WILL PROCEED IN DEPENDENCE UPON CHANGES IN PROPENSITIES THAT ARE OF THE SAME TYPE and independent of external objective conditions.[27]

C. SUFFERING AND THE ELEMENTS

Refuting [the idea] that [suffering] arises only from the elements [207]

[This is divided into:] (1) Giving a reminder of what already has been explained [208] and (2) Showing other reasons that refute [the idea] that body is the special basis of mind [209].

Giving a reminder of what already has been explained [208]

(158c)THIS [ALSO] REFUTES [THE IDEA] THAT [DEFILEMENTS] HAVE THE NATURE OF THE ELEMENTS;

---

tween the humors and defilements.

26 The "system of the rationalists" (*rigs pa smra ba gang gi lugs*) probably does not refer to a specific school of Buddhism, as, e.g., *rnam par shes pa smra ba* refers to Vijñānavāda, but simply to those who "speak reasonably," i.e., use reason properly in support of their doctrines.

27 The Buddhist position is that defilements arise in the mind on the basis of an assortment of conditions that arouse propensities or dispositions (*bag chags, vāsanā*) to a specific defilement. The substantial cause of a defiled state of mind will be the propensity, or seed, while its conditions will be whatever has the ability to awaken the propensity. The conditions may—but need not—include external or physical conditions, but in any case it will be the internal reaction to external conditions that will be the *indispensable* condition for the arousal of a propensity to a particular defilement. Thus, an increase in bile may *lead to* anger, or the sight of a beautiful woman may *lead to* attachment, but these are only indirect, assistant causes, and they no more invariably will lead to the defilement described than the defilement described need result only from them. Cf. TS 1954-56.

ALSO, THOSE [ELEMENTS ARE NOT] THE BASIS [OF DEFILEMENTS], BECAUSE THAT [THEY ARE] HAS BEEN REFUTED.

THIS reasoning that refutes [the idea] that attachment, etc., are the direct result of the three humors also REFUTES [the idea] THAT attachment, etc., HAVE THE NATURE of being the direct result OF THE ELEMENTS, because it is proven that [in the latter case, the assertion of] positive and negative concomitance is mistaken. It ALSO is not the case that [THOSE] four elements ARE THE BASIS of the abiding of an already existent attachment, etc., BECAUSE THAT HAS already BEEN REFUTED where it says: "Whether [substances are] existent or non-existent, there is no basis [substantially different from them]."[28]

Showing other reasons that refute [the idea] that body is the special basis of mind [209]

[This is divided into:] (1) Refuting the example [210] and (2) Refuting the meaning [211].

Refuting the example [210]

(159-160b) WHITENESS, ETC., ARE NOT BASED
UPON EARTH AND OTHER [ELEMENTS],
BECAUSE THE PHRASE "BASED UPON THOSE" MEANS "CAUSE";
OR, ALTERNATIVELY, THAT [WHITENESS'S] OWN BASES
ABIDE INSEPARABLY: SOMETHING ELSE
CANNOT BE ACCEPTED AS ITS BASIS.
(160c-161) IF YOU SAY THAT IT IS JUST LIKE THE CAPACITY TO INTOXICATE, ETC.,
WHICH ARE INSEPARABLE [FROM LIQUOR, WE REPLY:] THE CAPACITY [TO INTOXICATE]
IS NOT OBJECTIVELY SEPARATE FROM THE [LIQUOR] ENTITY.

---

28 Defilements cannot be the result of the elements any more than they can be the result of the humors, for the uncertainty that there is an invariable concomitance between the alleged cause and result is equally strong in both cases. Causality involves existence at different times. If the opponent argues, as they will attempt to, that the elements and defilements exist *simultaneously* as basis and based, rGyal tshab rje will refute them on the grounds that a basis and based only can exist simultaneously if they are substantially identical, and that substantially different qualities that exist simultaneously (such as the sweetness and color of sugar) cannot be described as basis and based. This argument has been applied above to the discussion of the mind-body relation (section III:3:B). The verse cited is PV 63a.

THE ENTITY IS DESTROYED [BY HEATING]; WHEN THE BASIS, THE LIQUOR,[29]
REMAINS [HEATED], THE BASED WILL BE DESTROYED [TOO].
IF YOU SAY THAT [ELEMENTS AND MIND] EQUALLY [ARE SUBSTANTIALLY IDENTICAL, WE REPLY:] IT IS NOT [THE SAME],
(162) BECAUSE THE ELEMENTS AND MIND ARE DIFFERENT,
SINCE THEY ARE COGNIZED AS HAVING DIFFERENT APPEARANCES.

[OPPONENT:] Just as you accept that secondary qualities are based upon the elements, so [must you accept that] attachment is [based upon the elements]. Otherwise, there will be a contradiction in what you accept.[30]

[RGYAL TSHAB RJE:] The secondary qualities of WHITENESS, ETC., ARE NOT BASED ON EARTH AND OTHER already existent and abiding elements, BECAUSE they are objectively separate from [the elements]. Also, it follows that the meaning of THE PHRASE, "explained as BASED UPON THOSE [elements]," IS that in a single simultaneous collection, [what abides together] is [merely] designated as the basis; it is taught as the basis by way of its previous generation. Something [substantially] other that already exists and abides [with it] cannot be accepted as the [real] basis, because either the *previous* elements are MEANT as THE [cooperative] CAUSE OR, ALTERNATIVELY, [if the elements are simultaneous,] they are merely designated as [whiteness's] OWN BASES because they ABIDE INSEPARABLY in a single simultaneous collection. [SOMETHING OTHER (THAN THESE) CANNOT BE ACCEPTED AS ITS BASIS.][31]

---

29 rGyal tshab rje reads PV161b-c as *dngos po 'jig 'gyur chang par / gnas na rten pa 'jig pa yin*. Both the Sanskrit and Tibetan of Miyasaka's edition support *chad* ("destroyed" = S. *nāśritam,* "unremaining") rather than *chang* ("liquor"). An alternative reading of the lines thus is: "The entity is what is destroyed; when the basis is destroyed, if it remains thus, the based will be destroyed." The sense is basically the same in either reading, since the liquor's "remaining heated"is tantamount to its "remaining destroyed."

30 The opponent attempts to argue that because the Buddhist accepts that secondary qualities (lit., "transformed elements," *'byung 'gyur, upādāya*) co-exist with and are based upon the primary elements (*'byung ba, bhūta*), they also must accept that defilements co-exist with and are based upon the elements, or contradict their own position.

31 The opponent has drawn their version of the Buddhist position from a passage in the *bhāṣya* to AK i:35a-c (Poussin [1923-31] I, 65), where the Buddha is cited as saying that secondary qualities are based upon the elements with which they co-exist. In fact, however, Dharmakīrti and rGyal tshab rje insist, the Buddhist does not assert the elements and secondary qualities as being simultaneous, substan-

[OPPONENT:] JUST AS liquor and its CAPACITY TO INTOXICATE, ETC., are objectively separate basis and based, so also attachment, etc., are based on separately existing elements. Alternatively, there [can be] no basis and based where there IS only an INSEPARABLE collection; liquor and its intoxicating power are a basis that exists separately.[32]

[RGYAL TSHAB RJE:] It follows that THE CAPACITY to intoxicate IS *NOT* OBJECTIVELY SEPARATE FROM THE liquor-ENTITY, because those two exist as substantially identical. Since that is the case,[33] it follows that when liquor is heated, THE liquor-ENTITY IS DESTROYED, because its capacity to intoxicate has been destroyed. WHEN THE BASIS, the liquor, REMAINS hot, it follows that the based, the capacity to intoxicate, WILL BE DESTROYED, and will not return.[34]

[OPPONENT:] The elements and mind equally are substantially different in the same way as liquor and its intoxicating power.[35]

---

tially different basis and based. Elements and secondary qualities may conventionally be *designated* as basis and based, but in fact they do not have such a relation, for simultaneous, substantially different entities cannot exist as cause and result, and the real meaning of basis and based is precisely such a causal relation. This relation obtains in the case of the elements and secondary qualities to the degree that a previous moment of an element serves as a cooperative condition for the subsequent moment of the secondary quality, and vice versa. Thus, the elements and secondary qualities have a causal relation, and in that sense are basis and based, but since one cannot establish an invariable causal relation between the elements and defilements, one cannot describe them as basis and based in any sense.

32 The opponent attempts to counter with an example of simultaneous but substantially *different* entities that are accepted as basis and based, namely liquor and its power to intoxicate.

33 In GT, read *de lta yin na* for *de lta min na.*

34 rGyal tshab rje, however, denies that liquor and its capacity to intoxicate are substantially different: if they exist simultaneously and do not have each other as immediately preceding conditions, then they must be substantially identical. Generally, two terms are said to be substantially identical when they arise, exist and are destroyed together, as the Buddhist holds liquor and it capacity to intoxicate to do.

35 The opponent counters that liquor and its capacity to intoxicate cannot be substantially identical on the Buddhist's definition, because we observe that heated liquor has lost its power to intoxicate, but the liquid remains. If they were substantially identical, the absence or presence of one should automatically entail the absence or presence of the other. Thus, even when liquor was heated, its capacity to intoxicate should remain, because the liquor remains; or, conversely, if one asserts that the capacity to intoxicate has been destroyed, then the liquor should have disappeared as well. While arguing for a differ-

[RGYAL TSHAB RJE:] It follows that [the cases] are NOT the same, BECAUSE THE ELEMENTS AND MIND ARE substantially DIFFERENT. This follows, because THEY ARE COGNIZED by an unmistaken mind AS HAVING DIFFERENT APPEARANCES, because they appear [respectively] as having the aspect of a tangible element and having the aspect of a pleasant sensation, etc.[36]

Refuting the meaning [211]

(162c-164b) [IF BODY AND MIND ARE BASIS AND BASED], THEN UNTIL THE BODY IS TRANSFORMED,
THE NATURE OF MIND WILL BE THE SAME,
LIKE FORM, ETC. CONCEPTUAL THOUGHT
IS UNDER THE CONTROL OF SOME OBJECT.
THUS, ANY [COGNITION ARISES] FROM SOME [PREVIOUS COGNITION],
WITHOUT EVER DEPENDING ON THE BODY;
ANY COGNITION WILL HAVE AS ITS CAUSE
THE AWAKENING OF THE PROPENSITY [LEFT] BY SOME [PREVIOUS COGNITION].

---

ence between liquor and its capacity to intoxicate, the opponent still is willing to accept a close connection, i.e., that between "element"(liquor) and "secondary quality"(capacity to intoxicate), since this connection is the basis for the relation they seek to establish between the elements and mental qualities.

36 The Buddhist would most likely argue that heated liquor cannot *entirely* lose its capacity to intoxicate, because if it does, it no longer is "liquor,"but merely a liquid. Since "liquor"is *defined* by its capacity to intoxicate, the two *are* identical, so one cannot use them as an example demonstrating the relation between the elements and the defilements, because the elements and the defilements are substantially different. We know that this is so because an unmistaken mind cognizes them thus; one is an external, observable phenomenon, the other an internal event, not intersubjectively observable. Two such disparate phenomena cannot be substantially identical. This very important argument is, in effect, based on the common-sense observation that the physical and the mental cannot be substantially identical because they seem to be irreducibly different *types* of phenomena. This common-sense view, the basis of our instinctive mind-body dualism, is asserted by Dharmakīrti to be supported by the observation of an unmistaken cognition. That an unmistaken cognition would thus cognize has presumably been established above, in the course of the discussion of the mind-body problem. A further problem, of course, is whether *that* discussion in some cases appealed to the distinction represented here. If it did, then the question was begged, for it is precisely such a distinction that Dharmakīrti sought to establish.

It follows [by your view] that UNTIL THE BODY IS TRANSFORMED, THE NATURE OF MIND WILL BE THE SAME [in] aspect, because any mind is based upon [body] as its special principal condition. [Mind, then,] is just LIKE the secondary qualities of FORM, ETC., which increase and decrease following on the elements.[37]

[OPPONENT:] [Mind's] aspect is transformed by the power of an objective condition.

[RGYAL TSHAB RJE:] It follows that it cannot in any way be accepted that CONCEPTUAL THOUGHT IS UNDER THE CONTROL OF SOME [external] OBJECT, because it arises through the appearance of a mere generic image. THUS, body and mind are unsuitable to be special basis and based; ANY later cognition originates FROM SOME previous cognition WITHOUT EVER DEPENDING UPON THE BODY [made] of elements, because without ever depending upon it, SOME subsequent COGNITION thus WILL HAVE AS ITS CAUSE THE AWAKENING OF THE PROPENSITY [left by] SOME previous cognition.[38]

Refuting [the idea that saṃsāra] has a beginning [212]

[This is divided into:] (1) Refutation by reason of the non-pervasion [of the reason proving] that saṃsāra has a beginning [213] and (2) Refutation by reason of the contradiction in pervasion [214].

---

37 rGyal tshab rje argues that the body cannot be the principal condition of mind, because a variation in the result, mind, must entail prior variation in the condition, body—yet we observe that the body does not alter as much as the mind; hence, it cannot be the mind's principal condition. The validity of this argument hinges on the opponent's assertion of an unchanging body. If the body is held to be momentary in the same way that mind is, then the body is constantly (though subtly) changing all the time, and thus can—at least in theory—serve as the mind's principal condition. A modern opponent would maintain that the brain, as the particular organ that is mind's principal condition, is, in fact, changing just as rapidly as is the mind, so there is no fallacy such that the principal condition is held to "remain" while the result changes.

38 Mental cognition, or conceptual thought, cannot possibly be invariably directly influenced by an external object, because if it were, then e.g., memory, imagination and dreaming all would be impossible, for these are mental phenomena that occur in the *absence* of any corresponding external object. The intentional object of a memory, imagination or dream is a generic image of some object, not the object itself. Indeed, *any* mental cognition has *mental* objects as its intentional objects, and has as its cause a previous mental cognition, either actual or latent—since mind must be preceded by a substantial cause that is homogeneous.

Refutation by reason of the non-pervasion [of the reason proving] that saṃsāra has a beginning [213]

(164c) IT ALSO CAN BE PROVEN BECAUSE THE NON-MENTAL
IS NOT THE SUBSTANTIAL [CAUSE] OF THE MENTAL.
(165-167b) IF YOU SAY, "BECAUSE ALL ENTITIES
POSSESS THE CAPACITY [TO GENERATE] MIND, WE ACCEPT THAT [ASSERTION OF YOURS],"
[WE REPLY:] WHO BUT A BOVINE SĀṂKHYA WOULD [MAKE] AN ARGUMENT
EXPRESSING [THE IDEA]—FOR SHAME!—THAT ON THE TIP
OF A BLADE OF GRASS, ETC.—THE PRIOR [CAUSE]—
WE COULD SEE A HUNDRED ELEPHANTS?
HOW WILL THOSE EXIST THERE?
EVEN IF WE DIVIDE THE CAUSE A HUNDRED TIMES,
THAT FORM THAT IS TO APPEAR [LATER]
AS SOME [RESULTANT] FORM WILL NOT APPEAR PREVIOUSLY.

Saṃsāra ALSO CAN BE PROVEN beginningless by other reasons, because it is not reasonable that sentient beings are newly born, without previous [lives]. Such is not the case, BECAUSE THE NON-MENTAL IS NOT suitable to be THE SUBSTANTIAL [cause] OF THE MENTAL.[39]

[OPPONENT:] BECAUSE ALL ENTITIES POSSESS an unclear mind that has THE CAPACITY to be the substantial cause generating MIND, WE ACCEPT THAT it is proven that it is already established that the non-mental is not the substantial cause of the mental.[40]

---

39 This is another form of the common-sense argument used above: mind and body are not only substantially different, but substantially different *types* of phenomena, so it is inconceivable that one be the substantial cause of the other, since a substantial result must have as its substantial cause a phenomenon of the same type, or genus. Because the mental cannot, as a consequence, result from the non-mental, e.g., at the moment of birth, there must be previous mental cause of the mind at the moment of birth (or, strictly speaking, conception), namely, a mind-moment associated with a previous life, whether in the intermediate state or in one of the six realms of saṃsāra.

40 The opponent is arguing that *they* do not accept that the mental arises from the non-mental, either, because they assert that to some degree *everything* has mentality, hence the capacity to generate mind. This view, akin to what is known in the West as panpsychism, was held by both Jainas (who attributed actual or latent mentality to all phenomena) and Sāṃkhyas (who maintained that all entities, both sentient and non-sentient, are transformations of a primordial stuff, prakṛti, that has the capacity to generate mind—though not the ultimate pure awareness that is puruṣa). Dharmakīrti reads the position as

[RGYAL TSHAB RJE:] WHO BUT A BOVINE SĀṂKHYA WOULD [make] AN ARGUMENT EXPRESSING [the idea] THAT all results exist potentially in the cause? It follows that it is unacceptable [so to argue], because you Lokāyatas pride yourselves on your sense of SHAME.[41] It follows that this [reason] pervades, because saying that ON THE TIP OF A BLADE OF GRASS, ETC.—THE PRIOR [cause]—WE COULD SEE A HUNDRED ELEPHANTS, the [eventual] result, the bovine Sāṃkhya makes that assertion. The reason this is bovine is this: HOW WILL THAT result EXIST in [some] form in the cause? It follows that it is unacceptable [that it so exist], because when [we seek the result that] exists in [some] form in the cause, then EVEN IF WE DIVIDE THE CAUSE A HUNDRED TIMES and analyze it, THAT FORM THAT IS suitable TO APPEAR AS some resultant FORM WILL NOT APPEAR PREVIOUSLY, at the time of the cause.[42]

---

that of the Sāṃkhyas.

41 The Lokāyatas, or materialists, who are the principal hypothetical opponents in the defense of the truth of suffering, apparently prided themselves on their commonsensical approach to life, and rGyal tshab rje wonders how they can sustain such pride while at the same time positing an explanation of causality as apparently nonsensical as that of the Sāṃkhya.

42 The reason the Sāṃkhya view of causality is nonsensical or, in Dharmakīrti's word, "bovine,"is that it implies that the result in some sense already "exists" in the cause. Thus—given that all phenomena are transformations of prakṛti—a blade of grass that is temporally prior to a hundred elephants is in some sense the cause of those elephants, because a transformation of the same substantial cause, prakṛti, at some point will result in a hundred elephants. Since, however, the effect is always said to pre-exist in the cause, the hundred elephants should be visible on the tip of the blade of grass. No matter how minutely we analyze the blade of grass, however, we do not find there the hundred elephants whose visibility should be entailed by the effect's pre-existence in the cause. In fact, of course, it is impossible for the effect to pre-exist in the cause; by the Buddhist view, the effect only can exist when the cause has ceased to exist, for two simultaneously existing entities cannot be cause and effect—cause and effect being a temporal relation. Alternatively, the exemplary case described by Dharmakīrti may be interpreted as that of a hundred *insects* on the tip of a blade of grass, who should be visible as the hundred elephants that they may be in a future rebirth. This interpretation of the example would seem to accord more closely with an attack on the Jainas, who did not posit that all phenomena are simply transformations of a basic stuff, but nonetheless maintained a substance-mode way of speaking of the careers of transmigrating beings—thereby implying the result's pre-existence in the cause. Incidentally, since the Jainas maintained that mind is present in all entities, a blade of grass could as easily as an insect someday be an elephant, so the first interpretation of the example could be taken as criticism of the Jainas

Refutation by reason of the contradiction in pervasion [214]

[This is divided into:] (1) Expressing a consequential [argument] that entails an independent [syllogism] [215] and (2) Refuting the reply to that [216].

Expressing a consequential [argument] that entails an independent [syllogism][43] *[215]*

(167c) IT WILL FOLLOW THAT [A BEING MIGHT] NOT BE ASCERTAINED AS ATTACHED, ETC.,
BECAUSE [THEY] ORIGINATE WITHOUT PRECEDENT.

IT WILL FOLLOW THAT it is possible that some ordinary, newborn sentient being might be born as a detached being, and NOT BE ASCERTAINED to originate AS an ATTACHED being, ETC., BECAUSE [by your argument] it is necessarily the case that all sentient beings have a lineage that ORIGINATEs newly, WITHOUT PRECEDENT. What is entailed by that is a reason [based on] apprehension of contradictory pervasion.[44]

---

as well as of the Sāṃkhyas. The Buddhist here refutes "panpsychism" on the basis of its association with substance-mode theories of causality. A panpsychism based on momentariness (which seems not to have existed in India) could not be rejected on these grounds. Indeed, the dispute between a Buddhist and a panpsychist who accepted momentariness simply would boil down to a disagreement over how generously the word "mind" should be attributed to entities that do not usually display traits that we usually associate with the word. (This is assuming that the panpsychist does not make the mistake of attributing to, e.g., a blade of grass, the "potential" for mind—but simply asserts that the grass *actually has* mind, but in an "unclear" form.)

43 A consequential argument that entails an independent syllogism (*rang rgyud 'phen pa'i thal ba*) is a syllogism that states the absurd consequences of an opponent's view in such a way that if the reason and predicate are reversed and their logical opposites supplied, a correct independent syllogism reflecting one's own view will result. For example, the consequential syllogism that stems from an opponent's assertion that sound is permanent is: "It follows that sound is non-produced, because it is permanent." If one reverses the reason and predicate and supplies their logical opposites, one is left with an independent syllogism: "Sound is impermanent, because it is produced." See, e.g., Tharchin (1979) 193ff.

44 In skeletal form, the opponent's assertion is that ordinary beings' minds arise newly at conception or birth, without homogeneous precedent. The consequential syllogism framed by rGyal tshab rje on the basis of this is: "Ordinary beings may be born as non-attached beings, because their minds arise newly at birth, without precedent." The implicit assumption, of course, is that if attachment does not come from homogeneous causes, it may not occur at all.

Refuting the reply to that [216]

[This is divided into:] (1) Its unacceptability because of the impossibility of detachment [if] the substantial [causes], the elements, are initially equal [217], (2) Its unacceptability because of the impossibility of later detachment [218] and (3) Refuting the example of that [219].

Its unacceptability because of the impossibility of detachment [if] the substantial [causes], the elements, are initially equal [217]

(168) IF [YOU SAY THAT] BECAUSE ALL [BEINGS] DO NOT TRANSCEND
THE NATURE OF THE ELEMENTS, THEY ARE ATTACHED, ETC.,
[WE REPLY:] ATTACHMENT WILL BE EQUAL IN ALL.
IF [YOU SAY THAT ATTACHMENT] IS FROM VARIATIONS IN THE ELEMENTS,
(169) [WE REPLY:] WHATEVER ARE THE BASES OF THIS VARIATION,
[ATTACHMENT WILL VARY] AS THEY INCREASE AND DECREASE;
FOR LIVING BEINGS WITH [EQUAL] ELEMENTS, THERE IS NO VARIATION [IN LIFE-FORCE].
[IF THAT IS ASSERTED,] THAT [ATTACHMENT] COULD PROCEED FROM EXISTENCE TO NON-EXISTENCE.

[OPPONENT:] BECAUSE ALL persons DO NOT TRANSCEND THE NATURE OF their causal ELEMENTS, it is necessarily impossible that those [born] ATTACHED, ETC., become detached.

[RGYAL TSHAB RJE:] It follows that the amounts of ATTACHMENT WILL BE EQUAL [in] ALL, because its substantial causes, the elements, are equal [in all beings].[45]

When one reverses the reason and predicate of the consequential syllogism and supplies their opposites, one is left with an independent syllogism that expresses the Buddhist view: "Ordinary beings do not have minds that arise newly at birth, without homogeneous precedent, because they are born as attached beings."The same assumption as above applies. A reason based on apprehension of contradictory pervasion (*'gal khyab dmigs pa'i rtags*) is one of eleven different types of reasons based on non-apprehension, or negation. See Tharchin (1979) 77-107.

45 The opponent holds that the elements are the substantial cause of the defilements. Since beings are known to be born with defilements such as attachment, and since the elements do not change their nature, there is no reason to believe that attachment ever can be eliminated. rGyal tshab rje points out that if the elements are the substantial cause of the defilements, then, since the elements are roughly equal in all people, then the defilements should be, too, which manifestly they are not.

[OPPONENT:] The amount of attachment, etc., IS [derived] FROM VARIATIONS IN THE amounts of the ELEMENTS.

[RGYAL TSHAB RJE:] It follows that among living beings there will be a distinction between those who are living and those who are "very living," because there are variations in the amounts of the elements that are their substantial causes. If that is asserted, it can be refuted by perception. Thus, it follows that WHATEVER elements ARE THE BASIS OF THIS VARIATION in the amount of attachment, etc., will increase and decrease AS THEY INCREASE AND DECREASE, because IN LIVING BEINGS in whom the ELEMENTS that are the substantial cause are equal, THERE IS NO VARIATION [from] living to "very living," but there is a variation [from] attached to very attached.[46] If that is asserted, it follows that THAT attachment, etc., COULD PROCEED FROM prior EXISTENCE TO [subsequent] NON-EXISTENCE, because of that assertion.[47]

Its unacceptability because of the impossibility of later detachment [218]

(170) [IF YOU SAY THAT] EVEN IF THERE ARE DIFFERENT [AMOUNTS] OF ATTACHMENT, ETC.,
IT IS NOT [NON-EXISTENT], BECAUSE THE NATURE OF THE EQUAL CAUSES [THE ELEMENTS]
IS IRREVERSIBLE, [WE REPLY:] ATTACHMENT WILL BE SIMILAR
IN ALL, BECAUSE THE CAUSE IS THE SIMILAR NATURE [OF THE ELEMENTS].
(171) "COW" IS A COGNITION THAT ORIGINATES FROM [SEEING]

---

46 If the opponent claims that the amount of one's defilement varies with the amount of one's elements, they find themselves in the position of implying that it might be possible for some beings to be "more alive" than others, because of their greater quantities or intensities of the elements that are the cause of life. In fact, of course, we do not observe that there is any difference in "aliveness" between one being and another—a being is either alive or it is not. On the other hand, we do observe a difference in the degree of defilement manifested by various beings. Defilement, therefore, must not come from the elements, but from a previous homogeneous cause. Thus, the causes of the defilements are quite independent of the elements, and the question of whether or not the defilements can be eliminated does not depend on the status of the elements.

47 In other words, if variations in the "intensity" of the elements is responsible for the degree of defilement, then in a case where there is *no* intensity in the elements, or the elements are not playing an active role, there would be no defilement. This kind of correlation clearly does not obtain—and if it did, ridding oneself of defilement might be as easy as, say, lowering one's metabolism, or losing weight! Compare the view criticized here with that of the Jainas, discussed below, section III:11:C.

THE ENTITY THAT IS THE SAME [AS OTHER COWS]; OR, IN THIS CASE,
THERE WILL NOT BE
IN EARTH AND OTHER [ELEMENTS] ANY LEVELS
OF DIFFERENTIATION OF "LIVINGNESS," ETC.

[OPPONENT:] EVEN IF THERE ARE DIFFERENT amounts of ATTACHMENT, ETC., in sentient beings, IT IS NOT possible that there is anyone in whom attachment, etc., will become non-existent, BECAUSE THE EQUAL NATURE OF THE CAUSES, the elements, necessarily IS IRREVERSIBLE.

[RGYAL TSHAB RJE:] It still follows that the amount of ATTACHMENT WILL BE SIMILAR IN ALL, BECAUSE the substantial CAUSE of the similar amount of attachment IS THE SIMILAR NATURE of the elements.[48]

For example, it follows that the visual cognition that apprehends a cow does not successively apprehend arising aspects that are specified as "COW," "very cow," "extremely cow," etc., because that [visual cognition] IS A COGNITION THAT ORIGINATES FROM taking as its apprehended object the self-nature that is the same as the opposite of what is a non-cow. It follows that the word "OR" [indicates that] IN THIS CASE of the Lokāyata system, THERE WILL NOT BE IN THE EARTH AND OTHER elements ANY LEVELS OF DIFFERENTIATION OF "LIVINGNESS," "very living," ETC., because of the equality among the elements that are the substantial cause.[49]

---

48 The opponent argues that there *are* differences in the amount of attachment in various beings, but that detachment *still* is impossible because the nature of the causal elements does not permit it. If they continue to maintain that the elements are the cause of attachment, however, then they cannot escape the consequence that the equality of the elements should entail the equality of attachment in all beings. If they wish to explain the obvious *in*equality in the amount of attachment manifested by beings, then they must abandon their contention that the elements are the substantial cause of attachment, and thereby open themselves to other possible explanations of attachment, including that of the Buddhist.

49 These sorts of differentiations of intensity, entailed by the opponent's attempt to account for the difference in the amount of attachment displayed by various beings by claiming that there are differences in the elements, are not observed to be present in actual living beings. Furthermore, although such distinctions do not apply within the realm of the living, there *is* a difference between non-living entities composed of the elements and living beings composed of the elements. If the opponent claims that the elements are the substantial cause of life and its properties, then they cannot explain why some collections of elements are living and others are not. Cf. above, p.226 ff.

Refuting the example of that [219]

[This is divided into:] (1) The actual [refutation] [220] and (2) The consequence that attachment is impossible [221].

The actual [refutation] [220]

(172) IF YOU SAY THAT, ALTHOUGH THERE ARE VARIATIONS
IN THE LEVELS OF HEAT, THERE DOES NOT EXIST ANY FIRE
THAT IS NOT HOT, SO ALSO IN THIS CASE; [WE REPLY:] NOT SO,
BECAUSE [THE IDEA] THAT FIRE IS OTHER THAN [HEAT] HAS BEEN REFUTED.
(173) THOSE QUALITIES THAT EXIST AS SEPARATE FROM SOME [THING]
CAN BE CUT OFF IN THOSE CASES, [EVEN WHEN] THEIR
VARIATIONS [ARE RELATED TO THAT THING'S] HAVING VARIATIONS
IN LEVEL, JUST LIKE WHITE AND OTHER [COLORS ARE SEPARABLE FROM A BLANKET].
(174) [ATTACHMENT, ETC.] ARE NOT ASCERTAINED [AS CONNECTED WITH ELEMENTS] AS FORM, ETC., [ARE CONNECTED WITH THE ELEMENTS],
BECAUSE [FORM EXISTS] INSEPARABLY WITH THE ELEMENTS.
IF YOU SAY THAT THEY ARE EQUAL, [WE REPLY:] THEY ARE NOT,
BECAUSE IT WOULD FOLLOW THAT ATTACHMENT, ETC., WOULD ARISE SIMULTANEOUSLY [WITH THE ELEMENTS].
(175) ALSO, [ATTACHMENT, ETC.,] DO NOT ASCERTAIN [EXTERNAL] OBJECTS,
BECAUSE THEY HAVE OBJECTS THAT ARE IMPUTED.

[OPPONENT:] ALTHOUGH THERE ARE VARIATIONS IN THE LEVELS of intensity OF HEAT, THERE DOES NOT EXIST ANY FIRE THAT IS NOT HOT. SO ALSO IN THIS CASE, although there are [distinctions in] the amount of attachment, it is impossible that attachment become non-existent.

[RGYAL TSHAB RJE:] It follows that the objects in the example are NOT equivalent, BECAUSE [the idea] THAT FIRE IS substantially OTHER THAN heat HAS BEEN authoritatively REFUTED.[50]

50 The opponent argues that just as fire, although of various temperatures, always is hot, so attachment, although of various amounts, always remains. rGyal tshab rje's reply is that the opponent has drawn an incorrect analogy, for fire and its heat are substantially identical, and thus inseparable, while attachment and the elements have *not* been shown to be substantially identical—or, for that matter, invariably causally related. Incidentally, a modern materialist, especially an "identity theorist," would maintain that the examples *are* similar, although they would argue that it is not the elements, but brain states, that are

It follows that it is possible that THOSE QUALITIES of attachment, etc., THAT EXIST AS objectively SEPARATE FROM SOME body, WILL BE CUT OFF IN THE CASE of some elements, because THEIR VARIATIONS of increase and decrease [come] from the elements' POSSESSING VARIATIONS IN the LEVELS of their [own] increase and decrease; [but] they are objectively separate and suitable for separation [from the elements], JUST LIKE the WHITE AND OTHER colors of a blanket.[51]

It follows that attachment, etc., ARE NOT ASCERTAINED to abide in the elements AS do such secondary qualities as FORM, ETC., BECAUSE IT IS unsuitable that they be connected INSEPARABLY WITH THOSE ELEMENTS, [and because] they are objectively separate and suitable to be separated from [the elements].[52]

[OPPONENT:] Those two ARE EQUAL in unsuitability for connection with the elements.[53]

[RGYAL TSHAB RJE:] It follows that THEY ARE NOT equivalent [cases], BECAUSE if [what you have asserted] were the case, IT WOULD FOLLOW THAT ATTACHMENT, anger, ETC., WOULD ARISE SIMULTANEOUSLY [with the elements]. It follows that they would arise simultaneously and together, because they arise from a single substantial cause, the elements.[54]

---

identical to attachment and other mental states.

51 A more appropriate analogy, rGyal tshab rje argues, is between the elements and "tertiary qualities" (such as a specific color, white) on the one hand and the elements and the defilements on the other. Just as the elements invariably will have secondary qualities, such as color, but need not have one or the other instance of a secondary quality (a blanket must have color, but that color need not be white), so too the elements may be associated with some sorts of mental qualities, but those qualities need not be defiled.

52 Since the defilements are not inseparably connected with the elements any more than whiteness is inseparably connected with a blanket, it is possible that elements continue to exist *without* association with attachment or other defilements.

53 The "two" referred to are whiteness and the defilements. The implication is that the appropriate analogy is between the secondary quality, color in general, and the defilements, i.e., just as the elements always have color of some sort, so the elements of a living being always are the cause of some sort of defilement.

54 The idea that defilements are related to the elements in the same way as secondary qualities are has been refuted above (PV 159-160b and commentary). Here, rGyal tshab rje simply reiterates the fact that, if the cases were the same, then the defilements invariably would co-exist with the elements, just as secondary qualities do, because in either case the similarity of substantial cause,

[OPPONENT:] They arise through the power of an objective condition, not simultaneously.

[RGYAL TSHAB RJE:] It follows ALSO that anger, attachment, etc., are sometimes NOT ASCERTAINed to arise with external OBJECTS as their apprehended objects, BECAUSE THEY [ARE minds that] can apprehend OBJECTS [THAT ARE merely] IMPUTED by the mind.[55]

The consequence that attachment is impossible [221]

(175c) ATTACHMENT, ETC., WOULD NOT BE ASCERTAINED OR [EXISTENT], BECAUSE THEY ARE SEPARATE FROM A CORRESPONDING CAUSE.

(176) [A CONSEQUENCE OF YOUR VIEW IS THAT] ALL MINDS WILL ARISE AT ALL

TIMES, BECAUSE THEIR CAUSES [THE ELEMENTS] ARE PRESENT.

It follows that in ordinary beings, ATTACHMENT, ETC., WOULD NOT BE ASCERTAINED to originate, OR would become non-existent, BECAUSE THEY ARE SEPARATE FROM A CORRESPONDING CAUSE.[56]

[OPPONENT:] The elements are the substantial causes.

[RGYAL TSHAB RJE:] It follows that ALL MINDS of attachment, etc., WILL ARISE IN ALL sentient beings AT ALL TIMES, BECAUSE the permanent elements that are THEIR CAUSES ARE PRESENT.[57]

---

the elements, assures the invariable co-existence of the two. Yet, although we do not see any instances in which elements do not entail secondary qualities, we *do* see instances in which the elements do not entail defilements—e.g., in non-living beings, not to mention liberated living beings (though the latter, not having yet been proved, cannot be cited as a probative example).

55 One cannot assert that defilements are generated in dependence upon some external object, because if that were so, one never could have a defiled attitude toward an imagined, dreamed or remembered object (or a generic image)—which, obviously, one can.

56 rGyal tshab rje maintains that the defilements cannot exist (indeed nothing can exist) without a previous homogeneous (or "corresponding," *skal mnyam, sabhāga*) substantial cause. If the opponent insists that at the moment of birth or any other time such a homogeneous cause is not present (as it *never* will be if the elements, asserted by the Buddhists to be *hetero*geneous vis à vis mind, are the substantial cause), then they cannot properly argue that the defilements can result. Thus, everyone should be detached. There is a fundamental disagreement between Buddhists and their opponent about the nature of causality. Buddhists maintain that only like can come from like; the opponent implies that *un*like can come from like. The Buddhist account gives a sounder basis for assuring continuity in the cosmos; the opponent's account seems more open to novelty.

57 If the opponent asserts once again that the elements *are* the substantial cause

Explaining the definition [of the truth of suffering] [222]

(176c-177) [SUFFERING] IS IMPERMANENT, BECAUSE IT IS SEEN
OCCASIONALLY; IT IS SUFFERING, BECAUSE IT IS THE BASIS
OF FLAWS AND ALSO BECAUSE IT IS UNDER THE POWER OF ITS CAUSES;
IT IS WITHOUT SELF, AND NOT CONTROLLED [BY A SELF], EITHER.
IT IS NOT CONTROLLED [BY A SELF]; THAT IS NOT [ITS] CAUSE—
HOW COULD A PERMANENT [ENTITY] BE A GENERATOR?
(178-179b) THEREFORE, IT IS NOT [THE CASE] THAT THE MULTIPLE
WILL ARISE AT DIFFERENT TIMES FROM ONE [PERMANENT CAUSE];
[SOMETHING] MAY BE INFERRED TO HAVE ANOTHER CAUSE,
BECAUSE WHEN SOME CAUSES ARE COLLECTED,
THE RESULT DOES NOT ARISE;
THAT [SITUATION] DOES NOT EXIST WHEN PERMANENT [ENTITIES ARE INVOLVED].

The first of the four particular qualities: THAT suffering IS IMPERMANENT, BECAUSE IT IS SEEN to arise OCCASIONALLY. Second: suffering IS SUFFERING, BECAUSE IT IS THE BASIS of the collection of present FLAWS AND ALSO BECAUSE IT IS UNDER THE external POWER of previous CAUSES, karma and defilements.[58] The third: [suffering] IS WITHOUT an essential independent SELF, because it is impermanent and under external power. The fourth: [suffering] is void, because IT IS NOT CONTROLLED by any independent self, EITHER.[59]

---

of the defilements, then they must accept one of three possible consequences, depending on how the "presence"of the elements is interpreted. (1) If they are impermanent but present from moment to moment, then defilements are continually present, because their causes, the elements, are continually present. (2) If they are eternal, in the sense of never being utterly terminated (other than moment-to-moment), then the defilements also would have to be eternal. Thus, a corpse could still be asserted to be defiled, or, in the extreme instance, a rock could be, too. (3) If they are permanent, then the defilements that are related to them could not change any more than the elements themselves could.

58 In other words, suffering both causes and results from previous suffering. For further discussion of the four aspects of suffering, see above, pp. 344-45.

59 The difference between the aspects of no-self and voidness is this: the fact that suffering is without self means that suffering itself cannot be described as a permanent, partless, independent substance of any sort, because a permanent entity cannot have impermanent extrinsic causes, and suffering, because it arises occasionally, obviously must have such causes. The fact that suffering is *void* means that suffering cannot be caused by a permanent, partless, independent substance that is extrinsic to it (e.g., God or some permanent self as-

The aggregates are NOT CONTROLLED by a self, because THAT [self] IS NOT their CAUSE. This follows, because that [self] is permanent. It follows that [this reason] pervades, because HOW COULD A PERMANENT [entity] also BE A GENERATOR? It is unacceptable that it could. It follows, THEREFORE, that IT IS NOT acceptable THAT THE MULTIPLE aggregates WILL ARISE AT DIFFERENT—earlier and later—TIMES FROM ONE permanent self, because a permanent [entity] is not a cause.[60]

A sense-cognition that apprehends form WILL BE able to be INFERRED TO HAVE ANOTHER CAUSE than just the faculties and mind, BECAUSE we see that in some instances WHEN SOME CAUSES, the faculties and mind, ARE COLLECTED, THE RESULT DOES NOT ARISE, and in some [other] instances it does arise. It follows that it is unsuitable that a permanent [entity] be a cause, because THAT absence of cause and result DOES NOT EXIST WHEN PERMANENT [entities are involved].[61]

---

sociated with the individual), because it is a result that is observed to arise occasionally, and thus to be impermanent, and an impermanent result (i.e., *any* result) cannot arise from a permanent cause. Indeed, a permanent entity cannot be shown to have any causal efficiency at all.

60 Again, a permanent entity, if it is causal, must produce all its results at once or not at all, while the results with which we are concerned, the aggregates, are extended from moment to moment, and hence inexplicable by a permanent cause.

61 At least part of the definition of a cause is a factor in whose absence a result will *not* arise and in whose presence a result *will* arise. For example, an object can be determined to be a "cause" of a sense-cognition, because we observe that when a faculty and mind are present but an object is not, there is no sense-cognition; while where a faculty and mind are present and an object is, too, a sense-cognition *does* arise. A "cause," in short, is a factor whose presence or absence makes a difference. A permanent cause will always be present, so it never can be absent. Thus, it cannot be ascertained to make a difference. Cf. above, section III:2:C.

8. *The Truth of Origination*

The truth of origination [223]

[This is divided into: (1) The aspect of cause [224], (2) The aspect of all-origination [225], (3) The aspect of strong arising [226] and (4) The aspect of condition [229].]

The aspect of cause [224]

(179c) THIS SUFFERING IS PROVEN TO HAVE A CAUSE,
BECAUSE IT IS OCCASIONAL.
(180-181) [SOMETHING] INDEPENDENT OF OTHER [ENTITIES] BECAUSE IT IS UNCAUSED
IS EITHER A PERMANENT EXISTENT OR WILL BE NON-EXISTENT.[1]
SOME EXPRESS [THE IDEA] THAT
JUST AS THE SHARPNESS
OF A THORN, ETC., ARE WITHOUT A CAUSE,
SO THESE [SUFFERINGS] WILL BE WITHOUT CAUSE.
[WE REPLY:] WHEN SOME [ENTITY] EXISTS, SOME [RESULT] ARISES, OR
WHEN SOME [ENTITY] IS TRANSFORMED, THEN SOME [OTHER ENTITY] IS TRANSFORMED.
(182) THAT [FORMER] IS EXPRESSED AS THE CAUSE OF THAT [LATTER];
THOSE [QUALITIES OF SHARPNESS, ETC.,] ALSO HAVE [A CAUSE].
TANGIBILITY IS [JUST] A CONDITION
FOR SEEING, BECAUSE IT IS A [MINOR] CAUSE OF THE FORM [THAT IS SEEN].

THIS aggregation of SUFFERING IS PROVEN TO HAVE A CAUSE, BECAUSE IT [IS something that] arises OCCASIONALly.

---

1 An alternative reading of PV 180a-b (*rgyu med gzhan la mi ltos phyir / rtag tu yod pa'am med par 'gyur*) yields: "That which is uncaused, because it is independent of other [entities], is either a permanent existent or will be non-existent."

Proof that [the reason] pervades:

"It follows that [suffering] originates INDEPENDENT OF OTHER causes and conditions, BECAUSE IT IS UNCAUSED." If that is asserted, it follows that [suffering] IS EITHER A PERMANENT EXISTENT OR WILL BE forever NON-EXISTENT, because of the assertion [that it is uncaused].[2]

SOME Lokāyatas, Mīmāṃsakas, etc., EXPRESS [the idea] THAT JUST AS THE SHARPNESS OF A THORN and the roundness of a pea, ETC., ARE WITHOUT any CAUSE that is their producer, SO THESE [suffering] entities WILL arise WITHOUT A CAUSE.

It follows that the sharpness of a thorn, etc., *do* have a cause, because [we see that] WHEN SOME objectively separate previous [entity] EXISTS, THEN some subsequent [entity] ARISES; OR, WHEN SOME previous [entity] IS TRANSFORMED, THEN THAT previous [entity], when it IS TRANSFORMED, IS EXPRESSED AS THE CAUSE OF THAT subsequent [entity that arises in its place]. It follows through positive and negative concomitance that those [qualities], the sharpness of a thorn, etc., ALSO HAVE [a cause].[3]

[OPPONENT:] Well, then, it follows that the tangibility of a single composite is the cause of a sense-cognition that sees form, because if [tangibility] did not exist, there would be no [sense-cognition].

[RGYAL TSHAB RJE:] The TANGIBILITY of the elements is merely A CONDITION FOR the sense-cognition SEEING form; it does not directly bring it about, BECAUSE it is the corresponding or simultaneously occurring CAUSE OF that FORM. It is imputed merely as the simultaneously occurring cause of a single simultaneous composite. Thus, the tangibility of the elements is a cause of the sense-cognition that sees a

---

2 It already has been established that the only entities that can be described as "uncaused" are those that are either permanent or non-existent—neither of which is a predication that can be applied to suffering.

3 The view represented by the "Lokāyatas, Mīmāṃsakas, etc.," is the *svabhāvavāda*, the view that certain things simply happen "naturally" (*svabhāvena*), without any specific cause, and that the sharpness of a thorn and the roundness of a pea are such things. The Buddhist view is that such things do not come about causelessly, because, in the examples, the qualities are dependent on the existence of the thorn or pea, which is, in turn, dependent on a number of causes and conditions: seed, soil, water, sunlight, etc. The presence or absence of these factors will affect the presence or absence of the thorn or pea, which, in turn, will affect the presence or absence of the quality of sharpness or roundness. Generally, rGyal tshab rje observes, such qualities as sharpness or roundness must be considered caused because they can be described in terms of the formula "If *x*, then *y*; if no *x*, then no *y*."

form, which is a secondary quality that is its own result, [only] because it is the corresponding cause of such form.[4]

The aspect of all-origination[5] [225]

(183) IT ALSO IS NOT POSSIBLE [THAT SUFFERING ORIGINATES] FROM GOD,
ETC., BECAUSE [THESE] ARE UNABLE [TO PRODUCE], AND PERMANENT [ENTITIES]
HAVE BEEN REFUTED. . . .

IT ALSO IS NOT POSSIBLE that suffering originates FROM a unique cause, such as GOD, ETC., BECAUSE [God, etc.,] ARE NOT ABLE to generate a result. This follows, BECAUSE WE HAVE already REFUTED [the idea] that PERMANENT [entities] can be causes. Having refuted [the idea] that individual sufferings have an independent [entity] as their cause, we have shown that they are necessarily all originated from a collection of causes.[6]

The aspect of strong arising [226]

[This is divided into:] (1) The nature of strong arising [227] and (2) Disposing [of the objection] that [our description] contradicts scripture [228].

---

4 Tangibility is a quality that exists simultaneously with form in a collection. Therefore, it and form serve as mutually assistant cooperative (or simultaneously arising) conditions. It is not, however, tangibility that is the actual objective condition for a sense-cognition—the form itself functions thus. Tangibility is a "cause" of a sense-cognition only to the degree that it is a cooperative condition of the form that is an indispensable condition; it is not itself indispensable. The term "corresponding cause" (*sabhāgahetu*) is used differently here than above (PV 175), where it meant a previous homogeneous causal moment. Here, it is being used as synonymous with "cooperative condition" or "simultaneously arising cause" (*lhan cig byed rkyen, sahakāriyapratyaya*).

5 The Tibetan term *kun 'byung* here is fully glossed; the Sanskrit *samudaya* does not usually suggest the origination (*udaya*) of all (*sam*) suffering, since *sam* does not have the force of the Tibetan *kun*.

6 Suffering cannot have a unique cause, such as God, because (a) a unique cause could not account for the variety of sufferings that are observed to arise and (b) such a unique cause usually is conceived of as permanent, and a permanent entity cannot have any causal efficiency at all. Therefore, all suffering must originate from a collection of various causes.

The nature of strong arising [227]

(183c) . . . BECAUSE OF THAT,
THE CAUSE IS THE CRAVING FOR EXISTENCE, BECAUSE OF WHICH
(184) PEOPLE GRASP COMPLETELY AT PARTICULAR
OBJECTS, WITH A THOUGHT TO OBTAIN THEM.

BECAUSE OF THAT impossibility that [anything] arise without a cause or from a permanent [entity], THE CAUSE of [resultant] suffering IS THE CRAVING FOR EXISTENCE that manifestly craves [saṃsāric] existence, BECAUSE OF WHICH PEOPLE GRASP COMPLETELY AT PARTICULAR OBJECTS, such as abodes, bodies and enjoyments, and they crave them WITH A THOUGHT desiring TO OBTAIN THEM. The expressions "grasping completely" and "all-grasping" here refer to [actually] obtaining, so the phrase "obtained by the condition that is craving" shows a cause and result that manifestly accomplish [one another].[7]

Disposing [of the objection] that [our description] contradicts scripture [228]

(184c-185b) BECAUSE OF THAT, WE ASSERT THAT THAT IS THE CRAVING
FOR EXISTENCE; THOSE THAT RELATE TO LIVING BEINGS'
DESIRE TO OBTAIN PLEASURE AND AVOID SUFFERING
ARE THE CRAVING FOR SENSE-PLEASURE AND ANNIHILATION,
[RESPECTIVELY].

[OPPONENT:] This contradicts the scriptural [teaching] that the cause [of suffering] is the threefold craving, [indicated] in such passages as: "What is the noble truth of the origination of suffering? Whatever is craving. . . ."

[RGYAL TSHAB RJE:] It follows [BECAUSE OF THAT] that there is no contradiction between the scriptural [teaching] that the cause is the threefold craving and the explanation that the cause is [the desire] to obtain such objects as abodes, bodies and enjoyments, because WE ASSERT THAT THAT craving that is intent on particular objects is the craving for existence that IS THE DESIRE FOR [saṃsāric] EXISTENCE, while THOSE cravings THAT RELATE TO objects by way of LIVING BEINGS' DESIRE TO OBTAIN PLEASURE AND their desire TO AVOID SUFFERING ARE, respectively, THE CRAVING FOR SENSE-PLEASURE AND the craving for ANNIHILATION.[8]

---

7 Here, rGyal tshab rje gives the traditional Buddhist explanation of the cause of suffering: it is craving (*sred pa, tṛṣṇa*) or desire (*'dod pa, iṣṭa*) of various sorts, which can be reduced to the craving for existence (*srid sred, bhāvatṛṣṇa*). That craving has a causal efficiency such that it invariably obtains its result. Thus, saṃsāra rolls on and on, impelled by beings' desire for continued existence.

The aspect of condition [229]

[This is divided into:] (1) Showing that craving is a condition [230], (2) Setting forth a demonstration of that [231] and (3) Disposing [of the objection] that [the consequences apply] equally [to us] [232].

Showing that craving is a condition [230]

(185c-186b) THEREFORE, CRAVING IS THE BASIS OF [SAṂSĀRIC] EXISTENCE;
BY PERCEIVING AS PLEASURABLE WHAT IS NOT PLEASURABLE,
ONE WILL ENTER INTO ALL [SAṂSĀRIC SPHERES],
THROUGH A CAUSE THAT IS ATTACHMENT TO SELF.

[THEREFORE,] CRAVING has the aspect of condition, because it IS THE cooperative BASIS OF its own result, a subsequent [saṃsāric] EXISTENCE. It follows that craving is thus, because BY PERCEIVING AS PLEASURABLE WHAT IS NOT PLEASURABLE, those who are degenerate WILL ENTER INTO ALL lower spheres. That distorted perception is not causeless, because it arises THROUGH A CAUSE THAT IS ATTACHMENT TO SELF.[9]

---

8 At numerous places in the sūtras (e.g., D, ii, 308) and śāstras (e.g., AK v:29), craving is described as threefold: craving for existence, craving for annihilation (or non-existence, or destruction) and craving for sense-pleasure. Dharmakīrti points out that his description of craving chiefly in terms of the craving for existence does not contradict these passages, for the craving for existence (the main force impelling the continuation of saṃsāra) entails the other two: the desire for objects in general is roughly synonymous with the craving for existence, the specific desire to *enjoy* objects is the craving for sense-pleasure and the specific desire to avoid objects that cause suffering (or to avoid the suffering connected with objects we desire) is the craving for annihilation. Thus, the two cravings that operate most of the time in ordinary life are the craving for pleasure and the craving for non-pain (=annihilation). One mistakenly believes that some sort of ultimate pleasure and ultimate absence of pain can be found within saṃsāra, so one generates the craving for further existences. One gets one's wish, further rebirths, and therefore continues to suffer.

9 Craving is a "condition"for the origination of suffering, because it is the indispensable cooperative condition for rebirth into a subsequent existence. Craving for existence involves the mistaken assumption that what is not pleasurable (*duḥkha*) is pleasurable (*sukha*), and thus becomes the basis for continued rebirth in realms whose nature ultimately is suffering. The root of the mistaken assumption, in turn, is self-grasping, or attachment to self (*bdag 'dzin, ātmagraha*). Because one either intuitively or philosophically posits a self, one posits an entity whose pleasure and pain one ultimately cares about, i.e., an entity to which one is attached. Because it is based on a misapprehension

Setting forth a demonstration of that [231]

(186c) ["THIS IS SO] BECAUSE WE DO NOT SEE A DETACHED ONE BORN"—
THIS HAS BEEN TAUGHT BY THE ĀCĀRYAS.

It follows that craving is the cause of a subsequent [saṃsāric] existence, BECAUSE WE DO NOT SEE A DETACHED ONE, an arhant, BORN into a subsequent [saṃsāric] existence, by virtue of their having utterly abandoned craving, BECAUSE THIS HAS BEEN TAUGHT BY THE earlier ĀCĀRYAS.[10]

Disposing [of the objection] that [the consequences apply] equally to us [232]

(187) [IF YOU SAY THAT] ATTACHMENT ALSO ORIGINATES FROM THE BODY,
BECAUSE WE DO NOT SEE ATTACHMENT IN ONE WHO IS BODILESS,
[WE REPLY:] WE HAVE ACCEPTED THE ASSERTION THAT [THE BODY] IS A CONDITION;
WE HAVE CLEARED AWAY [THE IDEA] THAT IT IS THE SUBSTANTIAL [CAUSE].
(188) [THE LOKĀYATAS] THEMSELVES WILL DAMAGE THEIR OWN ASSERTION
BY FOLLOWING THE REASONING ASSERTED [BY THE BUDDHISTS].
IF YOU SAY THAT BECAUSE WE SEE ATTACHMENT
AT BIRTH, IT HAS ORIGINATED SIMULTANEOUSLY WITH BIRTH,
(189) [WE REPLY:] IT IS PROVEN TO BE [FROM] PREVIOUS [ATTACHMENT], BECAUSE IT ARISES FROM A CORRESPONDING [CAUSE].

---

of the nature of reality, this attachment seeks the wrong object in the wrong manner, and thus succeeds only in frustrating one's ultimate desire—the elimination of all suffering.

10 This is a crucial argument—that craving is the cause of rebirth because there is no rebirth for one who has no craving, i.e., an arhant. It might be objected that this argument appears to beg the question, for the existence of a being such as an arhant has not yet conclusively been shown (only a proof of the truths of cessation and path can do that), so the opponent need not accept the arhant's attainment as probative of anything, since the arhant has yet to be proved. This objection seems cogent, though the Buddhist might reply that the possibility of the arhant has been demonstrated in the forward system of explanation, which showed how a buddha arrives at his goal via some path. Still, the arhant has not been proven in detail, so the objection retains some of its force. Incidentally, Nagatomi ([1957] 183-84) takes this verse together with the next one, and makes it part of an opponent's objection that because of what the Nyāya ācāryas have said, the *body* is the source of attachment.

NESCIENCE ALSO IS A CAUSE OF [SAṂSĀRIC] EXISTENCE;
IT IS NOT EXPRESSED [AS THE CAUSE HERE]. CRAVING IS EXPLAINED [AS THE CAUSE HERE]
BECAUSE IT INCITES THE CONTINUUM [OF EXISTENCES] AND
(190) BECAUSE IT IS IMMEDIATE. NOR IS KARMA [THE CAUSE],
BECAUSE EVEN IF THERE IS [KARMA], THERE WILL BE NO BIRTH [WHEN CRAVING IS ABSENT].

[OPPONENT:] Well, then, ATTACHMENT ALSO ORIGINATES FROM THE BODY, BECAUSE WE DO NOT SEE ATTACHMENT IN ONE WHO IS BODILESS. For example, [you yourself assert that] since we do not see a detached one take birth, attachment [must be] the cause for the arising of a [subsequent saṃsāric] existence.[11]

[RGYAL TSHAB RJE:] If you prove just that the body is a cause of attachment, then you prove what is already proven, because the Buddha has asserted that it is just a cause. This follows, BECAUSE WE HAVE already ACCEPTED [THE ASSERTION] THAT IT IS just A cooperative CONDITION.[12]

[OPPONENT:] Well, then, this contradicts your previous refutation [of the idea that the body is] the cause [of attachment].

[RGYAL TSHAB RJE:] We have not refuted [the idea] that the body is merely *a* cause of attachment, because WE HAVE CLEARED AWAY [the idea only] that [the body] IS THE SUBSTANTIAL [cause] or the special cooperative condition.[13]

It follows that the Lokāyatas THEMSELVES WILL DAMAGE THEIR OWN ASSERTION that there are no past or future lives, because they are FOLLOWING THE Buddhist REASONING [proving] that attachment is the cause of the body, and have set forth a correct example and ASSERTED the body as the cause of attachment.[14]

---

11 The opponent argues that one can take the Buddhist proof that attachment is the cause of rebirth and derive from it the notion that the body is the cause of attachment, because someone who has no body has no attachment, a fact that indicates a causal concomitance between the two.

12 The Buddhist will accept that the body is *a* cause of attachment—specifically a cooperative condition—but not that it is *the* cause, or an indispensable cause.

13 This idea has been "cleared away"in the lengthy discussion of the mind-body problem above, especially in section III:3.

14 The Lokāyatas threaten to undercut their own position when they attempt to turn the Buddhist proof around, for (1) they have asserted generally what the Buddhists already have proven, i.e., that the body is a cause of attachment and (2) they have been willing to carry on their discussion in terms of the example

[OPPONENT:] BECAUSE WE do not SEE any other [source of] visible ATTACHMENT in a body AT BIRTH, attachment that HAS not ARISEN before is SIMULTANEOUS WITH the BIRTH of the body, and so the body is *not* the result of attachment.

[RGYAL TSHAB RJE:] Well, then, it also follows that attachment is not the result of the body, because [the two] are asserted to originate simultaneously. If that is asserted, it follows that the attachment immediately after birth IS PROVEN AS coming from PREVIOUS attachment, BECAUSE IT ARISES from its CORRESPONDING cause.[15]

[OPPONENT:] If [you assert that] craving alone is the cause, then you contradict the explanation that the cause of suffering is threefold: ignorance, craving and karma.

[RGYAL TSHAB RJE:] NESCIENCE and ignorance are ALSO A CAUSE generating subsequent [saṃsāric] EXISTENCEs; the reason they are not explicitly expressed as the cause in this case is because they are not the *immediate* cause of [subsequent saṃsāric existences]—thus, [ignorance] IS NOT EXPRESSED [as the cause here]. The reason CRAVING IS EXPLAINED as the cause of a subsequent [saṃsāric] existence is BECAUSE IT INCITES THE CONTINUUM of a subsequent [saṃsāric] existence as its own result and is the projecting cause that projects [the subsequent saṃsāric existence]; AND BECAUSE IT IS the efficient cause that effects the IMMEDIATE [result]. NOR IS KARMA the principal cause of a subsequent [saṃsāric] existence, BECAUSE if there is craving, then there automatically is karma, while if there is no craving, then EVEN IF THERE IS [THAT] karma, THERE WILL BE NO birth into a [subsequent saṃsāric] existence, because if there is no craving, even a royal existence earned by karma will be avoided.[16]

---

of an arhant, accepted by the Buddhists, but not by them. For a similar instance, cf. above, PV 46 and commentary.

15 The opponent argues that the body of, say, this rebirth cannot result from attachment because when we consider the moment of birth we only see the simultaneous co-existence of body and attachment. rGyal tshab rje points out that simultaneously existing factors cannot be causally related, so (a) one can as easily expect that attachment causes a body as the other way around and (b) because two simultaneouly existing factors cannot be causally related, the first moment of attachment cannot be derived from the body, and so must be derived from a previous moment of attachment.

16 As before, rGyal tshab rje is most interested in the *immediate* cause for the continuation of saṃsāra, and only craving, or attachment, functions thus. Ignorance (or nescience: *mi shes, ajñāna*) is at the root of craving, but is not itself the projecting or impelling cause of a subsequent rebirth. Karma may predis-

pose one toward ignorance or craving, but one may (as in nirvāṇa "with remainder") have "left-over" resultant karma even when one has abandoned craving, so the presence of karma does not necessarily entail the taking of rebirth. For example, an arhant, at death, still may have karmic seeds left over, e.g., for rebirth as a king, but since they have utterly abandoned craving (and, of course, ignorance), there no longer is any basis for the presence of a cause that would project a subsequent rebirth, so these karmic seeds are forever prevented from ripening. Incidentally, this helps to explain why the fact that we have accumulated an infinity of karmic seeds in the past does *not* mean that we cannot ever be liberated because we have an infinity of karma to dispose of. Karmic seeds only will ripen under the proper conditions, the most important general condition being the presence of craving. If craving is eliminated, then no matter how many karmic seeds lie unripened in the mindstream, they have forever lost the opportunity of fruition. For similar discussions, cf. below, section III:11:C.

9. *The Truth of Cessation*

A. PROVING LIBERATION AND OMNISCIENCE

The truth of cessation [233]

[This is divided into:] (1) The aspect of cessation [234], (2) The aspect of peace [244] and (3) The aspect of sublimity [248]. The aspect of definitive emergence is explained together with the aspect of definitive removal of the truth of path, so it is not directly discussed at this point.

The aspect of cessation [234]

[This is divided into:] (1) Setting forth the reason that proves the truth of cessation [235] and (2) Disposing of objections [240].

Setting forth the reason that proves the truth of cessation [235]

[This is divided into:] (1) The meaning of the word [236] and (2) A detailed investigation [237].

The meaning of the word [236]

(190c) THAT [SUFFERING] IS NOT FIXED,
BECAUSE IT IS POSSIBLE THAT THE CAUSE STOP, ETC.

THAT aggregation [of suffering] of an ordinary being IS NOT an [eternal] continuum FIXED as unsuitable for cessation, BECAUSE IT IS POSSIBLE THAT [THE aggregation's] own CAUSE can [cease] through the STOPping power of the contradictory condition and the incompletion of the appropriate conditions, ETC.[1]

---

1 The suffering endemic to the aggregates of sentient beings, then, *can* be stopped, for it has identifiable causes and conditions that perpetuate it, and these causes and conditions are subject to counteraction by the appropriate antidote. The antidote has the power to eliminate the causes and conditions of sufferings and hence contribute to the elimination of suffering itself.

A detailed investigation[2] *[237]*

[This is divided into:] (1) The way of proving liberation [238] and (2) The way of proving omniscience [239].

The way of proving liberation [238]

There necessarily exists some type of elimination of one's own [suffering] continuum by the power of an antidote, since [there is an antidote] that is powerfully destructive of the type of cause [that causes] one's [suffering]. For example, when we see [a cause] having the power to counteract a cold touch, we see that there is an elimination of the continuum of horripilation. Similarly, we see that [an antidote] is powerfully destructive of the type of cause that [causes] this aggregation [of suffering] of an ordinary being. This is a correct, objectively impelled reason; its pervasion is proven by perceptual authority.[3]

Proof of the reason's relevance to the subject:

It is necessarily the case that there exists [an antidote] that is powerfully destructive of the type [of attitude] that is a distorted attitude toward the actuality of entities. For example, there is the [mistaken] superimposition that apprehends that there is no fire at a smoky pass. Similarly, [the view] that apprehends a self of persons is a distortion of the actuality of entities.[4]

---

2 The following discussions of liberation and omniscience are interpolated by rGyal tshab rje, and do not correspond to anything in Dharmakīrti's root-text.

3 The process whereby suffering comes to cease can be likened to the process whereby *any* condition comes to cease. A given condition, such as horripilation, is ascertained to result from contact with cold. The application of the "antidote"to cold, heat, is seen to end the horripilation. Similarly, the suffering of sentient beings has been ascertained through the truth of origination to be due to craving rooted in self-grasping. Therefore, the application of the antidote (the wisdom realizing no-self) should entail the cessation of the suffering resulting from self-grasping. rGyal tshab rje is maintaining that the "psychological"case is no different from the "physical": where we can ascertain specific causes for the generation of a particular result, the removal of those causes must entail the non-generation of the result.

4 rGyal tshab rje here uses "superimposition" (*sgro 'dogs, āropa*) in the same rather general sense that Dharmakīrti usually does. Thus, it has not the particular sense of *ātmavāda*, but the general sense of *any* mistaken apprehension of reality, *any* cognition involving a belief in what is not the case. Thus, the belief that there exists a self of persons is an "inversion,"or distortion, of the way things actually are as regards the self-question in the same way that the belief

[OPPONENT:] When we see that there is [an antidote] destructive of grasping at a self of persons, how does that prove that the cause of suffering can be destroyed?

[RGYAL TSHAB RJE:] From the authority that ascertains that those two are [respectively] cause and result.[5]

[OPPONENT:] How is that?

[RGYAL TSHAB RJE:] There is [this] passage[6]:

> IN SOMEONE [ORDINARY], saying "I" will [entail] desire
> For the permanent, for THEY SEE A SELF. (217)
> They will crave happiness, since they desire [the self], and
> The craving will hide the flaws [in the self];
> When they see the good qualities [of the self], they utterly crave them, [and]
> Saying "Mine," they seek the accomplishment of that. (218)
> Thus, they will circle [in saṃsāra]
> As long as there is manifest attachment to self.
> [Self-grasping] is the source of all faults:
> When there is self, there is recognition of other;
> From the parts, self and other, one will come into contact
> With [the attitudes of] grasping and anger, from which [all faults arise]. (219-220b)

[This] shows that it is proven by perception that craving for non-separation from self is drawn by its own power from grasping at a self of persons. It is proven by perceptual authority that from that [arises] craving for the pleasures of the self. From that [arises] craving for the sense-faculties and such externals as food and clothing, which accomplish the pleasures of the self. From that, in order to accomplish the pleasures of the self, there [arise] mental formations [tending toward] karma of the three doors. From that arise the suffering sensations of not obtaining desired objects and of obtaining undesired objects. [Thus,] we have proven by perceptual authority that present suffering and self-grasping are result and cause.[7]

---

that there is no fire at a smoky pass is an inversion of the way things actually are as regards instances of smoky passes.

5 In other words, that grasping at a self of persons is the cause of one's resultant suffering.

6 Here, and throughout this section, passages from the *Pramāṇavārttika* actually quoted by rGyal tshab rje are placed in small capitals; I have filled in the rest of the relevant verses so as to make the discussion more comprehensible.

If we [wish to] prove by objectively impelled inference that from death-time grasping there is connection to a subsequent homogene, [then the argument is as follows:] Since we designate the subsequent homogene to which there is a connection as "suffering," it is ascertained by objectively impelled inference that the subsequent suffering is in a cause-result relation [with the previous grasping].[8]

[OPPONENT:] Even if the subsequent homogene has the *meaning* of suffering, how, on the basis merely of ascertaining that present karma and defilements and [a subsequent event] are cause and result, can you ascertain through objectively impelled [inference] that that [result] should have the *name* "suffering"?[9]

[RGYAL TSHAB RJE:] We can ascertain by objectively impelled [inferential] authority that the *meaning* of suffering is that which is produced by karma and defilement. If you have not forgotten what has already been ascertained, it has been proven by perceptual authority that there exist up until death time karma and craving. Since it has been proven by inference that from that [karma and craving] there is a connection to a subsequent homogene, it is proven that the subsequent homogene is under the power of karma and defilement, so it is well proven that [that result] has the *meaning* of suffering. [Therefore,] one can understand that it also can be designated [with the *name* "suffering"].[10]

---

7 rGyal tshab rje is satisfied that the sequence he has described demonstrates adequately the degree to which belief in a self is the root of our sufferings within this life, i.e., that there is psychological cogency in the Buddhist notion that self-grasping is the root of suffering.

8 Since every suffering moment of this life (i.e., every moment) has been conditioned by self-grasping, and since it already has been proven that the last mind-moment of this life has the capacity to connect to a subsequent mind-moment in another life, the first mind-moment of the subsequent life must involve suffering, since the last mind-moment of this life will—all things being equal—involve self-grasping.

9 The opponent is willing to accept that the first moment of the next life will have the sense, or meaning (*don ldog*) of suffering, but argues that this does not mean that we can apply to it the *name* (*rang ldog*) "suffering."This argument seems at first utterly sophistic, but perhaps is based on the idea that we may take rebirth in a state in which there is no *term* "suffering,"hence perhaps no suffering in any meaningful sense.

10 rGyal tshab rje points out, simply, that if the first moment of the next life is accepted to have the "meaning"of suffering, then certainly the "name" "suffering" can be appropriately applied. For a discussion of the relation between word and meaning, cf., e.g., above, PV 18-20.

[OPPONENT:] Well, then, how do you prove that grasping at a self of persons is a distorted attitude toward the actuality of entities?

[RGYAL TSHAB RJE:] It is proven from the ascertainment that there is no self of persons. This is divided into: identifying the object of refutation, the reasoning refuting that [object of refutation] and the way of meditating on no-self.

Identifying the object of refutation:

This is taught in a later verse,[11] [where it says:]

A person knows that they have a different
Self-nature from their sense-faculties,
BECAUSE THEY WILL STRIVE FOR OTHERS THAT ARE SUPERIOR,
And because they have a mind subject to arising and destruction.
(247c-248b)

Innate to one's mind, there is desire for the ownership of an independent self of persons that is not the collection of aggregates, a single [aggregate] or the continuum. The desirous [mind] does not impute only this collection of aggregates as the person, because [we know that] if one could exhange one's present aggregates for special aggregates, such as those of a god, then clearly one would definitely desire to reject the former and accept the latter. Nor, thus, does one impute just mental cognition as exhaustive of the person, because if one could exchange one's present unclear mind for something like an omniscient mind, then, like a merchant [trading] goods, one clearly would desire whatever exhange one could manage. If a merchant thinks that [the meaning of] "merchant"is exhausted merely by an imputation on his goods, and holds that it is not otherwise, then [there result] the contradictions that they will be perplexed as to whether they can extract the goods of another; and if they [should wish to] obtain the goods of another, which are superior to their own goods, they will be perplexed as to whether they can substitute [the other merchandise for their own].[12]

---

11 See above, p. 391 n. 6.

12 The object of refutation for someone who is attempting to understand whether or not there is a self is not the "self of the philosophers,"but the self in which we all instinctively believe. The fact that we all *do* instinctively believe in a personal self that is neither coterminous with the aggregates nor identi-

Thus, there exists desire for an independent person that is not exhausted merely by its imputation on either the collection of aggregates or some single [aggregate], and that independent person for which there is desire, designated as the "self of persons,"is the object of refutation.[13]

The reasoning refuting that [object of refutation]:

The person does not exist as an independent [entity] that is not merely an imputation on the aggregates, because if it were, it would not be seen as other than suitable as the intentional object of an authority. It is definitely proven by just this statement.[14]

Alternatively, [the reason,] that which is neither naturally identical with nor different from the aggregates, does not pervade [the predicate,] a naturally existing [entity], as the horns of a hare [do not]. It also should be known that there does not exist anywhere an independent person that is naturally identical with or different from the aggregates. It is easy to ascertain pervasion. As for the relevance of the reason to the subject: there is no natural identity between an independent person [and the aggregates], because [the aggregates] are under the power of external causes. [The person] does not exist as naturally different from [the aggregates], because if it did, then it would not be seen as other than suitable as an intentional object.[15]

---

ified merely with one of them is shown by the fact that we entertain such thoughts as, "If only I could be in his shoes,"or "If only I could have a mind like hers."A merchant makes a similarly instinctive distinction between a merchant (= the self) and their goods (= the aggregates). If they did not make such a distinction, then they would have no notion of how to obtain the goods belonging to another or to exchange their own goods for those of another, because there would then be no "other"with whom to do business.

13 In Mahāyāna traditions, especially Madhyamaka, the self of persons (*gang zag gi bdag*) is generally paired with the self of dharmas (*chos kyi bdag*) as the two possible types of self to be refuted. The most detailed discussions usually are applied to identifying and refuting the former, since it is the more pernicious and difficult to excise.

14 In other words, if there *did* exist a self that was more than simply an imputation on the aggregates, an authoritative cognition would recognize it. Something that will be cognized by an authority, however, must stand up to analysis, and the concept of an independent self will not, when we search for it, be found.

15 The actual syllogism proving no-self will read: "An independent person that is naturally identical with or different from the aggregates is not a naturally existing [entity], because it is neither naturally identical with nor different from

Based on those two reasons, we have proven the voidness and no-self that are the special qualities of the truth of suffering, and which cut off the attachment grasping at an imputed self. Based on the fundamental reason, we have proven the no-self that cuts off the innate attachment grasping at a self.[16]

The way of meditating on no-self:

Having well identified the object of refutation, based on the appropriate reasoning one should contemplate one-pointedly again and again [the fact] that there is not the slightest existent [that exists] in the way of an independent self. When one has meditated thus, and rises from contemplation, by [the meditation's] power one should become mentally certain that the so-called "person" is merely an

---

the aggregates. Its non-natural existence is like that of the horns of a hare." The syllogism is correct because an independent self cannot, in fact, exist in relation to the aggregates in either of the two possible ways, i.e., as identical to or different from them. It cannot be identical to the aggregates because the aggregates are known to be impermanent and under the power of extrinsic causes and conditions, whereas a permanent self cannot be under the power of anything but itself. It cannot be different from the aggregates, because then the analysis investigating "persons"would discover it as an intentional object separate from the aggregates; in fact, however, analysis reveals that all the qualities and characteristics that we usually attribute to a "person"are covered by the five aggregates. Therefore, there cannot be any additional factor that "really"is the person. Thus, the person is simply a designation or imputation on the aggregates, nothing more, nothing less, and the search for any other "person"or "self"is bound to be futile. In the analogy often used by Tibetan teachers, a farmer believes that he has lost a cow, but knows that there are only two places where she might be found; looking in both places, he fails to find her, and therefore concludes that he has not, after all, lost a cow. The argument framed here by rGyal tshab rje is based on such Mādhyamika texts as Candrakīrti's *Madhyamakāvatāra* (sixth chapter) and Śāntideva's *Bodhicaryāvatāra* (ninth chapter). See the citations for these works in the bibliography. See also, e.g., The Dalai Lama (1985) chapter 6, Thurman (1981) III:b and Hopkins (1983) parts one and two, for fuller expositions of these arguments. For a concise exposition of Theravādin arguments about the self, see Collins (1982) II:3.2. Incidentally, though the arguments cited by rGyal tshab rje are rooted in the Madhyamaka, there is nothing in them that contradicts anything in Dharmakīrti. In this case, therefore, rGyal tshab rje's proof simply adumbrates and adds rigor to Dharmakīrti's own discussions.

16 The proof that there cannot exist a self independent of the aggregates provides one with a basis for extirpating the innate self-grasping that is the root of saṃsāra, and therefore with the basis for attaining a cessation of suffering.

imputation on the aggregates. One should remind oneself of this again and again.[17]

Therefore, in summary, it is proven by objectively impelled reasoning that there is a total elimination of the continuum of suffering by virtue of an antidote. That elimination is called "the truth of cessation" and "liberation."[18]

The way of proving omniscience [239]

There necessarily exists a type of powerful destroyer [that exists] in simultaneous combination with the elimination of all destructibles of [the appropriate] type, just as we see that a powerful fire exists in simultaneous combination with the elimination of all kinds of destructible cold to which it is proximate. The mind that realizes the actuality of the four noble truths, [in such aspects as] no-self, etc., is a powerful destroyer. It is proven by reason of this statement that the mind that understands the actuality of the four noble truths exists in simultaneous combination with the elimination of all destructible stains that [result from] straying from the actuality of the four noble truths. That mind that realizes the actuality of the four noble truths in combination with being devoid of all stains is known as omniscient.[19]

---

17 It is through the power of assiduous meditation on no-self that defilements actually will be eradicated. One contemplates it discursively on the paths of accumulation and application. One realizes it directly on the path of seeing, thereby beginning the actual eradication of defilements, and continues to develop this realization on the path of development. Throughout these higher paths, the gap between one's direct meditative awareness of no-self and one's conceptual recognition of it when not meditating narrows, until finally, when one is enlightened, one directly realizes no-self at all times.

18 Thus, liberation is proved by the fact that (a) suffering results from misapprehension of reality, (b) the belief in self is a misapprehension of reality, (c) belief in self leads to suffering and (d) the application of the opposite of a particular attitude entails the opposite of its results. As a consequence, (e) application of the opposite to a belief in self entails an end to the results of a belief in self, hence an end to suffering, which is liberation.

19 The actual syllogism on which is based the proof of omniscience will read: "The mind realizing the actuality of the four noble truths [in such aspects as] no-self, etc., is the type [of entity that exists] in simultaneous combination with the elimination of all destructibles of [the appropriate] type, because it is a powerful destroyer, like a powerful fire, which exists in simultaneous combination with the elimination of all kinds of destructible cold to which it is proximate." Contradictory conditions, such as the view of no-self and self-grasping, can be related in one of two possible ways. The first, "symmetrical"

Since it is also proven that one can take [as a logical subject] a mind realizing the no-self of dharmas, it is proven that there is a mind realizing the no-self of dharmas that exists in combination with the elimination of all [instances of] self-grasping. That mind is omniscient. This [latter] discussion is incidental in this section.[20]

---

relation is like that between day and night, one of which inevitably succeeds the other, but also invariably will itself be replaced in turn. An "asymmetrical" relation is like that between heat and cold: heat steadily applied will eliminate all cold to which it is proximate, and once the cold has been eliminated, it has no power to return—as long as the heat is present. It is a fundamental assumption of Buddhist soteriology that the relation between the realization of no-self and self-grasping is of the second, "asymmetrical"kind, i.e., that once no-self has been "directly"realized, it has the power to eliminate any instance of self-grasping to which it is applied. It is, in short, a powerful destroyer. This view may be—although it is not necessarily—related to the equally fundamental Buddhist assumption that the mind is naturally luminous and free from defilements, which are merely adventitious (below, PV 208c-d). The prevailing Western view is considerably different: the mind is considered to be fundamentally imperfect and "defiled,"capable of development but not perfection. Thus, the relation between the realization of no-self and self-grasping is more likely to be considered "symmetrical,"i.e., ultimately cyclical. There is a fundamental disagreement between the Buddhist and the Westerner over the salvific power of "truth,"much of which is, in turn, rooted in the differing sorts of "empirical"criteria accepted as having confirmatory power: Western assumptions are based more on the observation of "ordinary"psychological states, while Buddhist assumptions take into account "extraordinary"meditative states. For a discussion of these issues, see R. Jackson (1990). In any case, based on the foregoing assumptions, rGyal tshab rje is able to conclude that the "powerfully destructive"realization of no-self is able in principle to eliminate all instances of self-grasping, and therefore all defilements and residual "stains"based upon it. A mind that is free of all possible stains or obstacles is, by definition, omniscient.

20 As rGyal tshab rje already has pointed out, Dharmakīrti takes the "lowest common denominator"in the *Pramāṇasiddhi* chapter, and therefore discusses only the no-self of persons. In the *Pratyakṣa* chapter, however, he discusses an object's voidness of substantial difference from the subject that cognizes it, which rGyal tshab rje takes to be his analysis of the no-self of dharmas—from a Cittamātrin standpoint, of course. Thus, the realization of the no-self of dharmas, a prerequisite for omniscience, is only implied in the *Pramāṇasiddhi* chapter. If the no-self of dharmas is implied, then so too by extension is "full" omniscience, which Dharmakīrti nowhere in his writings specifically upholds. Thus, rGyal tshab rje has found in the *Pramāṇasiddhi* chapter at least two "implicit"proofs of omniscience: (1) because the Buddha has knowledge of what is to be rejected and what adopted by those intent on freedom, he knows every detail of saṃsāra and nirvāṇa, for those are what are to be rejected and

Inferring along these lines, one should [be able to] know extensively the way of proving liberation and omniscience through objectively impelled reasoning. [Some people] grow impatient if they see or hear even a little elaboration of words and meaning; since I want to satisfy even them, I have not elaborated.

B. ASPECTS OF CESSATION

Disposing of objections [240]

[This is divided into:] (1) Disposing of the consequence that liberation is impossible [241], (2) Disposing of the consequence that it is impossible to strive for liberation [242] and (3) Disposing of the consequence that once liberation is attained it is impossible to abide in [saṃsāric] existence for even a moment [243].

Disposing of the consequence that liberation is impossible [241]

> (191) IF YOU SAY THAT THERE IS NO LIBERATION BECAUSE OF SAṂSĀRA,
> [WE REPLY:] NOT SO, BECAUSE WE ASSERT [LIBERATION, AND YOUR
> REASON] IS UNPROVEN.

[OPPONENT:] If there is no permanent person who is objectively separate from saṃsāra and nirvāṇa, and if that person has a nature subject to saṃsāra, then it follows that THERE IS NO previous LIBERATION or subsequent liberation, BECAUSE OF that person's being subject to SAṂSĀRA.

[RGYAL TSHAB RJE:] This is argued by other schools that accept [the possibility of] liberation. Alternatively, those who are skeptical

---

adopted by those intent on freedom, and since saṃsāra and nirvāṇa are categories exhaustive of all phenomena, the Buddha must be omniscient (see above, section III:2:D) and (2) because any practitioner is in principle able to eliminate every instance of self-grasping, and therefore every defilement or defilement-stain based on that self-grasping, a state is possible in which no more stains or obstacles remain, and this state is regarded as omniscience. In each case, the proof of omniscience is arrived at through a process of extrapolation, taking "basic" enlightened awarenesses such as (a) what to reject and what adopt or (b) no-self, and assuming that to be "complete" these must be extended to all possible objects to be rejected and adopted or all possible objects to which a self might be attributed. Once they have been extended that far, all phenomena have been included, so omniscience is entailed. The crucial assumption is that "complete" knowledge is necessary; it might be argued by one skeptical about omniscience that it is only "essential" knowledge that is necessary (or possible). For further discussion, see R. Jackson (1987).

about liberation, such as the Mīmāṃsakas, say: "There is no liberation from saṃsāra, because the mind is naturally stained, so a person cannot transcend being subject to saṃsāra."

Just because one is subject to saṃsāra, it is NOT SO that it follows that one can prove that there is no liberation, BECAUSE WE ASSERT [liberation] regarding a different [kind of] person, and [because] the reason IS UNPROVEN. Alternatively, it follows that there does not exist a permanent person who is the basis of bondage and freedom, because we have replied to assertions regarding [the existence of] that person, and [shown that] the reason is unproven.[21]

Disposing of the consequence that it is impossible to strive for liberation [242]

(191c-192) AS LONG AS ONE HAS NOT DESTROYED ATTACHMENT TO SELF,
ONE WILL NOT ABIDE IN THE NATURE [OF LIBERATION];
JUST THAT LONG, HAVING SUPERIMPOSED [A] SUFFERING [SELF ON THE AGGREGATES],
ONE WILL BE UTTERLY TORMENTED.
ALTHOUGH THERE IS NO LIBERATED BEING,
THERE IS STRIVING SO AS TO DESTROY DISTORTED SUPERIMPOSITION.

---

21 The objection that a person cannot be liberated because they are a "saṃsāric subject" may be made by both believers and non-believers in liberation. A skeptic, such as a materialist or Mīmāṃsaka, will hold that liberation is impossible because beings are essentially saṃsāric, i.e., because their minds are inherently defiled. A believer in liberation, such as a Sāṃkhya, will hold that liberation is impossible without a "self" or "person" to be bound or liberated, and that if aggregates such as those described by the Buddhists are considered to be bound, it is inconceivable that they ever be freed—what *will* be freed, then, is a principle transcendent to the aggregates. Dharmakīrti does not refute the skeptic here, though he will attempt to do so below (PV 208ff.), when he argues that the mind is, in fact, intrinsically free of defilement. The Sāṃkhya is refuted by the observation that the Buddhist is describing an *impermanent* self (that is equivalent to the aggregates), and that while it may be certain that a *permanent* self described as bound never could be freed, there is no such certainty in the case of an impermanent self. Furthermore, of course, there can be no permanent self that is the basis of bondage and freedom, because the existence of such a self cannot be proven. Incidentally, Nagatomi ([1957] 187-88), following Prajñākaragupta, takes the Buddhist reply to be that the objection is irrelevant because the Buddhist does not assert that there ultimately exists anyone who is bound or liberated.

[OPPONENT:] If there is no self that first is bound in saṃsāra and [later] is freed, then it is pointless to exert oneself on the path to liberation.

[RGYAL TSHAB RJE:] An ordinary being, AS LONG AS THEY HAVE NOT in the least DESTROYED THEIR ATTACHMENT TO SELF, WILL NOT ABIDE happily IN THE NATURE of a liberated mindstream, because JUST THAT LONG, HAVING SUPERIMPOSED [on their aggregates] a SUFFERING self, WILL THEY BE UTTERLY TORMENTED by suffering. SINCE THERE IS NO self that is the LIBERATED BEING, THERE definitely IS a purpose in STRIVING on the path to liberation, BECAUSE, since there is no [self], it is necessary TO DESTROY THE DISTORTED SUPERIMPOSITION of a self.[22]

Disposing of the consequence that once liberation is attained, it is impossible to abide in [saṃsāric] existence for even a moment [243]

(193) ONE WHO IS FREE FROM ATTACHMENT REMAINS
THROUGH COMPASSION, OR, ALTERNATIVELY, [BECAUSE OF] PROJECTION
BY KARMA, BECAUSE THEY DO NOT DESIRE TO TURN AWAY [FROM SAṂSĀRA].
ONE WHO IS BEYOND CRAVING FOR EXISTENCE
(194) CANNOT BE PROJECTED INTO ANOTHER [LIFE] BY KARMA,
BECAUSE THE COOPERATIVE CONDITION HAS BEEN DESTROYED.

[OPPONENT:] If there is no self of persons, then an arhant will not remain in saṃsāra for even a moment, because they have realized no-self, and [thus] have no hope for the happiness of the self.

[RGYAL TSHAB RJE:] An arhant WHO IS FREE FROM ATTACHMENT to the three realms has the cause for REMAINING a little while in [saṃsāric] existence, BECAUSE they are under the power of COMPASSION that has sentient beings as its intentional objects; OR, ALTERNATIVELY, because the body PROJECTED BY previous KARMA has not completed the remainder of its life-span, BECAUSE it abides [when the arhant] DOes NOT DESIRE im-

---

22 The opponent argues that if there is no self that first is bound and later freed, there is no point in striving for liberation, since "no one" is freed. The reply is that it is precisely the belief in a (permanent) self that prevents liberation (of the impermanent self), for our instinctive belief in a self is the basis of saṃsāric suffering, while it is precisely the recognition that there is no permanent self independent of the aggregates that permits those aggregates, i.e., a person, to attain liberation. Alternatively, the Buddhist might argue, as Nāgārjuna does (MMK xxiv:20), that it is precisely because there is no permanent self that liberation is possible, and that if there did exist a permanent self that was "bound," it never could change, and therefore never could be liberated.

mediately TO TURN AWAY [from saṃsāra], and sees some purpose [in remaining].[23]

[OPPONENT:] Well, then, since the arhant is under the power of karma, that karma will project them into a subsequent [saṃsāric] existence.

[RGYAL TSHAB RJE:] An arhant WHO IS BEYOND CRAVING FOR EXISTENCE CANNOT BE PROJECTED INTO ANOTHER [saṃsāric] existence BY the KARMA in their mindstream, BECAUSE THE COOPERATIVE CONDITION of that [subsequent existence], craving, HAS BEEN DESTROYED.[24]

The aspect of peace [244]

[This is divided into:] (1) Disposing of the consequence that a detached one does not eliminate faults [245], (2) Disposing of the consequence that they are not freed from [saṃsāric] existence [246] and (3) Disposing of [alleged] extreme consequences in regard to self-grasping's being the cause of [saṃsāric] existence [247].

Disposing of the consequence that a detached one does not eliminate faults [245]

(194c-195) [AN ARHANT'S] COMPASSION IS NOT CONNECTED WITH [A WRONG VIEW TOWARD]
SENTIENT BEINGS, BECAUSE THERE IS NO CONTRADICTION IN THEIR KNOWING
SUFFERING, AND [BECAUSE] THEY HAVE ARISING A DHARMA-ENTITY
THAT FOLLOWS ON A PREVIOUS MENTAL FORMATION.
ATTACHMENT [ARISES] FROM [ATTRIBUTING SELF TO] DHARMAS THAT DO NOT HAVE
SELF, AND THE SUPERIMPOSITION OF A SELF OTHER [THAN THE AGGREGATES].

---

23 There are two possible reasons why a being who has eliminated all faults through an application of the wisdom realizing no-self may continue to exist in saṃsāra: (1) because the life-span karmically allotted to their body has not been exhausted and/or (2) because—even though they could leave the body—they choose not to, because they are compassionate, and see that there is some purpose conducive to the aims of others to be served by their remaining embodied.

24 Cf. above, PV 190a-b. An arhant who remains embodied is simply finishing out the terms of the karma that projected that body. They have eliminated ignorance, and therefore craving, and since they lack craving, they no longer have the cooperative condition necessary for the ripening of karma into a future rebirth. Therefore, they will not take rebirth, and cannot really be described as "under the power of karma," although in a technical sense they still have karma "remaining."

(196-197b) COMPASSION WILL ARISE
JUST FROM THE COGNITION OF THE CONTINUUM OF SUFFERING.
THERE IS NO ANGER BECAUSE OF ANY FAULT, FOR [THE ARHANT] IS WITHOUT THAT.
IGNORANCE IS THE ROOT OF FAULTS,
AND ALSO ENTAILS GRASPING AT SENTIENT BEINGS;
WE ASSERT THAT COMPASSION IS FAULTLESS.

[Disposing of] the consequence that they have not abandoned the self-view:

[OPPONENT:] It follows that an arhant has not abandoned the self-view, because they have a view toward sentient beings. If they did not, it would be contradictory that they be compassionate.

[RGYAL TSHAB RJE:] The COMPASSION of an arhant IS NOT CONNECTED WITH the view that there are independently [existing] SENTIENT BEINGS, BECAUSE THERE IS NO CONTRADICTION IN THEIR KNOWING by perception that sentient beings are tormented by SUFFERING, AND [because] THEY HAVE ARISING A DHARMA-ENTITY THAT FOLLOWS ON A PREVIOUS MENTAL FORMATION that represents the accustomation of equanimity.

An alternative reason for the foregoing thesis: [The compassion of an arhant is not connected with the view that there are independently existing sentient beings,] BECAUSE THEY directly KNOW the impermanence, etc., of SUFFERING AND HAVE ARISING A DHARMA-ENTITY THAT FOLLOWS ON A PREVIOUS MENTAL FORMATION that [represents] the accustomation in their mindstream of [compassion] THAT LACKS ITS own CONTRADICTORY [condition], anger.

In brief, the meaning of the verse is that since [an arhant] has abandoned all grasping at a self of persons, they see that what is imputed as a sentient being is merely the qualities [referred to as the aggregates], and compassion arises.[25]

---

25 The opponent maintains that if an arhant is held to be compassionate, then they must have objects of their compassion, and that they must therefore have "selves" as their objects of compassion. In fact, however, it is not necessary to believe in a permanent, independent self in order to have compassion for the suffering of those collections of aggregates that are conventional "selves." Indeed, it is precisely the recognition that the sufferings of various collections of aggregates are based on the belief that there is a self where there is not, that impels the arhant or bodhisattva to generate compassion, based on previously accustomated equanimity or compassion.

Disposing of the consequence that they are attached:

[OPPONENT:] It follows that they are attached, because they strive for the sake of sentient beings.

[RGYAL TSHAB RJE:] It follows that compassion and attachment do not at all have the same causes and aspects, etc., because ATTACHMENT arises [FROM] holding as [pure, pleasurable, etc.,] those DHARMAS THAT DO NOT HAVE the SELF-nature of purity, pleasure, etc., AND from THE SUPERIMPOSITION OF A present SELF existing as something OTHER than [the aggregates]; and COMPASSION WILL ARISE JUST FROM THE COGNITION OF THE CONTINUUM OF the SUFFERING aggregates, those formations devoid of a self.[26]

Disposing of the consequence that a detached one has anger:

[OPPONENT:] [An arhant] must have anger, because when others harm the objects of their benevolence, anger will arise.

[RGYAL TSHAB RJE:] For an arhant THERE IS NO ANGER arising BECAUSE OF ANY FAULT, because THEY DO NOT in the slightest HAVE THAT self-grasping. It follows that this [reason] pervades, because IGNORANCE IS THE ROOT OF the FAULTS of attachment, [anger,] etc., AND [ignorance] ALSO ENTAILS GRASPING AT a self of persons in SENTIENT BEINGS. It is reasonable [when WE] ASSERT THAT the COMPASSION in [the arhant's] mindstream IS FAULTLESS, because they have removed all defilements.[27]

---

26 Maintaining the same line of attack, the opponent claims that an arhant must be "attached" to sentient beings because they *desire* their welfare. rGyal tshab rje points out that an arhant's "desire" for the welfare of sentient beings is not a desire like that rooted in self-grasping (since an arhant has abandoned self-grasping), but one rooted in a recognition of and response to the suffering of other beings. Indeed, precisely because they have abandoned self-grasping, arhants are able more easily and spontaneously to sympathize with others, for there are no "personal" considerations to interfere.

27 Nor can an arhant grow "angry" in the usual sense of the word, since the basis of anger is self-grasping, and they have abandoned self-grasping. If they display "anger," or "upset," it is either as a result of empathy or, more often in the case of a bodhisattva, out of a compassionate application of skill-in-means. Skill-in-means is applied when a bodhisattva recognizes that a display of "anger" will be beneficial for a given being in a given situation, as, for instance, when a parent displays anger toward a child to emphasize the dangers of touching an electric socket into which the child is about to insert a finger.

Disposing of the consequence that they are not freed from [saṃsāric] existence [246]

(197c) IT IS NOT THE CASE THAT THEY ARE NOT FREED, BECAUSE, SINCE THEY HAVE ELIMINATED
PREVIOUS FORMATIONS, THERE WILL BE NO CONNECTION TO ANOTHER [LIFE].
(198) ALTHOUGH THEY HAVE NOT ELIMINATED WHAT IS BROUGHT ABOUT BY THE FORMATIONS,
THEY ARE WITHOUT ANY FAULT REMAINING.
[ŚRĀVAKAS, ETC.,] DO NOT MAKE A GREAT EFFORT TO REMAIN [IN SAṂSĀRA],
BECAUSE THEIR COMPASSION IS SMALL.
(199) [BODHISATTVAS] WILL DWELL THERE FOR THE SAKE OF OTHERS
[BECAUSE] THEY ARE ONES WHO HAVE GREAT COMPASSION.

[OPPONENT:] Since the arhant's body, projected by karma, is [included in] the truth of suffering, [an arhant] is not free from suffering.

[RGYAL TSHAB RJE:] IT IS NOT THE CASE THAT [an arhant] IS NOT FREED from [saṃsāric] existence, BECAUSE, SINCE THEY HAVE ELIMINATED the results of PREVIOUS karmic FORMATIONS through utterly destroying the defilements, THERE WILL BE NO CONNECTION TO ANOTHER [saṃsāric] existence. ALTHOUGH THEY HAVE NOT ELIMINATED this remaining aggregate BROUGHT ABOUT BY previous karmic FORMATIONS, it is not the case that THEY are not free from [saṃsāric] existence, because theirs IS an abandonment WITHOUT even the slightest FAULT of defilement presently REMAINING.

Alternatively, as long as the buddhas abide in [saṃsāric] existence, they are not covered by faults, as a lotus [is not covered with] mud, because the complete power of the two stores has not been exhausted, and will not be.[28]

---

28 Whether or not one is subject to saṃsāric suffering is determined ultimately by whether or not one has abandoned self-grasping. If one has, then one no longer will create karma conducive to further suffering, nor need one experience the results of past karma that has not yet ripened. One's present body is an instance of karma that has already ripened, so it cannot be reversed. Thus, while an arhant's body, as the result of past defiled karma, is included in the truth of suffering, "they"no longer suffer in saṃsāra, because their mind is utterly free of the defilements that are the force behind saṃsāra's perpetuation. From the Mahāyāna point of view, a buddha's body is not included in the truth of suffering, because it is the result not of past karma but of their completion of the two stores, of merit and gnosis. As a result of the storage of gnosis, there

[OPPONENT:] If they remain in [saṃsāric] existence because of compassion, then since the continuum [of compassion] is not cut, they will remain [in saṃsāra] forever.

[RGYAL TSHAB RJE:] Śrāvakas, pratyekabuddhas and arhants, even if they remain in [saṃsāric] existence for a little while, DO NOT MAKE A GREAT EFFORT TO REMAIN indefinitely, BECAUSE even though they accustomate COMPASSION, their accustomation [of it] IS SMALL. THOSE bodhisattvas who dwell on the great stages WILL DWELL THERE for the duration of the existence [of saṃsāra] FOR the sake of OTHERS, because THEY ARE ONES WHO HAVE accustomated GREAT COMPASSION continually and have increased it infinitely.[29]

Disposing of [alleged] extreme consequences in regard to self-grasping's being the cause of [saṃsāric] existence [247]

(199c) IF [YOU SAY THAT] WHEN ONE FIRST [REACHES] THE PATH [OF SEEING], ONE SHOULD HAVE NO [FURTHER] EXISTENCE,
BECAUSE ONE IS SEPARATED FROM THE VIEW OF [SELF IN] THE PERISHABLE,

---

arises a buddha's Dharma Body, and as a result of the storage of merit, there arises the Form Body, consisting of the Enjoyment and Transformation Bodies. The body in which the Buddha appeared on earth in the sixth century B.C.E., underwent his career and preached the Dharma, was an instance of the Transformation Body, its impurity only apparent. In fact, as a result of the storage of all possible merit, it was utterly pure, "unclothed" or uncovered by faults any more than a lotus is covered by the mud out of which it has risen.

29 The opponent's contention, that because of their unending compassion enlightened beings will remain in saṃsāra forever, is wrong in some cases and misleading in others. It is wrong where śrāvaka and pratyekabuddha arhants are concerned, because their compassion is not sufficient to insure that they feel compelled to remain in existence for long. Bodhisattvas on the "great stages" (the eighth, ninth and tenth *bhūmis*), who have abandoned all defilements, but not all subtle stains of the defilements, have compassion sufficiently strong to "compel" them to remain in saṃsāra until that elusive day when it is utterly emptied. To say that they are "in saṃsāra" is misleading, however, for as āryas they are able to take rebirth at will and by choice, and their physical involvement with saṃsāra does not in the least affect their minds, which are free of self-grasping and therefore of all defilements. They are, then "in saṃsāra," but not "of it." Note, incidentally, that rGyal tshab rje has supplied a clear distinction between Hīnayāna and Mahāyāna practitioners that is not stated in Dharmakīrti's verse.

(200) [WE REPLY: NOT SO,] BECAUSE ONE HAS NOT ABANDONED THE INNATE [VIEW];
IF ONE *HAS* ABANDONED [THE INNATE VIEW], WHERE IN EXISTENCE WILL ONE BE [BORN]?
WHEN ONE DESIRES, SAYING, "MAY I BE HAPPY,"
OR "MAY I NOT SUFFER,"
(201-202b) ANY THOUGHT WITH THE CONCEPTION OF "I"
IS THE INNATE VIEW OF [SELF IN] SENTIENT BEINGS.
ANYONE WITHOUT ATTACHMENT TO SELF
DOES NOT SEE AN "I", [AND]
WILL NOT RUN [TOWARD REBIRTH] THROUGH DESIRE FOR HAPPINESS,
[SINCE] THERE IS NO CRAVING FOR SELF.

[OPPONENT:] If the view of [self in] the perishable composites[30] is the root of saṃsāra, then it follows that AS SOON AS a streamwinner FIRST arises ON THE PATH of seeing, THEY SHOULD HAVE NO connection to a subsequent [saṃsāric] EXISTENCE, BECAUSE THEY ARE SEPARATED, without there being a remainder, FROM THE VIEW OF [SELF IN] THE PERISHABLE composites.

[RGYAL TSHAB RJE:] This is an objection by those who do not assert [the existence of] an innate view of [self in] the perishable. It follows that it is not the case that a streamwinner does not obtain a subsequent [saṃsāric] existence by reason of their utterly having abandoned the view of [self in] the perishable, BECAUSE THEY HAVE NOT utterly ABANDONED THE INNATE view of [self in] the perishable.[31]

---

30 Here, and in what follows, I translate according to the Tibetan term, *'jigs tshogs lta ba*, literally, the "view of [or toward] the perishable,"the "perishable"connoting composites in general and the aggregates in particular. The sense, then, is that one has the view that there exists, in such perishable composites as the aggregates, a permanent self, hence: "view of [self in] the perishable."The Sanskrit term, *satkāśyadṛṣṭi*, means literally "view of a true body"; the implication is: "belief in a truly, or permanently existing body of aggregates,"i.e., again, belief in a self in the aggregates. For a discussion of the term, see, e.g., Collins (1982) 93-94. Collins translates it as "Personality Belief."

31 The opponent's contention, that one who has attained the path of seeing and become a streamwinner should immediately leave saṃsāra because they have abandoned the view of self in perishable composites, or aggregates, fails to distinguish the conceptual belief in a self from the innate belief in a self. It is true that a streamwinner on the path of seeing has overcome the conceptual or philosophical belief in a self, but they have not yet overcome the innate belief in a self, and until that innate belief is uprooted, they cannot be free from saṃsāra—into which they will be reborn at most seven times.

If you say that the reason is unproven, and that [the streamwinner] HAS utterly ABANDONED [even the innate view of self in the perishable], then WHERE, it follows, IN [saṃsāric] EXISTENCE WILL THEY BE born? It follows [that they would be born nowhere]. Alternatively, it follows that a streamwinner [who has reached the path of] seeing and [will attain final] peace [in this lifetime] will not be born anywhere in [saṃsāric] existence, because an ārya, having utterly abandoned the view of [self in] the perishable at the time of the path of seeing, will actualize nirvāṇa in this lifetime.[32]

[OPPONENT:] There is [in such a streamwinner] no [more] defiled ignorance that is the cause of [saṃsāric] existence, but that view of [self in] the perishable is not the cause of [saṃsāric] existence. Since a conceptual [view] alone arises from the teachings of another, it is impossible that one be born into [a further saṃsāric] existence without one's mind being changed by a system of tenets.[33]

[RGYAL TSHAB RJE:] It is not the case that there is no innate view of [self in] the perishable, because WHEN ONE DESIRES objects, SAYING, "MAY I BE HAPPY," or "MAY I NOT SUFFER," [that "I"] is imputed without regard to systems of tenets; and ANY THOUGHT that grasps at the CONCEPTION OF AN independent "I" without merely imputing on the aggregates, IS THE INNATE VIEW OF a self in SENTIENT BEINGS.[34] The assertion that the view of [self in] the perishable and grasping at a self of persons are merely the thought that there is an "I" in sentient be-

---

32 If the opponent counters with the assertion that a streamwinner abandons even the *innate* belief in a self, then that streamwinner must be one of the highest type, who by virtue of their attainments on the path of seeing will attain final peace in this very lifetime. However, they will not attain nirvāṇa directly from the path of seeing, for, like all āryas, they must pass through the path of development before attaining the path of no-more-training. It is likely that because of their mental acuity they will traverse the path of development in the shortest possible time.

33 The opponent, possibly a Vaibhāṣika, argues that it is not the innate belief in a self that is the basis of saṃsāra, but the philosophical belief, derived from adhering to a system of tenets (*grub mtha', siddhānta*), and that one will not gain release from saṃsāra as long as one has not specifically changed one's philosophical views.

34 It certainly is the case that there is a belief in self that is philosophically based, but it is not the case that there is no belief in self *not* based on systems of tenets, because all beings instinctively wish to attain happiness and avoid suffering for them*selves*, thereby displaying an instinctive, untutored belief in a self that exists as more than just an imputation on their aggregates. It is this innate belief in a self that is, in fact, the basis of saṃsāra.

ings, is only the wrong idea that is skeptical regarding karma and its result, because an arhant who has utterly abandoned the view of [self in] the perishable has the thought conceiving "I" when they say "my begging bowl" or "my teaching cloak." Since it is not the case [that an arhant grasps at an "I"], it is impossible [even] when an arhant's begging bowl and teaching cloak are stolen, that they should become dejected. That is not all; the authors of the *Vinaya Piṭaka* and its commentaries cut off all doubt: when the wealth of the teacher was stolen after he had shown the way to nirvāṇa, it is impossible that he was the least bit dejected. Since he said "I" and "mine" before showing the way to nirvāṇa, doubt in this matter can be cut off. I will leave this [matter] for the time being.[35]

Thus, the view of [self in] the perishable is a grasping at an independent "I" that is not [merely] imputed on some continuum of composite aggregates. Induced by the power of that are two [types of] grasping: grasping at an independent "I" and grasping at a "mine" to be controlled by that. The [sources of that are] two: conceptually imputed [grasping derived from] systems of tenets and the innate [grasping] that arises without regard to [systems of tenets].[36]

Without that being the case, if the view of [self in] the perishable is merely the holding of the conception of "I," then it follows that merely holding [the conception of] a person is grasping at a self of persons. If that is asserted, then since thinking "that person is Devadatta" or "[that person] is Yajan" is grasping at a self of persons, that person [so named] will be the self of persons. If that is asserted, it follows that the aggregates are impossible, because a [permanent] person is impossible.[37]

---

35 While ordinary beings' wish for happiness for them*selves* is indicative of the presence of an innate belief in an independent self, the mere use of the word "I" does not prove that the person using the word believes in a self of persons, since the word is used as a conventional designation of their aggregates by arhants and buddhas, whose behavior otherwise reveals them to be utterly free of any self-grasping.

36 Since liberated beings use the word "I" as a designation of their own aggregates, yet are not suffering in saṃsāra, the belief in a self that is the basis of saṃsāra must be something other than just a designation of the aggregates. In fact, the "I" belief in which is the basis of saṃsāra is an "I" independent of the aggregates, which entails belief in both an independent "I" and a "mine" that is controlled by that self. Such belief in "I" and "mine" can be either philosophical or innate—it is the innate belief that is the actual basis of saṃsāra, for, although abandoning the philosophical belief in a self is a necessary condition for freedom, it is not a sufficient condition.

37 If belief in a self, or the view of [self in] the perishable, is simply the designa-

If there is some flaw in holding the thought of "I," then it follows that there is some flaw in thinking "I give charity" or "I guard morality." Thus, if it is proven that the grasping at a self of persons is the mistaken cognition of a desired object, then the mere holding of "I" will be [mistaken], too. Thinking that if one accepts a mere "I" one must necessarily accept a self of persons, one's mind will be well disposed toward the system that accepts a permanent self.[38] Objectifying another person, one has the desire to prove that it is independent, not just an imputation on the aggregates—that is grasping at a self of persons, but not the view of [self in] the perishable.[39]

It follows that ANY streamwinner IS WITHOUT ATTACHMENT TO SELF, because they DO NOT SEE AN "I" as independent. If that is asserted, it follows that THEY WILL NOT RUN toward a subsequent [saṃsāric] existence THROUGH DESIRE FOR HAPPINESS, because THERE IS NO CRAVING FOR [the happiness of] THE SELF.[40]

---

tion "I" or "him," then the aggregates so designated would be the self of persons. Since a self of persons is a philosophically incoherent concept, so too would the concept of aggregates be; thus, the aggregates would be an impossibility in the same way that a self of persons is.

38 Again, if merely designating the aggregates as "I" is tantamount to holding a self of persons, then saying "I give charity" or "I guard morality" (or even "I realize no-self"!) will involve belief in a self of persons, and thus will only serve to perpetuate one's suffering. Such close identification between the conventional designation "I" and the self of persons, rGyal tshab rje claims, shows that one is actually well disposed toward belief in a permanent self, since any instance of the word "I" will entail such a belief.

39 Finally, it must be noted that grasping at a self of persons is a broader category than the view of [self in] the perishable, for self-grasping involves belief in the existence of an independent self not only in ourselves but in others, too, while the view of [self in] the perishable involves the belief in "I" and "mine" only in relation to oneself. Grasping at a self of others presupposes the view of [self in] the perishable, but it is not that view.

40 Thus, at whatever point a streamwinner has eliminated the innate view that there is a self in but independent of the aggregates, they will abandon the craving for existence—since they no longer deludedly seek the happiness of a phantom "I." When they have abandoned the craving for existence, they no longer will have the cooperative condition for future rebirth. The foregoing discussion of the relations among grasping at a self of persons, the view of [self in] the perishable, and the mere designation of the aggregates as "I" may be indicated diagrammatically:

The aspect of sublimity [248]

(202c) BONDAGE IS THE CAUSE OF THE ARISING
OF SUFFERING; HOW COULD A PERMANENT [ENTITY BE BOUND]?
(203) LIBERATION IS THE CAUSE OF THE NON-ARISING
OF SUFFERING; HOW COULD A PERMANENT [ENTITY BE LIBERATED]?
WHATEVER IS NOT THE CAUSE OF ANY [RESULT]
HAS NOT BEEN EXPRESSED AS IMPERMANENT.
(204) IT ALSO DOES NOT EXIST IN SUCH A WAY
AS TO BE BOUND OR FREED, [SINCE] IT IS NOT EXPRESSIBLE [AS PERMANENT OR IMPERMANENT].
THE WISE CALL "PERMANENT"
THAT WHOSE NATURE IS INDESTRUCTIBLE.
(205) THUS, YOU SHOULD ABANDON THIS SHAMEFUL
VIEW, AND CALL THAT [PERSON] "PERMANENT."

[OPPONENT:] If a self exists, then when one has been freed from prior bondage, one obtains a particular satisfaction of the self, so that liberation is sublime. Since it is impossible that there be such if no-self is the case, there exists a permanent person who is the basis of bondage and freedom.

[RGYAL TSHAB RJE:] The defilements are what effect BONDAGE in [saṃsāric] existence, because they are THE CAUSE OF THE ARISING OF their own result, the SUFFERING of further [saṃsāric] existence. HOW COULD A PERMANENT [entity] be a binder or bound? It follows that it is

---

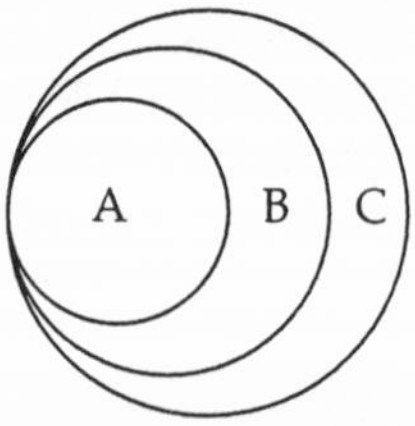

A= those with the view of [self in] the perishable composites. This view holds that independent of the aggregates there exists an independent "I" and a "mine" that is controlled by it. It may be either conceptual or instinctive, with the latter being more fundamental.

B= those who grasp at a self of persons in regard to both themselves and others. B in regard to others is not A, but presupposes it, and no one with B in regard to others lacks A.

C= those who designate the aggregates as "I." Some of C (ordinary persons) grasp at a self of persons, others (āryas) do not.

unacceptable that it could be, because it is unsuitable to be a cause. The wisdom directly realizing no-self is what effects LIBERATION from [saṃsāric] existence, because it IS THE supreme method that is the very CONDITION[41] FOR THE NON-ARISING OF the SUFFERING of further [saṃsāric] existence. HOW COULD A PERMANENT [entity] be a liberator or what is liberated? It follows that it is unacceptable that it could be, because it is unsuitable to be a result.[42]

[VĀTSĪPUTRĪYA OPPONENT:][43] *We* are not at fault, since we assert that the person is not expressed as either permanent or impermanent.

[RGYAL TSHAB RJE:] It follows that [WHATEVER] person [you assert] IS NOT THE CAUSE OF ANY result, because it HAS NOT BEEN EXPRESSED AS IMPERMANENT. IT ALSO follows that it DOES NOT EXIST IN SUCH A WAY THAT IT IS BOUND OR FREED, because IT IS NOT EXPRESSIBLE as either permanent or impermanent. It follows that it is permanent, because it is the basis of bondage and freedom, and is indestructible. It follows that [this reason] pervades, because THE WISE CALL "PERMANENT" THAT dharma WHOSE own NATURE IS INDESTRUCTIBLE. Having shown that it is acceptable that something lacking destructibility is permanent, this [reasoning] also well refutes the assertion that if something is permanent it must necessarily be a functioning entity and that a non-existent [entity] is permanent.[44]

---

41 The root-text (PV 203a) has *rgyu*, which is *hetu*, "cause."rGyal tshab rje glosses this as *rgyu mtshan, nimitta*, "condition."

42 The opponent argues that if there is no self, then bondage and freedom become meaningless, because there is no one who is bound and then freePd. The reply, of course, is that only a permanent, independent person is denied, not a collection of impermanent aggregates in which defiled states of mind can induce suffering and the wisdom realizing no-self can induce liberation. Indeed, it is only on the basis of impermanent aggregates that bondage and freedom can be meaningfully explained, since a permanent self can be neither cause nor result, and therefore neither binder and freer nor bound and freed.

43 dGe 'dun grub identifies the opponent as a Saṃmitīya. Both Vātsīputrīyas and Saṃmitīyas are upholders of the quasi-heretical view known as "Personalism" (*pudgalavāda*). The earliest sources consider the Vātsīputrīyas to be the original personalist spin-off from the Sthavīras, and the Saṃmitīyas to be a subsequent spin-off from the Vātsīputrīyas. See Bareau (1955) 16ff. and chapters XV and XVI; and Dutt (1970) 197ff.

44 The Personalist claims that the "person" is neither permanent nor impermanent. This assertion, however, involves the assertion that the person is *not impermanent*. If the person is not impermanent, then it cannot be either a cause or a result, so it cannot partake of the processes involved in bondage and free-

It follows, [THUS,] that the Vātsīputrīya SHOULD ABANDON THIS SHAMEFUL VIEW that accepts a third possibility where only [mutually exclusive] direct opposition is possible, AND CALL THAT person "PERMANENT"; it is reasonable that they so call it, because by [their reasoning] it is an indestructible entity.[45]

Alternatively, that [discussion of the truth of cessation] can be applied only to covering the aspect of cessation, without being divided individually into the two remaining aspects.[46]

---

dom. Furthermore, since it is asserted to be indestructible, the person must, in fact, be permanent, since indestructibility is synonymous with permanence, and the meaning conveyed by one's words is more important than the words themselves in determining one's actual philosophical assertion. Previous analyses have already determined that a permanent entity cannot be a functioning, or causally efficient entity, so the "person"described by the Personalist cannot have any relevance to bondage or freedom.

45 Two entities are directly opposed, or mutually exclusive and exhaustive (*dngos 'gal*) when one is the contradictory of the other and the assertion of both covers all phenomena. Permanent and impermanent are *dngos 'gal* because nothing that is permanent is impermanent, and vice versa, and an entity must be either permanent or impermanent. The Personalist fails to appreciate the logical relation between permanence and impermanence, and so illegitimately attempts to maintain that there can be an entity that pertains to neither, when, in fact, there is *nothing* that is not one or the other.

46 rGyal tshab rje has already noted (at the very outset of the chapter) that Dharmakīrti's discussion of the truth of cessation at most covers the first three aspects of that truth. Here, he notes that it also is possible to view the discussion as covering only a single aspect, that of cessation. This is Devendrabuddhi's view.

10. *The Truth of Path (1)*

A. A REFUTATION OF SKEPTICISM: THE NATURAL PURITY OF MIND

The truth of path [249]

[This is divided into:] (1) Proving that the wisdom realizing no-self is the path to freedom from [saṃsāric] existence [250] and (2) Proving that self-grasping is the root of craving [267].

Proving that the wisdom realizing no-self is the path to freedom from [saṃsāric] existence [250]

[This is divided into:] (1) Identifying the path to freedom [251] and (2) Disposing of objections to that [252].

Identifying the path to freedom [251]

(205c-d) THE PATH ALREADY EXPLAINED [IS THE PATH, SINCE] THROUGH ACCUSTOMATING IT,
[ONE ATTAINS] A TRANSFORMED STATE....

THE PATH ALREADY EXPLAINED BEFORE, which is the direct realization of no-self, is the path to freedom from [saṃsāric] existence, because THROUGH ACCUSTOMATING IT as the direct antidote to self-grasping, one eliminates all faults and attains a completely TRANSFORMED STATE.[1]

---

1 A "completely transformed state" or "fundamental transformation," or "reversion in the basis" (*gnas 'gyur, āśrayaparāvṛtti*) is that change (*parāvṛtti*) that occurs in the mental "basis" (*āśraya*)—often identified as the storehouse consciousness (*ālaya vijñāna*)—when one directly realizes the nature of reality. The concept is central to the *Laṅkāvatāra Sūtra* and much subsequent Yogācāra soteriology. It is one of the few passages in the *Pramāṇasiddhi* chapter that hints at Dharmakīrti's Yogācāra affiliation, and is one of the few references anywhere in his work to an explicitly Mahāyāna soteriology. As we saw in section I:9, Dharmakīrti generally is considered by Tibetan scholiasts to be a Cittamātrin Following Reasoning, hence not to accept an *ālaya vijñāna;* this

Disposing of objections to that [252]

[This is divided into:] (1) Disposing of the objection that abandonments are reversible [253], (2) Disposing of the objection that stains are unsuitable to be removed [265] and (3) Disposing of the objection that even if they can be removed a little, it is impossible that they be thoroughly removed [266].

Disposing of the objection that abandonments are reversible [253]

[This is divided into:] (1) The impossibility of a complete abandonment's being reversed [254], (2) The impossibility of there being a method of reversing [a complete abandonment] [260] and (3) Disposing of [the idea that] the wisdom realizing no-self is unacceptable as an antidote to self-grasping [261].

The impossibility of a complete abandonment's being reversed [254]

[This is divided into:] (1) The impossibility of generating faults in a mind in a transformed state [255] and (2) Even if there is [a fault], the impossibility of its remaining long [259].

The impossibility of generating faults in a mind in a transformed state [255]

[This is divided into:] (1) A brief demonstration [256], (2) An extensive explanation [257] and (3) Summary [258].

A brief demonstration [256]

(205d-206b) IF YOU SAY: "EVEN IF ONE TRANSFORMS
ONE'S STATE, JUST AS A PATH [ORIGINATES, SO] FLAWS WILL ORIGINATE [AGAIN],"
[WE REPLY:] NOT SO, BECAUSE THE CAPACITY [FOR GENERATING FAULTS] IS NON-EXISTENT [IN SUCH A STATE].

[OPPONENT:] EVEN IF for a short time ONE TRANSFORMS ONE'S STATE so that faults are non-existent, still, JUST AS an unprecedented

---

passage could be taken as evidence that he did accept the notion if and only if the *āśraya* referred to is the *ālaya*—and of this there is no clear evidence. rGyal tshab rje (who, as a Mādhyamika, does not accept an *ālaya vijñāna*) glosses the "fundamental transformation" as the change that occurs when one reaches the path of seeing, realizes no-self directly, becomes an ārya, and begins to uproot defilements that previously one only had been able to suppress.

PATH originates newly, so attachment and other FLAWS WILL ORIGINATE again.

[RGYAL TSHAB RJE:] This is the objection that it is unacceptable that [the truths of] cessation and path [have, respectively, the aspects of] definitive emergence and definitive removal. A mind that is in a completely transformed state will NOT have faults originate again in it, BECAUSE in it the wisdom realizing no-self renders THE CAPACITY for generating faults NON-EXISTENT.[2]

An extensive explanation [257]

(206c) COGNITION APPREHENDS [AN OBJECT] JUST AS IT EXISTS;
APPREHENDING AN OBJECT IS THE DHARMA OF [COGNITION], AND
(207) [FORM] ALSO IS THE GENERATOR
[OF] THAT [COGNITION] THAT HAS [AS AN OBJECT AN OBJECT THAT HAS] THE SELF-NATURE OF [ACTUALLY] EXISTING:
THE NATURE [OF FORM] IS [LIKE] THIS. [BEINGS] ARE DIVERTED
FROM THIS [CORRECT COGNITION] BY OTHER CONDITIONS.
(208) ABSENCE [OF FAULTS] DEPENDS ON CONDITIONS;
[WHEN THE CONDITIONS ARE PRESENT, FAULTS] WILL BE BASELESS, LIKE THE MIND [THAT SEES A ROPE AS] A SNAKE.

Demonstrating the natural purity of mind:

The sensory COGNITION that apprehends form has a nature such that it APPREHENDS the actuality of THAT form JUST as the object EXISTS, because APPREHENDING the actuality of AN OBJECT just as it exists IS THE DHARMA, or nature, OF [cognition]; AND, similarly, form ALSO has a nature such that it IS THE GENERATOR OF this cognition that apprehends just as it exists the nature of THAT object THAT HAS THE SELF-NATURE OF EXISTING in actuality, because THE NATURE possessed by form IS like THAT.[3]

---

2 The opponent attempts to argue that if the path, i.e., the wisdom realizing no-self, can arise where there never was occasion for it to arise before, then defilements ought to be able to arise in a transformed mind, because that transformation is only temporary, and the conditions preventing the arising of defilements will not, thus, always obtain. The Buddhist reply is that the mental transformation signalled by the attainment of a direct realization of no-self is *not* temporary, but everlasting, and that in such a mind the conditions conducive to defilement never will arise again, because the opposing condition to the self-grasping at the root of defilement, namely, wisdom, will continually be present. Cf. above, sections III:9:A-B.

3 This epistemological observation is tremendously important for Buddhist

[OPPONENT:] It is taught that stains are adventitious; the actuality of objects is impermanence, no-self, etc. If that is seen from the beginning by an unmistaken mind, then one will be freed without effort.

[RGYAL TSHAB RJE:] It follows that there is not the problematic consequence that sentient beings are freed without effort, because THEY ARE DIVERTED FROM THIS actuality BY OTHER CONDITIONS, such as self-grasping.[4]

[OPPONENT:] Since stains arise through sudden conditions, they will return, like the heat of water [reboiled].

[RGYAL TSHAB RJE:] It is not the case that faults will return, because their ABSENCE necessarily DEPENDS UPON accustomation of the [contradictory] CONDITION, the wisdom realizing no-self. If one accustomates that, it is not the case that it will be unsuitable that [faults] be absent, because THEY WILL BE BASELESS, since they have self-grasping as their root. It is LIKE THE MIND [that sees] a rope as A SNAKE.[5]

---

soteriology, for if the ultimate nature of the mind is such that it cognizes phenomena as they actually are, one will be able to argue that any cognition of phenomena as they are *not* is not natural to the mind, and thus adventitious and capable of ultimate and complete correction. Thus, it can be said that "fundamentally,"the mind knows things as without self, or even that it knows all things, and thus is omniscient. This observation is closely correlated with the traditional Buddhist account of perception, in which the very first moment of cognition of an object is unmediated and pure, then subject to *a posteriori* conceptual construction. It is what might be called an "optimistic"epistemology, since it allows that direct cognition of ultimates *is* possible for beings. A "pessimistic"epistemology (e.g., that of Kant or Wittgenstein) would maintain that although the mind is capable of forming useful approximate representations of reality, its cognitions never are unmediated by conceptions, and thus not "pure."Indeed, a pure cognition would be regarded in such an epistemology as impossible, for it is the nature of cognizers to have a point of view and to be limited by the fact of being an organism. Such an epistemology is clearly somewhat materialistic in orientation, whereas Buddhist epistemology assumes the mind's ultimate independence of particular bodies. For further discussion of the issues raised in this section of PV, see R. Jackson (1990).

4 The opponent raises the understandable objection that if the mind's nature is the cognition of objects as they actually are, then we all should already be freed, since we all have minds. The reply is that the mind's fulfillment of its basic function is dependent on the presence of the correct conditions—or, better, the absence of the conditions that prevent it from fulfilling that function. The conditions that prevent the mind from fulfilling its natural function are the defilements, the most basic of which is self-grasping. As long as self-grasping is present, a being's cognitions will be colored by an attitude that flies in the face of reality, and thus those cognitions will not be "pure."

Summary [258]

(208c) THE NATURE OF MIND IS CLEAR LIGHT;
THE STAINS ARE ADVENTITIOUS.
(209) THERE IS, [IN ONE WHO] HAS BECOME THE NATURE [OF THE ANTIDOTE] NO CAPACITY FOR THOSE [FAULTS] LATER,
BECAUSE EVEN EARLIER THEY HAVE NO CAPACITY.

THE NATURE OF THE MIND IS CLEAR LIGHT, because however much it is covered by the darkness of self-grasping, etc., that [self-grasping, etc.,] does not partake of the nature of mind, and because mind has the nature of being perishable, etc.[6] The nature of mind is not an ob-

---

5 The opponent argues that if mental stains are adventitious, i.e., occasional, they must be capable of regeneration, just as the heating of water can be resumed when a stove has been cold for awhile. rGyal tshab rje replies that although stains are adventitious, their generation is not capricious: it depends on the presence of certain conditions, the most important of which is self-grasping. If self-grasping is absent, there can be neither defilements nor stains, just as, once water has been boiled away, it cannot be heated any more, because there is nothing to heat. Or, to use another stock image from Indian philosophy, the mind that realizes no-self and has been transformed is like that that understands that a rope at first thought a snake is in fact only a rope: once the initial false cognition has been replaced by a true one, the false cognition no longer will arise, since truth can replace falsity, but falsity cannot replace a truth that has become well established. It is, of course, the Buddhist view that truth in general and the realization of no-self in particular are such that they utterly uproot the falsehoods to which they are contrary. Just as Buddhist epistemology is "optimistic"regarding the nature of the mind, so the Buddhist theory of truth is "optimistic"in its conception of the soteriological value a realization of the truth may have. A more "pessimistic"view of truth might grant that even if there are fundamental truths the realization of which may greatly alter the way we approach the world, those realizations will not have the power utterly to eradicate all falsehoods, or perpetually to be present in one's mindstream. The disagreement between the optimistic and pessimistic views is derived in part from the differing kinds of evidence used to support each: pessimists rely on observations of "ordinary"psychological states, while optimists rely on observations gleaned from meditative states that are not commonly accessible, but which are, nevertheless, regarded by the optimist as more normative (if not ordinary) than other, more accessible states.

6 If the mind were not perishable, i.e., impermanent, then its delusions would be everlasting. Since it is impermanent, it need not in principle always be deluded, since the condition obtaining at one moment need not necessarily obtain at some future moment in which conditions have changed. It is, of course, conceivable that even though the mind is impermanent, every cognition will partake of delusion because delusion or self-grasping is intrinsic to the mind.

ject that is not *covered* by stains, but the darkness of self-grasping that has come over the mind does not partake of the nature of [mind]. If it did so partake, then the manner of grasping that grasps a self would be in accord with how the mind actually exists. If that were the case, there would be no no-self, and a self would exist.[7]

THE STAINS of attachment, etc., ARE ADVENTITIOUS, because they are [based upon] minds that partake of the inverse of the actual nature of mind. THERE IS, IN a mind THAT HAS BECOME THE NATURE of the antidote that negates those flaws, NO CAPACITY FOR generating [THOSE] flaws at a LATER time, BECAUSE EVEN EARLIER, when one is training in study and reflection about the aggregates, THAT self-grasping HAS NO CAPACITY to destroy the wisdom realizing no-self.[8]

Even if there is [a fault], the impossibility of its remaining long [259]

(209c-210b) EVEN IF THERE DOES EXIST [IN AN ĀRYA'S MIND] THE CAPACITY [FOR FAULTS, FAULTS] DO NOT HAVE
THE CAPACITY TO REMAIN LONG, [BECAUSE THAT MIND EXISTS] AS AN ENTITY
THAT HAS THE NATURE SUCH THAT IT HAS THE CAPACITY TO GENERATE

Buddhists claim that self-grasping is *not* intrinsic to the mind, precisely because the nature of mind is the *correct* cognition of objects, and cognition tainted by self-grasping does not cognize its object correctly. The image of the mind as "clear light" (*'od gsal, prabhāsvara*) goes back at least as far as A, i, 10 (for *nikāya* references, see Collins [1982] 246 and notes), and is, of course, central to the tradition of discussion of tathāgatagarbha in Mahāyāna (see Ruegg [1969])—a tradition that seems to have originated primarily in circles that would be described as Yogācāra.

7 Indeed, if self-grasping were intrinsic to the mind, then no-self would have to be false and the view that there is a self true, for it is the intrinsic nature of mind to cognize objects correctly, and the mind's intrinsic cognition in this case would be that there is a self. The effectiveness of this argument, obviously, depends on the effectiveness of the assertion that it is the nature of mind to cognize correctly.

8 Once a mind has attained a state where its cognitions are invariably under the influence of the realization of no-self, i.e., when the realization of no-self is perfectly "natural" to the mind, there will be no room for self-grasping, for the mind will have attained its "real" nature, and cannot be diverted from that. rGyal tshab rje adds the observation that even before one has attained a direct realization of no-self, one can observe that even one's philosophical consideration of the topic helps to generate states of mind that cannot be damaged by self-grasping.

WHAT DAMAGES [ITS OPPOSITE], LIKE FIRE [WHICH WILL NOT BURN
LONG] ON DAMP GROUND.

A non-returner's mind, EVEN IF THERE DOES EXIST in it THE CAPACITY for generating faults, DOES NOT HAVE THE CAPACITY TO make them REMAIN A LONG TIME, because it exists AS AN ENTITY THAT HAS THE force and NATURE THAT HAS THE CAPACITY, has the power, TO GENERATE the wisdom realizing no-self, WHICH DAMAGES self-grasping. For example, it is LIKE FIRE, [which] cannot remain [burning] for a long time ON DAMP GROUND.[9]

The impossibility of there being a method of reversing a [complete abandonment] [260]

(210c-211b) EVEN IF ONE DOES TRY, ONE IS NOT [ABLE] TO RESTORE
MISTAKEN ATTITUDES, BECAUSE THOUGHT [THAT COGNIZES]
NATURALLY THE CORRECT OBJECT APPREHENDS
IN THAT WAY [COMPLETELY], WITHOUT BEING HARMED [BY
CONTRADICTORY CONDITIONS].[10]

An arhant does not try to restore the faults of attachment, etc., and EVEN IF THEY DO TRY, THEY DO NOT have the capacity to RESTORE [those MISTAKEN ATTITUDES], BECAUSE the independent THOUGHT in their mindstream that realizes perceptually [and NATURALLY] THE CORRECT OBJECT, no-self, APPREHENDS IN THAT WAY in all respects, WITHOUT BEING HARMED at all by the proximity of its contradictory condition, saṃsāra. The literal meaning of that is as explained in the first chapter.[11]

---

9 Even if an occasional fault should arise or a stain persist in the mind of one not yet liberated, such as a non-returner, those will not last long, because the conditions in which they can thrive, the presence of self-grasping, do not obtain. Faults cannot last in such a mind any longer than can fire when it is lit on damp ground, or in wet logs. The "power"of the ārya's mind is the destructive force of the wisdom realizing no-self, which can eradicate defilements. The "nature" of their mind is the wisdom itself, which has become completely natural to them, and thus is ever-present, allowing virtually no defilement to arise.

10 An alternate, somewhat more straightforward reading of the verse (*'tshe ba med dang yang dag don / rang bzhin la ni phyin log gis / 'bad du zin kyang mi zlogs te / blo ni de phyogs 'dzin phyir ro*) yields: "What is not harmful and [cognizes] a correct object cannot be reversed by mistaken attitudes even if one tries, because mind apprehends in that way."

11 In an arhant's mindstream, the wisdom realizing no-self is so utterly natural and uninterrupted that defilements simply cannot arise at all. Even if, for some strange reason, the arhant should attempt to generate a defilement,

Disposing of [the idea that] the wisdom realizing no-self is unacceptable as an antidote to self-grasping [261]

[This is divided into:] (1) The unsuitability, as an antidote, of the mere opposite to the mode of apprehension [that is self-grasping] [262], (2) Proving that defiled ignorance is not substantially different from the view of [self in] the perishable [263] and (3) Showing that the wisdom realizing no-self is the antidote through its opposition to the mode of apprehension [that is self-grasping] [264].

The unsuitability, as an antidote, of the mere opposite to the mode of apprehension [that is self-grasping] [262]

(211c-212) ALTHOUGH ATTACHMENT AND ANGER ARE MUTUALLY
DIFFERING, THEY DO NOT DESTROY [EACH OTHER],
BECAUSE THEY HAVE A SINGLE CAUSE, SELF-GRASPING,
AND THEY ARE [RELATED AS] DIRECT CAUSE AND RESULT.
LOVE, ETC., DO NOT EXTIRPATE
FAULTS, BECAUSE THEY DO NOT OPPOSE IGNORANCE.
(213) ALL FAULTS HAVE A ROOT THAT IS THAT [IGNORANCE],
WHICH ALSO IS THE VIEW OF [SELF IN] THE PERISHABLE COMPOSITES.

[OPPONENT:] If the mode of apprehension [that is self-grasping] is destroyed merely by its opposite, then self-grasping also will destroy [*its* opposite, as] attachment and anger destroy one another.

[RGYAL TSHAB RJE:] ALTHOUGH ATTACHMENT AND ANGER ARE merely MUTUALLY DIFFERING modes of apprehension, it follows that THEY are NOT [related as] DESTROYer and destroyed, BECAUSE THEY equally HAVE [a nature so as] to arise by the power A SINGLE CAUSE, SELF-GRASPING, AND because those two ARE DIRECT CAUSE AND direct RESULT.[12]

---

they could not do so, for they cannot do something that is contrary to the true nature of their mind, which now is well established. Of course, the desire to generate a defilement would itself be defiled, and so itself could never arise, so the question is academic. Since one's spiritual attainment is determined by one's mental state, it does not matter where an arhant finds themselves since although they may be "in"saṃsāra physically, their mind is immune to its allures. rGyal tshab rje's reference is to PV *Svārthānumāna*: 224ff., where Dharmakīrti refutes the authoritativeness of the Vedas.

12 Attachment and anger are opposing conditions, but their opposition is not the same as the opposition between between wisdom and self-grasping, for wisdom and self-grasping come from utterly different causes, while attachment and anger come from the same cause, self-grasping. Attachment and anger do

[OPPONENT:] Isn't meditation on the four immeasurables, etc., another antidote?

[RGYAL TSHAB RJE:] It follows that LOVE, ETC., are NOT the supreme direct antidotes that EXTIRPATE FAULTS, BECAUSE THEY DO NOT directly OPPOSE defiled IGNORANCE and the mode of apprehension [that is self-grasping]. It follows that this [reason] pervades, because attachment and ALL the [other] FAULTS HAVE A ROOT THAT IS THAT defiled ignorance, WHICH ALSO IS of the nature of THE VIEW OF [SELF IN] THE PERISHABLE COMPOSITES.[13]

Proving that defiled ignorance is not substantially different from the view of [self in] the perishable [263]

(213c) BECAUSE [IGNORANCE] IS AN OPPOSING FACTOR TO KNOWLEDGE, AND
BECAUSE BY THE VERY FACT THAT IT IS A MENTAL FACTOR, IT HAS AN INTENTIONAL OBJECT,
(214) IT IS NOT REASONABLE THAT [THE VIEW OF SELF IN THE PERISHABLE] BE OTHER [THAN IGNORANCE], BECAUSE [SCRIPTURE] SAYS THAT
IGNORANCE IS INVERTED SEEING.
WHATEVER [APPARENT] CONTRADICTION THERE IS HERE, IS TO BE EXPLAINED [AS NON-CONTRADICTORY].

[OPPONENT:] Ignorance is a mental factor that has the aspect of unclearness. The view of [self in] the perishable is a mental factor that has the aspect of definite determination, so it is unacceptable that those have one nature.[14]

---

replace one another, but the one is not capable of cutting the root of the other, for neither will disappear until its cause, self-grasping, is eliminated. Wisdom replaces self-grasping, but it will not, in turn, be replaced by it, because it is the opposing condition that has the power to uproot its opposite.

13 Thus, love, compassion, sympathetic joy and equanimity are able to replace or suppress such negative states of mind as malice, ill-will, envy or partiality, but they cannot uproot such attitudes, because they do not strike directly at the root of such states of mind, which is self-grasping. Only the wisdom realizing no-self is able to strike directly at the root of all negative states of mind, which is described also as defiled ignorance or the view of [self in] the perishable.

14 The opponent argues that ignorance and the self-view cannot be considered synonymous, because the self-view is the definite determination that there exists a self independent of the aggregates, and is, thus, a mental state with a specific intentional object, while ignorance is merely mental unclearness, a privative state with no intentional object.

[RGYAL TSHAB RJE:] Defiled ignorance IS AN OPPOSING FACTOR TO the KNOWLEDGE that is the wisdom realizing no-self. It follows that from among the three [types of opposing conditions], ignorance is neither the opposing factor of nescience nor some other opposing factor, BECAUSE BY THE VERY FACT THAT ignorance IS A MENTAL FACTOR it must necessarily apprehend an aspect of AN INTENTIONAL OBJECT.[15]

[OPPONENT:] [Only ignorance] is a contradictory opposing factor [to the wisdom realizing no-self].

[RGYAL TSHAB RJE:] It follows that IT IS NOT REASONABLE THAT THE VIEW OF [SELF IN] THE PERISHABLE composites, which is defined as the view of "I" and "mine," BE OTHER THAN IGNORANCE, BECAUSE A SÁTRA SAYS THAT defiled IGNORANCE is directly INVERTED SEEING [through] a mode of apprehension [opposite] to the wisdom realizing no-self, and because [the view of self in the perishable, too,] is a cognition that is the opposing factor contradicting that wisdom realizing no-self.[16] The *Candrapradīpa Sūtra* says, "What is it that is separate from ignorance? Whatever is separate from extra superimposition on the true, ultimate nature of dharmas."[17] Accordingly, it also says in the *Daśabhūmika*

---

15 There are, in fact, three types of opposing factors to a particular mental state, e.g., the wisdom realizing no-self: (1) Nescience, or the simple lack of knowing what is known in that mental state. This is the function of ignorance according to the opponent. (2) Other opposing conditions, i.e., anything that is *not* the mental state in question, such as a chair or an orangutan. (3) A contradictory opposing condition, which is a mode of apprehension directly in opposition to the mode of apprehension involved in the mental state in question. Unlike nescience, it has a specific intentional object, a self. Unlike other opposing conditions, it is a state of mind.

16 The opponent's claim that in that case only ignorance—but not the self-view—is the contradictory opposing factor to the wisdom realizing no-self, is refuted by the fact that ignorance is defined in the sūtras as a mode of apprehension opposite to the mode of apprehension entailed by the wisdom realizing no-self, and the view that there exists an "I" or "mine" independent of the aggregates also entails a mode of apprehension that is the opposite of wisdom's. Thus, the two must be identical. Nagatomi ([1957] 210-11) supplies the unidentified "sūtra-passage" in question, from Prajñākaragupta: *yaḥ kāścana lokavyavahāropapattayaḥ sarvās tā ātmābhiniveśato bhavanti ātmābhiniveśavigamato na bhavanti:* "All occurrences of worldly conventions originate from attachment to self; they do not originate when one has passed beyond attachment to self."

17 The *Candrapradīpa Sūtra,* better known as the *Samādhirāja,* is extant in Sanskrit (and is found in Tibetan translation in PTT vol. 31). It is described by Warder ([1980] 395) as "usually reckoned to stand closest to the Perfection of Understanding in doctrine, but expresses this primarily as the knowledge of the 'sameness' or 'equality' (*samatā*) of own-nature of all principles, the realiza-

Sūtra: "All conventional faulty actions arising in the world originate from manifest desire for self. If there is separation from manifest desire for self, they will not occur."[18]

Since we have shown that defiled ignorance is the apprehension of the direct opposite of the object of the wisdom realizing no-self, it is clear that we have shown that self-grasping is ignorance, because it is impossible that one apprehend the direct opposite [of wisdom] without grasping at a self.[19]

It follows that [the above passage from] the *Daśabhūmika Sūtra* also shows that self-grasping is ignorance, because if it were otherwise, then when the teacher [considered whether to] establish the factor of ignorance among the twelve factors of dependent origination, he would have left it out, and there would be no connection [between ignorance and] his teaching on self-grasping. [Since he *did* specify that ignorance was self-grasping,] it is unreasonable [to attempt] to show that that sūtra has a view other than that ignorance is self-grasping.[20]

[OPPONENT:] Since ignorance and the view of [self in] the perishable are [said in the *Daśabhūmika* to be] concomitant factors, ignorance is shown as a concomitant factor by entailment. If it were otherwise, [the assertion that] those two [are simultaneous concomitant factors] would contradict the explanation of concomitant factors in scripture.[21]

---

tion of which is the object of the practice of concentration. This 'sameness' is nothing but the emptiness of principles of any own-nature."

18 The *Daśabhūmika Sūtra* also is extant in Sanskrit (its Tibetan translation is found at PTT vol. 25). According to Warder ([1980] 424) it sometimes is reckoned as the twenty-second or twenty-fourth chapter of the *Avataṃsaka Sūtra*. It is concerned chiefly with a detailed accounting of a bodhisattva's progress through the ten stages leading to buddhahood.

19 Thus, it is clear that ignorance is, in fact, synonymous with self-grasping. Since it apprehends a specific intentional object, ignorance is not just non-knowledge, nescience or an unclear cognition: it is the specific "active" apprehension of phenomena in a manner opposite to wisdom's mode of apprehending phenomena.

20 Furthermore, if ignorance did not entail self-grasping, the Buddha would not have specified that it does when he set forth the twelve factors of dependent origination (see above, p. 70, n. 9). It is, after all, the self-grasping entailed by ignorance that permits the generation of karmic formations (*saṃskāras*), which, in turn, ripen as the first cognition (*vijñāna*) of a particular rebirth when the appropriate conditions are present. We already have seen that the indispensable cooperative condition of rebirth in saṃsāra is craving, which is rooted in self-grasping.

[RGYAL TSHAB RJE:] Since we accept that the view of [self in] the perishable is ignorance, it follows that, WHATEVER argument [is made] that there is a CONTRADICTION with the [scriptural] explanation that those two are concomitant factors, THERE IS no problem of contradiction HERE, because the scriptural passage that shows them as "concomitant" does not show those two as separate objects; it is reasonable that it IS TO BE EXPLAINED as showing that the view of [self in] the perishable *partakes of* ignorance, as when one says, "a *pālāśa* forest." Although the view of [self in] the perishable is pervaded by defiled ignorance, [ignorance] is not pervaded by the view of [self in] the perishable, because the innate grasping at permanence, etc., are concomitant with ignorance.[22] Acārya Candrakīrti also comments that it is the intention of the Protector Nāgārjuna [to assert] that the view of [self in] the perishable is ignorance.[23]

---

21 The opponent still is attempting to establish that ignorance and the view of [self in] the perishable are different factors. Thus, they cite a passage from the *Daśabhūmika* where ignorance and the self-view are said to be "concomitant factors" (*mtshungs ldan*). The opponent takes this to mean that they are concomitant factors in the most technical sense, i.e., that they are mental factors (*sems byung, caitta*) that are concomitant with a primary cognition in terms of basis, time, aspect, object and substance (see, e.g., Rabten [1980] 65). Since, however, a cognition only can be concomitant with one non-constant mental factor at a time, one cannot assert that both ignorance and the self-view are mental factors associated with the same primary cognition without contradicting the definition of concomitant factors. Thus, ignorance and the self-view must be different, with ignorance *entailing* the self-view, but not being the same as that view.

22 rGyal tshab rje replies that when the *Daśabhūmika* describes ignorance and the view of [self in] the perishable as "concomitant," it does not mean that they are "concomitant factors" in the technical sense used in epistemology, but simply that they are the same. They are not absolutely identical, because ignorance is the broader category and self-view the narrower: every instance of the self-view is an instance of ignorance, but not every instance of ignorance is an instance of the self-view, since there also is ignorance regarding such matters as permanence, pleasure, etc. Still, it is conventionally acceptable to describe ignorance as the self-view, because the self-view is the most basic and important type of ignorance. Similarly, one may speak of "a *pālāśa* forest," because even though the area known as the "forest" will contain instances of trees other than *pālāśas*, *pālāśas* predominate.

23 Candrakīrti's discussion is found in the sixth chapter of his *Madhyamakāvatāra*. The verse rGyal tshab rje has in mind probably is vi:120.

Showing that the wisdom realizing no-self is the antidote through its opposition to the mode of apprehension [that is self-grasping] [264]

> [(214c) WHATEVER CONTRADICTION THERE IS HERE, IS TO BE EXPLAINED.][24]
> BECAUSE THE VIEW OF VOIDNESS[25] OPPOSES THAT [IGNORANCE],
> (215) IT IS CLEARLY PROVEN TO OPPOSE
> THE NATURE OF THAT AND [HENCE] ALL FAULTS.

[OPPONENT:] If love, etc., do not oppose confusion, then what *does* oppose it?

[RGYAL TSHAB RJE:] It is to be explained here as whatever directly opposes defiled ignorance and the mode of apprehension [that is self-grasping], BECAUSE THE VIEW that realizes VOIDNESS directly OPPOSES [THAT] mode of apprehension [that is self-grasping]. The meaning of the first line must be explained in this way; if it shows only the avoidance of contradiction [rather than a contradictory condition], then it is unreasonable to make this the way of interpreting the words.[26] The wisdom realizing voidness IS CLEARLY PROVEN TO OPPOSE and destroy THE NATURE OF THAT ignorance and ALL THE attachment and other FAULTS that are its results, because [wisdom] destroys that ignorance through directly opposing the mode of apprehension [that is self-grasping].[27]

Disposing of the objection that stains are unsuitable to be removed [265]

> (215c) [IF YOU SAY THAT STAINS] CANNOT BE ELIMINATED BECAUSE THEY ARE NATURAL TO LIVING BEINGS,

---

24 PV 214c is repeated here, with a slightly different translation, because rGyal tshab rje refers to an alternate interpretation of it, applicable to the subject-matter of this section. Cf. above, p. 421.

25 This marks one of Dharmakīrti's rare references to "voidness" rather than "no-self." He is, however, still employing the concept of voidness—as he does throughout the *Pramāṇasiddhi* chapter—as referring to the no-self of persons and not to the no-self of dharmas.

26 In other words, the second way of reading PV 214c is as promising the explanation of a contradictory condition, rather than denying an apparent contradiction with scripture, which was the sense in which it was interpreted in the previous section (p. 424).

27 This reiterates a point that has been made several times before: wisdom and self-grasping are irremediably opposed manners of apprehending phenomena, in fundamental conflict, with the former able to destroy the latter because it is a *correct* apprehension of phenomena.

LIKE FORM, ETC., [TO A POT, WE REPLY:] IT IS NOT THE CASE, BECAUSE [THE REASON] IS UNPROVEN,
(216) BECAUSE WE HAVE SEEN THAT WHEN THEY COME INTO CONTACT
WITH THE ANTIDOTE, THEY ARE REMOVED.

[OPPONENT:] The faults CANNOT BE thoroughly ELIMINATED, BECAUSE THEY ARE NATURAL TO LIVING BEINGS, LIKE FORM, ETC., [are natural] to a pot.

[RGYAL TSHAB RJE:] It follows that IT IS NOT THE CASE that faults are unsuitable to be eliminated, BECAUSE [the reason] IS UNPROVEN. It follows that this is so, BECAUSE WE HAVE SEEN through authority THAT WHEN THEY COME INTO CONTACT WITH THE ANTIDOTE, the wisdom realizing no-self, THEY ARE utterly REMOVED.[28]

Disposing of the objection that even if they can be removed a little it is impossible that they be thoroughly removed [266]

(216c) WHEN THE FAULTS ARE STOPPED,
THEY WILL NOT ARISE AGAIN AS DOES [THE] SOLIDITY [OF MOLTEN GOLD],
(217) BECAUSE [THE MIND WITHOUT FAULTS] IS NOT SEPARATE FROM THE SELF-NATURE [OF THE ANTIDOTE]
AND [THE EXAMPLE] IS UNCERTAIN, AS ASHES [WILL NOT REVERT TO WOOD].

[OPPONENT:] Even if the faults are eliminated for awhile, they can return, like the solidity of gold [that has been melted].

[RGYAL TSHAB RJE:] [WHEN] THE FAULTS ARE STOPPED and eliminated by the power of the antidote, it follows that THEY WILL NOT ARISE AGAIN AS DOES the SOLIDITY of [melted] gold, BECAUSE a mind that is in a completely transformed state IS NOT SEPARATE FROM the wisdom realizing no-self, and by the fact that THAT [wisdom] has become of one nature with the SELF-NATURE of that [transformed mind]. It follows

---

28 rGyal tshab rje here considers the opponent's reason unproven because he maintains that faults are *not* natural to living beings, for it has been demonstrated that the mind is intrinsically pure and that its stains are adventitious, and can be removed by application of the appropriate "cleansing agent," the wisdom realizing no-self. Note that the appeal is to an authoritative observation of the effect of the wisdom realizing no-self on faults; it might be argued, of course, that an opponent would dispute that such an observation is possible, for they dispute that the wisdom realizing no-self is the opposing factor to faults. Thus, the ultimate issue is whether the Buddhist analysis of self and no-self is the proper key to saṃsāric faults.

that there is no certainty that when the destroyer is removed what has been damaged will return, because [your example] IS UNCERTAIN, AS [shown by the counter-example:] even when fire is removed, it does not follow that ASHES will revert to wood.[29]

B. SELF AND SUFFERING

Proving that self-grasping is the root of craving [267]

[This is divided into:] (1) Showing that self-grasping is the root of all faults [268] and (2) The impossibility of being freed from [saṃsāric] existence when one accustomates other methods without abandoning self-grasping [271].

Showing that self-grasping is the root of all faults [268]

[This is divided into:] (1) Showing that it is the root of suffering [269] and (2) Showing that it is the root of all defilements [270].

Showing that it is the root of suffering [269]

(217c) IN SOMEONE [ORDINARY], SAYING "I" WILL [ENTAIL] DESIRE
FOR THE PERMANENT, FOR THEY SEE A SELF.
(218) THEY WILL CRAVE HAPPINESS, SINCE THEY DESIRE [THE SELF], AND
THE CRAVING WILL HIDE THE FLAWS [IN THE SELF];
WHEN THEY SEE THE GOOD QUALITIES [OF THE SELF], THEY UTTERLY
CRAVE THEM, [AND]
SAYING "MINE,"THEY SEEK ACCOMPLISHMENT OF THAT.
(219) THUS, THEY WILL CIRCLE [IN SAṂSĀRA]
AS LONG AS THERE IS MANIFEST ATTACHMENT TO SELF.

IN SOMEONE who is an ordinary person, a common individual, SAYING "I" WILL [entail] the arising of DESIRE FOR THE PERMANENT non-separation

---

29 The opponent attempts to argue that faults can be restored to the mind because transformations are reversible. Gold, for instance, can be melted, but then can be restored to its solid state. In fact, however, the opponent has cited an inappropriate example, for there also are transformations that *cannot* be reversed, such as that wrought on wood by a fire. The transformation of the mind that occurs when one directly realizes no-self is of the irreversible kind, because that wisdom becomes utterly natural to the mind, and thus ever-present. Since it is ever-present, self-grasping cannot arise, because wisdom is true and the self-view false, and truth inevitably is stronger than falsehood. The same examples are used above, PV 55-57, in the discussion of the mind-body problem.

from the self, BECAUSE THEY SEE A SELF of persons and desire it. If that is asserted, [it follows that] THEY WILL CRAVE the HAPPINESS of the self, SINCE THEY DESIRE not to be separated from the self. Since that is the case, [the CRAVING] HIDES from the sense-faculties, etc., THE FLAWS that exist in what pertains to the self. WHEN THEY SEE THE GOOD QUALITIES of the non-existent [self], it follows that THEY UTTERLY CRAVE THEM, SINCE THEY CRAVE the happiness of the self. Thus, SAYING "MINE,"THEY will engage in SEEKing ACCOMPLISHMENT OF THAT self, because of the prior consequence [that they crave the good qualities of the self]. THUS, THEY WILL CIRCLE in saṃsāra, because they are therefore an ordinary being attached to a self. It follows that [this reason] pervades, because even if there is a little manifest attachment to a self, they will circle in saṃsāra AS LONG AS they have not abandoned [that MANIFEST ATTACHMENT TO SELF].[30]

Other schools [are guilty of] two contradictions, based on [their discussions of] (1) defilements and (2) purification. The first contradiction: It is contradictory to assert [on the one hand] that the continuum of suffering that comprises birth and death in saṃsāra is interruptible and to assert [on the other hand] that the root of those [sufferings] is a permanent self or principle, because without the cause being absent, it is impossible that the result be removed, and it is impossible that a permanent entity ever be absent. The contradiction based on purification: It is contradictory to assert [on the one hand] that one can attain a liberation that is the cessation of the suffering aggregates and to prove by reasoning [on the other hand that there exists] a self of persons, because when one grasps at a self of persons one forcefully generates the undesirable suffering of saṃsāra.[31]

Showing that it is the root of all defilements [270]

(219c-220b) [SELF-GRASPING] IS THE SOURCE OF ALL FAULTS:
WHEN THERE IS SELF, THERE IS THE RECOGNITION OF OTHER;
FROM THE PARTS, SELF AND OTHER, ONE WILL COME INTO CONTACT

---

30 This rather succinct account of the way in which belief in a self leads to suffering is cited and paraphrased by rGyal tshab rje in his discussion of the truth of cessation, above, p. 391.

31 This paragraph is interpolated by rGyal tshab rje as a sort of preface to the discussion, to follow shortly, on the impossibility of relating the concepts of bondage and freedom to a permanent self—for a permanent self cannot be a cause and, indeed, grasping at it actually is the cause of suffering.

WITH [THE ATTITUDES OF] GRASPING AND ANGER, FROM WHICH [ALL FAULTS ARISE].[32]

It follows that that [self-grasping] IS THE SOURCE OF attachment and ALL FAULTS, because if there is even a little self-grasping, [the faults] will not be undermined. It follows that [this reason] pervades, because WHEN THERE IS [SELF-grasping] THERE occurs THE RECOGNITION OF OTHER. FROM that, one analyzes out separate categories and PARTS having the nature of SELF AND OTHER. From that, ONE's mindstream WILL COME INTO CONTACT WITH the attachment and anger that [respectively] are GRASPING at and attached to one's own interests AND have ANGER toward the interests of others [FROM WHICH attitudes all faults arise].[33]

The impossibility of being freed from [saṃsāric] existence when one accustomates other methods without abandoning self-grasping [271]

[This is divided into:] (1) The unacceptability, as a path to freedom, of accepting a self and merely abandoning desire for what pertains to a self [272], (2) The unacceptability, as a path to freedom, of just the word of God [304] and (3) The unacceptability, as a path to freedom, of merely eliminating karma and the body [314].

The unacceptability, as a path to freedom, of accepting a self and merely abandoning desire for what pertains to the self [272]

[This is divided into:] (1) The impossibility of being separated from attachment to what pertains to the self without abandoning self-grasping [273], (2) If it is possible [to be separated from attachment to what pertains to the self without abandoning self-grasping], the pointless-

---

32 An alternative, somewhat more straightforward, reading of the verse (*bdag yod na ni gzhan du shes / bdag gzhan cha las 'dzin dang sdang / 'di dag dang ni yongs 'brel las / nyes pa thams cad 'byung bar 'gyur*) yields: "When there is self, there is recognition of other; from the parts, self and other, there will be grasping and anger, from which all faults originate."

33 The previous verse showed how grasping at a self inevitably leads to continued saṃsāric suffering. This verse elaborates, showing how self-grasping brings about a conceptual division of the world into the realms of "self" and "other," with the natural attitude toward one's own interests being attachment and the natural attitude toward the interests of others being resentment. Attachment and resentment are equivalent to desire and anger, which are, along with the ignorance on which they are based, the fundamental defilements—the "three poisons."

ness of accepting that a self is freed [302] and (3) Showing that it thus is necessary to abandon the self-view [303].

The impossibility of being separated from attachment to what pertains to the self without abandoning self-grasping [273]

[This is divided into:] (1) Setting forth the reason [274], (2) Disposing of objections to that [275] and (3) Summary [301].

Setting forth the reason [274]

(220c) ONE WILL NOT BE FREED FROM ATTACHMENT TO WHAT PERTAINS TO THE SELF
[WHEN] THERE IS DEFINITIVE ATTACHMENT TO THE SELF;
(221) THE CAUSE OF SEPARATION FROM ATTACHMENT
TO SELF WILL NOT EXIST, [SINCE THE SELF IS SEEN TO HAVE] NO FAULT.

A person who proves that there is a self of persons WILL NOT BE FREED FROM ATTACHMENT TO WHAT PERTAINS TO THE SELF without rejecting that tenet [that there exists a self], because even by virtue of the tenet THERE IS DEFINITIVE ATTACHMENT TO and desire for THE SELF. It follows that as long [as the tenet is held], THE CAUSE OF SEPARATION FROM ATTACHMENT TO SELF WILL NOT EXIST, because the person [will see] in that self not the slightest FAULT for the harm wrought in saṃsāra.[34]

Disposing of objections to that [275]

[This is divided into:] (1) Even if the self is flawless, the unacceptability, as a path to freedom, of abandoning desire for it [276] and (2) The unacceptability, as a path to freedom, of meditating on the suffering of suffering [279].

Even if the self is flawless, the unacceptability, as a path to freedom, of abandoning desire for it [276]

[This is divided into:] (1) Refutation by replying to a question [277] and (2) Refuting the reply to that [278].

---

34 The discussion to follow revolves around the division of one's concerns into the self (*bdag, ātman*), that of which one says "I"; and what pertains to the self (*bdag gi ba, ātmīya*), that of which one says "mine."The fundamental premise of all non-Buddhists who discuss freedom and bondage is that, at the very least, the self is permanent and flawless. It will be Dharmakīrti's basic contention that as long as one believes in such a self, either conceptually or instinctively, one cannot possibly be detached from it, because it is considered good, and one inevitably strives for what is considered good, even if it is a phantom.

Refutation by replying to a question [277]

(221c) IF [YOU SAY:] "ATTACHMENT [MUST BE SEEN] AS FLAWED;
FROM THAT, WHAT OCCURS? ONE WILL ABANDON THAT [DESIRE]";[35]
(222) [WE REPLY:] THIS [ATTACHMENT] CANNOT BE ABANDONED
WITHOUT THE OBJECT'S BEING CONFUTED;
AS FOR ABANDONING THE ATTACHMENT AND ANGER, ETC.,
CONNECTED WITH [SEEING] GOOD QUALITIES AND FLAWS:
(223) THERE IS [SUCH ABANDONMENT] WHEN ONE DOES NOT SEE IN THE OBJECT
THOSE [QUALITIES AND FLAWS], BUT ONE DOES NOT [ABANDON THEM] IN THE WAY [ONE ABANDONS] EXTERNALS.
ATTACHMENT DOES NOT [ORIGINATE] WHEN [ONE SEES] ATTACHMENT AS HAVING GOOD QUALITIES, BUT
WHEN ONE SEES THE OBJECT [OF ATTACHMENT] AS HAVING GOOD QUALITIES,
(224) HOW WILL ONE EFFECT REMOVAL OF THE RESULT
WHEN [ONE HOLDS AS FLAWLESS] THE CAUSE WITHOUT WHICH [THE RESULT] IS INCOMPLETE?

[OPPONENT:] Although the self and what pertains to the self are flawless, if one desires them, one will be bound in saṃsāra, so one must think about *ATTACHMENT* to self AS FLAWED. FROM thinking THAT, WHAT OCCURS? Seeing that desire and attachment are flawed, ONE WILL ABANDON THAT desire and attachment.

[RGYAL TSHAB RJE:] It follows that THIS attachment to self CANNOT BE ABANDONED merely by meditation on it as flawed, because that self that is the object desired is not eliminated WITHOUT [THE OBJECT'S] BEING CONFUTED by reasoning, because [attachment to something] originates from establishing it as flawless. It follows that [this reason] pervades, because AS FOR ABANDONING THE ATTACHMENT AND ANGER, ETC., CONNECTED WITH seeing the GOOD QUALITIES AND FLAWS in that object, THERE IS abandonment WHEN ONE DOES NOT SEE IN THE OBJECT THOSE flaws and good qualities that have been apprehended, BUT ONE DOES NOT abandon them IN THE WAY one pulls out AN EXTERNAL thorn.

---

35 An alternative reading of PV 221c-d (*gal te chags pa skyon bcas na / de las cir 'gyur de spong 'gyur*) takes only the first line as the opponent's position, with the second representing the beginning of the Buddhist response: "If [you say]: 'Attachment [must be seen] as flawed,' [we reply:] 'How will one change from that or abandon that?'"

It follows that attachment to self cannot be abandoned merely by its being viewed as flawed, because ATTACHMENT does NOT originate merely when one apprehends ATTACHMENT AS HAVING GOOD QUALITIES; BUT it originates WHEN ONE SEES THE self that is its own OBJECT of desire AS HAVING GOOD QUALITIES. For example, one may see attachment to liquor as a flaw that interrupts the Dharma, but since one grasps the taste of liquor as good, one will not reject attachment to it.

HOW, [by what] means, will a person who accepts a self EFFECT REMOVAL OF THE RESULTant attachment to self? It follows that they will not be able to, because it is reasonable that they hold as flawless THAT self-view that is the direct CAUSE WITHOUT WHICH [the result] IS INCOMPLETE.[36]

Refuting the reply to that [278]

(224c) WHAT FLAW COULD BE SEEN IN ATTACHMENT?
IF YOU SAY THAT IT IS THE BASIS OF SUFFERING,
(225) [WE REPLY:] ALTHOUGH THIS [ATTACHMENT ACTS] THUS, ONE WILL NOT BE FREED FROM ATTACHMENT,
BECAUSE ONE SEES WHAT PERTAINS TO A SELF AS, FOR EXAMPLE, [ONE SEES] THE SELF.
IF [YOU SAY THAT] THE SELF DOES NOT CAUSE SUFFERING
WITHOUT THAT [ATTACHMENT], [WE REPLY:] THAT [ATTACHMENT] WOULD BE [FLAWLESS] LIKE THAT [SELF];
(226) THERE IS SEPARATION FROM ATTACHMENT TO NEITHER, BECAUSE
BOTH THUS ARE [SEEN AS] FLAWLESS.

ALSO, WHAT FLAW COULD BE SEEN IN ATTACHMENT to self? It follows that it is impossible that [a flaw] could be seen, because there is a yearning that is intent upon the self.[37]

---

36 One cannot blithely maintain that simply by seeing the flaws in attachment to self one will get rid of attachment to self, for as long as one continues to see good qualities in the self itself—or, for that matter, even to believe in its existence—one cannot abandon attachment to it, any more than a drunkard can cure themselves of alcoholism simply by agreeing that the desire for alcohol is bad, but insisting that alcohol itself is good. What is good inevitably will be considered desirable, and thus will be desired—and whereof one has desire, therefrom one will not be detached. One only will be rid of attachment to self when one has come to recognize the self as flawed—not flawed in the sense that a real object is flawed, but flawed in the sense that it is a non-existent object the very concept of which leads to all mental faults.

37 It is inconceivable that one who believes the self to be flawless really be detached from it, particularly when one's soteriology revolves around the at-

[OPPONENT:] Attachment to self is flawed, because it acts as THE BASIS OF the SUFFERINGs of [saṃsāric] existence.

[RGYAL TSHAB RJE:] It follows that ALTHOUGH THIS attachment to self acts THUS as the basis of suffering, ONE WILL NOT BE FREED FROM ATTACHMENT, BECAUSE ONE SEES "my mind" as WHAT PERTAINS TO A SELF; AS, FOR EXAMPLE, when one grasps at a self, one is not freed from attachment, even though THE SELF is the basis of saṃsāric suffering. Alternatively, the reason is "because one sees the subject as a flawless self."[38]

[OPPONENT:] There is no flaw in the self, since THE SELF DOES NOT CAUSE SUFFERING independently, WITHOUT THAT desire and attachment and virtuous and non-virtuous karma.

[RGYAL TSHAB RJE:] It follows that THAT desire for and attachment to the self, etc., WOULD BE flawless LIKE THAT self, because they do not cause suffering independently, without the self that is the foundation of bondage and freedom. If that is asserted, it follows that THERE IS SEPARATION FROM ATTACHMENT FROM NEITHER the self nor desire for it, BECAUSE BOTH THUS ARE [seen as] FLAWLESS.[39]

---

tempt to "free" the self from its identification with what pertains to it. As long as one desires the freedom of the self, one is attached to the self, and therefore by definition unable to see the flaws in attachment to that self.

38 Attachment to self may, in fact, be the basis of saṃsāric suffering (such certainly is the Buddhist view), but recognizing that such attachment entails suffering is useless as long as one persists in accepting the existence—let alone the value—of a self that is in some sense the ultimate subject, the mind in its truest sense, for detachment from such a self is virtually impossible.

39 If the non-Buddhist argues that the self itself is flawless, but that suffering in relation to the self arises from the self's association with various mental qualities, then it can just as easily be argued, conversely, that the various mental qualities, including negative ones, must be flawless, because they are associated with a flawless self—how, after all, could "desire" for what is ultimately flawless really be flawed? Buddhists do not consider the "desire" to attain enlightenment to be a negative mental attitude, nor, by the same token, should non-Buddhists consider "desire" for the flawless self to be negative, let alone the basis of suffering. The Buddhist, of course, does believe that the desire for the self is the basis of suffering, but that is because they do not accept that that self exists. Their point is that if one accepts something as real and good, it is impossible to consider desire for it to be undesirable.

The unacceptability, as a path to freedom, of meditating on the suffering of suffering [279]

[This is divided into:] (1) Refuting the Vaiśeṣika system [280], (2) Refuting the Sāṃkhya system [296] and (3) Disposing of [the idea that our position] contradicts the [Buddha's] teaching on the meditation on suffering [300].

C. A REFUTATION OF VAIŚEṢIKA SOTERIOLOGY

Refuting the Vaiśeṣika system [280]

[This is divided into:] (1) Refuting the example [281] and (2) Refuting the meaning [286].

Refuting the example [281]

[This is divided into:] (1) The acceptability of our own system's reason for rejecting desire for what pertains to the self [282] and (2) The unacceptability of the other system's [reasons] [283].

The acceptability of our own system's reason for rejecting desire for what pertains to a self [282]

(226c) IF [YOU SAY THAT IT IS] JUST AS LIMBS BITTEN BY A SNAKE, [WHICH]
WILL BE ABANDONED WHEN ONE MEDITATES ON THE SUFFERING [THEY CAUSE],
(227-228b) [WE REPLY:] [ONE] REJECTS THIS BY DESTROYING THE THOUGHT
OF WHAT PERTAINS TO SELF, NOT OTHERWISE.
HOW WILL ONE REMOVE THE THOUGHT OF [WHAT PERTAINS TO] ONE'S OWN [SELF IN THE SENSE-FACULTIES],
WHEN THE SENSE-FACULTIES ARE GRASPED
AS THE VERY BASIS OF ENJOYMENT?
HOW COULD ONE BE DETACHED FROM THEM?
(228c-229b) IT IS THE PERCEPTION OF ALL
THAT THERE WILL ARISE A RENOUNCED MIND
TOWARD HAIR, ETC., REMOVED FROM THE BODY,
WHILE THERE WILL ARISE A DESIROUS [MIND] TOWARD OTHER [NON-REMOVED HAIR, ETC.]

[VAIŚEṢIKA OPPONENT:] According to us, JUST AS LIMBS, digits, etc., BITTEN BY a poisonous SNAKE [WILL BE ABANDONED], so one will abandon [suffering] WHEN ONE MEDITATES ON attachment to what pertains to the self, and to the self [itself], in the sense-faculties as the cause of SUFFERING. [Saying that] if one does not reject the object then one cannot abandon desire for it involves an unproven reason.[40]

[RGYAL TSHAB RJE:] This is the system that asserts as the path to liberation not meditation [that develops] a mind renouncing the suffering [pervading] formations, but just [meditation that develops] a mind renouncing the suffering feeling of suffering. It follows that just as one will not reject desire for the digits bitten by a poisonous snake other than through desirelessness toward what pertains to a self in them, so one will not become detached from flaws merely by seeing them, because it is necessary to REJECT THIS desire for [self] BY DESTROYING THE THOUGHT that grasps at WHAT PERTAINS TO A SELF; [one does NOT do so OTHERWISE].[41]

---

40 Heretofore, the Buddhist arguments have been directed against the *ātmavāda* in general, particularly against the view of self held by the Nyāya-Vaiśeṣikas and Sāṃkhyas. (Since Dharmakīrti lived either contemporaneously with or, more likely, before Śaṅkara, Vedānta does not seem to have been the important school during his time that it became later.) Now the Buddhist argument is turned against specific soteriologies. The Vaiśeṣika view, as summarized by Buddhist critics, is that "Through having practiced yoga for some time in accordance with the quintessential instructions of a guru, a yogī comes to know the self as a thing other than the senses and so forth, and thereby sees reality. He understands the nature of the six categories of existents, and he knows the self to be an all-pervasive entity that lacks activity. He does not accumulate either virtuous or non-virtuous actions or the predispositions they establish. Because he does not accumulate new actions but extinguishes old ones, the self separates from the body, senses, mind, pleasure, pain, desire, hatred and so forth, and does not assume a new body and senses. Thereby, the continuum of births is severed like a fire which has consumed its fuel. When the self is alone (without any of its nine qualities—desire, hatred, effort, pleasure, pain, consciousness, virtue, non-virtue and activity), this is said to be the attainment of liberation" (Sopa and Hopkins [1976] 57). See also Radhakrishnan and Moore (1957) chapter XI, Dasgupta (1975) I, Chapter VIII, Potter (1977) *passim* and Koller (1970) chapter 6. The Vaiśeṣika takes disassociation of the self from what pertains to it as the path to liberation; thus, they do *not* accept the Buddhist's contention that an object must be rejected if desire for it is to be rejected, holding as they do that the self need not be rejected, but that desire for it should be.

41 The Buddhist argues that the Vaiśeṣika's contemplation and rejection of the suffering of what pertains to the self springs from an insufficiently profound analysis of suffering, i.e., from a concern with the suffering of suffering rather than the suffering pervading the formations. The attempt to abandon suffering merely by disposing of what pains one is bound to fail, because one has not thus abandoned the attachment, to the pleasures of the self, that is the primary force binding one in saṃsāra. As long as one believes in a self, one will be attached to the pleasures of the self, and therefore incapable of utterly reject-

HOW, [by what] method, as long as one does not reject them as useful to the self, WILL ONE REMOVE THE THOUGHT grasping at what pertains to ITS OWN self with regard to the eye and other sense-faculties? It follows that it is unacceptable that one will, because [THE SENSE-FACULTIES, ETC.,] ARE GRASPED AS THE VERY BASIS OF the ENJOYMENT of the pleasures of the self. HOW, thus, COULD ONE BE DETACHED FROM [the sense-faculties]? It follows that it is unacceptable that one could be, because there is no reason for it.

It follows that grasping at what is useful to the self is the cause of desire for what pertains to the self; while *not* grasping [something as useful to the self] is not the cause of desire for [what pertains to the self], because IT IS proven by THE PERCEPTION OF ALL people THAT THERE WILL ARISE A RENOUNCED MIND TOWARD HAIR, nails, ETC., that have been REMOVED FROM THE BODY and are not taken as useful to the self, WHILE THERE WILL ARISE A DESIROUS [mind] TOWARD OTHER [hair and nails] still on the body, which are taken as useful.[42]

The unacceptability of the other system's [reasons] [283]

[This is divided into:] (1) The unacceptability of inherence and other relations as a cause of the arising of desire [284] and (2) Refuting the reply to that [285].

---

ing what pertains to the self, since what pertains to the self is naturally seen as a contributor to the pleasure of the self.

42 Thus, one cannot really become detached from one's sense-faculties, because they are instinctively felt to contribute to the pleasure of the self, and most of us naturally consider even defective faculties to be preferable to no faculties at all. The basic criterion by which we instinctively judge whether something is worthy of our concern is its "usefulness"or "uselessness"to the self. Thus, hair and nails that have been cut off are no longer of concern to us, because they no longer can affect the self's happiness, whereas hair and nails still on our bodies can affect our sensations, and thus remain of concern to us. A possible Vaiśeṣika response to many of the foregoing Buddhist objections might be to point out that the Buddhist is insightful in their psychological analysis, but that it still is possible for a yogin to overcome their instinctive identification of the self with what pertains to it, and thus to gain a "higher"realization of what is conducive to the *ultimate* happiness of the self, which is its separation from all that one once considered potentially beneficial to it. This would become psychologically compelling at the point where one recognized that the self (which is permanent and utterly blissful) is utterly different from those impermanent and suffering things to which one habitually has been attached. The issue of the possible existence of a permanent self would then—once again—become the focus of discussion.

The unacceptability of inherence and other relations as a cause of the arising of desire [284]

(229c-230) EVEN HAVING ALREADY SEEN [WHAT PERTAINS TO THE SELF AS SUFFERING], ONE WILL NOT ABANDON [DESIRE],
BECAUSE THE THOUGHT "MINE" WILL ARISE
FROM INHERENCE AND OTHER RELATIONS, AND
THOSE RELATIONS REMAIN AS THEY ARE.
EVEN IF THERE IS NO INHERENCE, ETC.,
IN ALL [THINGS], THERE EXISTS BENEFIT [TO THE SELF].

It follows that, EVEN HAVING ALREADY SEEN what pertains to the self as suffering, ONE WILL NOT and cannot ABANDON desire, BECAUSE THE THOUGHT that the sense-faculties, etc., are "MINE" WILL ARISE FROM the existence in the self of INHERENCE AND OTHER RELATIONS, AND THOSE RELATIONS REMAIN permanent, AS THEY ARE, before one meditates on [what pertains to the self] as suffering.[43]

[The Vaiśeṣikas] assert that there exist (1) inherence, which [relates] happiness and suffering to the self; (2) the conjunction relation, which [relates] the aural faculty and the body; (3) conjunction inherence, which [relates] form and other [qualities] to the body that is their ba-

---

43 According to Koller ([1970] 74), "The category of inherence reflects the fact that different things, such as substance, quality, action, etc., appear as one whole. Thus, the size of the man, his color, his nature as man and his particularity as this man, all appear so unified that we think of one thing appearing, rather than a collection of things appearing to us. Thus, the whole inheres in its parts; the jug in the clay, the pencil in the wood, etc. The basis for the unity of different categories must, like other categories, have a foundation in reality, as different from other kinds of things. Otherwise, it would appear as one of the other kinds of things, and not as separate. Therefore, the category of inherence is recognized as an independent kind of reality." "Conjunction" (*ldan pa, saṃyoga*), which has been discussed above (PV 89ff.) is that quality which is responsible for "connecting" two instances of the same category, i.e., two substances when "the pen is on the table" or two qualities when sugar is "sweet and white." Conjunction is impermanent, lasting only as long as the "connection" of which it is an expression. Inherence, on the other hand, relates instances of different categories (*padārtha*), and is considered permanent. For a Buddhist, this is its crucial characteristic, for if it is permanent, it must be indestructible. Thus, if it is asserted that the idea of "mine" or the quality of "suffering" "inhere" in the self, that inherence must be permanent, and the idea of "mine" or of "suffering" incapable of elimination. Nagatomi ([1957] 221) finds this analysis of inherence "high-handed," noting that the permanence asserted of inherence is a permanence that lasts only as long as related entities last.

sis; (4) inherence in the conjunction, which [relates general] form to [particular forms] and (5) the conjunction-relation in the conjunction, which [relates] the self to the visual and other faculties other than the aural.[44]

It follows that there will not arise the thought of what pertains to the self in relation to external food, clothing, etc., because those [items are] not [included in] the two [types of relations that relate things] to the self.[45] Thus, it follows that only its being related to the self does not [make something] the cause of desire, because EVEN IF THERE IS NO relation of INHERENCE, ETC., [connecting] ALL external food, clothing, etc., to the self, the thought [of "mine"] arises from seeing that THERE EXISTS A BENEFIT to the self.[46]

Refuting the reply to that [285]

(231) IF [YOU SAY:] BECAUSE [WE SEE THAT] IT GENERATES SUFFERING, THE THOUGHT
OF "ONE'S OWN" WILL NOT [ARISE], AS [IT DOES NOT WITH REGARD TO] A [POISONED] FINGER,
[WE REPLY:] IT IS NOT SOLELY SUFFERING.
[IF YOU SAY THAT] LIKE POISON IN FOOD, IT IS MOSTLY [SUFFERING],[47]

---

44 For further discussion of inherence, see Dasgupta (1975) I, 319; and Radhakrishnan and Moore (1957) 422-23. The list of types of inherence is supplied by rGyal tshab rje.

45 Since the two types of inherence that relate things other than the self to the self (numbers 1 and 5 above) only relate to the self such "internal" qualities as pleasure and pain and the sense-faculties, rGyal tshab rje argues that the Vaiśeṣika eliminates from identification with the self such obvious items as external food, clothing, housing, etc. It might, however, be pointed out in the Vaiśeṣika's defense that the self, as a substance, would be related to such other substances as food and clothing not by inherence (which is *inter*-categorial) but by conjunction, which relates items *intra*-categorially, so the exclusion of food and clothing from the list of items related to the self by inherence does not imply that no relation is possible.

46 In any case, according to rGyal tshab rje, the Vaiśeṣika's failure to account for all possible objects to which the word "mine" might be applied shows that what is considered "related" to the self, i.e., as pertaining to the self, is inadequate as a basis for explaining attachment. One must, therefore, adopt the rather broader Buddhist explanation, which is that anything considered beneficial to the self, whether internal or external, is in fact what pertains to the self and is, thus, an object of the word, "mine," hence an object of attachment. Nagatomi ([1957] 222) attributes the position expressed here to the Sāṃkhyas.

47 It also is possible to read PV 231d as a part of the Buddhist reply to the

(232) [WE REPLY:] ONE WHO IS ATTACHED TO A SPECIAL PLEASURE
WILL BE DETACHED FROM [AN ORDINARY PLEASURE] THAT CONTRASTS WITH THAT;
OUT OF CRAVING FOR THAT SPECIAL PLEASURE,
ONE WILL UTTERLY ABANDON A MINOR PLEASURE.
(233) [AN ORDINARY BEING] WILL ENGAGE AS MUCH [PLEASURE] AS THEY CAN ACQUIRE,
BECAUSE THEY DO NOT HAVE INTELLGENCE, AND HAVE ATTACHMENT TO THE SELF.
FOR EXAMPLE, WE SEE THAT IF THEY DO NOT ACQUIRE
FEMALES, [HUMAN MALES] ACT DESIROUSLY TOWARD ANIMALS.

[OPPONENT:] BECAUSE even though we see that the sense-faculties, etc., benefit the self, THEY still GENERATE SUFFERING, THE THOUGHT OF "ONE'S OWN" WILL NOT arise [when they are removed], AS [it does not arise regarding] A poisoned FINGER.

[RGYAL TSHAB RJE:] It follows that THOSE sense-faculties, etc., ARE NOT SOLELY the cause just of SUFFERING, because they sometimes act as the cause of pleasure.[48]

[OPPONENT:] Since, LIKE POISON IN FOOD, desire is MOSTLY a cause of suffering, it can be rejected.

[RGYAL TSHAB RJE:] Although desire is mostly a cause of suffering, it does not necessarily follow that it will not arise, because ONE WHO IS ATTACHED TO A SPECIAL PLEASURE WILL BE DETACHED FROM an ordinary pleasure THAT CONTRASTS WITH THAT, but we see that if they do not acquire [the special pleasure], they will be attached to the ordinary pleasure. It follows that this is so, because we see that if someone acquires food, etc., that generates special pleasure, OUT OF CRAVING FOR THAT [SPECIAL PLEASURE] THEY WILL UTTERLY ABANDON that which generates only MINOR PLEASURE. If one does not acquire [good food], one still [will eat] poisoned food [rather than starve].[49]

Vaiśeṣika objection raised in 231a-b.

48 The Vaiśeṣika argues that we can transcend attachment to the sense-faculties and other things that pertain to the self by recognizing that they are flawed and generate suffering. The Buddhist reply is that the recognition that something can cause *some* suffering is an inadequate basis for detachment from that thing, because as long as there remains the belief that that thing can provide some pleasure, too, one will not want to be rid of it.

49 Furthermore, even if one recognizes something as being primarily a cause of suffering, one will continue to be attached to it as long as one conceives that it is in the least bit necessary. Thus, even if we cannot have great pleasure, we

An ordinary being, if they do not acquire special [pleasures], WILL ENGAGE the cause of AS MUCH pleasure AS THEY CAN ACQUIRE, BECAUSE THEY DO NOT HAVE the INTELLIGENCE to distinguish [as the supreme pleasure] the pleasure of liberation, AND because they are a person who has not in the least abandoned ATTACHMENT TO THE SELF. FOR EXAMPLE, WE SEE THAT desirous [human males], IF THEY DO NOT ACQUIRE A FEMALE, ACT DESIROUSLY TOWARD ANIMALS.[50]

Refuting the meaning [286]

[This is divided into:] (1) The impossibility of a permanent person's meditating on suffering [287], (2) Extreme consequences if one is freed merely by meditating on suffering [290] and (3) Showing a perceptually based confutation [of the idea] that merely by seeing the sense-faculties, etc., as flawed one can remove desire for them [293].

The impossibility of a permanent person's meditating on suffering [287]

[This is divided into:] (1) The consequence that the self is impermanent [288] and (2) [Showing that] if the self exists, there can result no reliable antidote to desire [289].

The consequence that the self is impermanent [288]

(234-235b) HOW [FOR] SOMEONE WHO ASSERTS
A SELF CAN THAT [SELF] BE ASSERTED AS DESTRUCTIBLE?
HOW COULD THAT BE ASSERTED TO BE DESIRED?
IT IS THE OPPOSITE OF THE BASIS OF ALL EXPERIENCES,
CONVENTIONS OR GOOD QUALITIES;
IT IS NOT THE SAME AS [THE SELF] WHOSE NATURE IS DESIRED.[51]

---

happily will accept small and transient pleasures rather than no pleasures at all, just as we will eat potentially bad food rather than starve. Thus, even if, e.g., the sense-faculties are considered "primarily" a source of pain, we still prefer to live with them than to be utterly without them, for they still can supply a small amount of the pleasure considered essential to the self.

50 Most beings, in short, continue to pursue the pleasures of a phantom self, unaware of the unsurpassable pleasure that is involved in liberation—attained, of course, at the price of abandoning the concept of self. They continue to garner what small pleasures they can—to the point of utter debasement—rather than give up the idea of trying to please them"selves."

51 An alternative reading of PV 235b (*zhen pa'i rang bzhin de 'dra min*) yields: "The nature of what is desire is not like that." In other words, the nature of desire is not such as to wish the destruction of what is considered to be good.

HOW CAN SOME person WHO ASSERTS A SELF of persons, no matter how much they meditate on suffering, be freed from attachment to self? It follows that it is impossible [that they be freed], because it is unreasonable that THAT self BE ASSERTED AS DESTRUCTIBLE. HOW COULD the self THAT is freed, the self described, BE ASSERTED BY THE Ātmavādins TO BE like the self that is DESIRED? It follows that it could not, because [the self that is freed] IS THE OPPOSITE OF THE BASIS OF ALL EXPERIENCES of pleasure and pain, of CONVENTIONS to be adopted and rejected, OR of GOOD QUALITIES, such as compassion, wisdom, etc. It follows that this [reason] pervades, because the self described is accepted by the Ātmavādins as a permanent basis of all bondage and freedom that IS NOT THE SAME AS the self WHOSE NATURE IS DESIRED.[52]

[Showing that] if the self exists there can result no reliable antidote to desire [289]

(235c-236b) ONE WILL CONTINUE IN THAT SITUATION, GRASPING
THE SELF IN ALL ITS ASPECTS;
[GRASPING] ACTS TO SUPPORT ATTACHMENT TO SELF, AND
JUST THAT [GRASPING] IS THE SEED OF DESIRE FOR WHAT PERTAINS TO THE SELF.
(236c-237b) EVEN IF [A PERSON] EXERTS THEMSELVES, [SELF-GRASPING] PREVENTS
DETACHMENT AND COVERS UP THE FLAWS
IN WHAT PERTAINS TO THE SELF; BASED ON THE GOOD-QUALITY PART
OF WHAT PERTAINS TO THE SELF, ONE ENGAGES [IN ATTACHMENT].
(237c) IF [YOU ASSERT THAT] ONE ALSO IS FREED FROM ATTACHMENT TO SELF,
[WE REPLY:] NOW, [SINCE] THERE DOES NOT EXIST ANY [SELF] FREED FROM ATTACHMENT,
(238) IT WILL BE POINTLESS TO MEDITATE ON SUFFERING, [FOR]

---

52 There necessarily is a disjunction between the self that is freed and the self that is desired, even though it seems that the self that is desired is, in fact, the self that is freed. The self that is desired is a self that experiences and moves from bondage to freedom. The self that is freed is said to be the basis of all experience, including bondage and freedom. A permanent self, however, cannot reasonably be asserted to "experience" anything, or to move from one state (e.g., bondage) to another (e.g., freedom), since experience and transition presuppose change, and a permanent entity cannot change. Thus, the Vaiśeṣika desires the freedom of the self, but because the self is seen as permanent, it cannot "become free," for to "become" anything requires a mode of existence impossible for a permanent entity.

HOW COULD THAT [PERSON] REJECT THE SELF?

It follows that that self that is freed WILL CONTINUE to desire what pertains to a self [even] IN THAT SITUATION [i.e., when freed], because one does not change from GRASPING THE SELF IN ALL ITS ASPECTS. It follows that this [reason] pervades, because that [grasping] is the cause that ACTS TO SUPPORT ATTACHMENT TO SELF, and because JUST THAT IS THE potent SEED OF DESIRE FOR WHAT PERTAINS TO THE SELF.[53]

It follows that a person who desires liberation, EVEN IF THEY EXERT THEMSELVES in meditation on the suffering of what pertains to the self, will not thoroughly eliminate attachment if they do not abandon self-grasping, because the power of the self-view in their own mindstream WILL PREVENT their DETACHMENT from what pertains to the self, [AND] because it COVERS UP THE FLAWS IN [what pertains to the self]. It follows that this is the case, because by the power of that [self-view], BASED UPON seizing THE GOOD-QUALITY PART OF WHAT PERTAINS TO THE SELF, ONE ENGAGES in manifest attachment [to self], and will be reborn.[54]

[OPPONENT:] At the time of liberation, just as [one is freed from attachment to] what pertains to the self, so ONE ALSO IS FREED FROM ATTACHMENT TO SELF.

[RGYAL TSHAB RJE:] NOW, it follows that at the time of liberation THERE DOES NOT EXIST ANY self that is FREED FROM ATTACHMENT, because, since desire for it has been rejected, it is not cognized by anyone. If this is asserted, it follows that IT IS POINTLESS TO MEDITATE ON SUFFERING for the sake of obtaining a freed self, because HOW COULD [THAT] one who desires liberation even REJECT THE SELF later, any more than what pertains to the self?[55]

---

53 As long as there remains some desire for what pertains to the self, there must necessarily remain attachment to the self whose "needs" are served by what pertains it. Conversely, as long as there exists attachment to self, there will follow desire for what pertains to the self, because one naturally will seek out that which pleases the self.

54 In short, then, as long as one does not abandon self-grasping, one will continue to seize on whatever good one can find in what pertains to the self, assuming that "good" will contribute to the happiness of the self. In fact, however, one's attitude is based on a distorted understanding of reality, and entails a grasping that only serves to lengthen one's term in saṃsāra.

55 The opponent attempts to argue that at the time of liberation, attachment to both what pertains to the self and the self itself is overcome. This is absurd in the light of Buddhist assumptions about liberation. On the other hand, if one really is liberated, then one must have come to understand that there is no self, so one no longer can speak of a self to which one is or is not attached. On

Extreme consequences if one is freed merely by meditating on suffering [290]

[This is divided into:] (1) Actual extreme consequences [291] and (2) The impossibility of others being freed from attachment [292].

Actual extreme consequences [291]

(238c-239b) THOSE [VAIŚEṢIKAS], EVEN BY MEDITATING ON SUFFERING,
WILL NOT THUS BECOME DETACHED:
[IT IS KNOWN BY] DIRECT PERCEPTION THAT COGNIZANCE
OF SUFFERING ALREADY EXISTS BEFORE.
(239c-240b) IF [YOU ASSERT THAT ONE GAINS DETACHMENT] WHEN THE FAULTS IN THAT [WHICH PERTAINS TO SELF ARE SEEN],
[WE REPLY:] ONE WILL NOT BECOME DETACHED IN RELATION TO THAT:
EVEN IF THAT [ATTACHED] THOUGHT IS ABSENT FOR A MOMENT, [IT MAY RETURN,]
AS A DESIROUS [MALE MAY REJECT A LOVER, THEN TURN] TO ANOTHER WOMAN.
(240c) ONE DISTINGUISHES WHAT IS TO BE ADOPTED AND WHAT IS TO BE REJECTED;
WHATEVER ATTACHMENT ORIGINATES FROM A SINGLE [OBJECT],
(241) JUST THAT IS THE SEED OF ALL ATTACHMENT
WHEN [ATTACHMENT] IS GENERATED BY ITS SPECIFIC [CONDITIONS].[56]

It follows that THOSE [Vaiśeṣika] yogins, EVEN if they know [suffering] BY MEDITATING ON the SUFFERING of what pertains to the self, WILL NOT THUS BECOME thoroughly detached by that [meditation] alone, because we see by DIRECT PERCEPTION THAT COGNIZANCE OF SUFFERING ALREADY EXISTS BEFORE one meditates, as when one is sick.[57]

---

the other hand, if, prior to liberation, one's meditative efforts are directed toward freeing a flawless self, it is unlikely that at the time of liberation one will suddenly cease to be attached to it, for one's "liberation" is thoroughly tied in with the existence of that self.

56 An alternative reading of PV 240c-241b (*blang dang dor bya'i khyad yod na / gcig las byung ba'i chags gang yin / de nyid rnam grangs kyis bskyed tshe / chags pa kun gyi sa bon yin*) yields: "When one distinguishes what is to be adopted from what is to be rejected, whatever attachment arises from one [of the two]—just that is the seed of all attachment when it is generated in turn."

57 Meditation merely on the suffering or flaws of what pertains to the self hardly can be considered sufficiently profound to lead to one's detachment from all suffering, because even non-yogins, simply by being ill, directly realize that what pertains to the self involves some suffering. Thus to understand the suffering of suffering, however, is not to understand the fact or process of the

[OPPONENT:] Because we see that one becomes detached WHEN one sees FAULTS IN THAT which has previously been a cause generating pleasure, meditation on suffering *is* the cause of detachment.

[RGYAL TSHAB RJE:] It follows that a person who is attached to the self WILL NOT BECOME thoroughly DETACHED by seeing faults IN RELATION TO THAT object, because EVEN IF THAT attached THOUGHT IS ABSENT just FOR THE MOMENT when one sees the fault, attachment to that [object] can arise again. FOR EXAMPLE, although A DESIROUS [male] is free from attachment at the time when he sees faults in one woman, attachment *can* arise in relation TO ANOTHER WOMAN, and it *will* arise in relation to that other.[58]

It follows that that [person attached to the self] does not thoroughly eliminate attachment toward any object, because HE DISTINGUISHES, in regard to a single object, on the one hand desire for WHAT IS TO BE ADOPTED AND [on the other, aversion for] WHAT IS TO BE REJECTED. It follows that [this reason] pervades, because WHATEVER ATTACHMENT originates FROM one's intending ONE object, JUST THAT IS THE SEED OF ALL ATTACHMENT that will result WHEN GENERATED BY THE SPECIFIC [appropriate] condiitons.[59]

---

subtler and more pervasive sort of suffering (that of formations) that infects all saṃsāric beings. Even the suffering of suffering cannot be eradicated unless one understands and eliminates the more fundamental suffering, which is rooted in self-grasping. Thus, an appreciation of the suffering of suffering does nothing to dispel that suffering as long as one continues to be attached to the self, and thus to generate the grasping that is the real cause of suffering rebirths.

58 To become thoroughly detached from an object or type of object, it is not sufficient that we see that what once was a source of pleasure now is a source of suffering. As Dharmakīrti notes, the fact that a man may come to see the flaws in a woman to whom he has been attached does not mean that he sees all women as flawed; indeed, most men who have rejected one woman will attach themselves to another. Even if a man should come to see attachment to women in general as flawed because of his unhappy experiences with one woman, he still will seek pleasure for his phantom self through attachment to other objects or activities, e.g., drink, or travel, or art. As long as he persists in his innate attachment to the self, he will continue to seek some type of pleasure for that self, and thus to grasp at one or another object that pertains to the self. Thus grasping, he will continue to be reborn in saṃsāra.

59 As long as attachment to self continues, one will be concerned with obtaining that which "benefits"the self and avoiding that which "harms"it. One will, thus, generate desire and aversion, which are, in turn, the basis of our creation of the karma that leads to our various suffering experiences and rebirths.

The impossibility of others being freed from attachment [292]

(241c) ATTACHMENT HAS AN OBJECT [THE SELF] THAT IS FLAWLESS;
[WHAT PERTAINS TO THE SELF] ALSO MUST BE FLAWLESS, [AS IT] ACCOMPLISHES [THE PLEASURES OF THE SELF].
(242) NOW, TOWARD WHAT WILL THERE BE FREEDOM FROM ATTACHMENT?
JUST THAT [BELIEF IN FLAWLESSNESS] ALSO IS [THE CAUSE OF] TRANSMIGRATING.
IF [YOU SAY THAT] IN THAT [CASE], THAT [WHICH PERTAINS TO THE SELF] IS INDEED FLAWED,
[WE REPLY:] THAT IS THE SAME AS THE SELF.
(243) NOW, IN RELATION TO WHAT WILL ONE BE DETACHED?
[SEEING] THE FLAWS OF THAT [WHICH PERTAINS TO THE SELF] IN THAT [CASE] DOES NOT FREE ONE FROM ATTACHMENT.

It follows that ATTACHMENT to self does not in the end act to free one from attachment, because THE OBJECT for which it strives IS a FLAWLESS self, as when one strives for buddhahood. It follows ALSO that the sense-faculties, too, MUST BE FLAWLESS, because THEY ACCOMPLISH the pleasures of that flawless self, as offerings to please the Conquerors. NOW, TOWARD WHAT WILL THERE BE, for a Vaiśeṣika, FREEDOM FROM ATTACHMENT? It follows that it is unacceptable that there be detachment from anything, because the self, its objects, and what pertains to the self are, all three, flawless, and [because] it is [nevertheless] certain that JUST THAT [belief in flawlessness] ALSO IS the cause binding TRANSMIGRATING beings in saṃsāra.[60]

[OPPONENT:] In that abode that is saṃsāra, THAT which pertains to the self IS INDEED FLAWED, because it generates suffering.

---

60 It is impossible that a Vaiśeṣika free themselves from attachment to either the self or what pertains to the self. Just as a Buddhist does not consider desire and striving for flawless buddhahood to be "saṃsāric" desire or striving, the Vaiśeṣika must consider their desire for the self to be good, because the object that they desire and strive for is good. By the same token, just as a Buddhist will consider that which "gives pleasure" to the buddhas, offerings, to be "good,"so too the Vaiśeṣika must consider that which contributes to the pleasure of the "good" self—the sense-faculties and whatever else pertains to the self—to be "good,"too. Thus, a Vaiśeṣika must instinctively believe that the self and what pertains to it (as well as the subject that cognizes both) are flawless, and be attached to them. The Buddhist, of course, believes that such attachment is the root of saṃsāra, so they assume that the Vaiśeṣika not only can never be detached, but never can be freed, either, since freedom depends on detachment from self-grasping.

[RGYAL TSHAB RJE:] It follows that the self is also flawed, because THAT which generates suffering IS THE SAME AS THE SELF [in status]. NOW, IN RELATION TO WHAT object WILL THAT person BE DETACHED? It follows that they will not be [detached in regard to any], because they see THE FLAWS OF THAT self IN THAT abode that is saṃsāra, [but] DO NOT [act] to FREE themselves FROM ATTACHMENT to that [self].[61]

Showing a perceptually based confutation [of the idea] that merely by seeing the sense-faculties, etc., as flawed one [can] remove desire for them [293]

[This is divided into:] (1) [Showing that] just seeing flaws is not the cause for removing desire [294] and (2) [Showing] the impossibility of seeing flaws as they are in the sense-faculties, etc. [295].

Showing that just seeing flaws is not the cause for removing desire [294]

(243c) [IF YOU ASSERT THAT DESIRE] IS DESTROYED WHEN ONE SEES FAULTS [IN AN OBJECT],
[SINCE] DESIRE ARISES FROM SEEING ITS GOOD QUALITIES,
(244-245) [WE REPLY:] THAT [DESIRE] FOR THE SENSE-FACULTIES, ETC., IS NOT THUS,
BECAUSE EVEN IN CHILDREN, ETC., WE SEE [DESIRE];
BECAUSE WE HAVE [DESIRE] EVEN FOR A FLAWED [SENSE-FACULTY];
BECAUSE WE DO NOT [DESIRE] THE GOOD-QUALITY [TRAITS]
OF OTHERS; AND BECAUSE WHAT HAS BEEN SHED, ETC.,
WILL NOT BE [SEEN AS] PERTAINING TO THE SELF.
IT IS NOT THE CASE THAT SEEING GOOD QUALITIES IS THE CAUSE OF THE THOUGHT
OF WHAT PERTAINS TO THE SELF, BECAUSE OF THAT [PREVIOUS ASSERTION].
(246) ONE WILL NOT ABANDON THAT [DESIRE]
THROUGH SEEING NON-GOOD QUALITIES, BECAUSE OF THAT [PREVIOUS ASSERTION].

[OPPONENT:] Attachment to liquor, etc., will be DESTROYED and rejected WHEN ONE SEES THAT THERE absolutely ARE FAULTS in liquor, be-

---

61 Just as believing the self to be flawless entails one's belief that what pertains to the self must be flawless, so, conversely, holding what pertains to the self to be flawed will entail believing that the self is flawed, for the two are inextricably interrelated. If, however, one sees the self as flawed but continues to believe in it, one will not strike at the self-grasping that is the root of saṃsāra, and so will not be freed from it.

cause [attachment] is a DESIRE that ARISES FROM SEEING THE GOOD QUALITIES of the liquor.[62]

[RGYAL TSHAB RJE:] Thus, it follows that THAT desire FOR THE SENSE-FACULTIES, ETC., does NOT originate [THUS], simply from one's having seen their good qualities, BECAUSE EVEN IN CHILDREN, ETC., who do not know how to distinguish flaws from good qualities, WE SEE desire; BECAUSE WE HAVE desire EVEN FOR A FLAWED sense-faculty; BECAUSE WE DO NOT desire THE GOOD-QUALITY eyes, etc., OF OTHERS as our own eyes, etc.; AND BECAUSE hairs THAT HAVE BEEN SHED, ETC., which previously were apprehended as having good qualities when they pertained to the self now WILL NOT BE desired AS PERTAINING TO THE SELF.

Thus, it follows that IT IS NOT THE CASE THAT just SEEING THE GOOD QUALITIES of sense-faculties, etc., IS THE CAUSE OF THE THOUGHT desirous OF WHAT PERTAINS TO THE SELF, BECAUSE THAT [assertion] that there is positive and negative concomitance is mistaken. If that is asserted, it follows that ONE WILL NOT ABANDON THAT desire THROUGH SEEING as faulty what does NOT have GOOD QUALITIES, BECAUSE OF THAT assertion.[63]

[Showing] the impossibility of seeing flaws as they are in the sense-faculties, etc. [295]

(246c) WE ALSO SEE THOSE THROUGH ATTACHMENT THAT SUPERIMPOSES
GOOD QUALITIES THAT DO NOT EXIST OTHERWISE.
(247) HOW CAN ONE DAMAGE THAT [DESIRE] BY MEDITATING [ON THE SUFFERING OF WHAT PERTAINS TO THE SELF]?
[SUCH MEDITATION] DOES NOT DAMAGE THE CAUSE OF THAT [DESIRE].

---

62 rGyal tshab rje fails to indicate that this sentence is an expression of the opponent's position, but it is read most reasonably thus.

63 The opponent attempts to argue that, just as attachment arises from seeing the good qualities in a particular object, so detachment will arise from seeing the flaws in an object. The Buddhist reply centers on a demonstration that attachment and a recognition of an object's good qualities are *not* invariably concomitant, for (a) one may be attached without consciously recognizing good qualities, as children are; (b) one may be attached while recognizing something's flaws, as when one has a defective, but nonetheless serviceable, sense-faculty; (c) one may recognize the good qualities of an object without being attached to or craving it, as when one recognizes that another person has good eyes but does not desire them because one's own eyes are good, too; and (d) one who is utterly detached does not consider either the good or bad qualities of what pertains to the self to be worthy of further concern, understanding that the designation of good and bad qualities is based chiefly on self-grasping, which they have transcended.

It follows that it is not certain that by meditating on the suffering of the sense-faculties, etc., one will see them as flawed, because WE ALSO SEE THOSE [sense-faculties] as having good qualities THROUGH ATTACHMENT THAT SUPERIMPOSES GOOD QUALITIES THAT DO NOT EXIST in them OTHERWISE.[64]

Summary:

HOW, by meditating on the suffering of suffering of what pertains to the self, CAN ONE DAMAGE THAT desire for what pertains to the self? It follows that it cannot be accepted that [one can], because BY MEDITATING on that, [one performs] a meditation that just DOES NOT DAMAGE THE CAUSE OF THAT desire, because through that [meditation] there is no damage to self-grasping in the least.[65]

---

64 Thus, regardless of one's attempts to see what pertains to the self as flawed, one invariably will superimpose some desirable qualities on what pertains to the self, because one continues to believe in a self whose needs must be served by the sense-faculties and anything else of which the word "mine" may be used.

65 Cf. above, p. 437, n. 42, for a possible Vaiśeṣika defense against the sorts of arguments raised by Buddhists. Even if a Vaiśeṣika were able to argue that Buddhist *psychological* analyses failed to take into account the sublimity of yogic experiences, as a result of which one might seem to have transcended attachment to what pertains to the self, it is questionable that the Vaiśeṣika concept of the self would be able to stand up to criticism—at least from the Buddhist perspective. If, as Dharmakīrti claims, religious accomplishment is to be preceded by correct cognition of reality, and the Vaiśeṣika's understanding is proven false, it is impossible that the Vaiśeṣika really accomplish what they claim to.

11. *The Truth of Path (2)*

A. A REFUTATION OF SĀṂKHYA SOTERIOLOGY

Refuting the Sāṃkhya system [296]

[This is divided into:] (1) The unacceptability, as a path to freedom, of just knowing that prakṛti and puruṣa are different [297], (2) The unacceptability, as a cause of detachment, of having a mind afflicted by the suffering of suffering [298] and (3) Identifying the nature of detachment [299].

The unacceptability, as a path to freedom, of just knowing that prakṛti and puruṣa are different [297]

(247c-248) A PERSON KNOWS THAT THEY HAVE A DIFFERENT
SELF-NATURE FROM THEIR SENSE FACULTIES,
BECAUSE THEY WILL STRIVE FOR OTHERS THAT ARE SUPERIOR,
AND BECAUSE THEY HAVE A MIND SUBJECT TO ARISING AND
DESTRUCTION.
ONE ALSO IS NOT ATTACHED THROUGH SEEING [PRAKṚTI AND PURUṢA]
AS IDENTICAL,
BECAUSE OF THAT. THAT ATTACHMENT TO SELF—
(249) ATTACHMENT WILL BE NATURALLY [DRAWN]
TO THE INTERNAL FACTORS THAT INTEND [FORM, ETC.].

[SĀṂKHYA OPPONENT:] According to us, it cannot be accepted that seeing the sense-faculties, etc., as having good qualities is the cause of saṃsāra, or that seeing them as flawed is the path to liberation. If you ask what [our view is, it is this:] Because the attached mind that apprehends prakṛti, which is pleasure, etc., and puruṣa as one is the cause of saṃsāra, and [because] by knowing those two as separate one rejects [the belief] that [prakṛti is] puruṣa, then since the puruṣa is free from attachment, that direct knowledge that prakṛti, which is pleasure, etc., and puruṣa are different is the path to freedom.[1]

[RGYAL TSHAB RJE:] It follows that one is not freed from [saṃsāric] existence merely by direct knowledge that prakṛti and puruṣa are different, because [even] A foolish PERSON inexperienced on the path KNOWS that puruṣa HAS A DIFFERENT SELF-NATURE FROM THEIR SENSE-FACULTIES and prakṛti, which is pleasure, etc. It follows that this is so, BECAUSE [that foolish person], desiring to be a striver for the puruṣa itself, WILL STRIVE FOR OTHER objects, sense-faculties, pleasure, etc., THAT ARE SUPERIOR to those that they have at present; AND BECAUSE, apprehending the fact that the self is identical in earlier and later [moments], THEY HAVE A MIND that cognizes that their own pleasure, etc., are SUBJECT TO ARISING AND DESTRUCTION. It follows that ONE ALSO IS NOT ATTACHED to [saṃsāric] existence just THROUGH THE MIND'S seeing prakṛti and puruṣa AS IDENTICAL and by desiring [their identity], BECAUSE it is unacceptable THAT just knowing those two as different be the cause of freedom.[2]

Prakṛti is said to be chiefly a hidden phenomenon, but if one knows that puruṣa and pleasure [and other qualities of prakṛti] are different, one can also know that prakṛti, which [has the qualities] of pleasure, etc., is different [from puruṣa]. The desirous mind and prakṛti are both ascertained to be physical, and [puruṣa] to be conscious.[3]

---

1 For further discussion of the Sāṃkhya position, see Radhakrishnan and Moore (1957) 424-52; Dasugpta (1975) I, chapter VIII; Koller (1970) chapter 5, Larson and Bhattacharya (1987); and Sopa and Hopkins (1976) 58-62.

2 This is the passage cited by rGyal tshab rje above (section III:9:A) in his discussion of the innate belief in a self independent of the aggregates, which is the object of refutation of a meditation on no-self. Here, the Sāṃkhya is ridiculed for asserting as the basis of their soteriology a fact that not only is instinctively believed by all beings, but which, if accepted, actually is the basis of all suffering, not liberation. The Sāṃkhya argues that puruṣa (the "person,"or self) is utterly different from prakṛti (the "procreatrix,"or nature), which includes the intellect (*buddhi*), the I-principle (*ahaṃkāra*), the sense-faculties, and the elements: in short, everything that we ordinarily list as comprising the cosmos. According to the Buddhist, it is precisely the belief that there is a permanent "person"or "self"independent of the impermanent aggregates that is the ignorant view that leads to the self-grasping that insures our continued rebirth in saṃsāra. That such a belief is instinctive is shown by two facts: (1) we instinctively desire to exchange "defective"aggregates for better ones, without fearing that thereby we would become a different "person"or have a different "self"and (2) we recognize that our pleasures and the sense-faculties through which they are enjoyed are transient, yet we continue to strive for perpetual, unchanging pleasure. That such belief is false is shown by the fact that no such self can be found to exist either within or independent of the aggregates, which are, in fact, exhaustive of the "person": in Sāṃkhya terms, the Buddhist conclusion is that there is *only* prakṛti.

3 Prakṛti itself is not a manifest phenomenon, but must be inferred from the various items that evolve from it, such as the faculties, elements, intellect, etc.

Thus, THAT ATTACHMENT TO SELF is the cause of resultant saṃsāric suffering, because by its own power ATTACHMENT WILL BE NATURALLY drawn TO THE INTERNAL FACTORS, the visual and other faculties THAT INTEND form, etc., and because it is drawn by the power of self-grasping itself.[4]

The unacceptability, as a cause of detachment, of having a mind afflicted by the suffering of suffering[5] [298]

(249c) RENUNCIATION LIKE THAT [ARISING] THROUGH
SOME PRESENT SUFFERING IS AVERSION, BUT
(250-251b) IT IS NOT DETACHMENT; AT THAT TIME
THERE EXISTS ATTACHMENT, BECAUSE [CRAVING] ANOTHER OCCASION [FOR HAPPINESS], ONE SEEKS IT.
THAT [AVERSION] REMAINS ONLY AS LONG AS [THE SUFFERING];
WHEN THAT IS ABSENT, ONE WILL REVERT
TO ONE'S OWN NATURE,
BECAUSE AVERSION HAS SUFFERING AS ITS CAUSE.

[OPPONENT:] One *will* be freed by meditating on suffering, because we see that when one is afflicted by suffering and becomes renounced, having regretted [the suffering], one becomes renounced.

Through knowing that the various items that comprise, or are evolutes of, prakṛti are separate from puruṣa, one will be able to infer that prakṛti itself is separate from puruṣa. Further, prakṛti is said to be inanimate, i.e., ultimately physical, while puruṣa is said to be conscious. The Buddhist, of course, divides the physical from the conscious differently, disposing of the "person" altogether, and finding that within "nature," i.e., the aggregates, form is physical, while sensation, recognition, formations and cognition are to one degree or another non-physical. The "pure consciousness" of the Sāṃkhya puruṣa is most closely approximated by the aggregate of cognition, whose nature is the apprehension of objects as they actually exist (cf. above PV 206-208).

4 Thus, as long as one accepts the existence of a "person,"one will be attached to self and to what may benefit the self. Thus, one will continue instinctively to believe that what pertains to the self, i.e., prakṛti, is necessary to the self, and one thus will continue to identify the two. From the Sāṃkhya perspective, of course, as long as one continues to associate puruṣa with prakṛti, one cannot be liberated, so the Sāṃkhya agrees with the Buddhist about the problems entailed by identifying the two. Where there is disagreement, obviously, is over the question whether there even exists a "person" that one might mistakenly associate with prakṛti.

5 The remaining part of this section deals not with Sāṃkhya, but with general issues of attachment, detachment and freedom.

[RGYAL TSHAB RJE:] It follows that a RENUNCIATION LIKE THAT arising THROUGH SOME person's PRESENT feeling of affliction by the SUFFERING of suffering IS concomitant with AVERSION, or it is the cause of [aversion], BUT IT IS NOT DETACHMENT, because AT THAT TIME that [renunciation] arises, THERE EXISTS ATTACHMENT in the person whose mindstream [includes "renunciation"]. It follows that this is so, BECAUSE, greatly attached to ANOTHER OCCASION for happiness, ONE SEEKS it.[6]

[OPPONENT:] When aversion arises continually, one will have destroyed [any possible] occasion for the arising of attachment, so one will be detached.

[RGYAL TSHAB RJE:] It follows that an averse person will *not* become detached merely through[7] the arising of aversion, because THAT aversion REMAINS ONLY SO LONG AS the suffering feeling; WHEN [the feeling] IS ABSENT, ONE WILL REVERT TO ONE'S OWN attached NATURE. It follows that the previous reason [pervades], BECAUSE that [AVERSION] HAS the SUFFERING feeling AS ITS CAUSE.[8]

Identifying the nature of detachment [299]

(251c-252b) ONE IS SAID TO BE DETACHED
[WHEN] ONE HAS GAINED EQUANIMITY IN ALL CASES,
[AND] IT IS THE SAME WHETHER [ONE IS ANOINTED BY] SANDAL OR [STRUCK BY] AN AXE,
BECAUSE ONE HAS ABANDONED WHAT IS TO BE ADOPTED AND WHAT IS TO BE REJECTED.

---

6 The Buddhist argument is, in effect, that aversion and detachment are not the same. Our affliction by some type of suffering generates *aversion* to or renunciation of that suffering, but it is not detachment from it, because aversion actually is an example of anger, which is a defilement, and because one in whom there is aversion continues to be attached to regaining the "happiness" they had enjoyed before the onset of their suffering. Cf. above, PV 211c-212, for an analysis of why anger and attachment are opposing conditions without the absence of one entailing the absence of the other.

7 In GT, read *gyis*, rather than *gyi*.

8 A presumably hypothetical opponent argues that if aversion is generated continually, then attachment never need arise again. Such an argument is absurd, however, for the suffering of suffering has been shown to arise *occasionally*. Thus, particular instances of suffering sensation must cease, and when they have ceased, one inevitably will be comparatively "happy," and thus once more under the manifest sway of attachment. Even in *avīci* hell, presumably, there are moments of respite.

[OPPONENT:] Well, then, according to you, what is detachment?

[RGYAL TSHAB RJE:] An arhant IS SAID TO BE "DETACHED," because they are a person who HAS GAINED EQUANIMITY through utterly abandoning attachment and anger IN ALL CASES, and IT IS THE SAME WHETHER they are respectfully anointed with SANDAL paste or cut by AN AXE. It follows that this is so, BECAUSE they are a person who has utterly ABANDONED attachment to WHAT IS TO BE ADOPTED AND WHAT IS TO BE REJECTED.[9]

Disposing of [the idea that our position] contradicts the [Buddha's] teaching on the meditation on suffering [300]

(252c) [THE BLESSED ONE] TAUGHT THE MEDITATION ON SUFFERING
WITH THE SUFFERING OF THE FORMATIONS IN MIND.
(253) ALSO, THAT [SUFFERING PERVADING] OUR [FORMATIONS] ARISES FROM CONDITIONS;
[MEDITATION ON] IT HAS AS ITS BASIS THE VIEW OF NO-SELF;
ONE IS FREED BY THE VIEW OF VOIDNESS—
THE REMAINING MEDITATIONS ARE FOR THE PURPOSE OF THAT.
(254) THUS, [THE BLESSED ONE] TAUGHT THAT FROM IMPERMANENCE [COMES]
SUFFERING, AND FROM SUFFERING, NO-SELF.

[OPPONENT:] Well, then, how is it that the Blessed One TAUGHT THE MEDITATION ON SUFFERING?

[RGYAL TSHAB RJE:] He did not teach it with only the suffering of suffering in mind, because he taught the meditation on suffering for the sake of the renunciation of a [saṃsāric] existence, WITH THE pervasive SUFFERING OF THE FORMATIONS IN MIND. ALSO, THAT suffering [pervading] OUR formations is not based on a permanent self, because IT ARISES FROM its own causes and from defiled CONDITIONS.[10]

---

9 What is to be adopted and what rejected by worldly beings (objects of attachment and anger) is conceived in relation to a self. An arhant no longer believes in such a self, and thus is indifferent to what is ordinarily sought or avoided on its behalf. Thus their equanimity in the face of pleasure and pain—which they may continue to feel, but to which they are quite indifferent, since they do not (excuse the word-play) "I"-dentify with it.

10 As we have seen above (p. 351 ff.), suffering is identified with the five aggregates that are under the control of karma and the defilements, and thus with the third type of suffering, that pervading all formations—not merely with the suffering of suffering or the suffering of change. The latter two types of suffering cover, respectively, what we usually call pain and pleasure, while the suffering of formations describes the suffering that pervades all saṃsāric existence. It is not, as we have

ALSO, that mind that meditates on suffering like that is not asserted to be a path that directly frees one from [saṃsāric] existence, because [freedom] HAS AS ITS BASIS or highest method the generation of THE VIEW that realizes NO-SELF. It also is necessarily the case that the meditation [on suffering] is not the path that directly frees one from [saṃsāric] existence, because ONE IS directly FREED from [saṃsāric] existence BY accustomating THE VIEW that realizes VOIDNESS, and [because] THE REMAINING MEDITATIONS, realizing composites to be impermanent and realizing contaminated phenomena to be suffering, ARE necessarily contemplated FOR THE PURPOSE OF effecting THAT wisdom realizing no-self. THUS, the reason the Blessed One TAUGHT THAT FROM the realization of composites as IMPERMANENT originates the realization of contaminated phenomena as SUFFERING, and that FROM the realization of SUFFERING [originates] the realization of NO-SELF, is because—as just explained—he taught that the method and the result of the method exist thus. According to the sūtra:

> "O, monks, is form permanent or is it impermanent?"
> "It is impermanent, Lord."
> "Is what is impermanent suffering or is it happiness?"
> "It is suffering, Lord, and what is impermanent has the nature of changing to suffering."
> "Is it proper to say of that, 'This is mine,' 'This is I,' or 'This is myself'?"
> "It is not, Lord."[11]

---

seen, based on a permanent self, because it arises through causes and conditions.

11 The passage is found at, e.g., M, i, 232. It is not furnished by Dharmakīrti, but by his various commentators, who see it as a scriptural basis for ordering the three "marks of existents" according to Buddhism: all composites are impermanent, all contaminated phenomena are suffering and all dharmas are without self. (A fourth, nirvāṇa is peace, sometimes is added.) Only the direct realization of no-self can directly effect the peace of nirvāṇa, but the realization of no-self can be assisted by the prior recognition of impermanence and suffering. The realization that all composites are impermanent leads to the realization that no saṃsāric happiness can endure, and thus that there is suffering. The suffering of contaminated phenomena, however, is seen to be under the power of various defilements and karma, and thus not to be a permanent self—for a self could not thus be under the power of causes and conditions. Thus, the aggregates that are identified with suffering are seen to be empty of self. On the three marks, see, e.g., Collins (1982) 227 and notes.

The reason for ascertaining the ordering thus:

In the wake of the realization of the suffering [composites] as impermanent, one turns away from [the idea that those composites] are ultimately reliable for the accomplishment of one's own aims, and the realization of contaminated phenomena as suffering induces a renounced mind. Formerly, from the combination of grasping at the happiness of self as obtainable and grasping at it as permanent, one grasped at the happiness as unalterably reliable. When one realizes that happiness is impermanent, the realization induces a suffering mind. Also, in the samādhi on the contamination of the upper realms, there arises the renounced mind that sees [birth in the upper realms] as like entering into a burning house—this definitely depends on the prior realization of subtle impermanence. When one sees that one is under the power of karma and defilements, one also understands that there is no independent person. The ordering of rough impermanence, suffering and no-self is thus comprehensible.[12]

Summary [301]

(254c-255b) ONE WHO HAS CRAVING, IS NOT FREE FROM ATTACHMENT,
DEPENDS ON ALL EFFORTS, [AND]
IS NOT FREE FROM THE DEFILEMENTS AND KARMA—
SUCH A [BEING] IS CALLED "SAṂSĀRIC."

It follows that the self that is "freed" HAS CRAVING, because IT IS NOT FREE FROM ATTACHMENT to self. If that is asserted, it follows that [the self] DEPENDS ON ALL karmic EFFORTS at attainment and avoidance. If that is asserted, it follows that [that self] IS NOT FREE FROM THE DEFILEMENTS AND KARMA, because of the two previous assertions. If [the latter] is asserted, it follows that SUCH A [self] IS CALLED "saṃsāric," because that [is the sort of] person that has been asserted.[13]

---

12 The upper realms, whose suffering nature only can be understood when one understands subtle impermanence, are the form and formless realms, which correspond to the god realm among the six types of saṃsāric rebirth. Generally, it is sufficient to recognize that one's happiness is impermanent and that it therefore is suffering, and that the conditionality of suffering insures that that which suffers is without self. One cannot, of course, utterly renounce saṃsāra until even the sublimest divine existence is understood to have a suffering nature, but the general recognition of one's impermanence and suffering provides a sufficient basis for a preliminary appreciation of the fact of no-self.

13 The chain of reasoning is this: when a self is "freed," a self still is conceived to

If it is possible [that one be detached from what pertains to the self without abandoning self-grasping], the pointlessness of accepting that a self is freed [302]

(255c-256b) AT THAT TIME THERE IS NO EXPERIENCER OF THAT [WHICH PERTAINS TO THE SELF],
SINCE YOU DO NOT ASSERT THAT WHICH PERTAINS TO THE SELF;
IF [THAT IS THE CASE], THAT SELF DOES NOT EXIST, EITHER,
[SINCE THE SELF] IS DEFINED AS THE ACTOR AND ENJOYER [OF WHAT PERTAINS TO THE SELF].

It follows then that AT THAT TIME THERE ALSO IS NO EXPERIENCER OF THAT which pertains to the self, BECAUSE YOU DO NOT ASSERT that THAT WHICH PERTAINS TO THE SELF exists to be experienced. IF that is asserted, it follows THAT THAT SELF DOES NOT EXIST, EITHER, because of that assertion. It follows that that [reason] pervades, because that one permanent self IS DEFINED AS the cause, THE ACTOR that creates karma AND THE ENJOYER of the result.[14]

Showing that it is necessary to abandon the self-view [303]

(256c-257b) THEREFORE, YOU WHO DESIRE FREEDOM! YOU SHOULD DIG OUT
FROM THE VERY ROOT THE VIEW OF [SELF IN] THE PERISHABLE

---

exist. There is, thus, attachment to self. Since there is attachment to self, one will continue to strive for that which benefits the self and avoid that which harms it. One will, thus, continue to commit defiled actions based on craving, and thereby to circle in saṃsāra. In short, then, when the opponent asserts that a "self"is freed, they are, in fact, asserting an impossibility, for where a self is asserted there can be no freedom, and only where there is a recognition of no-self can there actually be freedom. This argument is reminiscent of that found in Candrakīrti's *Madhyamakāvatāra*, chapter vi.

14 Although the view opposed here is not clearly identified, it may be that of Vedānta, which maintains that only the self is real, and that what pertains to the self is ultimately non-existent or illusory. If that is asserted, however, then the self, too, must be non-existent, for the self is said to be the experiencer of what pertains to the self, and if what pertains to the self is non-existent, then so too must be the self, since the experiencer and the experienced must have the same ontological status, or their interaction cannot be explained. Furthermore, a permanent self such as posited by all Ātmavādins cannot possibly be both the creator of karma and the experiencer of karmic results, because such a self would have to change its nature from the time it was a "creator"to the time it was an "experiencer,"but only an impermanent entity can change its nature.

COMPOSITES, WHICH BEGINNINGLESSLY ORIGINATES
FROM THE SEEDS OF APPROPRIATE HOMOGENEOUS CAUSES.

We call benevolently: [THEREFORE,] YOU WHO DESIRE FREEDOM! If you desire to attain liberation, YOU SHOULD DIG OUT FROM THE VERY ROOT THE VIEW OF [SELF IN] THE PERISHABLE COMPOSITES. It follows that it is reasonable to dig it out, because the self-view is the root of saṃsāra and [because] it is proven that the wisdom realizing no-self is the direct antidote to that. The self-view does not originate causelessly or from inappropriate causes, because it BEGINNINGLESSLY ORIGINATES FROM THE SEEDS OF APPROPRIATE HOMOGENEOUS CAUSES.[15]

B. A REFUTATION OF THEIST-RITUALIST SOTERIOLOGY

The unacceptability, as a path to freedom, of just the word of God*[16] *[304]

[This is divided into:] (1) Refuting [the attempt to] prove that a ritual empowered by God as a path to liberation is [in fact] a path to freedom [305], (2) Expressing [a further] rejection [306] and (3) Showing that the wisdom realizing no-self is the path to freedom [313].

---

15 This concludes the main part of Dharmakīrti's attack on Ātmavādin soteriology, which has been marked by two major thrusts: (1) the *psychological* observation that belief in the existence of a permanent self independent of the aggregates can be seen to be the basis of all our defiled actions and consequent sufferings, and (2) the *philosophical* observation that the existence of such a self cannot stand up to analysis, and thus must be false, and since successful action cannot be preceded by false understanding, spiritual accomplishments alleged to be based on the self-view cannot actually come to pass. Dharmakīrti makes it clear here that delusion has no beginning, but has been with us eternally, perpetuated from moment to moment by appropriate homogenes rooted in ignorance. Though beginningless, delusion is not endless: application of the appropriate antidote will result in a state in which wisdom is natural to the mind, homogeneously proceeding from moment to moment, in unending liberation.

16 The following section, concerned chiefly with refuting the idea that liberation can be attained through divinely empowered rituals recorded in scripture, seems to be aimed chiefly at the practices of the Nyāya school, rather than at the better-known ritualism of Mīmāṃsā, for the rituals criticized by Dharmakīrti are empowered by *īśvara*—in which most Mīmāṃsakas did not believe—and involve the "Unseen," a concept central to Nyāya cosmology. See, e.g., Dasgupta (1975) I, chapter VIII.

Refuting [the attempt to] prove that a ritual empowered by God as a path to liberation is [in fact] a path to freedom [305]

(257c-258) THE STATEMENT THAT ONE IS FREED MERELY BY
SACRED AUTHORITY DOES NOT AT ALL SATISFY THE INTELLIGENT;
WE DO NOT SEE ANY REASON WHY
SACRED AUTHORITY IS SUCH AN ENTITY.
A RITUAL ACCOMPLISHES [THE NON-GENERATION] OF A SPROUT, ETC.;
IT WILL NOT BE ABLE [TO EFFECT] A PERSON'S NON-GENERATION [OF REBIRTH],
(259) BECAUSE IT WOULD FOLLOW THAT ONE COULD BE FREED EVEN THROUGH
[THE BODY'S] ANOINTMENT WITH SESAME OIL OR BEING BURNED BY FIRE, ETC.
THOSE VICES ARE NOT DESTROYED [BY SUCH RITUALS],
BECAUSE THOSE WHO WERE HEAVY BEFORE WILL LATER BE LIGHTER,
(260) BUT IT IS NOT THE CASE THAT THROUGH THE LIGHTENING OF THIS [BODY]
VICE WILL BE LIGHTENED, BECAUSE IT IS NON-PHYSICAL.

It follows that THE STATEMENT THAT ONE IS FREED MERELY BY a ritual explained by SACRED AUTHORITY DOES NOT AT ALL SATISFY THE INTELLIGENT, because WE DO NOT SEE ANY REASON WHY the SACRED AUTHORITY that teaches that one is freed merely by a ritual empowered [by God] IS SUCH AN ENTITY that is not mistaken in its express meaning.[17] The plural marker implies alternative [objectors].[18]

Extreme consequences:

[OPPONENT:] When the mantra explained by sacred authority affects a seed, the sprout is not generated, so we are not mistaken about our express meaning.

[RGYAL TSHAB RJE:] When we see that A RITUAL ACCOMPLISHES the non-generation of a sprout by A SEED, ETC., it follows that IT WILL NOT BE ABLE to effect THE NON-GENERATION of further [saṃsāric] existences

---

17 The fact that "sacred authority" (*lung, āgama*) asserts that liberation is said to be attained through ritual is not sufficient grounds for accepting that this is in fact the case, because "sacred authority" may be in error or misinterpreted, and its assertions must be checked by generally accepted perceptual and inferential tests.

18 The plural marker is the *rnams* on those who "do not see (*mthong ba rnams, apaśyatāṃ*) any reason why sacred authority is such an entity," and may refer to other schools that, like Buddhism, do not hold scripture inherently to be inerrant.

[for] A PERSON directly affected [by that ritual] empowered by God, BECAUSE if that were the case, IT WOULD FOLLOW THAT ONE COULD BE FREED EVEN THROUGH the body's ANOINTMENT WITH SESAME OIL, BEING BURNED BY FIRE, ETC.

Likewise, it follows that mental VICES ARE NOT DESTROYED by a fire of burnt offerings, BECAUSE THOSE WHO WERE HEAVY BEFORE WILL LATER BE LIGHTER because their bodies have been heated by the fire of burnt offerings, [but] it does NOT follow THAT merely THROUGH THE LIGHTENING OF THIS person [making] burnt offerings the weight of VICE IS LIGHTENED, too, BECAUSE [vice] IS NON-PHYSICAL.[19]

Expressing [a further] rejection [306]

[This is divided into:] (1) [Showing that] just sacred words cannot damage the cause of future rebirths [307], (2) Refuting the reply to that [308] and (3) Disposing of [the attempt to] damage our refutation [309].

[Showing that] just sacred words cannot damage the cause of future rebirths [307]

> (260c-261) AN INTENTION [CONCOMITANT WITH] CRAVING ORIGINATES
> FROM DISTORTED COGNITION; WHEN CUT, IT WILL NOT LEAD [TO REBIRTH],
> BECAUSE IT IS BY THE COMPULSION [OF THAT INTENTION]
> THAT TRANSMIGRATORS TAKE BIRTH IN LOWER ABODES.
> WHEN ONE IS BORN, ONE IS ENABLED [BY] THAT VERY [INTENTION],
> BECAUSE [BIRTH] ORIGINATES FROM JUST THAT.
> (262) BECAUSE INTENTIONS ARE THEMSELVES
> KARMA, [RITUALS THAT DO NOT AFFECT INTENTION] DO NOT UNDERMINE THE CAUSE OF BIRTH.

---

19 On the one hand, if rituals alone can lead to liberation, then any ritual with some sort of discernible physical effect ought to be soteriologically valid, so not only should mantras be able to eradicate defilements, but so too should any of the various practices that have been enjoined at one time or another on Hindus: smearing the body with special oils or unguents, burning oneself, bathing in the Ganges, etc. On the other hand, it is not, in fact, the case that defilements can be destroyed by ritual means, because the various ritual practices have only physical effects, while defilements are a mental matter. Thus, one can sweat or scorch or starve oneself to the point of emaciation, shedding a great deal of physical weight, but one will not, thereby, lighten in the least the weight of the defilements that pollute the mindstream—for only *mental* changes will be able to lessen one's defilements.

THE INTENTION concomitant with the attached CRAVING to obtain happiness that ORIGINATES FROM the DISTORTED COGNITION apprehending suffering as happiness, [when] CUT by the power of its antidote in some mindstream, WILL NOT LEAD to future rebirths, BECAUSE IT IS BY THE COMPULSIONS of that [intention] THAT TRANSMIGRATORS effect grasping for BIRTH IN THE LOWER ABODES. WHEN an ordinary being IS BORN, they are enabled to be assisted by THAT VERY intention concomitant with distorted cognition and craving, BECAUSE [birth] ORIGINATES FROM JUST THAT as its cause.[20]

[OPPONENT:] Isn't karma also necessary as a cause of rebirth?

[RGYAL TSHAB RJE:] It follows that for rebirth into [saṃsāric] existence it is not necessary to have some karma objectively separate from that intention, BECAUSE the INTENTIONS concomitant with distorted cognition and craving ARE THEMSELVES the KARMA that generates future rebirths.[21]

Thus, just empowered rituals are not the path to freedom from [saṃsāric] existence, because just by obtaining that empowerment, a

---

20 Intention (*sems pa, cetanā*), sometimes translated as "volition,"is in Buddhist psychology one of the five (or more) mental factors invariably concomitant with a primary cognition. In Rabten's words ([1978] 69), "Intention is both the conscious and automatic motivating elements of consciousness that cause the mind to involve itself with and apprehend its objects. Just as a magnet by nature moves any iron that comes into contact with it, likewise by the mere existence of intention the mind is moved to various beneficial and detrimental objects. In addition, intention is the actual principle of activity. It is karma itself. Whether an action is mental, vocal or physical, the formative element that is primarily responsible and that accumulates tendencies and imprints on the mind is intention. Thus it acts as a basis for conditioned existence."Thus, any cognition will have concomitant with it some kind of intention. In all sentient beings, in turn, intention invariably will be concomitant with the craving that arises from ignorance. When intention is concomitant with craving, saṃsāric rebirth will continue; when intention no longer is concomitant with craving, as in the mind of an arhant, rebirth need no longer occur.

21 Thus, when a Buddhist says that karma is a cause of continued saṃsāric existence, they actually are saying that an intention concomitant with both craving and a distorted cognition of reality is a cause of continued saṃsāric existence. The qualification that intention must be concomitant with craving and distorted cognition is important, because it is not intention as such that is saṃsāric, since a buddha's cognitions invariably will be concomitant with intention. A buddha's intentions, however, no longer will be concomitant with craving or distorted cognition; they *will* be concomitant with such factors as the wisdom realizing no-self, great compassion, etc.

person DOES NOT in the least UNDERMINE THE CAUSE OF BIRTH into [saṃsāric] existence.

Refuting the reply to that [308]

(262c) [YOU MAY ASSERT:] THE BASIS OF MOVEMENT AND COGNITION IS [THE SENSES, ETC.];
THAT ACTIVITY IS FROM THE UNSEEN.
(263-264b) BECAUSE THE UNSEEN IS DESTROYED,THERE IS NO MOVEMENT;
THUS [KARMA] IS A FORMATION [OF THE SELF], NOT AN INTENTION.
[WE REPLY:] WE SEE THAT MINDS ARE CAPABLE IN THE GENERATION
OF ACTIVITY, BUT OTHER [FACTORS] ARE NOT,
BECAUSE OF CONCOMITANCE [IN CASES OF] EXISTING AND NOT EXISTING.
HOW CAN THOSE NOT LEAD [TO REBIRTH, SINCE] THAT [INTENTION] EXISTS?

[OPPONENT:] It follows that a person who has obtained empowerment will not have future rebirths, because [when] a person moves toward some object, THE BASIS OF their MOVEMENT toward that object AND of their COGNITION of form, etc., is visual activity, etc. THAT ACTIVITY WILL arise FROM the Dharmic and non-Dharmic action of THE UNSEEN, and the action of THE UNSEEN IS DESTROYED by the empowerment, [SO THERE IS NO MOVEMENT]. THUS, karma IS A FORMATION of qualities of the self and NOT—as you have asserted—INTENTION.[22]

[RGYAL TSHAB RJE:] WE SEE THAT intentional MINDS concomitant with distorted cognition and craving ARE CAPABLE to assist IN THE GENERATION OF the ACTIVITY of the sense-faculties, etc., in the womb, BUT it follows that rituals, etc., OTHER [causes], DO NOT, BECAUSE only those [intentions] are [proven] by positive and negative CONCOMITANCE AS

---

22 The opponent replies that karma is not, as the Buddhist claims, identical with intention, but that it is, rather, the formation, or complex, of activities that begins with actions by the invisible but nevertheless physical Unseen (*ma mthong ba, adṛṣṭa*), and eventually issues in the mental, verbal and physical actions observed in the world. The Unseen is described by Dasgupta ([1975] I, 72) as the "potency" of any action, and is believed to be affected by ritual performance. Thus, Dharmakīrti's opponent claims that since karma is bound up with the Unseen, which is ultimately physical, an empowerment that affects the Unseen will affect karma, too—to the point where an empowerment that utterly destroys the power of the Unseen will by definition remove all karma, including that which impels one to take saṃsāric rebirths.

EXISTING as assistants [when present] AND NOT EXISTING [as assistants when absent]. HOW CAN THOSE empowerments one has obtained NOT LEAD to future rebirth? It follows that they will lead [to them], because THAT cause of that [rebirth] EXISTS, without having been undermined.[23]

Disposing of [the attempt to] damage our refutation [309]

[This is divided into:] (1) The unacceptability [of the idea] that the power of mind can be destroyed by an empowerment [310], (2) Extreme consequences [311] and (3) A permanent self's unsuitability as a creator [312].

The unacceptability [of the idea] that the power of mind can be destroyed by an empowerment [310]

> (264c-265b) IF [YOU SAY THAT EMPOWERMENT RENDERS] THOSE POWERLESS,
> [WE REPLY:] THOSE [WHO HAVE BEEN EMPOWERED], IMMEDIATELY UPON EMPOWERMENT
> WILL NOT APPREHEND, RELATE,
> WANDER OR STOP [VIS À VIS OBJECTS, ALL OF WHICH ACTIONS ARE] BY VIRTUE OF INTENTIONS.

[OPPONENT:] Because the empowerment has rendered THOSE distorted [cognitions] and craving POWERLESS to generate further rebirths, one who has obtained empowerment does not take rebirth.

[RGYAL TSHAB RJE:] It follows that THOSE persons who have obtained empowerment, IMMEDIATELY UPON EMPOWERMENT, WILL NOT willingly APPREHEND objects of the visual and other faculties, will not RELATE specifically to a desired object, and will not [mentally] WANDER from object to object OR STOP [wandering] through the appropriate conditions—[all of which actions occur] BY VIRTUE OF INTENTIONS in [the person's] own mindstream—because the power of the intentions that [so] act was destroyed by the empowerment. Alternatively, [one will not, because of the empowerment, encounter a situation where] the

---

23 The first Buddhist reply is a general counter-assertion: it is only intention that can be observed to be invariably concomitant with actions and experiences of body, speech and mind; rituals are not thus concomitant. Thus, ultimate control of the quality of one's actions cannot be gained through ritual, but only through transformation of the intentions that *are* the seed of all that we experience. Indeed, far from undermining saṃsāra, most rituals simply perpetuate it, because they are based on a mistaken apprehension of reality, and do not profoundly affect the actual causes of saṃsāra.

sense-faculties [at first] cannot relate to their objects because one is overly distracted and then are restored [to their objects] by means of [an intention] that ends [the distraction].[24]

Extreme consequences [311]

(265c-266b) [IF YOU SAY:] WHAT? WHEN [AT DEATH] THERE IS NO THOUGHT,
THERE WILL BE NO [REBIRTH]; [WE REPLY:] THE STAINS WILL CONNECT
WITH A [SUBSEQUENT] MIND. IF [YOU SAY:] THE CAPACITY [TO CONNECT] DOES NOT EXIST,
[WE REPLY:] THEN A LIVING PERSON ALSO WILL NOT HAVE THE CAPACITY [TO CONNECT THOUGHTS EVEN WHEN ALIVE].
(266b-267c) THE CONTINUUM OF FAULTS, WITH ITS OWN SEEDS,
IS NOT REMOVED THROUGH EMPOWERMENT,
BECAUSE WHEN THE ANTIDOTE INCREASES,
[FAULTS] DECREASE, AND [THEY] INCREASE [WITH THE INCREASE] OF WHAT FAVORS THEM.

[OPPONENT:] What? At death-time, WHEN THERE IS NO THOUGHT, THERE WILL BE NO origination of saṃsāric dharmas.

[RGYAL TSHAB RJE:] THE STAINS of attachment, etc., [adhering to] a dying person who has obtained empowerment WILL CONNECT WITH A subsequent homogeneous MIND, because of the completion of the uninterruptable direct cause with the capacity [to effect] that result.[25]

---

24 The opponent claims that an empowerment or ritual has the power to neutralize craving and ignorance, and thus prevent rebirth. The Buddhist reply is that if that is the case, then intention must have been neutralized as well, for craving and ignorance will invariably accompany intention in any mindstream that lacks a direct realization of no-self. Thus, intention's capacity to focus upon a particular object also will be neutralized as soon as the empowerment has been received—which clearly does not happen in those who have received empowerment. A possible opponent's reply to this alleged absurdity, not considered by Dharmakīrti or rGyal tshab rje, is that the empowerment has the power not to destroy intention as such, but simply to disassociate intention from craving and ignorance. The Buddhist reply to this contention would, of course, be to point out again that a ritual that does not presuppose or entail a direct realization of no-self simply will not have the power to disassociate intention from craving and ignorance.

25 The opponent shifts their tack slightly, arguing that an empowerment has the capacity to assure that *at death-time* there will be no more intention and thus no craving or rebirth. The Buddhist reply is that each mental moment in which craving is involved has the capacity to generate a subsequent mental moment

[OPPONENT:] Since the [final mind's] CAPACITY to connect with subsequent homogenes has been destroyed by the empowerment, [such connection] DOES NOT EXIST.

[RGYAL TSHAB RJE:] THEN it follows that [the mind] of A LIVING PERSON who has obtained empowerment ALSO WILL NOT HAVE THE CAPACITY to connect with subsequent homogenes even during life itself, because that ability has been destroyed by the empowerment. Thus, THE CONTINUUM OF the FAULTS of attachment, etc., WITH ITS OWN homogeneous SEEDS, IS NOT REMOVED THROUGH EMPOWERMENT, BECAUSE WHEN THE ANTIDOTE [to the faults], the wisdom realizing no-self, INCREASES, [the faults] DECREASE; [AND the faults] INCREASE when there is an increase OF WHAT FAVORS [the faults], inappropriate mental directionality.[26]

A permanent self's unsuitability as a creator [312][27]

(267c-268) IT IS CONTRADICTORY FOR [A PERMANENT SELF]
SUCCESSIVELY TO EFFECT
GENERATION, BECAUSE A PERMANENT [SELF]
IS INDEPENDENT, AND [BECAUSE] IT WOULD ACT WITH A NATURE

---

in which craving also is involved, and that the sequence perforce must continue until an antidote to the craving is applied. Thus, an empowerment should have the capacity immediately to destroy craving, or not at all. If craving has been observed to persist in a person who has received empowerment, we can safely conclude that the empowerment has not eradicated their craving, and that craving thus will be present at death-time, and will help impel them into a subsequent saṃsāric existence.

26 If the opponent argues that an empowerment specifically destroys the mind's ability to connect with a subsequent mind at death-time, the consequence is the same: if the empowerment *does* have such capacity, then mind should cease immediately after empowerment; since mind does not cease immediately after empowerment, we may conclude that the empowerment does not have the capacity to prevent mind from connecting with its subsequent homogenes. In fact, there is no concomitance between empowerment and the presence or absence of mental faults; the concomitance is between the faults and different types of mental directionality: negative, ignorance-based directionality leads to an increase in faults, while positive directionality, based upon wisdom, leads to a decrease in faults. Mental directionality, or attention (*yid la byed pa, manaskāra*) is, like intention, an omnipresent mental factor. See, e.g., Rabten (1978) 70.

27 The following two sections return to rather more general concerns: an attack on the basic premises of Ātmavāda and an attempt to establish that the wisdom realizing no-self is the path to freedom.

SUCH THAT IT IS A PRODUCER AND A NON-PRODUCER [AT THE SAME TIME];
ALSO, CAUSE AND RESULT WILL BE IDENTICAL.
IF [YOU SAY THAT] THOSE ARE DIFFERENT FROM THAT [SELF],
(269) [WE REPLY:] THIS WILL UNDERMINE THEIR BEING THE PRODUCER *AND* THE EXPERIENCER;
[ALSO,] IT IS NOT EVEN PROVED THAT [A PERMENENT SELF] IS ABLE [TO EFFECT RESULTS].
[IF YOU SAY THAT WITHOUT A SELF, ONE PERSON WOULD HAVE AN EXPERIENCE AND] ANOTHER WOULD REMEMBER AND ENJOY IT, ETC.,
[WE REPLY: OUR POSITION] IS NOT DAMAGED BY THIS CONSEQUENCE,
(270) BECAUSE THERE IS NOT ANYONE WHO REMEMBERS;
THUS, MEMORY ORIGINATES FROM EXPERIENCE.

[OPPONENT:] It is unacceptable that you Anātmavādins be liberated.[28]

[RGYAL TSHAB RJE:] It *is* acceptable for us, but it is not acceptable for those who speak of a permanent self, and it follows that IT IS CONTRADICTORY FOR a permanent self SUCCESSIVELY TO EFFECT GENERATION of the states of bondage and liberation, BECAUSE A PERMANENT [entity] IS INDEPENDENT of conditions. It follows that it also is contradictory that [a permanent self] even effect the generation of a result, because the permanent would then [ACT WITH] A NATURE SUCH THAT IT IS able to be [both] A PRODUCER AND A NON-PRODUCER of results. It follows that CAUSE AND RESULT WILL BE IDENTICAL, because that same self is the accumulator of karma and the experiencer of the result.[29]

---

28 This is a standard Ātmavādin retort to the Anātmavādin: if there is no "self" or "person" who first is bound and then liberated, one cannot say that anyone is liberated, so one cannot speak meaningfully of the Anātmavādin's "liberation."

29 The Buddhist reply is that, in fact, bondage and liberation only can be meaningfully predicated when there is no permanent self, for (a) a permanent self cannot generate both bondage and liberation, since the two are situations requiring utterly different conditions, but a permanent entity cannot be dependent on varying conditions, and thus cannot generate different types of situations; (b) a permanent self cannot, in fact, be held to generate any result, since if it generates one result, it simultaneously is the non-generator of other results, and thus simultaneously possesses two contradictory qualities—but whether it is a producer or a non-producer, it should remain thus forever, because it is permanent; and (c) a permanent self that is both the creator of karma and the experiencer of the result only can experience a result that is identical with the cause, because such a self neither changes nor is changed by con-

[OPPONENT:] THOSE causes and results ARE substantially DIFFERENT FROM THAT permanent self.

[RGYAL TSHAB RJE:] It follows that THIS WILL UNDERMINE [the idea] THAT THE PRODUCER of karma AND the EXPERIENCER of the result is that permanent self. It follows that IT IS NOT EVEN PROVEN THAT a permanent [self] IS ABLE to assist in [bringing about] the result, because a permanent [self] does not have complete ability to [show] positive and negative concomitance.[30]

[OPPONENT:] If there is no self, then one [person] would have an experience and ANOTHER WOULD REMEMBER it; AND one [person] would accumulate [karma] and another WOULD ENJOY ITs [fruits,] ETC.

[RGYAL TSHAB RJE:] Those who say the aggregates are momentary by reason of the no-self[31] of the experiencer and rememberer, do NOT have their [position] DAMAGED BY THE CONSEQUENCE that one [person] has an experience and another remembers it, or that one accumulates [karma] and another enjoys [the fruit], BECAUSE THERE IS NOT ANY permanent person WHO first has an experience and later REMEMBERS it. [THUS,] it follows that there is no fault such that one wastes karma that has been created or meets [the result of karma] not created, because MEMORY ORIGINATES FROM the EXPERIENCE of an object [similar to one encountered before], in accordance with conditions.[32]

---

ditions.

30 If the permanent self is said to be different from cause and result, then it no longer is meaningful to say that the self creates karma and experiences the result, for cause and result have become extrinsic to the self—and the Ātmavādin's entire argument has been based on positing a substantial self that could be the basis of bondage and freedom. Furthermore, a permanent self cannot even be asserted to be an assistant cause in the generation of some result, because an assistant cause must be such that its presence is correlated with the result's arising, and its absence with the result's non-arising, and a permanent self never can be absent. Thus, it cannot meaningfully be described as a cause. Cf. above, PV 21ff.

31 In GT, amend *bdag yod* to *bdag med*.

32 The Buddhist account of the operations of karma and memory neither requires a permanent self nor entails that a karmic result or memory will pertain to someone utterly different from the person who created the karmic cause or had a previous similar experience. Rather, the karmic causes and original experiences are events in a particular impermanent mindstream. Their seeds or impressions exist from moment to moment, outside the range of conscious awareness, as mental formations (*saṃskāras*). When the specific conditions that are necessary for the ripening of the karmic seed are present, that karma will "ripen" as the appropriate result. Similarly, memory occurs when one has

Showing that the wisdom realizing no-self is the path to freedom [313]

(270c-271b) WHEN ONE HAS SUPERIMPOSED ON THE FOUR [NOBLE] TRUTHS THAT
[SUFFERING] IS STABLE OR PLEASURABLE OR "I"
AND "MINE"—INCORRECT [INTERPRETATIONS]
OF THE SIXTEEN ASPECTS—THEN THERE IS CRAVING.
(271c-272b) THE CORRECT VIEW, OF NO-SELF—
CONTEMPLATED WELL WITH A REALIZATION OF THOSE [SIXTEEN CORRECT] ASPECTS,
THE OBJECTS THAT ARE THE OPPOSITES OF THOSE [MISINTERPRETATIONS LISTED ABOVE]—
DESTROYS CRAVING TOGETHER WITH WHAT FOLLOWS UPON IT.
(272c-273b) ONE CANNOT POSSIBLY BE BORN [AGAIN]
EVEN IF KARMA AND THE BODY REMAIN,
BECAUSE ONE [CRUCIAL CAUSE, CRAVING] DOES NOT EXIST; [REBIRTH, AFTER ALL,] HAS *THREE* CAUSES;
FOR EXAMPLE, WITHOUT THERE BEING A SEED, A SPROUT [WILL NOT ARISE, EVEN IF EARTH AND WATER ARE PRESENT].

Craving is the root of saṃsāra, because, WHEN ONE HAS SUPERIMPOSED their inverses ON THE FOUR NOBLE TRUTHS—such as that suffering is permanent, IS STABLE, OR PLEASURABLE, OR IS "I" AND "MINE," along with the remaining INCORRECT [interpretations] OF THE SIXTEEN ASPECTS—THEN THERE IS CRAVING, and by force of craving there is continued birth. Only the wisdom realizing no-self is the path to freedom, because THE CORRECT VIEW that IS realization OF NO-SELF—CONTEMPLATED WELL WITH a perfect REALIZATION OF THOSE sixteen ASPECTS, impermanence, etc., THE OBJECTS THAT ARE THE OPPOSITES OF THOSE inverses of the four noble truths—DESTROYS from the root CRAVING TOGETHER WITH WHAT FOLLOWS UPON IT.[33]

---

an experience or set of experiences that appear similar to a previous experience or set of experiences of which one continues to carry an impression. There is no *permanent* person who both experiences and remembers, but there is a person: the five impermanent aggregates. If the "person" is understood to be no more than the aggregates, then it *is* meaningful to speak of the same person experiencing and remembering—it simply always must be borne in mind that the person is impermanent.

33 Thus, the opposites of the sixteen aspects of the four noble truths are not an arbitrary listing, but comprise a description of the attitudes toward reality that contribute to the continued generation of craving and, thus, rebirth; while the sixteen aspects themselves comprise a description of attitudes toward reality

[OPPONENT:] Even if there is no craving, if karma and the body [still] exist, one will not be freed from saṃsāra.

[RGYAL TSHAB RJE:] An arhant CANNOT POSSIBLY BE BORN again into saṃsāra EVEN IF KARMA AND THE BODY REMAIN, BECAUSE ONE of the chief causes, craving, DOES NOT EXIST. This [reason] pervades, because birth into [saṃsāric] existence HAS THREE CAUSES. FOR EXAMPLE, WITHOUT THERE BEING A SEED, A SPROUT will not originate.[34]

C. A REFUTATION OF JAINA SOTERIOLOGY

The unacceptability, as a path to freedom, of merely eliminating karma and the body [314]

[This is divided into:] (1) The actual refutation [315] and (2) Disposing of objections [316].

The actual refutation [315]

(273c-274b) ONE WILL NOT ABANDON KARMA AND THE BODY,
BECAUSE THERE ARE NO ANTIDOTES,
AND BECAUSE ONE IS UNABLE, BECAUSE WHEN THERE IS
CRAVING, THERE IS RENEWED ORIGINATION.

[DIGAMBARA OPPONENT:] Even by the elimination of [just] karma and the body, one will be freed from [saṃsāric] existence, because rebirth has three causes. Thus, it is reasonable to rely on the antidotes only to karma and the body.[35]

---

that are conducive to the elimination of craving—the most important, of course, being no-self and voidness (the last two aspects of the truth of suffering), for direct realization of *them* is the basis for the elimination of all craving. Cf. above, p. 344 ff.

34 Rebirth is asserted to have three causes: craving, karma and the body. (Sometimes ignorance is listed instead of the body; cf. above, section III:7.) If any of these is absent, the resultant rebirth will not occur. Thus, even if an arhant still has a body and residual karmic seeds in their mindstream, if they lack craving they no more can be reborn than a sprout can appear when there no longer is a seed. Although rGyal tshab rje includes this objection-and-answer (= PV 272c-273b) in his discussion of wisdom as a path to freedom, it might easily be included in the following section, since the opponent seems to reflect a Jaina point of view.

35 The Digambara is one of the two major traditions within Jainism, the other being the Śvetāmbara. Digambara means "sky-clad" (= naked) and Śvetāmbara means "white-clad"—and, in fact, the differences between the traditions are little more than skin-deep, based as they are more on disagreements over par-

[RGYAL TSHAB RJE:] Without abandoning craving, ONE WILL NOT be able to ABANDON KARMA AND THE BODY, BECAUSE THERE ARE NO ANTIDOTES for abandoning karma and the body, AND BECAUSE without abandoning craving ONE IS NOT ABLE utterly to abandon [karma and the body]. It follows that this is so, BECAUSE WHEN THERE IS CRAVING, THERE IS RENEWED karma, and from that the ORIGINATION of a body.[36]

Disposing of objections [316]

[This is divided into:] (1) Refuting reliance on equally strong antidotes for destroying both karma and craving [317], (2) Refuting [the idea] that austerities combine the potencies of [many] karmas and eliminate them [318] and (3) Refuting [the idea] that karma and craving are equally to be abandoned [319].

Refuting reliance on equally strong antidotes for destroying both karma and craving [317]

(274c) IF [YOU SAY THAT] ONE MUST STRIVE FOR THE SAKE OF ELIMINATING BOTH [KARMA AND CRAVING],
[WE REPLY:] IT IS POINTLESS TO FATIGUE ONESELF [IN ORDER TO] ELIMINATE KARMA;

---

ticular types of observances than on fundamental doctrinal disputes. All Jainas, certainly, would agree that the primary goal of religious striving is the exhaustion and elimination of karma, particularly through physical austerities. The exhaustion of previous karma and the non-creation of new karma leaves one liberated and omniscient, for the soul (*jīva*) is intrinsically pure but soiled by karma, and the elimination of karma allows the soul to shine forth with all its natural radiance. Compare this view to that above, PV 208, where an impermanent mind (rather than a permanent soul) is said to be obscured by defilement (rather than karma). On Jainism, see, e.g., Sopa and Hopkins (1976) 62-63, Dasgupta (1975) I, chapter VI, Radhakrishnan and Moore (1957) chapter VIII and, e.g., P. Jaini (1979) and J. Jaini (1979).

36 Here, there simply is a disagreement on soteriology. The Jaina believes that the elimination of karma through, e.g., physical austerities, will entail the elimination of craving. The Buddhist, on the other hand, believes that both karma and the body are rooted in craving, and that as long as craving remains there will be karma and continued rebirth, while if craving is eliminated there will be no further basis for rebirth or the fruition of previously created karma. The Buddhist will be unable to accept that the Jaina path can eliminate craving, karma or the body, because craving is the basis of the other two, and craving only can be eliminated through a direct realization of no-self, a doctrine not held by the Jainas (who maintain that the soul's states are impermanent, but that its nature is permanent).

(275) ONE CAN INFER THAT KARMAS HAVE MANY DIFFERENT
POTENCIES, BECAUSE WE SEE VARIOUS
RESULTS. THUS, BY ONE AFFLICTION
[RESULTING FROM] AUSTERITY, ONE WILL NOT ELIMINATE [ALL KARMAS]:
(276) ONE WILL NOT [ELIMINATE ALL] HETEROGENEOUS [RESULTS]
THROUGH SOME [TORMENT],
THOUGH THE RESULT GENERATED WILL BE LESSER.[37]

[OPPONENT:] If that is the case, then it is reasonable that ONE STRIVE FOR THE SAKE OF ELIMINATING individually BOTH karma and craving, because both are causes of saṃsāra.

[RGYAL TSHAB RJE:] It follows that IT IS POINTLESS TO FATIGUE ONESELF [for the sake of] an antidote that will separately ELIMINATE KARMA, because without abandoning craving, one will not abandon [karma]; it is not necessary to abandon [karma] separately. By abandoning the one root of the defilements, one can abandon all the others. There is [however] no way that [the abandoning of just one] karma will have such [a result], because ONE CAN INFER THAT people's KARMAS HAVE MANY DIFFERENT POTENCIES, [BECAUSE] WE SEE that the VARIOUS RESULTS of karma are pleasant or unpleasant. [THUS,] it follows that BY the ONE AFFLICTION inflicted by pulling out hairs or [by] some other specific AUSTERITY, ONE WILL NOT ELIMINATE all karma, because by abandoning one karma, one will not [abandon] all karma that will be abandoned, since karmas are infinite.[38]

---

37 An alternative reading of PV 276a-b (*rnam 'gas de bskyed 'bras bu ni / chung 'gyur rigs mi mthun can min*) yields: "The results generated by some [karma] will be lessened, but one will not [eliminate all] heterogeneous [karmic results]."

38 Craving and karma are both causes of rebirth, but they are not equally responsible, for there can be karma without craving, but there cannot be craving without karma. Since craving is the more fundamental cause, one can eliminate karma through eliminating craving, but one cannot eliminate craving simply through the elimination of karma. Furthermore, because craving demonstrably is the basis of all other defilements and of the creation of all negative karma, the elimination just of craving will insure the elimination of all other defilements and the prevention of the fruition of previously created karma. One cannot, on the other hand, argue that one karma or type of karma is the basis of all other karmas, for different karmic results presuppose utterly different types of karmic causes. Thus, the experience, hence "exhaustion," of one karmic result does not entail the exhaustion of other, heterogeneous karmas, in part because karmas are infinite. An infinity of karmas never can be exhausted one by one: they only can be rendered impotent by the destruction of

One can infer through objectively impelled reasoning (a) from pleasant results, that they were preceded by good karma, (b) from unpleasant results, [that they were preceded by] bad karma and (c) from a mixture of pleasant and unpleasant [results] that they were preceded by a mixture of good and bad karma—but where, when and how the karma that preceded the body was created, are very hidden [phenomena].[39]

It follows that ONE WILL NOT eliminate all homogeneous and HETEROGENEOUS results [just] THROUGH SOME [specific] torment [of] the body with austerities, because by experiencing, e.g., the torment that is THE RESULT of previous karma GENERATED BY austerities, one will eliminate only [the fruition of] some [results], which are LESSER.[40]

Refuting [the idea] that austerities combine the potencies of [many] karmas and eliminate them [318]

(276c) IF [YOU SAY:] WHAT? AUSTERITIES HAVE A POWER.
BY THIS COMBINING POWER [THERE OCCURS THE] ELIMINATION [OF THE RESULTS OF MANY KARMAS];

---

the condition indispensable to their ripening, which is, according to Buddhism, craving based on self-grasping.

39 rGyal tshab rje adds the observation here that the invariable concomitance between types of experiences and types of karmic causes can be inferred from observation, and thus that the *general* validity of karma can be proven logically, whereas the relation between particular results and particular causes—especially where multiple lives are involved—only can be known perceptually by a highly developed or omniscient mind. *If* we grant that psychological observation validates karma within this life, and if we have accepted Dharmakīrti's earlier arguments proving past and future lives, then karma in general will have been proven. On the other hand, a skeptical opponent might contend that (a) it is not necessarily the case—even in this life—that everything that happens to us is a result of causes we and we alone have created and/or (b) it is arguable that every intentional act of body, speech and mind has a specifically moral quality that someday will fructify in further experiences for the agent. The argument then would turn on issues of causality and its relation to mentality and morality, on which the Buddhist and their opponent may have irreconcilable differences.

40 In any case, the great variety and number of karmic causes we have created beginninglessly assures that the experience of just one type of karmic result eliminates only the karma or type of karma that is the seed of *that* particular result. Other types of karma remain intact in the mindstream, their results still to be experienced, although perhaps with lessened effect.

(277) [WE REPLY:] YOU MUST ASSERT THAT AUSTERITIES ARE OTHER THAN
AFFLICTION OR THAT THEY ARE THE AFFLICTION ITSELF:
IF [THE FORMER, THEN] THROUGH SOME MINOR AFFLICTION ONE WILL AVOID [MAJOR SUFFERING], OR
WITHOUT AFFLICTION ONE WILL ABANDON ALL [KARMIC RESULTS];
(278-279b) [IF THE LATTER,] THIS [AUSTERITY] WILL NOT COMBINE
POTENCIES, BECAUSE IT IS THE RESULT OF KARMA.
THAT WHICH EFFECTS THE CESSATION OF ANY FLAWS
HAS POWER IN RELATION TO THE KARMA CREATED BY THAT [FLAWED DESIRE],
BECAUSE IT DESTROYS THE FAULT OF DESIRE FOR REBIRTH;
HOW WILL IT UNDERMINE [KARMA] ALREADY ACTIVATED?

[OPPONENT:] WHAT? AUSTERITIES HAVE a *combining* POWER to remove various suffering and pleasurable results. BY THIS, when one experiences one torment, just that one result which has COMBINING POWER will entail the ELIMINATION of many [karmic results].

[RGYAL TSHAB RJE:] YOU [must] ASSERT either (a) THAT AUSTERITIES ARE OTHER THAN [just] bodily torment and the AFFLICTION of suffering, [and include, e.g.,] generosity, morality, etc.; OR (b) THAT [austerities] ARE the AFFLICTION ITSELF.

If (a), it follows that it is pointless to strive intently for the sake of eliminating karma and its result [through such] torments as setting the five fires, etc., because THROUGH SOME MINOR AFFLICTION such as pulling out only one hair, ONE WILL be able to AVOID all the remaining results. The word "OR" [in the root-text[41] means that] it follows that WITHOUT austerities [that involve] the AFFLICTION of torment ONE WILL be able to ABANDON ALL karmas and their results, because an austerity has the power to combine into one the potencies of all karmas.

If (b) it follows that THIS austerity WILL NOT COMBINE THE POTENCIES of [all] karmas or [even] effect a rough elimination of their potency, ETC., BECAUSE THAT austerity IS THE RESULT OF bad KARMA, LIKE THE karma of a bullock who plows the fields.[42]

---

41 The "or"at the conclusion of PV 277a (*nyon mongs cha 'ga' spong ba* 'am) does not appear to reflect a corresponding *vā* in the Sanskrit.

42 If the Jaina maintains that an austerity has the power to exhaust many different types of karmas, then they are faced with a dilemma. If, on the one hand, austerity is something different from painful torment, then mild austerities should suffice for the elimination of all sorts of karma. If, on the other hand, austerity is identical to painful torment, then austerity is nothing but a karmic

[OPPONENT:] Well, then, you contradict your assertion that developing compassion, etc., and reciting dhāraṇīs purifies karmic obstacles. Further, when you destroy craving you also destroy all karmas, so you also contradict [your assertion] that there is no antidote to karma.

[RGYAL TSHAB RJE:] The wisdom realizing no-self, THAT WHICH EFFECTS THE CESSATION OF attachment and ANY other FLAWS, HAS THE destructive POWER to remove [the seeds of] the results of KARMA CREATED BY THAT defiled desire for future rebirth, BECAUSE IT DESTROYS THE FAULTS OF DESIRE FOR future REBIRTH. HOW WILL IT UNDERMINE such results of ALREADY-ACTIVATED karma as already exist, such as physical defects or crookedness? It follows that it will not, because it is unable [to prevent] the arising of results that already exist. Accordingly, by reciting dhāraṇīs, etc., one is able to render some karmic obstacles suitable to arise [as a different] resultant ripening, but without abandoning craving, no one has an antidote able to eliminate all karmas.[43]

Alternatively, the [third, fourth and fifth] lines [of verse 278-279b] show that if there is an abandonment without craving, then after that, one will be able to negate the ripening of even the smallest karmic potency; and the [last] line shows that without abandoning craving, one will be unable to render [karma] impotent to bring about the results of any previously created [karma]. [Some explain the third, fourth and fifth] lines [as saying that] one is able to abandon karma [whose results] one need not definitely experience and [the last as saying] that one cannot abandon karma [whose results] one must definitely expe-

---

result, and a bad one at that, the experience of which will entail the elimination only of the seed of that specific experience. In other words, if one asserts that many karmas of differing strength and quality can be eliminated by a single austerity, then if austerity is not identical with pain, a mild austerity or even a pleasant experience that is a result of one of the karmas to be eliminated should suffice as an "austerity." If austerity is identical with pain, then the Jaina faces the same problem as before: austerity only can eliminate the single karma of which it is a result.

43 The abandonment of craving through the realization of no-self *can* prevent the generation of further defilements and the experience of the results of defiled karmas already created (since craving is the basis for either of these, and now is absent). It *cannot* "repeal" karma whose results already have been experienced. Thus, an arhant whose body was crooked before their enlightenment will remain crooked afterwards, but they no longer create karma for future crooked bodies, nor need they experience the results of future-body karma created but unripened before their enlightenment, because their enlightenment represents the utter destruction of the craving that is the indispensable condition for defiled karma's creation or fruition.

rience. This explanation is not the meaning of the verse, and is rationally unacceptable, because it is said by many Mahāyānists that a full confession with the four [opponent] powers prevents the ripening [even] of karma that one must definitely experience, and that it purifies one.[44]

[OPPONENT:] Well, then, this contradicts [the idea] that [there is karma whose result] definitely must be experienced.

[RGYAL TSHAB RJE:] [Mahāyānists] say that the meaning of "definitely must be experienced" is that [the karmic result will definitely be experienced] if one does not meet the antidote.[45]

Refuting [the idea] that karma and craving are equally to be abandoned [319]

(279c-280b) THE FAULTS ARE NOT FROM KARMA;
ONE WILL EFFECT [KARMA THROUGH] HAVING THE FLAW [OF CRAVING],
NOT FROM THE REVERSE [WHERE THERE IS NO CRAVING];

---

44 The lines in question are PV 278c-279b: *skye 'dod nyes pa bcom pa'i phyir / gang yang skyon rnams 'gog byed pa / des skyed las la nus 'gyur gyi / ji ltar byas pa nyams par 'gyur*. An incorrect interpretation takes them to mean that the realization of no-self will insure that weak karmas, the experience of whose results is uncertain, will be eliminated, but that those stronger karmas, whose results definitely must be experienced, will not be eliminated. If this interpretation were correct, then enlightenment would be impossible, since there are in the mindstream infinite karmas whose result "definitely must be experienced." The correct interpretation sees the entire verse as referring to all karmas, both weak and strong. The meaning then is that (a) if craving is eliminated, all karma (except that whose results already have been experienced) can be prevented from ripening and (b) if craving is not eliminated, no other karma can be prevented from ripening. Mahāyānists hold that a full "confession" involving (1) recognition of the non-virtue committed, (2) regret for its commission, (3) a vow never to repeat the offense and (4) application of an antidote, has the power to prevent the experience of the results of the negative action, be it "strong" or "weak." Antidotes vary, but the most potent—as we might expect—is considered to be a meditation on no-self or voidness.

45 Thus, the designation of some karma as that whose results definitely must be experienced does not mean that there is karma whose results absolutely cannot be avoided—again, that would make enlightenment impossible. Karma whose results "definitely must be experienced" simply is karma sufficiently forceful that its fruition cannot be prevented unless mitigated or destroyed by the power of an antidote. A mitigating antidote is, e.g., a dhāraṇī, which can alter the manner in which a karmic result will be experienced. A destructive antidote is the direct realization of no-self, which uproots craving and thus eliminates the indispensable condition for the ripening of previously created karma.

[IN THE LATTER CASE,] THERE WILL NOT BE ATTACHMENT EVEN FROM HAPPINESS,
[SINCE] ONE IS WITHOUT DISTORTED IMPUTATIONS.

[OPPONENT:] Since karma occurs when there is craving and craving occurs when there is karma, each is equally to be abandoned.

[RGYAL TSHAB RJE:] The FAULTS of attachment, etc., ARE NOT arisen FROM KARMA that is without craving, because ONE WILL EFFECT accumulation [of karma] through HAVING THE FLAW of craving; but one does NOT accumulate [karma] FROM THE REVERSE [type of action, where there is] no craving.[46]

[OPPONENT:] Since happiness originates from virtuous karma, [from happiness] will originate the craving to attain the [pleasurable] object again.

[RGYAL TSHAB RJE:] It follows that for an arhant, THERE WILL NOT BE the arising of ATTACHMENT EVEN FROM HAPPINESS, because they ARE WITHOUT THE DISTORTED IMPUTATIONS of inappropriate mental judgments.[47]

Thus, we have identified and refuted the four principal factors opposing the truth of path, which are analyzed as paths to freedom by others: (1) meditating on the sense-faculties and other things that pertain to the self as suffering, (2) cognizing prakṛti and puruṣa as separate, (3) [practicing] rituals in which one has been empowered and (4) eliminating karma and tormenting the body.[48]

---

46 There may be a correlation between craving and karma, but the concomitance is not invariable, for karma can still exist (although impotent) where there is no craving; nor are the two equally fundamental as causes of saṃsāra, since craving is the invariable basis of the creation of negative karma, while negative karma is *not* necessarily the basis of craving—for residual negative karma will not generate craving in the mindstream of a person who has eliminated craving.

47 An arhant cannot possibly be attached to the pleasure they experience, because they are free from any notion of a self to whose pleasure they could be attached. Their pleasure is a genuine pleasure, unlike the spurious and transient pleasures of ordinary beings, but their enjoyment of it is unsullied by grasping or desire, which, after all, are based on the belief in a self.

48 These correspond, of course, to the Vaiśeṣika, Sāṃkhya, Nyāya and Jaina soteriologies. They do *not* correspond to the opposites of the four aspects of the truth of path, nor, for that matter, do the four aspects themselves seem to be explicitly discussed by Dharmakīrti. The section on the truth of path may perhaps best be seen as an extended discussion of the aspect of path, with the

To summarize: It is unacceptable that those others are paths to freedom from [saṃsāric] existence, because they are wholly founded on taking a permanent self as the foundation of bondage and freedom.[49] Thus, it should be known that any śāstra that is not founded on no-self does not show the chief path to freedom from [saṃsāric] existence.[50]

---

other three aspects (reasonableness, accomplishment and definitive removal) implicitly covered at one or another place in the discussion. The aspect of definitive removal, for instance, seems to be covered by the refutation of the idea that the wisdom realizing no-self cannot utterly eliminate mental stains. The other two aspects are covered in passing.

49 However arguable the details of the various soteriologies refuted, the central fact that each of them is based on the belief in a permanent self that is the basis of bondage and freedom is itself sufficient in Buddhist eyes to make them inconsistent, contradictory and, quite simply, false. Since false cognition cannot be the basis of the successful attainment that one expects, the liberation expected by those who believe in a self never will come to pass. The realization of no-self, on the other hand, is rational and true, and thus *can* be the basis of the attainment to which it points. Thus, Ātmavādin liberation is impossible, while Buddhist liberation is possible.

50 This presumably would include various Western systems, as well: Judaism, Christianity, Islam, and any philosophical system that posits any sort of unchanging substance. For discussion of these issues cross-culturally, see, e.g., Dharmasiri (1974) and Griffiths (1991).

12. Conclusions

The way of proving from that that he is the sugata [320]

(280c) [THE BUDDHA] IS PROVEN TO HAVE KNOWLEDGE THAT IS OF REALITY, IS FIRM,
AND IS SPECIALLY COMPLETE—[THIS IS] FROM THE FACT THAT HE IS THE SAVIOR;
(281) *SUGATA* HAS THE MEANING OF A COGNITION:
THUS, HE IS SUPERIOR TO NON-BUDDHISTS,
[BUDDHISTS ON] THE TRAINING PATHS AND [BUDDHISTS ON THE PATH OF] NO-MORE-TRAINING, BECAUSE OF THAT.

The *muni*, the Blessed One, [IS PROVEN] TO HAVE KNOWLEDGE THAT IS OF REALITY, because he sees by perception all ways in which the four noble truths exist. His knowledge IS FIRM, because he demonstrates the actuality of the four noble truths, and because in all texts where he demonstrates that, there is not the slightest contradiction between earlier and later and direct and interpretable teaching. [AND,] his knowledge is proven to be SPECIALLY COMPLETE, because he sees by direct perception every method for [attaining] high rebirths and the definitive good. He is the sugata FROM THE FACT THAT HE IS THE SAVIOR of those intent on freedom.

In this section on the reverse explanation, there is a reason for explaining [the meaning of] the word *SUGATA* as having THE MEANING OF A COGNITION, because it is said to be thus [on the basis of] the assertion that the purity of his knowledge is deduced from his being the savior. When it was to be proven in the section on the forward explanation that he is the savior of those intent on freedom, it was necessary to set forth a proof that he had eliminated all stains; in this section, we infer the purity of his knowledge from the reason, "he is the savior," so it is reasonable to explain the word *sugata* as having the meaning of cognition.[1]

---

1 This is permissible because *gata* is derived from the Sanskrit verbal root *gam*, which in such forms as *avagacchati* and *adhigacchati* denotes understanding,

THUS, his cognition IS SUPERIOR TO that of NON-BUDDHISTS, [Buddhists] ON THE TRAINING PATHS AND [Buddhists] on the paths of NO-MORE-TRAINING, such as śrāvaka and pratyekabuddha arhants, BECAUSE OF THAT knowledge of reality, etc., by stages.[2]

The way of proving from that that he is the teacher [321]

(281d) THE TEACHER IS APPLICATION TOWARD KNOWLEDGE FOR THE SAKE OF OTHERS.

[OPPONENT:] By what cause is he the sugata?

[RGYAL TSHAB RJE:] [The sugata] is preceded by THE TEACHER, which IS APPLICATION TOWARD complete KNOWLEDGE FOR THE SAKE OF OTHERS and which is the accustomation [of wisdom], because he possesses excellence of realization. It follows that this [reason] pervades, because the path that is the cause of his applying himself thus is demonstrated in this case to be the teacher. If it is not for the sake of others, it is impossible that his knowledge be proven special.[3]

---

or knowledge. See Nagatomi (1957) 254.

2 Since in the forward system of explanation, the emphasis was on proving the Buddha's accomplishment, the three special characteristics of the sugata were described in terms of abandonments of various sorts of obstacles (cf. above, PV 139c ff.). In the reverse system, the emphasis is on the Buddha's knowledge, which is *saving* knowledge. Thus, from the fact that the four noble truths are true, we can infer that the Buddha must be a sugata who is *cognitively* special in three ways: (1) unlike non-Buddhist yogins, he knows the truth about saṃsāra and nirvāṇa, encoded in the four noble truths; (2) unlike Buddhist practitioners who are not yet rid of all mental faults or stains, he has knowledge that is utterly firm and coherent, and not in the least conducive to further rebirth; (3) unlike ordinary arhants, he has knowledge that is complete, for he knows all possible paths to liberation and all saṃsāric dharmas that are to be rejected. Dharmakīrti's characterization of the Buddha's knowledge as "complete" (*ma lus, aśeṣa*) comes close to an assertion of his omniscience, but it is not *explicitly* so; it may merely imply that the Buddha knows all that is necessary for salvation, not that he knows all phenomena. Similarly, while rGyal tshab rje sees the completeness of the Buddha's knowledge as surpassing that of "Hīnayāna śrāvakas and pratyekabuddhas," Dharmakīrti's meaning may not be so relentlessly Mahāyānist: it may simply be that the Buddha, as the supreme arhant, has knowledge more complete than that of other arhants—a view common in Hīnayāna scholasticism.

3 If the Buddha is the sugata, with the knowledge needed by those intent on freedom, he also must be the teacher who, altruistically motivated, has discovered the truth and developed its salvific power to the utmost. More abstractly, of course, the "teacher" is one's excellence in application of the wisdom real-

The way of proving from that that he is the compassionate one [322]

(282) HE IS COMPASSIONATE THROUGH THAT, BECAUSE [ALTHOUGH] HE HAS ACCOMPLISHED
HIS [OWN] AIMS, HE DOES NOT REFUSE THE AIMS OF OTHERS.

[His being the teacher] IS preceded by his being greatly COMPASSIONATE and sympathetic, because he accustomates the path THROUGH THAT striving to apply himself toward complete knowledge.

[OPPONENT:] Doesn't he become an authoritative person merely by his complete knowledge of the four noble truths? What need is there to prove him greatly compassionate?

[RGYAL TSHAB RJE:] It is definitely necessary that the proof that he is an authoritative person be preceded by proof that he is greatly compassionate, BECAUSE by virtue of his complete accustomation of compassion, even when HE HAS ACCOMPLISHED HIS own AIMS, HE DOES NOT REFUSE to show the Dharma directed toward THE AIMS OF OTHERS; and because without compassion, even if he has knowledge, he will not instruct others in it.[4]

The way of proving from all those that he is an authority [323]

(282c) HE TEACHES WHAT IS GOOD SINCE HE HAS COMPASSION;
AND THE TRUTH FROM HIS GNOSIS—AN ACCOMPLISHMENT THAT COINCIDES [WITH COMPASSION].[5]

---

izing no-self, the completion of which is presupposed by the assertion that the Buddha has true, firm and complete knowledge. Thus, he is the teacher because he is the sugata.

4 If he is a teacher whose development of wisdom issues in a complete knowledge by virtue of which he both can and does act as a savior of sentient beings, the Buddha must necessarily be motivated by compassion. If he were not thus motivated, he would be content to understand the four noble truths with sufficient profundity to extricate himself from saṃsāra, but not to develop his wisdom to the utmost. Without developing his wisdom to the utmost, he cannot possess the "complete" knowledge that is the third characteristic of a sugata. Without being a sugata, he cannot be a savior. Without being a savior, he cannot be an authority for those intent on freedom. Thus, it is necessary that he be motivated by altruism. Thus, we must infer: "The Buddha is the compassionate one, because he is the teacher" with "teacher" signifying the *complete* accustomation of the wisdom realizing no-self. In rGyal tshab rje's reading, to accustomate completely the wisdom realizing no-self is to cognize the no-self of every possible object, which entails cognizing every object, which is, of course, omniscience. That this is Dharmakīrti's intention is, as already noted, not unambiguously clear. Cf. above, pp. 396-398.

(283) THAT [GNOSIS] IS DIRECTLY APPLIED TOWARD TEACHING;
THUS, HE IS AN AUTHORITY, BECAUSE OF THAT.

The *muni*, the Blessed One, TEACHES only GOOD and useful [truths] to disciples; he does not teach what is useless, SINCE HE HAS completed the accustomation of great COMPASSION and sympathy. This demonstrates that he is worthy to be [considered] the savior of those intent on freedom and that he does save them. He teaches THE TRUTH undistortedly because that [comes] FROM one's possessing the complete GNOSIS that knows [all things undistortedly], and he possesses it. This demonstrates that he is able to save. The gnosis that knows [all things undistortedly] does not originate causelessly or from inappropriate causes, because it originates from accustomating AN ACCOMPLISHMENT THAT COINCIDES with compassion. The *muni* is the savior of those intent on freedom, because THAT knowledge is knowledge of one who effects a complete endeavor DIRECTLY APPLIED TOWARD TEACHING it to others. [THUS,] it is well proven that HE IS A non-deceptive AUTHORITY for those intent on freedom, BECAUSE OF THAT fact, i.e., that he is the teacher who has completed the two aims.[6]

The purpose of praising him for his authoritativeness [324]

(283c-285b) IT IS MEANINGFUL, PRAISING HIM AS SUCH AN ENTITY:
IT IS FOR THE SAKE OF ESTABLISHING THE NATURE OF AUTHORITY
THROUGH WHAT IS TAUGHT BY HIM,
BECAUSE HE DID NOT REJECT INFERENCE,

---

5 An alternative, somewhat more straightforward, reading of PV 282c-d (*brtse bas legs dang ye shes las / bden pa gsung mdzad sgrub byed bcas*) yields: "He teaches what is good since he has compassion; and the truth, together with its accomplishment, from his gnosis."

6 Thus, once again the Buddha is shown to be soteriologically authoritative because he can and does save beings. That he *can* save beings is shown by his completion of his own aim, i.e., by the fact that he is a sugata with true, firm and complete knowledge of all that is to be adopted and rejected by those intent on freedom. That he *does* save beings is shown by the fact that his knowledge is combined with an infinite accustomation of the compassion that desires to take responsibility for the salvation of all beings. Thus, he has completed his own aim through the storage of wisdom and he completes the aims of others through the storage of merit from actions motivated by compassion. The store of wisdom (or gnosis: *ye shes, jñāna*) results (from a Mahāyāna perspective) in the Dharma Body; the store of merit results in the Enjoyment and Transformation Bodies (= Form Body).

AND BECAUSE WE SEE THAT [THE MEANING] OF [INFERENCE] ALSO IS APPLIED
IN MANY ASPECTS, IN PASSAGES SUCH AS:
"ANY [ENTITY] THAT HAS A SELF-NATURE SUCH THAT
IT ARISES, HAS A QUALITY SUCH THAT IT WILL CEASE."
(285c) THE REASON THAT HAS THE CHARACTERISTIC OF NOT OCCURRING
WHEN [THE PREDICATE] IS ABSENT IS THE BASIS OF INFERENCE;
THAT ALSO IS CLEARLY EXPLAINED [BY THE BUDDHA,] BECAUSE IT CAN BE SHOWN [IN AN EXAMPLE LIKE THAT ABOVE]
THAT THERE IS PERVASION BETWEEN A PREDICATE AND A REASON.

There is a [MEANINGFUL] purpose IN PRAISING the *muni*, the Blessed One, through showing that he is SUCH AN ENTITY as became an authority, because he is praised thus FOR THE SAKE OF ESTABLISHING a perfect demonstration of THE NATURE OF AUTHORITY THROUGH THOSE texts TAUGHT BY THAT teacher. This shows that the definition, investigation and way of relating to authority, which establishes liberation and omniscience, are extensively discussed in those texts. Therefore, when what is to be established, liberation and omniscience, are demonstrated, one is able to analyze the meanings of all texts by way of the foregoing key.[7]

[The assertion, that] "Seeing that one cannot understand those things without first hearing those texts together with their commentaries and having them explained, it also is necessary that liberation

---

7 The "key" referred to by rGyal tshab rje is the five-epithet interpretive schema supplied by Dignāga, on which, of course, the entire *Pramāṇasiddhi* chapter is based. The assertion here is that, contrary to what some have supposed, authority (*tshad ma, pramāṇa*) is discussed in all its many aspects even in sūtras that do not seem to have anything to do with it. We already have seen that it is meaning, not words, that is of primary importance in philosophical analysis, and it thus is both possible and necessary to maintain that all Buddhist scriptures touch on the problem of authority. It is possible because the meanings embedded in, e.g., the sūtras, can be shown to presuppose or entail understandings of authority that only are made explicit in a few places. It is necessary because without presupposing or entailing a correct understanding of authority, the texts cannot be the basis for correct understanding by those who hear or read them, since all correct understanding is based on authoritative cognition. Dignāga's "key" is particularly useful when authority and knowledge are put into a specifically religious context—as Dharmakīrti has done in the *Pramāṇasiddhi* chapter.

and omniscience are proven scripturally," is the assertion only of liars, who are ignorant of reasoning and believe in mere words.[8]

[OPPONENT:] How do [the texts] show the definition of authority, etc.?

[RGYAL TSHAB RJE:] "A person who has a cognition of blue (a) cognizes blue, but (b) not blueness." This quote shows the definition of perception. (a) [shows] unmistakenness and (b) shows non-conceptuality.[9]

Inference also is shown to be authoritative, BECAUSE if [the Buddha] had not desired to show [inference] as authoritative, it stands to reason that he would have refuted [the idea] that it is authoritative, but HE DID NOT REJECT [the idea] that INFERENCE is authoritative; AND BECAUSE WE SEE that the *basis* OF THIS inference IS ALSO APPLIED and discussed IN MANY ASPECTS IN such PASSAGES as "ANY [entity] THAT HAS A SELF-NATURE SUCH THAT IT ARISES HAS A QUALITY SUCH THAT IT WILL CEASE," ETC. Such passages as "Knowing fire from smoke" show a reason of result. Since [the Buddha] used perfectly probative words, we can understand implicitly that he desired [to teach] inference [as authoritative], because THE REASON THAT HAS THE CHARACTERISTIC OF NOT OCCURRING WHEN the predicate IS ABSENT IS THE BASIS OF INFERENCE. THAT relation whereby [the reason] does not occur if [the predicate] does not exist ALSO IS CLEARLY EXPLAINED, BECAUSE IT CAN clearly BE SHOWN THAT THERE IS PERVASION BETWEEN A PREDICATE, that which is subject to cessation, AND A REASON, that which is subject to arising.[10]

---

8 Those who assert that liberation and omniscience are proven simply by the fact that they are scripturally taught are derided for their ignorance of reasoning and their unreasonable faith in mere words. It may, in fact, be the case that everything taught in Buddhist scripture is true, but a Buddhist will maintain that this is the case not simply because it is *scriptural*, but because it is *reasonable*. Such validity as scripture may have derives not from its being a special or separate source of knowledge, but from its conformity to what can be understood perceptually and through objectively impelled inference. Thus, scriptural testimony is not itself an independent authority, for it cannot be accepted unless it conforms to what already is established by perceptual and inferential authority. See Cabezón (1981).

9 The fact that a perceptual authority is unmistaken, or unsublated, establishes the fact that it fulfills the definition of authority discussed by Dharmakīrti above, PV 1; the fact that it is non-conceptual establishes that it cannot involve inference, and thus must be perceptual. I have not been able to locate the quotation, which presumably is contained in the *Sūtrapiṭaka* (for the point in this section is to prove that authority is discussed in the sūtras).

10 It is wrong to argue that although the Buddha clearly recognized the impor-

[Dignāga and Dharmakīrti] are not expounding scriptural arrangements of the two [types of] authority that are discussed only occasionally rather than frequently; since it is impossible that [all] the texts not show the definition of authority, the basis of inference, etc., we have given examples that demonstrate that they are discussed in all the texts.[11]

Final remarks [325]

Thus, having understood through objectively impelled reasoning the way of proving the Buddha-teacher, the holy Dharma that is the [truths of] cessation and path, and the ārya saṅgha that accomplishes [religious goals] according to the Buddha's teaching], one is induced to go for refuge to the three jewels; and, having gone for refuge, one must accomplish perfect enlightenment for the sake of all sentient beings. Having well established by authority that one has both the potential and the ability [to attain enlightenment], one should take the vows for the generation of the thought of enlightenment; and also, having seen that obtaining perfect enlightenment originates from accustomating the mind that realizes the actuality of the four noble truths, one should undistortedly, through objectively impelled reason-

tance of perceptual authority, he did not believe that inference was an authority, for (a) he nowhere explicitly *denies* that inference is authoritative and, more importantly, (b) the sūtras show evidence of syllogistic thinking, if not of syllogisms. Indeed, syllogisms merely formalize and give coherence to cognitive procedures in which we all engage constantly. Thus, the presence of inference is established not by the presence of a formal inference itself, but by the presence of the *basis* of inference, which is a reason or mark that is relevant to a subject and positively and negatively concomitant with a predicate. With this criterion in mind, the sūtras can be shown to contain all recognized types of syllogisms. Thus, the statement that "Any entity that has a self-nature such that it arises has a quality such that it will cease"can be recast as a syllogism based on synonymy: "Any entity (subject) will cease (predicate), because it has a self-nature such that it arises (reason)."The reason is relevant to the subject because any entity must have arisen; the reason is positively and negatively concomitant with the predicate because generation entails destruction and non-generation entails non-destruction. The statement that "we know fire from smoke,"of course, can be restated as the classic syllogism based on causality, or result: "In that place (subject) there is fire (predicate), because there is smoke (reason)."

11 One might, thus, paraphrase the Buddha: "Whether or not śāstras are written to explain them, the two types of authority necessarily are dealt with in *all* the Buddha's teachings."

ing, investigate the four noble truths, whose gist is reversing engagement with saṃsāra, and one must be undistorted in rejecting and adopting again and again the objects [spoken of in the truths].[12]

It is not in the least the case that the beginning, end, and everything [in between in] this [chapter] do not suggest going for refuge. It is not in the least the case that [the chapter] does not show the method for cutting off superimposition; and, to the degree that one's continuum is free from superimposition, to that degree one lays the foundation of the Dharma-jewel. From [the point where] one [begins to be] free from the seeds of superimposition to [the point where] freedom is complete—that is the Dharma-jewel. From [the point where] one [begins] to strive for freedom from present superimposition, all minds that strive for freedom from any superimposition are a part of going for refuge.[13]

---

12 Implicitly, then, the *Pramāṇasiddhi* chapter describes the three jewels of refuge. On the basis of having taken refuge and become convinced of the possibility of attaining enlightenment, one should vow to attain enlightenment for the sake of all sentient beings. The surest way to fulfill that vow is to understand the four noble truths, practicing what is to be adopted and avoiding what is to be rejected, until one reaches the stage where no-self is realized directly and defilements are actually uprooted. When all defilements and their stains have been eliminated, of course, one is oneself a sugata, able and willing to be a savior of beings. Thus, this chapter should inspire the reader to strive to become an authoritative person.

13 rGyal tshab rje here rather imaginatively relates the Dharma-jewel to a more general theory of knowledge. Knowledge in Buddhist usage involves cutting off incorrect superimpositions on what really exists or really is the case. Thus, the Dharma-jewel, most often spoken of as the wisdom realizing no-self, can be described epistemically as any correct cognition that eliminates the seeds of further superimposition. Furthermore, any attempt to cut off superimposition, even in present mundane matters, may be considered as a "part" (*yan lag*) of refuge, since it is a mental action that exists on the same continuum as such exalted instances of cutting-off-superimposition as the wisdom realizing no-self. Thus, to the degree that "all human accomplishment is preceded by correct cognition," correct cognition is necessary in every sphere, from the mundane to the sublime. To the degree that the most sublime "accomplishment," enlightenment, is preceded by the same condition—the cutting off of superimposition—as is the most mundane, the most mundane can as reasonably be considered a part of the Dharma-jewel as the most sublime—for in every instance falsehood is binding and restricting, while truth is what is believed to make us free. Note that rGyal tshab rje's analysis rests on the assumption of a strong continuity between conventional and ultimate modes of knowledge, a characteristic of the epistemology and soteriology of the dGe

Proving well through reason the teacher's teaching,
One gains one-pointed faith in the three jewels.
Those who strive to accomplish their goal [in the Buddhist] way—
Those persons should be known as the wise.

From *Elucidating the Path to Liberation Explained in the Pramāṇavārttika,* this has been the commentary on the second chapter, "The Establishment of Correct Authority."[14] By [virtue of] this, may the *muni*'s precious teaching go out [through] all doors and spread in all directions, and may it be empowered to be widespread for a long time to come.

---

lugs—if not of all Buddhist systems.

14 The chapter generally is referred to as *Pramāṇasiddhi* (*tshad ma'i grub pa*), "establishment of authority." The "establishment of correct authority" (*tshad ma yang dag par grub pa*) would in Sanskrit be *samyakpramāṇasiddhi.*

Appendix, Glossary, Bibliography and Index

Appendix: rGyal tshab rje's Text Divisions

Section numbers reflect the consecutive enumeration provided in the translation and indicated there in parentheses after the section title. Outline numbers reflect rGyal tshab rje's actual divisions and subdivisions of the text. Asterisk (*) indicates the root verse or verses grouped together for discussion by rGyal tshab rje.

PV = verses in the *Pramāṇasiddhi* chapter of the *Pramāṇvārttika,* Miyasaka's edition.
GT = pages in rGyal tshab rje's *rNam 'grel thar lam gsal byed,* vol. I of the Sarnath edition.
TR = pages in my translation.

Section Number	Outline Number and Title	PV	GT	TR
	[1. Introductory]			
1	1. The general meaning	______	226-228	168-174
2	11. Setting forth the explanation of ācārya Dignāga	______	226-227	168-170
3	12. The way [Dignāga's] meaning was arranged by the author of the *Pramāṇavārttika*	______	227-228	170-172
4	13. The intention of [Dignāga and Dharmakīrti]	______	228	172-174
	[2. Definition and Examples of Authority]			
	[A. THE DEFINITION OF AUTHORITY]			
5	2. The meaning of the limbs	1-285	228-366	175-485
6	21. Proving the *m uni*to be an authority	1-283b	228-363	175-480
7	211. Showing through the forward system the way in which the teacher arrived [at his goal] via some path	1-146c	229-302	175-338

36	211.122.212.121.122. Extreme consequences if that is the case	13*	242	202
37	211.122.212.121.123. Disposing of [the objection that] it follows that the argument rebounds	14*	242-243	202-204
38	211.122.212.121.2. The unsuitability of the word "shape"as a reason	15-16	243-244	204-205
39	211.122.212.121.21. An example of the unreasonableness of seeing the mere word "shape"as a reason	15*	244	204-205
40	211.122.212.121.22. Extreme consequences	16*	244	205
41	211.122.212.122. Refuting other similar [arguments] through that	17*	244	206
42	211.122.212.123. The aim that is accomplished by those refutations	18-20[b]*	244-247	206-209
43	211.122.212.2. Showing that [the existence of] a creator of all knowledge-objects is confuted by authority	21-28	247-248	210-214
44	211.122.212.21. [God's] unsuitability as a permanent cause	21-24*	247-248	210-212
45	211.122.212.22. Disposing [of the idea that our objections apply] equally to us	25-28*	248	212-214

[D. WHY THE BUDDHA IS AN AUTHORITY]

46	211.122.22. Proving as omniscient the one who knows by perception how all [knowledge-objects] really exist	29-33	248-251	214-219
47	211.122.221. Objections	29*	248-249	214-216
48	211.122.222. Refuting those [objections]	30-33	249-251	216-219
49	211.122.222.1. The reason for seeking an omniscient one	30*	250	216-217
50	211.122.222.2. The way of seeking him	31*	250-251	217-218
51	211.122.222.3. Identifying the omniscient one	32-33*	251	218-219

[3. The Mind-Body Problem: A Refutation of Materialism (1)]

[A. INTRODUCTORY]

52	211.2. Defining the authoritative person through the four remaining [epithets]	34-146c	251-302	221-338
53	211.21. Proving the four particular qualities	34-145b	251-302	221-335
54	211.211. Identifying the excellence of intention	34-131	251-293	221-318
55	211.211.1. Showing initial proof of the excellence of intention	34a*	252	221-222
56	211.211.2. Disposing [of the objection] that that is unproven	34b-131	252-293	222-318
57	211.211.21 The objection	34b-c*	252	223
58	211.211.22. The refutation of that	34d-131	252-293	223-318
59	211.211.221. Refuting [the idea] that it is impossible to accustomate [compassion] through many lives	34d-119	252-288	223-308
60	211.211.221.1. A brief demonstration	34d*	252-253	224-225
61	211.211.221.2. An extensive explanation	35-119	252-288	226-308
62	211.211.221.21. Setting forth proof of the existence of past and future lives	35-44	253-257	226-234
63	211.211.221.211. Setting forth the reason	35-41b*	253-256	226-231

92	211.211.221.222.111.211. Setting forth the consequences	63a*	265	254
93	211.211.221.222.111.212. Refuting the reply to that	63b-66b*	265-266	254-256
94	211.211.221.222.111.213. Disposing [of the objection that our position] contradicts perception	66c-68*	266	256-258
95	211.211.221.222.111.22. Refuting other syllogisms through that	69*	266-267	258-259
96	211.211.221.222.111.23. Summary	70-72*	267	260-261

[C. WHY THE BODY IS NOT MIND'S SPECIAL COOPERATIVE CONDITION]

97	211.211.221.222.112. Refuting [the idea] that [the body] acts as the special cooperative condition [of mind]	73-83	267-270	261-268
98	211.211.221.222.112.1. The actual refutation	73-78	268-269	261-264
99	211.211.221.222.112.11. Refuting [the idea] that the body is the principal condition of wisdom, etc.	73-74*	268	261-262
100	211.211.221.222.112.12. Refuting [the idea] that it is the principal condition of attachment, etc.	75-78	268-269	263-264
101	211.211.221.222.112.121. [Proof that] attachment, etc., do not directly arise from the body, together with an example	75-77*	268-269	263-264
102	211.211.221.222.112.122. Summary	78*	269	264
103	211.211.221.222.112.2. Refuting [the idea] that body and mind are substantially identical	79*	269	264-265
104	211.211.221.222.112.3. Identifying the cause of saṃsāra	80-83	269-270	265-268
105	211.211.221.222.112.31. Identifying the cause of taking birth in a womb	80-81*	269-270	265-266
106	211.211.221.222.112.32. Disposing of objections to that	82-83*	270	266-268

[4. The Mind-Body Problem: A Refutation of Materialism (2)]

[A. PARTS AND WHOLES]

107	211.211.221.222.12. Refutation through an analysis of the essential aspect of the body that is the basis of [mind]	84-113	270-282	269-295
108	211.211.221.222.121. Refuting [the idea] that there is a partless gross body that is the special basis of mind	84-102	270-279	269-288
109	211.211.221.222.121.1. Refuting the idea that there is a partless whole	84-86a	271-272	269-272
110	211.211.221.222.121.11. Proving the reason	84-85*	271	270-271
111	211.211.221.222.121.12. Setting [the conclusion] forth	86a*	271-272	272
112	211.211.221.222.121.2. Disposing of [objections alleged to] damage that refutation	86b-102	272-279	273-288
113	211.211.221.222.121.21. Disposing of the [alleged] consequence that an external object cannot be cognized by a sense-cognition	86b-87b*	272-273	273-275

134	211.211.221.222.122.221.21. Refuting [the idea] that just individual minds are generated by many successively occurring breaths	107-109*	281	292-293
135	211.211.221.222.122.221.22. Refuting [the idea] that one mind is generated by many simultaneously occurring breaths	110-111*	281-282	293-294
136	211.211.221.222.122.221.3. Refuting [the assertion of] fault in our position	112*	282	294-295
137	211.211.221.222.122.222. Refuting [the idea] that even if mind arises simultaneously from the body at first, later it only arises successively from its homogenes	113*	282	295

[C. SUMMARY]

138	Showing a summary of the foregoing explanations	______	282-285	296-299

[D. ANSWERING OBJECTIONS]

139	211.211.221.222.2. Disposing of the attempt to damage our refutation	114-119	285-288	300-308
140	211.211.221.222.21. Objection	114 a-c*	285	300
141	211.211.221.222.22. Reply	114c-119	285-288	300-308
142	211.211.221.222.221. Investigating that and giving an answer	114c-115a*	285	300-301
143	211.211.221.222.222. Identifying the substantial cause of a future life's body	115b-118	285-287	301-307
144	211.211.221.222.222.1. Identification	115b-c*	285-287	301-305
145	211.211.221.222.222.2. Disposing of damaging [objections]	116*	287	305-306
146	211.211.221.222.222.3. Setting forth the proof	117-118*	287-288	306-307
147	211.211.221.223. Summary	119*	288	307-308

[5. The Buddha's Qualities]

[A. HIS INFINITE ACCUSTOMATION TO COMPASSION]

148	211.211.222. Refuting [the idea] that, even if such accustomation is possible, its infinite increase cannot be accepted	120-131	288-293	309-318
149	211.211.222.1. The argument	120a-c*	288-289	309
150	211.211.222.21. The answer	120d-131	289-293	310-318
151	211.211.222.21. [Showing why] jumping ability and boiling water do not have the particular mark [such that they can increase infinitely]	120d-123	289-290	310-311
152	211.211.222.211. Identifying the particulars of the mark and [showing why] they do not exist in the two examples	120d-123b*	289	310-311
153	211.211.222.212. [Showing that] if there exist such particulars, then it follows that there is infinite development	123b-d*	289-290	311
154	211.211.222.22. [Showing that] compassion, etc., do have [the particular mark such that they can increase infinitely]	124-126*	290-291	311-313
155	211.211.222.23. Disposing of objections to that	127-131	291-293	313-318

[B. THE BUDDHA AS TEACHER, SUGATA AND SAVIOR]

[6. The Four Noble Truths in General]

[7. The Truth of Suffering]

[A. THE NATURE OF SUFFERING]

[B. SUFFERING AND THE HUMORS]

[C. SUFFERING AND THE ELEMENTS]

[8. The Truth of Origination]

[9. The Truth of Cessation]

[A. PROVING LIBERATION AND OMNISCIENCE]

[B. ASPECTS OF CESSATION]

241	212.112.231.21. Disposing of the consequence that liberation is impossible	191a-b*	326-327	398-399
242	212.112.231.22. Disposing of the consequence that it is impossible to strive for liberation	191c-192*	327	399-400
243	212.112.231.23. Disposing of the consequence that once liberation is attained, it is impossible to abide in [saṃsāric] existence for even a moment	193-194b*	327-328	400-401
244	212.112.232. The aspect of peace	194c-202b	328-332	401-409
245	212.112.232.1. Disposing of the consequence that a detached one does not eliminate faults	194c-197b*	328-329	401-403
246	212.112.232.2. Disposing of the consequence that they are not freed from [saṃsāric] existence	197c-199b*	329-330	404-405
247	212.112.232.3. Disposing of [alleged] extreme consequences in regard to self-grasping's being the cause of [saṃsāric] existence	199c-202b*	330-332	405-409
248	212.112.233. The aspect of sublimity	202c-205b*	332-333	410-412

[10. The Truth of Path (1)]

[A. A REFUTATION OF SKEPTICISM: THE NATURAL PURITY OF MIND]

249	212.112.24. The truth of path	205c-280b	333-361	413-476
250	212.112.241. Proving that the wisdom realizing no-self is the path to freedom from [saṃsāric] existence	205c-217b	333-339	413-427
251	212.112.241.1. Identifying the path to freedom	205c-d*	333	413
252	212.112.241.2. Disposing of objections to that	205d-217b	333-339	414-427
253	212.112.241.21. Disposing of the objection that abandonments are reversible	205d-215b	333-339	414-425
254	212.112.241.211. The impossibility of a complete abandonment's being reversed	205d-210b	334-336	414-419
255	212.112.241.211.1. The impossibility of generating faults in a mind in a transformed state	205d-209b	334-335	414-418
256	212.112.241.211.11. A brief demonstration	205d-206b*	334	414-415
257	212.112.241.211.12. An extensive explanation	206c-208b*	334-335	415-416
258	212.112.241.211.13. Summary	208c-209b*	335	417-418
259	212.112.241.211.2. Even if there is [a fault], the impossibility of its remaining long	209c-210b*	335-336	418-419
260	212.112.241.212. The impossibility of there being a method of reversing a [complete abandonment]	210c-211b*	336	419
261	212.112.241.213. Disposing of [the idea that] the wisdom realizing no-self is unacceptable as an antidote to self-grasping	211c-215b	336-339	419-425
262	212.112.241.213.1. The unsuitability, as an antidote, of the mere opposite to the mode of apprehension [that is self-grasping]	211c-213b*	336	420-421
263	212.112.241.213.2. Proving that defiled ignorance is not substantially different from the view of [self in] the perishable	213c-214c*	336-338	421-424
264	212.112.241.213.3. Showing that the wisdom realizing no-self is the antidote through its opposition to the mode of apprehension [that is self-grasping]	214c-215b*	338-339	425

288	212.112.242.211.221.211. The consequence that the self is impermanent	234-235b*	345-346	440-441
289	212.112.242.211.221.212. [Showing that] if the self exists there can result no reliable antidote to desire	235c-238b*	346	441-442
290	212.112.242.211.221.22. Extreme consequences if one is freed merely by meditating on suffering	238c-243b	346-348	443-446
291	212.112.242.211.221.221. Actual extreme consequences	238c-241b*	346-347	443-444
292	212.112.242.211.221.222. The impossibility of others being freed from attachment	241c-243b*	347-348	445-446
293	212.112.242.211.221.23. Showing a perceptually based confutation [of the idea] that merely by seeing the sense-faculties, etc., as flawed one [can] remove desire for them	243c-247b	348-349	446-448
294	212.112.242.211.221.231. Showing that just seeing flaws is not the cause for removing desire	243c-246b*	348	446-447
295	212.112.242.211.221.232. [Showing] the impossibility of seeing flaws as they are in the sense-faculties, etc.	246c-247b*	348-349	447-448

[11. The Truth of Path (2)]

[A. A REFUTATION OF SĀṂKHYA SOTERIOLOGY]

296	212.112.242.211.222. Refuting the Sāṃkhya system	247c-252b	349-351	449-453
297	212.112.242.211.222.1. The unacceptability, as a path to freedom, of just knowing that prakṛti and puruṣa are different	247c-249b*	349-350	449-451
298	212.112.242.211.222.2. The unacceptability, as a cause of detachment, of having a mind afflicted by the suffering of suffering	249c-251b*	350	451-452
299	212.112.242.211.222.3. Identifying the nature of detachment	251c-252b*	350-351	452-453
300	212.112.242.211.223. Disposing of [the idea that our position] contradicts the [Buddha's] teaching on the meditation on suffering	252c-254b*	351-352	453-455
301	212.112.242.211.3. Summary	254c-255b*	362-353	455
302	212.112.242.212. If it is possible [that one be detached from what pertains to the self without abandoning self-grasping], the pointlessness of accepting that a self is freed	255c-256b*	353	456
303	212.112.242.213. Showing that it is necessary to abandon the self-view	256c-257b*	353	456-457

[B. A REFUTATION OF THEIST-RITUALIST SOTERIOLOGY]

304	212.112.242.22. The unacceptability, as a path to freedom, of just the word of God	257c-273b	353-358	457-468
305	212.112.242.221. Refuting [the attempt to] prove that a ritual empowered by God as a path to liberation is [in fact] a path to freedom	257c-260b*	353-354	458-459
306	212.112.242.222. Expressing [a further] rejection	260c-270b	354-357	459-466

[12. Conclusions]

Glossary

This is a list of most of the important technical terms that occur in rGyal tshab rje's commentary on the *Pramāṇasiddhi* chapter of the *Pramāṇavārttika*. I have, through cross-references, tried to indicate all variant English translations for Tibetan terms, but my listing of Sanskrit equivalents is not a complete one. I have tried to find the most common Sanskrit equivalent (where possible citing that used most often by Dharmakīrti), but for a complete index of Dharmakīrti's Sanskrit and Tibetan terminology, the reader should consult Nagatomi (1957) part D and Steinkellner (1967ref). An asterisk (*) after a Sanskrit term indicates that it is conjectural.

English	**Tibetan**	**Sanskrit**
abandonment	spangs pa	prahāṇa, hāna
abider	gnas pa po	sthātṛ
abiding	gnas pa (cf. existence) sthiti	
ability	nus pa (cf. capacity, potency, power)	śakti
absent	ldog pa	nivṛtta
absorption	bsam gtan	dhyāna
accomplishment (cf. proof)	sgrub pa	sādhana
accordant example	mthun dpe	sādharmyadṛṣṭānta
accustomation	goms pa	abhyāsa
action	las	karman
activity	spyod pa	caryā
actuality	gnas lugs	bhutārtha
adventitious	glo bur	āgantuka
aggregate	phung po	skandha
already arisen	byung zin (cf. past)	————
already existent	grub zin	————
anger	zhe sdang (cf. hatred)	dveśa
	khong khro	pratigha

antidote	gnyen po	pratipakṣa (cf. opposing factor)
apparent object	snang ba'i yul	*pratibhāsaviṣaya
appearance	snang ba	pratibhāsa
application	sbyor ba	prayoga
		yukti
appropriate conditions	mthun rkyen	————
apperception	rang rig	svasaṃvedanā
arhant	dgra bcom pa	arhant
arising	skyes ba (cf. life)	utpatti
ārya	'phags pa	ārya
ascertainment (cf. determination)	nges pa byed pa	niścaya
aspect	rnam pa	ākāra
assertion	'dod pa (cf. desire)	mata
assistant	phan 'dogs pa	upakārin
Ātmavādin	bdag smra ba	ātmavādin
atom	rdul phran	paramāṇu
attached mind	chags can gyi rig pa	————
attachment	chags pa	sneha (cf. desire)
	'dod chags	rāga
aural cognition	nyan shes	śrotavijñāna
austerity	dka' thub	tapas
authority, authoritative	tshad ma	pramāṇa
authority-object	gzhal bya	prameya
authoritative person	tshad ma'i skyes bu	*pramāṇapuruṣa
aversion	yid log	ghṛṇā
	zhe sdang (cf. anger)	dveśa
āyatana	skye mched	āyatana
balance	snyoms pa	sāmya (cf. equilibrium)
based	brten pa	āśrita
basis	rten (cf. support)	āśraya
beginningless	thog med	anādi
bile	mkhris	pitta
Blessed One	bcom ldan 'das	bhagavan
bodhisattva	byang chub sems dpa'	bodhisattva
body	lus	deha
body-cognition	lus kyi rnam par shes pa	kāyavijñāna
bondage, bound	bcing ba	bandha
breathing, breath	dbugs	prāṇa
the Buddha	sangs rgyas	buddha
capacity (cf. ability, potency, power)	nus pa	śakti
cause	rgyu	hetu, kāraṇa

cause of abiding	gnas kyi rgyu	sthitikāraṇa
cessation	'gog pa	nirodha
change (cf. excellence, variation)	'khyad pa	viśeṣa
characteristic (cf. definition)	mtshan nyid	lakṣaṇa
circumstances	gnas skabs	avastha
clarity, clear	gsal ba	prakāśa
cleared away (cf. confuted)	bsal ba	nirākṛta
co-existence	lhan cig gnas pa	sahasthāna
cognition	rtogs pa (cf. realization)	gati
	shes pa	jñāna (cf. gnosis)
	rig pa	vidyā (cf. mind)
collection	tshogs	sambhāra
collection-expression	tshogs brjod pa'i sgra	————
compassion	thugs rje	karuṇā
	brtse ba	kṛpā, dayā
compassionate one	brtse ldan	dayāvan
completion	mthar phyin pa	niṣṭāgata
conceptual thought	rnam par rtog pa	vikalpa
concern	dogs pa	śaṅka (cf. perplexity)
concomitant factors	mtshugs ldan	saṃprayoga
condition	rkyen	pratyaya
conditional intentional object (cf. objective condition)	dmigs rkyen	ālambanapratyaya
	rgyu mtshan (cf. reason)	nimitta
confession	bshags pa	deśanā
confusion	rmongs pa	moha
confuted (cf. cleared away)	bsal ba	nirākṛta
	sun phyung	duṣita
conjunction	ldan pa	saṃyoga
conjunction-inherence	ldan pa la 'du ba'i 'brel ba	————
conjunction-relation	ldan 'brel	————
conjunction relation in the conjunction	ldan pa la ldan pa'i 'brel ba	————
connection	mtshams sbyor	sandhāna, pratisandhāna
consequence	thal ba (cf. it follows)	prasaṅga
contaminated	zag bcas	sāsrava
continuum	rgyun	santāna (cf. mindstream)
	rigs 'dra (cf. homogene)	svajāti
contradiction	'gal ba	viruddha

contradictory condition	'gal rkyen	*viruddhapratyaya
convention	kun rdzob	saṃvṛti
	tha snyad pa (cf. designation)	vyavahāra
cooperative condition (cf. simultaneously occurring condition)	lhan cig byed rkyen	sahakāripratyaya
corresponding cause	skal mnyam gyi rgyu	sabhāgahetu
counteracts	gnod pa (cf. damage)	bādhyate
craving	sred pa	tṛṣṇa
craving for annihilation	'jig sred	vibhāvatṛṣṇa
craving for existence	srid sred	bhāvatṛṣṇa
craving for sense-pleasure	'dod sred	kāmatṛṣṇa
creativity	bzo	śilpa
creator	bzo ba	śilpin
damage	gnod pa (cf. counteracts)	bādhā
death-time	'chi kha'i dus	maraṇakāla
defilement	nyon mongs	kleśa
defilement-obstacle	nyon sgrib	kleśāvaraṇa
definiendum	mtshan gzhi	———
definitive good	nges legs	niḥśreyasa
definitive release	nges par 'byung ba	niḥsaraṇa
definitive removal	nges par 'byin pa	nairyānika
definition (cf. characteristic)	mtshan nyid	lakṣaṇa
demonstration	go bar byed pa	gamaka
	bstan pa (cf. teachings)	upadeśa
dependence	bltos pa	apekṣā
dependent origination	rten 'brel 'byung ba	pratītyasamutpāda
designation (cf. conventional)	tha snyad pa	vyavahāra
desire	'dod pa	icchā, kāma (cf. attachment)
	zhen pa	sneha (cf. attachment)
desire realm	'dod khams	kāmadhātu
destructive cause	'jig pa'i rgyu	nāśahetu
detached	chags bral	virāga, vairāgya
determination (cf. ascertainment)	nges pa byed pa	niścaya
Devendrabuddhi	lha dbang blo	devendrabuddhi
dharma	chos	dharma
dharmatā (cf. nature)	chos nyid	dharmatā
Dharmakīrti	chos grags	dharmakīrti
different	tha dad	bheda
direct opposition	dngos 'gal	———
direct results	ma chod pa'i 'bras bu	———
disadvantage	nyes dmigs	upālambha
disciple	gdul bya	vineya

disease (cf. humor, fault)	nyes pa	doṣa
distorted	log pa	mithyā
	phyin ci log pa, logs pa zhugs pa (cf. inverted)	viparyāsa
doubt	the tshom	vicikitsā
earth	sa	bhūmi
efficiency	don byed nus pa	arthakriyatva
efficient cause	'grub byed kyi rgyu	————
element	'byung ba	bhūta
elimination	zad pa	kṣaya
elucidation	gsal byed	prakaśa (cf. clarity)
embodied being	lus can	dehin
empowerment	dbang bskur	dikṣa, abhiṣeka
enlightenment	byang chub	bodhi
entity	dngos po	vastu, bhāva(cf. existent)
entitylessness void of efficiency	don byed nus stong dngos med	————
equanimity	btang snyoms	upekṣā
equilibrium	cha myam pa	sāmya (cf. balance)
essence (cf. nature)	ngo bo	rūpa (cf. form)
essential	snying po (cf. nature)	hṛdaya
etymological definition	skad dod kyi sgra	————
example	mtshon bya	lakṣman
	dpe	dṛṣṭānta
excellence (cf. change, variation)	khyad pa	viśeṣa
excellence in causes	rgyu phun tshogs	hetusampat
excellence in results	'bras bu phun tshogs	phalasampat
excellence of application	sbyor ba phun tshogs	prayogasampat
excellence of intention	bsam pa phun tshogs	āśayasampat
excellence of one's own aims	rang don phun tshogs	svārthasampat
excellence of others' aims	zhan don phun tshogs	parārthasampat
excellence of realization	rtogs pa phun tshogs	*jñānasampat
existence	gnas pa (cf. abiding)	sthāna
	yod pa, srid pa (cf. saṃsāric existence)	bhāva (cf. existent)
existent	yod pa	bhāva (cf. entity)
experience	myong ba	anubhava
expression (cf. verbal expression)	brjod pa'i sgra	————
external object	phyi rol gyi don	bahyārtha
extreme consequence	ha cang thal ba	atiprasaṅga
faculty (cf. sense)	dbang po	indriya
faith	yid dpyod	āraddhā

fallacy	ltar snang	ābhasa
fault (cf. flaw, disease, humor)	nyes pa	doṣa
fetter	btags pa	upacāra
final mind	tha ma'i sems	antyacetas
flaw	skyon (cf. problem)	doṣa (cf. fault, disease, humor)
form (cf. matter)	gzugs	rūpa (cf. essence, nature)
formation	'du byed	saṃskāra
form realm	gzugs khams	rūpadhātu
formless realm	gzugs med khams	ārūpyadhātu
forward system of explanation	bshad pa'i lugs 'byung	————
four-cornered analysis	mu bzhi	catuṣkoṭi
four immeasureables	tshad med bzhi	caturapramāṇāni
four noble truths	'phags pa'i bden bzhi	caturāryasatyāni
four [opponent] powers	stobs bzhi	*caturbalāni
freedom	grol ba	mukti
future	'byung 'gyur (cf. yet-to-arise, secondary quality)	————
	phyi ma (cf. later, subsequent)	uttara
generality (cf. universal)	spyi	sāmānya
generation	bskyed pa	utpatti
generation of the Mahāyāna thought	theg chen sems bskyed	mahāyānacittotpāda
generic image	don spyi	*arthasāmānya
generosity	sbyin pa	dāna
genus-expression	rigs brjod pa'i sgra	————
gnosis	ye shes	jñāna (cf. cognition, knowledge)
goal (cf. meaning, object)	don	artha
God	dbang phyug	īśvara
good quality (cf. quality)	yon tan	guṇa
great compassion	thugs rje chen po	mahākaruṇā
gross	rags pa	sthūla
happiness (cf. pleasure)	bde ba	sukha
has become an authority	tshad mar gyur pa	pramāṇabhūta
hatred (cf. anger)	zhe sdang	dveśa
hedonist	tshu rol mdzes pa	————
hidden phenomenon	lkog gyur	parokṣa
high rebirth	mngon mtho	*abhyudaya
homogene	rang gi rigs 'dra	svajāti
humor (cf. fault, disease)	nyes pa	doṣa
ignorance	ma rig pa	avidyā
immediate cause	de ma thag pa'i rgyu	samanantarahetu
immediately preceding condition	de ma thag pa'i rkyen	samanantarapratyaya

impermanent	mi rtag pa	anitya
impossible	mi srid	abhāva
imprint	lag rjes	————
imputation	kun brtags	vikalpa (cf. conceptual thought)
imputing name	btags ming	————
inappropriate	mi mthun pa	————
independent	rang stobs	svabala
	bltos pa med pa can	————
independent [syllogism]	rang rgyud [gtan tshigs]	svatantra [hetu]
indestructible	'jig pa med pa	avināśa
indispensable cause (cf. special indispensable cause)	ldog byed kyi rgyu	————
indirect results	chod pa'i 'bras bu	————
inference	rjes dpag	anumāna
inferential authority	rjes dpag gi tshad ma	anumānapramāṇa
infinite regress	thug pa med pa	anavasthā
inherence	'phrod pa 'du ba, 'du 'brel	samavāya
inherence in the conjunction	ldan pa la 'dus par 'du ba	————
innate	lhan skyes	sahaja
intentional object	dmigs yul	*ālambanaviṣaya
intermediate state	bar do	antarābhava
internal tangible object	nang gi reg bya'i don gzung yul	————
inverse pervasion	'gal khyab	*virodhavyapti
inverted (cf. distorted)	phyin ci log pa	viparyāsa
investigation	dpyad pa	vicāra
irreversible	slar mi ldog pa	*aprativiparyaya
it follows that. . .	. . .thal	. . .prasajyate
just-born	skyes ma thag	————
karma (cf. action)	las	karman
knowledge	mkhyen pa	jñāna (cf. gnosis)
knowledge-object	shes bya	jñeya
knowledge-obstacle	shes bya'i sgrib pa	jñeyāvaraṇa
later (cf. future, subsequent)	phyi ma	uttara
liberation	thar pa	mokṣa
	rnam thar	vimokṣa
life	skye ba (cf. arising)	janman
limb	yan lag	aṅga
lineage (cf. type)	rigs (cf. universal)	gotra
listening (cf. study)	thos pa	śruti
living being	srog chags	prāṇin
Lokāyata	rgyang 'phen pa	lokāyata
love	byams pa	maitri

lower abodes	dman gnas	———
lower realms	ngan 'gro	durgati
maker	byed pa po	kartṛ
manifest phenomenon	mngon gyur	abhimukhī
matter (cf. form)	gzugs	rūpa (cf. essence, nature)
meaning (cf. goal, object)	don	artha
meditate	nyams su len pa	āsthitikriyā
meditation	sgom pa	bhāvanā
mental cognition	yid kyi rnam par shes pa	manovijñāna
mental directionality	yid la byed pa	manaskāra
mental factor	sems byung	caitta
method	thabs	upāya
mind	blo	buddhi
	yid	manas
	rig pa (cf. cognition)	vidyā
mindstream	rgyud	santāna (cf. continuum)
mistaken	'khrul pa	vyabhicāra
moisture-born being	drod gsher las skyes pa skyes bo	saṃvedaja
moment	skad cig	kṣaṇa
morality	tshul 'khrims	śīla
movement	g-yo ba	kampa
the *muni*	thub pa	muni
mutual cause	phan tshun rgyu	parasparahetu
mutually successive	phan tshun rjes su byed pa	———
naturally	chos nyid du	dharmatvena
	ngang can	śālin
nature	ngo bo (cf. essence)	rūpa
	rang bzhin	svabhāva, prakṛti (q.v.)
	de kho na nyid (cf. reality)	tattva
	chos nyid	dharmatā (q.v.)
	snying po (cf. essential)	garbha
negative concomitance	ldog khyab	vyatireka
negative purpose	rnam bcad kyi dgos pa	———
nescience	mi shes	ajñāna
new	gsar	nava
nirvāṇa	mya ngan las 'das pa	nirvāṇa
no-self	bdag med pa	anātman, nairātmya
no-self of dharmas	chos kyi bdag med	dharmanairātmya
no-self of persons	gang zag gi bdag med	pudgalanairātmya
non-associated compositional factor	ldan min 'du byed	viprayuktasaṃskāra
non-conceptuality	rtog bral	kalpanāgoḍha

non-deceptive	mi slu ba	avisaṃvāda
non-dual	gnyis med	advaya
non-existent	med pa	abhāva (cf. impossible)
	ye med pa	————
non-returner	phyir mi 'ong ba	anāgāmin
number	grangs	saṃkhyā
object	don (cf. goal, meaning)	artha
	gzung	gṛhīta
	yul	viṣaya
object of refutation	dgag bya	niṣedhya
objection	rgol ba	————
	rtsod pa	codya
objective condition (cf. conditional intentional object)	dmigs rkyen	ālambanapratyaya
objective name	dngos ming	————
objectively impelled inference	dngos stobs rjes dpag	vastubalapravṛttānumāna
objectively separate	don gzhan	arthāntara
obstacle	sgrib	āvaraṇa
occurrence (cf. origination)	'byung ba	sambhava
omniscience	thams cad mkhyen pa	sarvajña
opposing factor	mi mthun phyogs	pratipakṣa (cf. antidote)
opposite of the negative	ldog pa (cf. absent)	————
ordinary being	tha mal pa	prākṛta
origination (cf. occurrence)	'byung ba	sambhava, samudaya
other-ascertainment	gzhan nges	paraniścaya
own-mark	rang gi mtshan nyid	svalakṣaṇa
pain	sdug	duḥkha (cf. suffering)
part	cha	aṃśa
	yan lag (cf. limb)	aṅga
particular mental inclination	blo'i khyad pa g-yer bag	————
particular quality	khyad par kyi chos	viśeṣadharma
partless	cha med	niraṃśa
past	byung zin (cf. already arisen)	————
	'das	atikrama
	snga ma (cf. previous)	pūrva
past and future lives	skye ba snga phyi	*pūrvottarajanma
path	lam	mārga
path of accumulation	tshogs lam	sambhāramārga
path of application	sbyor lam	prayogamārga
path of development	sgom lam	bhāvanāmārga
path of no-more-training	mi slob lam	aśaikṣamārga

path of seeing	mthong lam	darśanamārga
peace	zhi ba	śānti
perception	mngon sum	pratyakṣa
perceptual authority	mngon sum tshad ma	pratyakṣapramāṇa
permanent	rtag pa	nitya
perplexity	dvogs pa	śaṅkā (cf. concern)
person	skyes bu	puruṣa (q.v.)
	gang zag	pudgala
pervasion	khyab pa	vyāpti
phlegm	bad kan	kapha
pleasure (cf. happiness)	bde ba	sukha
pointless	don med	anartha
positive and negative concomitance	rjes su 'gro ldog	anvayavyatireka
positive concomitance	rjes khyab	anvaya
positive purpose	yongs gcod kyi dgos pa	———
potency (cf. ability, capacity, power)	nus pa	śakti
power (cf. ability, capacity, potency)	nus pa	śakti
	stobs	bala
powerful destroyer	stobs ldan gyi gnod byed	———
Prajñākaragupta	rgyan mkhan po	alaṃkārācārya
prakṛti	rang bzhin (cf. nature)	prakṛti
pratyekabuddha	rang sangs rgyas	pratyekabuddha
predicate (grammatical)	chos	dharma (q.v.)
predicate (logical)	bsgrub bya'i chos	sādhyadharma
predicate-expression	chos brjod pa'i sgra	———
present	da ltar ba	pratyutpanna
previous (cf. past)	snga ma	pūrva
previous homogene	rang gi rigs 'dra snga ma	pūrvasvajāti
principal condition	bdag rkyen	adhipatipratyaya
problem (cf. flaw)	skyon	doṣa
projecting cause	'phen byed kyi rgyu	ākṣepanahetu
proof (cf. accomplishment)	sgrub byed	sādhana
propensity	bag chags	vāsanā
pure	gtsang ba	śuddha
purification	rnam byang	vyavadāna
puruṣa (cf. person)	skyes bu	puruṣa
purpose	dgos	prayojana
quality (cf. good quality)	yon tan	guṇa
Ravigupta	nyi ma'i sbas	ravigupta
real nature	gnas gyur	bhutārtha (cf. actuality)

real object	don gyi de nyid	arthatattva
reality	de kho na nyid (cf. nature)	tathatā
realization (cf. cognition)	rtogs pa	gati
reason (causal)	rgyu mtshan (cf. condition)	nimitta
reason (logical)	rtags	liṅga
	gtan tshigs (cf. syllogism)	hetu (cf. cause)
reason based on result	'bras bu'i rtags	tadutpattihetu
reason based on negation	ma dmigs pa'i rtags	anupalabdhihetu
reason based on synonymy	rang bzhin gyi rtags	svabhāvahetu
reasoning	rigs pa	yukti
	rtog ge	tarka
reason's relevance to the subject	phyogs chos	pakṣadharma
rebounding argument	'bras mtshungs	kāryasama
redundant	rnam grangs pa	paryāya
reflection	bsam pa	cintā
refuge	skyabs pa	śarana
refutation	dgag pa	pratiṣedha
renunciation	yid 'byung	nirveda
result	'bras bu	phala
reverse system of explanation	bshad pa'i lugs ldog	————
ritual	cho ga	vidhi
sacred authority (cf. scripture)	lung	āgama
samādhi	ting nge 'dzin	samādhi
Sāṃkhya	grangs can pa	sāṃkhya
saṃsāra	'khor ba	saṃsāra
saṃsāric existence (cf existence)	srid pa	bhāva
saṅgha	dge 'dun	saṅgha
śāstra	bstan bcos	śāstra
savior	skyob pa	tāyin
science	rigs pa (cf. reasoning)	vidyā (cf. mind)
scripture (cf. sacred authority)	lung	āgama
secondary quality	'byung 'gyur (cf. future, yet-to-arise)	upādāya
self	bdag	ātman
self-ascertainment	rang nges	svaniścaya
self-grasping	bdag 'dzin	ātmagraha
self-nature	bdag nyid	ātmatā
self-view	bdag lta	ātmavāda
semen	khu ba	mada
sensation	tshor ba	vedanā
sense, sense-faculty	dbang po	indriya
sense-cognition	dbang shes	indriyavijñāna
sentient being	sems can	sattva

shape	dbyibs	saṃsthāna
sickness	nad	jvara
similarity	mtshungs pa	tulya
simultaneous basis	dus mnyam gyi rten	————
simultaneous	cig car	sakṛt
simultaneously occurring condition (cf. cooperative condition)	lhan cig byed rkyen	sahakāripratyaya
sound (cf. word)	sgra	śabda
special basis	rten khyad par can	*viśeṣāśraya
special cooperative condition	lhan cig byed rkyen khyad par can	*viśeṣasahakāri-pratyaya
special indispensable cause (cf. indispensable cause)	ldog byed gyi rgyu khyad par can	————
speech	ngag	vāk
śrāvaka	nyan thos	śrāvaka
stage	rim	krama
stain	dri ma	mala
streamwinner	rgyun zhugs	śrotāpanna
strongly arising	rab tu skyes ba	prabhava
study (cf. listening)	thos pa	śruti
subject (epistemological)	'dzin	grahaka
subject (logical, gram.)	chos can	dharmin
subject-expression	chos can brjod pa'i sgra	————
sublime	gya nom	praṇīta
subsequent (cf. future, later)	phyi ma	uttara
subsequent cognition	bcad shes	*paricchinnajñāna
substance	rdzas	dravya
substantial cause	nyer len gyi rgyu	upādānakaraṇa
substantially different	rdzas tha dad	*dravyabheda
substantially identical	rdzas gcig pa	*ekadravya
subtle momentariness	phra ba'i skad cig ma	sūkṣmakṣaṇikatva
successively	rim gyis, rim can	krameṇa
sudden condition	'phral gyi rkyen	*ākasmikapratyaya
suffering	sdug bsngal	duḥkha (cf. pain)
suffering of change	'gyur ba'i sdug bsngal	vipariṇāmaduḥkhatā
suffering of suffering	sdug bsngal gyi sdug bsngal	duḥkhaduḥkhatā
suffering of formations	'du byed kyi sdug bsngal	saṃskāraduḥkhatā
sugata	bde shegs	sugata
suitable	rung	yogya
superimposition	sgro 'dogs	āropa
support	rten (cf. basis)	ādhāra

syllogism (cf. reason [log.])	gtan tshigs	hetu
system	lugs	naya
system of tenets (cf. tenet)	grub mtha'	siddhānta
teacher	ston pa	śāstṛ
teaching (cf. demonstration)	bstan pa	upadeśa
tenet (cf. system of tenets)	grub mtha'	siddhānta
those intent on freedom	grol ba don gnyer rnams	*muktiprārthāni
thought of enlightenment	byang chub sems	bodhicitta
three final vehicles	mthar thug theg pa gsum	————
to be adopted	blang bya	upadeya
to be rejected	dor bya	heya
too broad	khyab ches pa	ativyāpti
too narrow	ma khyab	avyāpti
topic	brjod bya	vācya
trace-faults	gnas ngan len	dauṣṭulya
training	slob pa	śikṣa
training-path	slob lam	śaikṣamārga
transformation	'gyur ba	vikāra
transformed state	gnas 'gyur	āśrayaparāvṛtti
transmigrator	'gro ba	jagat
truth of cessation	'gog pa'i bden pa	nirodhasatya
truth of origination	kun 'byung gi bden pa	samudayasatya
truth of path	lam gyi bden pa	mārgasatya
truth of suffering	sdug bsngal gyi bden pa	duḥkhasatya
type (cf. lineage)	rigs (cf. universal)	gotra
ultimate	mthar thug	niṣṭa
	don dam	paramārtha
unacceptable	mi 'thad	viśleṣa
uncertain	ma nges	anekānta
universal	spyi	sāmānya
	rigs (cf. type, lineage) jāti	
undistorted	phyin ci ma log pa	aviparyāsa
universality (cf. generality)	spyi	sāmānya
unproven	ma grub	asiddha
unreasonable	mi rigs	anyāya
unseen	ma mthong ba	adṛṣṭa
unstable basis	rten mi brtan	asthirāśraya
Vaiśeṣika	bye brag pa	vaiśeṣika
variation (cf. change, excellence)	khyad pa	viśeṣa
Vātsīputrīya	gnas ma bu pa	vātsīputrīya
Veda	rig byed	veda
verbal expression (cf. expression)	brjod pa'i sgra	————
very hidden phenomenon	shin tu lkog gyur	atyantaparokṣa

vice	sdig pa	pāpa
view of [self in] the perishable	'jig tshogs lta ba	satkāyadṛṣṭi
virtuous friend	bshes gnyen	kalyānamitra
voidness	stong pa nyid	śūnyatā
volition	sems pa	cetanā
what pertains to the self	bdag gi ba	ātmīya
whole	yan lag can	*aṅgin
wind	rlung	prāṇa (cf. breath)
wisdom	shes rab	prajñā
wisdom of meditation	sgom pa'i shes rab	bhāvanāmāyiprajñā
wisdom of reflection	bsam pa'i shes rab	cintamāyiprajñā
wisdom of study	thos pa'i shes rab	śrutamāyiprajñā
wisdom realizing no-self	bdag med rtogs pa'i shes rab	———
word	sgra (cf. sound)	śabda
	tshig	vāk (cf. speech)
yet to arise (cf. future)	'byung 'gyur (cf. secondary quality)	———
yogin	rnal 'byor pa	yogin
yogic perception	rnal 'byor mngon sum	yogipratyakṣa

Bibliography

ABBREVIATIONS

A = *Aṅguttara Nikāya*, Morris edition (1958)
AK = Vasubandhu, *Abhidharmakośa*
AS = Asaṅga, *Abhidharmasamuccaya*
D = *Dīgha Nikāya*, Rhys Davids and Carpenter edition (1949-60)
GT = rGyal tshab rje, *rNam 'grel thar lam gsal byed*, Sarnath edition (1974)
JIABS = *The Journal of the International Association of Buddhist Studies*
M = *Majjhima Nikāya*, Trenckner and Chalmers edition (1948)
MK = Nāgārjuna, *Madhyamakakārikā*, Inada edition (1970)
NB = Dharmakīrti, *Nyāyabindu*
P. = Pāli
PS = Dignāga, *Pramāṇasamuccaya*
PTT = *Tibetan Tripiṭaka, Peking Edition*, D.T. Suzuki edition (1957-61)
PV = Dharmakīrti, *Pramāṇavārttika*, Miyasaka edition (1972-77)
PVA = Prajñākaragupta, *Pramāṇavārttikālaṃkāra*
PVVṛ = Ravigupta, *Pramāṇavārttikavṛtti*
PVn = Dharmakīrti, *Pramāṇaviniścaya*
PVP = Devendrabuddhi, *Pramāṇavārttikapañjikā* (PTT translation)
RGV = *Ratnagotravibhāgamahāyānottaratantraśāstra*, Johnston and Chowdhury edition (1950)
S = Saṃyutta Nikāya, Feer edition (1960)
Sk. = Sanskrit
T. = Tibetan
TS = Śāntarakṣita, *Tattvasaṃgraha*
TSP = Kamalaśīla, *Tattvasaṃgrahapañjikā*
VV = Nāgārjuna, *Vigrahavyāvartanī*, Johnston and Kunst edition, in Bhattacharya (1978)

Reference Works

Andersen, Dines (1979). *A Pali Reader, with notes and glossary*. 2 vols. Rpt., New Delhi: Award Publishing House.

Apte, Vaman Shivram (1979). *The Student's Sanskrit-English Dictionary*.

Chandra, Lokesh (1963). *Materials for a History of Tibetan Literature*. 3 parts. New Delhi: International Academy of Indian Culture.

________ (1976). *Tibetan-Sanskrit Dictionary*. 2 vols. Rpt., Kyoto: Rinsen Book Co.

Childers, R.C. (1979). *A Dictionary of the Pali Language*. Rpt., New Delhi: Cosmo Publications.

Dagyab, L.S. (1966). *Tibetan Dictionary (Bod brda'i tshig mdzod)*. Dharamsala: Imperial Printing Press.

Das, Sarat Chandra (1979). *Tibetan-English Dictionary*. Rpt., Kyoto: Rinsen Book Co.

Edgerton, Franklin (1972). *Buddhist Hybrid Sanskrit Grammar and Dictionary*. 2 vols. Rpt., Delhi: Motilal Banarsidass.

Fukuda, Yoichi and Yumiko Ishihama. *A Comparative Table of* sa bcad *of the Pramāṇavārttika Found in Tibetan Commentaries on the Pramāṇavārttika*. Studia Tibetica, no. 12. Tokyo: Toyo Bunko, 1986.

Jackson, Roger (1982). "Terms of Sanskrit and Pāli Origin Acceptable as English Words."JIABS 5,2: 141-42.

Jäschke, H.A. (1972). *Tibetan-English Dictionary*. Rpt., London: Routledge and Kegan Paul.

Kanakura, Yensho, Ryujo Yamada, Tokan Tada and Hakuyu Hadano (1953). Editors. *A Catalogue of the Tohoku University Collection of Tibetan Works on Buddhism*. Sendai, Japan: Tohoku University.

Monier-Williams, Sir Monier (1974). *A Sanskrit-English Dictionary*. Rpt., Delhi: Motilal Banarsidass.

Potter, Karl (1983). *Bibliography of Indian Philosophies*. 2nd edition. Princeton: Princeton University Press.

Rhys Davids, T.W. and William Stede (1972). *The Pali Text Society's Pali-English Dictionary*. Rpt., London: Routledge and Kegan Paul.

R. Sasaki (n.d.). Compiler. *Mahāvyutpatti*. 2 vols. n.p.

Steinkellner, Ernst (1967ref). *Verse-Index of Dharmakīrti's Works*. Wien: Arbeitskreis für Tibetische und Buddhistische Studien Universität Wien.

Editions and Translations of Pāli, Sanskrit and Tibetan Sources

Abhisamayālaṃkāra: see Conze (tr.: 1954)

Aṅguttara Nikāya: see Morris (ed.: 1958), Woodward and Hare (tr.: 1951-55).

Asaṅga, *Abhidharmasamuccaya*: see Rahula (tr.:1971).

Aṣṭasāhasrikāprajñāpāramitā Sūtra: see Vaidya (ed.:1963a), Conze (tr.:1973).

Atīśa (1983). *A Lamp for the Path and Commentary*. Tr. and annot. Richard Sherburne, S.J. The Wisdom of Tibet Series—5. London: George Allen & Unwin.

Aung, Shwe Zan and C.A.F. Rhys Davids (1960). (tr.) *Points of Controversy or Subjects of Discourse, being a translation of the Kathā-Vatthu from the Abhidhamma-Piṭaka*. Pali Text Society Translation Series, no. 5. Rpt., London: Luzac & Co.

Batchelor, Stephen (1979). (tr.) Shantideva, *A Guide to the Bodhisattva's Way of Life*. Dharamsala: Library of Tibetan Works and Archives.

Bhattacharya, Kamaleshwar (1978). (tr.) *The Dialectical Method of Nāgārjuna (Vigrahavyāvartanī)*. Text critically edited by E.H. Johnston and Arnold Kunst. Delhi: Motilal Banarsidass.

Buddhaghosa, Bhadantācariya (1976). *The Path of Purification*. Tr. Bhikku Ñāṇamoli. 2 vols. Rpt. Berkeley and London: Shambhala.

Candrakīrti, *Madhyamakāvatāra*: PTT no. 5261-2, vol. 98. See Poussin (tr.: 1907-1911), Rabten (tr.: 1983), Huntington (tr.: 1989).

Chalmers, Lord (1926-27). (tr.) *Further Dialogues of the Buddha. Translated from the Pāli of the Majjhima Nikāya*. 2 vols. Sacred Books of the Buddhists, vols. 5-6. London: Humphrey Milford.

Chattopadhyaya, Debiprasad (1972). (ed.) *Tārānātha's History of Buddhism in India*, tr. Lama Chimpa and Alaka Chattopadhyaya. Simla: Indian Institute of Advanced Study.

Conze, Edward (1972). (tr.) *Buddhist Wisdom Books, containing the Diamond Sutra and the Heart Sutra*. Rpt. New York: Harper & Row.

_________ (1954). (tr.) *Abhisamayālaṅkāra*. Serie Orientale Roma, vol. 6. Roma: Istituto Italiano per il Medio ed Estremo Oriente.

_________ (1973). (tr.) *The Perfection of Wisdom in Eight Thousand Lines and Its Verse Summary. (Aṣṭasāhasrikāprajñāpāramitā)*. Bolinas: Four Seasons Foundation.

Daśabhūmika Sūtra: see Vaidya (ed.: 1967).

Devendrabuddhi, *Pramāṇavārttikapañjikā*: PTT no. 5717b, vols. 130-131.

dGe 'dun grub pa (n.d.). *Tshad ma rnam 'grel legs par bshad pa*. Woodblock print.

Dharmakīrti. *Hetubindu*: PTT no. 5712, vol. 130. See Steinkellner (tr.:1967).

_________. *Nyāyabindu*: PTT no. 5711, vol. 130. See Śāstri (ed.:1954) and Stcherbatsky (tr.:1962, vol. II).

_________. *Pramāṇavārttika*: [PTT no. 5709, vol. 130]. See Miyasaka (ed.:1972-77), Saṅkṛtyāyana (ed.:1938-40), Shastri (ed.:1968), Gnoli (ed.:1960), Frauwallner (ed. & tr.: 1930-36), Mookerjee and Nagasaki (tr.:1968), Nagatomi (tr.:1957), Vetter (tr.:1984), Tillemans (tr.:1986) and van Bijlert (tr.:1989).

_________. *Pramāṇaviniścaya*: PTT no. 5710, vol. 130. See Vetter (ed. & tr.:1956) and Steinkellner (ed. & tr.:1979)

_________. *Sambandhaparīkṣā*: PTT no. 5713, vol. 130. See Frauwallner (tr.:1934).

_________. *Santānāntarasiddhi*: PTT no. 5716, vol. 130. See Kitagawa (tr.:1955).

_________. *Vādanyāya*: PTT no. 5715, vol. 130. See Shastri (ed.:1972).

Dīgha Nikāya: see Rhys Davids and Carpenter (ed.:1949-60) and Rhys Davids (tr.:1951).

Dignāga, *Pramāṇasamuccaya*: PTT no. 5700, vol. 130. See Hattori (tr.:1968).

Feer, M. Leon (1960). (ed.) *The Saṃyutta-Nikāya of the Sutta-Piṭaka*. 5 vols. Rpt., London:Luzac & Co.

Frauwallner, E. (1934). (tr.) *Sambandhaparīkṣā*. Wiener Zeitschrift für des Kundes Morgenlandes (41) 261-300.

_________ (1930-36). (ed. & tr.) "Beiträge zur Apohalehre." Wiener Zeitschrift für des Kunstes Morgenlandes. 37 (1930) 259-83; 39 (1932) 247-85; 40 (1933) 51-94; 42 (1935) 93-102; 44 (1936) 233-87.

Gangopadhyaya, Mrinalkanti (1978). (ed. & tr.) *Vinītadeva's Nyāyabindu-ṭīkā*. Calcutta: Indian Studies Past and Present.

Gelek Demo, Ngawang (1980). (ed.) *The Collected Works (Gsung 'Bum) of rGyal-rtshab-rje dar-ma rin-chen*. 2 vols. Delhi.

Gnoli, Raniero (1960). (ed.) *The Pramāṇavārttikam of Dharmakīrti* [*Svārthānumāna* chapter]. Serie Orientale Roma, 23. Roma: Istituto Italiano per il Medio ed Estremo Oriente.

Hattori, M. (1968). *Dignāga, On Perception, Being the Pratyakṣapariccheda of Dignāga's Pramāṇasamuccaya*. Harvard Oriental Series, XLVII. Cambridge: Harvard University Press.

Heart Sūtra: see Conze (tr.:1972)

Huntington, C.W., Jr. (1989). (tr.) *The Emptiness of Emptiness*. With Geshé Namgyal Wangchen. Honolulu: University of Hawaii Press.

Inada, Kenneth K. (1970). (ed. & tr.) *Nāgārjuna: A Translation of His Mūlamadhyamakakārikā*. Tokyo: The Hokuseido Press.

Jha, Ganganatha (1937-39). (tr.) *The Tattvasaṃgraha of Śāntarakṣita with the Commentary of Kamalaśīla*. 2 vols. Baroda: Oriental Institute.

Jig-me-ling-pa (1982). *The Dzogchen Innermost Essence Preliminary Practice*. Tr. Ven. Tulku Thondup. Dharamsala: Library of Tibetan Works and Archives.

Johnston, E.H. and T. Chowdhury (1950). (eds.) *The Ratnagotravibhāga Mahāyānottaratantraśāstra*. Patna: Bihar Research Society.

Kamalaśīla, *Tattvasaṃgrahapañjikā*: see Shastri (ed.:1968a) and Jha (tr.:1937-39).

Kathāvatthu: see Aung and Rhys Davids (tr.:1960).

Kern, H. (1963). (tr.) *Saddharma-Puṇḍarīka or the Lotus of the True Law*. Rpt., New York: Dover.

Kitagawa, H. (1955). (tr.) *Santanāntarasiddhi. Journal of the Greater India Society* (14).

Lamotte, Étienne (1935). (ed. & tr.) *Saṃdhinirmocana Sūtra: L'explication des mystères*. Université de Louvain, receuil de travaux, 2e série, 34e fasc. Paris: Maisonneuve.

Laṅkāvatāra Sūtra: see Vaidya (ed.: 1963) and Suzuki (tr.: 1978).

Majjhima Nikāya: see Trenckner and Chalmers (ed.: 1948), Chalmers (tr.: 1926-27) and Sīlācāra (1924).

Manorathanandin, *Pramāṇavārttikavṛtti*: see Saṅkṛtyāyana (ed.:1938-40) and Shastri (ed.:1968).

Mi pham rgya mtsho (n.d.). *Tshad ma rnam 'grel gyi rgya chen bshad pa rigs pa'i rgya mtsho*. Dehradun: Nyingmapa Monastery.

Milindapañhā: See Rhys Davids (tr.: 1963).

Miyasaka, Y. (1972-77). (ed.) *Pramāṇavārttika-kārikā. Sanskrit and Tibetan. Acta Indologia* (2-4).

mKhas grub dge legs bzang po (n.d.). *rGyas pa'i bstan bcos tshad ma rnam 'grel gyi rgya chen bshad pa rigs pa'i rgya mtsho*, in Mongolian Lama Gurudeva, (ed.), *mKhas grub rje gSung 'bum*. vol. *da*. Delhi: Mongolian Lama Gurudeva.

Mookerjee, Satkari and Hojun Nagasaki (1968). (tr.) *The Pramāṇavārttikam of Dharmakīrti* [*Svārthānumāna* chapter, verses 1-51]. Patna: Nava Nālandā Mahāvihāra.

Morris, R. (1958). (ed.) *The Aṅguttara Nikāya*. 5 vols. Rpt., London: Luzac & Co.

Nāgārjuna, *Madhyamakakārikā*: see Inada (ed. & tr.: 1970) and Streng (tr.: 1967).

_________. *Vigrahavyāvartanī*: see Bhattacharya (ed. & tr.:1978).

Nagatomi, Masatoshi (1957). (tr.) "A Study of Dharmakīrti's *Pramāṇavārttika*: An English Translation and Annotation of the *Pramāṇavārttika*, Book I." Unpublished dissertation, Harvard University.

Obermiller, E. (1931). (tr.) "The Sublime Science of the Great Vehicle to Salvation, being a Manual of Buddhist Monism: the Work of Ārya Maitreya with a Commentary by Āryāsaṅga." *Acta Orientalia* (IX) 81-306.

_________. (1931-32). (tr.) Bu-ston, *A History of Buddhism*. 2 parts. Heidelberg.

Poussin, Louis de la Vallée (1907-11). (tr.) *Madhyamakāvatāra. Le Muséon*. Louvain.

_________ (1923-31). (tr. & annot.) *L'Abhidharmakośa de Vasubandhu*. 6 vols. Paris: Paul Geuthner.

Pradhan, P. (1975). (ed.) *Abhidharmakośabhāṣyam*. Patna: K.P. Jayaswal Research Institute.

Prajñākaragupta, *Pramāṇavārttikālaṃkāra* [or *-bhāṣya*]: PTT no. 5917, vol. 132. See Saṅkṛtyāyana (ed.:1953).

Rabten, Geshé (1983). *Echoes of Voidness*. Tr. & ed. Stephen Batchelor. London: Wisdom Publications.

Rahula, Walpola (1971). (tr.) *Le compendium de la super-doctrine (philosophie) (Abhidharmasamuccaya) d'Asaṅga*. Publications de l'École Française d'Extrême-Orient, vol. LXXVIII. Paris: École Française d'Extrême-Orient.

Ratnagotravibhāgamahāyānottaratantraśāstra: see Johnston and Chowdhury (ed.: 1950), Obermiller (tr.:1931).

Ravigupta, *Pramāṇavārttikavṛtti*: PTT no. 5726, vol. 136.

rGyal tshab dar ma rin chen (1974). *rNam 'grel thar lam gsal byed: Tshad ma rnam 'grel gyi tshig le'ur byas pa'i rnam bshad phyin ci ma log par gsal bar byed pa*. 2 vols. Sarnath: Pleasure of Elegant Sayings Press (Tibetan Monastery). See also Gelek (1980).

Rhys Davids, C.A.F. and F.L. Woodward (1950-56). (tr.) *The Book of Kindred Sayings (Saṃyutta Nikāya) or Grouped Suttas*. 5 vols. Pali Text Society Translation Series, nos. 7, 10, 13, 14, 16. Rpt., London: Luzac & Co.

Rhys Davids; T.W. (1963). (tr.) *The Questions of King Milinda*. 2 vols. Rpt., New York: Dover.

Rhys Davids, T.W. and C.A.F. (1951). (tr.) *Dialogues of the Buddha. (Dīgha Nikāya*. 3 vols. Sacred Books of the Buddhists, vols. II-IV. Rpt., London: Luzac & Co.

Rhys Davids, T.W. and J. Estlin Carpenter (1959-60). (ed.) *The Dīgha Nikāya*. 3 vols. Rpt., London: Luzac & Co.

Sa skya paṇḍita kun dga' rgyal mtshan (1968). *Tshad ma rigs pa'i gter*, in bSod-rNams-rGya-mTsho, ed., *The Complete Works of the Great Masters of the Sa-skya Sect of Tibetan Buddhism*, vol. 5. Biblioteca Tibetica 1-5. Tokyo: The Tokyo Bunyo.

Saddharmapuṇḍarīka Sūtra: see Vaidya (ed.:1960) and Kern (tr.:1963).

Śākyabodhi [or Śākyamati], *Pramāṇavārttikavṛtti*: PTT no. 5718, vol. 131.

Samādhirāja Sūtra: see Vaidya (ed.: 1961).

Saṃdhinirmocana Sūtra: see Lamotte (ed. & tr.: 1935).

Saṃyutta Nikāya: see Feer (ed.:1960) and Rhys Davids and Woodward (tr.:1950-56).

Saṅkṛtyāyana, Rāhula (1938-40). (ed.) *Dharmakīrti's Pramāṇavārttika, with a Commentary by Manorathanandin. The Journal of the Bihar and Orissa Research Society* (Patna).

_________ (1953). (ed.) *Pramāṇavārttikabhāshyam or Vārtikālaṃkāra of Prajñākaragupta*. Patna: Kāshi Prasad Jayaswal Research Institute.

Śāntarakṣita, *Tattvasaṃgraha*: see Shastri (ed.: 1968a) and Jha (tr.:1937-39).

Śāntideva, *Bodhicaryāvatāra*: see Vaidya (ed.: 1960b) and Batchelor (tr.: 1979).

Śāstri, Chandrashekhara (1954). (ed.) *The Nyāyabindu of Śrī Dharmakīrti, with a Sanskrit Commentary by Śrī Dharmottarācharya*. The Chowkhambha Sanskrit Series, no. 1. Varanasi: Chowkhambha.

Sgam po pa, *Jewel Ornament of Liberation*. Tr. Herbert V. Guenther. Rpt., London: Rider & Co.

Shastri, Dwarikadas (1968). (ed.) *Pramāṇavārttika of Acharya Dharmakīrti, with the Commentary "Vritti" of Acharya Manorathandin*. Varanasi: Bauddha Bharati.

________ (1968a). (ed.) *Tattvasaṃgraha, with the Commentary 'Pañjikā' of Śrī Kamalaśīla*. 2 vols. Varanasi: Bauddha Bharati.

Shastri, S.D. (1972). (ed.) *Vādanyāyaprakaraṇam ācārya-Śāntarakṣitakṛta-Vipañcitārthavyākhyāyutam evaṃ ācārya-Prabhācandrakṛtavyākhyāsanāthā Sambandhaparīkṣā*. Bauddha Bharati Series, VIII. Varanasi.

Sīlācāra, Bhikku (1924). (tr.) *The Majjhima Nikāya: The First Fifty Discourses from the Collection of the Medium-Length Discourses of Gotama the Buddha*. 2nd edition. München: Oskar Schloss Verlag.

Steinkellner, E[rnst] (1967). (tr.) *Hetubindu, reconstructed into Sanskrit and translated by E. Steinkellner*. Sitzungberichte der Österreichische Akademie der Wissenschaften 252, Band 1 & 2. Wien: Böhlaus.

________ (1979). *Dharmakīrti's Pramāṇaviniścayaḥ. Zweites Kapitel: Svārthānumāna*. Sitzungberichte der Österreichische Akademie der Wissenschaften, Band 358, Hest 15. Wien.

Streng, Frederick L. (1967). *Emptiness: A Study in Religious Meaning*. Nashville: Abingdon Press.

Suzuki, Daisetz Teitaro (1978). (tr.) *The Laṅkāvatāra Sūtra*. Rpt., Boulder: Prajñā Press.

Tibetan Tripiṭaka, Peking Edition. Ed. Daisetz T. Suzuki. Tokyo-Kyoto: Tibetan Tripiṭaka Research Foundation, 1957-61.

Trenckner, V. and Lord Chalmers (1948). (ed.) *The Majjhima Nikāya*. 3 vols. Rpt., London: Oxford University Press.

Tsong kha pa blo bzang grags pa (1961). *Byang chub lam rim chen mo:* PTT no. 6001, vol. 152.

Udāna: see Woodward (tr.:1948).

Vaidya P.L. (1960a). (ed.) *Saddharmapuṇḍarīkasūtra*. Buddhist Sanskrit Texts, no. 6. Darbhanga: The Mithila Institute.

________ (1960b). (ed.) *Bodhicaryāvatāra*. Buddhist Sanskrit Texts, no. 12. Darbhanga: The Mithila Institute.

________ (1961). (ed.) *Samādhirājasūtram*. Buddhist Sanskrit Texts, no. 2. Darbhanga: The Mithila Institute.

________ (1963a). (ed.) *Aṣṭasāhasrikāprajñāpāramitā*. Buddhist Sanskrit Texts, no. 4. Darbhanga: The Mithila Institute.

________ (1963b). (ed.) *Saddharmalaṅkāvatārasūtram*. Buddhist Sanskrit Texts, no. 3. Darbhanga: The Mithila Institute.

________ (1967). (ed.) *Daśabhūmikasūtram*. Buddhist Sanskrit Texts, no. 7. Darbhanga: The Mithila Institute.

van Bijlert, Vittorio A. (1989). *Epistemology and Spiritual Authority: The Development of Epistemology and Logic in the Old Nyāya and the Buddhist School of Epistemology with an Annotated Translation of Dharmakīrti's Pramāṇavārttika II (Pramāṇasiddhi) VV. 1-7.* Wiener Studien zur Tibetologie und Buddhismuskunde, vol. 20. Wien: Arbeitskreis für Tibetische und Buddhistische Studien Universität Wien.

Vasubandhu, *Abhidharmakośa*: see Pradhan (ed.:1975) and Poussin (tr.:1923-31).

Vetter, F. Tillman (1966). (ed. & tr.) *Dharmakīrti's Pramāṇaviniścaya Pratyakṣam*. Sitzungberichte der Österreichische Akademie der Wissenschaften 250, Band 3. Wien: Böhlaus.

________ (1984). (tr.) *Der Buddha und Seine Lehre in Dharmakīrtis Pramāṇavārttika* [*Pramāṇasiddhi* chapter, verses 146c-287]. Wiener Studien zur Tibetologie und Buddhismuskunde, Heft 12. Wien.

Vinītadeva, *Nyāyabinduṭīkā*: see Gangopadhyaya (ed. & tr.: 1971).

Wangchen, Namgyal (1980). *kLad sems kyi 'brel ba la brtag pa'i gtam legs bshad tshad ma'i dgongs rgyan*. Sarnath.

Wang-ch'uk dor-je, the Ninth Karmapa (1978). *The Mahamudra Eliminating the Darkness of Ignorance*. Tr. Alexander Berzin. Dharamsala: Library of Tibetan Works and Archives.

Warren, Henry Clarke (1970). (tr.) *Buddhism in Translations*. Rpt., New York: Atheneum.

Wayman, Alex and Hideko (1974). (tr.) *The Lion's Roar of Queen Śrīmālā: A Buddhist Scripture on the Tathāgatagarbha Theory*. New York: Columbia University Press.

Woodward, F.L. (1948). (tr.) *Minor Anthologies of the Pali Canon, part 2*. Sacred Books of the Buddhists, vol. 8. London: Oxford University Press.

Woodward, F.L. and E.M. Hare (1951-55). (tr.) *The Book of Gradual Sayings (Aṅguttara-Nikāya) or More-numbered suttas*. 5 vols. Pali Text Society Translation Series, nos. 22, 24-27. Rpt., London: Luzac & Co.

Yamāri, *Pramāṇavārttikaṭīkā*: PTT no. 5723, vols. 134-35.

Secondary Sources

Ashby, R.W. "Verifiability Principle." In Edwards (1967) 8: 240-46.

Bambrough, Renford (1978). "Intuition and the Inexpressible." In Katz (1978).

Barbour, Ian (1974). *Myths, Models and Paradigms: A Comparative Study in Science and Religion*. New York: Harper & Row.

Bareau, André (1955). *Les sectes bouddhiques du petit véhicule*. Publications de l'École Française d'Extrême-Orient, vol. XXXVIII. Paris: École Française d'Extrême-Orient.

Basham, A.L. (1959). *The Wonder That Was India. A Survey of the Culture of the Indian Subcontinent Before the Coming of the Muslims.* New York: Grove Press.

Bastian, Edward W. (1980). "Mahāyāna Buddhist Religious Practice and the Perfection of Wisdom According to the *Aṣṭasāhasrikāprajñāpāramitā* and the *Pañcaviṃśatisāhasrikāprajñāpāramitā*." Unpublished Ph.D. dissertation, University of Wisconsin-Madison.

Batchelor, Stephen (1983). *Alone With Others: An Existential Approach to Buddhism.* New York: Grove Press.

Berger, Peter and Thomas Luckmann (1966). *The Social Construction of Reality: A Treatise in the Sociology of Knowledge.* Garden City: Doubleday.

Bierce, Ambrose (1979). *The Devil's Dictionary.* New York: Thomas Y. Crowell.

Blakemore, Colin (1977). *Mechanics of Mind.* New York: Cambridge University Press.

Bodhi, Bhikku (1978). *The Discourse on the All-Embracing Net of Views: The Brahmajala Sutta and Its Commentarial Exegesis.* Kandy: Buddhist Publication Society.

Bruner, Jerome and Carol Fleischer Feldman (1986). "Under Construction." *The New York Review of Books.* March 27, 1986.

Bucknell, Rod (1984). "The Buddhist Path to Liberation: An Analysis of the Listing of Stages." JIABS 7, 2:10-40.

Bultmann, Rudolf (1951-55). *The Theology of the New Testament.* Tr. Kendrick Gobel. New York: Scribner.

Burns, Douglas M. (1971). "Nirvana, Nihilism and Satori," in Ven. Nyanaponika, ed., *Pathways of Buddhist Thought: Essays from "The Wheel".* Selected by M.C. O'Walshe. London: George Allen & Unwin.

Cabezón, José I. (1981). "The Concepts of Truth and Meaning in the Buddhist Scriptures." JIABS 4, 1:7-23.

Campbell, Joseph (1962). *The Masks of God: Oriental Mythology.* New York: Viking Press.

Chi, Richard S.Y. (1969). *Buddhist Formal Logic.* London: Royal Asiatic Society of Great Britain and Ireland.

Collins, Steven (1982). *Selfless Persons: Imagery and Thought in Theravāda Buddhism.* Cambridge: Cambridge University Press.

Conze, Edward (1967). *Buddhist Thought in India.* Ann Arbor: University of Michigan Press.

Culler, Jonathan (1982). *On Deconstruction: Theory and Criticism after Structuralism.* Ithaca: Cornell University Press.

Dalai Lama, The (1985). *Opening the Eye of New Awareness.* Tr. Donald S. Lopez, Jr., with Jeffrey Hopkins. London: Wisdom Publications.

Dasgupta, Surendranath (1975). *A History of Indian Philosophy.* 6 vols. Rpt., Delhi: Motilal Banarsidass.

Dayal, Har (1970). *The Bodhisattva Doctrine in Buddhist Sanskrit Literature.* Rpt., Delhi: Motilal Banarsidass.

Daye, Douglas Dunsmore (1972). "Metalogical Studies in Sixth Century Buddhist Proto-metalogic from the Sanskrit and Chinese Texts of the Nyāyapraveśa, or Unpacking Ordinary Sanskrit." Unpublished Ph.D. dissertation, University of Wisconsin-Madison.

Demiéville, Paul (1952). *Le concile de Lhasa: Un controverse sur le quiétisme entre Bouddhistes de l'Inde et de la Chine au VIIIe siècle de l'ère chrétienne.* Bibliothèque de l'institut des hautes études chinoises, vol. VII. Paris: Imprimerie Nationale de France.

Dennett, Daniel C. *Brainstorms: Philosophical Essays on Mind and Psychology.* Cambridge: The MIT Press.

Derrida, Jacques (1974). *Of Grammatology.* Tr. Gayatri Chakravorty Spivak. Baltimore: The Johns Hopkins University Press.

Dhargyey, Geshe Ngawang (1974). *Tibetan Tradition of Mental Development.* Dharamsala: Library of Tibetan Works and Archives.

Dharmasiri, Gunapala (1974). *A Buddhist Critique of the Christian Concept of God.* Colombo: Lake House Investments.

Donovan, Peter (1976). *Religious Language.* London: Sheldon Press.

Dreyfus, Georges (1991). "Ontology, Philosophy of Language and Epistemology in Buddhist Tradition: A Study of Dharmakīrti's Philosophy in Light of Its Reception in the Later Indo-Tibetan Tradition." Unpublished Ph.D. dissertation, University of Virginia.

_________ and Christian Lindtner (1989). "The Yogācāra Philosophy of Dignāga and Dharmakīrti." *Studies in Central and East Asian Religions* (2) 27-52.

Dutt, Nalinaksha (1970). *Buddhist Sects in India.* Calcutta: Firma K.L. Mukhopadhyay.

Eckel, Malcolm David (1987). *Jñānagarbha's Commentary on the Distinction Between the Two Truths.* New York: State University of New York Press.

Edwards, Paul (1967). (ed.) *The Encyclopedia of Philosophy.* 8 vols. New York: Macmillan.

Ergardt, Jan T. (1977). *Faith and Knowledge in Early Buddhism: An Analysis of the Contextual Structures of the Arahant-Formula in the Majjhima Nikāya.* Studies in the History of Religions, no. XXXVII. Leiden: E.J. Brill.

Evans, Donald (1974). "Differences Between Scientific and Religious Assertions." In Norbert O. Schedler, ed., *Philosophy of Religion: Contemporary Perspectives.* New York: Macmillan.

Ezorsky, Gertrude (1967). "Pragmatic Theory of Truth." In Edwards (1967) 6:427-30.

Fenner, Peter (1982). *Liberative Philosophy—A Madhyamika View: Some Supportive Arguments and Foundational Requirements for a Dharma Philosophy.* Melbourne: Spectrum.

Feyerabend, Paul (1975). *Against Method.* London: New Left Books.

Flew, Antony (1979). *A Dictionary of Philosophy*. New York: St. Martin's Press.

Forman, Robert K.C. (1990). (ed.) *The Problem of Pure Consciousness*. New York: Oxford University Press.

Frauwallner, E. (1953). *Geschichte der indischen Philosophie*. Salzburg: O. Müller. [English translation: *History of Indian Philosophy*. Tr. V.M. Bedekar. 2 vols. Delhi: Motilal Banarsidass, 1973.]

_________ (1954). "Die Reihenfolge und Entstehung der Werke Dharmakīrtis." In *Asiatica: Festschrift F. Weller*. Leipzig.

_________ (1961). "Landmarks in the History of Buddhist Logic." Wiener Zeitschrift für die Kunde Süd- und Ostasiens (5) 125-148.

Gadamer, Hans-Georg (1975). *Truth and Method*. New York: Seabury Press.

Gimello, Robert (1978). "Mysticism and Meditation." In Katz (1978).

Goodman, Nelson (1978). *Ways of Worldmaking*. Indianapolis: Hackett.

Griffiths, Paul J. (1986). *On Being Mindless: Buddhist Meditation and the Mind-Body Problem*. La Salle, IL: Open Court.

_________ (1991). *An Apology for Apologetics: A Study in the Logic of Interreligious Dialogue*. Faith Meets Faith Series. Maryknoll, NY: Orbis Books.

Guenther, Herbert V. (1971). *The Life and Teaching of Nāropa*. Rpt., New York: Oxford University Press.

Gyatso, Geshe Kelsang (1980). *Meaningful to Behold*. Tr. Tenzin Norbu, ed. Jonathan Landaw. Ulverston, U.K.: Wisdom Publications.

Hayes, Richard P. (1984). "The Question of Doctrinalism in the Buddhist Epistemologists." *Journal of the American Academy of Religion* (LII, 4) 645-70.

_________ (1986). Review of Amar Singh, *The Heart of Buddhist Thought: The Philosophy of Diṅnāga and Dharmakīrti*. JIABS (9, 2) 166-72.

_________ (1988a). *Dignāga on the Interpretation of Signs*. Boston: D. Reidel.

_________ (1988b). "Principled Atheism in the Buddhist Scholastic Tradition." *Journal of Indian Philosophy* (16) 5-28.

Hellerstein, David (1988). "Plotting a Theory of the Brain." *The New York Times Magazine*, May 22, 1988, p. 17ff.

Hick, John (1989). *An Interpretation of Religion: Human Responses to the Transcendent*. New Haven and London: Yale University Press.

Hoffman, Frank (1982). "The Buddhist Empiricism Thesis." *Religious Studies* (18).

_________ (1987). *Rationality and Mind in Early Buddhism*. Delhi: Motilal Banarsidass.

Hofstadter, Douglas R. and Daniel C. Dennett (1981). (eds.) *The Mind's I: Fantasies and Reflections on Self and Soul*. New York: Basic Books.

Hollis, Martin and Steven Lukes (1982). (eds.) *Rationality and Relativism*. Cambridge: The MIT Press.

Hookham, Susan (1991). *The Buddha Within: Tathagatagarbha Theory According to the Shentong Interpretation of the Ratnagotravibhaga*. Albany: State University of New York Press.

Hopkins, Jeffrey (1980). *Compassion in Tibetan Buddhism*. Valois, NY: Gabriel/Snow Lion.

_________ (1983). *Meditation on Emptiness*. London: Wisdom Publications.

Horner, I.B. (1936). *The Early Buddhist Theory of Man Perfected: A Study of the Arahan*. London: Williams and Norgate.

Hospers, John R. (1967). *An Introduction to Philosophical Analysis*. 2nd ed. Englewood Cliffs, NJ: Prentice-Hall.

Houston, Gary W. (1980). *Materials for a History of the bSam yas Debate*. Monumenta Tibetica Historia, Abteilung I, Band 2. Sank Augustin: VGH Wissenschaftsverlag.

Inami, Masahiro and Tom J.F. Tillemans (1986). "Another Look at the Framework of the Pramāṇasiddhi Chapter of the Pramāṇavārttika." *Wiener Zeitschrift für die Kunde Südasiens und Archiv für Indische Philosophie*, Band XXX, 123-42.

Jackson, David P. (1987). *The Entrance Gate for the Wise (Section III): Sa-skya Paṇḍita on Indian and Tibetan Traditions of Pramāṇa and Philosophical Debate*. Wiener Studien zur Tibetologie und Buddhismuskunde (Vienna), vol. 17, 2 parts.

Jackson, Roger R. (1983). "Is Enlightenment Possible? An Analysis of Some Arguments in the Buddhist Philosophical Tradition, with Special Attention to the *Pramāṇasiddhi* Chapter of Dharmakīrti's *Pramāṇavārttika*." Unpublished Ph.D. dissertation, University of Wisconsin-Madison.

_________ (1985). "For Whom Emptiness Prevails: An Analysis of the Religious Implications of Nāgārjuna's *Vighrahavyāvartanī* 70." *Religious Studies* (21) 407-14.

_________ (1986). "Dharmakīrti's Refutation of Theism." *Philosophy East and West* (36, 4) 315-48.

_________ (1987). "Dharmakīrti's Attitude Toward Omniscience." In M.A. Dhaky, ed., *Bacherdas Doshi and Dalsukh Malvaniya Felicitation Volume*. Ahmedabad.

_________ (1988). "The Buddha as *Pramāṇabhūta*: Epithets and Arguments in the Buddhist 'Logical' Tradition." *Journal of Indian Philosophy* (16) 335-65.

_________ (1989). "Matching Concepts: Deconstructive and Foundationalist Tendencies in Buddhist Thought." *Journal of the American Academy of Religion* (LVII/3) 561-89.

_________ (1990). "Luminous Mind Among the Logicians: An Analysis of *Pramāṇavārttika* II:205-211." In Paul J. Griffiths and John P. Keenan, eds., *Buddha Nature: A Festschrift in Honor of Minoru Kiyota*, 95-123. Las Vegas: Buddhist Books International.

James, William (1955). "What Pragmatism Means." In Morton White (ed.), *The Age of Analysis*, 154-73. New York: Mentor.

_________ (1961). *The Varieties of Religious Experience*. New York: Collier.

Jaini, Jagmanderlal (1979). *Outlines of Jainism.* Ed. F.W. Thomas. Indore: J.L. Jaini Trust.

Jaini, Padmanabh S. (1974). "On the *Sarvajñatva* (Omniscience) of Mahāvīra and the Buddha." In L. Cousins, A. Kunst and K.R. Norman, eds., *Buddhist Studies in Honour of I.B. Horner*, 71-90. Dortrecht: D. Reidel.

________ (1979). *The Jaina Path of Purification.* Berkeley: University of California Press.

Jayatilleke, K.N. (1980). *Early Buddhist Theory of Knowledge.* Rpt., Delhi: Motilal Banarsidass.

Kalupahana, David J. (1976). *Causality: The Central Philosophy of Buddhism.* Honolulu: The University Press of Hawaii.

Karunadasa, Y. (1967). *Buddhist Analysis of Matter.* Colombo: Department of Cultural Affairs.

Katsura, Shoryu (1984). "Dharmakīrti's Theory of Truth." *Journal of Indian Philosophy* (15) 57-70.

Katz, Steven T. (1978). (ed.) *Mysticism and Philosophical Analysis.* New York: Oxford University Press.

Kaufmann, Walter (1972). *Critique of Religion and Philosophy.* Princeton: Princeton University Press.

Klein, Anne (1986). *Knowledge and Liberation: Tibetan Buddhist Epistemology in Support of Transformative Religious Experience.* Ithaca: Snow Lion.

________ (1991). *Knowing, Naming and Negation: A Sourcebook on Tibetan Sautrāntika.* Ithaca: Snow Lion.

Koller, John (1970). *Oriental Philosophies.* New York: Scribner's.

Krausz, Michael (1989). (ed.) *Relativism: Interpretation and Confrontation.* Notre Dame: Notre Dame University Press.

________ and Jack W. Meiland (1982). (eds.) *Relativism: Cognitive and Moral.* Notre Dame: University of Notre Dame Press.

Kuhn, Thomas S. (1962). *The Structure of Scientific Revolutions.* Chicago: University of Chicago Press.

Lamotte, Étienne (1958). *Histoire du bouddhisme indien des origines à l'ère Saka.* Bibliothèque du Muséon, no. 43. Louvain: Publications universitaires.

Larson, Gerald and Ram Shankar Bhattacharya (1987). (eds.) *Sāṃkhya: A Dualist Tradition in Indian Philosophy.* Princeton: Princeton University Press.

Lati Rinbochay (1980). *Mind in Tibetan Buddhism.* Tr. & ed. Elizabeth Napper. Valois, NY: Gabriel/Snow Lion.

Lindbeck, George A. (1984). *The Nature of Doctrine.* Philadelphia: The Westminster Press.

Lindtner, Christian (1980). "Apropos Dharmakīrti - Two New Works and a New Date." *Acta Orientalia* (41) 27-37.

Lopez, Donald S., Jr. (1987). *A Study of Svātantrika.* Ithaca: Snow Lion.

Matilal, Bimal K. (1986). *Perception*. Oxford: Clarendon Press.

_________ and Robert D. Evans (1986). (eds.) *Buddhist Logic and Epistemology: Studies in the Buddhist Analysis of Inference and Language*. Dordrecht: D. Reidel.

McDermott, A.C. Senape (1970). *An Eleventh-Century Buddhist Ontology of "Exists"*. Dordrecht: D. Reidel.

Mookerjee, Satkari (1980). *The Buddhist Doctrine of Universal Flux: An Exposition of the Philosophy of Critical Realism as Expounded by the School of Dignāga*. Rpt., Delhi: Motilal Banarsidass.

Moore, Peter (1978). "Mystical Experience, Mystical Doctrine, Mystical Technique." In Katz (1978).

Nagatomi, Masatoshi (1959). "The Framework of the *Pramāṇavārttika*, Book I." *Journal of the American Oriental Society* (79) 263-66.

_________ (1967-68). "Arthkriyā." *The Adyar Library Bulletin: Dr. V. Raghavan Felicitation Volume*. Adyar, Madras.

_________ (1980). "Mānasa-pratyakṣa: A Conundrum in the Buddhist Pramāṇa System." In M. Nagatomi et al. (eds.) *Sanskrit and Indian Studies*. Boston: D. Reidel.

Napper, Elizabeth (1989). *Dependent Arising and Emptiness: A Tibetan Buddhist Interpretation of Madhyamika Philosophy Emphasizing the Compatibility of Emptiness and Conventional Phenomena*. London and Boston: Wisdom.

Obermiller, E. (1933, 1936). *Analysis of the Abhisamayālaṃkāra*. 2 fascicles. London: Luzac & Co.

O'Flaherty, Wendy D. (1984). *Dreams, Illusions and Other Realities*. Chicago: University of Chicago Press.

Pande, G.C. (1974). *Studies in the Origins of Buddhism*. Delhi: Motilal Banarsidass.

Passmore, John (1970). *A Hundred Years of Philosophy*. London: Penguin.

Perdue, Daniel (1992). *Debate in Tibetan Buddhism*. Ithaca: Snow Lion.

Phillips, Stephen H. (1987). "Dharmakīrti on Sensations and Causal Efficiency." *Journal of Indian Philosophy* (15) 231-59.

Place, U.T. (1964). "Is Consciousness a Brain Process?" In Antony Flew, ed., *Body, Mind, and Death*. New York: Macmillan.

Popper, Karl R. (1963). *Conjectures and Refutations*. London: Routledge & Kegan Paul.

_________ and John C. Eccles (1978). *The Self and Its Brain: An Argument for Interactionism*. New York: Springer International.

Potter, Karl H. (1976). *Presuppositions of India's Philosophies*. Rpt., Westport, CT: Greenwood Press.

_________ (1977). (ed.) *Encyclopedia of Indian Philosophies: Indian Metaphysics and Epistemology: The Tradition of Nyāya Vaiśeṣika up to Gangeśa*. Princeton: Princeton University Press.

Prior, A.N. (1967). "Correspondence Theory of Truth." In Edwards (1967) 2:223-32.

Quine, W.V. (1969). *Ontological Relativity and Other Essays.* New York: Columbia University Press.

_________ and J.S. Ullian (1970). *The Web of Belief.* New York: Random House.

Rabten, Geshé (1978). *The Mind and Its Functions: A Textbook of Buddhist Epistemology and Psychology.* Tr. Stephen Batchelor. Mt. Pelerin, Switzerland: Tharpa Choeling.

_________ (1984). *The Essential Nectar: Meditations on the Buddhist Path.* London: Wisdom Publications.

Radhakrishnan, Sarvepalli (1929). *Indian Philosophy.* 2 vols. London: G. Allen & Unwin.

_________ and Charles A. Moore (1957). (eds.) *A Sourcebook in Indian Philosophy.* Princeton: Princeton University Press.

Rahula, Walpola (1978). *What the Buddha Taught.* Rpt., London: Gordon Fraser.

Robinson, Richard H. (1967). *Classical Indian Philosophy.* Madison: Department of Indian Studies, University of Wisconsin.

_________ (1971-72). "Implications of the Human Sciences for Buddhism." *World Buddhism.* October 1971-April 1972.

Rorty, Richard (1979). *Philosophy and the Mirror of Nature.* Princeton: Princeton University Press.

_________ (1982). *Consequences of Pragmatism.* Minneapolis: University of Minnesota Press.

Rose, Steven (1976). *The Conscious Brain.* Updated edition. New York: Vintage.

Ruegg, D[avid] S[eyfort] (1966). *The Life of Bu Ston Rin Po Che, with the Tibetan Text of the Bu ston rNam thar.* Serie Orientale Roma, XXXIV. Roma: Istituto Italiano per il Medio ed Estremo Oriente.

_________ (1969). *La Théorie du Tathāgatagarbha et du Gotra: Études sur la sotériologie et gnoséologie du Bouddhisme.* Publications de l'École Française d'Extrême-Orient, vol LXX. Paris: École Française d'Extrême-Orient.

Russell, Bertrand (1961). *My Philosophical Development.* London: Unwin Books.

Ryle, Gilbert (1949). *The Concept of Mind.* New York: Barnes and Noble.

Sangharakshita, Bhikshu (1980). *A Survey of Buddhism.* 5th ed. Boulder: Shambhala.

Shaffer, Jerome (1967). "Mind-Body Problem."In Edwards (1967) 5: 336-46.

Shah, Nagin J. (1967). *Akalaṅka's Criticism of Dharmakīrti's Philosophy.* L.D. Series, no. 11. Ahmedabad: L.D. Institute of Indology.

Singh, Amar (1984). *The Heart of Buddhist Thought: The Philosophy of Diṅnāga and Dharmakīrti.* New Delhi: Munshiram Manohalal.

Sinha, Jadunath (1934). *Indian Psychology.* London: K. Paul, Trench, Trubner & Co.

Smart, Ninian (1978). "Understanding Religious Experience."In Katz (1978).

_________ (1979). *The Philosophy of Religion.* New York: Oxford University Press.

Solomon, Esther (1976-78). *Indian Dialectics: Methods of Philosophical Discussion.* Ahmedabad: Gujarat Vidya Sabha.

Sopa, Geshe Lhundup and Jeffrey Hopkins (1976). *Practice and Theory of Tibetan Buddhism.* New York: Grove Press.

Staal, Frits (1975). *Exploring Mysticism.* Berkeley: University of California Press.

Stcherbatsky, F. Th. (1962). *Buddhist Logic.* 2 vols. Rpt., New York: Dover.

_________ (1970). *The Central Conception of Buddhism and the Meaning of the Word "Dharma".* Rpt., Delhi: Motilal Banarsidass.

Steinkellner, Ernst (1968-69). "Die Entwicklung des *kṣaṇatvānumānam* bei Dharmakīrti." Wiener Zeitschrift für die Kunde Süd- und Ostasiens, (12-13) 361-67.

_________ (1982). "The Spiritual Place of the Epistemological Tradition in Buddhism." Nanto Bukkyo (49) 1-18.

_________ (1983). "*Tshad ma'i skyes bu.* Meaning and Historical Significance of the Term." In E. Steinkellner and H. Tauscher, eds., *Contributions on Tibetan and Buddhist Religion and Philosophy,* 274-84. Proceedings of the Csoma de Kórös Symposium, vol. 2. Wiener Studien zur Tibetologie und Buddhismuskunde, Heft 11. Wien.

_________ (1990). "Is Dharmakīrti a Mādhyamika?" In David Seyfort Ruegg and Lambert Schmithausen, eds., *Early Buddhism and Madhyamaka.* Panels of the VIIth World Sanskrit Conference, vol. II. Leiden: E.J. Brill.

Sweet, Michael (1979). "*Bodhicaryāvatāra* 9:2 as a Focus for Tibetan Interpretations of the Two Truths in the Prāsaṅgika Mādhyamika." JIABS (2, 2) 79-89.

Tarthang Tulku (1977). *Time, Space and Knowledge: A New Vision of Reality.* Emeryville, CA: Dharma Publishing.

Tharchin, Geshe Lobsang (1979). *The Logic and Debate Tradition of India, Tibet and Mongolia: History, Reader, Resources.* Howell, NJ: Rashi Gempel Ling.

Thurman, Robert A.F. (1981). (ed.) *Life and Teachings of Tsong kha pa.* Dharamsala: Library of Tibetan Works and Archives.

_________ (1984). *Tsong Khapa's Speech of Gold in the "Essence of True Eloquence": Reason and Enlightenment in the Central Philosophy of Tibet.* Princeton Library of Asian Translation. Princeton: Princeton University Press.

Tillemans, Tom J.F. (1986). "*Pramāṇavārttika* IV (1)." *Wiener Zeitschrift für die Kunde Südasiens und Archiv für Indische Philosophie.* Band XXX, 143-62.

Tracy, David (1987). *Plurality and Ambiguity: Hermeneutics, Religion, Hope.* New York: Harper & Row.

Trungpa, Chögyam (1973). *Cutting Through Spiritual Materialism.* Berkeley: Shambhala.

Tucci, Giuseppe (1958). *Minor Buddhist Texts II.* Roma: Istituto Italiano per il Medio ed Estremo Oriente.

van der Kuijp, Leonard W.J. (1983). *Contributions to the Development of Tibetan Buddhist Epistemology.* Alt- und Neu-Indische Studien, no. 26. Wiesbaden.

_________ (1987). "An Early Tibetan View of the Soteriology of Buddhist Epsitemology: The Case of 'Bri-gung 'Jig-rten mGon-po." *Journal of Indian Philosophy* (15) 57-70.

Vattanky, John (1984). *Gangeśa's Philosophy of God*. Madras: The Adyar Library and Research Centre.

Vetter, Tilmann (1964). *Erkenntsnisprobleme bei Dharmakīrti*. Wien: Österreichische Akademie der Wissenschaften.

Vidyabhusana, S. Chandra (1978). *A History of Indian Logic*. Rpt., Delhi: Motilal Banarsidass.

Vroom, Hendrik M. (1989). *Religions and the Truth: Philosophical Reflections and Perspectives*. Tr. J.W. Rebel. Grand Rapids, MI: William B. Eerdmans.

Warder, A.K. (1971). *Outline of Indian Philosophy*. Delhi: Motilal Banarsidass.

_________ (1980). *Indian Buddhism*. 2nd ed. Delhi: Motilal Banarsidass.

Watts, Alan (1961). *Psychotherapy East and West*. New York: Ballantine Books.

Wayman, Alex (1980). "The Sixteen Aspects of the Four Noble Truths and Their Opposites." JIABS (3, 2) 67-76.

White, Alan R. (1967). "Coherence Theory of Truth." In Edwards (1967) 2:130-133.

Williams, Paul (1989). *Mahayana Buddhism: The Doctrinal Foundations*. London and New York: Routledge.

Willson, Martin (1984). *Rebirth and the Western Buddhist*. London: Wisdom Publications.

Winternitz, Moritz (1972). *A History of Indian Literature*. Tr. S. Kelkar and H. Kohn. Vol. II: *Buddhist Literature and Jaina Literature*. Rpt., Delhi: Oriental Reprint.

Wittgenstein, Ludwig (1958). *Philosophical Investigations*. Tr. G.E.M. Anscombe. Third edition. New York: Macmillan.

Wolfe, David L. (1982). *Epistemology: The Justification of Belief*. Downer's Grove, IL: InterVarsity Press.

Zwilling, Leonard (1975). "Some Aspects of Dharmakīrti's Ontology Reconsidered." *Kailash* (III, 3) 303-13.

_________ (1976). "Dharmakīrti on *Apoha*: The Ontology, Epsitemology and Semantics of Negation in the *Svārthānumānapariccheda* of the *Pramāṇavārttikam*." Unpublished Ph.D. dissertation, University of Wisconsin-Madison.

_________ (1981). "Saskya Paṇdita's Version of *Pramāṇavārttikam* III.3—A Case Study on the Influence of Exegesis upon Translation in Tibet." In *Studies in Indian Philosophy, A Memorial Volume in Honour of Pandit Sukhalaji Sanghvi*. L.D. Series 84, Dalsukh Malvaniya and Nagin J. Shah, general editors. Ahmedabad: L.D. Institute of Indology.

Index

tangible, 366
tertiary qualities of: *See* qualities: tertiary
embodied beings, 267
emotions, 356n
empirical evidence, 28-29, 36, 83-84, 85, 90, 397n. *See also* observation
empowerment, 460-464, 475
Enjoyment Body, 78, 334n, 405n
cause of, 480n
characteristics of, 74, 155
enlightenment, 9, 21, 50, 61, 63, 73, 77, 126, 161, 172n, 190n, 238n, 331n, 348n, 473n. *See also* buddha; buddhahood; cessation; nirvāṇa; truth of cessation
accomplishment of, 483, 484n
altruistic aspiration to, 156, 192n, 222n, 325n, 396n. *See also bodhicitta;* thought of enlightenment
causes of, 117
gzhan stong pa concept of, 195
innate, 80
Mahāyāna ideal of, 73, 74-75
path to, 156, 217, 325n
possibility of, 10, 13, 81, 93-94, 95, 96, 130, 143, 144-145, 474n, 483, 484n
entity/entities, 173n, 192, 193, 197n, 198n, 288n, 336, 364, 365, 368, 373, 383n, 418, 419, 458, 480, 481
actuality of, 390
all-pervasive, 435
arising and ceasing of, 481, 482, 483n
auxiliary, 305
causal, 209, 210-212, 294, 379-380
dharma-, 401, 402
definition of, 195n
existent and non-existent, 254n, 259n, 411
functioning, 411
general, 206-207
impermanent, 456n
in relation to words, 201-202, 206-209, 280-288
natural destructibility of, 254-261, 410-412
naturally existing, 394
objectively separate: *See* objectively separate [entities]
permanent, 199, 210-212, 259n, 260, 261n, 352n, 377, 378, 380n, 381, 382, 428, 441n, 465
unsuitability of for bondage or freedom, 410-412
proof of, 207, 208-209
transformation of, 252
unreal, 281n
entitylessness void of efficiency, 236-237
entrances, 118. *See also āyatana*
epiphenomenalism, 223n
epistemology/epistemological, 104, 106, 110, 115n, 163, 170n, 188n, 424n, 484n
Buddhist, 75, 87-88, 101-107, 150, 178n, 185n, 415-416n, 484n
Dharmakīrti's, 122-126, 138, 158, 173n
Indian, 100, 101-107, 149-150
optimistic and pessimistic, 416n, 417n
problems of, 142-145, 267-268n
equanimity, 402, 421n, 452, 453
eschatology, 66
E.S.P.: *See* perception: extra-sensory
essence, 279
Essential Body, 74n
eternalism, 195n
ether, 118. *See also* space
Evans, Donald, 95-96, 97
evil, 87
problem of, 219n
example(s) (logical), 92, 103, 198, 223, 243-244n, 250, 252, 256-257, 263-264, 277n, 299, 310-311, 317, 351, 363, 374, 376n, 385, 434, 467, 468, 481. *See also* analogy
accordant, 103, 104, 235
non-accordant, 103, 104, 311
uncertain, 426, 427
unproven in subject, 198-199, 200n, 234, 235-243
excellence(s) (of a buddha), 128-129, 309, 310-311, 337n
of application, 128-129, 169-172, 221, 318-326, 330n, 337n, 478n
of causes, 128-129, 169-172, 326n, 337n
of intention, 128-129, 169-172, 221-318, 318, 326, 337n
basic proof of, 221-222
of one's own aims, 129, 169-172, 325n, 326n, 327-335, 337n, 479, 480n
of others' aims, 129, 169-172, 324-325, 326n, 327, 335-338, 337n, 401n, 479, 480n
of realization, 172, 478
of results, 129, 169-172, 221, 326n, 327-338, 337n
existence, saṃsāric, 68, 79, 156, 331n, 400, 401, 449-450, 453, 454. *See also* saṃsāra; suffering
cause(s) of, 382-386, 405-412, 460, 461, 464n, 468
freedom from, 401-405, 413, 458, 468, 476n
existence, substantial. *See* substantial existence

178n, 299, 308, 357n, 481, 482, 483n. *See also* concomitance: negative, positive and negative; pervasion
of result, 482
overanalaysis of, 202-204
particular, 206, 207
perfect, 339
pervasion by: *See* pervasion
relation of to words and entities, 206-209, 215
relevance of to subject, 103, 104, 125, 178, 207n, 208, 299, 308, 357n, 358n, 390, 394, 483n
uncertain, 125, 200n, 201, 202n, 203, 205, 234, 236, 238n, 240, 333-334, 354n, 360n
uncommon, 204
unproven, 125, 200n, 201, 203, 204, 206, 207, 221, 222, 240-241, 255, 270, 273, 274, 280, 290, 293, 294, 304, 357, 357n, 358, 398, 399, 407, 426, 435
reasoning/reason, 169, 170, 172, 194, 206, 233, 238, 239, 270, 280, 281, 320, 323, 330, 334, 344, 348, 363, 384, 385, 393, 395, 412, 428, 431, 471, 482, 485. *See also* rationality
objectively-impelled: *See* objectively impelled inference/reasoning
rebirth, 9, 21, 23, 24, 43, 44, 45, 48, 52, 65, 66, 67, 68-71, 77, 80, 92, 133, 141, 161, 226n, 336n, 343n, 384n, 392n, 405n, 406, 423n, 442, 458, 478n. *See also* birth; lives: future; lives, past and future; saṃsāra
cause(s) of, 265-266, 383n, 384-387, 409n, 444n, 450n, 459-464, 467-468, 469n, 470n. *See also* saṃsāra: cause of; suffering: cause of; truth of origination
desire for, 472, 473
high, 156, 172-173, 176, 178, 224, 225, 477
human, 156, 157
proof of: *See* lives, past and future: Dharmakīrti's proof of
rebounding argument. *See* argument: rebounding
reciprocal dependence (*anyonyāśraya*), 102
recognition, 68, 118, 230, 322n, 351n, 391, 451n
Red mda' ba, 115, 153
reductio, 100n, 234
reflection, 265
refuge, 483-484
inducement to as purpose of *Pramāṇasiddhi* chapter, 483
reincarnation, 66. *See also* lives, future; rebirth
relativism, 31, 33, 35n, 39, 40n, 83, 85, 96, 97, 107, 143
religion, 12, 35-42, 86n, 143
and science, 83-85, 86n, 95-98, 144n
as cultural system, 38
as fact, 40-41
as fiction, 37, 40, 53
as rule-governed, 38
as story, 37, 54
metaphysicality of claims of, 36, 39, 40
place of argument in 81-85
problem-solution framework in, 61, 65-66
universality of claims of, 36, 38, 39-40, 143
religious language, 40-41, 54, 81-82, 85-86
renunciation, 348, 451, 452, 453, 455
res cogitans, 138
res extensa, 138
result, 121, 200, 202, 203, 204, 210-212, 242n, 248, 261n, 303n, 304, 336, 340, 344, 359, 381, 383, 386, 391, 392, 410, 411, 465, 466. *See also* cause: and result/effect
definition of, 294
direct, 356, 358n, 363, 420
factors required for non-production of, 390n, 428, 431, 466n
factors required for production of, 212-214
heterogeneous, 470, 471
homogeneity of with cause, 226-227, 231, 294, 357, 358
impermanence of, 378, 410-412
karmic, 404, 408, 456, 465, 466, 470-474
necessity of when causes complete, 196-197n, 295n, 299n, 303n, 463, 464
of arhant's final mind, 236-237
of craving, 382n
of method, 454
pre-existence of in cause, 368-369
substantial, 238n, 252, 301n, 305n, 368n
suffering and pleasurable, 472
resurrection, 36, 37, 38, 40, 42
reverse system of explanation, 128, 132-134, 170, 172, 175, 221n, 222n, 296, 327n, 338, 339, 340, 477, 478n
exposition of, 339-480
rGyal dpog pa, 333. *See also* Mīmāṃsā
rGyal tshab rje (rGyal tshab dar ma rin chen), 12, 13, 126, 144
as author of *Pramāṇavārttika* commen-